BORGO CATALOGING GUIDES
Number Four
ISSN 0891-9615

WORLD WAR I

A Cataloging Reference Guide

by

Buckley Barry Barrett

California State University, San Bernardino

BORGO PRESS / WILDSIDE PRESS

www.wildsidepress.com

*   *   *   *   *   *   *

Library of Congress Cataloging-in-Publication Data

Barrett, Buckley Barry, 1948-
  World War I : a cataloging reference guide / by Buckley Barry Barrett.
    p. cm. — (Borgo cataloging guides, ISSN 0891-9615 ; no. 4)
  Includes bibliographical references and index.
  ISBN 0-89370-824-0 (cloth). — ISBN 0-89370-924-7 (pbk.)
  1. Subject headings—World War, 1914-1918.   2. Classification—
Books—World War, 1914-1918. 3. Classification, Library of Congress.
4. Classification, Dewey decimal. I. Title. II. Title: World War one. III.
Series.
Z695.1.W7B37 1995   93-19745
025.4'99403—dc20   CIP

FIRST EDITION

CONTENTS

ACKNOWLEDGMENTS

Primary thanks to Nannette, Ross, and Elizabeth, for their patience and support during the six years needed to complete both the World War I and World War II (forthcoming from Borgo Press) phases of this project. Gratitude also goes out to my publisher for granting extra time to work on the books, and to Jim Scanlon, Katherine Carlson, and other Cal State San Bernardino Computer Center staff for help with the laser-printed master copy. Finally, with appreciation for the encouragement and lodging given by Ross and Rita Barrett during my many visits to the Graduate Research Library at the University of California, Los Angeles.

INTRODUCTION

This guide seeks to improve the subject access to World War I information stored in most academic and public libraries in the United States. By describing and listing the classification or shelving schemes and controlled descriptors used by these libraries for cataloging the literature, I would hope to provide researchers with enough specific examples and overriding principles to find more materials than otherwise possible.

The scope of the work includes primarily the First World War as well as the preceding decades leading up to and pointing toward the conflict. A few entries move past the Great War and toward the global conflict of the 1930s and '40's for comparative purposes, although the researcher should consult my forthcoming volume on World War II for full coverage of that era and its origins. Since this is mostly an historical tool, I have also included many of the countries involved, and have rounded out the coverage with pertinent engineering, military, and naval concepts and facts.

Two main divisions make up the work: 1. Subject classification systems used for shelving and; 2. Controlled subject, biographical, and corporate headings used in electronic, card. or microform catalogs.

The first division contains two sections listing and describing Library of Congress and Dewey Decimal call numbers, with each section providing selected cross-references to the other system. Most academic or research libraries catalog by L.C., whereas public libraries tend toward the Dewey system. Numbers given in this guide concentrate heavily on the world war; but overall outlines of both schemes are given as well, for the sake of context and because the global war under study influenced or was influenced by matters of society, politics, economics, literature, and science in addition to history and other areas.

With a better comprehension of the major classification arrays utilized in the United States, researchers can look in a greater number of shelf locations and can find similar materials located in proximity. Certain library electronic or card catalogs may also allow for a type of remote subject browsing by call number or classification, which can prove a valuable complement to subject-term searching in the catalog.

The second primary section of the book contains Library of Congress subject headings along with proper biographical and corporate agency names. These are all placed in alphabetical order as might occur in libraries' separate subject or unified dictionary catalogs.

Most public and academic libraries in the United States look to the Library of Congress for authorized subject words and phrases; so, the search vocabulary need not change from library to library. The subject headings of this division of the book represent events, places, people, government departments, armies, navies, air forces, weapons, strategies, and other objective and subjective matters related to the war, its historical period, and the process of studying this era. Researchers may find that some of the biographical entries listed herein can be found in particular li-

1

braries as authors or topics. In a similar fashion one may find some of the government or other agency headings utilized as corporate authors or subjects.

I have given L.C. and/or Dewey call numbers or class ranges for a large sample of main and peripheral headings in order to assist with intelligent browsing of the stacks or shelf inventory records. The principal purpose here, however, is to improve catalog search results through the listing of a large volume of pertinent subject and corporate quasi-subject terms and types.

To summarize, this work attempts to provide readers with a library subject control system for use in World War I research in academic, public, and special libraries. With greater knowledge of both classified storage patterns and controlled indexing terminology, one can find a greater number of materials and can also pinpoint more specific items that might otherwise remain lost or buried.

—Buckley Barry Barrett
California State University, San Bernardino

I. LIBRARY OF CONGRESS CLASSIFICATION SYSTEM (LC)

The Library of Congress classification system divides knowledge and history into groups of alphanumeric symbols. Single, double, or triple letters are followed by numbers from 1 through 9999. These numbers are sometimes broken down into more specialized topics by decimalization and/or letter-number symbols. Libraries finish LC call numbers with alphanumeric combinations generally derived from author's last names and sometimes from titles.

Each class letter section or schedule devised, published, and employed by LC represents a different discipline or area of information, and LC has developed each section more or less independently from the other sections through the years from around the early 20th Century.

As a result of this somewhat autonomous growth, patterns of usage vary from schedule to schedule. For example, the 'D' class covering Old World, Eastern, and Oceanic history features double and even triple letters for certain areas. Great Britain is represented by 'DA' and Eastern Europe by 'DJK'. On the other hand, the 'E' and 'F' schedules cover North and South America without any multiple letters. Number spans also vary from class to class and even within. For instance, the 'VK' section of Naval Science ('V') goes up to around VK1660 or so in covering navigation and merchant marine, whereas 'VM' only reaches about VM990 in classifying naval architecture.

The LC system differs from the Dewey classification in a number of ways. The most obvious, of course, is the use of letters rather than numerals as the primary means of division. As will be seen in more detail in the next segment of this book, Dewey divides knowledge up into ten basic sets of 100 numbers each. For instance, history may often be found in the 900-999 section. Subdivisions are handled by the use of tens, digits, or decimals. Thus, much of the specific World War One material may be in the 940.3-940.499 area, while LC places equivalent items in the D501-D680 range in using letters followed by numbers in combination in order to separate different subjects or historical periods.

Call numbers built from either system can prove involved and lengthy, although complex DDC numbers may appear longer due to their general lack of breaks or pauses. LC schedules present more specific and more required choices, whereas DDC (Dewey Decimal Classification) specifies less and allows libraries to tack on one or more standardized decimal additions if desired for a more thorough description.

The Library of Congress array does not appear as intrinsically logical as the Dewey method because LC has neither the consistency nor the mnemonic hierarchy of its rival. LC's variable use of one, two, or three letters to begin different topical areas (e.g. 'D', 'DA-DX', and 'DJK' versus 'E' and 'F') does not stem from any pattern, and neither does its sometimes application of alphabetic subdivisions for greater subject detail (e.g. V858 for U.S. submarines as opposed to V859.G3 for German subs.).

In practice, LC brings similar titles together in useful groups just as well as Dewey, while usually allowing for more range expansion room and shorter, less crowded numbers. In some subject sections, LC has indeed left space for the future addition of entirely new and unused number sets out to 9999. For Dewey, however, new topics more often lead to longer, more awkward call numbers or to continued employment of the same old numbers. In the latter cases, new and prior meanings may share the same numbers regardless of differing intent or definition.

Because of some of the reasons stated herein, most academic and some (generally larger) public libraries in the United States have chosen the Library of Congress system to catalog their resources. In summary, LC appears preferable for larger collections as well as for special ones due to its provision of more detail with less clutter.

This section of the guide first outlines the overall LC scheme and then gives a specific listing of the divisions most pertinent to world war and military research. LC alphanumerics are accompanied by descriptions and Dewey equivalents where feasible. Be aware of continuing changes and additions made to LC and Dewey in order to keep them as dynamic methods of classification. Some of these changes are noted as possible.

Both of the class systems allow for a certain amount of choice in matching topics with numbers, and yet each method also takes a somewhat different view of the universe and its knowledge. Hence, as in comparing and contrasting two languages, we see that each offers its own variety of internal synonyms and that these do not always precisely equal particular words in the other language.

A unified alphabetic index follows the conclusion of the Dewey class listing and contains both LC and Dewey numbers. Some topics do not have exact possibilities for call-number assignment and may seem to belong in more than one area, and sometimes perfectly equated LC/Dewey translations do not appear to exist. Accordingly, researchers should use the LC/Dewey index plus LC headings sections in order to determine the most classification numbers.

LC CLASS NUMBERS: DESCRIPTIONS: POSSIBLE DEWEY NUMBERS

A	General works (gen. almanacs, encyclopediae, etc.)	000-099
B	Philosophy, psychology, religion	100-299
C	History (auxiliary: civilization, gen. archaeology, heraldry, gen. biography)	900-909, 920-929, 930-939+
D	History (general, Eastern Hemisphere, Oceania)	909, 930-969, 990-996
D-DX	World history, Europe, Africa, Asia, Oceania	900-949, 990's
DA-DR	Europe and Turkey	940's, 956.1
D25	Military history (world)	355.48, 904.7, 909
D501-680	WORLD WAR I	940.3-940.499
D731-838	WORLD WAR II	940.53-940.5499
E	America & North America (gen.), United States	970, 973
F	United States (local history), Canada, Latin America	971-972, 974-989
G	Geography, anthropology, sports, & recreation	910-919, 301, 790's
H	Social sciences (economics, commerce, sociology, communism)	300-319, 330-389
J	Political science, international law	320-329, 341
K	Law	340, 342-349
L	Education	370-379
M	Music	780-789
N	Arts & architecture (visual, decorative & applied)	700-709, 720-769
P	Languages & literatures	400-499, 800-899
PN	Literature (gen. & gen. collections)	800-809
PR	English literature	820-829
PS	American literature in English	810-819
Q	Sciences (pure), math, & computer science	500-599, 611-612
R	Medicine, psychiatry, & nursing	610-619, 649
S	Agriculture, forestry, hunting	630-639, 574, 581, 799
T	Technology, photography, manufacturing, handicrafts, home economics	600-609, 620-629, 640-650, 660-699, 770-779
U	Military science & engineering	355-358, 623
V	Naval science, navigation, & naval architecture	359, 623, 629
Z	Bibliography & library science (bibliog's. sometimes classed with A-Z subject #s)	010-028+

D	History (general, Eastern Hemisphere, Oceania)	909, 930-969, 990-996
D25	World military history	355.48, 904.7, 909
D51-838, D901+	Europe (gen.)	940-949
D501-680	World War I & Aftermath	940.3-940.499
DA	Great Britain	941-942
DB	Austria, Czechoslovakia, Hungary	943.6-943.9
DC	France	944
DD	Germany	943
DG	Italy	945
DJK	Eastern Europe (after about 1977-78)	943.7-943.9, 947, 947.8, 949.6-949.84
DK	Russia, Finland, Poland	
DL	Scandinavia	
DP	Iberian Peninsula	
DQ	Switzerland	949.4
DR	Balkan Peninsula, Eastern Europe (prior to about 1978-79)	949.6-949.8, 943.7-943.9, 947, 947.8, 956

```
DS          Asia    950-959
DT          Africa    960-969
DU          Oceania, Australia, New Zealand    990-996
D1-1075+    HISTORY (gen., world wars, Eur. overall, etc.)    909, 940, 950
D25         Military history (world)    355.48, 904.7, 909
D25.A2      Dictionaries, chronologies, etc. (military history: world)
D27         Naval history (world)    359, 904.7
D208        Modern history (1453-)    901.93, 909.8+, 940
D215        Naval history (1453-)
D299        Modern history (1789-)    909.8+
D358        Modern history (1801-1914/20)    909.81
D359        Europe (1801-1914)    940.28
D361        Military history (1801-1914/20)    355.033003+
D362        Naval history (1801-1914/20)
D371-379    Eastern question (1801-1914/20)    949, 320.956, 327.41-42
D374        Eastern question (general: 19th c)
D377        Slavs (Eastern question: 19th c.)
D377.3-5    Panslavism (Eastern question: 19th c.)
D378        Central Asian question (19th c.)
D394-400    World history (1871-late 19th c.)    909.81, 327.0904
D394        Primary sources (1871-late 19th c.)
D395        Modern history (1871-late 19th c.)
D396        Military history (1871-late 19th c.)    359.009
D397        Politics and diplomacy (1871-late 19th c.)
D399-399.8  Biography (1871-late 19th c.: collected)
D400.A-Z    Biography (1871-late 19th c.: individual)
D410-460+   WORLD HISTORY (20th c.: overall)
D410        Periodicals, associations, yearbooks (20th c.)
D410.5      Current events yrbks. (20th c.: nonserial: includes pictorial titles: by
                time then author)
D411        Primary sources (20th c.: collections)
D412-412.8  Biography (20th c.: memoirs and collective)
D412        Biography (20th c.: collective: gen.)    920.02
D412.5      Women (20th c.: collective biography)
D412.6      Public figures (20th c.: collective biog.: men)    920.02, 909.82,
                                                                940.50922
D412.7      Rulers, kings, etc. (20th c.: collective biography)    929.7
D412.8      Queens, princesses, etc. (20th c.: collective biography)
D413.A-Z    Biography (20th c.: individual or memoir by name)
D414-415    World history (20th c.: collected)
D414        World history (20th c.: several authors)
D415        World history (20th c.: single-author collections)
D416        Pamphlets, minor works (20th c.)
D419        Dictionaries (20th c. history)    909.8203, 320.03, 320.904
D421-425    World history (20th c.: general titles)
D421        World history (20th c.: gen.)    909.82
D422        Popular histories (20th c.)
D424        Europe (20th c.)    940.288-5
D425        Popular histories (20th c.: Europe)
D426        Pictorial and graphic histories (20th c.)    779.990194, 909.82
D427        Chronologies, outlines, syllabi, tables, etc. (20th c.)    909.82, 940.28
D429        Civilization, customs, social life (20th c.: SEE ALSO CB415, GT146)
                                                    940.5, 320.904, 327.09
```

6

D431	Military history (20th c.)	355.020904, 355.009, 355,033+
D436	Naval history (20th c.)	359.409, 904.7, 359.47
D437	Air warfare	358.41409, 358.41447
D440-460	Politics and diplomacy (20th c.)	
D440	Annual registers (20th c.: politics and diplomacy)	
D441	Primary sources (20th c.: politics and diplomacy)	
D442	Politics and diplomacy (20th c.: collected works)	
D443	Politics and diplomacy (20th c.: gen.: world pol., Triple Alliance & Entente, etc.) 940.5, 320.904, 327.09	
D445	Politics and diplomacy (20th c.: gen. special: projected, possible wars, other polit. events)	
D446	Anglo-Saxon supremacy	
D447	Pangermanism	
D448	Panlatinism	
D448.5	Panceltism	
D449	Panslavism	
D450	Pamphlets, minor works (20th c.: politics and diplomacy)	
D451-457	Diplomacy (20th c.)	
D451	Primary sources (20th c.: diplomacy)	
D453	Diplomacy (20th c.: gen.) 909.82, 327.3-9, 320.9	
D455	Diplomacy (20th c.: gen. special)	
D457	Pamphlets, minor works (20th c.: diplomacy)	
D458	Triple Alliance (1882: SEE ALSO D397, D443, D511)	
D459	Triple Entente (1907: SEE ALSO D443, D511)	
D460	Little Entente (1919)	
D461-475	Eastern question (20th c.) 320.95, 956.03, 325.342	
D463	Eastern question (20th c.: gen.)	
D469.A-Z	Eastern question (20th c.: by country)	
D471-72	Central Asian question (20th c.)	
D471	Central Asian question (1914-)	
D472.A-Z	Central Asian question (20th c.: by country)	
D475	Moroccan question (20th c.: PREFER DT317)	
D501-680	WORLD WAR I (1914-1918) 940.3-940.499	
D501	Periodicals, collected serials (WWI)	
D502	Associations, societies (WWI)	
D503	Museums, exhibitions, etc. (WWI)	
D504	Conferences (WWI)	
D505	Primary sources, documents (WWI)	
D507	Biography (WWI: collective) 940.3092, .481-2. Also use country #'s	
D509	World War I (collected works)	
D510	Dictionaries & encyclopedias (WWI: includes 'Times' index and chronology)	
D511-520	CAUSES, AIMS, RESULTS (WWI) 940.31-2	
D511	Causes, aims, results (WWI: gen.) 940.311, .314	
D512	Austria (WWI: causes, aims, results)	
D513	Serbia (WWI: causes, aims, results)	
D514	Russia (WWI: causes, aims, results: includes Panslavism)	
D515	Germany (WWI: causes, aims, results)	
D516	France (WWI: causes, aims, results)	
D517	Great Britain (WWI: causes, aims, results)	
D518	Belgium (WWI: causes, aims, results)	
D519	Japan (WWI: causes, aims, results)	
D520.A-Z	Causes, aims, results (WWI: misc. countries)	
D520.I7	Italy (WWI: causes, aims, results: includes Treaty of London, 1915)	

D520.S8	South America & Latin America (WWI: causes, aims, results)
D520.T8	Turkey & Islam (WWI: causes, aims, results)
D520.U6-7	United States (WWI: causes, aims, results)
D521	WORLD WAR I (GENERAL) 940.3, 940.4
D522	Pictorials (WWI: SEE ALSO D527)
D522.22	Documentary films, slides, etc. (WWI: catalogs)
D522.23	Movies (WWI)
D522.25	Posters (WWI: SEE ALSO D527.5)
D522.3	Maps & atlases (WWI: PREFER G1037)
D522.4	Instruction (WWI)
D522.42	Historiography (WWI)
D522.5	Tables, outlines, etc, (WWI)
D522.6	Examinations, questions, etc. (WWI)
D522.7	Juvenile works (WWI)
D523	World War I (gen. special)
D524	Ethics, prophecy, religious questions (WWI)
D525	Pamphlets, minor works, sermons (WWI)
D526-526.7	Poetry, satire, etc. (WWI: PREFER PQ-PT)
D526	Satire, poetry, etc. (WWI: gen.)
D526.2	English poetry, satire, etc. (WWI: PREFER PR, PS)
D526.3	French poetry, satire, etc. (WWI)
D526.5	German poetry, satire, etc. (WWI)
D526.7.A-Z	Poetry, satire, etc. (WWI: languages besides Eng., Fr., Ger.)
D527	Views (WWI: SEE ALSO D522)
D527.3	Films, lantern slides, etc.: (WWI)
D527.5	Posters (WWI: SEE ALSO D522.25)
D527.8	Ribbons (WWI: commemorative)
D528	Battlefield guides (WWI: gen.: SEE ALSO specific battles)
D528.5	Mobilization and beginnings (WWI)
D529	Reports, Official (WWI: military)
D529.3-9	Reports, Official (WWI: military: special branches or modes)
D529.3	Infantry (WWI: official reports)
D529.4	Cavalry (WWI: official reports)
D529.5	Artillery (WWI: official reports)
D529.7	Engineers (WWI: official reports)
D529.9.A-Z	Reports, Official (WWI: military: misc. branches or modes)
D530-549	WESTERN FRONT (WWI)
D530	Military ops. (WWI: West: gen.) 940.41+, .421, .424, .4272, .431, .434
D531-538	German military ops. (WWI: West & overall)
D531	German military ops. (WWI: West & gen.: includes Hindenburg, Ludendorff memoirs) 940.343, .40943, .413+, 943.084-085
D532-538	GERMAN MILITARY OPS. (WWI: West: special by area, type)
D532-532.9	Prussian military ops. (WWI)
D532	Prussian military ops. (WWI: gen.)
D532.1	Armies (WWI: Prus.)
D532.3	Infantry (WWI: Prus.)
D532.4	Cavalry (WWI: Prus.)
D532.5	Artillery (WWI: Prus.)
D532.6	Machine-gun regiments (WWI: Prus.)
D532.7	Gas regiments (WWI: Prus.)
D532.8	Engineers (WWI: Prus.)
D532.9	Prussian military ops. (WWI: misc. regiments)
D533	Baden military ops. (WWI)
D534-534.9	Bavarian military ops. (WWI: divided like Prussian #'s at D532)

D535	Hessian military ops. (WWI)
D536	Saxon military ops. (WWI)
D537	Württemberg military ops. (WWI)
D538.A-Z	German military ops. (WWI: by misc. place)
D538.5.A-Z	Local history (WWI: Ger.: by place)
D538.5.S76	Straubing, Ger. (WWI)
D539	Austrian & Austro-Hungarian military ops. (WWI)
D539.5.A-Z	Austrian & Austro-Hungarian military ops. (WWI: special divisions)
D539.5.C8	Czechoslovakian military ops. (WWI)
D539.7.A-Z	Local history (WWI: Austria: by place)
D540	Hungarian military ops. (WWI)
D541	Belgian military ops. & battles in Belgium (WWI: gen.)
D542.A-Z	BATTLES, campaigns, sieges (WWI: BELGIUM: by place)
D542.A6	Antwerp, Siege of (1914)
D542.B7	Bruges, Bel. (WWI)
D542.C4	Charleroi, Bel. (WWI)
D542.D4	Dinant, Bel. (WWI)
D542.L5	Liege, Bel. (WWI)
D542.L7	Louvain, Bel. (WWI)
D542.M7	Mons, Bel. (WWI)
D542.Y5	Ypres, Bel. (WWI: gen.)
D542.Y6	Ypres, 1st Battle of (1914)
D542.Y7	Ypres, 2d Battle of (1915)
D542.Y72	Ypres, 3d Battle of (1917)
D542.Y8	Yser, Battle of the (WWI)
D544-549+	ANGLO-FRENCH & ALLIED MILITARY OPS. (WWI)
D544	ALLIES & Allied military ops. (WWI: gen.) 940.412+, .414, .42-3, 944.0814
D545.A-Z	BATTLES, campaigns, sieges (WWI: FR.: by place)
D545.A5	Aisne, Fr. (WWI)
D545.A55	Alsace, Fr. (WWI: SEE ALSO DD801.A57)
D545.A6	Argonne, Battle of the (1915)
D545.A63	Argonne, Battle of the (1918)
D545.A7	Arras, Fr. (WWI)
D545.B4	Belleau Wood, Fr. (WWI)
D545.C37	Champagne, Fr. (WWI)
D545.C4	Château-Thierry, Battle of (1918)
D545.C7	Compi`egne, Fr. (WWI)
D545.L5	Lille, Fr. (WWI)
D545.L7	Lorraine, Battle of (1914)
D545.M3	Marne, Battle of the (1914)
D545.P5	Picardy, Fr. (WWI)
D545.R4	Reims, Fr. (WWI)
D545.S7	Somme, Battle of the (1916)
D545.S75	Somme, 2d Battle of the (1918)
D545.V25	Verdun, Battle of (WWI: 1914)
D545.V3	Verdun, 2d Battle of (WWI: 1916)

```
D546-547.8+      BRITISH MILITARY OPS., British Empire, & England (WWI)
D546             British military ops. (WWI: gen.)      354.42066, 940.48341, .412+,
                                                        941.083
D546.A1-19  Associations, societies (WWI: G.B.)
D546.A12    Comrades of the Great War (G.B.)
D546.A2-Z        British military ops. (WWI: gen.)
D546.3-547.8+    British military ops. & British Empire (WWI: special)
D546.3           Officers Training Corps (WWI: G.B.)
D546.5.1st-  Armies etc. (WWI: G.B.: by #)
D546.5.5th   Great Britain. Fifth Army (WWI)
D546.52          Artillery (WWI: G.B.)
D546.53          Infantry (WWI: G.B.)
D546.54          Cavalry (WWI: G.B.)
D546.55          Engineers (WWI: G.B.)
D547.A-Z-547.8+       British military ops., The Empire, & Great Britain (WWI)
D547.A-Z    BRITISH EMPIRE & BRITAIN (WWI: by place or name)
D547.A1          Colonies (WWI: G.B.: gen.)
D547.A4          South Africa (WWI)
D547.A5          West Africa (WWI)
D547.A8          Australia & Anzacs (WWI)
D547.B6          Black Watch (WWI)
D547.C2          Canada (WWI)
D547.C6          Coldstream Guards (WWI)
D547.G5     Glasgow Highlanders (WWI)
D547.G7     Grenadier Guards (WWI)
D547.G8     Guards Division (WWI: G.B.)
D547.I5          India (WWI)
D547.I6          Ireland (WWI)
D547.J3          Jamaica (WWI)
D547.K43    King's Liverpool Regiment (WWI)
D547.K47    King's Own Scottish Borderers (WWI)
D547.L6          London Regiment (WWI)
D547.N4          Blacks (WWI: negroes: G.B.)
D547.N5          New Zealand (WWI)
D547.N7          Northumberland Fusiliers (WWI)
D547.O7     Oxford University (WWI)
D547.Q3     Queen's Westminster and Civil Service Rifles (WWI)
D547.R4          Remount Service (WWI: G.B.)
D547.R5          Royal Artillery Regiment (WWI)
D547.R6          Royal Fusiliers (WWI)
D547.R63    Royal Highlanders of Canada (WWI)
D547.R7          Royal Naval Division (WWI)
D547.R8          Royal Scots (WWI)
D547.S4          Scots Guard (WWI)
D547.S5          Sherwood Foresters (WWI)
D547.T3          Tasmania (WWI)
D547.W4     Wales (WWI)
D547.W5     West Riding Territorials (WWI: G.B.)
D547.8.A-Z  Local history (WWI: England: by place)
D547.8.E3   East Anglia, Eng. (WWI)
D547.8.H6   Hornchurch, Eng. (WWI)
D547.8.L7   London, Eng. (WWI)
```

D548-549	FRENCH MILITARY OPS. & France (WWI)	
D548	France & French military ops. (WWI: gen.)	940.344, .412+
D548.1	Army corps (WWI: Fr.)	
D548.2	Divisions (WWI: Fr.)	
D548.3	Infantry (WWI: Fr.)	
D548.35	French Foreign Legion (WWI)	
D548.4	Cavalry (WWI: Fr.)	
D548.5	Chasseurs (WWI: Fr.: includes Blue Devils & Chasseurs alpins)	
D548.6	Artillery (WWI: Fr.)	
D548.75	Gas regiments (WWI: Fr.)	
D548.9.A-Z	French military ops. (WWI: misc.: includes colonial)	
D548.9.C	Colonies (WWI: Fr.)	
D549.A-Z	French military ops. (WWI: special groups by name)	
D549.C5	Chinese troops (WWI: Fr. ops.)	
D549.C7	Colored troops (WWI: Fr. ops.)	
D549.5	Western front (WWI: misc. countries: gen.)	
D549.52.A-Z	Western front (WWI: misc. countries: by place)	
D549.52.P8	Portugal (WWI)	
D549.52.P82.A-Z	Local history (WWI: Port.: by place)	
D550-569	EASTERN FRONT (WWI)	
D550	RUSSIAN MILITARY OPS. and Eastern Front (WWI: gen.)	
		940.4147, .40947
D551	Russo-German conflict (WWI: gen.)	
D552.A-Z	Battles, campaigns, sieges (WWI: Russo-German)	
D552.L5	Lithuania (WWI)	
D552.T3	Tannenberg, Battle of (1914)	
D556-557	Russo-Austrian conflict (WWI)	
D556	Russo-Austrian conflict (WWI: gen.)	
D557.A-Z	Battles, campaigns, sieges (WWI: Russo-Austrian: by place)	
D557.P7	Przemysl, Siege of (1914)	
D558	Siberia (WWI)	
D559	Archangel & northern Russia (WWI)	
D560-565	Balkan conflict (WWI)	
D560	Balkan conflict (WWI: gen.)	940.4147
D561	Serbia (WWI)	
D562.A-Z	Battles, campaigns, sieges (WWI: Serbia)	
D563.A2	Bulgaria (WWI: gen.)	
D563.A3-Z	Battles, campaigns, sieges (WWI: Bulg.)	
D564.A2	Montenegro (WWI: gen.)	
D564.A3-Z	Battles, campaigns, sieges (WWI: Montenegro)	
D565.A2	Rumania (WWI)	
D565.A3-Z	Battles, campaigns, sieges (WWI: Rum.)	
D566-569	NEAR EAST, TURKEY, ITALY, GREECE (WWI)	
D566	Turkey & Near East (WWI: gen.)	940.415, .4145
D567.A2	Turco-Russian conflict (WWI)	
D567.A3-Z	Battles, campaigns, sieges (WWI: Turco-Russian: by place)	
D568.A2	Turco-Egyptian conflict (WWI)	
D568.A3-Z	Battles, campaigns, sieges (WWI: Turco-Egyptian)	
D568.2	Egypt (WWI)	
D568.3	Gallipoli & the Dardanelles (WWI)	
D568.4	Arabia (WWI)	
D568.5	Assyria & Mesopotamia (WWI)	
D568.6	Syria (WWI)	
D568.7	Palestine (WWI)	
D568.8	Persia (WWI)	

D568.9	West Turkestan & Khurasan (WWI)	
D569	Italy (WWI)	940.4145
D569.A2	Italian military ops. (WWI: gen.)	940.4145
D569.A25	Armies etc. (WWI: Ital.)	
D569.A3-Z	Battles, campaigns, sieges (WWI: Italy)	
D569.G7	Gorizia, It. (WWI)	
D569.P4	Piave, 1st Battle of the (1917)	
D569.P5	Piave, 2d Battle of the (1918)	
D569.V4	Venice, Defense of (WWI)	
D569.V5	Vittorio Veneto, Battle of (1918)	
D569.2	Greece & Macedonia (WWI)	
D569.3.A-Z	Battles, campaigns, sieges (WWI: Greece)	
D569.5	Albania (WWI)	
D570-570.9+	UNITED STATES MILITARY ops. & U.S. (WWI)	940.373, .41273, .40973, 327.73
D570	United States (WWI: gen.)	940.373
D570.A1-15	Associations, societies (WWI: U.S.)	
D570.A1-14.Z9	American Legion (WWI)	
D570.A1	American Legion (WWI: gen.)	
D570.A12.A-Z	American Legion (WWI: by state)	
D570.A13.A-Z	American Legion (WWI: by city)	
D570.A135	American Legion (WWI: France)	
D570.A14-A14.A6-W	American Legion (WWI: Auxiliary, publications, by state)	
D570.A14.Z9	Pamphlets, minor works (WWI: American Legion)	
D570.A15.A-Z	Associations, societies (WWI: misc. American military)	
D570.A15.D5	Disabled American Veterans of the World War (WWI)	
D570.A2	Bulletins, misc. collections, serials (WWI: U.S.: official)	
D570.A3	Legislative compendia (WWI: U.S.)	
D570.A4	Histories, Official (WWI: U.S.)	
D570.A5-Z	American military ops. & U.S. (WWI: gen. unofficial)	940.373, 41273, .40973, 327.73
D570.15	Pamphlets, minor works (WWI: U.S.)	
D570.2-.79	United States military ops. (WWI: organiz. units: land, sea, air: SEE D570.A4-Z, D545 etc. for overall participation, battles, etc.)	
D570.2	United States military ops. (WWI: gen. special)	
D570.25-.358	ARMIES ETC. (WWI: U.S.)	940.412+, .44973, .45
D570.25.A-Z	General staff & headquarters (WWI: U.S.)	
D570.27.A-Z	Army corps (WWI: U.S.)	
D570.27.A1.A-Z	Army corps (WWI: U.S.: gen.: newer titles)	
D570.27.1st-	Army corps (WWI: U.S.: specific units: newer titles)	
D570.3.A-Z	Divisions (WWI: U.S.: newer bks. may use A1 or #'s like D570.27)	
D570.3.R3	Rainbow Division (WWI: U.S.)	
D570.309-.31	Engineers (WWI: U.S.)	
D570.315	Antiaircraft artillery (WWI: U.S.)	
D570.32	Field artillery (WWI: U.S.)	
D570.325	Coast artillery (WWI: U.S.)	
D570.327	Trench artillery (WWI:U.S.)	
D570.33	Infantry (WWI: U.S.: newer bks. may use A1 or #'s as in D570.27)	
D570.34	Machine-gun battalions (WWI: U.S.)	
D570.345	Gas regiments (WWI: U.S.)	
D570.348	Marines (WWI: U.S.: inland ops.)	
D570.35	Military police (WWI: U.S.)	
D570.355	Ambulance companies (WWI: U.S.)	940.4753

D570.36	Training camps (WWI: U.S.: gen.)	
D570.37.A-Z	Training camps (WWI: U.S. in Europe: SEE U294.5 for those in U.S.)	
D570.37.B7	Brest, Fr. (WWI: U.S. training camp)	
D570.4-.5	United States naval ops. (WWI)	940.45+, .41273
D570.4	United States naval ops. (WWI: gen.: PREFER D589.U5-6)	
D570.45	United States naval ops. (WWI: special: land batteries, Marine Corps landings, etc.)	
D570.5.A-Z	United States naval ops. (WWI: by battle, ship, etc.: PREFER D589.U6-7)	
D570.6	United States aerial ops. (WWI: PREFER D606 for general works)	940.44973
D570.7	Squadrons (WWI: U.S. aerial)	
D570.72-.73	Transport service (WWI: U.S.)	
D570.8.A-Z	UNITED STATES (WWI: SPECIAL TOPICS: SEE D639 for outside U.S.)	
D570.8.A6	Alien enemies (WWI: U.S.)	
D570.8.C4	Civil liberties (WWI: U.S.)	
D570.8.C8.A-Z	Councils of Defense (WWI: U.S.: by state)	
D570.8.E8	Executions (WWI: U.S.)	
D570.8.I6	Indians as soldiers (WWI: U.S.)	
D570.8.M5	Missions to the U.S. (WWI: overall)	
D570.8.M6.A-Z	Missions to the U.S. (WWI: by country)	
D570.8.M6.B5	British mission to U.S. (WWI)	
D570.8.M6.F4	French mission to U.S. (WWI)	
D570.8.M6.I8	Italian mission to U.S. (WWI)	
D570.8.M6.J4	Japanese mission to U.S. (WWI)	
D570.8.M6.R7	Russian mission to U.S. (WWI)	
D570.8.P7	Political prisoners (WWI: U.S.)	
D570.8.R4	Registration (WWI: U.S.)	
D570.8.S4	Seizure & disposition of German ships (WWI: U.S.)	
D570.8.S5	Service flags (WWI: U.S.)	
D570.85.A-W	States of the U.S. (WWI)	974-979
D570.85.C2	California (WWI: gen.)	
D570.85.C21.A-Z	Local history (WWI: Calif.)	
D570.85.C21.L52	Los Angeles, Calif. (WWI)	
D570.85.D6	District of Columbia (WWI)	
D570.85.F5-51	Florida (WWI)	
D570.85.I3-31	Illinois (WWI)	
D570.85.M4-41	Massachusetts (WWI)	
D570.85.M8-81	Missouri (WWI)	
D570.85.N4-5	New York (WWI)	
D570.85.P4-41	Pennsylvania (WWI)	
D570.87.A-Z	Possessions of the U.S. (WWI)	
D570.87.H3	Hawaii (WWI)	
D570.88.A-Z	Nationalities (WWI: U.S.)	
D570.9.A-Z	Personal accounts, expeditionary experiences (WWI: U.S.: SEE ALSO E745 for military biog.)	
D571	Japanese military ops. (WWI: gen.)	
D572.A-Z	Battles, sieges, etc. (WWI: Jp.)	

D573-578	COLONIES (WWI)	
D573	Colonies (WWI: gen.)	
D574-576	German colonies (WWI)	
D574	German colonies (WWI: gen.)	
D575	African colonies (WWI: Ger.: gen.)	940.416
D576.A-Z	African colonies (WWI: Ger.: by place)	
D576.C3	Cameroons (WWI)	
D576.G3	German East Africa (WWI)	
D576.G5	German Southwest Africa (WWI)	
D576.G7	Gold Coast (Ghana: WWI)	
D576.T7	Togoland (WWI)	
D577	Pacific, Asiatic, & other colonies (WWI: Ger.: gen.)	
D578	Pacific, Asiatic, & other colonies (WWI: Ger.: by place)	
D578.N4	New Guinea (WWI)	
D578.S2	Samoa (Western: WWI)	
D580-595	NAVAL OPS. (WWI)	940.45
D580	Freedom of the seas & naval ops. (gen.: WWI)	
D582.A-Z	British naval ops. & Anglo-German naval conflict (WWI: by battle, ship, etc.)	
D582.D8	Dresden (WWI: cruiser)	
D582.F2	Falkland Islands, Battle of (1914)	
D582.G7	Goeben & Breslau (WWI: cruisers)	
D582.J8	Jutland, Battle of (1916)	
D582.K6	Konigsberg (WWI: cruiser)	
D583	French naval ops. & Franco-Austrian naval conflict (WWI)	
D584.A-Z	Austrian-Franco naval conflict (WWI: by battle, ship, etc.)	
D585	Russian naval ops. (WWI)	
D586	Egyptian naval ops. (WWI)	
D587	Turkish naval ops. (WWI)	
D588	Italian naval ops. (WWI)	
D589.A-Z	Naval ops. (WWI: misc. countries: by place)	
D589.U5-8	United States naval ops. (WWI: SEE ALSO D570.4-5)	
D589.U5	Primary sources (WWI: U.S. naval)	
D589.U6	United States naval ops. (WWI: gen.)	
D589.U7.A-Z	United States naval ops. (WWI: by battle, ship, etc.)	
D589.U8	Medals (WWI: U.S. naval)	
D590-595	SUBMARINE OPS. & submarine chasers (WWI)	940.451+
D590	Anti-submarine & submarine ops. (WWI: gen.)	
D591	German submarine ops. (WWI: gen.)	940.4512
D592.A-Z	German submarine ops. (WWI: by ship, engagement, etc.)	
D592.D4	Deutschland (WWI: submarine)	
D592.L8	Lusitania (WWI: steamship)	
D593	British submarine ops. (WWI: gen.)	940.451341
D594.A-Z	British submarine ops. (WWI: by battle, ship, etc.)	
D594.Z4	Zeebruge-Ostend raids (WWI: 1918)	
D595.A-Z	Submarine ops. (WWI: misc. countries besides Ger., G.B.)	
D595.U6-7	United States submarine ops. (WWI)	
D600-607	AIR FORCE OPS. (WWI)	940.44
D600	Aerial ops. (WWI: gen.)	
D602	British aerial ops. (WWI)	940.44941
D603	French aerial ops. (WWI)	940.44944
D604	German aerial ops. (WWI)	940.44943
D605	Russian aerial ops. (WWI)	
D606	United States aerial ops. (WWI)	940.44973
D607.A-Z	Aerial ops. (WWI: misc. countries)	

D607.3	Engineering ops. (WWI)	
D607.5	Gas warfare (WWI: PREFER UG447)	
D608	Tank warfare (WWI)	358.18, 940.4+
D609	LISTS & REGISTERS (WWI: decorated, dead, wounded)	940.467
D609.A2	Registers & lists (WWI: decorated, dead, wounded: gen.)	
D609.A3-Z	Registers & lists (WWI: decorated, dead, wounded: by country)	
D609.F8-82	Dead, wounded, decorated (WWI: lists: Fr.)	
D609.G7	Dead, wounded, decorated (WWI: lists: G.B.)	
D609.U6-7	Dead, wounded, decorated (WWI: lists: U.S.)	
D610-621	DIPLOMACY (WWI)	940.32
D610	Diplomacy (WWI: gen.)	
D611	Neutrality, other special diplomatic history (WWI)	
D613	Peace efforts (WWI: ongoing: gen.)	
D613.5	Ford Peace Expedition (WWI)	
D614.A-Z	Treaties (WWI: misc. separate)	
D614.A2	Treaties (WWI: misc. separate: collections)	
D614.B5	Brest-Litovsk, Ukraine (WWI: treaty: 9 Feb. 1918)	
D614.B6	Brest-Litovsk, Russia (WWI: treaty: 3 Mar. 1918)	
D615	Belgium & Belgian neutrality (WWI: dipl. history)	
D616	Greece (WWI: dipl. hist.)	
D617	Italy & Italian neutrality (WWI: dipl. history)	
D618	South America (WWI: dipl. hist.)	
D619	United States (WWI: neutrality & dipl. history)	940.32273, .373
D619.3	Espionage, conspiracies, propaganda in U.S. (WWI: German)	
D619.5.A-Z	Espionage in U.S. (WWI: Ger.: by case)	
D619.5.A7	Archibald, James Frances J. (WWI: Ger. spy in U. S.)	
D619.5.M3	Martens, Ludwig (WWI: Ger. spy in U. S.)	
D619.5.P2	Papen, Franz von (WWI: Ger. spy in U. S.)	
D620	German-Americans (WWI)	
D621.A-Z	Diplomatic history (WWI: misc. countries)	
D621.A8	Argentina (WWI: dipl. hist.)	
D621.S3	Scandinavia (WWI: dipl. hist.)	
D621.S4	Denmark (WWI: dipl. hist.)	
D621.S45	Norway (WWI: dipl. hist.)	
D621.S5	Sweden (WWI: dipl. hist.)	
D622-639	WORLD WAR I (SPECIAL TOPICS)	
D622	Catholic Church (WWI)	
D623.A2	Occupied territories (WWI: gen.: includes laws)	
D623.A3-Z	Occupied territories (WWI: by country)	
D623.B4	Belgium (WWI: occupation)	
D625-626	ATROCITIES, war crimes, trials (WWI)	
D625	War crimes, atrocities, trials (WWI: gen.)	940.405, .472
D626.A-Z	Trials (WWI: atrocities, war crimes: by country accused)	
D626.A9	Atrocities, war crimes, trials (WWI: Austria)	
D626.G3	Atrocities, war crimes, trials (WWI: Ger. & Central Powers)	
D626.G4	Trials (Leipzig: 1921)	
D627.A1	Periodicals & associations (WWI: prisons)	940.472+
D627.A2	Prisons & prisoners (WWI: gen.)	
D627.A3-Z	Prisons & prisoners (WWI: by country)	

D628-630	MEDICAL SERVICES, HOSPITALS, RED CROSS (WWI)	940.475+, .477+

D628   Hospitals, medical services, Red Cross (WWI: gen.)
D629.A-Z   Red Cross & medical services (WWI: by country)
D629.G7   Medical services & Red Cross (WWI: G.B.)
D629.U6   Medical services & Red Cross (WWI: U.S.: gen.)
D629.U62.A-W   United States medical services (WWI: by state)
D629.U7.A-Z   United States medical services (WWI: by place in U.S.)
D629.U8.A-Z   United States medical services (WWI: by overseas locale)
D629.U8.F5-9   United States medical services (WWI: in Fr.)
D630.A-Z   Biography & memoirs (WWI: medical: by name)
D630.C3   Cavell, Edith (WWI: medical biog.)
D631   Censorship, press, publicity (WWI: gen.: SEE ALSO D639.P6-7 for propaganda)   940.315097
D632   Press, publicity, censorship (WWI: U.S.)
D633   Publicity, press, censorship (WWI: special topics)
D635   Economic matters (WWI: commerce, finance, mail: SEE ALSO HC56, HF3030, HJ236,HJ8011)
D636   Alien enemies (WWI)
D636.A2   Alien enemies (WWI: gen.)
D636.A3-Z   Alien enemies (WWI: by country)
D636.G7   Alien enemies (WWI: G.B.)
D637   Charities, refugees, relief work (WWI: gen.)   940.477+
D638.A-Z   Refugees, relief work, charities (WWI: by country or area)
D638.A7   Relief work, refugees, etc. (WWI: Armenia)
D638.E2   Relief work, refugees, etc. (WWI: Near East)
D638.U5   Relief work, refugees, etc. (WWI: U.S.)
D639.A-Z   WORLD WAR I (MISC. SPECIAL: SEE D570.8 for U.S.)
D639.A6   Amnesty (WWI)
D639.A64   Anarchism & anarchists (WWI)
D639.A65   Animals (WWI: use of)
D639.A7   Racial problems, ethnology, anthropology (WWI)
D639.A75   Astrology (WWI)
D639.A8   Automobiles (WWI)
D639.B6   Boy Scouts (WWI)
D639.C4   Children & orphans (WWI)   940.53161
D639.C5   Christian Science (WWI)
D639.C54   Church of England (WWI)
D639.C75   Cryptography (WWI)
D639.D4   Dead (WWI: burial, cemeteries, etc.)
D639.D45   Democracy (WWI)
D639.D6   Dogs (WWI)
D639.D7   Dreams (WWI)
D639.E2-6   Education (WWI)
D639.E2   Education (WWI: gen.)
D639.E3-42   Education (WWI: U.S.)
D639.E3   Education (WWI: U.S.: gen.: inclu. Student Army Training Corps)
D639.E35   American Expeditionary Force Univ. (WWI)
D639.E4.A-Z   College, school, etc. (WWI: U.S.: by name)
D639.E4.H3   Harvard Univ. (WWI)
D639.E4.S3   St. Louis public schools (WWI)
D639.E42.A-Z   Fraternities (WWI: U.S. educ.: by name)
D639.E42.S5   Sigma Alpha Epsilon (WWI: U.S. educ.: fraternity)
D639.E47   Education (WWI: Ger.)
D639.E5-53   Education (WWI: G.B.)

D639.E8	Entertainment & recreation for soldiers (WWI)
D639.F3	Fashion (WWI)
D639.F8	Freemasons (WWI)
D639.F9	Friends, Society of (WWI)
D639.G6	Governments in exile (WWII)
D639.G8	Gynecology (WWI)
D639.H5	Historic monuments (WWI)
D639.I2	Idealism (WWI)
D639.I5	Illegitimate war babies (WWI)
D639.J4	Jews (WWI: includes Ukrainian pogroms: SEE DS145.P5-7 for Protocols of the Wise Men of Zion)
D639.L2	Labor (WWI)
D639.L4	Lawyers (WWI)
D639.L5	Libraries (WWI: PREFER Z675.W2)
D639.M37	Mennonites (WWI)
D639.M4-5	Merchant marine (WWI)
D639.M8	Mutinies (WWI)
D639.M82.A-Z	Mutinies (WWI: by country)
D639.N2-3	Naturalized subjects in belligerent lands (WWI)
D639.N4	Blacks (WWI: Negroes)
D639.P45	Pigeons (WWI)
D639.P5	Population (WWI)
D639.P6	Propaganda (WWI: gen.: SEE ALSO D631-633 for press) 940.488+
D639.P7.A-Z	Propaganda (WWI: by country)
D639.P7.G3	Propaganda, German (WWI)
D639.P77	Protest movements (WWI)
D639.P8	Psychical phenomena (WWI)
D639.P87	Public opinion (WWI: gen.)
D639.P88.A-Z	Public opinion (WWI: by place)
D639.R4	Religion, Christianity (WWI) 940.478
D639.S15	Salvation Army (WWI)
D639.S2	Science & technology (WWI)
D639.S3	Sex (WWI)
D639.S4	Slavs (WWI)
D639.S5	Snowshoeing (WWI)
D639.S6	Socialism (WWI)
D639.S7-8	Espionage, secret service, spies (WWI)
D639.S7	Secret service, spies (WWI: gen.)
D639.S8.A-Z	Spies, espionage (WWI: by name)
D639.S8.Z4	Mata Hari (WWI: spy: Zelle)
D639.S9	Supplies (WWI)
D639.T35	Telegraph & radio (WWI)
D639.T4	Telephone (WWI)
D639.T6	TocH (WWI)
D639.T8	Transportation (WWI)
D639.W7	Women & women's work (WWI) 940.315042
D639.Y7	Y.M.C.A., Y.W.C.A. (WWI)
D640	Personal accounts (WWI: SEE ALSO D570.9 for U.S. soldiers) 940.481+
D640.A2	Personal accounts (WWI: collective)

D641	Armistice (WWI)	940.439
D642-651	PEACE (WWI)	940.312, .3141
D642	Primary sources, documents (WWI: peace: collections)	
D643	TREATIES (WWI: Allies-Central powers)	940.3141
D643.A2-A7	Treaties (WWI: Ger.: 28 June 1919)	
D643.A2	Treaty of Versailles (WWI: 28 June 1919: collected texts)	
D643.A3-4	Treaty of Versailles (WWI: preliminary discussions)	
D643.A5.1919+	Treaty of Versailles (WWI: texts by date)	
D643.A51	Treaty of Versailles (WWI: protocol)	
D643.A55	Treaty of Versailles (WWI: reservations by date)	
D643.A6	Treaty of Versailles (WWI: official discussions by date)	
D643.A65	Treaty of Versailles (WWI: other official by date)	
D643.A67	Resolution of peace (WWI: U.S. Congress by date)	
D643.A68	Treaties (WWI: U.S.-Ger.)	
D643.A7.A-Z	Treaty of Versailles (WWI: unofficial talks)	
D643.A8-Z	Treaties (WWI: countries other than Ger.)	
D643.A8-A9	Treaties (WWI: Austria: 10 Sept. 1919)	
D643.A8	Treaty of St. Germain (WWI: texts by date)	
D643.A83	Treaties (WWI: U.S.-Austria)	
D643.B5	Treaties (WWI: Bulg.: 27 Nov. 1919)	
D643.B6	Treaty of Neuilly-sur-Seine (WWI: texts)	
D643.H7-9	Treaties (WWI: Hungary: 4 June 1920)	
D643.H7	Treaty of Trianon (WWI: non-U.S. texts)	
D643.H8	Treaties (WWI: U.S.-Hung.)	
D643.T8	Treaties (WWI: Turkey: S`evres: 10 Aug. 1920)	
D644	Peace (WWI: gen.)	940.312
D645	Peace (WWI: special topics)	
D646	Pamphlets, minor works (WWI: peace)	
D647.A2	Peace commissions (WWI: gen.)	
D647.A3-Z	Commissions, Peace (WWI: by country)	
D647.U6	Commissions, Peace (WWI: U.S.)	
D648	Indemnity & reparations (WWI: gen.)	940.31422
D649.A-Z	Reparations & indemnity (WWI: by country)	
D649.G3	Reparations (WWI: Ger.)	
D649.G3.A4-5	Dawes Plan (WWI)	
D649.G3.A6-7	Young Plan (WWI)	
D650.A-Z	Peace (WWI: other special topics)	
D650.B7	Bridges of the Rhine (WWI: peace topic)	
D650.D5	Disarmament (WWI: Ger.)	
D650.I6	Inter-allied Military Commission of Control in Germany (WWI)	
D650.J4	Jews (WWI: peace topic)	
D650.M5	Occupation, Military (WWI: Rhineland)	
D650.R8	Ruhr Valley (WWI: peace topic)	
D650.T4	Territorial questions (post-WWI: gen.: SEE D651 for specific places) 940.31424	
D651.A-Z	TERRITORIAL QUESTIONS (post-WWI: by place)	
D651.A4	Africa (post-WWI territorial ?s)	
D651.A41	German East Africa (post-WWI territorial ?s)	
D651.A42	German Southwest Africa (post-WWI territorial ?s)	
D651.A5	Albania (post-WWI territorial ?s)	
D651.A7	Armenia (post-WWI territorial ?s)	
D651.A95	Austria (post-WWI territorial ?s)	
D651.A98	Azerbaijan (post-WWI territorial ?s)	
D651.B2	Baltic provinces (post-WWI territorial ?s)	
D651.B3	Belgium (post-WWI territorial ?s)	

D651.B4	Bessarabia (post-WWI territorial ?s)
D651.B8	Bulgaria (post-WWI territorial ?s)
D651.C3	Cameroons (post-WWI territorial ?s)
D651.C4-7	China (post-WWI territorial ?s)
D651.C5	China (post-WWI relns.: U.S.)
D651.C6	China (post-WWI relns.: Japan)
D651.C78	Croatia (post-WWI territorial ?s)
D651.C8	Cuba (post-WWI territorial ?s)
D651.C9	Czechoslovakia (post-WWI territorial ?s)
D651.D3	Dalmatia (post-WWI territorial ?s)
D651.E3	Estonia (post-WWI territorial ?s)
D651.E8	Estonia (post-WWI territorial ?s)
D651.F5-7	France (post-WWI territorial ?s)
D651.F5	France (post-WWI territorial ?s: gen.)
D651.F6.A2-Z	France (post-WWI relns.: U.S.: inclu. defensive alliance bet. Fr., U.S., G.B.)
D651.G18	Galicia (post-WWI territorial ?s)
D651.G2	Georgia, Transcaucasia (post-WWI territorial ?s)
D651.G3	Germany (post-WWI territorial ?s)
D651.G5-7	Great Britain (post-WWI territorial ?s)
D651.G5	Great Britain (post-WWI territorial ?s: gen.)
D651.G6	Great Britain (post-WWI relns.: U.S.: inclu. defensive alliance w. Fr., U.S.)
D651.G7	Great Britain (post-WWI relns.: countries other than U.S.)
D651.G8	Greece & unredeemed Greeks (post-WWI territorial ?s)
D651.H7	Hungary (post-WWI territorial ?s)
D651.I5	Istria (post-WWI territorial ?s)
D651.I6-8	Italy (post-WWI territorial ?s: inclu. Fiume)
D651.I6	Fiume & Italy (post-WWI territorial ?s: gen.)
D651.I7	Italy (post-WWI relns.: U.S.)
D651.J3-5	Japan (post-WWI territorial ?s)
D651.J4	Japan (post-WWI relns.: U.S.)
D651.L4	Latvia (post-WWI territorial ?s)
D651.L45	Lebanon (post-WWI territorial ?s)
D651.L5	Lithuania (post-WWI territorial ?s)
D651.L8	Luxemburg (post-WWI territorial ?s)
D651.M3	Macedonia (post-WWI territorial ?s)
D651.M4	Mesopotamia (post-WWI territorial ?s)
D651.M7	Montenegro (post-WWI territorial ?s)
D651.N3	Nauru (post-WWI territorial ?s)
D651.N5	Nicaragua (post-WWI territorial ?s)
D651.P2	Pacific Islands, German (post-WWI territorial ?s)
D651.P3	Palestine (post-WWI territorial ?s)
D651.P4	Persia (post-WWI territorial ?s)
D651.P7	Poland (post-WWI territorial ?s)
D651.P75	Portugal (post-WWI territorial ?s)
D651.P89-9	Prussia, East & West (post-WWI territorial ?s)
D651.P8	Posen (post-WWI territorial ?s)
D651.R6	Rumania (post-WWI territorial ?s)
D651.R8	Russia (post-WWI territorial ?s)
D651.R9	Ruthenia (post-WWI territorial ?s)
D651.S13	Saar Valley (post-WWI territorial ?s)
D651.S3	Samoa, Western (post-WWI territorial ?s)
D651.S4	Schleswig (post-WWI territorial ?s)
D651.S5	Silesia, Upper (post-WWI territorial ?s)

D651.S53	Slovenia (post-WWI territorial ?s)	
D651.S9	Syria (post-WWI territorial ?s)	
D651.T5	Thrace (post-WWI territorial ?s)	
D651.T7	Togoland (post-WWI territorial ?s)	
D651.T8	Transylvania (post-WWI territorial ?s)	
D651.T85	Trieste (post-WWI territorial ?s)	
D651.T9	Turkey (post-WWI territorial ?s)	
D651.T95	Tyrol (post-WWI territorial ?s)	
D651.U6	Ukraine (post-WWI territorial ?s)	
D651.Y8-9	Yugoslavia (post-WWI territorial ?s)	
D652-659	POST-WAR ERA & RECONSTRUCTION (WWI)	940.3144, .34-39
D652	Primary sources, documents, collections (WWI: Reconstruction)	
D653	Reconstruction & post-war era (WWI: gen.)	
D657	United States (WWI: Reconstruction: gen.)	
D658.A-Z	United States (WWI: Reconstruction: by state)	
D658.C2-21	California (WWI: Reconstruction)	
D658.G4-41	Georgia (WWI: Reconstruction)	
D658.M5	Michigan (WWI: Reconstruction)	
D659.A-Z	Reconstruction (WWI: countries outside U.S.)	
D659.F8	France (WWI: Reconstruction)	
D659.G3	Germany (WWI: Reconstruction)	
D659.G7	Great Britain (WWI: Reconstruction)	
D659.I8	Italy (WWI: Reconstruction)	
D663-680	MONUMENTS, MEMORIALS, CELEBRATIONS (WWI)	940.46+
D663	Memorials, monuments, celebrations (WWI: gen.: SEE ALSO D503 for museums & NA9325 for fine arts)	
D665	Celebrations, memorials, monuments (WWI: misc.)	
D670-675	Services, memorials, monuments, celebrations (WWI: U.S.)	
D671	Veteran's or Armistice Day addresses, services (WWI: U.S.)	
D673.A-W	Monuments, memorials, celebrations (WWI: U.S.: by state)	
D675.A-Z	Monuments, memorials, celebrations (WWI: U.S.: by city)	
D675.A74 or .W2	Tomb of the Unknown Soldier (WWI: U.S.: Arlington, Va. or Washington, D.C.)	
D680.A-Z	Monuments, memorials, celebrations (WWI: countries other than U.S.)	
D680.G7	Monuments, memorials, celebrations (WWI: G.B.)	
D720-728	World history (1919-39)	
D726	Civilization, customs, social life (1919-39: sometimes Europe alone)	
D727	Politics & diplomacy (1919-39)	327.0904, .4, 909.822-23, 940.51-52
D731-838	WORLD WAR II (1939-1945)	940.53-940.5499
D739	World War II (collected works)	
D740	Dictionaries & encyclopedias (WWII)	940.5303
D741	CAUSES, AIMS, RESULTS (WWII: gen.)	940.5311, 327+
D742.A-Z	Causes, aims, results (WWII: by country)	940.534-539
D742.C5	China (WWII: causes, aims, results)	
D742.F8	France (WWII: causes, aims, results)	
D742.G3	Germany (WWII: causes, aims, results)	
D742.G7	Great Britain (WWII: causes, aims, results)	
D742.J3	Japan (WWII: causes, aims, results)	
D742.R9	Russia (WWII: causes, aims, results)	
D742.U5-6	United States (WWII: causes, aims, results)	
D743	World War II (gen.)	940.53, .54
D743.3	Maps & atlases (WWII: PREFER G1038)	
D743.42	Historiography (WWII)	

D747	Battlefield guides (WWII: gen.: particular battles at D756.5 etc.)	
D748-754	Diplomacy (WWII)	940.532+, 327.+
D756	MILITARY OPS. (WWII: West: gen.)	
D757	German military ops. (WWII: gen.)	940.5343, .54013, .5413, .5421, 943.086
D759	British military ops. & Great Britain (WWII: gen.)	940.54091, .5341-5342, 942.084
D761	French military ops. & France (WWII: gen.)	940.5344, .540944, 944.0815-0816
D763.I8-82	Italy & Italian military ops. (WWII)	940.40945, .41345, 945.091
D764	Russia & Eastern Front (WWII: gen.)	940.540947, .532247, .5347, .541247, 947.0842
D767.8-82	Australia & Australian military ops. (WWII)	
D769-769.99	United States military ops. & U.S. (WWII)	940.532273, .5373, .540973, .541273, .5428
D770-784	NAVAL & SUBMARINE OPS. (WWII)	940.545
D770	Battle of the Atlantic, freedom of the seas, general naval ops. (WWII)	940.545
D780-784	Submarine & anti-submarine ops. (WWII)	940.5451
D785-792	AIR FORCE OPS. (WWII)	940.544
D803-804	Atrocities, war crimes, trials (WWII)	
D805	Prisons & prisoners (WWII: inclu. internment, extermination, & concentration camps)	940.5472+
D806-807	Medical services, hospitals, Red Cross (WWII)	
D808-809	Relief work, refugees, displaced persons, charities (WWII)	
D810.W7	Women & women's work (WWII)	
D820.T4	Territorial questions (post-WWII: gen.: SEE D821 for specific places)	
D821.A-Z	Territorial questions (post-WWII: by place)	
D825	Reconstruction (WWII: gen.)	940.53144
D830-838	Monuments, memorials, celebrations (WWII: memorials dedicated to special divisions classed with them)	
D921	Description & travel (Europe: 1901-1950)	914.045
DA	GREAT BRITAIN	941-942
DA10-18	British Empire & colonies (SEE ALSO JV1000-1099 for other collective works & D-F for specific colonies)	
DA11	Description & travel (Brit. Empire)	
DA16	British Empire (gen.)	909.824+
DA20-690	England	
DA25	Primary sources, documents (Eng.)	
DA30	England (gen.)	941, 942
DA34	Dictionaries, chronologies, etc. (G.B.)	
DA40	Politics (Eng.: gen.)	
DA42	Politics (Eng.: modern)	
DA45	Diplomacy (G.B.: gen.)	327.41+
DA47	Foreign relns. (G.B.-other countries)	327.410+
DA47.1	Foreign relns. (G.B.-Fr.)	327.41044
DA47.2	Foreign relns. (G.B.-Ger.)	327.41043
DA47.65	Foreign relns. (G.B.-Rus.)	327.41047
DA47.9.A-Z	Foreign relns. (G.B.-misc. countries: SEE E183.8 for U.S.)	

DA50-69.3	Military history (G.B.)	
DA50	British military history (gen.)	355.00941
DA52	Dictionaries, Military (G.B.)	
DA54	Biography, Military (G.B.: collective)	
DA68	Military history (G.B.: 19th c.)	
DA68.32.A-Z	Biography, Military (G.B.: 1850-1900: inclu. memoirs: by name)	
DA68.32.A1	Biography, Military (G.B.: 1850-1900: collective)	
DA68.32.G6	Gordon, Charles Alexander, Sir (G.B.: 19th c. mil. biog.)	
DA68.32.K6	Kitchener, Horatio Herbert K., 1st Earl (G.B.: 19th c. mil. biog.)	
DA68.32.R6	Roberts, Frederick Sleigh Roberts, 1st Earl (G.B.: 19th c. mil. biog.)	
DA68.32.Y8	Ypres, John Denton P. F., 1st Earl of (G.B.: 19th c. mil. biog.)	
DA69	Military history (G.B.: 20th. c.: gen.)	355.00941, .033041, .033241, .033541
DA69.3.A-Z	Biography, Military (G.B.: 20th c.: inclu. memoirs)	355.3310922-24
DA69.3.A1	Biography, Military (G.B.: 20th c.: collective)	
DA69.3.A57	Alexander, Harold Rupert (G.B.: 20th c. mil. biog.)	
DA69.3.A6	Allenby, Edmund Henry H. Allenby, 1st Viscount (G.B.: 20th c. mil. biog.)	
DA69.3.H3	Haig, Douglas Haig, 1st earl (G.B.: 20th c. mil. biog.)	
DA70-89	Naval history (G.B.)	
DA70	British naval history (gen.)	359.00941
DA72	Dictionaries, Naval (G.B.)	
DA74	Biography, Naval (G.B.: collective)	
DA89	Naval history (G.B.: 20th c.)	359.00941, .4741
DA89.1.A-Z	Biography, Naval (G.B.: 20th c.: by name)	
DA89.1.A1	Biography, Naval (G.B.: 20th c.: collective)	
DA89.1.B4	Beatty, David Beatty, 1st Earl (G.B.: 20th c. naval biog.)	
DA89.1.F5	Fisher, John Arbuthnot Fisher, Baron (G.B.: 20th c. naval biog.)	
DA89.1.J4	Jellicoe, John Rushworth Jellicoe, 1st Earl (G.B.: 20th c. naval biog.)	
DA89.5-6	Air force history (G.B.)	
DA89.5	British air force history (gen.)	358.400941
DA89.6.A-Z	Biography, Air force (G.B.: inclu. memoirs)	
DA89.6.A1	Biography, Air force (G.B.: collective)	
DA89.6.J6	Joubert de la Ferté, Philip Bennet, Sir (G.B.: air force biog.)	
DA300	England (1485-)	
DA470	England (1702-)	
DA530	England (19th. c.)	
DA550-565	England (1837-1901: Queen Victoria)	941.08
DA550	Great Britain (1837-1901: gen.)	941.08
DA554	Victoria (G.B.: Queen: 1837-1901)	
DA563	Gladstone (G.B.: 19th c.: Prime Min.)	
DA564.A-Z	Biography (G.B.: 1850-1901: prime ministers besides Gladstone)	
DA564.B3	Disraeli, Benjamin, 1st Earl of Beaconsfield (G.B.: 19th c.: Prime Min.)	
DA565.A-Z	Biography (G.B.: 1837-1901: except prime ministers: inclu. memoirs)	941.0810924
DA565.C4	Chamberlain, Joseph (G.B.: 1837-1901 time period)	
DA565.C6	Churchill, Randolph Henry Spencer, Lord (G.B.: 1837-1901 era)	
DA565.C95	Curzon, George Nathaniel Curzon, 1st Marquis (G.B.: 1837-1901 biog.)	
DA565.L9	Lytton, Edward George E. Lytton Bulwer-Lytton, Baron (G.B.: 1837-1901 time)	

DA566-566.9	England (20th c.: misc. overall)	
DA566	Great Britain (20th c.: gen.)	941.082
DA566.4	Civilization, customs, social life (G.B.: 20th c.)	
DA566.5	Military & naval history (G.B.: 20th c.)	
DA566.7	Foreign relns. & politics (G.B.: 20th c.)	
DA566.8	Satire, caricature (G.B.: 20th c.)	
DA566.9.A-Z	Biography (G.B.: 20th c.: inclu. memoirs)	941.0820922-24
DA566.9.A1	Biography (G.B.: 20th c.: collective)	
DA566.9.B15	Baldwin, Stanley, 1st Earl (G.B.: 20th c.)	
DA566.9.B2	Balfour, Arthur James Balfour, 1st Earl of (G.B.: 20th c.)	
DA566.9.B37	Beaverbrook, William Maxwell Aitken, Baron (G.B.: 20th c.)	
DA566.9.B5	Birkenhead, Frederick E. S., 1st Earl of (G.B.: 20th c.)	
DA566.9.C43	Chamberlain, Austen, Sir (G.B.: 20th c.)	
DA566.9.C5	Churchill, Winston Leonard Spencer, Sir (G.B.: 20th c.)	
DA566.9.G8	Grey, Edward (G.B.: 20th c.)	
DA566.9.L5	Lloyd George, David (G.B.: 20th c.)	
DA566.9.M25	MacDonald, James Ramsay (G.B.: 20th c.)	
DA566.9.N7	Northcliffe, Alfred C. W. Harmsworth, 1st Viscount (G.B.: 20th c.)	
DA566.9.O7	Oxford and Asquith, Herbert Henry Asquith, 1st Earl of (G.B.: 20th c.)	
DA567-570	England (1901-10: King Edward VII)	941.082
DA567	Edward VII (G.B.: King: 1901-1910)	
DA568.A-Z	Biography (G.B.: 1901-10)	
DA570	Great Britain (1901-10: gen.)	
DA573-578	England (1910-36: King George V)	941.083
DA573	George V (G.B.: King: 1910-36)	
DA574.A-Z	Biography (G.B.: 1910-36: inclu. memoirs)	
DA574.A1	Biography (G.B.: 1910-36: collective)	
DA574.A2-45	Biography (G.B.: 1910-36: various royalty)	
DA576	Great Britain (1910-36)	
DA577	Great Britain (1914-19: WWI era)	
DA578	Great Britain (1920-39)	
DA630	Description & travel (G.B.: 1901-45)	914.1-2, 914.10482
DA650	Guidebooks (G.B.)	
DA670.A-Z	Local history (G.B.: counties, regions, etc.: by name)	942+
DA670.C4	Channel Islands (G.B.)	942.34
DA675-689	Local history (London, Eng.)	942.1
DA677	London, Eng. (gen.)	942.1
DA679	Guidebooks (London, Eng.)	914.21
DA684	London, Eng. (1901-50)	942.1082
DA685.A-Z	London, Eng. (boroughs, streets, etc.)	
DA686-687	Buildings (London, Eng.)	
DA687.A-Z	Buildings (London, Eng.: by name)	
DA687.D7	Downing St. (London, Eng.: No. 10)	
DA688	Social life, culture, customs (London, Eng.)	
DA689.A-Z	Scenic places (London, Eng.: bridges, parks, etc.)	
DA689.B8	Bridges (London, Eng.: inclu. London Bridge)	
DA689.M7	Monuments, statues, memorials (London, Eng.)	
DA689.P17	Palaces (London, Eng.)	
DA689.P6	Port of London (Eng.)	
DA690.A-Z	Local history (Eng.: towns besides London)	942.2+
DA690.C75	Coventry, Eng.	

DA722	WALES (19th & 20th c.)	942.908+
DA821	SCOTLAND (20th c.)	941.1082
DA880.A-Z	Local history (Scotland: counties, regions, etc.)	
DA880.O5-6	Orkney Islands (Scot.)	
DA880.S5	Shetland Islands (Scot.)	
DA959	IRELAND (20th c.)	941.5082
DA960	Ireland (1901-22)	
DA962	Ireland (1914-21)	
DA964.A-Z	Diplomacy (Ire.: 20th c.)	
DA964.A2	Foreign relns. (Ire.: 20th c.: gen.)	
DA964.G3	Foreign relns. (Ire.-Ger.: 20th c.)	
DA964.G7	Foreign relns. (Ire.-G.B.: 20th c.)	

DB	AUSTRIA, HUNGARY, CZECHOSLOVAKIA	943.6-9
DB1-860	AUSTRIA	943.6
DB17	Austria & Austro-Hungarian Empire (gen.)	
DB26	Description & travel (Austria: 1901-45)	
DB38	Austria (1801-)	943.604
DB46-49	Politics & diplomacy (Austria)	
DB48	Austrian question (20th c.)	
DB49.A-Z	Foreign relns. (Austria: by other country)	
DB85-90	Austria (1848-1916: Emp. Franz Joseph I)	
DB85	Austria (1848-1916: gen.)	
DB86.7	Austria (1914-18: WWI era)	
DB87	Franz Joseph I (Austria: Emp.: 1848-1916)	
DB89.A-Z	Biography (Austria: misc. royalty)	
DB89.F7	Franz Ferdinand (Austria: Archduke)	
DB89.R8	Rudolf (Austria:1848-1916 era: Crown Prince)	
DB90.A-Z	Biography (Austria: 1848-1916)	
DB91	Austria (20th c.: gen.)	
DB91-99+	Austria (20th c.) 943.605	
DB92	Austria (1916-18: Emp. Karl I: gen.)	
DB96	Austria (1918-: Republic) 943.6051	
DB98.A-Z	Biography (Austria: 20th c.: by name: inclu. memoirs)	
DB191-217	CZECHOSLOVAKIA (PREFER DB2000-3150 for titles cataloged after 1979) 943.7	
DB215	Czechoslovakia (20th c.) 943.7024-703+	
DB250	Bosnia & Bosnia-Herzegovina (20th c.)	
DB280	Bukowina (20th c.)	
DB378.5	Croatia & Slavonia (1848-1918)	
DB420	Dalmatia (20th c.)	
DB500	Galicia (20th c.)	
DB540	Herzegovina (20th c.)	
DB540.5	Liechtenstein (SEE ALSO DB881-898 for newer books)	
DB660	Silesia (20th c.)	
DB678	Slovakia (1800-1918: PREFER DB2000+)	
DB740	Transylvania (1801-1918: SEE DR281.T7 for 1918-)	
DB780	Tyrol & Vorarlberg (20th c.)	
DB847	Vienna, Austria (gen. hist. & descr.)	
DB855	Vienna (20th c.)	

DB861-975+   HUNGARY, Liechtenstein
DB872   Budapest (20th c.)
DB881-898 LIECHTENSTEIN (SEE ALSO DB540.5 for older titles)
DB886, 891 Liechtenstein (gen. hist. & descr.)
DB893   Diplomacy (Liech.: gen.)
DB894.A-Z Foreign relns. (Liech.: by country)
DB894.G3   Foreign relns. (Liech.-Ger.)
DB906   Hungary (gen.)   943.9
DB925   Hungary (gen.: pubn. dates 1801+)
DB926   Diplomacy (Hung.: gen.)
DB926.3.A-Z   Foreign relns. (Hung.-other lands)
DB926.3.G3   Foreign relns. (Hung.-Ger.)
DB926.3.S65   Foreign relns. (Hung.-Sov. Un.)
DB947-957+   Hungary (20th c.)   943.9043+
DB947   Hungary (20th c.: gen.)
DB950.A-Z   Biography (Hung.: 20th c.: by name, inclu. memoirs)
DB950.H6   Horthy, Miklós (Hung.: 20th c.)
DB953   Hungary (1914-1918: WWI era)   943.9043
DB2000-3150+   CZECHOSLOVAKIA (inclu. Bohemia, Moravia, Slovakia: SEE
                                 ALSO DB191-217 for earlier titles)
DB2000-2299   Czechoslovakia   943.7+
DB2011   Czechoslovakia (gen.)
DB2020   Description & travel (Czech.: 1901-45)
DB2062   Czechoslovakia (1801-1976 pubns.)
DB2078.A-Z   Foreign relns. (Czech.: by country)
DB2176   Czechoslovakia (1815-1918: gen.)   943.7024
DB2185-2232+   Czechoslovakia (1918-)
DB2200-2201.A-Z   Biography (Czech.: 1918-39)
DB2415-2421   Moravia (20th c.)
DB2416   Moravia (20th c.: gen.)
DB2629   Prague, Cz. (20th c.)
DB2795-2822+   Slovakia (1800-1945)
DB2796   Slovakia (1800-1918)

DC   FRANCE   944
DC3   Primary sources, documents (Fr.)
DC17   France (gen. hist., culture)
DC28   Description & travel (Fr.: 1871-1945)
DC33.7   Civilization, customs, social life (Fr.: 1901-)
DC38   France (gen. hist.: pubn. 1815-)
DC44-47   Military history (Fr.)
DC45   French military history (gen.)   355.00944, .033044
DC47   Military history (Fr.: 19th-20th c.)
DC49-53   Naval history (Fr.)
DC50   French naval history (gen.)
DC53   Naval history (Fr.: 19th-20th c.)
DC55-59   Politics & diplomacy (Fr.)
DC55   Diplomacy (Fr.: gen.)
DC58   Foreign relns. (Fr.: 19th-20th c.)
DC59.8.A-Z Foreign relns. (Fr.: by country)   327.440+
DC59.8.G3 Foreign relns. (Fr.-Ger.)   327.44043
DC59.8.G7 Foreign relns. (Fr.-G.B.)   327.44041
DC59.8.R9   Foreign relns. (Fr.-Rus.)
DC59.8.S65   Foreign relns. (Fr.-Sov.Un.)

```
DC110          France (1515-)
DC281-326      Franco-Prussian War (1870-71)
DC289          Franco-German War (1870-71: gen.)
DC334-354+        France (1871-1940: 3rd Repub.)
DC334          Primary sources, documents (Fr.: 1871-1940)
DC335          Third Republic (Fr.: 1871-1940)
DC339          Military history (Fr.: 1871-1940)
DC342              Biography (Fr.: 1871-1940: collective)
DC342.8.A-Z        Biography (Fr.: 1871-1940: by name: inclu. memoirs & autobiog.)
DC342.8.C6             Clemenceau, Georges (Fr.: 1871-1940 era)
DC342.8.F6             Foch, Ferdinand (Fr.: 1871-1940 era)
DC342.8.G3             Gambetta, Léon Michel (Fr.: 1871-1940 era)
DC342.8.J6         Joffre, Joseph J. (Fr.: 1871-1940 era)
DC342.8.P4         Pétain, Henri Philippe (Fr.: 1871-1940 era)
DC361-373      France (20th c.: overall)
DC361          France (20th c.: gen.)              944.081
DC365          Civilization, customs, social life (Fr.: 20th c.)
DC367          Military history (Fr.: 20th c.)
DC368          Naval history (Fr.: 20th c.)
DC369          Foreign relns. & politics (Fr.: 20th c.)     944.08
DC371              Biography (Fr.: 20th c.: collective)
DC373.A-Z          Biography (Fr.: 20th c.: by name)
DC373.B7               Briand, Aristide (Fr.: 20th c.)
DC373.L33              Lattre de Tassigny, Jean Joseph (Fr.: 20th c.)
DC373.M3              Maurras, Charles M. (Fr.: 20th c.)
DC380          France (1906-13: time of Clément Fallières)       944.0813
DC385          France (1913-20: era of Pres. Raymond Poincaré)
DC387          France (1914-18: WWI era)          944.0814
DC389-396      France (1919-40: Reconstruc.)
DC601-609+        Local history (Fr.: north, east, Riviera, etc.)
DC611.A-Z         Local history (Fr.: regions, prov.'s, depts., etc.: by name)
DC701-790+        Local history (Paris, Fr.)         944.36
DC707          Description & travel (Paris, Fr.: ALSO gen. hist.)
DC708          Guidebooks (Paris, Fr.)
DC715          Social life, culture, customs (Paris, Fr.)
DC735          Paris, Fr. (1871-1914)
DC736          Paris, Fr. (1914-21)
DC801.A-Z      Local history (Fr.: towns besides Paris)
DC801.B83      Brest, Fr.
DC801.C11      Caen, Fr.
DC801.L96-988  Lyons, Fr.
DC801.V45      Verdun, Fr.
DC801.V55-57   Versailles, Fr. (ALSO Trianon)
DC890          Colonies, French (PREFER D-F for individual colonies or JV1800-1899
                    for collective works)
```

DD	GERMANY & Prussia	943
DD16	Guidebooks (Ger.)	
DD17	Germany (gen. hist., culture, etc.)	
DD41	Description & travel (Ger.: 1871-1918)	
DD67	Civilization, customs, social life (Ger.)	
DD68	German culture (in other lands: gen.)	
DD74	Races & ethnography (Ger.)	
DD76	National characteristics (Ger.)	
DD89	Germany (gen.: pubn. 1801-)	
DD99-105	Military history (Ger.)	
DD100.A2	Biography, Military (Ger.: collective: gen.)	
DD100.A3-Z	Biography, Military (Ger.: collective: officers)	
DD101	German military history (gen.)	355.00943
DD104	Military history (Ger.: 20th c.)	355.00943, .033043, .033242, .033543
DD106	Naval history (Ger.)	359.00943, .4743
DD110-120	Politics & diplomacy (Ger.)	
DD110	Primary sources, documents (Ger.: for. relns. & politics)	
DD112	Diplomacy & politics (Ger.: gen.)	320.943, 327.43+
DD117	Foreign relns. (Ger.: 19th-20th c.)	327.43+
DD119.3	Germans (in other lands: gen.)	
DD119.5	Propaganda, German	
DD120.A-Z	Foreign relns. (Ger.: by country)	327.430+
DD120.F8	Foreign relns. (Ger.-Fr.)	327.43044
DD120.G7	Foreign relns. (Ger.-G.B.)	327.43041
DD120.I6	Foreign relns. (Ger.-Ire.)	
DD120.I8	Foreign relns. (Ger.-It.)	
DD120.J3	Foreign relns. (Ger.-Japan)	327.43052
DD120.R9	Foreign relns. (Ger.-Rus.)	327.43047
DD120.S65	Foreign relns. (Ger.-Sov. Un.)	
DD120.U6-7	Foreign relns. (Ger.-U.S.)	
DD175	Germany (1519-)	
DD217-231	Germany (1871-1918: New Empire)	943.08
DD217	Primary sources, documents (Ger.: 1871-1918)	
DD218	Bismarck, Otto von (inclu. family)	
DD219.A-Z	Biography (Ger.: mostly pre-WWI: by name)	
DD219.M7	Moltke, Helmuth (Ger.: 1871-1918 era)	
DD220	Germany (1871-1918: New Empire: gen.)	
DD221	Foreign relns. & politics (Ger.: 1871-1918)	
DD223	Germany (1871-1888: Kaiser Wilhelm I era)	
DD228-231	Germany (1888-1918: Kaiser Wilhelm II era)	943.084
DD228	Germany (1888-1918: Kaiser Wilhelm II era: gen.)	
DD228.3	Civilization, customs, social life (Ger.: 1888-1918)	
DD228.5	Politics (Ger.: 1888-1918)	
DD228.6	Diplomacy (Ger.: 1888-1918: gen.)	327.43+
DD228.7.A-Z	Foreign relns. (Ger.:1888-1918: by country)	
DD228.7.F8	Foreign relns. (Ger.-Fr.: 1888-1918)	
DD228.7.G7	Foreign relns. (Ger.-G.B.: 1888-1918)	
DD228.7.R8-9	Foreign relns. (Ger.-Rus.: 1888-1918)	
DD228.7.U6-7	Foreign relns. (Ger.-U.S.: 1888-1918)	
DD228.8	Germany (1914-1918: WWI period)	943.08
DD228.9	Wilhelm II (Ger.: Kaiser, 1888-1918: abdication & flight)	
DD229	Wilhelm II (Ger.: Kaiser, 1888-1918: biog. inclu. family)	

DD231.A-Z	Biography (Ger.: 1888-1918+: by name)
DD231.A2	Biography (Ger.: 1888-1918+: collective)
DD231.H5	Hindenburg, Paul von (Ger.: 1888-1918+ period)
DD231.L8	Ludendorff, Erich (Ger.: 1888-1918+ period)
DD231.R3	Rathenau, Walther (Ger.: 1888-1918+ period)
DD231.S83	Stresemann, Gustav (Ger.: 1888-1918+ period)
DD231.T5	Tirpitz, Alfred von (Ger.: 1888-1918+ period)
DD232	Germany (20th c.: gen.)
DD233-251+	Germany (1918-: revolution & Republic) 943.085
DD237	Germany (1918-: revolution & Republic: gen.)
DD240-241	Diplomacy & politics (Ger.: 1918-)
DD241.A-Z	Foreign relns. (Ger.: 1918-: by country)
DD241.A9	Foreign relns. (Ger.-Austria: 1918-)
DD241.B4	Foreign relns. (Ger.-Bel.: 1918-)
DD241.F8	Foreign relns. (Ger.-Fr.: 1918-)
DD241.G7	Foreign relns. (Ger.-G.B.: 1918-)
DD241.I6	Foreign relns. (Ger.-Ire.: 1918-)
DD241.I8	Foreign relns. (Ger.-It.: 1918-)
DD241.J3	Foreign relns. (Ger.-Japan: 1918-)
DD241.P7	Foreign relns. (Ger.-Pol.: 1918-)
DD241.R9	Foreign relns. (Ger.-Rus.: 1918-)
DD241.U6-69+	Foreign relns. (Ger.-U.S.: 1918-)
DD247.A-Z	Biography (Ger.: 1918-48: inclu. memoirs: by name)
DD248	Germany (1918: Revolution)
DD249	Germany (1919-25: Ebert period)
DD251	Germany (1925-34: Hindenburg era) 943.085
DD252-256	Germany (1930-45, 1933-45: eras of Hitler & National Socialism)
	943.086
DD448	Prussia (1871-1918: gen.)
DD452-454	Prussia (1918-45)
DD491.A-Z	Local history (Prus.: provinces, regions, etc.)
DD491.R4-52	Rhine Province (Prus.)
DD491.S3-39	Saxony (Prus.)
DD491.W4-52	Westphalia (Prus.)
DD701-800	Local history (Ger.: large areas)
DD791-800	German Austria & Bavaria
DD801.A-Z	Local history (Ger.: provinces, regions, states, etc.)
DD801.A31-69	Alsace-Lorraine (Ger.)
DD801.B31-55	Bavaria 943.3
DD801.B422	Bavaria (1939-45)
DD801.R7-76	Rhine River (Ger.) 943.4
DD851-900	Berlin, Ger.
DD859	Guidebooks (Berlin, Ger.)
DD860	Berlin, Ger. (gen.) 943.155
DD866	Social life, culture, customs (Berlin, Ger.)
DD879	Berlin, Ger. (1914-21)
DD883	Berlin, Ger. (districts, sections)
DD887	Streets, bridges, etc. (Berlin, Ger.)
DD896	Buildings, Public (Berlin, Ger.)
DD901.A-Z	Local history (Ger.: areas, towns except Berlin)
DD901.A25-28	Aachen, Ger. (Aix-la-Chapelle)
DD901.B65	Brandenburg, Ger.
DD901.B71-79	Bremen, Ger.
DD901.D2-29	Danzig
DD901.D28	Danzig (19th-20th c.)

DD901.D71-79	Dresden, Ger.	
DD901.D95	Düsseldorf, Ger.	
DD901.E75	Essen, Ger.	
DD901.F71-79	Frankfurt, Ger.	
DD901.H55-59	Heidelberg, Ger.	
DD901.M71-95	Munich, Ger.	
DD901.M77	Munich, Ger. (gen.)	
DD901.M9	Munich, Ger. (1871-1950)	
DD901.S95-97	Stuttgart, Ger.	
DD905	Colonies, German (PREFER D-F #s for specific colonies or JV2000-2099 for collective titles)	

DF	Greece	949.5
DF701-951+	GREECE (Modern)	
DF751	Greece (gen.)	949.5
DF765	Military history (Greece)	
DF775	Naval history (Greece)	
DF785	Diplomacy (Greece: gen.)	
DF787.A-Z	Foreign relns. (Greece: by country)	
DF787.G3	Foreign relns. (Greece-Ger.)	
DF787.G7	Foreign relns. (Greece-G.B.)	
DF787.I8	Foreign relns. (Greece-It.)	
DF833	Greece (20th c.: gen.)	949.507
DF836.A-Z	Biography (Greece: 20th c.)	
DF838	Greece (1914-18: WWI)	949.506

DG	ITALY, Sicily, Sardinia, Malta	945
DG48-84	Military history (It.)	
DG401-579	Italy (476-)	
DG403	Primary sources, documents (It.)	
DG417	Italy (gen. hist., culture, etc.)	
DG428	Description & travel (It.: 1901-18)	914.5009
DG450	Civilization, customs, social life (It.: 1816-1945)	
DG467	Italy (gen.: titles dated after 1800)	
DG481	Biography, Military (It.: collective)	
DG482	Italian military history (gen.)	355.00945
DG484	Military history (It.: 1792-20th c.)	
DG486	Naval history (It.: gen.)	359.00945
DG491-499	Diplomacy & politics (It.)	
DG491	Politics & diplomacy (It.: gen.)	320.945, 327.45+
DG498	Foreign relns. (It.: 1861-1945)	
DG499.A-Z	Foreign relns. (It.: by country)	327.450+
DG499.E7	Foreign relns. (It.-Eth.)	
DG499.F8	Foreign relns. (It.-Fr.)	
DG499.G3	Foreign relns. (It.-Ger.)	
DG499.G7	Foreign relns. (It.-G.B.)	
DG499.R9	Foreign relns. (It.-Rus.)	
DG499.S65	Foreign relns. (It.-Sov.Un.)	
DG499.U6-7	Foreign relns. (It.-U.S.)	
DG499.Y8	Foreign relns. (It.-Yug.)	

DG555-575	Italy (1871-1947: United Italy: Monarchy)	
DG555	Italy (1871-1947: gen.)	945.09
DG556.A-Z	Biography (It.: 1871-1941)	
DG556.S6	Spaventa, Silvio (It.: 1871-1945 era)	
DG566-575	Italy (1900-46: times of Vittorio Emanuele III, Umberto II)	
DG566	Vittorio Emanuele III (It.: King, 1900-46: gen. inclu. times)	
DG570	Italy (1914-18: WWI)	945.0814
DG571	Italy (1919-45: Fascism)	945.0815-0816
DG574	Biography (It.: 1871-1947: collec.)	
DG575.A-Z	Biography (It.: 1900-46: by name, inclu. memoirs)	
DG575.B2	Badoglio, Pietro (It.: 1900-46 period)	
DG575.N5	Nitti, Francesco (It. 1900-46 period)	
DG600-980	Local history (It.: large areas, cities)	
DG651-662	Lombardy & Milan, It.	
DG670-679	Venice, It. (city state & modern)	
DG731-760	Tuscany & Florence, It.	
DG791-800+	PAPAL STATES	
DG799	Holy SEE (1870-)	
DG803-818	Rome, It. (modern era)	
DG806	Description (Rome, It.: 1861-1950)	
DG808	Rome, It. (476-: gen.)	
DG812	Rome, It. (1527-)	
DG813	Rome, It. (1871-)	
DG869	SICILY (20th c.)	
DG975.A-Z	Local history (It.: non-metro. towns, provinces, etc.)	
DH-DJ	Low Countries	
DH39	Description & travel (Bel. & Holl.: 1901-50)	
DH401-925	Belgium & Luxembourg	
DH418-811+	BELGIUM 949.3	
DH433	Description & travel (Bel.: 1831-1945)	
DH540	Military history (Bel.: gen.)	
DH545	Military history (Bel.: 1815-)	
DH566	Diplomacy & politics (Bel.: gen.)	
DH569.A-Z	Foreign relns. (Bel.: by country)	
DH569.F8	Foreign relns. (Bel.-Fr.)	
DH569.G3	Foreign relns. (Bel.-Ger.)	
DH677	Belgium (20th c.)	949.304
DH681	Belgium (1909-34: King Albert)	949.3041
DH682	Belgium (1914-18: WWI)	
DH685.A-Z	Biography (Bel.: 1909-34)	
DH801.A-Z	Local history (Bel.: provinces, regions, etc.)	
DH801.A6-69	Antwerp area (Bel.)	
DH801.F4-49	Flanders area (Bel.)	
DH801.N2-29	Namur area (Bel.)	
DH801.S6	Soignes Forest (Bel.)	
DH802-809	Brussels, Bel.	
DH807.5	Brussels, Bel. (20th c.)	
DH811.A-Z	Local history (Bel.: towns except Brussels)	
DH811.A55-68	Antwerp, Bel.	
DH811.L5	Li`ege, Bel.	

DH901-925	LUXEMBURG
DH905	Luxemburg (gen. hist., culture, etc.)
DH906	Description & travel (Lux.: to 1945)
DH908	Luxemburg (gen.) 949.35
DH908.5	Diplomacy & politics (Lux.)
DH908.6.A-Z	Foreign relns. (Lux.: by country)
DH908.6.G3	Foreign relns. (Lux.-Ger.)
DH916	Luxemburg (1815-)
DJ	NETHERLANDS (HOLLAND) 949.2
DJ39	Description & travel (Neth.: 1901-45)
DJ124	Military history (Neth.)
DJ142	Politics & diplomacy (Neth.: gen.)
DJ147	Diplomacy & politics (Neth.: 1795-20th c.)
DJ149.A-Z	Foreign relns. (Neth.: by country)
DJ149.G3	Foreign relns. (Neth.-Ger.)
DJ281-287	Holland (1890-1948: Queen Wilhelmina)
DJ281	Netherlands (1890-1948: gen. & biogs. of Queen Wilhelmina) 949.2071
DJ283.A-Z	Biography (Neth.: by name)
DJ285	Netherlands (1914-18: WWI) 949.2071
DJ401.A-Z	Local history (Neth.: islands, provinces, regions, etc.)
DJ411.A-Z	Local history (Neth.: towns, cities, etc.)
DJ411.A5-59	Amsterdam, Neth.
DJ500	Colonies, Dutch (PREFER D-F #s for indiv. colonies or JV2500-2599 for collective)
DJK	EASTERN EUROPE (gen.: pubns. after about 1977-78: SEE DR for earlier & for specific countries)
DJK17	Description & travel (Eastern Europe: 1901-50)
DJK38	Europe, Eastern (gen.)
DJK41	Primary sources, documents (Eastern Europe: politics)
DJK42	Politics (Eastern Europe: gen.)
DJK43-44	Foreign relns. (Eastern Europe)
DJK48	Eastern Europe (1815-1918)
DJK49	Eastern Europe (1918-45)
DJK61-66	Black Sea region
DJK71-75	Carpathian Mts. region
DJK76	Danube River Valley (gen.)
DK	Russia, Poland, Finland, Soviet Asia
DK1-275+	RUSSIA 947
DK3	Primary sources, documents (Rus.)
DK17	Russia (gen.)
DK27	Description & travel (Rus.: 1901-44) 914.70904
DK32	Civilization, customs, social life (Rus.: gen.)
DK33	Races & ethnography (Rus.)
DK36	Dictionaries, chronologies, etc. (Rus.)
DK50-54	Russian military history
DK50.5-8	Biography, Military (Rus.: collective)
DK53	Military history (Rus.: 1801-1917) 355.00947
DK54	Military history (Rus.: 1917-) 355.00947, .033+
DK58	Russian naval history (1801-1917)
DK59	Naval history (Rus.: 1917-) 359.00947

DK60-63	Politics & diplomacy (Rus.)	
DK60	Primary sources, documents (Rus.: politics & diplomacy)	
DK61	Politics & diplomacy (Rus.: gen.)	320.947
DK63	Politics & diplomacy (Rus.: 1894-1939)	
DK65-69	Diplomacy (Rus.)	
DK65	Primary sources, documents (Rus.: for. relns.)	
DK66	Foreign relns. (Rus.: gen.)	327.47
DK67-69	Foreign relns. (Rus.: particular areas)	327.470+
DK67	Foreign relns. (Rus.-Europe)	
DK67.3	Foreign relns. (Rus.-Cath. Church)	
DK67.4	Foreign relns. (Rus.-Balkan Penin.)	
DK67.5.A-Z	Foreign relns. (Rus.-specific Eur. countries)	
DK67.5.B8	Foreign relns. (Rus.-Bulg.)	
DK67.5.C95	Foreign relns. (Rus.-Czech.)	
DK67.5.F5	Foreign relns. (Rus.-Fin.)	
DK67.5.F8	Foreign relns. (Rus.-Fr.)	
DK67.5.G3	Foreign relns. (Rus.-Ger.)	
DK67.5.G7	Foreign relns. (Rus.-G.B.)	
DK67.5.G8	Foreign relns. (Rus.-Greece)	
DK67.5.H9	Foreign relns. (Rus.-Hung.)	
DK67.5.I8	Foreign relns. (Rus.-It.)	
DK67.5.P7	Foreign relns. (Rus.-Pol.)	
DK67.5.R8	Foreign relns. (Rus.-Rum.)	
DK67.5.S8	Foreign relns. (Rus.-Swe.)	
DK67.5.Y8	Foreign relns. (Rus.-Yug.)	
DK68.A3-Z	Foreign relns. (Rus.-Asia: gen.: pubns. 1801-)	
DK68.7.A-Z	Foreign relns. (Rus.-particular Asian countries)	
DK68.7.C5	Foreign relns. (Rus.-China)	327.47051
DK68.7.I55	Foreign relns. (Rus.-Iran)	
DK68.7.J3	Foreign relns. (Rus.-Japan)	327.47052
DK68.7.T8	Foreign relns. (Rus.-Tur.)	
DK69	Foreign relns. (Rus.-U.S.: PREFER E183.8.R9)	327.47073
DK69.3.A-Z	Foreign relns. (Rus. & non-U.S. Am. countries)	
DK234-243	Russia (1881-94: Czar Alexander III)	
DK235-236.A-Z	Biography (Rus.: 1881-94)	
DK240	Russia (1881-94: gen.)	
DK246	Russia (20th c.: gen.)	947.084
DK251-264	Russia (1894-1917: Czar Nicholas II)	
DK251	Primary sources, documents (Rus.: 1894-1917)	
DK253	Biography (Rus.: 1894-1917: collective)	
DK254.A-Z	Biography (Rus.: 1894-1917: by name, inclu. memoirs)	
DK254.L3-46	Lenin, Vladimir Ilich (Rus.: 1894-1917 : biog. & works)	
DK254.L3.A2-219	Lenin, Vladimir Ilich (Rus.: 1894-1917: collected works by)	
DK254.L3.A25-259	Lenin, Vladimir Ilich (Rus.: 1894-1917: selected works by)	
DK254.L4-46	Lenin, Vladimir Ilich (Rus.: 1894-1917: biogs.)	
DK254.R3	Rasputin, Grigory (Rus.: 1894-1917: biog.)	
DK254.T6	Trotsky, Leon (Rus.: 1894-1917: biog.)	
DK258-260	Russia (1894-1917)	947.083
DK258	Nicholas II (Rus.: Czar, 1894-1917)	
DK262	Russia (1904-17: empire status)	

```
DK263-264.3    Russian Revolution (1905-6)
DK263         Russia (1905-6: Revolution: gen.)
DK264         Russian Revolution (1905-6: special events)
DK264.1905     Treaties (Rus. Rev., 1905-6: Björkö)
DK264.2.A-Z    Local history (Rus. Rev., 1905-6: by place)
DK264.3        Russian Revolution (1905-6: reaction)
DK264.8        Russia (1914-18: WWI era)        947.083
DK265-265.9+   Russian Revolution (1917-21)
DK265.A56-Z    Russian Revolution (1917-21: gen.)
DK265.2        Russian military ops. (Rev., 1917-21)
DK265.3        Russian naval ops. (Rev., 1917-21)
DK265.4        Russian Revolution (1917-21: Allied intervention, 1918-20)
DK265.42.A-Z   Allied intervention (Rus. Rev.: by country)
DK265.8.A-Z    Local history (Rus. Rev., 1917-21: by place)
DK265.8.L195   Leningrad, Rus. (Rev., 1917-21)
DK265.8.M6     Moscow, Rus. (Rev., 1917-21)
DK265.8.S5     Siberia (Rev., 1917-21)
DK265.8.S63    Central Asia (Rus, Rev., 1917-21)
DK265.8.U4     Ukraine (Rev., 1917-21)
DK265.9.A-Z    Russian Revolution (1917-21: special topics)
DK265.9.A5       Anarchists (Rus. Rev., 1917-21)
DK265.9.A6       Politics (Rus. armed forces, 1917-21)
DK265.9.C62      Cossacks (Rus. Rev., 1917-21)
DK265.9.E2     Economic aspects (Rus. Rev., 1917-21)
DK265.9.F5     Russian Revolution (1917-21: foreign particip.: gen.)
DK265.9.F52.A-Z   Foreign participation (Rus. Rev., 1917-21: by country)
DK265.9.K73      Red Guard (Rus. Rev., 1917-21: Krasnaia Gvardiia)
DK265.9.S4       Spies, secret service, etc. (Rus. Rev., 1917-21)
DK265.9.S6       Soviets (Rus. Rev., 1917-21: councils)
DK265.9.W57    Women (Rus. Rev., 1917-21)
DK266         Soviet Union (1918-)  947.084
DK266.3        Soviet Union (1918-: special inclu. espionage, sabotage)
DK266.5        Soviet Union (1918-24: Lenin era)        947.0841
DK267-273     Soviet Union (1925-53: Stalin regime)
DK401-441+     POLAND (SEE ALSO DK4010-4800 for newer titles from perhaps
                       1976 on)        943.8
DK402         Primary sources, documents (Pol.)
DK404         Poland (gen. history, culture, etc.)
DK407         Description & travel (Pol.: 1867-1945)
DK411         Civilization, customs, social life (Pol.)
DK414.A3-Z    Poland (gen.: pubns. 1801+)
DK417         Military history (Pol.: SEE ALSO DK4170+ for newer titles)
DK417.7          Naval history (Pol.)
DK418         Diplomacy & politics (Pol.)
DK418.5.A-Z    Foreign relns. (Pol.: by country)
DK418.5.F8     Foreign relns. (Pol.-Fr.)
DK418.5.G3     Foreign relns. (Pol.-Ger.)
DK418.5.G7     Foreign relns. (Pol.-G.B.)
DK418.5.R9     Foreign relns. (Pol.-Rus.)
DK418.5.A-Z       Foreign relns. (Pol.: by country)
DK418.5.F8     Foreign relns. (Pol.-Fr.)
DK418.5.G3     Foreign relns. (Pol.-Ger.)
DK418.5.G7     Foreign relns. (Pol.-G.B.)
DK418.5.R9     Foreign relns. (Pol.-Rus.)
```

DK434.9   Poland (1795-1918)   943.803
DK436.4   Poland (1832-1914: gen.)
DK436.5.A-Z   Biography (Pol.: 1832-1914: by name)
DK438   Poland (1867-1914)   943.803
DK439   Poland (1914-18: WWI)   943.803
DK440   Poland (1918-: Republic: inclu. wars of 1918-21)   943.804
DK440.5.A-Z   Biography (Pol.: 1918-: inclu. memoirs)
DK440.5.P5   Pilsudski, Joseph (Pol.: 1918+ biog.)
DK440.3   Treaties (Pol., 1921: Riga)
DK445-465   FINLAND (PREFER DL1002-1180+ for pubns. from around 1970 on)
                                                          948.97
DK459   Finland (20th c.: inclu. Revolution, 1917-18)   948.9703
DK459.3   Treaties (Fin.: 1918)
DK461.A-Z   Biography (Fin.: 20th c.)
DK501-973+   Local history (Russia)
DK501   Russia, Northern
DK502.3-505 Baltic States
DK502.7   Baltic States (gen.)
DK503   Russia, Eastern & Estonia (SEE DK511.E4 for earlier pubns. on
                       Estonia)   947.41
DK503.73   ESTONIA (1800-1918)   947.41
DK504   LATVIA (SEE DK511.L15 for earlier pubns.)   947.43
DK504.73   Latvia (1800-1918)
DK505   LITHUANIA (SEE DK511.L2 for earlier pubns.)   947.5
DK505.73   Lithuania (1800-1918)
DK507   White Russia (Western Russia)
DK508-508.9+   UKRAINE
DK508.54   Military history (Ukr.)
DK508.55   Cossacks (Ukr.)
DK508.554   Politics (Ukr.: gen.)
DK508.56   Diplomacy (Ukr.: gen.)
DK508.57   Foreign relns. (Ukr.: by country)
DK508.772   Ukraine (1775-1917: gen.)
DK508.79-835   Ukraine (1917-44)
DK508.9.A-Z   Local history (Ukraine: regions, oblasts, etc.)
DK508.9.C37   Carpathian Mts. (Uk.)
DK508.9.D64   Dnepropetrovsk (Uk.)
DK508.92-939   Kiev (Uk.)
DK508.95.A-Z   Local history (Ukraine: towns etc.)
DK508.95.I24   Yalta, Uk. (Jalta)
DK508.95.K54   Kiev, Uk. (Kyiv)
DK508.95.O33   Odessa, Uk.
DK508.95.S49   Sevastopol, Uk.
DK509   Russia, Southern (Black Sea, Caucasus, Armenia, etc.)
DK510   Russian S.F.S.R. (Russia)
DK510.7-72   Russian S.F.S.R. (1917-45)
DK511.A-Z   Local history (Eur. Russia, Poland: provinces, governments,
                       regions, etc.)
DK511.A5   Archangel (Rus.)
DK511.B2   Baku (Rus.)
DK511.C1-35   Caucasus area (Rus.)
DK511.C7   Crimea (Rus.)   947.717
DK511.D7   Don River Valley (Rus.)

DK511.E4-8	ESTONIA (SEE DK503 for later pubns.)	947.41
DK511.G3-47	Georgia (Rus.: SEE DK670 for later pubns.)	
DK511.L15-18	LATVIA (SEE DK504 for later pubns.)	947.43
DK511.L178	Latvia (1914-18: WWI)	
DK511.L195	Leningrad area (Rus.)	
DK511.L2-28	LITHUANIA (SEE DK505 for later pubns.)	947.5
DK511.L26	Lithuania (1914-19)	
DK511.M6	Moscow area (Rus.)	
DK511.U7	Ural Mts. (Rus.)	947.87
DK511.V65	Volga River Valley (Rus.)	
DK511.W5	White Russia (Belorussia)	947.65
DK541-579	Leningrad, U.S.S.R.	947.45
DK561	St. Petersburg, Rus. (gen.)	
DK568	Petrograd, Rus. (1801-)	
DK591-609	Moscow, Rus.	947.31
DK600	Social life, culture, customs (Moscow, Rus.)	
DK601	Moscow, Rus. (to 1950)	
DK651.A-Z	Local history (Rus.: towns other than Moscow in Eur., Pol. areas)	
DK651.K37	Kiev, Rus.	
DK651.M5	Minsk, Rus.	
DK651.O2	Odessa, Rus.	
DK651.R5	Riga, Rus.	
DK651.R7	Rostov, Rus.	
DK651.S45	Sevastopol, Rus.	
DK651.S65	Smolensk, Rus.	
DK651.S7	Stalingrad, Rus.	947.4785
DK651.T28	Tallinn, Rus. (Reval)	
DK651.W2	Warsaw, Pol.	
DK651.Y25	Yalta, Rus.	
DK670-679	GEORGIA (Rus.: SEE DK511.G3 for earlier pubns.)	
DK676.5-6	Politics (Georgian S. S. R.: gen.)	
DK677.4-6	Georgian S. S. R. (1801-1921)	
DK680-689	ARMENIA (SEE ALSO DK509 for some gen. works, DS161-199 for earlier titles)	
DK689	Local history (Armenian S. S. R.)	
DK690-699	Azerbaijan S. S. R.	
DK699.2-39	Baku, Rus.	
DK750-973+	Russian Asia	957-958
DK750	Asia, Russian	
DK751-781	Siberia	957
DK753	Siberia (gen. hist., exploration, culture, etc.)	957
DK755	Description & travel (Siberia: 1801-1945)	
DK761	Siberia (gen.)	
DK766	Siberia (19th-20th c.)	957.08
DK771.A-Z	Local history (Siberia: provinces, regions, etc.)	
DK771.B3	Lake Baikal (Sib.)	
DK771.K2	Kamchatka (Sib.)	
DK771.S2	Sakhalin (Siberia)	
DK771.T8	Transbaikalia (Sib.)	
DK781.A-Z	Local history (Siberia: towns etc.)	
DK781.V5	Vladivostok, Rus.	
DK845-973	Asia, Soviet Central	958
DK858	Russian Central Asia (to 1920)	

DK4010-4800	POLAND (SEE ALSO DK401-441 for older titles prior to 1976-77)	
		943.8
DK4040	Poland (gen.)	
DK4070	Description & travel (Pol.: 1867-1944)	
DK4110	Social life, culture, customs (Pol.)	
DK4120	Races & ethnography (Pol.: gen.)	
DK4121.5.A-Z	Races & ethnography (Pol.: by specific element)	
DK4121.5.C9	Czechs (in Pol.)	
DK4121.5.G4	Germans (in Pol.)	
DK4121.5.T3	Tatars (in Pol.)	
DK4121.5.U4	Ukrainians (in Pol.)	
DK4121.5.W5	White Russians (in Pol.)	
DK4122	Poles (in other lands)	
DK4140	Poland (gen.: pubn. dates 1801+)	
DK4170-4178	Military history (Pol.)	
DK4170	Polish military history (gen.: SEE ALSO DK417 for older works)	
DK4173	Military history (Pol.: 1795-1918)	
DK4177-4178	Naval history (Pol.)	
DK4178.5-4185	Diplomacy & politics (Pol.)	
DK4179	Politics (Pol.)	
DK4180	Foreign relns. (Pol.: gen.)	
DK4182	Polish question	
DK4185.A-Z	Foreign relns. (Pol.: with particular countries)	
DK4185.F8	Foreign relns. (Pol.-Fr.)	
DK4185.G3	Foreign relns. (Pol.-Ger.)	
DK4185.R9	Foreign relns. (Pol.-Rus.)	
DK4349-4395	Poland (1795-1918)	
DK4349	Poland (1795-1918: gen.)	943.803
DK4380	Poland (1864-1918)	943.803
DK4382	Poland (20th c.)	
DK4383-4389	Poland (Revolution of 1905)	
DK4385	Poland (Revolution of 1905: gen.)	
DK4390	Poland (1914-18: WWI)	943.803
DK4392	Poland (1915-18: Austrian occupation)	
DK4397	Primary sources, documents (Pol.: 1918-45)	
DK4397-4420	Poland (1918-45)	943.804
DK4419	Biography (Pol.: 1918-45: collec.)	
DK4420.A-Z	Biography (Pol.: 1918-45: by name, inclu. memoirs)	
DK4420.P3	Paderewski, Ignacy Jan (Pol.: 1918-45 era)	
DK4420.P5	Pilsudski, Jozef (Pol.: 1918-45 time)	
DK4600-4800	Local history (Pol.)	
DK4600.A-Z	Local history (Pol.: provinces)	
DK4600.G34	Galicia (Pol.)	
DK4600.P67	Pomerania (Pol.)	
DK4600.P77	Prussia, East (Pol.)	
DK4600.V5	Vistula River & Valley (Pol.: Wisla)	
DK4610-4645	Warsaw, Pol.	
DK4630	Warsaw, Pol. (gen.)	
DK4632	Warsaw, Pol. (1795-1918)	
DK4650-4685	Danzig, Pol. (Gdansk)	
DK4670	Gdansk, Pol. (Danzig: gen.)	
DK4672	Danzig, Pol. (1793-1919)	
DK4700-4735	Krakow, Pol. (Cracow)	

DL	SCANDINAVIA, Northern Europe, Finland	
DL1-87+	Europe, Northern (plus Scandinavia and Finland)	
DL10	Description & travel (Scan., N. Eur., Fin.: 1901-50)	
DL55	Foreign relns. & politics (Scan., N. Eur., Fin.: gen.)	
DL83	Northern Europe, Scandinavia, Finland (1901-45)	948.08
DL101-291+	DENMARK	
DL109	Denmark (gen.) 948.9	
DL118	Description & travel (Den.: 1901-50)	
DL159	Diplomacy (Den.: gen.)	
DL159.5.A-Z	Foreign relns. (Den.-other lands)	
DL250	Denmark (20th c.) 948.905	
DL255-257	Denmark (1912-47: time of Christian X) 948.9051	
DL255	Christian X (Den.: 1912-47 period: ALSO gen. histories of time)	
DL256	Denmark (1914-18: WWI)	
DL271.A-Z	Local history (Den.: counties, islands, regions)	
DL276	Copenhagen, Den.	
DL301-398+	ICELAND 949.12	
DL401-596+	NORWAY 948.1	
DL458	Diplomacy & politics (Nor.: gen.)	
DL459.A-Z	Foreign relns. (Nor.-other specific countries) 327.4810+	
DL527	Norway (20th c.) 948.104	
DL529.A-Z	Biography (Nor.: 20th c.)	
DL530-533	Norway (1905-57: Haakon VII era) 948.1041-1045	
DL531	Norway (1914-18)	
DL581	Oslo, Nor. (Christiana) 948.2	
DL601-991+	SWEDEN 948.5	
DL658-659	Diplomacy & politics (Swe.)	
DL658.A3-Z	Politics & diplomacy (Swe.: gen.) 320.9485, 327.485	
DL658.8	Foreign relns. (Swe.: 1818-20th c.)	
DL659.A-Z	Foreign relns. (Swe.-other lands: by name) 327.485+	
DL659.F5	Foreign relns. (Swe.-Fin.)	
DL659.G3	Foreign relns. (Swe.-Ger.)	
DL659.G7	Foreign relns. (Swe.-G.B.)	
DL659.R9	Foreign relns. (Swe.-Rus.)	
DL659.S65	Foreign relns. (Swe.-Sov. Un.)	
DL659.U6-7	Foreign relns. (Swe.-U.S.)	
DL860	Sweden (20th c.) 948.505	
DL867	Gustav V (Swe.: King, 1907-50)	
DL867-870	Sweden (1907-50: Gustav V)	
DL867.5	Diplomacy & politics (Swe.: 1907-50) 948.5051-2	
DL868	Sweden (1914-18: WWI era)	
DL870.A-Z	Biography (Swe.: 1907-50: by name)	
DL976	Stockholm, Swe.	
DL1002-1180+	FINLAND (PREFER this but ALSO SEE DK445-465 for pre-1970 pubns. in some libs.) 948.97	
DL1005	Primary sources, documents (Fin.)	
DL1015.2	Description & travel (Fin.: 1901-44)	
DL1032	Finland (gen.) 948.97	
DL1036-1037	Military history (Fin.) 355.0094897	
DL1040-1042	Naval history (Fin.)	
DL1046	Diplomacy (Fin.: gen.) 327.4897	
DL1048.A-Z	Foreign relns. (Fin. & other partic. lands)	
DL1048.G3	Foreign relns. (Fin.-Ger.)	
DL1048.R9	Foreign relns. (Fin.-Rus.)	
DL1048.S65	Foreign relns. (Fin.-Sov. Un.)	

```
DL1065      Finland (1809-1917: Russian control)    948.9702
DL1066      Primary sources, documents (Fin.: 20th c.)
DL1066.5    Finland (20th c.)            948.9703
DL1084      Finland (1918-39)           948.97031
DL1088-1088.5  Biography (Fin.: 1918-39)
DL1170.A-Z  Local history (Fin.: regions, provinces, etc.)
DL1175      Helsinki, Fin.              948.971
DL1175.42   Helsinki, Fin. (gen.)
DL1175.48   Helsinki, Fin. (1917-)
DL1180.A-Z  Local history (Fin.: towns except Helsinki)


DP          Iberian Peninsula    946
DP1-402+    SPAIN       946
DP42        Description & travel (Sp.: 1901-50)
DP83-86         Diplomacy & politics (Sp.)
DP84        Politics & diplomacy (Sp.)
DP85.8      Diplomacy (Sp.: 1814-20th c.)
DP86.A-Z    Foreign relns. (Sp.: with partic. countries)     327.460+
DP233       Spain (1886-20th c.: gen.)       946.08
DP234-247   Spain (1886-1931: period of Alfonso XIII)
DP235-236   Biography (Sp.: 1886-1931)
DP238       Alfonso XIII (Sp.: King, 1886-1931)
DP240       Spain (1886-1931: gen.)
DP246       Spain (1914-18: WWI)
DP302.G31-41    GIBRALTAR
DP361           Madrid, Sp. (1801-1950)
DP501-900+      PORTUGAL  946.9
DP556       Politics & diplomacy (Port.: gen.)
DP672       Portugal (20th c.: gen.)     946.904
DP675       Portugal (1910-: Republic)      946.904
DP676.A-Z   Biography (Port.: 1910-)
DP677       Portugal (1914-18: WWI)  946.9041
DP802.A-Z   Colonies, Portuguese (SEE ALSO D-F for indiv. places & JV4200-4299
                for collective)


DQ          SWITZERLAND      949.4
DQ24        Description & travel (Swit.: 1901-50)
DQ59            Military history (Swit.)
DQ68-76         Diplomacy & politics (Swit.)    320.9494, 327.4940+
DQ68            Primary sources, documents (Swit.: dipl. & polit. hist.)
DQ69            Politics & diplomacy (Swit.: gen.)
DQ75        Diplomacy & politics (Swit.: 1798-20th c.)
DQ76.A-Z    Foreign relns. (Swit.-specific countries)     327.4940+
DQ76.F8     Foreign relns. (Swit.-Fr.)
DQ76.G3     Foreign relns. (Swit.-Ger.)     327.494043
DQ76.G7     Foreign relns. (Swit.-G.B.)
DQ76.I8         Foreign relns. (Swit.-It.)    327.494045
DQ76.R9         Foreign relns. (Swit.-Rus.)
DQ76.U6-7       Foreign relns. (Swit.-U.S.)     327.494073
DQ201       Switzerland (20th c.)       949.407
DQ206-207   Biography (Swit.: 20th c.)
```

DQ301-800	Local history (Swit.: cantons, cantonal capitals)
DQ401-420	Bern, Swit. 949.45
DQ441-460	Geneva, Swit. 949.45
DQ820-829	ALPS 949.47
DQ841.L8	Lucerne, Lake (Swit.)
DR	EASTERN EUROPE & Balkan Peninsula (SEE DJK for gen. bks. on E. Eur. after about 1977-78) 949.6-8
DR15	Description & travel (E. Eur. & Balkan Penin.: 1901-50)
DR45	BALKAN PENINSULA & Eastern Europe (1901-: gen.)
DR46	Balkan War (1912-13) 949.6
DR47	Balkan Peninsula (1913-19)
DR51-98	BULGARIA 949.77
DR52	Primary sources, documents (Bulg.)
DR60	Description & travel (Bulg.: 1879-1950)
DR70	Military history (Bulg.)
DR72	Diplomacy & politics (Bulg.)
DR73.A-Z	Foreign relns. (Bulg.-specific countries)
DR73.G3	Foreign relns. (Bulg.-Ger.) 327.4977043
DR73.R9	Foreign relns. (Bulg.-Rus.)
DR85	Bulgaria (1879-1943) 949.7702
DR85.5.A-Z	Biography (Bulg.: 1879-1943: inclu. memoirs)
DR87	Bulgaria (1887-1918: reign of Ferdinand)
DR87.7	Bulgaria (1912-13: Balkan War period)
DR87.8	Bulgaria (1914-18: WWI)
DR88.A-Z	Biography (Bulg.: 1887-1918: by name)
DR88.S77	Stamboliski, Alexander (Bulg.: 1887-1918 time)
DR89	Bulgaria (1918-43: Boris III era)
DR95-98	Local history (Bulg.)
DR97	Sofia, Bulg.
DR101-196+	MONTENEGRO 949.76
DR109	Description & travel (Montenegro: 1860-1950)
DR117	Montenegro (gen.)
DR154	Montenegro (1860-1918: Nicholas I era)
DR158	Montenegro (1914-18: WWI)
DR159	Montenegro (1918-: part of Yug.)
DR201-296	RUMANIA 949.8
DR203	Primary sources, documents (Rum.)
DR209	Description & travel (Rum.: 1866-1950)
DR219	Military history (Rum.)
DR225	Naval history (Rum.)
DR226	Diplomacy & politics (Rum.)
DR229.A-Z	Foreign relns. (Rum. & partic. countries)
DR229.G3	Foreign relns. (Rum.-Ger.) 327.498043
DR229.R9	Foreign relns. (Rum.-Rus.)
DR250-266	Rumania (1866-1944)
DR250	Rumania (1866-1944: gen.)
DR252-258	Rumania (1881-1914: Carol I) 949.802
DR252	Primary sources, documents (Rum.: 1881-1914)
DR253.A-Z	Biography (Rum.: 1881-1914)
DR255	Carol I (Bulg.: King, 1881-1914)
DR256	Rumania (1881-1914: gen.)
DR258	Rumania (1912-13: Balkan War era)

DR260-263	Rumania (1914-27: Ferdinand) 949.802
DR260	Primary sources, documents (Rum.: 1914-27)
DR261	Ferdinand (Rum.: King, 1914-27: ALSO works on era)
DR262.A-Z	Biography (Rum.: 1914-27)
DR263	Rumania (1914-18: WWI)
DR264-266	Rumania (1918-44) 949.802
DR281-296	Local history (Rum.)
DR286	Bucharest, Rum. 949.82
DR301-396	YUGOSLAVIA (Serbia: SEE ALSO DR1202+ for later pubns.) 949.7-71
DR309	Description & travel (Yug.: 1860-1944)
DR317	Yugoslavia (gen.)
DR319	Military history (Yug.)
DR326	Diplomacy & politics (Yug.)
DR327.A-Z	Foreign relns. (Yug.-specific countries)
DR357	Yugoslavia (20th c.) 949.702, .7102
DR359.A-Z	Biography (Yug.: 20th c.)
DR360-363	Yugoslavia (1903-21: Peter I) 949.701-702
DR360	Peter I (Yug.: King, 1903-21: ALSO covers era)
DR363	Yugoslavia (1914-18: WWI)
DR364-369	Yugoslavia (1918-45: inclu. Croatia, Serbia, Slovenia) 949.7021-7022, 949.7102 (Serbia)
DR381-396	Local history (Yug.)
DR381.A-Z	Local history (Yug.: provinces, regions, etc.)
DR386	Belgrade, Yug.
DR401-741	TURKEY & Albania (primarily Tur.)
DR403	Primary sources, documents (Tur.)
DR428	Description & travel (Tur.: 1901-50)
DR448	Military history (Tur.) 355.009561
DR451	Naval history (Tur.)
DR476	Politics & diplomacy (Tur.: 1876-1918: inclu. Panislamism)
DR477	Diplomacy & politics (Tur.: 1918-) 327.5610+, 320.9561
DR479.A-Z	Foreign relns. (Tur.-particular countries)
DR479.G3	Foreign relns. (Tur.-Ger.)
DR479.G7	Foreign relns. (Tur.-G.B.)
DR479.R9	Foreign relns. (Tur.-Rus.)
DR571-579	Turkey (1876-1909: Abdul Hamid II)
DR571	Abdul Hamid II (Tur.: monarch, 1876-1909: ALSO works on era)
DR575	Greco-Turkish War (1897)
DR577	Turkey (20th c.) 956.102
DR583-588	Turkey (1909-18: Mohammed V) 956.101
DR583	Mohammed V (Tur.: ruler, 1909-18: ALSO titles on era)
DR586	Turkey (1911-12: Turco-Italian War era)
DR587	Turkey (1912-13: Balkan War period)
DR588	Turkey (1914-18: WWI era)
DR589	Turkey (1918-22: Mohammed VI)
DR592.A-Z	Biography (Tur.: 1909-: inclu. memoirs)
DR592.E55	Enver Pasha (Tur.: 1909- period: ALSO '...Pasa')
DR592.K4	Kemal, Mustafa (Tur.: 1909- era)
DR701.A-Z	Local history (Tur.: Eur. regions: by name)
DR701.A5	Aegean Sea
DR701.D2	Dardanelles (Tur.)
DR701.G3	Gallipoli (Tur.)

DR701.S49-86   ALBANIA (Scutari: SEE ALSO DR941-979 for later titles)   949.65
DR701.S5   Scutari (Albania: gen.)
DR701.S6   Albania (1914-17: Kingdom)   949.6502
DR701.S7   Albania (1917-25)   949.6502
DR716-739   Istanbul, Tur. (Constantinople)   956.3
DR941-979+   ALBANIA (SEE ALSO DR701.S49-86 for earlier works)   949.65
DR941   Albania (gen.)
DR970-975   Albania (1912-44)
DR971   Albania (1912-44: gen.)
DR972   Albania (1912-18: SEE ALSO DR46+ for Balkan War etc.)
DR1214-1307+   YUGOSLAVIA (SEE ALSO DR301+ for earlier pubns.)   949.7
DR1214   Yugoslavia (gen., descrip., culture, hist.)   949.7
DR1221   Description & travel (Yug.: 1901-44)   914.971+
DR1245-1246   Yugoslavia (gen. hist.)   949.7
DR1251   Military history (Yug.: gen.)
DR1257-1258   Foreign relns. (Yug.: gen.)
DR1274   Yugoslavia (1800-1918)   949.701
DR1280   Yugoslavia (1914-18: WWI era: SEE ALSO DR301+ for earlier
                      pubns.)   949.7, .701
DR1288-1298   Yugoslavia (1918-45)   949.702
DR1288   Primary sources, documents (Yug.)
DR1295   Yugoslavia (1918-21: reign of Peter I)
DR1350.A-Z Local history (Yug.: regions not limited to partic. sections or old
                      republics)
DR1350.A35   Adriatic coast (Yug.)
DR1350.D35   Danube River Valley (Yug.)
DR1350.D55   Dinaric Alps (Yug.)
DR1352-2285+   Local history (Yug.: sections & old republics: Slovenia, Bosnia,
                      Montenegro, etc.)
DR1352-1485+   SLOVENIA   949.73
DR1370, 1376   Slovenia (gen.)
DR1423   Slovenia (1814-1918: gen.)
DR1431   Slovenia (1849-1918: gen.)
DR1434   Slovenia (1914-18: WWI)
DR1435-1443   Slovenia (1918-45)
DR1502-1645   CROATIA   949.72
DR1510, 1535   Croatia (gen.)
DR1579   Croatia (1849-1918)
DR1582   Croatia (1914-18: WWI)
DR1583-1591   Croatia (1918-45)
DR1620-1630   Dalmatia (Yug.: local Croatia)   949.72
DR1620-1636+   Local history (Croatia)
DR1633-1636   Slavonia (Yug.: local Croatia)   949.72
DR1652-1785   BOSNIA & Hercegovina (Herzegovina: SEE ALSO DR357 etc.)
                                                          949.742
DR1660, 1685   HERZEGOVINA (Hercegovina) & Bosnia (gen.)
DR1722-1732   Bosnia & Hercegovina (1878-1918: Austrian control)
DR1723   Hercegovina & Bosnia (1878-1918: Austrian rule: gen.)
DR1725   Politics & diplomacy (Bosnia & Herceg.: 1878-1918)
DR1732   Bosnia & Hercegovina (1914-18: WWI)
DR1733-1741   Bosnia & Hercegovina (1918-45)

DR1801-1928	Montenegro (SEE ALSO DR357+, DR1214)	949.745
DR1810, 1835	Montenegro (gen.)	
DR1878-1883	Montenegro (1878-1918: Nicholas I)	
DR1878	Montenegro (1878-1918: Nicholas I: gen.)	
DR1883	Montenegro (1912-18: Balkan wars & WWI)	
DR1884-1893	Montenegro (1918-45)	
DR1932-2125+	SERBIA (SEE ALSO DR301+ & DR1202 areas)	949.71-71022
DR1940	Serbia (gen., descrip., culture, history)	
DR1965	Serbia (gen. histories)	
DR1970	Military history (Serbia)	
DR1972	Politics (Serbia: gen.)	
DR1975	Diplomacy & politics (Serbia: gen.)	
DR1976.A-Z	Foreign relns. (Serbia-other specific places)	
DR2006-2032	Serbia (1804-1918)	949.71
DR2007	Serbia (1804-1918: gen.)	
DR2012	Biography (Serbia: 1804-1918)	
DR2030-2032	Serbia (1903-18: Peter I Karadordevic)	
DR2030	Peter I Karadordevic (Serbia: ruler, 1903-18: ALSO gen. works on period)	
DR2031	Biography (Serbia: 1903-18)	
DR2032	Serbia (1914-18: WWI)	
DR2033-2040	Serbia (1918-45: part of Yug.)	
DR2075-2125	Local history (Serbia)	
DR2106-2124	Belgrade, Serbia (Yug.)	
DR2152-2285+	MACEDONIA	949.76
DR2160, 2185	Macedonia (gen., descrip., culture, hist.)	
DR2214	Macedonia (1878-1912)	
DR2230	Macedonia (1912-45)	
DR2237	Macedonia (1912-19)	

DS	ASIA	950-959
DS9	Description & travel (Asia: 1901-50)	915.044
DS31	Dictionaries, chronologies, etc. (Asia)	
DS33.3	Politics & diplomacy (Asia: gen.)	320.95, 327.5+
DS33.4.A-Z	Foreign relns. (Asia-particular other areas or countries)	
DS35	Asia (20th c.)	950.4

DS41-329	MIDDLE EAST & Southwestern Asia	953, 955, 956
DS49	Description & travel (Mid. East, SW. Asia: 1901-50)	915.6044
DS62	SOUTHWESTERN ASIA & Middle East (gen. histories)	
DS62.4	NEAR EAST & Southwestern Asia (modern)	
DS63	Politics & diplomacy (Middle East, SW. Asia)	320.956, 327.56+
DS63.2.A-Z	Foreign relns. (Mid. East, SW. Asia: by specific country)	327.560+
DS67-79	IRAQ 956.7	
DS70.95	Diplomacy & politics (Iraq: gen.)	
DS70.96.A-Z	Foreign relns. (Iraq-other specific places)	
DS70.96.G3	Foreign relns. (Iraq-Ger.)	
DS70.96.G7	Foreign relns. (Iraq-G.B.)	
DS77	Iraq (1517-1918: Turkish period)	956.703
DS80-90	LEBANON 956.92	
DS85	Lebanon (1861-1918: close of Turkish era)	

```
DS92-99        SYRIA           956.91
DS95        Syria (gen.)
DS95.5        Diplomacy & politics (Syria: gen.)
DS95.6.A-Z  Foreign relns. (Syria-other countries)    327.56910+
DS95.6.F8   Foreign relns. (Syria-Fr.)
DS95.6.G3   Foreign relns. (Syria-Ger.)
DS95.6.G7   Foreign relns. (Syria-G.B.)
DS97.5        Syria (1517-1918: Turkish period)    956.9103
DS101-151  PALESTINE, Israel, & the Jews      956.94, 909.04924
DS102        Primary sources, documents (Palestine & the Jews)
DS107.3        Description & travel (Palestine: 1901-50)
DS109        Jerusalem, Pal.
DS109.93        Jerusalem, Pal. (1917-)
DS110.A-Z  Local history (Palestine: regions, towns, etc.)
DS110.J6   Jordan River (Pal.)
DS112-113  Civilization, customs, social life (Palestine & the Jews)
DS114        Dictionaries, chronologies, etc. (Palestine, the Jews)
DS117        Jews, Palestine, & Israel (gen. histories)
DS119-119.8     Politics & diplomacy (Palestine, Jews)
DS123        Israel (70 A.D.+)
DS125        Palestine (19th-20th c.)          956.9403-9404
DS125.3.A-Z     Biography (Palestine: 19th-20th c.)
DS125.3.A2     Biography (Palestine: 19th-20th c.: collective)
DS125.3.B37        Ben-Gurion, David (Palestine: 19th-20th c.)
DS125.3.W45     Weizmann, Chaim (Palestine: 19th-20th c.)
DS125.5        Palestine (1914-18: WWI)     956.9403-9404
DS133-151  Jews (outside Palestine)
DS134        Jews (outside Israel: gen.)          909.04924
DS135.A-Z  Jews (by country or area)  Usually 004924 after Dewey place #s
DS135.E5-6  Jews (Eng. and G.B.)
DS135.E8-9  Jews (Eur.)      940.04924 (single '0' after decimal in this case)
DS135.F8-9  Jews (Fr.)       944.004924
DS135.G3-5  Jews (Ger.)      943.004924
DS141        Jewish question
DS143        Jews, Modern
DS145        Anti-Semitism
DS145.P49-7        Protocols of the Wise Men of Zion (WWI: anti-Semitism)
DS149-151        Zionism, Restoration, Judenstaat
DS153-154  JORDAN           956.95
DS154.4        Jordan (1517-1918: Turkish rule)     956.9503
DS161-199  ARMENIA (SEE ALSO  DK509 for some gen. titles, DK680-689 for later
                works)          956.62
DS195        Armenia (1901-)       956.6202
DS201-248  SAUDI ARABIA & Arabian Peninsula          953
DS207        Description & travel (Arabian Penin.: 1801-1950)
DS223        Arabian Peninsula (gen.)
DS227        Diplomacy & politics (Saudi Arabia: gen.)
DS228.A-Z  Foreign relns. (Saudi Arabia-specific countries)
DS228.G3   Foreign relns. (Saudi Arab. Penin.: Ger.)
DS228.G7   Foreign relns. (Saudi Arab. Penin.: G.B.)
DS243        Saudi Arabia (1873-1914)        953.04
DS244        Saudi Arabia (1914-: gen.)        953.04-05
DS247.A-Z  Local history (Arabian Penin.: regions, sultanates, etc.: by place)
DS248.A-Z  Local history (Arabian Penin.: cities)
DS248.M4   Mecca, Saudi Arabia
```

```
DS251-325    IRAN (Persia)    955
DS251        Description & travel (Iran: 1801-1950)
DS274        Diplomacy & politics (Iran)
DS274.2.A-Z       Foreign relns. (Iran-other countries)       327.550+
DS274.2.G3        Foreign relns. (Iran-Ger.)    327.55043
DS274.2.G7        Foreign relns. (Iran-G.B.)    327.55042
DS274.2.R9   Foreign relns. (Iran-Rus.)        327.55047
DS274.2.U6-7      Foreign relns. (Iran-U.S.)    327.55073
DS298-316    Persia (1794-1925: Kajar dynasty)       955.04-051
DS298        Iran (1794-1925: Kajar dynasty: gen.)
DS315        Iran (1909-25: Ahmed era)    955.05-051
DS335-498    SOUTHERN ASIA & Indian Ocean Region     954, 958.1, 959.1
DS335        INDIAN OCEAN REGION & Southern Asia (gen.)
DS350-375    AFGHANISTAN      958.1
DS356        Afghanistan (gen.)    958.1
DS361        Afghanistan (19th-20th c.: gen.)        958.103-104
DS376-498    INDIA, Pakistan, Ceylon, Burma, etc.    954, 959.1
DS401-498    PAKISTAN (pre-1947), India, Ceylon, Burma, etc.    954
DS401-481    India (overall) & pre-1947 Pakistan    954
DS413        Description & travel (India, pre-1947 Pak.)
DS442.6        Military history (India: 1901-)
DS448        Diplomacy & politics (India, pre-1947 Pak.: 20th c.)
DS450.A-Z    Foreign relns. (India-other specific places)    327.540+
DS450.G3     Foreign relns. (India-Ger.)        327.54043
DS463-480.83    India (1761-1947: Brit. rule)    954.03
DS463        India (1761-1947: Brit. rule: gen.)
DS479        India (1862-1914)    954.035
DS479.1.A-Z     Biography (India: thru 1900: by name)
DS480.3      India (1910-16: Lord Hardinge)    954.0356
DS480.4      India (1914-19)    954.0356-0357
DS480.45     India (1919-47)    954.035+
DS480.5      India (1916-21: Viscount of Chelmsford)
DS481.A-Z    Biography (India: 1901-: inclu. memoirs)
DS481.S8     Sultan Muhammad Shah, Sir, Agha Khan (India: 1901+ era)
DS485-498    Local history (India, Pak., Burma, Ceylon, Indian Ocean islands, etc.)

DS501-935+     FAR EAST, Eastern & Southeastern Asia    950-952, 958-959
DS503        Primary sources, documents (Far East, E. & SE.Asia)
DS504        Dictionaries, guidebooks, etc. (Far East, E. & SE.Asia)
DS508        Description & travel (Far East, E. & SE.Asia: 1901-50)    915.0441
DS516-517    Russo-Japanese War (1904-5)        952.031, 947.083
DS516.5        Views (Russo-Japanese War, 1904-5)
DS516.A-Z    Primary sources, documents (Rus.-Jpn. War, 1904-5)
DS517        Russo-Japanese War (1904-5: gen.)
DS517.1        Naval history (Rus.-Jpn. War, 1904-5)
DS517.13     Diplomacy & politics (Rus.-Jpn. War, 1904-5)
DS517.15-5   Battles, campaigns, sieges (Rus.-Jpn. War, 1904-5: by name)
DS517.15     Yalu, Battle of (Rus.-Jpn. War, 1904-5)
DS517.3        Port Arthur, Siege of (Rus.-Jpn. War, 1904-5)
DS517.4        Mukden, Battle of (Rus.-Jpn. War, 1904-5)
DS517.5        Tsushima, Battle of (Rus.-Jpn. War, 1904-5)
DS517.7        Treaty of Portsmouth (Rus.-Jpn. War, 1904-5)
DS517.8        Pamphlets, minor works (Rus.-Jpn. War, 1904-5)
DS517.9        Russo-Japanese War (1904-5: reminiscences & misc.)
```

DS518-518.9	EASTERN ASIA (history & foreign relns.: inclu. SE. Asia)	
DS518	Far East (1904-45: inclu. Far Eastern question: SEE ALSO DU29)	
		327.5, 950.41
DS518.2	Far Eastern question (France)	
DS518.3	Far Eastern question (Ger.)	
DS518.4	Far Eastern question (G.B.)	
DS518.5	Far Eastern question (Netherlands)	
DS518.6	Far Eastern question (Port.)	
DS518.7	Far Eastern question (Russia)	
DS518.8	Far Eastern question (U.S.)	
DS518.9.A-Z	Far Eastern question (misc. countries: SEE DS845 for Japan,	
	DS740.63 for China)	
DS519	Yellow Peril	
DS521-689	SOUTHEAST ASIA, Dutch East Indies, Philippines	959
DS521-605	Southeast Asia 959	
DS521-560	INDOCHINA 959-959.7	
DS525	Southeast Asia (gen. histories: older titles have descrip. & travel)	
DS526.6	Southeast Asia (1900-45)	
DS531-560	FRENCH INDOCHINA 959.4, 959.6-7	
DS556	VIETNAM (Annam) 959.7	
DS556.5	Annam (Vietnam: gen.)	
DS556.58.F8	Foreign relns. (Viet.-Fr.)	
DS556.58.J3	Foreign relns. (Viet.-Japan)	
DS591-599	MALAY PENINSULA, Malaya, & the Straits 959.5	
DS598.S7	Singapore 959.52	
DS611-649	DUTCH EAST INDIES & Indonesia	
DS643	INDONESIA (1798-1942: colonial era) 959.8022	
DS651-689	PHILIPPINE ISLANDS 959.9	
DS653	Primary sources, documents (Philip.)	
DS659	Description & travel (Philip.: 1898-1945) 915.99043	
DS663-664	Civilization, customs, social life (Philip.)	
DS665-666	Races & ethnography (Philip.)	
DS668.A3-Z	Philippine Islands (gen.: pubn. 1801+) 959.9	
DS671	Military history (Philip.) 355.009599	
DS672	Naval history (Philip.)	
DS672.8	Politics & diplomacy (Philip.: gen.) 320.9599, 327.599	
DS673.A-Z	Foreign relns. (Philip.: by country) 327.5990+	
DS673.J3	Foreign relns. (Philip.-Japan) 327.599052	
DS673.U6-7	Foreign relns. (Philip.-U.S.) 327.599073	
DS676-684	Philippine Islands (1894-1901) 959.902-9031	
DS676	Philippine Islands (1894-1901: gen.) 959.903	
DS676.8.A-Z	Biography (Philip.: 1894-1901: by name)	
DS679	Philippine Islands (1898-1901: SEE ALSO E712-735 for	
	Span.-Am. War) 959.9031	
DS682-684	Military & naval history (Philip.: inclu. battles vs. Sp. & U.S.:	
	PREFER E717.7 for Battle of Manila Bay [1898] & U.S.-Sp.	
	naval confront.)	
DS685	Philippine Islands (1901+) 959.903	
DS688.A-Z	Local history (Philip.: islands, provinces, regions)	
DS688.L9	Luzon (Philip.) 959.91	
DS689.M2	Manila, Philip. 959.91	

DS701-796+   CHINA   951
DS710   Description & travel (China: 1901-48)   915.1043-1044
DS721   Civilization, customs, social life (China: gen.)
DS730-731   Races & ethnography (China)
DS732   Chinese (in other lands: gen.)
DS733   Dictionaries, chronologies, etc. (China)
DS735.A3-Z   China (gen.: pubn. 1801+)   951
DS740.4   Diplomacy (China: gen.)   327.51
DS740.5.A-Z   Foreign relns. (China & other lands: by name)   327.510+
DS740.5.G2-3 Foreign relns. (China-Ger.)   327.51043
DS740.5.G5-6 Foreign relns. (China-G.B.)
DS740.5.G6.H6 Foreign relns. (China-Hong Kong)
DS740.5.G6.J3 Foreign relns. (China-Japan)   327.51052
DS740.5.S65   Foreign relns. (China-Sov. Un.)   327.51047
DS740.5.U6-7 Foreign relns. (China-U.S.)   [PREFER E183.8.C5]
                                                          327.51073
DS740.63   Far Eastern question (China: 1861-1945)
DS754   China (1644-1912: Ch'ing Dynasty: gen.)   951.03
DS761   China (1861-1912)
DS764.4-767.7 Chinese-Japanese War (1894-5)   951.03, 952.031
DS765   Sino-Japanese War (1894-5: gen.)
DS770-772   Boxer Rebellion (China: 1899-1901)   951.03
DS773-773.23 China (1908-12: Hsuan-T'ung era)   951.03
DS773.32-6   Chinese Revolution (1911-12)   951.03
DS773.4   China (1911-12: Rev.: gen.)
DS773.5-52   Personal accounts (Ch. Rev., 1911-12)
DS773.83-776 China (1912-49 [Republic] & 20th c. overall)   951.03-04
DS773.83   Primary sources, documents (China: 20th c. & 1912-49)
DS774   China (1912-49 [Republic] & 20th c. overall: gen.)   951.04
DS775.2   Civilization, customs, social life (China: 20th c. & 1912-49)
DS775.4   Military history (China: 20th c. & 1912-49)
DS775.5   Naval history (China: 20th c. & 1912-49)
DS775.7   Politics (China: 20th c. & 1912-49)
DS775.8   Foreign relns. (China: 20th c. & 1912-49)
DS776   Biography (China: 20th c. & 1912-49: collective: SEE partic. era for
                   indiv.)
DS776.4   China (1912-28: gen.)   951.041
DS777.A2-567 Sun Yat Sen (China: 1912-49 era: writings of)
DS777.A3   Sun Yat Sen (China: 1912-49 era: autobiography)
DS777.A597.A-Z89   Sun Yat Sen (China: 1912-49 era: biograpy & criticism)
DS777.15.A-Z Biography (China: 1912-49 period: except Sun Yat Sen)
DS777.2   China (1913: 2d Rev.)
DS777.43   May 4th Movement (China: 20th c.)
DS781-784.2+ MANCHURIA   951.803-804
DS783.7   Manchuria (19th-20th c.)
DS783.7.L4-45 League of Nations Commission of Enquiry (Manchuria: Lytton
                   Commission)
DS783.7.L45   Lytton Commission (Manchuria: League of Nations Commission of
                   Enquiry: summary & var. reports)
DS785.A5-Z CENTRAL ASIA & Tibet (pubns. to 1950: gen.)   951.5, 958 (C. Asia)
DS793.M7 MONGOLIA (SEE ALSO DS19-23.1 for Mongols)   951.7

DS795   Peiping, China (Peking)   951.156
DS796.A-Z   Local history (China: cities & towns)
DS796.C2   Canton, China
DS796.H7   HONG KONG   951.25
DS796.S2   Shanghai, China   951.132
DS796.T7   Tsingtao, China
DS798.92-799.99+   FORMOSA (Taiwan: SEE ALSO DS895.F7-77 for many pre-
                                1970 pubns.)   951.249
DS799   TAIWAN (Formosa: gen. hist., culture, descrip.)
DS799.15   Description & travel (Formosa: to 1945)   915.1249044
DS799.5   Formosa (gen.)   951.249
DS799.625   Diplomacy (Formosa: gen.)
DS799.63.A-Z   Foreign relns. (Formosa-other places)
DS799.63.J3   Foreign relns. (Formosa-Japan)
DS799.69-72   Formosa (1895-1945)   951.24904
DS799.7   Taiwan (1895-1945: gen.)

DS801-897+   JAPAN   952
DS803   Primary sources, documents (Japan)
DS810   Description & travel (Japan: 1901-45)   915.2043
DS821   Civilization, customs, social life (Japan: gen.)
DS822.25   Civilization, customs, social life (Japan: 1868+)
DS822.3   Civilization, customs, social life (Japan: 1868-1912)
DS822.4   Civilization, customs, social life (Japan: 1912-45)
DS833   Dictionaries, chronologies, etc. (Japan)
DS834.1   Biography (Japan: Imperial family & rulers)
DS835   Japan (gen. history, descrip., culture)
DS838   Military history (Japan: overall)   355.00952
DS838.7   Military history (Japan: 1868+)   355.00952, .033052, .033252, .033552
DS839   Naval history (Japan: gen.)   359.00952
DS839.7   Naval history (Japan: 1868+)   359.00952, .4752
DS840-849   Diplomacy & politics (Japan)   320.952, 327.52
DS841   Politics & diplomacy (Japan: gen.)
DS845   Diplomacy (Japan: gen.)   327.52
DS849.A-Z   Foreign relns. (Japan-other places)   327.520+
DS849.A75   Foreign relns. (Japan-Asia)   327.5205
DS849.C5   Foreign relns. (Japan-China)   327.52051
DS849.G3   Foreign relns. (Japan-Ger.)   327.52043
DS849.G7   Foreign relns. (Japan-G.B.)   327.52041
DS849.I4   Foreign relns. (Japan-India)
DS849.I45   Foreign relns. (Japan-Indoch.)
DS849.I5   Foreign relns. (Japan-Indonesia)
DS849.I8   Foreign relns. (Japan-It.)
DS849.M3   Foreign relns. (Japan-Malayas)
DS849.P5   Foreign relns. (Japan-Philip.)   327.520599
DS849.R9   Foreign relns. (Japan-Rus.)   327.52047
DS849.S65   Foreign relns. (Japan-Sov. Un.)   327.52047
DS849.U6-7   Foreign relns. (Japan-U.S.)   327.52073
DS849.V5   Foreign relns. (Japan-Viet.)
DS881.85+   Japan (1868+: modern era)   952.03
DS881.9   Japan (1868+: modern era: gen.)
DS882-884   Japan (1868-1912: Meiji period: Mutsuhito)   952.031
DS882.6   Foreign relns. (Japan: 1868-1912)

DS885	Japan (20th c.)	952.03-04
DS885.5.A-Z	Biography (Japan: 20th c.: inclu. memoirs: SEE ALSO DS890)	
DS885.5.K6	Konoye, Fumimaro, Prince (Japan: 20th. c.)	
DS886	Japan (1912-26: Taisho time: Yoshihito) 952.032	
DS887	Japan (1914-18: WWI era) 952.032	
DS895.A-Z	Local history (Japan: islands, provinces, regions)	
DS895.F7-77	FORMOSA (Taiwan: SEE ALSO DS799 for many post-1969 pubns.)	
		951.249
DS895.F72	Taiwan (Formosa: gen.)	
DS895.F75	Formosa (19th-20th c.) 951.24903-24904	
DS895.K9	Kurile Islands (Japan) 957.7	
DS896	Tokyo, Japan (SEE DS897.T6 for earlier works) 952.135	
DS896.6	Tokyo, Japan (gen.)	
DS897.T6	Tokyo, Japan (SEE DS896 for later pubns.) 952.135	
DS901-935+	KOREA 951.9	
DS916	Korea (20th c.) 951.903-904	

DT	AFRICA 960-969	
DT1-38	Africa (overall) 960	
DT12	Description & travel (Africa: 1901-50) 916.0431-0432	
DT29	Africa (1884-1945: gen.) 960.23-31	
DT31-38	Politics & diplomacy (Africa: inclu. colonialism) 320.96, 327.6	
DT31.5	Diplomacy & politics (Africa: 19th-20th c.: gen.)	
DT32.5	Foreign relns. (Africa-G.B.: 19th-20th c.) 960.23-3, 325.3+	
DT33.5	Foreign relns. (Africa-Fr.: 19th-20th c.)	
DT34.5	Foreign relns. (Africa-Ger.: 19th-20th c.)	
DT35.5	Foreign relns. (Africa-It.: 19th-20th c.)	

DT43-154	EGYPT & the Egyptian Sudan 962	
DT43	Primary sources, documents (Egypt)	
DT55	Description & travel (Egypt & Egyp. Sudan: 1901-50) 916.2044-2045	
DT77	Egypt (gen.)	
DT81	Military history (Egypt)	
DT82	Politics & diplomacy (Egypt: gen.)	
DT82.5.A-Z	Foreign relns. (Egypt & various countries) 327.620+	
DT82.5.G3	Foreign relns. (Egypt-Ger.) 327.62043	
DT82.5.G7	Foreign relns. (Egypt-G.B.) 327.62041	
DT107	Egypt (1879-1952) 962.03-052	
DT107.2.A-Z	Biography (Egypt: 1879-1952)	
DT107.6	Egypt (1892-1914: Abbas II era)	
DT107.7	Egypt (1914-17: Hussein Kamil) 962.04	
DT107.8	Egypt (1917-36: Fuad I) 962.04-051	
DT108	EGYPTIAN SUDAN (inclu. Anglo-Egyptian: for newer titles SEE DT154.1-159) 962.4	
DT108.6	Anglo-Egyptian Sudan (1899-1955) 962.403	
DT124	Nile River (20th c.: descrip. & travel) 962.044-045	
DT137.A-Z	Local history (Egypt: provinces, regions, etc.)	
DT137.A7	Arabian Desert (Egypt)	
DT139-152	Cairo, Egypt 962.16	
DT143	Cairo, Egypt (gen. hist. & descrip.)	

DT154.1-159   SUDAN & Anglo-Egyptian Sudan (SEE DT108 for older works)
DT154.A-Z   Local history (Egypt: cities, towns, other)
DT154.A4   Alexandria, Egypt
DT154.K63   Khartoum, Egypt
DT154.S9   Suez Canal (Egypt: inclu. Isthmus)   962.15
DT155.6   Sudan (gen.)
DT156.7   Sudan (1900-1955)
DT160-177   NORTH AFRICA (Egypt & Barbary States)   961-962
DT165   Description & travel (N. Africa: 1901-50)   916.2043
DT176   North Africa (19th-20th c.)   961.023-03+
DT181-346   BARBARY STATES   961.1-2, 964-965, 966
DT190   Description & travel (Barbary States: 1901-50)
DT204   Barbary States (19th-20th c.)   961.023-03+
DT211-239   LIBYA   961.2
DT220   Description & travel (Libya: 1901-50)
DT227   Politics & diplomacy (Libya: gen.)
DT227.5.A-Z   Foreign relns. (Libya & other particular places)
DT227.5.G3   Foreign relns. (Libya-Ger.)
DT227.5.I8   Foreign relns. (Libya-It.)
DT233   Libya (1801-1912)
DT234   Turco-Italian War (1911-12: Libya)
DT235   Libya (1912-45)   961.203
DT238-239   Local history (Libya)
DT241-269   TUNISIA   961.1
DT257.5.I8   Foreign relns. (Tunisia-It.)
DT264   Tunisia (1881-1957: Fr. Protectorate)   961.104
DT271-299   ALGERIA   965
DT280   Description & travel (Algeria: 1901-50)
DT294.5-295.3   Algeria (1901-62: for older titles use DT295)
DT294.5-7   Algeria (1901-45)   965.04 (1900-62)
DT295   Algeria (1901+: for newer works SEE DT294.5-295.3)   965.04+
DT299.A-Z   Local history (Algeria: towns etc.)
DT301-330   MOROCCO   964
DT317.5.A-Z   Foreign relns. (Morocco-other specific places)
DT324   Morocco (19th-20th c.)   964.03-04
DT330   SPANISH MOROCCO   964.2
DT331-346   SAHARA DESERT   966
DT333   Sahara Desert (gen. hist., descrip. etc.)
DT351-364   CENTRAL AFRICA   967
DT365-469   EAST AFRICA   967.6, 963
DT365.7   East Africa (1884-1960: gen.)   967.6
DT367   ITALIAN EAST AFRICA & Northeast Africa   963
DT367.75   NORTHEAST AFRICA (1900-74)   963.05+
DT371-390   ETHIOPIA (Abyssinia)   963
DT378   Description & travel (Ethiopia: 1901-50)
DT386   ABYSSINIA (19th -20th c.)   963.03-05+
DT387-387.6   Ethiopia (1889-1928: inclu. 1895-6 conflict w. Italy)   963.043-054
DT401-420   SOMALILAND   967.7
DT406   BRITISH SOMALILAND   967.73-7305+
DT411   FRENCH SOMALILAND (Djibouti or Afars & Issas)   967.71-7104+
DT416   ITALIAN SOMALILAND   967.73-7305+

DT421-435   BRITISH EAST AFRICA & East Africa   967.6
DT431   EAST AFRICA (to 1960)
DT433.5-434   KENYA (newer books)
DT433.57-433.577   Kenya (1895-1963: Brit. era)
DT434.Z3   ZANZIBAR (Brit. colony: SEE DT449.Z2+ for newer)
DT436-449   TANGANYIKA (German East Africa)   967.82
DT444   German East Africa (gen.: later Tanganyika)
DT447   Tanganyika (to 1960: newer titles)
DT449.Z2-Z29   ZANZIBAR (SEE DT434.Z3 & DT435 for older titles)
DT451-465   MOZAMBIQUE (Portuguese East Africa)   967.9
DT469.A-Z   East African islands
DT469.M21-38   MADAGASCAR   969.1
DT471-720   WEST AFRICA   966-967, 968.8
DT491-518   BRITISH WEST AFRICA   966, 966.4-51, .7, .81, .9
DT521-553   FRENCH WEST AFRICA   966, 966.1-3, .52, .68, .81
DT561-584   CAMEROONS (German West Africa) & Togoland   966.6695, .81, 967.1
DT591-617   ANGOLA (Portuguese West Africa)   967.3
DT641-665   BELGIAN CONGO   967.5
DT671.A-Z   West African islands
DT701-720   SOUTHWEST AFRICA (German Southwest Africa)   967.1, 968.8
DT730-995   SOUTHERN AFRICA   968
DT751-848   BRITISH SOUTH AFRICA   968-968.7
DT769   Military history (S. Afr.)   355.00968
DT779   SOUTH AFRICA (1909-: Union)   968.05+
DT779.5   South Africa (1914-18: WWI period)
DT855   BRITISH CENTRAL AFRICA (1901-52)   968.97
DT946-965   RHODESIA

DU   OCEANIA (Pacific Ocean)   990-996, 909.0964
DU22   Description & travel (Pacific: 1898-1950)
DU28.3   PACIFIC OCEAN (Oceania: gen.)   990, 990.09, 909.0964
DU29   Diplomacy & politics (Pacific: gen.: inclu. colonial rule)
DU30   Foreign relns. (Pacific-U.S.)
DU40   Foreign relns. (Pacific-G.B.)
DU50   Foreign relns. (Pacific-Fr.)
DU60   Foreign relns. (Pacific-Ger.)
DU65   Foreign relns. (Pacific-Sp.)

DU80-480   AUSTRALIA, New Zealand, Tasmania
DU80-398   AUSTRALIA   994
DU80   Primary sources, documents (Australia)
DU104   Description & travel (Australia: 1901-50)   919.4044
DU107   Civilization, customs, social life (Australia)
DU110   Australia (gen.)   994
DU112.3   Military history (Australia) 355.00994, .033094
DU112.4   Naval history (Australia)   359.00994
DU113   Diplomacy (Australia: gen.)   327.94
DU113.5.A-Z   Foreign relns. (Australia-other specific lands)   327.940+
DU113.5.G7   Foreign relns. (Australia-G.B.)   327.94041
DU113.5.U6-7   Foreign relns. (Australia-U.S.)   327.94073
DU114.A2   Biography (Australia: collective)
DU114.A3-Z   Biography (Australia: by name: SEE ALSO DU116.2 for later works)
DU116   Australia (1901-45: Commonwealth)   994.04
DU116.2   Biography (Australia: 1901-45: SEE DU114 for earlier pubns.)
DU120-122   Races & ethnography (Australia)

DU145-398	Local history (Australia)	
DU145	Canberra, Australia (inclu. Capital Territory)	
DU150-180	New South Wales (Australia)	994.4
DU161	New South Wales (Australia: 1837-1950: gen.)	
DU178	Sydney, Australia	994.41
DU180.A-Z	Local history (New S. Wales, Aust.: towns, regions, etc. except Sydney)	
DU228	Melbourne, Australia	994.51
DU230.A-Z	Local history (Victoria, Aust.: all except Melbourne)	
DU250-280	Queensland (Australia)	994.3
DU278	Brisbane, Australia	994.31
DU280.A-Z	Local history (Queens., Aust.: all except Brisbane)	
DU300-330	South Australia	994.23
DU350-380	Western Australia	994.1
DU378	Perth, Australia	994.11
DU400-430	NEW ZEALAND	993.1
DU411	Description & travel (N. Zea.: 1840-1950)	919.31042-310435
DU420	New Zealand (gen.)	993.1-1037+
DU420.5	Military history (N. Zea.)	355.009931
DU421	Politics & diplomacy (N. Zea.: gen.)	
DU421.5.A-Z	Foreign relns. (N. Zea.-other specific places)	327.9310+
DU421.5.U6-7	Foreign relns. (N. Zea.-U.S.)	327.931073
DU422.A-Z	Biography (N. Zea.: inclu. memoirs: by name)	
DU423	Races & ethnography (N. Zea.)	
DU428	Wellington, N.Z.	993.127
DU430.A-Z	Local history (N. Zea.: regions, towns, dependencies, etc. except Wellington)	
DU430.A8	Auckland, N.Zea.	993.122
DU430.C5	Christchurch, N. Zea.	993.155
DU430.C6	COOK ISLANDS	996.23-24
DU490	MELANESIA (gen.: SEE DU520-950 for specific islands, groups, atolls, etc.)	993, 993.2-7, 996.1
DU500	MICRONESIA (gen.: SEE DU520-950 for particular islands, island groups, atolls, etc.)	996.5-68
DU510	POLYNESIA (gen.: SEE DU520-950 for specific island groups, individual islands, atolls, etc.)	996, 996.1-4, .9
DU520-950	SOUTH SEAS (Oceanica: islands, chains, groups, etc.)	
DU520	ADMIRALTY ISLANDS	993.7
DU550	BISMARCK ARCHIPELAGO (gen.) 993.6	
DU560-568	CAROLINE ISLANDS	996.6
DU590	ELLICE ISLANDS	996.81
DU600	FIJI ISLANDS	996.11
DU615	GILBERT ISLANDS (inclu. Tarawa & Makin Atolls)	996.81
DU620-629	HAWAIIAN ISLANDS	996.9
DU623	Description & travel (Hawaiian Is.: to 1950)	919.69043
DU627.4	Hawaiian Islands (annex. to U.S.)	
DU640-648	MARIANA ISLANDS (Ladrones)	996.7
DU710	MARSHALL ISLANDS (inclu. Kwajalein Atoll)	996.83
DU740-746	NEW GUINEA	995
DU742	German New Guinea (N.E.: SEE ALSO DU550+ for Bismarck Arch.)	993.6, 995
DU744-744.5	DUTCH NEW GUINEA (West)	995.1

```
DU810-819   SAMOAN ISLANDS    996.13-14
DU817.A6-Z  Samoa (modern hist.)
DU819.A1    American Samoa    996.13
DU819.A2    Western Samoa (was Ger. Samoa)      996.14
DU819.A3-Z      Local history (Samoan Is.: partic. islands, towns, etc.)
DU819.P3    Pago Pago, Samoa
DU850       SOLOMON ISLANDS (inclu. Guadalcanal, New Georgia, Choiseul,
                  Savo, Florida, Bougainville, etc.)        993.5
DU870       SOCIETY ISLANDS (inclu. Tahiti, Bora Bora, etc.)     996.21


DX1-301     GYPSIES
DX145       Gypsies in Europe (gen. & elsewhere)
DX211-275   European Gypsies (by place)
DX222       Gypsies in Czechoslovakia
DX229       Gypsies in Germany
DX241       Gypsies in Russia (inclu. Poland & Lith.)


E           WESTERN HEMISPHERE (gen.) & United States       970
E1-143      AMERICA (gen.)        970
E18.185         America (1901-)   970.05
E31-45      NORTH AMERICA      970
E45         North America (gen.)
E77-99      Indians (N. Am.)     970.00497, .1-5, 973.0497
E98.M5      Military skill (Indians of N. Am.)


E151-860+   UNITED STATES      973-979.9+
E151        United States (gen. & cultural, serials, societies, etc.)
E161        Civilization, customs, social life (U.S.: gen.)
E168        Description, travel, civilization, customs (U.S.: 1866-1913)
E169        Description, travel, civilization, customs (U.S.: 1914-45)       917.3049
E169.1      Americanization, civilization, etc. (U.S.)
E171            Periodicals & yearbooks (U.S.)
E172            Associations, societies (U.S.)
E173            Primary sources, documents (U.S.)
E174            Dictionaries & encyclopedias (U.S.)       973.03
E174.5          Chronologies (U.S.)
E178        United States (gen. hist.)  973
E181        Military history (U.S.)  355.00973, .033073
E182        Naval history (U.S.)  359.00973, .4773
E183        Politics (U.S.: gen.)  320.973
E183.7      Diplomacy (U.S.: gen.)      327.73
E183.8.A-Z  Foreign relns. (U.S.-other places)     327.730+
E183.8.C5       Foreign relns. (U.S.-China)     327.73051
E183.8.F8       Foreign relns. (U.S.-Fr.)       327.73044
E183.8.G3       Foreign relns. (U.S.-Ger.)      327.73043
E183.8.G7       Foreign relns. (U.S.-G.B.)  327.73041
E183.8.I8   Foreign relns. (U.S.-It.)     327.73045
E183.8.J3   Foreign relns. (U.S.-Japan)     327.73052
E183.8.R9   Foreign relns. (U.S.-Russia)     327.73047
E183.8.S65  Foreign relns. (U.S.-Sov.Un.)     327.73047
```

E184.A-Z	Races, ethnography, religious groups (U.S.)	973.04+
E184.A1	Races, ethnography, religious groups (U.S.: gen.)	
E184.B7	British (in U.S.)	
E184.F8	French (in U.S.)	
E184.G3	Germans (in U.S.)	
E184.I8	Italians (in U.S.)	
E184.J3	Japanese (in U.S.)	
E184.J5	Jews (in U.S.)	
E184.O6	Orientals (in U.S.)	
E184.R9	Russians (in U.S.)	
E185	Blacks (in U.S.)	973.0496
E185.63	Blacks as soldiers & seamen (U.S.)	
E660-738	United States (1865-1900+)	973.8-89
E660.A-Z	Statesmen (U.S.: collected works: inclu. some working through 1921: SEE E742.5 for rest of 20th c.)	
E660.B87-94	Bryan, William Jennings (U.S.: 1865-1900 era: works)	
E660.M14	McKinley, William (U.S.: 1865-1900 era: works)	
E660.R75-89	Roosevelt, Theodore (U.S.: 1865-1900 era: works)	
E660.T11-12	Taft, William Howard (U.S.: 1865-1900 era: works)	
E660.W7-75	Wilson, Woodrow (U.S.: 1865-1900 era: works)	
E661	United States (1865-1900: gen.)	973.8
E661.7	Foreign relns. (U.S.: 1865-1900: gen.: SEE ALSO E183.8.A-Z)	
E663	Biography (U.S.: 1865-1900: collective)	
E664.A-Z	Biography (U.S.: 1865-1900: by name)	
E664.L7	Lodge, Henry Cabot (U.S.: 1865-1900 era)	
E664.P15	Page, Walter Hines (U.S.: 1865-1900 era)	
E664.R3	Reed, Thomas Brackett (U.S.: 1865-1900 era)	
E664.R7	Root, Elihu (U.S.: 1865-1900 era)	
E706	United States (1893-7: Pres. Grover Cleveland)	973.85
E710-751	United States (1897-1901: Pres. Wm. McKinley)	973.88
E711	United States (1897-1901: gen.)	
E713	Foreign relns. (U.S.: 1897-1901: gen.)	
E714-735	Spanish-American War (1898)	973.89-898
E714.5-6.A-Z	Biography (Sp.-Am. War, 1898)	
E714.6.D51	Dewey, George, Adm. (Sp.-Am. War era)	
E715	Spanish-American War (1898: gen.)	973.89
E717	Military ops. (Sp.-Am. War, 1898: gen.)	973.89, .893, .895
E717.1	Cuba (Sp.-Am. War, 1898)	
E717.7	Philippine Islands (Sp.-Am. War, 1898: ALSO Battle of Manila Bay) 973.8937	
E723	Treaties (Sp.-Am. War, 1898)	973.892
E725	Armies etc. (Sp.-Am. War, 1898)	973.894, 946.08
E725.3-8	Armies etc. (Sp.-Am. War, 1898: U.S.)	973.894
E725.4.1st-	Infantry regiments (Sp.-Am. War: U.S.: by #)	
E725.45.1st	Rough Riders (Sp.-Am. War: U.S. cavalry)	
E725.45.1st-	Cavalry regiments (Sp.-Am. War: U.S.: by #)	
E725.5.J4	Jews (Sp.-Am. War, 1898: U.S.)	
E725.5.N3	Blacks (Sp.-Am. War, 1898: U.S.: Negroes)	
E725.9	Armies etc. (Sp.-Am. War, 1898: Sp.)	973.894, 946.08
E725.A-Z	Ethnic groups (Sp.-Am. War: U.S.: participation)	
E727-729	Naval ops. (Sp.-Am. War, 1898)	973.895
E727	United States naval ops. (Sp.-Am. War, 1898: ALSO gen. works on naval ops. of war: Manila Bay battle at E717.7) 973.895	

E740-749	United States (20th c.: overall)	973.9
E740	Associations, periodicals, societies (U.S.: 20th c.)	
E740.5	Primary sources, documents (U.S.: 20th c.)	
E741	United States (20th c.: gen.)	973.9
E742.5.A-Z	Statesmen (U.S.: collected works: 20th c.: SEE E660 for up to 1921)	
E742.5.R5-7	Roosevelt, Franklin Delano (U.S.: 20th c.: works)	
E743	Politics (U.S.: 20th c.)	320.973, .904
E743.5	Subversive activities (in U.S.: propaganda, espionage, 5th column, etc.)	
E744	Foreign relns. (U.S.: 20th c.: gen.)	327.73
E745	Military history (U.S.: 20th c.: inclu. biog.: more than 1 war)	
		355.00973, .033073, .033273, .033573
E746	Naval history (U.S.: 20th c.)	359.00973, .4773
E747	Biography (U.S.: 20th c.: collective)	
E748.A-Z	Biography (U.S.: 20th c.: by name)	
E748.B32	Baruch, Bernard (U.S.: 20th c.)	
E748.H93	Hull, Cordell (U.S.: 20th c.)	
E748.K55	Knox, W. Frank (U.S.: 20th c.)	
E748.S895	Stimson, Henry (U.S.: 20th c.)	
E756-760	United States (1901-9: Pres. Theodore Roosevelt)	973.911
E756	United States (1901-9: gen.)	
E757	Roosevelt, Theodore (U.S.: Pres., 1901-9)	
E761	United States (1909-13: Pres. Wm. Howard Taft: gen.)	973.912
E765-783	United States (1913-21: Woodrow Wilson period)	973.913
E765	Politics (U.S.: 1912 Pres. campaign)	
E766	United States (1913-21: gen.)	
E767	Wilson, Woodrow (U.S.: Pres., 1913-21)	
E768	Foreign relns. (U.S.: 1913-21)	
E769	Politics (U.S.: 1916 Pres. campaign)	
E772	Woodrow Wilson Foundation	
E780	United States (1914-18: WWI era: internal)	973.913
E784	United States (1919-33: inclu. Roaring Twenties)	973.913-916
E785	United States (1921-3: Warren G. Harding era: gen.: SEE JX235 ALSO for arms limitation conference, Pacific possessions treaty, etc.)	
		973.914
F	UNITED STATES (local), Canada, Newfoundland, Mexico, Central & South America	974-79+, 971-2, 980-89
F1-975+	United States (local: regions, states, towns, etc.)	974-79
F1-15	New England (overall)	974
F4	New England (gen. hist.)	974
F6-105	New England states	974.1-6
F9	New England (1865-1950)	974.04-042
F16-30	Maine	974.1
F19	Maine (gen.)	
F25	Maine (1865-1950)	
F61-75	Massachusetts	974.4
F70	Massachusetts (1865-1950: SEE D570.85.M4-41 for war years, 1914-18)	974.404-043
F73.5	Boston, Mass. (1865-1950)	
F106	Atlantic Coast (U.S.: Maine to Flor.)	974-975

F116-205	Middle Atlantic states & District of Columbia
F116-130	New York 974.7
F119	New York (gen.)
F124	New York (1865-1950: SEE D570.85.N4-5 for 1914-18 war years)
	974.704
F127.A-Z	Local history (New York: regions, counties, etc.)
F127.H8	Hudson River (N.Y.)
F127.L8	Long Island (N.Y.)
F128	New York City, N.Y. 974.71
F128.3	New York City, N.Y. (gen.)
F128.5	New York City area (N.Y.: 1901-50) 974.7104-043
F128.67.A-Z	New York City, N.Y. (streets, bridges, railroads)
F128.68.A-Z	New York City, N.Y. (sections, suburbs, rivers)
F129.A-Z	Local history (N.Y.: cities, towns, etc. except N.Y.C.)
F129.A3	Albany, N.Y.
F129.B8	Buffalo, N.Y.
F130.A-Z	Races, ethnography, religious groups (N.Y.)
F130.G3	Germans (in N.Y.)
F130.I8	Italians (in N.Y.)
F130.J5	Jews (in N.Y.)
F131-145	New Jersey 974.9
F139	New Jersey (1865-1950: SEE D570.85.N3-31 for 1914-18 war years)
F146-160	Pennsylvania 974.8
F154	Pennsylvania (1865-1950)
F158	Philadelphia, Penn. 974.811
F191-205	District of Columbia 975.3
F194	Washington, D.C. (gen.)
F196	Social life & politics (Washington, D.C.)
F199	Washington, D.C. area (1878-1950) 975.303-304
F203	Local history (Washington, D.C.: cemeteries, churches, hotels, statues, parks, circles, streets, etc.)
F203.4.A-Z	Monuments, statues, memorials (Washington, D.C.)
F203.7.A-Z	Washington, D.C. (streets, bridges, railroads)
F203.7.P4	Pennsylvania Ave. (Washington, D.C.)
F204.A-Z	Buildings (Washington, D.C.)
F204.W5	White House (Washington, D.C.)
F206-220	South Atlantic states & the South (U.S.: covers south of Mason-Dixon Line) 975-976
F215	South & South Atlantic states (1865-1950) 975.04, 976.04
F221-235	Virginia 975.5
F232.A-Z	Local history (Virginia: regions, counties, etc.)
F232.C43	Chesapeake Bay region (Va.)
F234.A-Z	Local history (Virginia: towns etc.)
F234.A7	Arlington National Cemetery (Arlington, Va.)
F234.N8	Norfolk, Va.
F251-265	North Carolina 975.6
F259	North Carolina (1865-1950)
F281-295	Georgia 975.8

F296-395	Gulf states, Mississippi Valley, Middle West, & Texas	975.9-976.4, 976.7-9
F296	Gulf states (U.S.: gen.) 976	
F306-320	Florida 975.9	
F316	Florida (1865-1950) 975.906	
F317.A-Z	Local history (Florida: regions, counties, etc.)	
F317.G8	Gulf Coast (Florida)	
F317.M7	Florida Keys (Monroe County, Fl.)	
F319.A-Z	Local history (Florida: towns etc.)	
F319.P4	Pensacola, Florida	
F321-335	Alabama 976.1	
F326	Alabama (to 1950)	
F336-350	Mississippi 976.2	
F351-355	Mississippi Valley & the Midwest 976-977	
F354	Middle West & Mississippi River Valley (1865-1950) 977.03	
F366-380	Louisiana 976.3	
F381-395	Texas 976.4	
F391	Texas (1846+: SEE D570.85.T4-41 for 1914-18 war years) 976.405-406	
F392.A-Z	Local history (Texas: regions, counties, etc.)	
F392.G9	Gulf Coast (Texas)	
F394.A-Z	Local history (Texas: towns etc.)	
F394.D2	Dallas, Texas	
F394.E4	El Paso, Texas	
F394.H8	Houston, Texas 976.41411	
F396-475	Southwest (Old) & lower Mississippi Valley (Ark., Tenn., Ken., Missouri)	976.7-9, 977, 977.8
F461-475	Missouri 977.8	
F474.S2	St. Louis, Mo. 977.866	
F476-590	Northwest (U.S.: Old) 977	
F484.5	Old Northwest (U.S.: 1865-1950) 977.03	
F486-500	Ohio 977.1	
F536-550	Illinois 977.3	
F546	Illinois (1865-1950) 977.303	
F548	Chicago, Ill. 977.311	
F548.5	Chicago, Ill. (1892-1950) 977.31103-033	
F551-556	Great Lakes (U.S.) 977	
F561-575	Michigan 977.4	
F591-705	West (U.S.) & Trans-Mississippi 978	
F595	Trans-Mississippi & the West (1880-1950) 978.02-033	
F601-615	Minnesota 977.6	
F631-645	North Dakota 978.4	
F676-690	Kansas 978.1	
F691-705	Oklahoma 976.6	
F721-785	Rocky Mts. area (Mont., Idaho, Wyo., Colo.) 978	
F726-740	Montana 978.6	
F771-785	Colorado 978.8	
F786-850	Southwest (New: New Mex., Ariz., Utah, Nev.) 978.9-979.3, 979	
F791-805	New Mexico 978.9	
F801	New Mexico (1848-1950)	
F804.A-Z	Local history (New Mex.: towns etc.)	
F804.L6	Los Alamos, New Mex.	

```
F851-915+    Pacific States & Alaska      979
F852         Pacific Northwest (1859-1950)      979.5
F856-870     California        979.4
F861         California (gen.)  979.4
F866         California (1869-1950: SEE D570.85.C2-21 for 1914-18 war years)
                                                         979.404-4053
F867         Southern California       979.49
F868.A-Z     Local history (Calif.: regions, counties, etc.)
F868.L8          Los Angeles County (Calif.)      979.493
F868.S156    San Francisco Bay area (Calif.)      979.46
F868.S23     Santa Barbara County (Calif.)        979.491
F869.A-Z     Local history (Calif.: towns etc.)
F869.L8          Los Angeles, Calif.   979.494
F869.S22     San Diego, Calif.        979.498
F869.S3          San Francisco, Calif.       979.461
F870.A-Z     Races, ethnography, religious groups (Calif.)
F870.A1          Races, ethnography, religious groups (Calif.: gen.)
F870.G3          Germans (in Calif.)
F870.J3          Japanese (in Calif.)
F870.J5          Jews (in Calif.)
F870.O6          Orientals (in Calif.)
F886-900     Washington (state)        979.7
F891         Washington (state: to 1950)
F897.A-Z     Local history (Wash. state: regions, counties, etc.)
F897.P9          Puget Sound (Wash.)
F899.A-Z     Local history (Wash. state: towns etc.)
F899.S4          Seattle, Wash.        979.777
F965         Territories (U.S.: inclu. Alaska & Hawaii: SEE ALSO DU620-629 for
                     Haw.)

F1001-1140+   CANADA     971
F1015        Description & travel (Can.: 1867-1950)      917.1045-1063
F1026        Canada (gen.)
F1027        French Canadians
F1028            Military history (Can.)      355.00971
F1028.5          Naval history (Can.)    359.00971
F1029            Diplomacy (Can.: gen.)      327.71
F1029.5.A-Z      Foreign relns. (Can.-other places)  327.710+
F1029.5.F8           Foreign relns. (Can.-Fr.)   327.71044
F1029.5.G3          Foreign relns. (Can.-Ger.) 327.71043
F1029.5.G7          Foreign relns. (Can.-G.B.)       327.71041
F1029.5.I8       Foreign relns. (Can.-It.)
F1029.5.R9       Foreign relns. (Can.-Rus.)       327.71047
F1029.5.U6-7     Foreign relns. (Can.-U.S.) 327.71073
F1033        Canada (1867+)        971.05+
F1034        Canada (1914+)                           971.061+
F1035.A-Z    Races, ethnography, religious groups (Can.)
F1035.G3     Germans (in Can.)
F1035.8          Maritime Provinces (Can.: Atlantic coast)      971.5-8
F1036-1040       Nova Scotia      971.6
F1041-1045       New Brunswick    971.5
F1056-1059.7     Ontario (Can.)   971.3
F1075-1080       Alberta  971.23
F1086-1089.7     British Columbia  971.1
```

```
F1121-1139  Newfoundland    971.8, .803 (1934-49)
F1135-1139  Labrador
F1170           Saint Pierre & Miquelon    971.88


F1201-3799+     LATIN AMERICA & the West Indies      972, 980-989
F1201-1392      MEXICO           972-972.7
F1227.5         Military & naval history (Mex.)
F1228           Diplomacy (Mex.: gen.)
F1228.5.A-Z     Foreign relns. (Mex.-other places)      327.720+
F1228.5.G3  Foreign relns. (Mex.-Ger.)      327.72043
F1228.5.R9  Foreign relns. (Mex.-Rus.)      327.72047
F1228.5.S65     Foreign relns. (Mex.-Sov.Un.)      327.72047
F1228.5.U6-7    Foreign relns. (Mex.-U.S.)      327.72073
F1234       Mexico (1910-46)          972.081-082
F1386       Mexico City area (Mex.)    972.53
F1392.A-Z   Races, ethnography, religious groups (Mex.)
F1392.G4    Germans (in Mex.)
F1401-1419  Latin America (gen.)       980
F1414       Latin America (1898-)      980.032+
F1415       Diplomacy (Latin Am.: gen.)    327.8
F1416.A-Z   Foreign relns. (Latin Am. & other places except U.S.)      327.80+
F1416.F8        Foreign relns. (Latin Am.-Fr.)
F1416.G3        Foreign relns. (Latin Am.-Ger.)      327.8043
F1416.G7        Foreign relns. (Latin Am.-G.B.)
F1416.I8    Foreign relns. (Latin Am.-It.)
F1416.R9    Foreign relns. (Latin Am.-Rus.)
F1418       Foreign relns. (Latin Am.-U.S.)      327.8073
F1421-1577  CENTRAL AMERICA          972, 972.8+
F1438       Central America (1821-1950)      972.804-805
F1561-1577      PANAMA          972.87


F1601-2175+     WEST INDIES    972.9
F1621       West Indies (gen. hist.)
F1621.5         Diplomacy (W.Ind.: gen.)
F1622       Foreign relns. (W.Ind.-U.S.)
F1622.5.A-Z     Foreign relns. (W.Ind.-partic. places)
F1622.5.G3  Foreign relns. (W.Ind.-Ger.)
F1622.5.G7  Foreign relns. (W.Ind.-G.B.)
F1623       West Indies (1898-)      972.904-905
F1629.A-Z       Races, ethnography, religious groups (W.Ind.)
F1630-1640      BERMUDA ISLANDS      972.99
F1650-1660      BAHAMA ISLANDS       972.96
F1741-1991      GREATER ANTILLES (Cuba, Haiti, Puerto Rico, Jamaica, etc.)
                                               972.9, .91-95
F1751-1849  CUBA        972.91
F1765       Description & travel (Cuba: 1898-)      917.291046
F1776.1         Military & naval history (Cuba)
F1776.2         Diplomacy (Cuba: gen.)
F1861-1896  JAMAICA        972.92
F1871       Description & travel (Jam.: 1811-1950)
F1886       Jamaica (1810-1953)        972.92034-9205
F1951-1983  PUERTO RICO            972.95
```

F2131-2133	BRITISH WEST INDIES	972.9, .973
F2136	VIRGIN ISLANDS (U.S.)	972.9722
F2141	DUTCH WEST INDIES	972.986
F2151	FRENCH WEST INDIES	972.976
F2161-2175	CARIBBEAN SEA AREA	972.9, 909.096365

F2201-3799+	SOUTH AMERICA	980-989
F2223	Description & travel (S.Am.: 1811-1950)	
F2231	South America (gen.)	980
F2236	South America (1830-)	980.03
F2239.A-Z	Races, ethnography, religious groups (S.Am.)	
F2239.B8	British (in S.Am.)	
F2239.F8	French (in S.Am.)	
F2239.G3	Germans (in S.Am.)	
F2251-2299	COLOMBIA	986.1+
F2301-2349	VENEZUELA	987
F2501-2659	BRAZIL	981
F2515	Description & travel (Brazil: 1890-1950)	918.1045-1061
F2521	Brazil (gen.)	
F2522	Military & naval history (Brazil)	
F2523	Diplomacy (Brazil: gen.)	327.81
F2523.A-Z	Foreign relns. (Brazil-other lands)	
F2523.G3	Foreign relns. (Brazil-Ger.)	
F2523.G7	Foreign relns. (Brazil-G.B.)	
F2535	Brazil (1822-)	981.04+
F2537	Brazil (1889-)	981.05+
F2541-2636+	Local history (Brazil: regions, states, etc.)	
F2611	Rio de Janeiro (Brazil: state)	
F2646	Rio de Janeiro, Br.	981.53
F2659.A-Z	Races, ethnography, religious groups (Brazil)	
F2659.A5	Americans (in Brazil)	
F2659.F8	French (in Brazil)	
F2659.G3	Germans (in Brazil)	
F2661-2699	PARAGUAY	989.2
F2682	Diplomacy (Paraguay)	
F2682.A-Z	Foreign relns. (Paraguay-other places)	
F2682.G3	Foreign relns. (Paraguay-Ger.)	327.892043
F2699.A-Z	Races, ethnography, religious groups (Paraguay)	
F2699.G3	Germans (in Paraguay)	
F2701-2799	URUGUAY	989.5
F2721	Uruguay (gen.)	
F2722.5.A-Z	Foreign relns. (Urug. & other partic. places: by name)	
F2722.5.G3	Foreign relns. (Urug.-Ger.)	327.895043
F2728	Uruguay (1904-)	989.5061-5063
F2799.A-Z	Races, ethnography, religious groups (Urug.)	
F2799.F7	French (in Urug.)	
F2799.G3	Germans (in Urug.)	

```
F2801-3021  ARGENTINA      982
F2815          Description & travel (Arg.: 1806-1950)   918.2043-2062
F2831          Argentina (gen.)
F2832          Military & naval history (Arg.)
F2833              Diplomacy (Arg.: gen.)
F2833.5.A-Z      Foreign relns. (Arg.-partic. lands)   327.820+
F2833.5.F8       Foreign relns. (Arg.-Fr.)
F2833.5.G3       Foreign relns. (Arg.-Ger.)       327.82043
F2833.5.G7       Foreign relns. (Arg.-G.B.)
F2833.5.I8       Foreign relns. (Arg.-It.)
F2833.5.U6-7     Foreign relns. (Arg.-U.S.)
F2846          Argentina (1810-)        982.03+
F2848          Argentina (1910-43)      982.06
F3001          Buenos Aires, Arg.        982.11
F3021.A-Z      Races, ethnography, religious groups (Arg.)
F3021.A5       Americans (in Arg.)
F3021.B86      British (in Arg.)
F3021.F8       French (in Arg.)
F3021.G3       Germans (in Arg.)
F3021.I8       Italians (in Arg.)
F3021.U5       Ukrainians (in Arg.)
F3031          FALKLAND ISLANDS        997.11
F3051-3285  CHILE        983
F3063          Description & travel (Chile: 1810-1950)      918.3044-30643
F3081          Chile (gen.)
F3083          Diplomacy (Chile: gen.)
F3083.5.A-Z      Foreign relns. (Chile-other places)
F3083.5.G3 Foreign relns. (Chile-Ger.)
F3083.5.U6-7     Foreign relns. (Chile-U.S.)
F3301-3359  BOLIVIA      984
F3401-3619  PERU         985
F3433          Diplomacy (Peru: gen.)
F3434.A-Z      Foreign relns. (Peru-other places)
F3434.G3       Foreign relns. (Peru-Ger.)
F3701-3799  ECUADOR        986.6


U              Military science (gen.)        355
U-UH           MILITARY SCIENCE, MILITARY ENGINEERING, & AIR FORCES
                                                             355-359, 623
UA             Armies (organization, descrip., status)
UB             Administration, Military
UC             Maintenance & transportation, Military
UD             Infantry
UE             Cavalry (armored & mechanized)
UF             Artillery
UG             Military engineering & air forces
UH             Military science (misc. services: medical etc.)
```

U1-900+	MILITARY SCIENCE (GEN.)	355
U1	Periodicals & associations (military: in English)	355.005-006
U9	Almanacs, annuals, etc., Military (U.S.)	
U10.A-Z	Almanacs, annuals, etc., Military (countries besides U.S.)	
U10.G7	Almanacs, annuals, etc., Military (G.B.)	
U13.A-Z	Museums, Military (inclu. exhibitions)	355.0074
U13.A1	Military museums & exhibitions (gen.)	
U13.A2-Z	Exhibitions & museums, Military (by country)	355.00740+
U13.F8	Museums, Military (Fr.)	
U13.G7	Museums, Military (G.B.)	
U13.G72.L69	Imperial War Museum (London, G.B.)	
U13.S65	Museums, Military (Sov.Un.)	
U13.U6-7	Museums, Military (U.S.)	355.0074073
U21.75	Women & the military (sociology)	
U24-25	Dictionaries & encyclopedias (mil. sci.) 355.003	
U27-45	Military science (history)	
U27	Military science (history: gen.)	355.009
U39	Military science (modern: 1800-)	
U41	Military science (19th c.)	
U42	Military science (20th c.) 355.00904	
U43.A-Z	Military science (history: by country or area)	
U51-55	Biography, Military (SEE ALSO D-F war & country #s)	
		355.3310922-0924, .00922-00924
U52	Military biography (U.S.: collective)	
U53.A-Z	Biography, Military (U.S.: individual)	355.330973
U54.A-Z	Biography, Military (except U.S.: group by place)	
U55.A-Z	Biography, Military (except U.S.: individual)	
U56	Military clubs (U.S.)	
U58	Clubs, Military (G.B.)	
U59.A-Z	Clubs, Military (by place, except U.S. & G.B.)	
U102	Military science (gen. titles: pubn. date 1789-)	355, .43
U110-145	Handbooks & manuals, Soldiers'	355.00202
U110	Soldiers' handbooks & manuals (gen.)	
U113	Manuals & handbooks, Soldiers' (U.S.)	
U115.A-Z	Handbooks & manuals, Soldiers' (by place except U.S.)	
U130-135	Handbooks, Officers'	
U150-155	Military planning	
U153	Planning, Military (U.S.)	
U162	Strategy (mil. sci.: pubn. 1789-)	355.43
U162.6	Deterrence	
U165	Tactics, Military (pubn. 1811-)	355.42
U167.5.A-Z	Military tactics (special topics: by name)	
U167.5.A35	Advanced guard	
U167.5.D4	Desert warfare	
U167.5.E57	Envelopment (mil. sci.)	
U167.5.F6	Forest fighting	
U167.5.H3	Hand-to-hand fighting	
U167.5.M3	Machine-gun warfare	
U167.5.M6	Motorized units (mil. sci.)	
U167.5.N5	Night fighting	
U167.5.R34	Raids (mil. sci.)	
U167.5.S7	Street fighting	
U167.5.W5	Winter warfare	

U168	Logistics (mil. sci.)	355.411
U170-175	Field service (mil. sci.)	
U180-185	Encampments	355.412
U200	Landing maneuvers & debarkation	
U215	Rearguard action	
U220	Reconnaisance & patrols 355.413, 358.45	
U225	Survival (combat: escape & evasion)	
U250-255	Maneuvers (mil. sci.)	
U250	Maneuvers (mil. sci.: gen.)	355.52
U253	Maneuvers (mil. sci.: U.S.)	
U255.A-Z	Maneuvers (mil. sci.: places besides U.S.)	
U260	Combined ops. (joint: air, army, navy)	
U261	Amphibious ops.	359.83, .96
U262	Commando tactics	355.425
U265	Military expeditions	
U290	Drill camps, instruction bases, maneuver grounds (gen.)	
U293	Instruction camps, maneuver grounds, etc. (U.S.)	
U294.5.A-Z	Drill camps, maneuver grounds, etc. (U.S.: by name)	
U300-305	Artillery & rifle ranges	
U303	Rifle & artillery ranges (U.S.)	
U310	War games	355.5
U311	Models, Military	
U312	Map maneuvers & problems	
U320-325	Physical training (mil. sci.)	355.54+
U323	Training, Physical (mil. sci.: U.S.)	
U327	Sports, Military (gen.)	
U328.A-Z	Military sports (by place)	
U390-395	Research, Military	355.07
U393	Military research (U.S.)	
U400-714	EDUCATION, MILITARY	355.07
U400	Military education & training (gen.)	355.07
U403	Training & education, Military (modern hist.)	
U405	Education, Military (gen.: pubns. 1801+)	
U407-439	Education, Military (U.S.)	
U408	Military education (U.S.: gen.)	355.0071073
U408.3	U.S. military education (gen. special)	
U410.A-R3+	U.S. Military Academy (West Point)	355.0071173
U410.C3-H8	U.S. Military Academy (admin.)	
U410.E1	Reports, Official (U.S. Mil. Acad. Superinten.: annual)	
U410.E5	Reports, Congressional (U.S. Military Academy: by date)	
U410.H2	Rosters, Officers' (U.S. Mil. Acad.)	
U410.H3-4	Registers, Official (U.S. Mil. Acad.)	
U410.H5-8	U.S. Military Academy (registers, unoff.)	
U410.H5	Cullum's Register (U.S. Mil. Acad.)	
U410.L1	U.S. Military Academy (gen. hist.)	
U410.L1.A1-5	West Point (U.S. Mil. Acad.: official hist's.)	
U410.L3	Pictorials (U.S. Mil. Acad.)	
U410.M1.A1-Z	Biography (U.S. Mil. Acad.: by name)	
U410.M1.P1	West Point (descrip. & life)	
U412	National War College (U.S.: Wash., D.C.)	
U413	Army War College (U.S.)	
U415	Military education (U.S.: Command & Gen. Staff Coll.)	
U428.5	Reserve Officers' Training Corps (U.S.: R.O.T.C.)	
U440-444	Military education (Can.)	

U505-630	Education, Military (Eur.)	355.007104+
U505	Military education (Eur.: gen.)	
U510-549.3	Education, Military (G.B.)	
U510	Military education (G.B.: gen.)	
U511	British military education (special time periods)	
U518.A-Z	Royal Military Academy (Woolwich: div'd like U410.A-Z)	
U518.L1	Royal Military Academy (Woolwich: gen. hist's.)	
U520.A-Z	Royal Military College (Sandhurst)	
U520.L1	Sandhurst (Royal Mil. Coll.: descrip. & life)	
U550	Education, Military (Austria-Hung.: gen.)	
U551	Military education (Austria-Hung.: special eras)	
U565-569	Education, Military (Fr.)	
U570-574	Education, Military (Ger.)	355.0071043
U570	Military education (Ger.: gen.)	
U571	German military education (special times)	
U572.A-Z	Military education (Ger.: special topics)	
U574.A-Z	Training, Military (Ger.: by school location)	
U585-589	Education, Military (It.)	
U600-604	Education, Military (Rus.)	355.0071047
U620-624	Education, Military (Tur.)	
U625	Education, Military (Balkan States)	
U635-660	Education, Military (Asia)	
U650-654	Education, Military (Japan)	355.0071052
U700-704	Education, Military (Australia)	355.0071094
U705-709	Education, Military (New Z.)	
U719-740+	Observations, Military	
U719	Military observations (collected: 2 or more wars)	
U729	Observations, Military (Franco-Prussian War, 1870-1)	
U730	Observations, Military (Russo-Turkish Conflict, 1877-8)	
U731	Observations, Military (Sp.-Am. War, 1898-9)	
U733	Observations, Military (S.Afr. Conflict, 1899-1902)	
U735	Observations, Military (Russo-Jpn. War, 1904-5)	
U738	Observations, Military (WWI)	
U750-773	MILITARY LIFE & CUSTOMS	355.1
U750	Customs, Military (gen.)	
U765	Life & customs, Military (modern: gen.) 355.1	
U766	Military life & customs (modern: U.S.) 355.10973	
U767	Military life & customs (modern: G.B.) 355.10941	
U768	Military life & customs (modern: Fr.)	
U769	Military life & customs (modern: Ger.) 355.10943	
U770	Military life & customs (modern: It.)	
U771	Military life & customs (modern: Rus.) 355.10947	
U773	Military life & customs (modern: misc. countries besides U766-771)	
U790	Curiosities, Military (inclu. collector's hdbks.)	

U799-897	ARMS & ARMOR (Hist.)	
U799	Periodicals & associations (arms & armor: hist.)	
U800.A3-Z	Arms (gen.: pubn. dates 1801+)	355.8, 623.4
U804	Museums, exhibitions, etc. (arms)	
U804.A2-Z	Museums, exhibitions, etc. (arms: by country)	
U815	Armament (modern: gen.)	
U818	Armament (modern: U.S.)	
U820.A-Z	Armament (modern: Eur.: by place)	
U820.G3	British armament (modern)	
U820.G7	German armament (modern)	
U821.A-Z	Armament (modern: Asia: by country)	
U880	Guns (gen.) 623.4	
U884	Small arms (gen.)	
U889	Small arms (19th-20th c.)	
U897.A-Z	Small arms (by region or country)	

UA	ARMIES (organiz. & world status)	355
UA10	Military status (world: gen.) 355.03	
UA10.5	National security (gen.)	
UA11	Policy, Military (gen.)	
UA14	Colonial troops	
UA15	Armies & navies (of the world)	
UA16	Military missions	
UA17	Costs, Military 355.622	
UA17.5.A2	Manpower (gen.) 355.22, .61	
UA17.5.A3-Z	Manpower (by country)	
UA18.A2	Mobilization, Industrial (gen.) 355.28	
UA18.A3-Z	Industrial mobilization (by country: SEE ALSO D-F for specific wars)	
UA21-876+	MILITARY STATUS (worldwide: place by place)	355.0330+
UA21-645	MILITARY STATUS (W. Hemis.)	
UA21	America (mil. status: gen.) 355.03301812	
UA22-602	MILITARY STATUS (N. Am.)	
UA22	North America (mil. status) 355.03307	
UA23-585	MILITARY STATUS (U.S.) 355.033273	
UA23.A1.A-Z	Periodicals & associations (military: U.S.)	
UA23.A2-Z	United States (mil. status: gen.)	
UA23.2-6	U.S. Dept. of Defense 353.6-7	
UA23.2	Reports, Official (U.S. Dept. Defense: formerly War Dept.)	
UA23.6	U.S. Dept. of Defense (gen. hist.)	
UA24-39	U.S. Army	
UA24.A1-7	Reports, Official (U.S. Army: War Dept., Dept. o/t Army, Adj. Gen., Inspec. Gen., etc.: annual)	
UA24.A1-149	U.S. War Dept. (ann. reports)	
UA25	U.S. Army (gen.) 355.00973, .30973, .310973	
UA26.A1-6	Army posts (U.S.: gen.)	
UA26.A7-Z	Army posts (U.S.: by place)	
UA27.3.1st-	Armies (U.S.: by #/author)	
UA27.5.1st-	Divisions (U.S.: by #/author)	
UA27.A-Z	Divisions (U.S. Army: by place)	
UA27.P5	Division of the Philippines (U.S. Army)	
UA28	Infantry (U.S.: gen.) 356.10973	
UA29.1st-	Infantry regiments (U.S.: by #/author)	
UA30	Armored units & cavalry (U.S.: inclu. mechanized: gen.) 357.10973	
UA31.1st-	Cavalry & armored regiments (U.S.: by #/author)	

```
UA32            Artillery (U.S.: gen.)      358.10973, .120973
UA33.1st-       Artillery batteries (U.S.: by #/author)
UA34.A-Z        U.S. Army (special troops: by name)
UA37            Lists & registers (U.S. Army: vets.)
UA42-560        RESERVES, ARMY (U.S.: Nat. Guard, militia, volunteers, etc.)
UA42.A1-59         Reports, Official (army reserves: U.S.)
UA42.A6.A-Z        Associations, periodicals, societies (U.S.: army reserves)      E740
UA42.A7-Z          U.S. National Guard (gen.)
UA45               Women's reserves (U.S.)
UA50-549        MILITIA (U.S.: inclu. Nat. Guard etc.: state by state)
UA90-99            Reserves, Army (U.S.: Calif.)
UA90               California National Guard (gen.)
UA91               Primary sources, documents (Calif. army reserves)
UA92               Lists & registers (Calif. Nat. Guard)
UA93-94         Infantry (U.S.: Calif. reserves)
UA95            Cavalry (U.S.: Calif. reserves)
UA96            Artillery (U.S.: Calif. reserves: gen., inclu. field)
UA97-97.5          Coast artillery (U.S.: Calif. reserves)
UA170-179          Volunteers (Nat. Guard, militia, etc.: Illinois)
UA290-299          Reserves, Army (U.S.: Missouri)
UA360-369       Reserves, Army (U.S.: N.Y.: militia, volunteers, Nat. Guard, etc.)
UA360           New York National Guard (gen.)
UA361           Primary sources, documents (N.Y. army reserves)
UA362           Lists & registers (N.Y. Nat. Guard)
UA363-364          Infantry (U.S.: N.Y. reserves)
UA365              Cavalry (U.S.: N.Y. reserves)
UA366-367.75       Artillery (U.S.: N.Y. reserves)
UA366              Field artillery (U.S.: N.Y. reserves: ALSO gen. artil.)
UA420-429       Reserves, Army (U.S.: Penn.)
UA470-479       Reserves, Army (U.S.: Texas)
UA565.A-Z       Auxiliaries, Army (U.S.)
UA600-602       Military status (Can.)
UA600           Canada (mil. status: gen.)      355.033271, .033571, .033071
UA602.3            Latin America (mil. status: gen.)      355.03328, .03308
UA612-645          Military status (S.Am.)
UA612              South America (mil. status: gen.)      355.03308, .03328
UA646-829       MILITARY STATUS (Eur.)
UA646           Europe (mil. status)      355.03304, .03324, .03354
UA646.53        Baltic Sea (mil. status)      355.033016334, .4716334, 359.4716334
UA646.55        Mediterranean Sea (mil. status)      355.03301638, 359.471638
UA646.6            North Sea (mil. status)      355.033016336
UA646.7            Scandinavia (mil. status)      355.033048, .033248, .033548
UA646.85        Northern Europe (mil. status)      355.033048
UA647-668       Military status (G.B.)      355.033041-033042, .033241, .033541
UA647           Great Britain (mil. status)  355.033041
UA648           Primary sources, documents (G.B.: War Dept., Parliament, other
                    re military)
UA649-668       G.B. Army
UA649           G.B. Army (gen.)      355.00941, .310941
UA650-653       Infantry (G.B.)
UA650           Infantry (G.B.: gen.)      356.10941
UA651.A-Z       Infantry regiments (G.B.: by name)
UA651.C6        Coldstream Guards (G.B.)
```

UA654-657	Cavalry (G.B.)	357.10941
UA658	Artillery (G.B.)	358.10941, .120941
UA663	Welsh troops (G.B.)	
UA664	Scottish troops (G.B.)	
UA665	Irish troops (G.B.)	
UA668	Colonial troops (G.B.: inclu. natives: gen.)	
UA670-679	Military status (Austria & Austria-Hung.)	
UA670	Austria & Austria-Hungary (mil. status)	355.0330436
UA672	Austria-Hungary. Army (gen.)	355.309436
UA673	Infantry (Austria & Austria-Hung.)	
UA674	Cavalry (Austria & Austria-Hung.)	
UA680-689	Belgium (mil. status)	355.0330493
UA690-699	Denmark (mil. status)	355.0330489
UA700-709	Military status (Fr.)	
UA700	France (mil. status: gen.)	355.033044
UA702	France. Army (gen.)	355.00944, .30944
UA702.3	Army posts (Fr.: gen.)	
UA702.32.A-Z	Army posts (Fr.: by place)	
UA703-705	France. Army (infantry, cavalry, armor, artillery)	
UA709	Colonial troops (Fr.)	
UA710-719	Military status (Ger.)	
UA710	Germany (mil. status: gen.)	355.033043, .033243, .033543
UA712	Germany. Army (gen.)	355.00943, .30943, .310943
UA713.A1-Z9.A-Z	Infantry (Ger.)	356.10943
UA713.A1-5	Primary sources, documents (Ger. infantry)	
UA713.A6-Z4	Infantry (Ger.: gen.)	
UA713.Z6.1st-	Infantry (Ger.: by regiment #)	
UA713.Z9.A-Z	Infantry (Ger.: by group name)	
UA714	Armored units & cavalry (Ger.)	357.10943, .50943, 358.180943
UA715	Artillery (Ger.)	
UA716.A-Z	Germany. Army (special units: by name)	
UA717	Militia (Ger.)	
UA718.A-Z	Germany. Army (local)	
UA719	Colonial troops (Ger.)	
UA720-729	Greece (mil. status)	355.0330495
UA730-739	Netherlands (mil. status)	355.0330492
UA740-749	Military status (It.)	
UA740	Italy (mil. status)	355.033045
UA742	Italy. Army (gen.)	355.30945
UA743	Infantry (It.)	
UA744	Armored units & cavalry (It.)	
UA745	Artillery (It.)	
UA745.5	Swiss Guards (Papal Guards)	
UA750-759	Military status (Norway)	
UA770-779	Military status (Rus. or Sov.Un.)	
UA770	Russia (mil. status)	355.033047, .033247, .033547
UA771	Primary sources, documents (Rus. military)	
UA772	Russia. Army (gen.)	355.30947, .00947
UA773.A1-Z9.A-Z	Infantry (Rus.)	
UA773.A1-5	Primary sources, documents (Rus.)	
UA773.A6-Z4	Infantry (Rus.: gen.)	
UA773.Z6.1st-	Infantry (Rus.: by regiment #)	
UA773.Z9.A-Z	Infantry (Rus.: by group name)	
UA774	Armored units & cavalry (Rus.)	
UA775	Artillery (Rus.)	

UA780-789	Spain (mil. status)	355.033046
UA790-799	Sweden (mil. status)	355.0330485
UA800-809	Switzerland (mil. status)	355.0330494
UA810-819	Military status (Tur.)	
UA810	Turkey (mil. status)	355.0330561
UA820-827	Military status (Balkan States)	
UA820	Balkan States (mil. status: gen.)	355.0330496
UA822	Balkan States (mil. status: descrip. & hist.)	
UA824	Bulgaria (mil. status)	355.03304977
UA826	Rumania (mil. status)	355.0330498
UA827	Yugoslavia (mil. status)	355.0330497
UA829.A-Z	Military status (misc. Eur. countries)	
UA829.C95	Czechoslovakia (mil. status)	355.0330437
UA829.H9	Hungary (mil. status)	355.0330439
UA829.P7	Poland (mil. status)	355.0330438
UA830-853	MILITARY STATUS (Asia)	
UA830	Asia (mil. status: gen.)	355.03305, .03325, .03355
UA835-839	Military status (China)	
UA840-844	India (mil. status)	355.033054
UA845-849	Military status (Japan)	
UA845	Japan (mil. status: gen.)	355.033052, .033252, .033552
UA853.A-Z	Military status (Asia: by country except India, China, Japan)	
UA855-868	Military status (Africa)	
UA855	Africa (mil. status: gen.)	355.03306
UA856	South Africa (mil. status)	355.00968, .033068
UA859	Cameroon (mil. status)	
UA860	Ethiopia (mil. status)	355.033063
UA860.5	Kenya (mil. status)	355.03306762
UA865	Egypt 355.033062	
UA867.5	Tunisia (mil. status)	355.0330611
UA868	Libya (mil. status)	355.0330612
UA870-874	Military status (Australia)	
UA870	Australia (mil. status)	355.033094, .033294, .033594
UA871	Primary sources, documents (Australia: military status)	
UA872	Australia. Army (descrip. & hist.)	355.00994, .30994, .310994
UA873.A-Z	Australia. Army (special branches by name)	
UA874.A-Z	Australia (mil. status: states, territories, localities)	
UA874.3-7	Military status (New Z.)	
UA874.3	New Zealand (mil. status: gen.)	355.0330931
UA874.5	New Zealand. Army (descrip. & hist.)	355.309931
UA874.6.A-Z	New Zealand. Army (special sections)	
UA875-876	Military status (Pacific islands)	
UA875	Oceania (mil. status) 355.03309	
UA910-915	Mobilization	
UA910	Mobilization (gen.)	355.28
UA913	Mobilization (U.S.)	355.280973
UA915.A-Z	Mobilization (except U.S.: by name of place)	
UA915.G7	Mobilization (G.B.)	355.280941
UA917.A2	Demobilization (gen.)	355.29
UA917.A3-Z	Demobilization (by country)	
UA920	Attack & defense plans (gen.)	355.0330+, .0332+, .0335+, .4+
UA923	Defense & attack plans (U.S.)	355.033073, .4773
UA925.A-Z	Plans, Attack & defense (countries except U.S.)	

UA926.A3-Z Civil defense (gen.: SEE ALSO numbers within wars, such as D810.C69 for WWII)
UA926.5 Bomb shelters (plus other special civil defense topics like psych. aspects)
UA927 Civil defense (U.S.: gen.)
UA928-928.5.A-Z Defense, Civil (U.S. states, cities, etc.)
UA929.A-Z Civil defense (countries besides U.S.)
UA929.G7 Civil defense (G.B.)
UA929.S65 Civil defense (Sov.Un.)
UA929.5 Industrial defense (gen.) 355.28, .26
UA929.6-8 Defense, Industrial (U.S.)
UA929.9.A-Z Industrial defense (places besides U.S.)
UA929.95.A-Z Industrial defense (by specific industry: SEE ALSO H industry #s)
UA929.95.A35 Agriculture (defense)
UA929.95.C5 Chemical industry (defense)
UA929.95.E4 Electric plants (defense)
UA929.95.G7 Grain industry (defense)
UA929.95.P4 Petroleum industry (defense)
UA929.95.P93 Public utilities (defense)
UA929.95.R3 Railroads (defense)
UA929.95.T4 Telecommunication (defense)
UA929.95.T7 Transportation (defense)
UA929.95.W3 Waterworks (defense)
UA930 Strategic lines, bases, etc. 355.43
UA940 Military communications (gen.) 355.27, .41, .6
UA943-944 Communications, Military (U.S.)
UA945.A-Z Military communications (except U.S.: by country)
UA950-979 Communication routes (mil. sci.)
UA950 Travel routes (mil. sci.: gen.)
UA953-954 Communication routes (U.S.)
UA955.A-Z Communication routes (except U.S.)
UA960 Roads & highways (gen.)
UA963-964 Highways (U.S.)
UA965.A-Z Roads (places outside U.S.)
UA970-975 Waterways
UA975.A-Z Waterways (outside U.S.)
UA975.G3 Waterways (Ger.)
UA979 Travel routes (misc.)
UA985-997 Military geography 355.47+, .0330+, 359.47+
UA990 Geography, Military (gen. inclu. Eur.) 355.47
UA993 Military geography (U.S.) 355.4773, 359.4773
UA995.A-Z Military geography (except U.S.)
UA997 Preservation of maps & charts

| UB | ADMINISTRATION, MILITARY (command, intelligence, law, etc.) |
| | 355, .6 |

UB1	Periodicals (mil. admin.)
UB15	Administration, Military (gen. hist.)
UB21-124	MILITARY ADMINISTRATION (by country)
UB23-25	Military administration (U.S.) 353.6, 355.60973
UB23	Administration, Military (U.S.: gen.)
UB24.A-W	Military administration (U.S.: by state)
UB26-27	Military administration (Can.)
UB27.5-54	Military administration (Lat.Am.)
UB55-95	Military administration (Eur.)
UB55	Administration, Military (Eur.: gen.)
UB57-64	Military administration (G.B.)
UB57	Administration, Military (G.B.: gen.) 355.60941, 354.41066
UB58.1900+	Military administration (G.B.: by time period)
UB59	Military administration (G.B.: Eng. & Wales)
UB61	Military administration (G.B.: Scot.)
UB65-66	Military administration (Austria)
UB67-68	Military administration (Belg.)
UB71-72	Military administration (Fr.) 354.44066
UB73-74	Military administration (Ger.) 354.43066, 355.60943
UB75-76	Military administration (Greece)
UB79-80	Military administration (It.)
UB85-86	Military administration (Rus.: Eur.) 354.47066
UB86.5	Military administration (Scan.: gen.)
UB95.A-Z	Military administration (misc. Eur. lands)
UB95.P7	Military administration (Pol.)
UB99-113	Military administration (Asia)
UB103-104	Military administration (India)
UB105-106	Military administration (Japan) 354.52066, 355.60952
UB109-110	Military administration (Rus.: Asia & Sib.)
UB111-112	Military administration (Tur.)
UB115-119	Military administration (Africa)
UB121-122	Military administration (Australia) 354.94066
UB122.5	Military administration (New Z.)
UB145	Military administration (gen.: pubn. 1801-1970) 355.6
UB146	Military administration (gen.: pubn. 1971+) 355.6
UB147	Military service as a profession
UB160-165	Accounting & accounts, Military (inclu. records, muster rolls, etc.)
UB160	Muster rolls & accounts, Military (gen.: inclu. gen. corresp.: admin.)
UB170-175	Adjutant generals' offices
UB180-197	Military administration (civil sections)
UB180	Civilian personnel (mil. admin.: gen.) 355.23
UB193	Personnel, Civilian (mil. admin.: U.S.)
UB200-245	Command control 355.41, .33, .6
UB200	Generals, marshals, commanders (admin.: duties etc.) 355.331
UB210	Leadership, Military
UB212	Command & control systems
UB220-225	Staffs, Army
UB220	Staffs, Military (gen.)
UB223	Army staffs (U.S.)
UB225.A-Z	Military staffs (countries besides U.S.)
UB230-235	Headquarters, Military
UB230	Military headquarters ops. (gen.: inclu. aides, adjutants, etc.)
UB240-245	Inspection, Military

UB246-249	Security (defense info.)	
UB246	Information security (mil. data: gen.)	
UB247	Military information (security: U.S.)	
UB248.A-Z	Military information (security: besides U.S.)	
UB249	Security, Industrial (defense purposes)	
UB250-271	Intelligence, Military	
UB250	Military intelligence (gen.)	355.3432
UB251.A-Z	Intelligence, Military (by country)	
UB251.G3	Military intelligence (Ger.)	355.34320943
UB251.G7	Military intelligence (G.B.)	
UB260	Attachés, Military	
UB270-271	Espionage & spies (mil. admin.)	
UB270	Spies (mil. admin.)	327.12
UB271.A-Z	Espionage (by country responsible: SEE D-F #s for other cases in particular countries or particular wars)	
UB271.G3	German espionage (gen.)	327.120943
UB271.G32.A-Z	Spies, German (by name)	
UB271.G7	British espionage (gen.)	327.120941
UB271.R9	Russian espionage (gen.)	327.120947
UB271.R92.A-Z	Spies, Russian (by name)	
UB271.U6	Espionage (U.S.: gen.)	327.120973
UB271.U62.A-Z	Spies, United States (by name)	
UB273	Sabotage (mil. sci.: gen.)	355.3437
UB274	Sabotage equipment (mil. sci.)	
UB275	Propaganda & psych. warfare (mil. sci.: gen.: SEE ALSO BF1045.M55 & HM263 for indiv. & social aspects)	355.3434
UB276	Propaganda & psych. warfare (U.S.)	355.34340973
UB277.A-Z	Psychological warfare & propaganda (countries except U.S.)	
UB277.G3	Propaganda & psych. warfare (Ger.)	355.34340943
UB277.R9	Propaganda & psych. warfare (Rus.)	355.34340947
UB277.S65	Propaganda & psych. warfare (Sov.Un.)	355.34340947
UB280-285	Orders, passes, field correspondence (mil. sci.)	
UB280	Passes, orders, field correspondence (mil. sci.: gen.)	
UB290	Cryptography & ciphers	358.24
UB320-325	Recruitment, enlistment, promotion, discharge (mil. sci.)	
UB320	Promotion, discharge, recruitment, enlistment (mil. sci.: gen.)	355.2, .61
UB323	Enlistment, recruitment, promotion, discharge (mil. sci.: U.S)	355.20973
UB325.A-Z	Discharge, promotion, recruitment, enlistment (mil. sci.: countries besides U.S.)	
UB330-336	Medical & mental examinations (mil. recruits)	
UB330	Mental & medical examinations (mil. recruits: gen.)	355.2236
UB337	Classification, Military	
UB340-345	Conscription & exemption (mil. service)	
UB340	Induction & exemption (mil.)	355.22363, .225
UB341	Conscientious objectors (gen.)	355.224
UB342.A-Z	Conscientious objectors (by country)	
UB343-344	Draft & exemption (mil.: U.S.)	355.2236306073
UB345.A-Z	Compulsory service & exemption (mil.: besides U.S.)	
UB345.G3	Exemption & draft (mil.: Ger.)	
UB345.J3	Draft & exemption (mil.: Japan)	
UB350-355	Universal service	

UB356-405	Veterans' benefits & services	355.115
UB356	Veterans' education, employment, etc. (gen.)	355.1152, .1154
UB357-358	Education & employment of veterans (U.S.)	355.1150973
UB359.A-Z	Employment & education of veterans (countries except U.S.)	
UB360	Rehabilitation of disabled veterans (gen.)	355.1156, .1154
UB363-364	Disabled veterans (U.S.: rehab.)	
UB365.A-Z	Veterans' rehabilitation (places besides U.S.)	
UB366.A-Z	Occupational rehabilitation of veterans (by occup.)	
UB368-369	Medical care of veterans	355.115
UB370-375	Pensions, Veterans'	355.64, .1151
UB380-385	Veterans' homes & hospitals	
UB380	Soldiers' & sailors' homes	
UB382-384	U.S. Veterans' Administration	
UB383	National Home & Vets' Admin. (U.S.: gen.)	
UB384.A-W	Soldiers' & sailors' homes (U.S.: state)	
UB385.A-Z	Veterans' homes & hospitals (besides U.S.)	
UB390-397	Cemeteries & graves, Military	
UB400-405	Pensions, Survivors' (mil.)	
UB407-409	Warrant officers (mil.)	
UB407	Officers, Warrant (mil.: gen.)	
UB410-415	Officers, Military (inclu. appt., promo., retire.)	
UB410	Rank, appointment, promotion, retirement, etc. (mil. officers: gen.)	
		355.332
UB412-414	Officers, Military (U.S.)	355.3320973
UB415.A-Z	Military officers (except U.S.: by country)	
UB415.G3	Officers, Military (Ger.)	355.3320943
UB415.G7	Officers, Military (G.B.)	355.3320941
UB416	Minorities & women in the armed forces (gen.)	355.22 (women), .3
UB417	Women & minorities in the armed forces (U.S.: gen.)	
UB418.A-Z	Minorities & women in the armed forces (U.S.: by group name)	
UB418.A47	Afro-Americans (armed forces)	
UB418.B69	Boys (armed forces)	
UB418.H57	Hispanic-Americans (armed forces)	
UB418.W65	Women (armed forces: U.S.)	
UB419	Minorities & women in the armed forces (places besides U.S.)	
UB420-425	Furloughs	
UB430-435	Military decorations, medals, rewards, etc.	355.1342
UB430	Decorations, Military (gen.)	
UB433	Medals, decorations, etc. (mil.: U.S.)	
UB440-445	Retired military	355.1342
UB448-449	Medical care for retired military	
UB461-736	MILITARY LAW	
UB465	Law, Military (gen.: pubn. 1801+)	343.01
UB481	International military law (PREFER JX areas)	341.6
UB485	Customs & laws of war (inclu. treatment of prisoners: SEE ALSO JX)	
UB500-504	Military law (U.S.: PREFER KF7201-7755)	343.010973, .0106073
UB505-509	Military law (Can.)	
UB590-684	European military law	
UB590	Military law (Eur.: gen.)	
UB600-604	Military law (Austria)	
UB615-619	Military law (Fr.)	
UB620-624	Military law (Ger.)	343.010943
UB625-629	Military law (G.B.: PREFER KD6000-6355)	343.010941

UB655	Military law (Rus.: gen.)	343.010947
UB655.A2	Military law (Rus.: statutes & compil's.)	
UB655.A7-Z	Law, Military (Rus.: commentaries, digests, etc.)	
UB655.9-656.5	Regulations, Army (Rus.)	
UB657	General orders (Rus. military: collections)	
UB657.A5	Orders, General (Rus. military: offic. compil's.)	
UB657.A6-7	Orders, Special (Rus. military: collec's. & compil's.)	
UB675-679	Military law (Tur.)	
UB680-683	Military law (Balkan states)	
UB685-710	Asian military law	
UB685	Military law (Asia)	
UB730-734	Military law (Australia)	
UB734.5	Military law (New Z.)	
UB780-789	Offenses & crimes, Military	
UB780	Crimes, Military (gen.)	355.1334
UB783	Military crimes (U.S.: SEE ALSO KF7615-7618)	
UB785.A-Z	Military crimes (countries outside U.S.)	
UB787	Mutiny (mil.)	
UB788	Desertion (mil.)	
UB789	Looting & other mil. crimes	
UB790-795	Military discipline	343.014, .13325
UB793	Discipline, Military (U.S.: SEE ALSO KF7590)	
UB800	Military prisons & prisoners (gen.)	365.48, 355.13325, 344.03548
UB803	Prisons, Military (U.S.: SEE ALSO KF7675)	
UB805.A-Z	Military prisons (outside U.S.)	
UB810	Corporal punishment & flogging (mil. sci.: gen.)	
UB813	Punishment, Corporal (U.S.)	
UB815.A-Z	Flogging & corp. punish. (countries besides U.S.)	
UB820	Military police (gen.)	355.13323
UB825.A-Z	Police, Military (by country)	
UB840	Military justice (admin.: gen.)	343.0143, .133
UB845.A-Z	Judiciary, Military (by country except U.S., for which SEE KF7601-7679)	
UB850	Courts-martial, Military (gen.)	343.0146, 355.13325
UB855.A-Z	Courts-martial, Military (besides U.S., for which SEE KF7625-7659)	
UB857.A-Z	Cases (courts-martial, mil.: by place: for U.S. SEE KF7642, 7652, etc.)	
UB860	Courts of inquiry, Military (gen.)	
UB865.A-Z	Inquiry, Courts of (mil.: by country)	
UB867.A-Z	Cases (courts of inquiry: by place: SEE KF7642 etc. for U.S.)	
UB870	Commissions, Military (gen.)	
UB875.A-Z	Military commissions (by country except U.S., for which SEE KF7661)	

UC	MAINTENANCE & TRANSPORT, MILITARY	
UC10	Military maintenance & transport (gen.)	355.6-8
UC12	Transport & maintenance (mil. sci.: gen. spec.)	
UC15	Requisitions, Military	
UC20-258	ORGANIZATION (mil. maint. & transport: by country)	
UC20-88	Maintenance & transport (mil.: U.S.)	
UC20	Military maintenance & transport (U.S.: gen.)	
UC23	Maintenance & transport (mil.: U.S.: by time period)	
UC23.1917-1918	Military maintenance & transport (U.S.: WWI era)	
UC30-34	Quartermaster's Dept. (U.S.)	355.8
UC40-44	Subsistence Dept. (U.S. Army)	
UC45	Construction Div. (U.S. Army)	
UC46	Military construction (U.S.: gen.: SEE ALSO UG for engineer., VC420+ & VG590+ for naval)	358.22
UC70-75	Paymaster's Dept. (U.S. Army)	
UC90-93	Maintenance & transport (mil.: Can.)	
UC158-233	Maintenance & transport (mil.: Eur.)	
UC158	Military maintenance & transport (Eur.: gen.)	
UC180-183	Maintenance & transport (mil.: Ger.)	
UC184-187	Maintenance & transport (mil.: G.B.)	
UC184	Supply & transport depts. (mil.: G.B.)	
UC185	Pay & allowances (mil.: G.B.)	
UC208-211	Maintenance & transport (mil.: Rus.)	
UC234-245	Maintenance & transport (mil.: Asia)	
UC255	Maintenance & transport (mil.: Australia)	
UC256.5	Maintenance & transport (mil.: New Z.)	
UC260-267	Supplies & stores, Military (inclu. procure., storage, specs., surplus, etc.)	
UC260	Military supplies & stores (gen.)	
UC263-264	Stores & supplies, Military (U.S.)	
UC265.A-Z	Procurement (mil. supplies: countries besides U.S.)	
UC267	Contracts, Military (supplies)	
UC270-360	Transport, Military	358.25, .44, 355.27
UC270	Transportation, Military (gen.)	358.25
UC273-274	Military transport (U.S.)	
UC275.A-Z	Transport, Military (besides U.S.: by place)	
UC277	Packing & shipment (mil. supplies)	
UC310	Railroads (mil. transp.: gen.)	623.63, 355.83
UC313	Military railroads (U.S.: gen.)	355.830973
UC314.A-Z	Railroads (mil. transp.: U.S. regions or states)	
UC315.A-Z	Transport, Railroad (mil.: places besides U.S.)	
UC320-325	Waterways & troopships (mil. transp.)	359.3264
UC320	Troopships & waterways (mil. transp.: gen.)	
UC330-335	Air transport, Military	358.44
UC340-345	Motor transport (mil. sci.)	355.83
UC343	Transport, Motor (mil. sci.: U.S.)	
UC347	Motorcycles (mil. transp.)	623.7472
UC349	Coolies (mil. transp.)	
UC350	Camels, elephants, etc. (mil. transp.)	
UC355	Dogs (mil. transp.: SEE ALSO UH100)	355.424
UC360	Snowshoes, skis, skates, etc. (mil. transp.)	

UC400-440	Camps & barracks, Military	
UC400	Barracks & camps, Military (gen.)	355.412, .7
UC403-404	Military barracks & camps (U.S.)	355.70973
UC405.A-Z	Military quarters & camps (besides U.S.)	
UC410	Billeting	
UC415	Furnishings (mil. qtrs.)	
UC420	Fuel & light (mil. qtrs.)	
UC425	Fires (mil. qtrs.)	
UC430	Latrines & sewers (mil. qtrs.)	
UC440	Laundries, Military	
UC460-535	Clothing & equipment, Military	
UC460	Equipment & clothing, Military (gen.)	
UC463-464	Military clothing & equipment (U.S.)	
UC465.A-Z	Clothing & equipment, Military (places besides U.S.)	
UC480	Uniforms, Military (gen.)	355.14
UC483-484	Military uniforms (U.S.)	355.140973
UC485.A-Z	Uniforms, Military (besides U.S.)	
UC490-495	Shoes, footwear, gloves (mil.)	
UC493	Military footwear (U.S.)	
UC500-505	Helmets, hats, etc. (mil.)	
UC500	Military headgear	
UC520	Equipment, Military (gen.)	355.8
UC523-524	Military equipment (U.S.)	355.80973
UC525.A-Z	Equipment, Military (countries except U.S.)	
UC529.A-Z	Equipment, Military (special: by name)	
UC529.C2	Canteens (mil. equip.)	
UC529.K6	Knapsacks (mil. equip.)	
UC530-535	Badges, insignia, etc. (mil.: SEE ALSO UB430+ for decorations)	
UC533	Insignia, badges, etc. (mil.: U.S.)	
UC540-585	Field kits & equip. (mil.)	
UC540	Military kits & field equip. (gen.)	355.81
UC543-544	Field kits & equip. (mil.: U.S.)	
UC550-555	Bunks & bedding (mil.)	
UC570-585	Tents, Military	
UC590-595	Flags, colors, standards (mil.)	
UC590	Military flags, colors, standards (gen.)	355.15
UC593-594	Colors, flags, standards (mil.: U.S.)	
UC595.A-Z	Standards, colors, flags (mil.: places besides U.S.)	
UC600-695	Horses & mules, Military	
UC600	Military horses & mules (gen.)	
UC603-604	Horses & mules, Military (U.S.)	
UC605.A-Z	Mules & horses, Military (places besides U.S.)	
UC700-780	Food, cooking, water, etc.	355.65-66, .81
UC700	Subsistence (mil.: gen.)	
UC703-704	Subsistence (mil.: U.S.)	
UC705.A-Z	Subsistence (mil.: countries besides U.S.)	
UC710-715	Rations (mil.)	
UC720	Cooking (mil.: gen.)	
UC723	Messing (mil.: cooking: U.S.)	
UC730-735	Bakeries (mil.)	
UC730	Field ovens (mil.)	
UC740-745	Clubs, Officers' (mil.)	
UC743	Officers' clubs & messes, Military (U.S.)	
UC750-755	Post exchanges & canteens, Military	
UC753	Canteens & post exchanges, Military (U.S.)	

UC760	Refrigerators, Military
UC770	Slaughterhouses, Military
UC780	Water supplies, Military
UD	INFANTRY (tactics, use, gen. hist's.: SEE ALSO UA for specific armies) 356
UD1	Periodicals & associations (infantry)
UD7	Infantry (collections)
UD10	Organization (infantry: gen.)
UD15	Infantry (gen. hist.) 356.09, 109, 355.009
UD21-124	INFANTRY (hist.: by area or country regardless of specific unit: SEE ALSO UA)
UD23	Infantry (U.S.) 356.10973
UD26	Infantry (Can.)
UD55-95	Infantry (Eur.)
UD55	European infantry (gen.) 356.1094
UD57-64	Infantry (G.B.)
UD57	British infantry (gen.) 356.10941
UD58	Infantry (G.B.: by date)
UD65	Infantry (Austria) 356.109436
UD71	Infantry (Fr.) 356.10944
UD73	Infantry (Ger.) 356.10943
UD79	Infantry (It.) 356.10945
UD85	Infantry (Rus.: Eur.) 356.10947
UD99-113	Infantry (Asia)
UD109	Infantry (Rus.: Asian)
UD121	Infantry (Australia) 356.10994
UD122.5	Infantry (New Z.)
UD145	Infantry (gen.: pubn. 1801+) 356.1
UD150-155	Manuals, Infantry
UD150	Infantry manuals (gen.) 356.10202
UD153	Handbooks, Infantry (U.S.)
UD155.A-Z	Manuals, Infantry (places besides U.S.)
UD157-302	TACTICS, MANEUVERS, & DRILLS (infantry)
UD157	Maneuvers, drills, & tactics (infantry: gen.) 356.18, 355.42
UD160-162	Drills, tactics, & maneuvers (infantry: U.S.)
UD160	Infantry tactics & maneuvers (U.S.: gen.)
UD161	Drill regulations (infantry: U.S. reserves)
UD215-269	Tactics, maneuvers, & drills (infantry: Eur.)
UD215	Infantry tactics & maneuvers (Eur.: gen.)
UD219-221	Tactics, maneuvers, & drills (infantry: Austria)
UD228-230	Tactics, maneuvers, & drills (infantry: Fr.)
UD231-233	Tactics, maneuvers, & drills (infantry: Ger.)
UD234-236	Tactics, maneuvers, & drills (infantry: G.B.)
UD243-245	Tactics, maneuvers, & drills (infantry: It.)
UD252-254	Tactics, maneuvers, & drills (infantry: Rus.)
UD270-280	Tactics, maneuvers, & drills (infantry: Asia)
UD270	Infantry tactics & maneuvers (Asia: gen.)
UD271-273	Tactics, maneuvers, & drills (infantry: China)
UD277-279	Tactics, maneuvers, & drills (infantry: Japan)
UD295-298	Tactics, maneuvers, & drills (infantry: Australia & New Z.)
UD310	Marching & guides (mil.: gen.)
UD313-314	Guides & marching (mil.)
UD315.A-Z	Marching & guides (countries except U.S.)
UD315.G3	German marching (mil.)

UD317	River & stream crossing (infantry)	
UD320-325	Arms manuals (infantry)	
UD323-324	Manual of arms (infantry: U.S.)	
UD330	Firing or sharpshooting (infantry: gen.)	
UD333-334	Sharpshooting (infantry: U.S.)	
UD340-345	Bayonet drill	
UD370-375	Equipment, Infantry	
UD380-425	Small arms (infantry)	355.824+, 623.44
UD380	Arms, Small (infantry: gen.)	
UD382	Inspection (small arms: infantry)	
UD383-384	Infantry arms (small: U.S.)	
UD385.A-Z	Small arms (infantry: countries besides U.S.)	
UD390-395	Rifles, carbines, etc. (infantry)	355.82425, 623.4425
UD390	Carbines, rifles, etc.	
UD395.A-Z	Rifles (infantry: by type)	
UD395.M3	Mauser rifle	
UD395.S8	Springfield rifle	
UD395.U6	United States magazine rifle	
UD396	Shotguns	
UD400	Bayonets	
UD410	Pistols & revolvers (gen.)	355.8243, 623.443
UD413-414	Revolvers & pistols, Infantry (U.S. models)	
UD420-425	Swords	
UD430	Reserves & militia, Infantry	
UD440-445	Field service, Infantry	
UD450	Mounted infantry (gen.)	
UD453-454	Infantry, Mounted (U.S.)	
UD460-465	Mountain warfare & troops	356.164
UD470-475	Ski troops	356.164

UE	ARMOR & CAVALRY (SEE ALSO UA for specific armies)	357-358.1
UE1	Periodicals & associations (armor & cavalry)	
UE7	Cavalry & armor (collections)	
UE10	Organization (armor & cavalry: gen.)	
UE15	Armor & cavalry (gen. hist.: inclu. several countries)	357.09, .109, 358.1809
UE21-124	CAVALRY & ARMOR (by place: SEE ALSO UA for specific units)	
UE23	Armor & cavalry (U.S.)	357.0973
UE55-95	Armor & cavalry (Eur.)	
UE55	Cavalry & armor (Eur.: gen.)	357.094
UE57-64	Armor & cavalry (G.B.)	
UE57	Cavalry & armor (G.B.: gen.)	357.0941
UE58	Armor & cavalry (G.B.: by date)	
UE65	Armor & cavalry (Austria)	357.109436
UE71	Armor & cavalry (Fr.)	357.0944
UE73	Armor & cavalry (Ger.)	357.0943
UE79	Armor & cavalry (It.)	
UE85	Armor & cavalry (Rus.: Eur.)	357.0947
UE99-113	Armor & cavalry (Asia)	
UE109	Armor & cavalry (Rus.: Asia)	
UE121-122.5	Armor & cavalry (Australia & New Z.)	357.099+
UE145	Horse cavalry (pubn. 1801+)	357.1
UE147	Mechanized & armored cavalry	357.5, 358.18
UE149	Armor & cavalry (essays & speeches)	

UE150-155	Manuals, Armor & Cavalry
UE153-154	Armor & Cavalry manuals (U.S.)
UE157-302	TACTICS, MANEUVERS, & DRILLS (armor & cavalry)
UE157	Tactics, maneuvers, & drills (horse cavalry: gen.)
UE158	Maneuvers & tactics (horse cavalry & artillery)
UE159	Tactics, maneuvers, & drills (armored & mechanized cavalry)
UE160-302	MANEUVERS & TACTICS (armor & cavalry: by place)
UE160	Tactics, maneuvers, & drills (armor & cavalry: U.S.: gen.)
UE161	Drill regulations (armor & cavalry: U.S. reserves)
UE215-269	Drills, tactics, & maneuvers (armor & cavalry: Eur.)
UE215	Tactics, maneuvers, & drills (armor & cavalry: Eur.: gen.)
UE219	Tactics, maneuvers, & drills (armor & cavalry: Austria)
UE228	Tactics, maneuvers, & drills (armor & cavalry: Fr.)
UE231	Tactics, maneuvers, & drills (armor & cavalry: Ger.)
UE252	Tactics, maneuvers, & drills (armor & cavalry: Rus.)
UE270-280	Maneuvers & tactics (armor & cavalry: Asia)
UE270	Tactics, maneuvers, & drills (armor & cavalry: Asia: gen.)
UE271	Tactics, maneuvers, & drills (armor & cavalry: China)
UE277	Tactics, maneuvers, & drills (armor & cavalry: Japan)
UE295	Tactics, maneuvers, & drills (armor & cavalry: Australia)
UE360	Reconnaisance, Cavalry 355.413, 358.45
UE400-405	Firing (armor & cavalry)
UE420-425	Sword exercises (cavalry)
UE430	Training camps (armor & cavalry: gen.)
UE433-434	Camps, Training (armor & cavalry: U.S.)
UE435.A-Z	Training camps (armor & cavalry: places besides U.S.)
UE460-475	Horses, Cavalry
UE460	Cavalry horses (gen.)
UE470-475	Training (cavalry horses)
UE500	Camel troops & camelry

UF	ARTILLERY (SEE ALSO UA for specific armies & units) 358.1+, 355.82+
UF1	Periodicals & associations (artillery)
UF6	Museums, Artillery (inclu. exhibitions)
UF6.A1.A-Z	Artillery museums & exhibitons (gen.) 358.12
UF6.A2-Z	Museums, Artillery (by country or region)
UF6.x2.A-Z	Museums, Artillery (by city within area, whose 1st letter & shelf # are shown by 'x' in 'x2')
UF7	Artillery (titles in collections)
UF9	Dictionaries & encyclopedias (artillery) 358.1203
UF10	Organization (artillery forces)
UF15	Artillery (gen. hist.) 358.109, .1209, 355.82, .821
UF21-121	ARTILLERY (by place: SEE ALSO UA for particular armies)
UF23	Artillery (U.S.) 358.120973, .10973, 355.820973
UF57	Artillery (G.B.: gen.) 358.120941
UF58	Artillery (G.B.: by date periods)
UF58.1914-18	Artillery (G.B.: WWI)
UF71	Artillery (Fr.) 358.120944
UF73	Artillery (Ger.) 358.120943
UF79	Artillery (It.)
UF85	Artillery (Rus.: Eur.)
UF99-113	Artillery (Asia)
UF111	Artillery (Turkey)
UF121-122.5	Artillery (Australia & New Z.)

UF130-135	Laws, Ordnance
UF133	Ordnance laws (U.S.: PREFER KF7335)
UF145	Artillery (pubn. 1801+) 358.12
UF148	Exercises, problems, etc. (artillery)
UF150-155	Manuals (artillery) 358.120202
UF153-154	Artillery manuals (U.S.)
UF157-302	TACTICS, MANEUVERS, & DRILLS (artillery)
UF157	Maneuvers, drills, & tactics (artillery: gen.)
UF160-302	DRILLS, MANEUVERS, & TACTICS (artillery: by place)
UF160	Tactics, maneuvers, & drills (artillery: U.S.: gen.)
UF162.A-W	Drill regulations (artillery: U.S. reserves: by state)
UF163	Tactics, maneuvers, & drills (artillery: Can.)
UF215-269	Maneuvers & tactics (artillery: Eur.)
UF215	Tactics, maneuvers, & drills (artillery: Eur.: gen.)
UF228	Tactics, maneuvers, & drills (artillery: Fr.)
UF231	Tactics, maneuvers, & drills (artillery: Ger.)
UF234	Tactics, maneuvers, & drills (artillery: G.B.)
UF243	Tactics, maneuvers, & drills (artillery: It.)
UF252	Tactics, maneuvers, & drills (artillery: Rus.)
UF264	Tactics, maneuvers, & drills (artillery: Tur.)
UF295-298	Tactics, maneuvers, & drills (artillery: Australia & New Z.)
UF320	Stream & river crossing (artillery)
UF340-345	Target practice
UF356	Reserves, Artillery
UF370	Horses, Artillery
UF380-385	Wagons & carts, Artillery
UF390	Motor transport, Artillery
UF400	Field artillery (gen.) 358.12
UF403-404	Artillery, Field (U.S.)
UF405.A-Z	Field artillery (places besides U.S.)
UF405.G3	German field artillery
UF410	Horse artillery
UF420	Camel batteries
UF430	Elephant batteries
UF440-445	Mountain artillery
UF443-444	Artillery, Mountain (U.S.)
UF450-455	Seacoast artillery
UF450	Coast artillery (gen.)
UF453-454	Artillery, Seacoast (U.S.)
UF460-465	Siege artillery
UF460	Artillery, Siege (gen.)
UF470-475	Howitzers & mortars
UF473	Mortars & howitzers (U.S.: gen.)
UF475.A-Z	Artillery, Howitzer & mortar (places besides U.S.)
UF475.F8	Howitzers & mortars (Fr.)
UF475.G7	Howitzers & mortars (G.B.)
UF475.J3	Howitzers & mortars (Japan)
UF480	Garrison & fortress artillery (gen.)
UF483	Fortress & garrison artillery (U.S.: gen.)
UF490	Railroad artillery (gen.)
UF493	Artillery, Railway (U.S.: gen.)
UF495.A-Z	Railway artillery (countries besides U.S.)
UF495.F8	Railway artillery (Fr.)
UF495.G3	Railway artillery (Ger.)
UF500-505	Weapons systems (artillery)

UF520-537	Ordnance & small arms	355.82, 623.4+, .44
UF520	Small arms & ordnance (gen.)	355.82
UF523	Ordnance & small arms (U.S.)	355.820973
UF525.A-Z	Small arms & ordnance (besides U.S.: by place)	
UF526	Research, Ordnance & small-arms	
UF526.3	Ordnance & small-arms research (U.S.)	
UF526.5.A-Z	Small-arms & ordnance research (places besides U.S.)	
UF527	Instruction (ordnance & small arms)	
UF530	Manufacture (ordnance & small arms: gen.)	623.4+, 338.476234
UF533	Small arms & ordnance (manufacture: U.S.: gen.)	338.4762340973
UF534.A-W	Manufacture (small arms & ordnance: U.S.: by state)	
UF537.A-Z	Manufacturers (small arms & ordnance)	
UF540	Armories, arsenals, magazines (gen.)	
UF543	Arsenals, armories, etc. (U.S.: gen.)	
UF545.A-Z	Magazines, armories, etc. (countries except U.S.)	
UF550	Ordnance stores, accounts, etc. (gen.)	
UF553	Stores, Ordnance (U.S.: gen.)	
UF560-780	ORDNANCE PROPER	
UF560-565.A-Z.A-Z(II-IV) etc.	Ordnance material (by type, mark #, ed. date, etc.)	
UF560-565... .B.L	Breech-loading ordnance	
UF560-565... .H	Hotchkiss ordnance	
UF560-565... .M.L	Muzzle-loading ordnance	
UF560-565... .N	Nordenfelt ordnance	
UF560-565... .Q.F	Quick-firing ordnance	
UF560	Ordnance material (gen.)	355.82+, 623.4+
UF563	Ordnance material (U.S.: gen.)	355.820973, 623.40973
UF563.A4-8	Handbooks, Gun (U.S.: artillery)	
UF563.A4.1+	Gun handbooks (U.S.: by mm. or cm. then date)	
UF563.A5	Handbooks, Gun (U.S.: by inches)	
UF563.A5.2.95in.Mt.	Mountain guns (U.S.: handbooks: 2.95)	
UF563.A6	Handbooks, Gun (U.S.: by pounds)	
UF563.A7-8	Handbooks, Gun (U.S.: by class or type: sometimes use UF563.A4-6 with measure. & alphab. symbol: e.g. UF563.A5.12 in.M for 12 mortar... or ... Mt. for mountain)	
UF563.A7	Coast guns (U.S.: handbooks)	
UF563.A75	Mortars (U.S.: handbooks)	
UF563.A76	Railway gun matériel (U.S.: handbooks)	
UF563.A77	Trench warfare matériel (U.S.: handbooks)	
UF563.A8	Subcaliber guns (U.S.: handbooks)	
UF563.A9-Z	United States ordnance (gen.)	
UF565.A-Z	Ordnance material (countries besides U.S.)	
UF565.F8	Ordnance material (Fr.)	
UF565.G3	Ordnance material (Ger.)	
UF565.G7	Ordnance material (G.B.)	
UF565.R9	Ordnance material (Rus.)	

UF620.A2	Machine guns (gen.)	623.4424
UF620.A3-Z	Machine guns (specific types)	
UF620.B6	Browning machine guns	
UF620.C6	Colt machine guns	
UF620.G3	Gatling machine guns	
UF620.G6	Goriunov machine guns	
UF620.H8	Hotchkiss machine guns	
UF620.L5	Lewis machine guns	
UF620.M4	Maxim machine guns	
UF620.N8	Nordenfelt machine guns	
UF620.S8	Sten machine guns	
UF620.T5	Thompson machine guns	
UF620.U6	United States automatic machine guns	
UF620.V4	Vickers machine guns	
UF625	Antiaircraft guns & defenses (SEE ALSO UG730+)	358.13
UF628	Antitank guns 623.42, .44, .4518	
UF630	Guns (misc. types: mil. sci.)	
UF640	Gun carriages, caissons, limbers, etc. (gen.) 623.43	
UF643	Caissons, gun carriages, etc. (U.S.: gen.)	
UF650	Gun carriages, Disappearing	
UF652	Gun carriages, Self-propelled (plus track-layer tractors & other self-contained)	
UF655	Railway gun cars (SEE ALSO UF563.A76, UF565) 358.22	
UF660	Cupolas, Revolving (& other portable gun shelters)	
UF670-675	Firing instructions, Artillery	
UF700	Ammunition, Artillery 358.825, 623.45	
UF740-745	Cartridges 623.455	
UF750-770	Projectiles, Artillery 623.451	
UF750	Artillery projectiles (gen.)	
UF753	Projectiles, Artillery (U.S.)	
UF760	Shells & shrapnel 623.4513-4518	
UF765	Grenades 623.45114	
UF767	Bombs & projectiles, Aircraft (inclu. std. & nuclear) 623.451	
UF770	Bullets 623.455	
UF780	Firing devices (primers, percussion caps, etc.)	
UF800	Gunnery, Artillery (gen.) 623.55	
UF805	Aerial observations (artillery)	
UF810	Firing tests (artillery)	
UF820-830	Ballistics 623.51+	
UF820	Projectile velocities & motions (gen.) 623.51	
UF823	Ballistics, Interior 623.513	
UF825	Ballistics, Exterior 623.514	
UF830.A-Z	Ballistic instruments	
UF840	Photography, Ballistic (inclu. photochronography)	
UF845	Binoculars & telescopes, Military	
UF848-856	Fire control, Artillery (inclu. instruments)	
UF848	Artillery fire control (inclu. instruments: gen.) 623.558	
UF849-856	Instruments, Artillery (specific types)	
UF849	Optical instruments & tools, Artillery	
UF850.A2	Range finders, Artillery (gen.) 623.46	
UF850.A3-Z	Artillery range finders (particular types)	
UF850.A9	Azimuth instrument (artillery)	
UF850.D4	Depression range finder	
UF850.W3	Watkin range finder	
UF853	Position finders (artillery) 623.46	

UF854	Sights, Firearm	
UF855	Telescopic sights (artillery)	
UF856.A-Z	Artillery instruments (misc.)	
UF857	Range tables, Artillery	
UF860-880	Military explosives, unguided rockets, etc.	
UF860	Explosives, Military (gen.)	623.452
UF870	Explosions, powder force, etc.	
UF890	Tests, Ordnance	
UF900	Resistance to projectiles (artillery)	
UF910	Bulletproof clothing, materials, etc.	
UG	MILITARY ENGINEERING, AIR FORCES, & AIR WARFARE	358.2, 623, 358.4 (air forces etc.)
UG1-620	ENGINEERING, MILITARY	
UG1	Periodicals & associations (mil. engineering)	
UG6	Museums & exhibitions (mil. engineering)	
UG7	Military engineering (collections)	
UG15	Engineering, Military (gen. hist.)	358.2, .209
UG21-124	Engineering, Military (by country or area)	
UG23-25	Engineering, Military (U.S.)	358.20973
UG23	Military engineering (U.S.: gen.)	
UG55-95	Engineering, Military (Eur.)	358.2094
UG55	Military engineering (Eur.: gen.)	
UG57	Engineering, Military (G.B.)	
UG57.Z6.1st+	Military engineering (G.B.: by #'d regiment)	
UG71	Engineering, Military (Fr.)	
UG73	Engineering, Military (Ger.)	
UG73.Z6.1st+	Military enginering (Ger.: by #'d regiment)	
UG85	Engineering, Military (Rus.: Eur.)	
UG99-113	Engineering, Military (Asia)	
UG101	Engineering, Military (China)	
UG105	Engineering, Military (Japan)	
UG121-122.5	Engineering, Military (Australia + New Z.)	
UG125.1st+	Military engineering (U.S.: by #'d regiment)	
UG127	Biography, Military engineering (collective)	
UG128.A-Z	Biography, Military engineering (indiv.: SEE ALSO UG21-124)	
UG130-135	Laws (engineer corps)	
UG133	Laws (engineer corps: U.S.: PREFER KF7335.E5)	
UG145	Engineering, Military (gen.: pubn. 1801+)	
UG150-155	Manuals (mil. engineering)	
UG153	Military engineering manuals (U.S.)	
UG156	Engineering, Military (essays & lectures)	
UG157	Instruction (mil. engineering)	
UG160-302	TACTICS & REGULATIONS (mil. engineering: by place)	
UG160	Tactics & regulations (mil. engineering: U.S.)	
UG163	Tactics & regulations (mil. engineering: Can.)	
UG215-269	Tactics & regulations (mil. engineering: Eur.)	
UG215	Regulations & tactics (mil. engineering: Eur.: gen.)	
UG228	Tactics & regulations (mil. engineering: Fr.)	
UG231	Tactics & regulations (mil. engineering: Ger.)	
UG234	Tactics & regulations (mil. engineering: G.B.)	
UG252	Tactics & regulations (mil. engineering: Rus.)	
UG270-280	Tactics & regulations (mil. engineering: Asia)	
UG295-298	Tactics & regulations (mil. engineering: Australia & New Z.)	
UG320-325	Maneuvers (mil. engineering)	
UG323	Military engineering maneuvers (U.S.)	

UG330	Roads (mil. engineering)	623.62
UG335	Bridges (mil. engineering)	623.67
UG340	Tunnels (mil. engineering)	623.68
UG343	Ice excavation, tunnels, rooms, etc. (mil. engineering)	
UG345	Railroads, armored trains, etc. (mil. engineering) 623.63	
UG350	Harbors, canals, dams (mil. engineering) 623.64	
UG360-390	Field engineering (mil.)	
UG360	Military engineering (field: gen.)	
UG365	Camp-making (mil. sci.) 355.412, .544, .71	
UG370	Demolitions (mil. engineering) 623.4545, 358.23	
UG375	Obstacles (mil. engineering) 355.544	
UG380	Intrenching tools (mil.)	
UG385	Ferrying (mil. engineering)	
UG390	Field engineering (misc. topics)	
UG400-442	Fortification	
UG401	Fortification (gen.: pubn. 1801+) 355.544, 623.1	
UG403	Field fortification	
UG405	Fortification, Permanent	
UG407	Entanglements & misc. fortification	
UG408-409	Steel & iron land defenses	
UG410-442	Fortifications (by place) 623.19+, 355.45-47+	
UG410-412	Fortified defenses (U.S.) 623.1973, 355.4773	
UG410	Defenses, Fortified (U.S.: gen.) 623.1973, 355.4773	
UG411.A-Z	Fortifications (U.S.: by state or region) 623.1974-1979+,	
	355.450974+, .4774+	
UG411.P2	Pacific Coast (U.S.: fortifications)	
UG412.A-Z	Fortifications (U.S.: by town or place)	
UG412.K4	Key West, Fl. (fortifications)	
UG412.N5	New York City (fortifications)	
UG412.P3	Panama Canal (fortifications)	
UG412.S3	San Diego, Calif. (fortifications)	
UG413-415	Fortified defenses (Can.)	
UG428-430	Fortified defenses (Eur.)	
UG428	Defenses, Fortified (Eur.: gen.) 623.194, 355.474	
UG429.A-Z	Fortifications (Eur.: by region or country)	
UG429.G3	Fortified defenses (Ger.)	
UG430.A-Z	Fortifications (Eur.: by town or place)	
UG431-433	Fortified defenses (Asia) 623.195	
UG432.A-Z	Fortifications (Asia: by country)	
UG432.J3	Fortified defenses (Japan) 623.1952	
UG437-439	Fortified defenses (Australia)	
UG440-442	Fortified defenses (Pacific islands)	

UG443-449	Attack, defense, & siege	
UG444	Defense, attack, & siege (gen.: pubn. 1789+)	355.4+
UG446	Trench warfare	355.44
UG446.5	Tanks, armored cars, etc. (attack, defense, & siege: SEE ALSO	
	UE159-302 for armored cavalry)	355.422, 357.5, 358.18
UG447-447.6	Chemical warfare (inclu. flames)	623.4516
UG447	Flame & chemical weapons (gen.)	358.34
UG447.5.A-Z	Gas warfare (by chem. name)	623.4516
UG447.5.M8	Mustard gas	623.4516
UG447.6	Gas masks (mil.)	
UG447.65	Incendiary weapons	
UG447.7	Smoke screens & tactics	
UG447.8	Biological & bacterial warfare	
UG448	Coast defenses (SEE UG410-442 for specific places)	358.16, 355.45
UG449	Camouflage (SEE ALSO V215 for naval)	358.3, 623.77
UG450	Mechanical engineering (mil. applications)	
UG455	Weights & measures (mil. metrology)	
UG460	Architecture, Military 623.1	
UG465-465.5	Geology & seismology, Military	
UG467	Meteorology, Military	
UG468	Hydrology, Military	
UG470-474	Military surveying, mapping, & topography	
UG470	Surveying, mapping, & topography (military: gen.)	623.71
UG472	Mapping & surveying, Military (U.S.)	
UG473.A-Z	Topography & mapping, Military (places except U.S.)	
UG475	Surveillance, Military 355.413, 358.45	
UG476	Photography, Military 623.72	
UG480	Electricity (mil. uses) 623.76	
UG485	Electronics, Military 623.732+	
UG490	Mines, Land (inclu. countermeasures) 623.45115	
UG500-565	Technical troops & other special corps	
UG500	Technical troops & artificers (gen.) 358.2-3	
UG503	Artificers, Military (U.S.: ALSO tech. troops)	
UG503	Sappers & bridge troops (U.S.)	
UG505.A-Z	Military artificers & technical troops (places besides U.S.)	
UG510	Bridge troops & sappers (gen.)	
UG520-525	Railroad troops	
UG530-535	Pioneer troops	
UG550-555	Mining & torpedo troops	
UG550	Torpedo & mining troops	
UG560-565	Electricians, Military	
UG570-582	Signaling, Military 358.24, 623.73+, 355.85	
UG570-575	Signal corps & troops	
UG573	Signal corps & troops (U.S.)	
UG580	Military signaling (gen.)	
UG582.A-Z	Signaling, Military (particular types)	
UG582.H2	Hand signaling (mil.)	
UG582.H4	Heliograph (mil. signal.)	
UG582.S4	Semaphores (mil.)	
UG582.S68	Sound signaling (mil.)	
UG582.V5	Visual signaling (mil.)	

UG590-613.5	Telecommunications, Military	
UG590	Telephone, radio, & telegraph (military: gen.)	623.732-7345
UG600-605	Telegraph, Military (inclu. telegraph troops)	
UG603	Military telegraph & troops (U.S.)	
UG607	Submarine cables (mil.)	
UG610	Telephone, Military (gen.)	
UG610.3	Military telephone (U.S.)	
UG610.5.A-Z	Telephone, Military (places besides U.S.)	
UG611	Radio, Military (gen.)	
UG611.3	Military radio (U.S.)	
UG612	Radar, Military (gen.) 623.7348	
UG612.3	Military radar (U.S.)	
UG612.5.A-Z	Radar, Military (places except U.S.)	
UG612.5.G7	Radar, Military (G.B.)	
UG615	Motor vehicles, Military (gen.)	623.747, 355.83, 357.5+
UG618	Vehicles, Motor (mil.: U.S.)	
UG620.A-Z	Military motor vehicles (places besides U.S.)	

UG622-1425	AIR FORCES & AIR WARFARE	358.4, 623.74-746
UG622	Periodicals & associations (air forces)	358.005-006
UG623	Conferences (air forces)	
UG623.3.A1	Museums, Air force (inclu. exhibitions: gen.)	623.74074, 358.40074
UG623.3.A2-Z	Air museums & exhibitions (by country or area)	
UG623.3.x2.A-Z	Exhibitions & museums, Air force (by place within country)	
UG624	Air warfare & forces (collected works: gen.)	
UG625	Air forces & warfare (hist.: gen.)	358.4009
UG626	Biography, Air force (collective)	358.400922
UG626.2.A-Z	Biography, Air force (individual)	358.400924
UG627	Air forces & warfare (essays & lectures)	
UG628	Dictionaries & encyclopedias (air forces & warfare) 358.4003	
UG630	Air warfare & forces (gen.) 358.4	
UG633	Air forces (U.S.: gen.) 358.400973	
UG634.5.A-Z	Air bases & fields (U.S.: by name)	
UG634.A-W	Air forces (U.S.: by state)	
UG635.A-Z	Air forces (places besides U.S.)	
UG635.A8	Air forces (Australia)	
UG635.F8	Air forces (Fr.)	
UG635.G3	Air forces (Ger.)	
UG635.G322.T3	Tempelhof Airfield (Berlin, Ger.)	
UG635.G7	Air forces (G.B.)	
UG635.I8	Air forces (It.)	
UG635.R9	Air forces (Rus.)	
UG635.S65	Air forces (Sov.Un.)	
UG635.x2.A-Z	Airfields & bases (countries besides U.S.: by name of base)	
UG637-639	Education & training, Air force 358.415+	
UG637	Training & education, Air force (gen.)	
UG638-638.8	Air force training & education (U.S.)	
UG638	Flight training, Air force (U.S.: gen.: inclu. other educ.)	358.4150973
UG639.A-Z	Training & education, Air force (places besides U.S.)	

UG640	Research, Aeronautical (mil.: gen.)	358.407, .40072+
UG643	Aeronautical research, Military (U.S.: gen.)	358.4070973
UG643.5.A-W	Military research, Aeronautical (U.S.: by state of origin)	
UG644.A-Z	Research, Aeronautical (mil.: by company or establishment)	
UG645.A-Z	Research, Aeronautical (mil.: places besides U.S.)	
UG645.G3	Aeronautical research, Military (Ger.)	
UG670	Manuals & regulations, Air force (gen.)	
UG673	Regulations & manuals, Air force (U.S.)	
UG675.A-Z	Air force manuals & regulations (places except U.S.)	
UG675.G3	Air force regulations & manuals (Ger.)	
UG700-705	Tactics, Air warfare (bombing, strafing, dog fighting, air mining, etc.)	
		358.4142, .43
UG700	Air force tactics (gen.)	
UG703	Bombing, dog fighting, other air tactics (U.S.)	
UG705.A-Z	Dog fighting, bombing, other air tactics (countries besides U.S.)	
UG730-735	Defenses, Air (SEE ALSO UF625 for antiaircraft & UA926+ for civil	
	defense)	358.4145, .13
UG733	Air defenses (U.S.)	358.41450973
UG735.A-Z	Defenses, Air (places besides U.S.)	
UG760-765	Reconnaisance, Aerial	358.45
UG763	Aerial reconnaisance (U.S.)	
UG770-1045	ORGANIZATION (air forces)	
UG770-775	Administration (air forces: structure & personnel: gen.)	
		358.41, .413, .416+
UG773	Personnel & administration (air forces: U.S.)	
UG790	Officers, Air force (gen.)	358.41331-41332
UG793	Officers, Air force (U.S.)	
UG795.A-Z	Air force officers (countries except U.S.)	
UG795.G3	Officers, Air force (Ger.)	
UG820-825	Airmen & non-commissioned air officers	358.41338
UG823	Officers, Non-commissioned (air: U.S.: inclu. airmen)	
UG825.A-Z	Non-commissioned officers, Air force (countries besides U.S.)	
UG880-885	Recruiting, enlistment, etc. (air forces)	
UG880	Enlistment, recruiting, etc. (air forces: gen.)	
UG940-945	Pay & benefits (air forces)	358.41135, .4164
UG943	Benefits, pay, allowances (air forces: U.S.)	
UG970	Leaves, furloughs, etc. (air forces: gen.)	
UG973	Furloughs, leaves, etc. (air forces: U.S.)	
UG980-985	Medical services (air forces)	358.41345
UG990-995	Recreation, social work, etc. (air forces)	
UG990	Social work, recreation, etc. (air forces: U.S.)	
UG1000-1005	Chaplains, Air force	
UG1020-1025	Police, Air force	
UG1040-1045	Prisons, Air force	
UG1100-1425	EQUIPMENT & SUPPLIES (air force)	
UG1100-1105	Supplies & equipment (air force: gen.)	358.418
UG1120	Procurement & contracts, Air force (gen.)	358.41621
UG1123	Contracts & procurement, Air force (U.S.)	
UG1130-1185	Personnel, Air force	
UG1130-1135	Air force personnel (gen.) 358.4161	
UG1140-1145	Barracks & quarters, Air force 358.4171	
UG1143	Quarters & barracks, Air force (U.S.)	
UG1160-1165	Uniforms, Air force 358.4114	
UG1180-1185	Insignia, badges, etc. (air force)	

UG1200-1405	Operational equipment, Air force (airplanes, bombs, guns, vehicles)
UG1200	Air force equipment (gen.: planes, bombs, etc.) 358.418, .412
UG1203	Equipment, Air force (gen.: planes, bombs, etc.: U.S.) 358.4180973
UG1220	Airships or dirigibles (gen.) 623.743
UG1225.A-Z	Dirigibles (places outside U.S.)
UG1225.G3	Dirigibles (Ger.)
UG1240-1245	Airplanes, Military 623.746, 358.418
UG1240	Airplanes (air force: gen.)
UG1242.A-Z	Airplanes (air force: by type)
UG1242.A25	Antisubmarine aircraft
UG1242.A28	Attack planes
UG1242.B6	Bombers (air force) 623.7463, 358.42
UG1242.F5	Fighter planes 623.7464, 358.43
UG1242.R4	Reconnaisance planes 623.7467, 358.45
UG1242.S3	Seaplanes (air force) 629.133347, 623.7466-7467
UG1242.T7	Transport planes (air force)
UG1243	Air force planes (U.S.: PREFER UG1242 for particular types) 358.40973, .4140973, .414773, 623.740973, .7460973
UG1245.A-Z	Air force planes (countries besides U.S.)
UG1245.F8	Air force planes (Fr.) 358.400944
UG1245.G3	Air force planes (Ger.) 358.400943, .414743, 623.740943
UG1245.G7	Air force planes (G.B.) 358.400941, .414741-414742, 623.740941, .7460941
UG1245.I8	Air force planes (It.) 358.400945
UG1245.J3	Air force planes (Japan) 358.400952, .414752, 623.740952
UG1245.R9	Air force planes (Rus.) 358.400947
UG1270-1275	Ordnance, Air force (gen.) 358.4182, 623.45+
UG1273	Air force ordnance (gen.: U.S.)
UG1280-1285	Bombs, Air force 358.418251, 623.451
UG1282.A-Z	Air force bombs (by specific type)
UG1282.F7	Fragmentation bombs (aerial) 623.4514
UG1282.I6	Incendiary bombs (aerial) 623.4516
UG1340-1345	Guns, Aircraft 623.7461
UG1340	Aircraft guns & small weapons (gen.)
UG1370-1375	Balloons & kites, Air force 623.741-744
UG1400-1405	Vehicles, Motor (air force: ground)
UH	MILITARY SERVICES (misc.)
UH20	Chaplains or religious officials, Military (gen.) 355.347
UH23	Chaplains, Military (U.S.) 355.3470973
UH25.A-Z	Religious officials, Military (countries except U.S.)
UH30-35	Cyclists, Military
UH30	Bicyclists, Military (gen.) 357.52
UH40-45	Bands & music, Military
UH40	Music & bands, Military (gen.)
UH60-65	Banking services, Military
UH80-85	Postal service, Military 355.69
UH87-100	Animals, Military
UH87	Military animals (gen.) 355.24
UH90	Pigeons, Military (for communications: SEE ALSO D639.P45 for WWI)
UH100	Dogs, Military

UH201-570	MEDICAL & RELIEF SERVICES, MILITARY
UH201-515	SANITARY & MEDICAL SERVICES, MILITARY
UH201	Periodicals & associations (military medical services)
UH206	Museums, Military medical (inclu. exhibitions)
UH215-324	MEDICAL SERVICES, MILITARY (hist., statistics, etc.: gen. & by place)
UH215	Military medical services (hist., statistics, etc.: includes sanitary services: gen.) 355.345
UH223-225	Medical services, Military (U.S.) 355.3450973
UH223.A1-29	Reports, Official (military medical: U.S.: serial)
UH223.A1-49	Medical services, Military (U.S.: official reports)
UH223.A3-39	Reports, Official (military medical: U.S.: monographic)
UH223.A4-49	Statistics, Official (military medical: U.S.)
UH223.A5	Statistics (militray medical: U.S.: unofficial)
UH223.A6-Z	Medical services, Military (U.S.: unofficial)
UH224	Military medical services (U.S.: by time period or date: SEE ALSO particular wars)
UH224.1917-18	Medical services, Military (U.S.: WWI)
UH226-227	Medical services, Military (Can.)
UH255-295	Medical services, Military (Eur.)
UH255	Medical services, Military (Eur.: gen.) 355.345094
UH256	Military medical services, Military (Eur.: by date or period)
UH256.1914-18	Medical services, Military (Eur.: WWI)
UH257	Medical services, Military (G.B.: gen.) 355.3450941
UH258	Military medical services (G.B.: by period or date)
UH271-272	Medical services, Military (Fr.)
UH273-274	Medical services, Military (Ger.) 355.3450943
UH285-286	Medical services, Military (Rus.)
UH299-313	Medical services, Military (Asia)
UH309-310	Medical services, Military (Rus.: Asia)
UH311-312	Medical services, Military (Tur.)
UH315-319	Medical services, Military (Africa)
UH317-318	Medical services, Military (Egypt)
UH321-322	Medical services, Military (Australia)
UH322.5	Medical services, Military (New Z.)
UH341	Biography, Military medical (collective, inclu. nurses) 355.3450922
UH347.A-Z	Medical biography, Military (indiv.: by name) 355.3450924
UH390-396	Medicine, Military (gen., hdbks., etc.)
UH390	Military medicine (gen.: inclu. hdbks., manuals, etc.) 616.98023
UH393	Medicine, Military (U.S.: official manuals etc.)
UH394	Medicine, Military (U.S.: unofficial manuals etc.)
UH395.A-Z	Medicine, Military (places besides U.S.: manuals etc.)
UH396	First-aid manuals, Soldiers' (SEE ALSO UH393-395)
UH398	Medical schools, Army (U.S.: gen.)
UH398.5.A-Z	Army medical schools (U.S.: by region or state)
UH399.5-7	Research & laboratories, Medical (mil.)
UH399.A-Z	Medical schools, Army (places besides U.S.)

UH400-485	Organization (mil. medical: inclu. services)	
UH400	Military medical services (gen.: inclu. organization, surgeons, etc.)	
UH420-425	Pharmacy services, Military	
UH430-435	Dentistry, Military	
UH440-445	Supplies, Medical & surgical (mil.)	355.88
UH450-455	Bacteriology, Military (inclu. vaccination)	
UH460-485	Hospital services, Military	
UH470	Hospitals, Military (gen.)	355.72
UH473-474	Military hospitals (U.S.: SEE ALSO D629.U6-8 for WWI)	
UH475.A-Z	Hospitals, Military (except U.S.)	
UH487	Cookery & diet, Medical (mil.)	
UH490	Nurses & nursing, Military (gen.)	355.345
UH493	Military nursing (U.S.)	
UH495.A-Z	Nursing & nurses, Military (besides U.S.)	
UH500-505	Ambulances, Military (plus transport)	623.74724
UH500	Transport, Medical (mil.: gen.)	
UH510-515	Equipment, Medical corps	
UH510	Medical corps equipment (gen.)	
UH520-560	Relief societies (mil.: inclu. care of sick & wounded)	361.05, .77
UH520	Wounded, Care of (mil.: inclu. relief societies: gen.)	361.05, .77, .9, 940.477+
UH523	Sick & wounded, Care of (mil.: relief societies, etc.: U.S.: gen.)	
UH524.A-Z	Relief societies (mil.: U.S. by state or region)	
UH525.A-Z	Relief societies (mil.: besides U.S.: by place)	
UH531-533	Geneva & Hague conventions (PREFER JX5136 & JX5243) 341.6+, .65	
UH531	Hague & Geneva conventions (official works: by date: PREFER JX5136 & 5243)	
UH533	Treatment of prisoners (Geneva & Hague conven.: unofficial: PREFER JX5136 & JX5243)	
UH534	Congresses, International (relief, sick, wounded, etc.: misc.: by date)	
UH535	Red Cross (gen.: wartime)	940.4771, .54771
UH537.A	American Red Cross	
UH537.A-Z	Red Cross (by country or region)	
UH543-545	Relief associations (besides U.S.)	
UH560	Employment for crippled soldiers & sailors (PREFER UB360-66)	355.1154-1156
UH570	Dead, Treatment of	
UH600-629	Hygiene & sanitation, Military	
UH600	Sanitation & hygiene, Military	
UH603	Military hygiene & sanitation (U.S.)	
UH605.A-Z	Hygiene & sanitation, Military (besides U.S.)	
UH611	Tropical hygiene (mil. sci.)	
UH623	Handbooks & manuals (mil. hygiene: Eng. & Am.)	
UH625	Manuals & handbooks (mil. hygiene: not Eng. or Am.)	
UH627	Research, Physiological (mil. hygiene)	
UH629	Mental health, psychiatry, etc. (mil.: gen.)	
UH629.3	Psychiatry, Military (U.S.: inclu. mental health)	
UH629.5.A-Z	Hygiene, Mental (besides U.S.)	
UH630	Moral & health protection (mil.: alcoholism, drug abuse, prostitution, venereal diseases, etc. & work vs.)	
UH650-655	Veterinary services (mil.)	355.345

UH700-705	Press & public relns. (mil.)
UH700	Media & public relns. (mil.: gen.)　　　070.433, .449, 355.342
UH703	War correspondents & public relns. (mil.: U.S.)
UH705.A-Z	Public relations & press (mil.: places besides U.S.)
UH705.G3	Radio, media, & public relns. (mil.: Ger.)
UH720-725	Nonmilitary use of armed forces
UH723	Civic programs (armed forces: U.S.)
UH750	Social work, Military (gen.)　　　355.34, .346-347
UH755	Welfare services, Military (U.S.: gen.)
UH760	Social welfare services, Military (U.S. Army)
UH769.A-Z	Military social & welfare services (countries besides U.S.)
UH800-910	Recreation & information services, Military
UH800	Military recreation & information services (gen.)　　　355.346
UH805	Information & recreation, Military (U.S.: gen.)　　　355.3460973
UH810-815	Recreation & information services, Military (U.S. Army)
UH819.A-Z	Recreation & information services, Military (besides U.S.)
UH900-910	Recreation, Military (off-post)
UH905	Canteens (Off-post mil. recreation: U.S.)
V	Naval science (gen.)　　　359, 623, 629
V-VM	NAVAL SCIENCE, NAVIGATION, & SHIPBUILDING
VA	Navies (organiz. & world status)
VB	Naval administration
VC	Maintenance, Naval
VD	Seamen, Naval
VE	Marines
VF	Ordnance, Naval
VG	Naval science (misc. services: medical etc.)
VK	Navigation & merchant marine
VM	Naval architecture & shipbuilding
V1-995+	NAVAL SCIENCE (gen.)　　　359, 623.8
V1	Periodicals & associations (naval: in English)　　　359.005, .006+
V7	Conferences (naval sci.)　　　359.0060+, .0063
V9	Almanacs, Naval (official)　　　359.00202
V10	Yearbooks, Naval (unofficial)
V11.A-Z	Yearbooks, Naval (official: ALSO lists: by country: SEE ALSO VA
	#s if dept. reports involved)　　　359.0025+, .005
V11.U6	Lists, Naval (U.S.: ALSO official yearbooks)
V13.A1	Museums, Naval (gen.: inclu. exhibitions)　　　359.0074
V13.A2-Z	Naval museums & exhibitions (by country)　　　359.00740+
V13.x2.A-Z	Exhibitions & museums, Naval (by country then city)
V15-17	Naval science (collected works: monographic)
V19	Speeches & essays (naval sci.: gen.)
V23	Dictionaries & encyclopedias (naval sci.: gen.)　　　359.003
V24	Dictionaries (naval sci.: multi-ling.)

V25-64	Naval science (history, antiquities, & biog.: gen., during peace & war: SEE ALSO D-F #s for specific countries, wars, etc.)	
V25	Philosophy, Naval (e.g. theory of naval sea power)	
V27	Navies (gen. hist.)	359.009, .409, .47
V29-41	Naval science (ancient hist.)	359.00901
V43-46	Naval science (medieval hist.)	359.00902
V47-53+	Naval science (modern hist.: 17th-20th c.)	359.00903
V51	Naval science (19th c.)	359.009034
V53	Naval science (20th c.)	359.00904, .40904
V55.A-Z	Naval science (by region or country)	359.47+
V55.A65	Navies (America)	359.477, .1812
V55.A75	Navies (Asia)	359.475
V55.E8	Navies (Europe)	359.474
V61-64	Biography, Naval (SEE ALSO D-F #s for indiv. biog's. from particular countries)	
V61	Naval biography (collective)	359.00922
V62	Naval biography (U.S.: collective)	359.00922
V63.A-Z	Biography, Naval (U.S.: by name)	359.00924, .3310924, 940.410924, .450924, .540924, .5420924, .5450924
V64.A-Z	Biography, Naval (places besides U.S.: by place)	
V64.x2.A-Z	Naval biography (places except U.S.: by person's name after country name)	
V66	Navy clubs (U.S.)	
V67.A-Z	Clubs, Navy (Am. besides U.S.)	
V68	Clubs, Navy (G.B.)	
V69.A-Z	Clubs, Navy (besides U.S. & G.B.: by country)	
V101	Naval science (gen.: pubn. thru 1800)	
V103	Naval science (gen.: pubn. 1801+)	
V107	Naval science (pop. works)	359
V110-145	Handbooks, Naval	
V110	Handbooks, Seamen's (gen.)	359.00202
V113	Seamen's handbooks (U.S. Navy)	
V115.A-Z	Naval handbooks (seamen's: places besides U.S.)	
V115.G3	Seamen's handbooks (Ger.)	
V115.G7	Seamen's handbooks (G.B.)	
V115.R9	Seamen's handbooks (Rus.)	
V120-125	Handbooks, Petty officers'	
V120	Petty officers' handbooks (gen.)	
V123	Naval petty officers' handbooks (U.S.)	
V130-135	Handbooks, Naval officers'	359.3320202
V133	Naval officers' handbooks (U.S.)	
V135.A-Z	Officers' handbooks, Naval (places besides U.S.)	
V140-145	Handbooks, Naval reserve	
V160	Strategy, Naval (gen.: pubn. thru 1800)	
V163	Naval strategy (gen.: pubn. 1801+)	359.03, .43
V165	Naval strategy (gen. special)	
V167	Tactics, Naval (gen.)	359.42
V169	Naval tactics (gen. particular)	
V175	Landing ops. & field service tactics (naval: inclu. shore srvc., small arms instruc., etc.)	355.41, .422
V178	Boat attack (naval tactics)	359.32, .42
V179	Logistics, Naval	359.41
V180	Blockades, Naval	355.44, 359.42-43, 940.452, .5452
V182	Convoys, Naval	359.4-43
V185	Security, Naval	

V190	Patrols & reconnaisance, Naval 359.413	
V200	Coast defense, Naval (SEE ALSO UG410-442) 359.45	
V210	Submarine warfare (gen.) 359.3257, .42-43	
V214	Antisubmarine warfare 359.3254, .42-43	
V215	Camouflage, Marine 623.77	
V220	Bases, ports, & docks (naval: gen.: SEE ALSO VA67-750 for specific countries) 359.7	
V230	Yards, Navy (gen.: SEE ALSO VA67-750 for particular places) 359.7	
V240	Coaling stations, Naval (gen.: SEE ALSO VA67-750)	
V245	Maneuvers, Naval (SEE U260-262 for combined — army, navy, air forces — or amphibious warfare ops.) 359.52	
V250	War games, Naval 359.52	
V252	Training, Simulated (navies)	
V253	Imaginary naval battles & wars 359.47	
V260	Training, Physical (navies: gen.) 359.54	
V263-264	Physical training (navies: U.S.)	
V265.A-Z	Training, Physical (navies: countries besides U.S.)	
V267-268	Sports in navies	
V270	Orders, Transmission of (navies) 359.27, .85	
V280-285	Signaling, Naval (gen.) 359.27, .983	
V283	Naval signaling (U.S.)	
V300	Flags, Naval & marine (gen.: SEE ALSO VK385) 359.15	
V303	Naval flags (U.S.: inclu. marine)	
V305.A-Z	Flags, Naval & marine (besides U.S.)	
V305.G7	Naval flags (G.B.)	
V310	Ceremonies, honors, & salutes (navies: gen.) 359.17, .1349	
V380-385	Safety measures, Naval (inclu. educ.)	
V390	Research, Naval (gen.) 359.07	
V393	Research, Naval (U.S.: gen.) 359.070973	
V393.5.A-W	Naval research (U.S.: by state)	
V394.A-Z	Naval research (U.S.: by special establishment locale)	
V395.A-Z	Research, Naval (countries besides U.S.)	
V396	Oceanography, Military (gen.) 359.982, 551.46, 620.4162	
V396.3-4	Military oceanography (U.S.)	
V396.5.A-Z	Oceanography, Military (places besides U.S.)	
V400-695	EDUCATION, NAVAL	
V400	Naval education & training (gen.) 359.007	
V401	Education, Naval (hist.: gen.)	
V404	Training & education, Naval (modern hist.: gen.)	
V409	Education, Naval (hist.: 20th c.)	
V411-438	Education, Naval (U.S.)	
V411	Naval education (U.S.: gen.) 359.0071073, .0071173, .50973, .550973	
V415.A1	U.S. Naval Academy (Act of incorp.: PREFER KF7353.55)	
V415.A1-R4+	U.S. Naval Academy (Annapolis) 359.0071173	
V415.C3-6	Regulations (U.S. Naval Acad.)	
V415.C3-H5	U.S. Naval Academy (admin.)	
V415.E1-4	Reports, Official (U.S. Naval Acad. Superinten.: annual)	
V415.E5	U.S. Naval Academy (Cong. docs.: gen.: by date)	
V415.E9	Hazing (U.S. Naval Acad.: Cong. docs.)	
V415.F3.A-Z	Commencement addresses (U.S. Naval Acad.: by speaker)	
V415.F5.A-Z	Speeches (U.S. Naval Acad.: misc.: by speaker)	
V415.F7	Reports, Official & unoff. (U.S. Naval Acad.)	
V415.H3-39	Registers, Official (U.S. Naval Acad.: annual)	
V415.H5	U.S. Naval Academy (registers, unoff.)	

V415.J1-7	Student publications (U.S. Naval Acad.)	
V415.K1-4	Publications, Graduate (U.S. Naval Acad.)	
V415.K4	Class histories (U.S. Naval Acad.: by date)	
V415.L1	Annapolis (U.S. Naval Acad.: gen. hist's. & other titles)	
V415.L1-P1	U.S. Naval Academy (hist. & descrip.)	
V415.L3	Pictorials (U.S. Naval Acad.)	
V415.M1.A-Z	Biography (U.S. Naval Acad.: by name)	
V415.P1	Annapolis (U.S. Naval Acad.: life & conditions)	
V415.R1-4	Examinations (U.S. Naval Acad.)	
V420	Naval War College (U.S.)	359.550973, .0071173
V425.A-Z	Training schools, Naval (misc.)	
V426	Naval Reserve Officers' Training Corps (U.S.: N.R.O.T.C.)	359.2232
V430	Schools, Private naval (U.S.)	
V433	Training stations, Naval (U.S.: gen.)	359.50973, .70973
V434.A-Z	Naval training stations (U.S.: by place)	
V434.G7	Great Lakes Naval Training Station (Ill.)	
V434.H2	Hampton Roads Naval Training Station (Va.)	
V435	Training ships (U.S. Navy: gen.)	
V436.A-Z	Naval training ships (U.S.: by name)	
V437	Training & education, Naval (U.S. Coast Guard)	359.9707
V440-444	Education, Naval (Can.)	
V500-623	Education, Naval (Eur.)	
V500	Naval education (Eur.: gen.)	
V510-530	Education, Naval (G.B.)	
V510	Naval education (G.B.: gen.)	359.0071141, .50941, .550941, .007041
V511-512	British naval education (special topics)	
V513	Examinations (G.B. Royal Navy)	
V515.A1	Dartmouth (Royal Naval College: Act of incorp.)	
V515.A1-R1+	Royal Naval College (Dartmouth)	
V515.C1-K3	G.B. Royal Naval College, Dartmouth (admin.)	
V515.E1-49	Reports, Official (Royal Naval Coll., Dart.: annual)	
V515.F3.A-Z	Speeches (Royal Naval Coll., Dart.: by speaker)	
V515.H1-5	Registers, Official & unoff. (Royal Naval Coll., Dart.)	
V515.K3	Class histories (Royal Naval Coll., Dart.: by date)	
V515.L1	Royal Naval College (Dartmouth: hist.)	
V515.M1.A-Z	Biography (Royal Naval Coll., Dart.: by name)	
V515.P1	Royal Naval College (Dartmouth: life, pictorials, etc.)	
V520.A1-R1+	Royal Naval College (Greenwich: set up like V515)	
V522-525	Training & education, Naval (G.B.: stations, ships, engin. schools, etc.)	
V522.5.A-Z	Training stations, Naval (G.B.: by place)	
V522.5.P6	Portsmouth, Eng. (Royal Naval Barracks)	
V565-569	Education, Naval (Fr.)	
V570-574	Education, Naval (Ger.)	
V570	Naval education (Ger.: gen.)	359.007043, .50943
V574.A-Z	Schools, Naval (Ger.)	
V574.A2-65	German naval education (main school)	
V574.A7-Z	Naval schools (Ger.: by name or place)	
V585-589	Education, Naval (It.)	
V600-604	Education, Naval (Rus.)	
V625-650	Education, Naval (Asia)	
V640-644	Education, Naval (Japan)	
V650.T9	Education, Naval (Turkey)	
V690-694	Education, Naval (Australia)	359.007094
V694.1-5	Education, Naval (New Z.)	

V701-716	Naval observations (wartime: PREFER D-F areas)	
V705	Observations, Naval (U.S. Civil War, 1861-5)	
V707	Observations, Naval (Franco-German War, 1870-1)	
V709	Observations, Naval (Span.-Am. War, 1898)	
V713	Observations, Naval (Russo-Japanese War, 1904-5)	952.031, 359.4752, .4747
V715	Observations, Naval (WWI)	940.45-453
V720-743	Naval life & customs	
V720	Customs, Naval (gen.)	359.1
V735-743	Naval life & customs (modern)	
V735	Life & customs, Naval (modern: gen.)	359.10904
V736	Naval life & customs (modern: U.S.)	359.10973
V737	Naval life & customs (modern: G.B.)	359.10941
V739	Naval life & customs (modern: Ger.)	359.10943
V741	Naval life & customs (modern: Rus.)	359.10947
V743.A-Z	Naval life & customs (modern: misc. countries)	
V745	Curiosities, Naval	359.00207, .002
V750-995+	WARSHIPS (construction, armament, types, etc.: SEE VA for status & organiz. of specific navies around the world)	
V750	Ships, Naval (gen.: SEE here for earlier works on battleships & V815 for later works)	
V765-767	Vessels, Naval war (modern period)	623.80904
V799	Construction of warships (1860-1900: armored vessels)	
V800	Construction of warships (1901+)	623.825, 359.325+
V805	Construction of warships (materials: gen.)	
V805.3	Construction of warships (materials: U.S.)	
V805.5.A-Z	Construction of warships (materials: besides U.S.)	
V810	Damage control (warships)	623.888
V815-895	Warships (types)	623.825-826, 359.83, .325-326
V815	Battleships (gen.: construc., armament, etc.: SEE V750 for earlier titles)	623.8252, .81252, 359.3252
V815.3	Battleships (U.S.)	623.82520973, 359.32520973
V815.5.A-Z	Battleships (besides U.S.: by place)	
V815.5.G3	Battleships (Ger.)	623.82520943
V815.5.G7	Battleships (G.B.)	623.82520941
V815.5.J3	Battleships (Japan)	623.82520952
V820	Cruisers (gen.: tech. info.)	623.8253, .81253, 359.3253
V820.3	Cruisers (U.S.)	
V820.5.A-Z	Cruisers (besides U.S.)	
V820.5.G7	Cruisers (G.B.)	
V825	Destroyers (gen.)	623.8254, .81254, 359.3254
V825.3	Destroyers (U.S.)	
V825.5.A-Z	Destroyers (besides U.S.: by place)	
V825.5.J3	Destroyers (Japan)	
V826	Frigates & corvettes (gen.)	623.8254
V826.3	Frigates (U.S.)	
V826.5.A-Z	Corvettes & frigates (besides U.S.)	

V830-838	Torpedo boats	623.8258, 359.3258
V830	P.T. boats (gen.)	
V833	Torpedo boats (U.S.)	
V835.A-Z	Torpedo boats (places besides U.S.)	
V835.G3	Torpedo boats (Ger.)	
V837-838	Torpedo boat service	
V840	Torpedo boat destroyers	623.8254
V850	Torpedoes (gen.: inclu. propelling or launching devices)	623.4517, 359.82517
V855.A-Z	Torpedoes (types or devices: by name)	
V855.G7	Graydon aerial torpedo thrower	
V855.W5	Whitehead torpedo	
V856	Minelaying, minesweeping, submarine mines, etc. (gen.)	623.2, .26, .263, .36, .45115, .8262, 359.825115, .3262
V856.5.A-Z	Minesweeping, minelaying, sub. mines, etc. (by place)	
V856.5.U6-7	Submarine mines, minelaying, minesweeping, etc. (U.S.)	
V857	Submarines (gen.: SEE ALSO V210-14 for sub warfare & VM365-7 for construc.)	623.8257, .82572, .81257, 359.3257
V858	Submarines (U.S.)	623.82570973, 359.32570973
V859.A-Z	Submarines (besides U.S.)	
V859.G3	Submarines (Ger.)	623.82570943
V859.J3	Submarines (Japan)	623.82570952
V860	Turrets, Revolving (naval sci.: inclu. monitors)	
V865	Naval vessels (auxiliary: fleet trains, repair & supply ships, etc.)	623.826, 359.326
V870	Naval vessels, Unarmored	
V874	Aircraft carriers (gen.)	623.8255, 359.3255
V874.5.G7	Aircraft carriers (G.B.)	623.82550941
V875.A36	Aircraft launching & recovery equipment (carriers)	
V880	Vedettes, scout & dispatch boats, other minor craft (gen.)	
V885	Minesweepers (SEE ALSO V856)	623.8262
V890	Floating batteries	
V895	Naval vessels (misc., non-major: inclu. landing craft)	
V900-925	Armor plate (naval sci.)	
V900	Armor plate (naval sci.: gen.)	623.81821, .8251
V903	Armor, Naval (U.S.)	623.82510973
V905.A-Z	Naval armor (places besides U.S.)	
V907.A-Z	Plating, Armor (naval sci.: special type)	
V907.K7	Krupp armor plating (naval sci.)	
V910-915	Testing (naval armor: SEE ALSO VF540)	
V913	Naval armor testing (U.S.)	
V950	Armament, Naval (gen.)	623.8251
V960	Naval armament (installation)	
V980	Equipment, Naval (misc.)	

VA	NAVIES (organiz. & world status)	
VA10	Naval status (world: gen.)	359, .03
VA20-25	Costs, Naval (budgets etc.)	
VA25	Budgets, Naval (gen.)	359.622
VA40	Navies (of the world: gen.)	359, .03, .009, 623.82509
VA41	World navies (pop. works)	
VA42	Pictorials (world navies)	
VA45	Reserves, Naval (gen.)	359.37+
VA48	Mobilizaton, Naval (gen.)	359.28
VA49-750+	NAVAL STATUS (worldwide: place by place)	
VA49	Periodicals & associations (naval: U.S.)	359.005-007+
VA50	Naval status (U.S.: gen.)	359.030973, .4773
VA52-395	NAVAL STATUS (U.S.)	
VA52-79	U.S. Navy (SEE ALSO E182)	
VA52.A1-89	Reports, Official (U.S. Navy Dept.)	
VA52.A1-19	U.S. Navy Dept. (official docs.: gen.)	
VA52.A2-29	Secretary of the Navy (U.S.: official docs.)	
VA52.A6-67	Reports, Official (U.S. Navy Bur's. of Navigation, Personnel)	
VA52.A68-69	Material, Naval (U.S. Navy. Office of: reports)	
VA52.A7-79	Naval ops. (U.S. Navy. Office of: reports)	
VA53	Reports, Congressional (U.S. Navy: official & others)	
VA54	Speeches (U.S. Navy)	
VA55	U.S. Navy (gen.)	359.00973, .30973, .4773
VA58	U.S. Navy (gen.: 1881-1970 coverage)	359.00973
VA59	Pictorials (naval: U.S.)	359.3250973
VA60	Budgets, Naval (U.S.)	359.6220973
VA61	Ships (U.S. Navy: lists)	359.32, .320222
VA62-74	U.S. Navy (placement & stations)	
VA62	U.S. Navy (distribution: gen.)	359.4773, .31
VA62.5	Naval districts (U.S.: gen.)	359.70973
VA62.7.1st+	Naval districts (U.S.: by #)	
VA63.A-Z	Fleets, squadrons, etc. (U.S. Navy: by name)	359.310973
VA63.A83	Atlantic Fleet (U.S.)	
VA63.N8	North Atlantic Fleet (U.S.)	
VA63.P2	Pacific Fleet (U.S.)	
VA65.A-Z	Ships (U.S. Navy: by name)	359.32520973-.32560973
VA65.A75	Arizona (battleship: U.S.)	
VA65.M2	Maine (battleship: U.S.)	
VA66.A-Z	U.S. Navy (misc. units: by name)	
VA66.C6-65	Construction Battalions (U.S. Navy)	359.33+, .90973
VA67-68	Naval bases, ports, docks, etc. (U.S.)	
VA67	Ports, bases, docks, etc. (U.S. Navy: gen.)	359.70973, 940.4530973 (WWI), .54530973 (WWII), .545973 (WWII)
VA68.A-Z	Bases, ports, etc. (U.S. Navy: by place)	
VA69	Naval yards & stations (U.S.: Dept.)	359.70973, 623.830973
VA70.A-Z	Yards & stations, Naval (U.S.: by place)	
VA70.N5	New London Naval Station (U.S.: Conn.)	
VA70.N7	Norfolk Navy Yard (U.S.: Va.)	
VA70.P5	Philadelphia Navy Yard (U.S.: Penn.)	
VA70.P8	Portsmouth Navy Yard (U.S.: N.H.)	
VA73	Naval coaling stations (U.S.: gen.)	359.70973, .750973
VA74	Coaling stations, Naval (U.S.: by place)	
VA77	Mobilization (U.S. Navy)	359.280973
VA79	Supply vessels, transports, service craft, etc. (U.S. Naval Auxiliary Service)	

```
VA80-390        RESERVES, NAVAL (U.S.)
VA80            Naval reserves (U.S.: gen.)        359.370973
VA90-387        MILITIA, NAVAL (U.S.: state by state)
VA100-107       Reserves, Naval (U.S.: Calif.)
VA100                Naval reserves (U.S.: Calif.: gen.)  359.3709794
VA101                Reports, Official (naval reserves: U.S.: Calif.)
VA102                Registers & lists (naval reserves: U.S.: Calif.)
VA103.1st+           Reserves, Naval (U.S.: Calif.: special groups by #)
VA104.A-Z            Reserves, Naval (U.S.: Calif.: special groups by name)
VA105.A-Z            Ships (Calif. naval reserves: by name)
VA107                Reserves, Naval (U.S.: Calif.: misc. topics)
VA140-147       Reserves, Naval (U.S.: Florida)
VA240-247       Reserves, Naval (U.S.: Mississ.)
VA280-287       Reserves, Naval (U.S.: N.Y.)
VA350-357       Reserves, Naval (U.S.: Texas)
VA370-377       Reserves, Naval (U.S.: Wash.)
VA390           Waves (U.S. naval reserves for women & other non-local U.S.
                    naval res.)
VA400-402       Naval status (Can.)
VA400           Canada (naval status: gen.)      359.030971, .4771
VA402.5            Latin America (naval status)
VA415-445          Naval status (S.Am.)
VA450-619       NAVAL STATUS (Eur.)
VA450           Europe (naval status: gen.)      359.03094, .474
VA452-467       Naval status (G.B.)
VA452               Periodicals & associations (naval: G.B.)
VA453               Primary sources, documents (naval: G.B.)
VA454           G.B. Royal Navy (gen.)     359.0309441, .30941, .4741-4742, .00941
VA455           Budgets, Naval (G.B.)
VA456           Ships (G.B. Royal Navy: lists)        359.325+, .320941
VA457.A-Z       Fleets, squadrons, etc. (G.B.: by name)      359.310941
VA458.A-Z       Ships (G.B. Royal Navy: by name)     359.320941, .3252+-.326+
VA459           Naval bases, ports, docks, etc. (G.B.)
VA459.A1        Ports, bases, docks, etc. (G.B. Royal Navy: gen.)       359.70941,
                                                   940.4530941 (WWI), .54530941 (WWII)
VA459.A3-Z Bases, ports, etc. (G.B. Royal Navy: by place)
VA459.H55          Hong Kong Naval Base (Royal Navy)
VA459.S5           Singapore Naval Base (Royal Navy)        940.5453095952,
                                                   .5453095957(WWII)
VA460           Naval yards & stations (G.B.)  359.70941
VA463           Mobilization, Naval (G.B.)     359.280941
VA464           Reserves, Naval (G.B.)
VA470-479       Austria (naval status)     359.2809436
VA480-489       Belgium (naval status)
VA500-509       Naval status (Fr.)
VA503.A1-49        Ships (Fr. Navy: lists)     359.320944, .3250944
VA503.A5-Z         France (naval status: gen.)     359.030944, .4744
```

```
VA510-519    Naval status (Ger.)
VA510          Periodicals & associations (naval: Ger.)
VA511            Budgets, Naval (Ger.)
VA512            Primary sources, documents (naval: Ger.)
VA513.A1-49      Ships (Ger. Navy: lists)        359.320943, .3250943
VA513.A5-Z         Germany (naval status: gen.)  359.030943, .00943, .30943, .4743
VA514.A-Z    Fleets, squadrons, etc. (Ger.: by name)     359.310943
VA515.A-Z    Ships (Ger. Navy: by name)        359.320943, .3252+-.326+
VA515.S      Scharnhorst (armored [WWI], battle [WWII] cruiser: Ger.)
VA516.A1     Naval bases, ports, docks, etc. (Ger.: gen.)        359.70943,
                                            940.4530943 (WWI), .54530943 (WWII)
VA516.A3-Z   Ports, bases, docks, etc. (Ger. Navy: by name)
VA516.K4     Kiel Naval Base (Ger.)
VA517          Coaling stations, Naval (Ger.)
VA518          Mobilization, Naval (Ger.)       359.290943
VA519          Reserves, Naval (Ger.)           359.370943
VA530-539        Netherlands (naval status)
VA540-549        Naval status (It.)
VA543.A5-Z       Italy (naval status: gen.)          359.030945, .00945, .30945, .4745
VA570-579        Naval status (Rus.)
VA573.A5-Z       Russia (naval status: gen.)     359.030947, .00947, .4747
VA590-599        Sweden (naval status)
VA620-667    NAVAL STATUS (Asia)
VA630-639        China (naval status)         359.030951
VA650-659        Naval status (Japan)
VA653.A1-49      Ships (Japan. Imper. Navy: lists)       359.30952, .320952,
                                            .3252+-326+
VA653.A5-Z       Japan (naval status: gen.)      359.030952, .00952, .30952, .4752
VA654.A-Z         Fleets, squadrons, etc. (Japan: by name)       359.310952
VA667.T9     Turkey (naval status)            359.0309561
VA670-700    Africa (naval status)
VA690          Egypt (naval status)              359.030962
VA700.S52      South Africa (naval status)       359.030968
VA710-719    Naval status (Australia)
VA713.A1-49    Ships (Australia. Navy: lists)   359.30994, .320994, .3250994
VA713.A5-Z     Australia  (naval status: gen.)      359.030994, .00994, .4794
VA715.A-Z        Ships (Australia. Navy: by name)   359.32520994-.3260994
VA716          Naval bases, ports, docks, etc. (Australia)   359.70994
VA720-729    Naval status (New Z.)
VA723.A1-49    Ships (New Z. Navy: lists)       359.309931
VA723.A5-Z     New Zealand (naval status: gen.)   359.0309931, .009931, .47931

VB           ADMINISTRATION, NAVAL (command, personnel, law, etc.)
VB15         Administration, Naval (gen. hist.)       359.6, .1-3
VB21-124     NAVAL ADMINISTRATION (by country)
VB23           Naval administration (U.S.)          359.60973
VB26           Naval administration (Can.)
VB55-96      Naval administration (Eur.)
VB55         Administration, Naval (Eur.: gen.)       359.6094
VB57           Naval administration (G.B.)     359.60941, .30941
VB71           Naval administration (Fr.)      359.60944
VB73           Naval administration (Ger.)     359.60943, .30943
VB79         Naval administration (It.)       359.60945
VB85         Naval administration (Rus.)      359.60947
```

VB99-113	Naval administration (Asia)	
VB105	Naval administration (Japan)	359.60952, .30952
VB121	Naval administration (Australia)	359.60994
VB122.5	Naval administration (New Z.)	
VB145	Naval administration (gen.: pubn. 1801-1970)	359.6, .3
VB170-187	Naval administration (civil sections)	
VB170	Civil depts. (naval admin.: gen.)	
VB180-187	Civilian personnel (naval admin.)	
VB180	Personnel, Civilian (naval admin.: gen.)	
VB183	Employees, Civilian (naval admin.: U.S.)	
VB185.A-Z	Civilian personnel (naval admin.: places besides U.S.)	
VB190	Admirals, commanders, etc. (admin.: inclu. duties)	
VB200-205	Naval command and leadership	
VB200	Command of ships (naval admin.: gen.)	359.33, .6, 158.4, 350.00323
VB203	Leadership (naval admin.: U.S.)	
VB205.A-Z	Leadership (naval admin.: besides U.S.)	
VB210	Headquarters, Naval (ops. inclu. aides)	
VB220-225	Inspection, Naval (inclu. inspectors)	
VB230-254	Intelligence, Naval	
VB230	Naval intelligence (gen.) 359.3432	
VB231.A-Z	Intelligence, Naval (by country) 359.343209+	
VB231.G3	Naval intelligence (Ger.) 359.34320943	
VB231.G7	Naval intelligence (G.B.) 359.34320941	
VB231.U6-7	Naval intelligence (U.S.) 359.34320973	
VB240	Attachés, Naval	
VB250	Espionage & spies (naval admin.) 359.3432-3433	
VB252	Propaganda & psych. warfare (naval sci.: gen.) 359.3434	
VB253	Propaganda & psych. warfare (naval sci.: U.S.) 359.34340973	
VB254.A-Z	Psychological warfare & propaganda (naval sci.: places besides U.S.)	
VB255	Orders, passes, field correspondence (naval admin.)	
VB257	Personnel administration (naval sci.: gen.) 359.61	
VB258	Naval personnel (admin.: U.S.) 359.610973	
VB259	Career guidance (naval sci.)	
VB260-275	Enlisted personnel (naval sci.: inclu. recruitment, enlistment, promotion, discharge, etc.)	
VB260	Recruitment, enlistment, promotion, discharge (naval sci.: enlisted personnel: gen.) 359.223, .338, .11+	
VB263	Promotion, discharge, recruitment, enlistment (naval sci.: enlisted personnel: U.S.) 359.2230973, .3380973	
VB264.A-Z	Enlistment, recruitment, promotion, discharge (Naval sci.: U.S.: by region or state)	
VB265.A-Z	Discharge, promotion, recruitment, enlistment (naval sci.: places besides U.S.)	
VB265.G3	Enlisted personnel (naval sci.: Ger.: inclu. enlistment, promotion, etc.) 359.2230943	
VB270-275	Recruits, Naval (inclu. medical & mental examinations) 359.2236	
VB277	Demobilization, Naval (inclu. civil employ.) 359.29, .1154	
VB278	Crippled sailors, Employment of (PREFER UB360-366)	
VB280-285	Pensions, disability benefits, etc. (naval admin.) 359.115-1156	
VB283	Disability benefits, pensions, etc. (naval admin.: U.S.)	
VB290-295	Homes, Sailors' (SEE ALSO UB380-385)	
VB300-305	Cemeteries (naval) 351.86, .866	
VB303-304	Naval cemeteries (U.S.)	

VB307	Warrant officers (naval: gen.) 359.332	
VB308	Officers, Warrant (naval: U.S.)	359.3320973
VB309.A-Z	Naval warrant officers (besides U.S.)	
VB310-315	Officers, Naval (inclu. appt., promo., rank, retire., etc.)	
VB310	Rank, appointment, promotion, retirement, etc. (naval officers: gen.) 359.332, .331	
VB313	Officers, Naval (U.S.: gen.) 359.3320973, .3310973	
VB314.A-Z	Biography, Naval (U.S.: by name) 359.3310973, .3310924	
VB315.A-Z	Naval officers (except U.S.)	
VB315.G7	Officers, Naval (G.B.) 359.3320941	
VB315.J3	Officers, Naval (Japan)	
VB315.R9	Officers, Naval (Rus.)	
VB320-325	Minorities & women (navies)	
VB320	Women & minorities (navies: gen.) 359.22	
VB323	Women & minorities (U.S. Navy: gen.)	
VB324.A-Z	Minorities (U.S. Navy: by group)	
VB324.A47	Afro-Americans (U.S. Navy)	
VB324.I5	Indians (U.S. Navy: native-Am's.)	
VB324.W65	Women (U.S. Navy)	
VB330-335	Badges, brevets, medals of honor, rewards, etc. (navies)	
VB330	Medals, badges, brevets, etc. (navies: gen.) 359.1342	
VB333	Brevets, badges, medals, etc. (U.S. Navy: inclu. Navy Cross) 359.13420973	
VB335.A-Z	Rewards, badges, brevets, medals (navies: except U.S.)	
VB340-345	Pensions, Survivors' (naval)	
VB350-785	NAVAL LAW	
VB350	Law, Naval (gen.) 359.13, 343.01+	
VB353	International naval law	
VB360-785	NAVAL LAW (by area or country)	
VB360-369	Naval law (U.S.: PREFER KF7345-7375)	
VB360	Law, Naval (U.S.) 343.7301	
VB363	Regulations, Naval (U.S.)	
VB365	General orders (naval: U.S.)	
VB370-379	Naval law (Can.)	
VB530-699	European naval law	
VB530	Naval Law (Eur.: gen.)	
VB570-579	Naval Law (FR.)	
VB580-589	Naval Law (Ger.)	
VB590-599	Naval Law (G.B.: PREFER KD6128-6158)	343.4101
VB650-659	Naval law (Rus.)	
VB700-799	Asian naval law	
VB700	Naval law (Asia: gen.)	
VB775	Naval law (Australia)	
VB777	Naval law (New Z.)	
VB790-925	Naval justice (admin. of)	
VB790	Justice, Naval (gen.: inclu. judiciary) 343.014, .0146	
VB793	Judiciary, Naval (U.S.: inclu. overall naval justice)	
VB795.A-Z	Naval justice (places besides U.S.)	

VB800	Courts-martial, Naval (gen.)	343.0146
VB803	Courts-martial, Naval (U.S.: PREFER KF7646-7650)	
VB805.A-Z	Courts-martial, Naval (besides U.S.: by place)	
VB806	Cases (courts-martial, naval: U.S.: PREFER KF7646-7650)	
VB807.A-Z	Cases (courts-martial, naval: besides U.S.: by place)	
VB810-815	Courts of inquiry, Naval	343.0143
VB813	Inquiry, Courts of (naval: U.S.: PREFER KF7646-7650)	
VB814.A-Z	Cases (courts of inquiry, naval: U.S.: PREFER KF #s)	
VB815.A-Z	Courts of inquiry, Naval (besides U.S.)	
VB840-845	Naval discipline	359.13
VB843	Discipline, Naval (U.S.)	359.130973
VB845.A-Z	Discipline, Naval (besides U.S.)	
VB845.G7	Discipline, Naval (G.B.)	
VB850-880	Offenses & crimes, Naval	
VB850	Crimes, Naval (gen.) 359.1334	
VB853	Naval crimes (U.S.)	
VB855.A-Z	Naval crimes (except U.S.)	
VB855.G3	Naval crimes (Ger.)	
VB855.G7	Naval crimes (G.B.)	
VB860	Mutiny (naval: gen.)	359.1334
VB863	Mutiny (naval: U.S.)	
VB865.A-Z	Mutiny (naval: except U.S.)	
VB867.A-Z	Naval mutiny (by ship)	
VB870-875	Desertion (naval)	359.1334
VB873	Naval desertion (U.S.)	
VB880	Looting & other naval crimes	
VB890-910	Prisoners, prisons, punishments (naval)	
VB890	Naval prisons & prisoners (gen.)	344.03548
VB893	Prisons & prisoners, Naval (U.S.)	344.035480973
VB895.A-Z	Prisons & prisoners, Naval (except U.S.: by place)	
VB895.G7	Prisons & prisoners, Naval (G.B.)	
VB895.R9	Prisons & prisoners, Naval (Rus.)	
VB910	Corporal punishment (naval) 364.67, 343.0146, 359.13325	
VB920	Shore patrol (gen.)	359.13323, .34
VB923	Shore patrol (U.S.)	
VB925.A-Z	Police, Naval (besides U.S.)	
VB925.G3	Shore patrol (Ger.)	
VB925.G7	Shore patrol (G.B.)	
VB955	Administration, Naval (misc. topics)	
VC	MAINTENANCE, NAVAL	359.6-8
VC10	Naval maintenance (gen.)	359.6
VC20-258	ORGANIZATION (naval maintenance: by place)	
VC20-65	Maintenance, Naval (U.S.)	
VC20	Naval maintenance (U.S.: gen.)	359.60973
VC25-38	Reports, Official (naval maint.: U.S.)	
VC39	Reports, Unofficial (naval maint.: U.S.)	
VC40-41	Reserves, Naval (U.S.: maint. & organ.)	359.370973
VC50-65	Pay & allowances (U.S. Navy)	359.135, .640973
VC54-60	Handbooks & tables (naval pay & allowances: U.S.)	
VC54	Allowances & pay (U.S. Navy: tables inclu. interest)	
VC60	Handbooks & manuals (U.S. Navy: Pay & allowances)	
VC64	Reports, Unofficial (naval pay etc.: U.S.)	
VC90-93	Maintenance, Naval (Can.)	

```
VC160-229   Maintenance, Naval (Eur.)
VC160       Naval maintenance (Eur.: gen.)
VC176-179      Maintenance, Naval (Fr.)
VC180-183      Maintenance, Naval (Ger.)      359.60943
VC180       Supplies, Naval (Ger.)      359.80943
VC181       Pay & allowances (Ger. Navy)
VC182       Reserves, Naval (Ger.: maint. & organ.)      359.370943
VC183.A-Z   Maintenance, Naval (Ger.: by region or area)
VC184-187   Maintenance, Naval (G.B.)      359.60941
VC196-199      Maintenance, Naval (It.)
VC208-211      Maintenance, Naval (Rus.)
VC230-245   Maintenance, Naval (Asia)
VC255-256   Maintenance, Naval (Australia)      359.60944
VC256.5     Maintenance, Naval (New Z.)
VC260-268   Supplies & stores, Naval (inclu. stds., procure., storage, etc.)
VC260          Naval supplies & stores (gen.)      359.8, .62
VC263-264      Stores & supplies, Naval (U.S.)      359.80973
VC265.A-Z      Procurement (naval supplies: except U.S.)
VC265.G7       Naval stores & supplies (G.B.)
VC266          Supplies & stores, Naval (management methods)      359.62
VC267.A-Z   Contracts & claims, Naval (supplies: by place)
VC267.U6-7  Naval contracts (supplies: U.S.)
VC268.A-Z   Commandeering, compensation, etc. (naval: by country or place)
VC270-279   Equipment, fuel, supplies, etc. (ships)
VC270          Naval equipment & supplies (gen.: for ships)      359.8
VC273-274      Ships' stores & equipment (U.S.)
VC275.A-Z      Ships' stores & equipment (except U.S.)
VC276          Fuel supplies & costs, Naval
VC276.A1       Naval fuel (gen.: ALSO costs etc.)  359.83, 623.874, .415
VC276.A3-49    Fuel, Naval (U.S.)      359.83
VC276.A5-Z     Fuel, Naval (other than U.S.)
VC279.A-Z   Supplies & stores, Naval (misc.)
VC279.C3    Cables (naval supplies)
VC279.H45   Hemp (naval supplies)
VC279.R6       Rope (naval supplies)
VC279.R8       Rubber (naval supplies)
VC279.T5       Timber (naval supplies)
VC279.T6       Tools (naval supplies)
VC280-345   Clothing, Naval (inclu. related items)
VC280-285   Naval clothing & personal equipment (overall)
VC300-345   Naval uniforms, badges, shoes, etc.
VC300       Uniforms, Naval (gen.)      359.14, .81
VC303       Naval uniforms (U.S.: gen.)      359.140973, .81
VC305.A-Z   Uniforms, Naval (besides U.S.)
VC307          Foul-weather gear, Naval (plus other special clothing)      359.81
VC310          Shoes & footwear, Naval
VC320          Headgear, Naval
VC330          Tailoring (naval clothing)
VC340       Binoculars (naval clothing: inclu. other misc. accessories)
VC345       Insignia & badges (naval clothing)      359.1342
```

VC350-410	Subsistence & provisions, Naval (inclu. rations, galleys, water, etc.)	
VC350	Provisions & subsistence, Naval (gen.)	359.81
VC353-354	Naval provisions & subsistence (U.S.)	359.810973
VC355.A-Z	Naval provisions & subsistence (countries besides U.S.)	
VC355.G3	Provisions & subsistence, Naval (Ger.)	
VC355.R9	Provisions & subsistence, Naval (Rus.)	
VC360-365	Rations, Naval	
VC370-375	Cookery, Naval	359.81
VC380-385	Officers' clubs & messes, Naval	
VC380	Messes & clubs, Naval officers' (gen.)	359.346
VC383	Naval officers' clubs (U.S.)	359.3460973
VC384.A-W	Naval officers' clubs (U.S.: by state)	
VC390-395	Canteens & ship exchanges	
VC390	Ship exchanges & canteens (gen.)	359.341
VC398	Galleys & equipment (naval sci.)	
VC400	Refrigeration (naval sci.)	623.8535
VC410	Water supplies, Naval (inclu. preservation, purification, etc.: SEE VM503 for onboard storage)	623.854
VC412-425	Navy yards, shore facilities, stations, etc.	
VC412	Shore facilities, yards, stations (navies: gen.)	359.7, 623.83
VC414	Yards, stations, shore facilities (navies: U.S.: gen.)	359.70973
VC415.A-W	Stations, shore facilities, yards (navies: U.S.: by state)	
VC415.C2	Naval stations & shore facilities (U.S.: Calif.)	
VC415.F5	Naval stations & shore facilities (U.S.: Fl.)	
VC415.H2	Naval stations & shore facilities (U.S.: Haw.)	
VC416.A-Z	Naval stations & shore facilities (countries besides U.S.)	
VC416.G3	Naval stations & shore facilities (Ger.)	
VC417	Maintenance & repair, Naval (yards etc.)	
VC417.5	Sanitation & refuse (naval sci.)	
VC418	Power systems, Electric (naval sci.)	
VC420-425	Barracks, quarters, housing (naval)	
VC420	Quarters & barracks, Naval (gen.)	359.71
VC423-424	Naval quarters & barracks (U.S.)	
VC425.A-Z	Housing & barracks, Naval (places besides U.S.)	
VC430	Laundries, Naval	
VC500-505	Accounting & accounts, Naval (inclu. ships' records)	359.622
VC503-504	Ships' records & accounts (U.S.)	
VC530-580	Transport, Naval	
VC530-535	Transportation, Naval (gen.)	359.83, .27
VC533	Naval transport (U.S.)	
VC537	Shipment & packing (naval sci.)	
VC550-555	Personnel transport (navies)	
VC553	Transport, Personnel (navies: U.S.)	
VC570-575	Motor transport (naval sci.)	
VC573	Transport, Motor (navies: U.S.)	
VC580	Railroads (naval transp.)	

VD	SEAMEN, NAVAL (enlisted personnel in gen.: drill, way of life, etc.)	
VD7	Enlisted personnel, Naval (gen.: nonperiodical collections)	
VD15	Naval seamen (gen. hist.: enlisted way of life etc.)	359.338, .12
VD21-124	NAVAL SEAMEN (by area or country)	
VD23-25	Sailors, Navy (U.S.)	
VD23	Seamen, Naval (U.S.: gen.)	359.3380973, .120973
VD24.A-W	Naval seamen (U.S.: by state)	
VD25.A-Z	Enlisted personnel, Naval (U.S.: by city)	
VD26-27	Sailors, Navy (Can.)	
VD55-96	Sailors, Navy (Eur.)	
VD55	Seamen, Naval (Eur.: gen.)	359.338094, .12094
VD57-64	Sailors, Navy (G.B.)	
VD57	Seamen, Naval (G.B.: gen.)	359.3380941, .120941
VD59	Naval seamen (G.B.: Eng. & Wales)	
VD61	Naval seamen (G.B.: Scot.)	
VD63	Naval seamen (G.B.: N. Ire.)	
VD64.A-Z	Enlisted personnel, Naval (G.B.: by city or other div.)	
VD71-72	Sailors, Navy (Fr.)	359.3380944
VD73-74	Sailors, Navy (Ger.)	
VD73	Seamen, Naval (Ger.: gen.)	359.3380943, .120943
VD74.A-Z	Naval seamen (Ger.: by locality)	
VD76.5	Sailors, Navy (Ire.)	
VD85-86	Sailors, Navy (Rus.)	359.3380947
VD99-113	Sailors, Navy (Asia)	
VD99	Seamen, Naval (Asia: gen.)	359.338095, .12095
VD101	Sailors, Navy (China)	
VD105-106	Sailors, Navy (Japan)	
VD105	Seamen, Naval (Japan: gen.)	359.3380952, .120952
VD121-122	Sailors, Navy (Australia)	359.3380994
VD122.5	Sailors, Navy (New Z.)	
VD145	Seamen, Naval (gen.: pubn. 1801-1970)	
VD146	Sailors, Navy (gen.: pubn. 1970+)	
VD150	Manuals (naval seamen: gen.: SEE ALSO V110+ & V120+)	
		359.00202, .40202
VD153	Manuals (naval seamen: U.S.)	359.402020973
VD155.A-Z	Manuals (naval seamen: places except U.S.)	
VD157	Tactics & maneuvers, Naval (PREFER V167-178 & V245)	
		359.415, .4152
VD160-302	NAVAL DRILLS (seamen: by country or area: includes watch, station, quarter, fire)	
VD160-162	Drills, Naval (U.S.)	
VD160	Watch drills, Naval (U.S.: gen.: ALSO quarter, station, other)	
		359.50973, .1330973, .133220973
VD163	Quarter drills, Naval (Can.: ALSO watch, station, other)	
VD215-269	Drills, Naval (Eur.)	
VD215	Station drills, Naval (Eur.: gen.: ALSO quarter, watch, etc.)	
VD228	Fire drills, Naval (Fr.: ALSO quarter, watch, station, etc.)	
VD231	Drills, Naval (Ger.)	359.50943
VD234	Drills, Naval (G.B.)	359.50941
VD252	Drills, Naval (Rus.)	
VD270-280	Drills, Naval (Asia)	
VD295	Drills, Naval (Australia)	359.50994
VD298	Drills, Naval (New Z.)	

VD320	Manual of arms (naval seamen)	359.5470202, .8240202
VD330-335	Shooting (naval seamen: inclu. marksmanship, regs., etc.)	
VD333	Marksmanship (naval seamen: U.S.)	
VD340-345	Bayonet drill (naval seamen)	
VD350-355	Equipment (naval seamen)	
VD360-365	Arms, Small (navies: gen. & by place)	359.824, .8242
VD360-390	Small arms (navies)	
VD363	Naval small arms (U.S.)	359.8240973
VD370	Rifles, carbines, etc. (navies)	359.82425
VD380	Bayonets (navies)	359.8241
VD390	Revolvers & pistols (navies)	359.8243
VD400-405	Small boat service (inclu. armament)	359.3258
VD430	Seamen, Naval (misc. subjects)	
VE	MARINES	359.96
VE7	Marines (collected, nonserial titles)	
VE15	Marines (gen. hist.)	359.96, .9609
VE21-124	MARINES (by geographic area)	
VE22	Marines (N. Am.)	
VE23	U.S. Marine Corps	359.960973
VE23.A1.A-Z	Periodicals (U.S. Marines)	359.96097305
VE23.A2-79	Reports, Official (U.S. Marines)	
VE23.A2	Reports, Official (U.S. Marines: annual)	
VE23.A25	Regulations, Marine (U.S.)	
VE23.A3-32	U.S. Marine Corps (official hist's.)	
VE23.A33	Registers (U.S. Marines)	
VE23.A48	Manuals (U.S. Marines)	
VE23.A5	U.S. Marine Corps (official monographs)	
VE23.A6	Recruiting literature (U.S. Marines: by date)	
VE23.A8-Z	U.S. Marine Corps (gen.)	
VE23.22.1st+	Divisions (U.S. Marines: by #)	
VE23.25.1st+	Marine regiments (U.S.: by #)	
VE25	Biography (U.S. Marines: PREFER E #s)	
VE55-96	Marines (Eur.)	
VE57-64	Marines (G.B.)	
VE57	British marines (gen.)	359.960941
VE59	Marines (Eng. & Wales)	
VE61	Marines (Scot.)	
VE73	Marines (Ger.)	
VE79	Marines (It.)	
VE85	Marines (Rus.)	
VE99-113	Marines (Asia)	
VE121-122.5	Marines (Australia & New Z.)	
VE145	Marines (gen.: pubn. 1801-1970)	359.9609
VE146	Marines (gen.: pubn. 1970+)	359.9609
VE150	Manuals & handbooks (marines: gen.)	359.960202
VE153	Handbooks & manuals (marines: U.S.)	
VE155.A-Z	Manuals & handbooks (marines: places besides U.S.)	
VE155.G7	Handbooks & manuals (marines: G.B.)	
VE157	Maneuvers & tactics (marines)	359.9642, .9652

VE160-302	MARINE DRILLS (by place)	
VE160-162	Drill regulations, Marine (U.S.)	
VE160	Drills, Marine (U.S.: gen.)	359.965, .9654
VE215-269	Drills, Marine (Eur.)	
VE215	Marine drills (Eur.: gen.)	
VE231	Drills, Marine (Ger.)	
VE234	Drills, Marine (G.B.)	
VE270-280	Drills, Marine (Asia)	
VE295	Drills, Marine (Australia)	
VE320	Manual of arms (marines)	359.968240202
VE330-335	Shooting (marines: inclu. marksmanship, training, etc.)	
VE340	Bayonet drill (marines)	359.96547
VE350-355	Equipment (marines)	
VE360-390	Small arms (marines)	
VE370	Rifles (marines)	359.9682425, 623.4425
VE380	Bayonets (marines)	623.441
VE390	Pistols & revolvers (marines)	359.968243
VE400-405	Uniforms, Marine	359.9614
VE420-425	Barracks & quarters, Marine	
VE420	Marine barracks & quarters (gen.)	359.961292, .9671
VE422	Quarters & barracks, Marine (U.S.: gen.)	359.96710973
VE430-435	Training camps, Marine	359.967+

VF	ORDNANCE, NAVAL	359.82, 623.8251
VF1	Periodicals & associations (naval ordnance)	
VF6.A1	Museums & exhibitions (naval ordnance: gen.)	
VF6.A2-Z	Exhibitions & museums (naval ordnance: by place or country)	
VF7	Naval ordnance (nonperiodical collections)	
VF15	Ordnance, Naval (gen. hist's.)	359.8209
VF21-124	NAVAL ORDNANCE (by country or place)	
VF23	Ordnance, Naval (U.S.)	359.820973, 623.82510973
VF55-96	Ordnance, Naval (Eur.)	359.82094
VF55	Naval ordnance (Eur.: gen.)	
VF57	Ordnance, Naval (G.B.)	359.820941
VF71	Ordnance, Naval (Fr.)	
VF73	Ordnance, Naval (Ger.)	359.820943
VF79	Ordnance, Naval (It.)	
VF85	Ordnance, Naval (Rus.)	
VF99-113	Ordnance, Naval (Asia)	
VF105	Ordnance, Naval (Japan)	359.820952
VF121	Ordnance, Naval (Australia)	
VF145	Ordnance, Naval (gen. pubns. 1801+)	359.82
VF147	Naval ordnance (special overall)	
VF150-155	Handbooks & manuals (naval ordnance)	
VF150	Ordnance, Naval (handbooks & manuals: gen.)	
VF153	Manuals & handbooks (naval ordnance: U.S.)	
VF155.A-Z	Manuals & handbooks (naval ordnance: places besides U.S.)	

VF160-302	NAVAL ORDNANCE DRILLS (by place)	
VF160	Drills, Naval ordnance (U.S.: gen.)	
VF215-269	Drills, Naval ordnance (Eur.)	
VF215	Ordnance drills, Naval (Eur.: gen.)	
VF228	Drills, Naval ordnance (Fr.)	
VF231	Drills, Naval ordnance (Ger.)	
VF234	Drills, Naval ordnance (G.B.)	
VF252	Drills, Naval ordnance (Rus.)	
VF270-280	Drills, Naval ordnance (Asia)	
VF277	Drills, Naval ordnance (Japan)	
VF295	Drills, Naval ordnance (Australia)	
VF310-315	Target practice, Naval	
VF310	Naval target practice (gen.)	623.553
VF313	Gunnery practice, Naval (U.S.)	623.5530973
VF315.A-Z	Naval gunnery practice (places except U.S.)	
VF315.G7	Gunnery practice, Naval (G.B.)	623.5530941
VF320-325	Artillery equipment, Naval	
VF323	Naval artillery equipment (U.S.)	
VF325.A-Z	Equipment, Naval artillery (places other than U.S.)	
VF330-335	Shore service	
VF346-348	Weapons systems, Naval	
VF347	Naval weapons systems	
VF350-375	Ordnance & arms, Naval (in sum)	
VF350-355	Arms & ordnance, Naval (gen.)	359.82, 623.418
VF350	Naval ordnance & arms (gen.)	
VF353	Naval arms & ordnance (gen.: U.S.)	
VF357	Instruction (naval ordnance)	
VF360	Research (naval ordnance: gen.)	359.82072
VF360.3	Ordnance research, Naval (U.S.)	
VF360.5.A-Z	Naval research (ordnance: places besides U.S.)	
VF370-375	Ordnance & arms, Naval (manufacture)	
VF370	Manufacture (naval ordnance & arms: gen.)	
VF373	Naval ordnance & arms (manufacture: U.S.)	
VF380-385	Ordnance magazines & facilities (navies)	
VF380	Magazines, Ordnance (navies: gen.)	359.75
VF390-395	Ordnance proper (navies)	
VF390	Naval ordnance material (gen.)	623.418
VF393	Ordnance material (navies: U.S.)	
VF393.A1-3	Ordnance proper (navies: U.S.: documents)	
VF393.A4-6	Manuals, Naval ordnance (U.S.: by mm., cm., inches, or lbs.)	
VF393.A5.5	5 in. guns, Naval (U.S.: manuals)	
VF393.A7-Z	Ordnance proper (navies: U.S.: gen.)	
VF395.A-Z	Naval ordnance material (besides U.S.)	
VF410.A2	Machine guns, Naval (gen.)	623.4424
VF410.A3-Z	Naval machine guns (special by name)	
VF420	Ordnance material (misc.)	
VF430	Gun carriages, Naval	623.43
VF440	Turrets & cupolas, Naval	
VF450-455	Firing instructions, Naval	
VF460	Ammunition, Naval	359.825, 623.45
VF470	Cartridges, Naval	359.8255
VF480-500	Projectiles, Naval	
VF480	Naval projectiles (gen.)	359.8251, 623.451
VF490	Shells & shrapnel, Naval	
VF500	Bullets (navies)	359.8255, 623.455

VF509	Depth charges, Naval	623.45115, .4517
VF520-530	Fire control, Naval gunnery (inclu. instruments)	
VF520	Instruments, Naval gunnery	623.558
VF530	Radar equipment, Naval	623.557
VF540	Tests, Ordnance & firing (navies)	
VF550	Range tables, Naval ordnance	623.5530212
VF580	Ordnance, Naval (misc. topics)	
VG	NAVAL SERVICES (misc.)	
VG20-25	Chaplains or religious officials, Naval	
VG20	Naval chaplains (gen.)	359.347
VG23	Chaplains, Naval (U.S.)	359.3470973
VG25.A-Z	Religious officials, Naval (places besides U.S.)	
VG30-35	Bands & music, Naval (SEE ALSO ML1300-1354)	
VG33	Music & bands, Naval (U.S.)	359.340973, .170973
VG50-55	Coast guard & coast signal service	359.97
VG50	Signal service, Coast (plus coast guard: gen.)	
VG53	U.S. Coast Guard	359.970973
VG55.A-Z	Coast guard & coast signal service (places besides U.S.)	
VG60-65	Postal service, Naval	359.341
VG70-85	Telecommunications, Naval	359.415, .85, 623.856, .73
VG70-75	Telegraph, Naval	
VG73	Naval telegraph (U.S.)	359.4150973
VG76-78	Telegraph, radar, & radio communications (navies: wireless)	
VG76	Communications, Naval (inclu. radio, radar, wireless telegraph: gen.)	
		623.8564, .734
VG80-85	Telephone, Naval	623.85645
VG86-88	Underwater demolition teams (navies)	
VG86	Frogmen (navies: gen.)	359.984
VG87	Naval underwater teams (U.S.: inclu. demolition) 359.9840973	
VG88.A-Z	Navy frogmen (besides U.S.)	
VG90-95	Air forces & warfare, Naval	359.94, 358.4
VG100-475	MEDICAL SERVICES, NAVAL (SEE ALSO UH201-515)	
VG100	Periodicals & associations (naval medical services)	
VG115	Naval medical services (gen.)	359.345, .72, 616.98024
VG121-224	NAVAL MEDICAL SERVICES (by place)	
VG123	Medical services, Naval (U.S.)	359.3450973
VG155-196	Medical services, Naval (Eur.)	
VG157	Medical services, Naval (G.B.)	
VG173	Medical services, Naval (Ger.)	
VG185	Medical services, Naval (Rus.)	
VG199-213	Medical services, Naval (Asia)	
VG221	Medical services, Naval (Australia)	
VG226	Biography, Naval medical (gen.)	
VG227.A1	Medical biography, Naval (U.S.: collective)	
VG227.A2-Z	Naval medical biography (U.S.: indiv.)	
VG228.A-Z	Biography, Naval medical (places besides U.S.)	
VG230-235	Instruction (naval medicine)	
VG240-245	Research & laboratories, Naval medical	
VG260-265	Surgeons, Naval 359.345, 616.98024, 617.99	
VG263	Naval surgeons (U.S.)	
VG270-275	Dispensaries, Naval	
VG280-285	Dentistry, Naval	
VG290-295	Supplies, Medical & surgical (navies)	

VG310-325	Hospital corps, Naval
VG310	Naval hospital corps (gen.)
VG320	Hospital corps, Naval (U.S.)
VG325.A-Z	Hospital corps, Naval (places besides U.S.)
VG350-355	Nurse corps, Naval
VG350	Naval nurse corps (gen.) 359.345, 610.7349, .7361, 616.98024
VG353	Nurse corps, Naval (U.S.)
VG410-450	Hospital services & hospitals, Naval (SEE ALSO D #s for particular wars)
VG410	Hospital services, Naval (gen.) 359.72
VG420-425	Hospital services, Naval (U.S.)
VG420	Hospitals, Naval (gen.)
VG424.A-Z	Naval hospitals (U.S.: by area or state)
VG425.A-Z	Hospitals, Naval (U.S.: by town)
VG430.A-Z	Naval hospitals (places except U.S.)
VG450	Hospital ships 623.8264, 359.3264
VG457	Red Cross at sea
VG460-466	Handbooks, Medical & surgical (navies)
VG460	Medical & surgical handbooks (navies: gen.) 359.3450202, 610.0202, 617.0260202
VG463	Surgical & medical handbooks (navies: U.S.)
VG465.A-Z	Manuals, medical & surgical (navies: besides U.S.)
VG466	First-aid handbooks, Naval
VG470-475	Health, hygiene, & sanitation (navies)
VG470	Naval health, hygiene, & sanitation (gen.)
VG471	Hygiene, health, & sanitation (navies: special: tropics, drinking water, alcohol problem, venereal diseases, diet, etc.)
VG473	Health, hygiene, & sanitation (navies: U.S.)
VG475.A-Z	Sanitation, health, & hygiene (navies: places besides U.S.)
VG478	Rehabilitation of disabled sailors (PREFER UB360+)
VG500-505	Press & public relns. (navies)
VG500	Media & public relns. (navies: gen.) 359.342, 070.433, .439
VG503	War correspondents & public relns. (navies: U.S.)
VG505.A-Z	Newspapers, media, & public relns. (navies: besides U.S.)
VG590-595	Civil engineering (navies: SEE ALSO VA66.C6+)
VG590	Engineering, Civil (navies: gen.)
VG593	Naval engineering (civil: U.S.)
VG600-605	Artisans, Naval (carpenters' mates, painters, etc.)
VG600	Artificers, Naval (gen.: inclu. carpenters' mates etc.)
VG603	Carpenters & other naval artisans (U.S.)
VG610-615	Aerographers (naval weather & surf forecaster)
VG610	Weather forecaster, Naval (gen.)
VG613	Forecaster, Weather (navies: U.S.)
VG800-805	Machinists, Naval
VG900-905	Yeomen & clerks, Naval
VG903	Clerks & yeomen, Naval (U.S.)
VG920-925	Surveyors, draftsmen, & engineering aids (navies)
VG920	Draftsmen & surveyors, Naval (gen.)
VG950-955	Boatswains
VG953	Boatswains' mates (U.S.)
VG1010-1015	Photographers, Naval
VG1020	Photographic interpretation (navies)
VG1030-1035	Instrumentmen, Naval

VG2000-2005	Social welfare services, Naval
VG2000	Social work, Naval (gen.)
VG2003	Welfare services, Naval (U.S.)
VG2005.A-Z	Naval welfare services (places besides U.S.)
VG2020-2029	Recreation & information services, Naval
VG2020	Naval recreation & information services (gen.) 359.346
VG2025-2026	Information & recreation services, Naval (U.S.: gen.) 359.3460973
VG2029	Recreation & information services, Naval (places besides U.S.)
VK	MARINE NAVIGATION & MERCHANT MARINE
VK1	Periodicals & associations (marine navig. & merch. marine)
VK5	Conferences (marine navig. & merch. marine)
VK6	Museums & exhibitions (marine navig. & merch. marine)
VK7-8	Nautical almanacs & yearbooks
VK7	Almanacs & yearbooks, Nautical (American: inclu. abridged)
VK8	Yearbooks & almanacs, Nautical (non-American)
VK15	Merchant marine & navigation (gen. hist's.)
VK18	Navigation, Marine (gen. hist's.: modern: inclu. merch. marine)
VK20	Merchant marine & navigation (20th c.: hist. & conditions)
VK21-124	Merchant marine & navigation (hist. & conditions: by area or country)
VK139-140	Biography (merch. marine)
VK145	Marine navigation & merchant marine (gen.: pubn. 1801+) 623.89
VK147	Merchant marine & navigation (gen. special)
VK149	Nautical life (merchant marine: pop. titles)
VK155	Handbooks & manuals (marine navig. & merch. marine) 623.890202
VK160	Merchant marine (occupation) 387.0023
VK199	Accidents, Marine
VK200	Safety, Marine
VK205	Masters' manuals (merch. marine: inclu. command of ships)
VK221	Manning of vessels (merch. marine)
VK233	Watch duty (merch. duty)
VK321-369+	Harbors & ports 387.1+
VK358	Terminals, Marine (bunkers, coal supplies, repairs, etc.)
VK371-378	Collisions & avoidance, High seas
VK381-397	Signaling, Merchant marine (flags, lights, codes, radio, etc.)
VK383	Fog signals (merch. marine)
VK385	Flag signals (merch. marine)
VK387	Light signals (merch. marine)
VK391	Code signals (merch. marine)
VK397	Wireless signals (merch. marine)
VK401-529	Instruction (merch. marine)
VK401	Merchant marine & navigation (study & teaching: gen.)
VK421-524	Marine navigation (instruction: by locale: inclu. merch. marine)
VK423	Merchant marine & navigation (instruction: U.S.)
VK457	Navigation, Marine (instruction: G.B.: inclu. merch. marine)
VK531-537	Training (marine navig. & merch. marine)
VK541-547	Seamanship (marine navig. & merch. marine) 623.88
VK545	Warship handling (plus other seamanship topics) 623.8825

VK549-572	Marine navigation science	
VK549	Navigation, Marine (science: hist.)	527.094, 387.155
VK555	Science of marine navigation (gen.: pubn. 1801+)	623.81
VK563-567+	Tables, Nautical 623.8920212	
VK563	Nautical tables (gen.: inclu. azimuth)	
VK565	Latitude & longitude (marine navig.: inclu. tables)	
VK567	Longitude & time at sea (marine navig.: inclu. tables)	
VK570	Optimum ship routing	
VK571	Great circle routing (marine navig.)	
VK572	Dead reckoning (naut. navig.)	623.8923
VK573-587	Instruments, Nautical	
VK573	Nautical instruments (gen.)	623.894, .863
VK575-584	Instruments, Nautical (special)	
VK575	Chronometers, Nautical (PREFER QB107)	
VK577	Compasses (sea, air, or land: inclu. gyro type)	623.82
VK579	Distance finders (inclu. tables etc.)	
VK581	Logs, Nautical	
VK583	Sextants & quadrants 527.028, 623.894	
VK584.A-Z	Nautical instruments (misc.)	
VK584.A7	Artificial horizon	
VK584.S6	Sounding apparatus	
VK587	Chart use, Nautical (plus other misc. topics on naut. instruments)	
VK588-597	Hydrography, Marine	
VK591	Marine hydrography & surveying (gen.)	
VK593	Surveying, Hydrographic (gen. special)	
VK600-794	TIDE & CURRENT TABLES	
VK602	Current & tide tables (gen.: pubn. 1801+)	623.8949
VK603	Tables, Tide & current (collections)	
VK607-794	TIDE & CURRENT TABLES (by area)	
VK610-680	Atlantic Ocean (all & east: tide & current tables)	
VK610	Tide & current tables (Atlantic Ocean: all & east: gen.)	
		623.894909163
VK611	North Atlantic (tide & current tables)	623.8949091631
VK615-626	North Sea & Baltic (tide & current tables)	
VK627-638	British Isles (tide & current tables)	
VK639-644	English Channel (tide & current tables)	
VK645	Coasts, French (gen. & Eng. Ch.: tide & current tables)	
VK651	Gibraltar Strait (tide & current tables)	
VK653-674	Mediterranean Sea (tide & current tables)	
VK759-792	Current & tide tables (Atlantic Ocean: west)	
VK781	East Coast (U.S.: tide & current tables)	623.8949091634
VK793	Coasts, United States (tide & current tables)	
VK798-997	SAILING DIRECTIONS & PILOT GUIDES	
VK799	Tables, Nautical navigation (distances etc.)	623.8920212
VK802	Pilot guides & sailing directions (gen.: pubn. 1801+)	623.8922, .8929+
VK803	Sailing & pilot guides (official: British)	
VK804-997	PILOT & SAILING GUIDES (by area)	
VK804	American waters (gen.: pilot & sailing guides)	623.89297
VK810-880	Atlantic Ocean (all & east: pilot & sailing guides)	
VK810	Pilot & sailing guides (Atl. Ocean: all & east: gen.)	623.8929163
VK811-814.5	North Atlantic (pilot & sailing guides)	
VK813	Convoy lanes (N. Atlantic: pilot & sailing guides)	
VK815-826	North Sea & Baltic (pilot & sailing guides)	

VK827-844	British Isles & English Channel (pilot & sailing guides)	
		623.892916336, .8929422
VK845	Coasts, French (gen. & Eng. Ch.: pilot & sailing guides)	623.8929442
	(Normandy)	
VK853-874	Mediterranean Sea (pilot & sailing guides)	623.89291638, .8929448
VK959-992	Atlantic Ocean (West: pilot & sailing guides)	
VK959	Pilot & sailing guides (W. Atlantic: gen.)	
VK981	East Coast (U.S.: pilot & sailing guides)	
VK985	Canada (E. coast: pilot & sailing guides)	
VK993	Coasts, United States (pilot & sailing guides)	
VK1000-1249	LIGHTHOUSES, BEACONS, FOGHORNS, ETC. (inclu. buoys & lightships)	
VK1010	Beacons, foghorns, lighthouses, etc. (gen.)	623.8942, 387.155
VK1015	Foghorns, beacons, lighthouses, etc. (hist's.)	
VK1021-1124	LIGHTHOUSES, BEACONS, FOGHORNS, ETC. (by area)	
VK1023-1025	United States (lighthouses, beacons, foghorns, etc.)	
VK1024	Lighthouses, beacons, foghorns, etc. (U.S.: by area)	
VK1055-1096	Europe (lighthouses, beacons, foghorns, etc.)	
VK1055	Lighthouses, beacons, foghorns, etc. (Eur.: gen.)	
VK1057-1064	Great Britain (lighthouses, beacons, foghorns, etc.)	
VK1071-1072	France (lighthouses, beacons, foghorns, etc.)	
VK1073-1074	Germany (lighthouses, beacons, foghorns, etc.)	
VK1079-1080	Italy (lighthouses, beacons, foghorns, etc.)	
VK1085-1086	Russia (Eur.: lighthouses, beacons, foghorns, etc.)	
VK1086.5	Scandinavia (lighthouses, beacons, foghorns, etc.)	
		623.89420948
VK1099-1113	Asia (lighthouses, beacons, foghorns, etc.)	
VK1109-1110	Russia (Asia: lighthouses, beacons, foghorns, etc.)	
VK1111-1112	Turkey & Asia Minor (lighthouses, beacons, foghorns, etc.)	
VK1150-1249	LISTS (beacons, foghorns, lighthouses, etc.)	
VK1150	Beacons, foghorns, lighthouses, etc. (lists: gen.: inclu. Br. Admiralty)	623.8944
VK1151-1185	Europe (lighthouses, beacons, foghorns, etc.: lists)	
VK1151	Lighthouses, beacons, foghorns, etc. (Eur.: gen.: lists)	
		623.8944094
VK1153-1159	Great Britain & Ireland (lighthouses, beacons, foghorns, etc.: lists)	
		623.89440941
VK1173	France (lighthouses, beacons, foghorns, etc.: lists)	
		623.89440944
VK1176	Mediterranean Sea (lighthouses, beacons, foghorns, etc.: lists)	
		623.8944091638
VK1190-1199	Africa (lighthouses, beacons, foghorns, etc.: lists)	
VK1198	Egypt (lighthouses, beacons, foghorns, etc.: lists)	
VK1203-1209	Asia (lighthouses, beacons, foghorns, etc.: lists)	
VK1243	United States (lighthouses, beacons, foghorns, etc.: lists)	
VK1250-1299	SHIPWRECKS & FIRES (PREFER D-F #s for specific wars)	
VK1250	Fires & shipwrecks (gen.)	910.453
VK1255.A-Z	Shipwrecks (by name)	
VK1257.A-Z	Fires, Nautical (by name of ship)	
VK1259	Abandoning ship (plus other misc. marine topics of disaster)	
VK1265	Disasters, Submarine	
VK1270-1294	Shipwrecks (by area)	
VK1270-1273	Shipwrecks (U.S.)	
VK1280-1282	Shipwrecks (Eur.)	
VK1299	Icebergs	

VK1300-1491	SAVING LIFE & PROPERTY (marine navig.)
VK1300-1481	Lifesaving, Marine
VK1315	Marine lifesaving (hist's.)
VK1321-1424	Nautical lifesaving (by area)
VK1445-1447	Survival after shipwrecks (plus other misc. lifesaving topics) 623.865
VK1460-1481	Lifesaving apparatus & stations (marine navig.)
VK1460-1461	Equipment, Lifesaving (marine navig.: gen.) 623.865
VK1462-1463	Lifesaving on ships
VK1473	Lifeboats 623.829
VK1477	Life preservers
VK1479	Rockets, signal (marine lifesaving)
VK1481.A-Z	Lifesaving equipment (special: by name)
VK1481.S4	Shark protection
VK1491	Salvage, Marine
VK1500-1661	PILOTS & PILOTING, NAUTICAL
VK1515	Nautical pilots & piloting (gen. hist's.) 623.8922, .892209
VK1521-1624	PILOTING & PILOTS, NAUTICAL (by area) 623.291-89299
VK1523-1525	Piloting, Nautical (U.S.) 623.2973
VK1555-1596	Piloting, Nautical (Eur.) 623.294
VK1645-1661	Pilots & piloting, Nautical (gen.)
VM	NAVAL ARCHITECTURE & MARINE ENGINEERING
VM1-565	NAVAL ARCHITECTURE & SHIPBUILDING (SEE ALSO V750-995+ for construction & armament of warships)
VM1	Periodicals & associations (naval architec.: Eng.)
VM5	Conferences (naval architec.)
VM6	Museums & exhibitions (naval architec.)
VM7	Architecture, Naval (collected, nonperiodical works)
VM12	Directories (naval architec.)
VM15-124	Naval architecture (hist.)
VM15	Shipbuilding, Naval (gen. hist.)
VM18	Naval architecture (hist.: modern: gen.)
VM19	Naval architecture (hist.: 19th c.)
VM20	Naval architecture (hist.: 20th c.)
VM21-124	Naval shipbuilding (hist.: by area or country)
VM23-25	Shipbuilding, Naval (hist.: U.S.) 623.80973
VM55-96	Shipbuilding, Naval (hist.: Eur.)
VM55	Naval shipbuilding (hist.: Eur.: gen.) 623.8094
VM57-64	Shipbuilding, Naval (hist.: G.B.) 623.80941
VM71-72	Shipbuilding, Naval (hist.: Fr.) 623.80944
VM73-74	Shipbuilding, Naval (hist.: Ger.) 623.80943
VM79-80	Shipbuilding, Naval (hist.: It.) 623.80945
VM85-86	Shipbuilding, Naval (hist.: Rus.) 623.80947
VM99-113	Shipbuilding, Naval (hist.: Asia)
VM99	Naval shipbuilding (hist.: Asia: gen.) 623.8095
VM105-106	Shipbuilding, Naval (hist.: Japan) 623.80952
VM121-122	Shipbuilding, Naval (hist.: Australia) 623.80994
VM122.5	Shipbuilding, Naval (hist.: New Z.)
VM139-140	Biography (naval architec.)
VM142-148	Naval architecture (gen.) 623.81
VM142-145	Wooden ships (naval architec.) 623.81
VM146-147	Metal ships (naval architec.) 623.8182

VM151	Handbooks, tables, etc. (ship calculations: naval architec.)	
		623.810202, .810212
VM153	Tonnage tables (naval architec.)	
VM155	Measurement of ships (naval architec.)	
VM156-163	Theory & principles (naval architec.)	
VM165-276	Instruction (naval architec.)	
VM165	Naval shipbuilding (instruc.: gen.)	623.8107
VM171-274	Instruction (naval architec.: by place)	
VM173	Shipbuilding, Naval (instruc.: U.S.)	
VM205	Shipbuilding, Naval (instruc.: Eur.: gen.)	
VM207	Shipbuilding, Naval (instruc.: G.B.)	
VM223	Shipbuilding, Naval (instruc.: Ger.)	
VM255	Shipbuilding, Naval (instruc.: Japan)	
VM271	Shipbuilding, Naval (instruc.: Australia)	
VM275-276	Schools (naval architec.: special)	
VM293	Standards (naval architec.)	
VM295-296	Contracts & specifications (naval architec.)	
VM295	Specifications & contracts (naval architec.: gen.)	
VM297	Designs, drawings, blueprints (naval architec.)	623.812
VM297.5	Blueprints, drawings, designs (naval architec.: laying out)	
VM298	Models, Ship	623.8201, 745.5928
VM298.5-301.	Shipbuilding industry	
VM298.5	Industry, Shipbuilding (gen.)	338.476238, 387.5+
VM298.6	Shipbuilding industry (U.S.)	387.50973
VM298.7.A-Z	Shipbuilding industry (places besides U.S.)	
VM298.7.G7	Shipbuilding industry (G.B.)	
VM301.A-Z	Shipyards & shipbuilding companies (by name)	
VM307	Pictorials (ships)	387.2+
VM308	Figureheads, ornaments, decorations on ships	
VM321-349	Small craft	
VM321	Small craft (gen.)	
VM321.5	Boatyards, Small craft (gen.)	
VM321.52.A-Z	Boatyards, Small craft (by name)	
VM322	Maintenance & repair (small craft)	
VM331	Yachts (small craft: gen.)	
VM341	Motorboats & launches (small craft: gen.)	
VM351	Rowboats, small sailboats, etc.	
VM365-367	Submarine boats	
VM365	Submarine boats (gen.)	359.3257, 623.8257
VM367.A-Z	Equipment (submarine boats: special)	
VM367.P4	Periscopes (submarine architec.)	
VM367.S7	Batteries, Storage (submarine architec.)	
VM378-466	Vessels (naval architec.: by use)	
VM380	Warships (naval architec.: PREFER V750-995+) 623.825, 359.32	
VM381-383	Passenger ships (naval architec.)	
VM383.A-Z	Liners, Passenger (by name)	
VM383.B7	Bremen (pass. ship)	
VM383.N6	Normandie (pass. ship)	
VM385.A-Z	Steamship lines (by co. name)	
VM391-395	Freighters (naval architec.)	623.8245, 387.544
VM397	Coast guard vessels (naval architec.: by type) 623.8245, 359.9732	
VM451	Icebreakers (naval architec.)	623.828
VM455	Tankers (naval architec.)	623.8245, 387.544
VM457	Ore carriers	623.8245, 387.544
VM469.5	Pontoons & pontoon gear (naval architec.)	

VM471-479	Electricity (naval architec. & engin.)	623.8503, .852, .8726
VM473	Electricity (naval architec. & engin.: U.S. Navy)	
VM480	Electronics, Marine (radar, radio, sonar, etc.: naval architec. & engin.)	
		623.8504, .734+, .8564-85648
VM481-482	Heating, ventilation, & sanitation (naval architec. & engin.)	
VM481	Sanitation, heating, & ventilation (naval architec. & engin.)	
		623.853-854
VM483	Disinfection & fumigation (naval engin.)	
VM485	Cold storage (naval architec. & engin.)	
VM491-493	Lighting (naval architec. & engin.)	
VM501	Plumbing (naval architec. & engin.)	
VM503-505	Water supply (naval architec. & engin.)	623.854
VM511	Hammocks, berths, etc. (naval architec.)	
VM521	Propulsion (naval architec. & engin.: gen.)	623.87
VM565	Steerage, Nautical	
VM600-989	MARINE ENGINEERING	
VM600-605	Engineering, Marine (gen.)	623.87
VM607	Handbooks, tables, etc. (marine engin.)	623.870202
VM615	Marine engineering (hist.: gen.)	
VM621-724	Engineering, Marine (hist.: by place)	
VM623-625	Marine engineering (hist.: U.S.)	
VM655	Marine engineering (hist.: Eur.)	
VM657	Marine engineering (hist.: G.B.)	623.870941-870942
VM671	Marine engineering (hist.: Fr.)	
VM673	Marine engineering (hist.: Ger.)	623.870943
VM679	Marine engineering (hist.: It.)	
VM685	Marine engineering (hist.: Rus.)	
VM721	Marine engineering (hist.: Australia)	
VM725-728	Instruction (marine engin.)	623.8707
VM727	Marine engineering (instruction: U.S.)	
VM728.A-Z	Instruction (marine engin.: places except U.S.)	
VM731-779	Marine engines	
VM731	Engines, Marine (gen.)	623.872
VM740	Turbines, Marine	623.87233
VM741-750	Boilers, Marine	623.873
VM751-759	Propulsion & resistance (marine engin.)	
VM751	Resistance & propulsion (marine engin.: gen.)	
VM753-757	Propellers (marine engin.)	623.81473
VM770	Diesel, oil, & gas engines (marine engin.)	623.8723
VM773	Electric propulsion (marine engin.)	623.8726
VM779	Fuels, Marine engine	623.874
VM781-861	Ships' appliances (engin.)	
VM781	Appliances, Ships' (engin.: gen.)	623.86
VM791	Anchors, cables, etc. (marine engin.)	
VM815	Lights, Ships' (engin.)	
VM821	Pumps, Marine (engin.)	
VM841-845	Steering gear, Marine (engin.)	
VM851	Hatchways, ladders, other special fittings (marine engin.)	
VM880	Ship trials (gen.)	
VM881.A-Z	Trials, Ship (by name of vessel)	

VM901-965	Maintenance & building devices & procedures, Marine (engin.)	
VM901	Shipbuilding & maintenance appliances & activities (engin.: gen.: SEE TC361 & 363 for dry & floating docks)	
VM951	Fouling, corrosion, etc. (marine engin.)	
VM961	Scraping, painting, etc. (marine engin.)	
VM965	Welding & cutting, Underwater (marine engin.)	
VM975-989	Diving (marine engin.: SEE GV840.S78 for skindiving)	
VM977	Diving (marine engin.: hist.)	627.7209, 623.8257 (subs.), 359.3257 (subs.—naval ops.), 797.23 (scuba)
VM980	Biography (divers: marine engin.)	
VM981	Diving (marine engin.: gen.)	627.72
VM985-989	Diving (marine engin.: special types)	

Z	BIBLIOGRAPHY 010	
Z1236	Bibliographies (U.S.: hist.)	016.97309
Z1244	Bibliographies (U.S.: hist.: 1900-45)	016.9730904, .97309044 (WWII)
Z1249.M5	Bibliographies (mil. hist.: U.S.)	016.3550973, .35500973,
Z1249.N3	Bibliographies (naval hist.: U.S.)	016.3590973, .35900973, .35930973, .3593310924
Z2016-2020+	Bibliographies (G.B.: hist.)	016.941-942
Z2021.N3	Bibliographies (naval hist.: G.B.)	016.3590941
Z2237	Bibliographies (Ger.: hist.)	016.94309
Z2241.M5	Bibliographies (mil. hist.: Ger.)	016.3550943
Z2506-2510+	Bibliographies (Rus.: hist.)	016.94709
Z3306-3308	Bibliographies (Japan: hist.)	016.95209
Z3308.M5	Bibliographies (naval hist.: Japan)	016.3590952
Z6207.E8 or .W7	Bibliographies (WWI)	016.9403
Z6616	Bibliographies (naval sci. & hist.)	016.35909, .35900722
Z6724	Bibliographies (mil. sci. & hist.)	016.35509, 355.009, .0009

II. DEWEY DECIMAL CLASSIFICATION SYSTEM (DDC)

Dewey Decimal Classification numbers consist of three digits followed in some instances by a decimal point and one or more digits beyond the decimal. These added numerals may represent divisions of the higher subject unique to that class. They may ALSO be repeating subdivisions taken from the ends of other specified numbers or from certain standard or geographic tables. The complete call numbers end with a letter and number usually for the author's last name.

The basic concept of the Dewey class system is to divide all knowledge into 1000 hierarchical categories running from 000 through 999. Each group of 100 numbers then represents a related area of research. For instance, the 900's belong to the class of History and Geography. Within each set of 100 or 10 or even within single numbers users can find associated material extending out to the third digit and beyond the decimal point as well.

Dewey numbers differ from Library of Congress numbers in several ways, some of which are discussed in the LC introduction. DDC uses digits sometimes succeeded by decimalized numbers for the classification scheme, whereas LC employs letters followed by numerals possibly followed by more letter-number subject subdivisions. Dewey has fewer basic numbers and tries to keep allied material closer together in a tighter overall schema. Further, DDC call numbers utilized in many libraries tend to have fewer identification lines than LC but may well have longer ones if many numbers past the decimal are applied. Incidentally, remember to look at the earlier digits past the decimal to keep proper order rather than going by total number of digits. Therefore, 355.34 shelves AFTER 355.338.

Since many DDC libraries try to avoid overlong numbers traveling six or more digits past the decimal, one can generally count on Dewey numbers to show less specificity in practice than their LC counterparts. The obvious hierarchical nature of the Dewey system, however, makes it more mnemonic for some people and may appear to bring related titles more closely together on the shelves.

Because of its relatively tight character, DDC has not always comfortably incorporated new subject concepts or historical developments. The hierarchical logic of the scheme and its available subdivisions has nevertheless made it a popular model of both sophistication and simplicity. Basic Dewey numbers are definitely easier than LC numbers to remember.

Most public libraries utilize the Dewey system of classification and shelving. In addition, some academic libraries use Dewey or have a split collection, with newer titles probably ordered by LC.

This part of the classification section consists of an outline of the primary Dewey groups followed by an extensive listing of pertinent military, engineering, and historical areas. Brief descriptions of each number are given, and similar Library of Congress numbers follow when available or relevant.

A single index to both Dewey and LC class numbers can be found after the Dewey listings. As mentioned before, certain topics do not easily translate from LC to DDC. Also, while each book or resource item can obviously receive only one call number in the cataloging process, every item may well receive several subject or other headings. Furthermore, subject and corporate headings may provide the greatest focus for certain specific matters. Therefore, readers should check the overall classification index as well as the LC headings section after it in order to find the most leads.

DEWEY CLASS NUMBERS: DESCRIPTIONS: POSSIBLE LC CLASS NUMBERS

000-099	General works	
010	Bibliography	Z; sometimes D-F, U-V, or other subject classes
016	Bibliographies (specific subjects)	Z; sometimes D-F, U-V, or other subject classes
100-199	Philosophy & psychology B-BD, BH-BJ, BF	
200-299	Religion	BL-BX
300-399	Social sciences G-H, J-L, U-V	
355-358	Military science	U
359	Naval science	V
400-499	Language	P
500-599	Sciences (pure) & math	Q
600-699	Technology, medicine, engineering, agriculture, management	
		T, R, QA76, S, H
620	Engineering	T
623	Military & marine engineering	UG, VM
629.13	Aeronautics	
700-799	Arts, architecture, music, sports, & recreation	N, NB-NX, NA, M, GV
800-899	Literature	P
900-999	Geography & history	G, D-F
940.3-.499	European War (1914-18)	D501-680
940.53-5499	World War II (1939-45)	D731-838

010-019	Bibliographies (inclu. partic. kinds, subjects, etc.)	Z
016	BIBLIOGRAPHIES [SEE ALSO subject #'s like 359+, 940+, etc.]	
016.355	Bibliographies (mil. sci. & hist.)	Z6724
016.359	Bibliographies (naval sci. & hist.)	Z6616
016.9403	Bibliographies (WWI)	Z6207.E8 or .W7
016.94053-94054	Bibliographies (WWII)	Z6207.W8
016.94109	Bibliographies (G.B.: hist.)	Z2016-2020+
016.94309	Bibliographies (Ger.: hist.)	Z2237
016.94709	Bibliographies (Rus.: hist.)	Z2506-2510+
016.95209	Bibliographies (Japan: hist.)	Z3306-3308
016.97309	Bibliographies (U.S.: hist.)	Z1236-1245+

300-399	Social sciences	G-H, J-L, U-V
300-309	Social sciences (gen.)	H1-99
320-329	Political science J	
330-339	Economics HB-HJ	
340-349	Law	K
350-359	Public administration	H-J
355-359	Military & naval science	U, V
370-379	Education	L
380-389	Commerce, communications, & transport	HF, HE

355-358	Military forces & science	U
356-359	Warfare & military forces (types)	UD-UG, V
358.41	Air warfare (gen.)	
359	Naval science	V

355	MILITARY SCIENCE & ORGANIZATION (ALSO armed forces, ground forces, etc.: officers' hdbks. here at 355)	U, U21+
355.003	Dictionaries & encyclopedias (mil. sci.)	U24-25
355.0082	Women in armed forces	
355.0092	Biography, Military	U51-55
355.02	War & warfare	U21, U21.2, U102
355.021	Warfare (summary topics)	U161-162, UA10
355.0213	Militarism & antimilitarism (inclu. mil.-indus. complex)	JX1952, JX1963, UA23, U21.5, JF195.C5
355.0215	Limited war (ALSO older titles on total war)	UA11+, U21+, UA11
355.022	Sociological factors of war [SEE ALSO 303.66 & 306.2]	
355.023	Economic factors of war [PREFER 355.02]	HB195, HC65, JX1953
355.027	War (causes)	U21.2, HB195, JX1952
355.0272	Causes of war (political)	
355.0273	Causes of war (economic)	HB195
355.0274	Causes of war (sociological)	
355.0275	Causes of war (psychological)	
355.028	War (aftermath: occupation, reconstruc., etc.)	
355.03	Military status (gen.: inclu. policy)	
355.031	Alliances, Military	
355.032	Military missions & attachés	
355.033	Military status (gen. hist.)	D25, U21+, U27, UA15
355.033001-033005	Military status (hist. periods)	
355.033004	Military status (20th c.)	U42
355.0330041	Military status (1900-1919)	
355.03301-03309	Military status (by area or country)	
355.03304	Europe (mil. status)	
355.033043	Germany (mil. status)	
355.033052	Japan (mil. status)	UA845+
355.033073	United States (mil. status)	UA23
355.033094	Australia (mil. status)	UA870+
355.0332+	Military capability	
355.033244	France (mil. capabil.)	
355.033251	China (mil. capabil.)	
355.033273	United States (mil. capabil.)	
355.0335+	Policy, Military	
355.033541-033542	Great Britain (mil. policy)	UA647+, UA647-668
355.033543	Germany & Central Europe (mil. policy)	UA710+, UA710-719
355.033547	Russia (mil. policy)	UA770+
355.033551 (China)-033552 (Japan)	Japan & China (mil. policy)	UA830, UA835+, UA845+
355.033573	United States (mil. policy)	
355.033594	Australia (mil. policy) UA870-874	
355.07	Research & development, Military	
355.1	MILITARY LIFE, CUSTOMS, & POSTMILITARY BENEFITS	U750, U22
355.11	Military life (service periods, promotion, vet. benefits, etc.)	
355.112	Promotion & demotion (mil.)	UB320+
355.113	Leaves, furloughs, other inactive periods (mil.)	
355.114	Discharge, retirement, other termination (mil.)	UB320+
355.115	Veterans' benefits	UB356-405, UB356-358
355.1151	Pensions, Veterans' [PREFER now 331.25291355]	

355.12	Living conditions, Military	U750-773, U750, U765
355.123	Morale, Military U22	
355.129	Military living conditions (partic. situations) U765+	
355.1292	Basic training (mil. living conditions: ALSO regular quarters)	
355.1293	Transport & maneuvers (mil. living conditions)	
355.1294	Combat conditions (mil. life)	
355.1295	Military prison life (SEE ALSO 365.48)	
355.1296	Prisoner-of-war camps (mil. life: SEE ALSO 365.45) UB800-805	
355.13	Conduct & rewards, Military U765+	
355.133	Discipline & conduct, Military (regulation)	
355.1332	Punishment & enforcement, Military	
355.13323	Military police & conduct enforcement	
355.13325	Military prisons (SEE ALSO 365.48) UB800-805	
355.1334	Mutinies & military offenses (SEE 364.138 for war crimes) UB780+	
355.1336	Etiquette, Military U765+	
355.134	Rewards & privileges, Military UB430-435	
355.1342	Medals, decorations, badges, etc. (mil. rewards)	
355.1349	Gun salutes & other military rewards (misc.: USE 355.134 with 1989+ pubn.)	
355.135	Salaries, Military (SEE ALSO 355.64) UC70-75 (U.S.), UC91-258 (other places), UC180-183 (Ger.), UC184-187 (G.B.), UC241 (Japan)	
355.14	Uniforms, Military (inclu. insignia, etiquette of, etc.) UC480-535, UC483 (U.S.)	
355.15	Colors & standards, Military UC590-595, U360-365	
355.16	Celebrations & commemorations, Military	
355.17	Ceremonies, Military U350-355	
355.2	RESOURCES, MILITARY UA18, UA10	
355.21	Military resources (prep., review, preserv.)	
355.22	Human resources (mil.) UA17.5, UB320+, UB340+	
355.223	Recruitment & enlistment, Military	
355.2232	Training, Reserve	
355.2234	Qualifications, Service (mil.)	
355.2236	Commissioning, registration, classification, exams, etc. (mil. manpower procure.) UB330+, U400+	
355.22362	Enlistment, Military UB320-325, UB323 (U.S.)	
355.22363	Draft, Military UB340-345, UB343 (U.S.)	
355.224	Conscientious objectors UB341-342	
355.225	Universal service & training (mil. resources) UB350-355	
355.23	Civilian personnel (mil. resources)	
355.24	Raw materials (mil. resources) HC110.A-Z, UA18, UA929.5+	
355.242	Metals (mil. raw materials)	
355.243	Minerals (non-metal: mil. raw materials)	
355.245	Agricultural products (mil. raw materials) UA929.95.A35	
355.26	Industrial resources (mil. use) UA18, UA929.5+, HC106+	
355.27	Communication & transport (mil. resources) UA940-945, UA929.95.T7, UC10+, UC270-275	
355.28	Mobilization (mil. resources: inclu. requisition, commandeering, voluntary, etc.) UA910-915, UA913 (U.S.)	
355.29	Demobilization (mil. resources: gen.) UA917	

355.3	MILITARY PERSONNEL (inclu. organization; readiness of partic. groups) UA15+, UA23-39+ (U.S.)
355.309	Organization (mil. personnel: hist. & geog. treatment)
355.31	Military units (types: armies, div's., regiments, co's., mil. districts, etc.) UA, UA23-39+ (U.S.), UA646-829 (Eur.), UA830-853 (Asia), UA870-876 (Australia-Pac.)
355.33	Hierarchy, Military (mil. personnel) UA, UB410-415, UB210
355.33041	Line functions (mil. organiz.)
355.33042	Staff functions (mil. organiz.)
355.331	General & flag officers (above army col. or navy capt.) UB200, UB210
355.332	Officers, Commissioned & warrant UB407-415
355.338	Enlisted personnel (inclu. non-coms) UB320, U765+
355.34	Noncombat services (mil.: inclu. soc. srvcs., dependent srvcs., civil activ's., etc.)
355.341	Supply & administrative services, Military (canteens, post-ex's., messes, etc.: SEE ALSO 355.6 & .71) UC, UC750-755, UH80-85
355.342	Public information & relations (mil.) UH700-705, UH703 (U.S.)
355.343	Espionage & unconventional warfare (mil.: SEE ALSO 327.12) UB250-290
355.3432	Intelligence & military espionage (inclu. cryptanalysis, data analysis, etc.) UB250-251, UB251.A-Z (by country), UB270-271, UB271.A-Z (by place), UB271.x2.A-Z (by spy)
355.3433	Counterintelligence (mil.)
355.3434	Psychological warfare & propaganda (mil.: ALSO use 355.34 for propag.) UB275-277, UB276 (U.S.), UB277.A-Z (except U.S.)
355.3437	Subversion & sabotage (mil.) UB273-274UB275-277, UB276 (U.S.), UB277.A-Z (except U.S.)
355.345	Medical & health services, Military UH201-629, UH215, UH223-225 (U.S.)
355.346	Recreation services, Military (inclu. sports, arts, music, libraries, clubs, etc.) UH800-910, UH800, UH805 (U.S.)
355.347	Religious & counseling services, Military UH20-25
355.348	Women's military units UA565.W6 (U.S. Wac's)
355.35	Combat units (by service field) UA
355.351	Home guards & frontier troops UA42 (U.S. Nat. Guard)
355.352	Expeditionary & colonial forces UA14, UA668 (G.B.), UA709 (Fr.), UA719 (Ger.), UA849 (Jp.)
355.356	Allied forces (inclu. various multi-nat. & combined ops.) UA12 (U.S.), UA15, U260 (comb. ops.)
355.357	International forces (PERHAPS PREFER 355.356)
355.359	Foreign legions
355.37	Reserves, Army UA, UA42 (U.S.), UA50-549 (U.S.: by state), UA661 (G.B.)

355.4	STRATEGY & MILITARY OPS. (plans, attack, defense, etc.)
	UA11, UA23 (U.S.), U27, U42-43, U102, U161-167
355.409	Military ops. (hist's. & types of persons: SEE ALSO 355.47 for
	geog. treat.) U27-43
355.41	Support & logistics, Military (logistics, camouflage, p.o.w. care, etc.)
	U168, UC260-270
355.411	Logistics & troop movement
355.412	Encampments U180-185
355.413	Reconnaisance & patrols U220
355.415	Troop support (communication, supply, medical, p.o.w.'s, etc.:
	ALSO use 355.41 for newer titles on p.o.w. care)
	UC260-267, UA940-945
355.42	Tactics, Military U164-167.5, U165
355.422	Military tactics (partic. kinds: commando, retreats, blitz, landings,
	attacks & counters, etc.)
355.423	Tactics, Military (in different terrains, climates, weathers)
	U167.D4 (desert), .F6 (forest), .W5 (winter)
355.424	Animals, Use of (mil. sci.)
355.426	Urban warfare tactics U167.5.S7
355.43	Nuclear ops., Military (also gen. strategy: USE 355.4 for post-'88 titles
	on gen. strategy) U161-163
355.44	Siege warfare UG443-449
355.45	Home defense (coasts, frontiers, other valuable redoubts)
	UA (gen.), UG410-442 (fortific's.), UG410-412 (U.S.),
	UG428-430 (Eur.), UG429.G7 (G.B.)
355.46	Combined ops., Military (2 or more types of forces)
355.47	Geography, Military (tactical & strategic) UA985-997
355.473	United States (mil. geog.) UA993
355.474	Europe (mil. geog.) UA990, UA995.E
355.4741-4742	Great Britain (mil. geog.) UA995.G7
355.4743	Germany & Central Europe (mil. geog.) UA995.G3
355.4747	Russia (mil. geog.) UA995.R9
355.4761-4762	Tunisia & Egypt (mil. geog.)
355.48	Analysis, Military (real & mock events) UA719-740+, U161-167+
355.49	Occupation & government, Military D802 (WWII)
355.5	TRAINING & EDUCATION, MILITARY U400-717, U400 (gen.),
	U403 (modern), U408 (U.S.), U410 (West Pt.), U510-549 (G.B.)
355.50973	Education & training, Military (U.S.)
355.52	Military maneuvers U250-255
355.54	Basic training (mil.: inclu. drills, survival exercises, etc.) U400-717,
	U765-773, U320-325
355.544	Encampment & field training (mil.) U180-185, UG400-409+
355.547	Small arms & bayonet training UD380-415, U169
355.548	Hand-to-hand combat & self-defense (training: inclu. unarmed &
	knife fighting) U167.5.H3, U262
355.55	Training, Officer (mil. sci.) U400-717 (educ.)
355.56	Training, Technical (mil. sci.)

355.6	MILITARY ADMINISTRATION	UB-UC
355.61	Personnel administration, Military (civilian & mil.)	UB160-165,
	UB180-197, UB410-415 (officers), UB320-338	
355.62	Administration, Military supply & finance	UC260-267, UA
355.621	Supply administration (mil.)	UC260-267
355.6211	Contract administration (mil.)	UC267
355.6212	Procurement (mil. supplies)	UC263-267, HD3858-3860
355.6213	Supplies, Military (use & disposal)	
355.622	Financial administration (mil.)	UB150-155, UC263-267,
	UA21-876, UA910-915	
355.63	Military inspection	UB240-245
355.64	Salaries & wages, Military (admin.: SEE ALSO 355.135)	UC70-75
355.65-66	Clothing, food, & equipment (mil. admin.: PREFER 355.81)	
	UC460-535, UC700-735	
355.67	Housing administration (mil.: SEE ALSO 355.71 & .12 [gen.])	
	UC400-440	
355.693	Mail, Military	
355.699	Graves registration & military burial	
355.7	MILITARY INSTALLATIONS & LAND (inclu. bases, forts, camps,	
	posts, etc.)	UA26+ (U.S.), UC400-405, UA600-876
355.709	Military bases, camps, forts, reservations, etc. (geog. & hist. applic.)	
355.71	Quarters, Military (barracks, p.o.w. camps etc. on-site)	UC400-405
355.72	Medical installations, Military	UH470-475
355.73	Artillery installations (arsenals, depots, target ranges, schools, etc.)	
	UF540-545	
355.74	Engineering installations, Military	
355.75	Supply depots, Military	UC260-269
355.79	Land (mil. bases, reservations, etc.)	
355.8	EQUIPMENT & SUPPLIES, MILITARY	U800+, UC260-267
355.81	CLOTHING, FOOD, CAMP EQUIPMENT, ETC. (SEE ALSO .65-66)	
	UC460-465+, UC700-705	
355.82	Ordnance	UF520-780, U800-823+
355.821	Artillery (gen.)	
355.8212	Artillery, Field	UF400-405
355.8217	Artillery, Coast	UF450-455
355.8218	Artillery, Naval (SEE ALSO 359.8218)	VF320-325
355.822	Artillery (specific pieces)	
355.823	Gun mounts	
355.824	Small arms	UF520-537+
355.82424	Automatic firearms (rifles, machine guns, etc.)	UF620
355.82425	Rifles	UD390-395
355.8243	Revolvers & pistols	UD410-415
355.825	Bombs, ammunition, etc.	
355.82511	Grenades, mines, etc.	
355.825114	Grenades, Hand & rifle	UF765
355.825115	Mines (mil. equip.)	UG490
355.82516	Chemical & biological weapons (projectiles etc.)	UG447-447.8
355.8252	Explosives	UF860-880
355.82542	Detonators	
355.82545	Demolition charges	
355.8255	Ammunition, Small arms	
355.82594	Biological agents (mil.)	
355.826	Sighting apparatus & other ordnance access.	UF848-856

355.83	Transport equipment & supplies, Military (vehicles, fuel, trains, etc.)
	UC270-360, UC270-275, UC340-345, UC260-267, UG615-620
355.85	Communication equipment, Military UG570-613, UA940-945
355.88	Medical supplies UH440-445

355.83   Transport equipment & supplies, Military (vehicles, fuel, trains, etc.)
    UC270-360, UC270-275, UC340-345, UC260-267, UG615-620

355.85   Communication equipment, Military   UG570-613, UA940-945

355.88   Medical supplies   UH440-445

356-357   Land forces warfare   UD-UF

356   FOOT FORCES WARFARE   UD, U14-43, UA

356.1   INFANTRY   UD, UD15, UD21-124 (by place), UD144-145+, UA

356.11   Motorized infantry (pubns. before 1989 may inclu. regular infan. also)
    U167.5.M6, UD15, UD21-124+, UA

356.15   Irregular troops (guerrillas, brigands, etc.)   U240, U167.5.A-Z

356.16   Troops, Special-purpose   U167.5.A-Z

356.162   Snipers, bazookamen, machine-gunners, & other special-weapon
    troops   U167.5.A-Z, UD390+, UF620

356.164   Troops, Ski & mountain   UD470-475, U167.5.W5

356.166   Paratroops   UD480-485, UD483 (U.S.), UG630-635

356.167   Rangers & commandos   U262

356.18   Infantry (gen.)   UD160-302, UD160 (U.S.)

356.181   Life & customs (infantry)

356.1814   Uniforms, Infantry

356.183   Tactics & operations, Infantry

356.184   Training (infantry)   U400-714 (educ.), U320-325

356.186   Equipment & supplies (infantry)   UD380+, UC260-267, UC460+

356.187   Installations, Infantry   UC400-405, U180-185

356.189   Organization & personnel (infantry)

357   MOUNTED FORCES & WARFARE   UE, UE15, UE21-124,
    UE23 (U.S.), UE57 (G.B.), UE65 (Austria), UD450-455

357.043   Organization & personnel (cavalry: inclu. specific units)

357.1   CAVALRY, HORSE   UE15, UE21-124, UE150+, UA

357.184   Horse cavalry (gen. & ops.)   UE150-475, UE150+, UE157+

357.185   Training, Horse cavalry   UE430-435, UE160-302 (by place)

357.187   Cavalry installations (horse)   UE350, UE430-435, UC400-405, UA

357.188   Equipment & supplies (horse cavalry)   UE440-445, UC260-267

357.2   REMOUNT & TRAINING SERVICES (cavalry: horse training, remount
    depots, care & breeding, etc.) UE460-475, UC600-695

357.5   CAVALRY, MECHANIZED   UE147-149, UE150-155 (manuals),
    UE159, UE160-302 (by place)

357.52   Bicycle troops (mech. cav.)   UH30-35

357.53   Motorcycle troops (mech. cav.)   UC347

357.54   Mechanized cavalry (jeep, truck, other large-motor vehicle troops)
    UC340-345, UG615-620

357.58   Mechanized cavalry (gen. & ops.)   UE147-155, UE159,
    UE160-302 (by place)

358	SPECIALIZED FORCES & WARFARE (armored land, technical land, & air)	UE-UG
358.1	ARTILLERY, LAND MISSILE FORCES, & ARMORED WARFARE UF, UF15, UF21-124, UE147, UA32-33 (U.S.), UA	
358.12	Army artillery (inclu. field & antitank) UF400-405, UF15, UF21-124 (by place), UF150-157+ (manuals & tactics)	
358.13	Artillery, Antiaircraft (land) UF625	
358.16	Artillery, Coast UF450-455	
358.18	Armored forces & warfare (tanks, armored cav., etc.) UG446.5, UE147	
358.2	ENGINEER FORCES, ARMY UG15, UG21-124 (by place), UG23 (U.S.), UG500-620	
358.22	Construction & maintenance (army engineers) UG360-390+, UG15-124	
358.23	Bomb disposal & demolition (army engineers) UG370, UG550-555	
358.24	Communications, signaling, & cryptography forces (mil. engineers) UG570-611.5, UA940-945, UB290 (cryp.)	
358.25	Transportation services (mil. engineers) UC270-275, UG345 (rail)	
358.3	TECHNICAL FORCES (chem., biol., & radiation warfare: pre-1989 titles may cover camouflage construc. & war matériel manufac.)	
358.34	Chemical warfare UG447-447.6	
358.38	Biological warfare UG447.8	
358.4	AERIAL WARFARE & AIR FORCES (inclu. naval av. for works prior to 1989--SEE 359.94 after 1988) UG622-1425, UG630, UG633-634 (U.S.), UG635.A-Z (places besides U.S.), VG90-95 (naval av.)	
358.403	Air forces (policy & status) UG630-635, UA	
358.407	Research & development (air forces equip. & supplies)	
358.41	Air warfare (gen.)	
358.411	Air force life & customs U750-773, UG770-775, UG1130-1135	
358.41112	Promotion & demotion (air forces) UB320-325, UB410-415	
358.4112	Living conditions (air forces)	
358.4113	Conduct, discipline, & reward (air forces: etiquette, enforcement, punishments, etc.) UB790-795, UB430-435	
358.4114	Uniforms, Air force UG1160-1165	
358.412	Resources, Air force UG630+, UG1100+	
358.4122	Human resources (air forces: enlistment etc.) UG880-885	
358.4124-4126	Industrial resources & raw materials (air forces) UG1100-1105, UG630+	
358.4127	Communication & transport (air force resources) UC330-335, UA940-945	
358.413	Structure & personnel, Air force UG770-775, UG1130-1135	
358.4131	Air force units (types)	
358.4133	Hierarchy, Air force UG770-775	
358.41331	General officers (air forces) UG790-795	
358.41332	Commissioned & warrant officers, Air force UG820-825	
358.41338	Enlisted personnel & non-coms, Air force UG820-825	
358.4134	Noncombat services (air forces)	
358.41343	Unconventional warfare (air forces: intelligence, propaganda, etc.)	
358.41345	Medical & health services, Air force UH201-655	
358.41348	Women in air forces	
358.41356	Allied forces (air) UG625, UG630+	

358.414	Air force ops. (gen.)	UG630, UG633-635, UG700-765

358.414   Air force ops. (gen.)   UG630, UG633-635, UG700-765
358.41409 Air warfare (hist.: gen.)   UG625
358.4141   Logistics & support, Air force   UG1100-1105
358.41415 Troop support (air forces)   UG700-705, UG260
358.4142   Tactics, Air force   UG700-705
358.4143   Strategy, Air force   U162-163, UG633-635
358.4145   Home defense, Air force   UG730-735, UG630-635
358.4147   Geography, Air warfare   UG633-635, UA
358.41474 Europe (air war geog.)
358.414741   Great Britain (air war geog.)   UG635.G7
358.414743   Germany (air war geog.)   UG635.G3
358.414747   Russia (air war geog.)
358.41475   Asia (air war geog.)
358.414773 United States (air war geog.)   UG633
358.4148   Analysis, Air warfare (real & imagined)   UG630-635
358.415   Training & education, Air force   UG637-639
358.4152   Maneuvers, Air force (training)
358.4155   Training, Officer (air forces)
358.4156   Training, Technical (air forces)
358.416   Air force administration   UG770-775, UG1100-1135, UG630-635
358.4161   Air force personnel   UG1130-1135
358.4162   Finances & supplies (air force admin.)   UG1100-1105, UG1100-1425
358.416212   Equipment & supply procurement (air forces)   UG1120-1125, UG1123 (U.S.)
358.4164   Wages & salaries, Air force   UG940-945, UC74 (U.S.), UC90+
358.4165-4166   Clothing, food, & equipment (air forces)   UG1100-1105, UG1160-1165, UC460-465, UC700-705
358.4167   Housing administration (air forces) UG1140-1145
358.417   Bases & fields, Air force   UG634.5.A-Z (U.S.: by name), UG635.A-Z (other countries)
358.4171   Barracks & quarters, Air force   UG1140-1145
358.418   Matériel & equipment, Air force   UG1100-1425+, UG1100-1105
358.4182   Ordnance, Air force   UG1270-1275
358.4183-4184   Combat & support aircraft   UG1240-1245, UG1242.A-Z (by type), UG1243 (U.S.), UG633-635, VG90-95 (naval), TL685+
358.42   Bomber forces & ops.   UG1242.B6, UG633-635, UG633 (U.S.), TL685.3, TL686.A-Z (by co. or name)
358.43   Pursuit & fighter forces & ops. (air)   UG1242.F5, UG633 (U.S.), UG635.A-Z (places except U.S.), TL685.3, TL686.A-Z (by co. or name)
358.44   Transport groups (air forces)   UC330-335, UG633-635, UG1242.T
358.45   Reconnaissance forces, Air (inclu. antisub. work)   UG760-765, UG1242.R4
358.46   Air force communications & ops.   UA940-945, UG611-612.5
358.47   Engineering services (air forces)

359	NAVAL FORCES & WARFARE	V-VM, V27-55, V101-109
359.001	Theory & philosophy (naval warfare)	
359.003	Dictionaries & encyclopedias (naval forces)	V23
359.009+	Sea forces & warfare (hist.)	VA, D-F, VA10, VA25-55
359.00941-00942	Great Britain (naval hist.)	VA452-467, DA70-89
359.00943	Germany (naval hist.)	VA510-519
359.00952	Japan (naval hist.)	VA650-659
359.0092	Biography, Naval	V61-64, V63.A-Z (U.S.: by name), V64.A-Z (other countries)
359.00973	United States (naval hist.)	VA49-395, VA50-70, E182, E746 (20th c.)
359.03+ (country #s follow)	Policy & status, Naval	VA
359.030941	Great Britain (naval policy & status)	
359.030952	Japan (naval policy & status)	
359.030973	United States (naval policy & status)	
359.07	Research & development (naval equip. & supplies)	V390-395
359.1	LIFE & CUSTOMS, NAVAL	V720-743, V110-145
359.11	Service periods (navies)	
359.112	Promotion & demotion (navies)	VB260-275, VB307-315
359.113	Furloughs, leaves, other inactive periods (navies)	VB260-275, VB307-315
359.114	Retirement, resignation, other service termination (navies)	
359.12	Living conditions (navies)	V720-743, V720 (gen.), V735 (modern), V736 (U.S.), V737 (G.B.)
359.123	Morale (navies)	
359.129	Living conditions (navies: partic. situations)	
359.1292	Naval living conditions (training or perm. bases)	
359.1294	Battle conditions, Naval	
359.13	Conduct & rewards, Naval	VB840-845, VB843 (U.S.)
359.133	Regulation of conduct, Naval	
359.1332	Discipline & enforcement (naval conduct)	VB850-855, VB890-925
359.13323	Enforcement (naval conduct)	
359.13325	Punishments (naval conduct)	
359.1334	Mutiny & other naval offenses	VB850-880
359.1336	Etiquette, Naval	V720-743, VB260-265, VB307-315
359.134	Rewards (navies: inclu. privileges, citations, medals, etc.)	VB330-335
359.1342	Medals, decorations, other reward insignia (navies)	
359.14	Naval uniforms (insignia, service, etiquette, etc.)	VC300-345
359.15	Colors & standards (navies)	V300-305
359.16	Commemorations & celebrations (navies)	V310
359.17	Naval ceremonies	V310
359.2	RESOURCES, NAVAL	VB, VB21-124 (by place), VB23 (U.S.), VB144-146, VA49-750 (by place), VA50-80+ (U.S.)
359.21	Naval resources (preparation, eval., preserv.)	
359.22	Human resources (navies)	
359.223	Recruitment & enlistment (navies)	VB260-315
359.2232	Training, Naval reserve	V400-695
359.2234	Qualifications (naval personnel)	
359.2236	Commissioning, draft, examination, registration, other methods of naval personnel procurement	VB260-275 (enlisted pers.), VB307-315 (officers)
359.22362	Voluntary enlistment (navies)	
359.22363	Conscription or draft (navies)	

359.229	Women in naval forces	VA49-750, VA390.W (U.S. Waves)
359.23	Civilian personnel (navies)	VB170-187
359.24	Raw materials (naval resources)	VC260-267, VF390+
359.26	Industrial resources (navies)	
359.27	Communication & transport (naval resources)	VC530-580 (trans.), VB255, VG70-85, V270
359.28	Naval mobilization	VA48, VA77-750, VA77 (U.S.)
359.29	Naval demobilization	VB277, UA917

359.3   ORGANIZATION & PERSONNEL, NAVAL   VA, VA50 (U.S.), VB21-124

359.31	Squadrons, fleets, flotillas, etc. (naval units)	VA, VA63.A-Z (U.S.), VB200-205
359.32	Ships & crews (naval forces)	V750-895, V750, VA (indiv. ships)
359.325	Ships, Powered (as units: group op. in squadrons etc., crew duties & life, hist's. of indiv. ships in most cases: SEE ALSO 359.83 & .835-836 for ships as equip.: PREFER .325+ when in doubt)	V750, V765-767, V799-800
359.3251	Naval armor & ordnance	V900-905, V950-980, VF, VF23 (U.S.)
359.3252	Battleships (units)	V750, V765-767, V799-800, VA, VA65.A-Z (U.S.: by name)
359.3253	Cruisers (in units)	V820-820.5, VA65.A-Z (U.S.: by name)
359.3254	Destroyer escorts & destroyers (units)	V825-825.5, VA65 (U.S.)
359.3255	Aircraft carriers (units: SEE ALSO 359.9435 for pubns. after 1988)	V874-875
359.3256	Landing craft (navies: units)	V895
359.3257	Naval submarines (units: SEE ALSO 359.933 after 1988) V857-859, V858 (U.S.), V859.A-Z (other countries), VA65.A-Z (U.S.: by name), VM365-367 (construc.)	
359.32572	Submarines, Diesel & electric (navies: units)	
359.3258	Combat vessels, Small (P.T.'s etc.: units)	V830-840, V880-885
359.326	Support vessels, Naval (units)	V865
359.3262	Minesweepers & minelayers (navies: units)	V885, V856+
359.3263	Coast guard vessels (units)	VM397
359.3264	Military transport vessels & hospital ships (units: SEE ALSO 359.9853 for transp. ships on pubns. after 1988)	VA79 (transports), VG450 (hosp. ships)
359.3265	Military supply ships (freighters, tankers, etc.: units: SEE ALSO 359.9853 after 1988)	VA79
359.33	Hierarchy, Naval	V110-145, VA, VB21-124, VB23 (U.S.), VB257-258.5, VB203
359.33041	Line positions (naval hier.)	
359.33042	Staff positions (naval hier.)	
359.331	Flag officers, Naval (above captain)	VB190, VB200-205, VB310-315
359.332	Officers, Commissioned & warrant (navies)	VB307-315
359.338	Enlisted personnel & non-coms, Naval	VB260-275
359.34	Non-combat services, Naval	VG1-2029+, VC10-580+
359.341	Supply services, Naval (canteens, post exch's, messes, etc.) VC, VC10, VC20-258 (overall by place), VC20-65 (U.S.), VC260-410	
359.342	Public relations & information (navies)	VG500-505
359.343	Unconventional warfare (navies)	VB230-250
359.3432	Intelligence, Naval	VB230-250, VB230, UB250-271
359.3433	Counterintelligence, Naval	
359.3434	Naval propaganda & psychological warfare	UB275-277
359.3437	Sabotage, Naval	VG86-88 (underwater demolition), UB273-274

359.345	Medical & nursing services (navies)	VG100-475, VG115, VG121-224 (overall by place), VG123 (U.S.), VG350-355 (nurse corps)
359.346	Recreation services, Naval (sports, arts, music, dancing, libraries, etc.)	VG2020-2029, UH800-910
359.347	Religious & counseling services, Naval	VG20-25, VG2000
359.348	Women's naval units (gen.)	VA
359.351	Home guard naval forces	VA45
359.356	Allied naval forces (inclu. various coalition forces)	VA40-42, VA, U260
359.37	Reserves, Naval	VA45, VA, VA80+

359.4   STRATEGY & NAVAL OPS. (SEE ALSO 359.43 for strategic works prior to 1989)   V27-55, V101-107, VA, VA10, VA50-750

359.409	Naval ops. (hist's.: gen.)	V27-55
359.41	Support & logistics, Naval	V179, VC10
359.411	Logistics, Naval	V179
359.413	Reconnaissance, Naval	V190
359.415	Troop support, Naval	
359.42	Tactics, Naval	V167-178
359.43	Strategy, Naval (PREFER 359.4 with titles after 1988)	V160-165
359.45	Home defense, Naval	VA45, V200
359.46	Combined ops., Naval (2 or more types of forces)	
359.47	Geography, Naval (strategic & tactical)	UA985-997, VA160-178, VA49-750 (by place)
359.474	Europe (naval geog.)	VA450
359.4741-4742	Great Britain (naval geog.)	VA452-467, VA454 (gen.)
359.4743	Germany (naval geog.)	VA510-519, VA513 (gen.)
359.4744	France (naval geog.)	VA500-509
359.4745	Italy (naval geog.)	VA540-549
359.4747	Russia (naval geog.)	VA570-579
359.4748	Scandinavia (naval geog.)	VA619.S, VA590599 (Sweden)
359.4749	Europe (naval geog.: misc. areas: Greece etc.)	
359.475	Asia (naval geog.)	VA620-639
359.4756	Turkey (naval geog.)	VA667.T9
359.47729	West Indies (naval geog.)	VA409-410
359.4773	United States (naval geog.)	VA49-395, VA50 (gen.)
359.4774-4779	United States (naval geog.: partic. states)	VA90-387
359.479	Pacific (naval geog.)	VA710-750, VA730
359.48	Analysis, Naval warfare (real & imagined battles, campaigns, etc.)	V25-55, V160-178

359.5   TRAINING & EDUCATION, NAVAL   V400-695 (by place), V411-438 (U.S.), V260-265

359.52	Maneuvers, Naval (training)	V245
359.54	Basic training (naval)	V260-265
359.55	Training, Officer (navies)	V400-695, V411-438 (U.S.: Annapolis etc.), VB307-315
359.56	Training, Technical (navies)	

359.6	ADMINISTRATION, NAVAL	VB, VB15, VB21-124 (by place),

359.6   ADMINISTRATION, NAVAL   VB, VB15, VB21-124 (by place), VB23 (U.S.), VC (maint.), VC10, VC20-258 (by place), VC20-65 (U.S.)

359.61   Personnel administration, Naval (civilian & mil.)   VB257-258.5

359.62   Administration, Naval supply & finance   VC10, VC20-258 (by place), VC20-65 (U.S.)

359.621   Supply administration (navies)   VC260-267, VC263 (U.S.)

359.6211   Contract administration (navies)   VC267

359.6212   Procurement (naval supplies &equip.)

359.622   Financial administration (navies)   VC20-258, VC500-505, VA

359.63   Naval inspection   VB220-225

359.64   Salary & wage administration, Naval   VC50-258, VC50-65 (U.S.)

359.65-66   Food, clothing, & equipment (naval admin.: SEE ALSO 359.81)   VC280-285+, VC283 (clothing: U.S.), VC350-355 (food etc.), VC353 (U.S.)

359.67   Housing administration (navies)   VC420-425

359.69   Burial services, graves registration, & naval military mail

359.693   Mail, Military (navies)

359.699   Graves registration & burial services (navies)

359.7   BASES & STATIONS, NAVAL   V220 (gen.), VA67-750 (by place), VA69-70 (U.S.), VA459-461 (G.B.), VA516-517 (Ger.), VA576-577 (Rus.), VA656-657 (Japan), VC412-425 (maint.: gen.)

359.709+   Naval installations (hist. & geog. works)

359.70941-70942   Naval bases & stations (in G.B.)

359.70943   Naval bases & stations (in Ger.)

359.70944   Naval bases & stations (in Fr.)

359.70945   Naval bases & stations (in It.)

359.70947   Naval bases & stations (in Rus.)

359.70973   Naval bases & stations (in U.S.)

359.70993   Naval bases & stations (in New Z.)

359.71   Quarters, barracks, etc. (navies)   VC420-425

359.72   Medical facilities, Naval   VG410-450, VG420 (U.S.), VG430 (G.B.)

359.73   Ordnance facilities, Naval   VF380-385

359.74   Engineering facilities, Naval   VM621-724, VM623 (U.S.), VC590-595

359.75   Supply depots, Naval   VC260-265

359.79   Land (naval bases etc.)   VC412-416

359.8   EQUIPMENT & SUPPLIES, NAVAL (develop., procure., issue, util., shipping, etc.)   VC, VF, VC10, VC20-258, VC20 (U.S.: gen.), VC260-267, VF145, VF21-124, VF23 (ordnance: U.S.), VF57 (G.B.), VF73 (Ger.), VF105 (Japan), VF71 (Fr.)

359.81   Clothing, equipment, food, & office supplies (navies: SEE ALSO 359.65-66)   VC280-345 (clothing & equip.), VC350-410 (food etc.)

359.82   Ordnance, Naval

359.8218   Artillery, Naval

359.825   Ammunition (navies)

359.8251   Delivery or charge-holding devices (naval ammun.)

359.825115   Mines (naval ammun.)

359.82513   Shells, Naval artillery

359.8254   Depth charges

359.826   Sighting & range apparatus (naval ordnance)

359.83	Transport equipment & supplies, Naval (inclu. fuel, vehicles, ships [gen.], etc.)	VC530-580, VC270-279, VC276, V750-895, UC320-325

359.835-836	Warships (as equip.: develop., operation, tech. effectiveness: SEE ALSO 359.32+ for ships as units or indiv. ships)
359.8351	Armor & weapons, Naval
359.8352	Battleships (as equip.)
359.8353	Cruisers (as equip.)
359.8354	Destroyers (as equip.)
359.8357	Submarines, Naval (as equip.: SEE ALSO 359.93832 for titles after 1988)

359.85	Communication equipment, Naval	VG70-85
359.88	Medical supplies, Naval	VG290-295

359.9	SPECIALIST FORCES, NAVAL
359.93	Submarine forces & warfare
359.933	Submarines, Naval (as units: SEE 359.3257 for titles prior to 1989)

359.938	Equipment & supplies (naval submarines)
359.93832	Submarines, Conventionally-powered (navies: as equip.: SEE 359.8357 for works before 1989)
359.9435	Carriers, Aircraft (as units: SEE 359.3255 for works before 1989)
359.94834	Aircraft, Naval

359.96 (add to .96 those #s after 355 in 355.1-.8)

	MARINES & marine warfare	VE, VE7-500+, VE15 (gen.), VE21-124 (by place), VE23 (U.S.), VE57 (G.B.), VE145-146
359.961	Life & customs (marines)	VE, VE21-124, V735-743
359.9612	Living conditions (marines)	VE420-425
359.962	Resources (marines)	VA-VC
359.963	Organization & personnel (marines)	VB21-124
359.9631	Military units (marines)	
359.9633	Hierarchy (marines)	
359.964	Marine military ops.	VE21-124 (by place)
359.9642	Tactics (marines)	VE157
359.9643	Strategy (marines)	VE21-124 (by place), VE144-146
359.9647+	Geography, Marine military (strategic & tactical) VE21-124, VA	
359.965	Training (marines)	VE430-435, V411-695, VE422 (U.S.)
359.966	Administration (marines)	VB21-124
359.967	Bases & camps (marines)	VE21-124, VE23-25 (U.S.), VA67-68, VG90-95 (marine av.)
359.968	Matériel & equipment (marines)	VE350-390, VF (ordnance)

359.97	Coast guard (SEE ALSO 363.286 for U.S.C.G.) VG50-55, VG53 (U.S.)
359.98	Technical forces, Naval (engineering, communic's., etc.)
359.9812	Artillery services, Naval
359.982	Engineering services, Naval
359.983	Communications services, Naval VG70-85
359.984	Underwater reconnaissance & demolition (navies: inclu. frogmen) VG86-88 (demo.), VG190 (recon.)

600-699	Technology, medicine, engineering, agriculture, management	
	T, R, QA76, S, H	
620	Engineering T	
623	Military & marine engineering	UG, VM
623.8	Naval engineering & seamanship	VM, VK
629.13	Aeronautics	

623	ENGINEERING, MILITARY & NAUTICAL	UG, VM (naval),
	V, UG15 (mil.: gen.), UG21-124 (mil.: by place),	
	UG23 (U.S.), V750-895 (vessels)	
623.003	Dictionaries & encyclopedias (mil. & naut. engineering: SEE	
	ALSO 603) UG144-147	
623.009+	Military & nautical engineering (hist. & biog. works: overall) UG400-401
623.04	Military & nautical engineering (overall topics)	
623.042	Engineering, Military & nautical (optical) UG476, UG487
623.045	Engineering, Military & nautical (mechanical) UG450
623.047	Engineering, Military & nautical (construction) UG460
623.1	Fortifications (mil. engineering) UG400-442
623.1-7	Military engineering UG
623.12	Military fortifications, Permanent (engineering: for titles after 1988 SEE
	ALSO 623.1) UG405
623.15	Military fortifications, Temporary (engineering) UG403
623.19	Fortifications (mil. engineering: by place: for works prior to 1989 SEE
	ALSO 623.109) UG410-442
623.262	Mine laying & sweeping (mil. engnrg.: land) UG490
623.263	Mine sweeping & laying (mil. engineering: marine) V856-856.5
623.27	Demolition (mil. engineering) UG37
623.3	Engineering, Defense UG400-442
623.31	Defenses, Direct-invasion (barriers, flooding, traps, etc.) UG375,
	UG403, UG407-409, UG448 (coast)
623.36	Countermining (defense engineering: SEE ALSO 623.3) UG490
623.37	Warning systems (defense engineering: SEE 623.737 for titles
	after 1988)
623.38	Bunkers, caves, shelters (defense engineering: protective construc.)
623.4	ORDNANCE (engineering & design) UF520-910+, UF520-
	525 (gen.), UF523 (U.S.), VF (naval), VF1-580, VF21-124 (by
	place), VF23 (U.S.)
623.41	Artillery (design) UF, UF1-910+, UF15 (gen.), UF144-145 (gen.),
	UF21-124 (by place), UF23 (U.S.), VF320-325 (naval)
623.412	Field & rail artillery (design) UF400-405, UF490-495 (rail)
623.417	Coastal artillery (design) UF450-455
623.418	Naval artillery (design) VF320-325, VF323 (U.S.)
623.419	Artillery (misc.: design: for space artil. after 1988)
623.42	Cannons, howitzers, mortars, small rockets, other specific
	artillery (design)
623.43	Gun mounts (design)

623.44	Side arms & misc. weapons (design)	UD380-425
623.441	Knives, bayonets, swords, etc. (design)	UD420-425, UD400 (bayonets)
623.442	Firearms, Portable (design)	UG520-525, UD380-385+
623.4424	Automatic weapons (machine & submach. guns, auto. rifles, etc.: design)	UD390-395, UF620 (mach. g's.)
623.4425	Rifles & carbines (design)	UD390-395
623.443	Military pistols & revolvers (design)	UD410-415
623.444	Sidearms, Modern (design: SEE ALSO 623.441 or .44)	UD420-425, UD400
623.445	Flame throwers, tear-gas devices, smoke mortars, other chemical weapons (design)	UG447-447.5
623.45	Ammunition & other ruinous media (design)	UF700-770
623.451	Shells, bombs, missiles, other delivery units with charges (design)	UF750-755
623.4511	Grenades, mines, nuclear weapons (design)	
623.45114	Grenades, Hand or rifle (design)	UF765
623.45115	Mines (design)	UG490, V856-856.5 (naval)
623.4513	Artillery shells & other projectiles (design)	UF750-760, VF480 (naval)
623.4514	Shrapnel & other antipersonnel devices (design)	UF760-765, VF490
623.4516	Chemical & biological weapons (design)	UG447-447.6 (chem.), UG447 (gen.), UG447.5.A-Z (type gas), UG447.8 (bio.)
623.4517	High-explosive devices (torpedoes, blockbusters, etc.: design)	V850-855 (torpedoes), UF860-870
623.4518	Armor-piercing shells & devices (design)	
623.4526	Gunpowder, cordite, & other explosives (design: inclu. propellant types)	UF870
623.4527	High explosives (design: inclu. dynamite, nitro, TNT)	TP285, TP270-295
623.4542	Detonators (design: fuses, percus. caps, primers, etc.)	UF780, VF510
623.4544	Charges, Demolition (destructors, bangalore torpedoes, etc.: design)	UG370, UF860
623.455	Small-arms ammunition (bullets, bazooka rockets, etc.: design)	UF700, UF740-745, UF770, TS538, VF500
623.459	Nonexplosive agents (tear gas etc.: design)	UF780
623.4592	Gases, poisons, other chemical agents (design)	
623.4594	Biological agents (ammunition: design)	
623.4595	Heat or other radiations (ammunition: design)	
623.46	Ranging & sighting apparatus (ordnance: design)	UF848-856, VF520
623.48	Maintenance & repair (ordnance)	UF350-355, UF550-560
623.5	BALLISTICS & GUNNERY (engineering)	UF800-830, UF820
623.51	Ballistics (engineering)	UF820-830
623.513	Ballistics, Interior (within bore)	UF823
623.514	Ballistics, Exterior (environmental)	UF825
623.516	Ballistics, Terminal (effects on targets)	

623.55	Gunnery (engineering)	UF800-805, VF144-302

623.55 Gunnery (engineering) UF800-805, VF144-302
623.551 Gunnery, Land (engineering) UF800-805
623.553 Gunnery, Naval (engineering) VF144-302, VF145 (gen.), VF150-155 (hdbks.), VF160-302 (drill bks.), VF160 (U.S.)
623.555 Gunnery, Aircraft (engineering)
623.557 Target detection & selection (inclu. radar & other methods: engineering: USE 623.46 for ranging & siting apparatae)
623.558 Firing & fire control (mil. engineering) UF848-856, UF848 (gen.), UF850.A-Z (range finders), VF520-530 (naval)
623.57 Recoil (mil. engineering)
623.6 MILITARY TRANSPORT ENGINEERING UC, UC10, UC270-360, UC270-275 (gen.)
623.61 Land transport (mil. engineering)
623.62 Construction, Road (mil. engineering) UG330
623.63 Military railroads & rolling stock (engineering) UC310-315, UF490-495 (r.r. artil.), UG345 (engnrg.)
623.64 Naval facilities (bases, docks, artificial harbors, etc.: design) V220-230, VA69-750 (by place), VA67-70 (U.S.), VM301
623.66 Air force facilities UG633-635, UG21-124 (engnrg. by place), UG360-390 (field engnrg.)
623.6613 Air bases (mil. design) UG633-634.5 (U.S.), UG635 (other lands)
623.666 Air traffic control (mil. engineering)
623.67 Military bridges (design) UG335, UC320-325
623.68 Military tunnels (design) UG340
623.7 MILITARY ENGINEERING (misc.)
623.71 Reconnaisance & intelligence topography (mil. engineering) UG470-474
623.72 Photography, Military (mil. engineering) UG476
623.73 Communications technology (mil. engineering) UG590-613.5, UG580, UG590, UG570-575
623.731 Signals, Visual (mil. engineering) UG582.V5
623.7312 Semaphore, flag signals, & heliograph (mil. engineering) UG582.S4, UG580, UG582, VK385, V300-305
623.7313 Pyrotechnic signal devices (mil. engineering) UG580, UF860
623.7314 Blinkers & electrooptical signal devices (mil. engineering) UG580, UG614-614.5, VK387
623.732 Telegraphy, Wire (mil. engineering) UG600-607
623.733 Telephony, Wire (mil. engineering) UG610-610.5
623.734 Radio & radar (mil. engineering) UG611-612.5
623.7342 Radiotelegraphy (mil. engineering) UG600-607, VG76-78
623.737 Air-raid warning systems (design: SEE 623.37 for titles prior to 1989) UG730-735
623.74 Vehicles, Military (design: inclu. combat & support v's. & neces. ordnance) UC270-275+
623.741 Aircraft (lighter-than-air: mil. design) UG1310-1375
623.742 Balloons, Military (design) UG1370-1375
623.743 Dirigibles (mil. engineering) TL659, UG1220-1225
623.7435 Airships, Rigid (mil. engineering)
623.7436-7437 Airships, Semirigid & nonrigid (mil. engineering)
623.744 Barrage ballons & nets (design) UG1370-1375, UG730-735, UF625

623.746	Aircraft (heavier-than-air: mil. engineering)	UG1240-1245, UG630-635, TL685.3, VG90-95
623.746042	Prop-driven aircraft (mil. design)	
623.746048	Piloting (gen.: mil. engineering: SEE ALSO 623.7463 [bombers] or other types)	TL710+, UG670-675 (manuals), UG700-705 (tactics)
623.746049	Aircraft components (cabins, engines, fuselages, instruments, wings, etc.)	TL672-683
623.7461	Ordnance, Aircraft (design)	UG1270-1275, UF530-537
623.7462	Training planes (design)	
623.7463	Bombers & fighter-bombers (mil. engineering)	TL685.3, TL686.A-Z (by manufac. or model), UG1242.B6
623.7464	Planes, Fighter (design)	TL685.3, TL686.A-Z (by manufac. or model), UG1242.F5
623.7466	Rescue aircraft (mil. engineering)	
623.7467	Planes, Reconnaisance (mil. design)	UG1242.R4
623.747	Land vehicles, Motorized (mil. design)	UC270-275, UC340-345
623.7472	Personnel transport vehicles (land: mil. design)	
623.74722	Jeeps (mil. design)	
623.74723	Buses (mil. design)	
623.74724	Ambulances (mil. design)	UH500-505
623.7474	Supply transport vehicles (land: mil. design)	
623.7475	Armored cars & other combat vehicles (land: design)	
623.74752	Tanks (design)	UG446.5
623.75	Safety & sanitation (mil. engineering)	UH600-629.5, U380-385, VC417.5, VG470-475, VM481-482, V380-386
623.751	Water supply (mil. engineering)	UC780, VC410, VM503-505
623.753	Sewage disposal (mil. design)	UC430, VM481, VM503
623.754	Garbage disposal (mil. engineering)	
623.76	Electrical engineering (mil.)	UG480, VM471-479
623.77	Engineering, Camouflage (mil.)	UG449, UG1240-1245 (air forces), V215 (ships)
623.8	NAUTICAL ENGINEERING & SEAMANSHIP	VM (architec.), VK (navig.)
623.81	Naval design	VM, V750-995 (warships), VM15-20 (hist.), VM21-124 (by place), VM23 (U.S.), VM57 (G.B.), VM146 (metal ships), VM156 (theory), V750, V765, V800
623.812	Ships (design)	VM297, V765
623.812045	Submersibles (naval design)	
623.8125	Warships (powered: design)	V750, V765-767, V799-800
623.81255	Carriers, Aircraft (design)	V874-875
623.81257	Submarines (naval: design)	V858-859, VM365-367
623.814	Naval design (components & details)	VM, VM156
623.8144	Hull design (naval architec.)	VM156
623.8147	Powerplants (naval design)	VM731+
623.817	Structural theory & design (naval architec.)	VM156-163
623.818	Structural design (naval architec.: specific materials)	
623.81821	Structural design (naval architec.: steel)	VM146
623.819	Tests (naval architec.)	

623.82	Nautical craft & types	VM, VM145
623.82001	Theory & philosophy (nautical craft)	VM156
623.8201	Model ships	
623.8202	Small craft (naut. engineering)	VM320-361, VM321, VM331, VM341
623.8203	Sailing vessels (naut. engineering)	VM156, VM142-145 (wooden), VM331, VM351
623.8205	Submersibles (naut. engineering)	VM365-367
623.8208	Maintenance & repair (naut. engineering: SEE ALSO 623.00288 after 1988)	VM763 (engines)
623.821-829	Seacraft, Modern (specific types: engineering)	
623.822	Sailing ships, Modern (engineering)	VM321, VM351
623.8225	Warships, Sail-driven (engineering)	V750-797, V750, V795
623.823	Power-driven craft (naut. engineering)	VM315
623.824	Merchant ships, Powered (engineering)	
623.8243	Passenger ships (engineering)	VM381-385, VM383.A-Z (by ship name), VM385.A-Z (by co.)
623.8245	Cargo ships, freighters, & tankers (engineering)	VM391-395, VM455-459, VM455 (tankers)
623.825	Warships, Fuel-powered (engineering)	V750, V765, V797-799
623.8251	Naval ordnance (engineering)	VF, VF21-124 (by place), VF23 (U.S.), VF350-355
623.8252	Battleships (engineering)	V750
623.8253	Cruisers (naval engineering)	V820-820.5
623.8254	Destroyer escorts (d.e.'s) & destroyers (naval engineering)	V825-825.3
623.8257	Submarines, Naval (engineering)	VM365-367, V857-859
623.82572	Naval submarines (diesel- & electric-powered: engineering)	
623.8258	Combat craft, Light (torpedo boats etc.: engineering)	V830-835 (p.t.'s), V880
623.826	Support ships (naval engineering)	V865
623.8262	Minelayers & minesweepers (naval engineering)	V885 (sweepers), V856-856.5 (both)
623.8263	Coast guard craft (engineering: also police boats, revenue cutters, etc.)	VM397
623.8264	Transport ships & hospital ships (naval engineering)	UC320-325, VG450 (hosp. ships)
623.8265	Supply ships (naval engineering)	V865
623.828	Lightships, icebreakers, other misc. ships (engineering)	VM451 (icebreakers)
623.829	Lifeboats & other manually-driven vessels (engineering)	VK1473, VM351, VM360 (inflatable)
623.83	Dry docks, shipyards, etc. (naval engineering)	VM301
623.84	Ship hulls (naut. engineering)	VM156
623.848	Hulls (special construc.: anti-fire & -shock, corrosion-resistant, etc.)	
623.85	Engineering systems (naut. craft: mech., electric, water, etc.)	VM471-505
623.8501	Mechanical systems (naut. craft: engineering)	
623.8503	Electrical systems (naut. craft: engineering)	VM471-475
623.852	Electric lighting (naut. craft: engineering)	VM491-493
623.853	Cooling & heating (naut. craft: engineering)	VM481
623.854	Water & sanitation (naut. craft: engineering)	VM503-505 (water), VM481-483 (san.)
623.8542	Water, Potable (naut. craft: engineering)	
623.8543	Water, Sea (naut. craft: engineering)	
623.8546	Sanitation (naut. craft: engineering)	VM481-483

623.856	Communications systems, Naval (engineering)	VG70-85, VB255
623.8561	Communication systems, Naval (visual: design)	V280-305
623.85612	Communication systems, Naval (flag & semaphore: design)	
		V280-285, V300-305 (flags), VK385
623.85613	Communication systems, Naval (pyrotechnical: design)	
623.85614	Communication systems, Naval (blinkers & electrooptical: design)	
623.85642	Communication systems, Naval (radio telegraph: design)	
		VG70-75
623.86	Gear, equipment, & outfitting (nautical: engineering)	VM781-861,
		VM781 (gen.)
623.862	Rigging & gear, Nautical (anchors, masts, rope, rudders, sails,	
	etc.: design)	VM791 (anchors), VC279.R6 (rope)
623.863	Instruments, Nautical (design)	VK573-587
623.865	Safety equipment, Nautical (fire-fighting, life-saving, etc.: design)	
		VK1258, VK1460-1481
623.866	Furniture (naut. design)	
623.87	Power plants (marine engineering)	VM600-779, VM600,
	VM623 (U.S.), VM657 (G.B.), VM673 (Ger.), VM705 (Japan)	
623.872	Engines, Marine (types: design)	VM731-779, VM731
623.8722	Steam engines (marine engineering)	VM741-749, TJ735-740
623.8723	Internal combustion engines (marine engineering)	VM770
623.87233	Gas-turbine engines (marine engineering)	VM740, TJ778
623.87234	Spark-ignition engines (marine engineering)	
623.87236	Diesel engines (marine engineering)	VM770
623.87237	Cylinders, valves, etc. (internal combustion engines: marine	
	engineering)	VM769
623.8726	Electric engines (marine engineering)	VM773
623.873	Engine auxiliaries (marine engineering: boilers, blowers, pumps,	
	propellers, etc.)	VM753-757 (propellers),
	VM741-750 (boilers), VM821 (pumps), VM781+	
623.874	Engine fuels, Marine	VM779
623.88	Seamanship	VK1-587+, VK541-547
623.881	Handling of nautical craft (gen.)	VK541
623.8812	Small craft (naut. handling)	VK543, GV811
623.8813	Sailing vessels (handling)	VK543
623.8814	Handling of nautical craft (powered)	VK541, VK145,
	VK205, VB200-205	
623.8825	Warships, Fuel-powered (handling)	VB200-205
623.88252	Battleships (handling)	V750
623.88253	Cruisers (handling)	V820-820.5
623.88254	Destroyers (handling)	V825-825.5
623.88257	Submarines (navies: handling)	V857-859, V210-214
623.888	Safety technology, Marine (plus other misc. topics)	
623.8881	Loading & unloading nautical craft (plus cargo handling)	VK235
623.8882	Knots & splices (naut. ropes & cables)	VM533
623.8884	Collision & grounding, Nautical (prevention)	VK371-378
623.8885	Wrecks, Nautical (research)	VK1250+
623.8886	Fire-fighting, Nautical (technology)	VK1258
623.8887	Rescue ops., Nautical	VK1321-1424, VK1323 (U.S.), VK1445 (gen.)

623.89	Course navigation (marine: inclu. celestial)	VK549-572+
623.892	Geonavigation, Marine	
623.8920212	Tables, formulae, statistics (marine geonavigation)	
623.8922	Piloting & pilot guides, Nautical	VK1500-1661, VK1523-1525 (U.S.), VK1645 (gen.), VK798-803
623.8923	Dead reckoning (naut. navig.)	VK572
623.8929	Harbor piloting (inclu. approach)	VK321-369.8
623.89291-89299	Pilot guides (geog. treatment)	VK804-997
623.892941-892942	British Isles (pilot guides)	VK827-838.5
623.892943	Germany (pilot guides)	VK822, VK824
623.892947	Russia (pilot guides)	VK809, VK821, VK870, VK910 (Siberia)
623.892973	United States (pilot guides: gen.)	VK993
623.892974-892979	United States (pilot guides: specific areas)	VK947-948 (W. Coast), VK981-982 (E. Coast)
623.894	Geonavigational aids, Marine (misc. non-electronic)	
623.8942	Lighthouses	VK1000-1249 (gen. & by place), VK1010, VK1021-1124, VK1023-1025 (U.S.), VK1243 (U.S.: lists)
623.8943	Lightships	VK1010, VK1021-1124
623.8944	Beacons, buoys, etc. (marine navig.)	VK1000-1249, VK1010, VK1021-1124, VK1023-1025 (U.S.)
623.8945	Light lists (marine navig.)	VK1150-1246, VK1150, VK1151-1185 (Eur.), VK1203-1209 (Asia), VK1211-1223 (Australia & Pac.), VK1241-1246 (N.Am.)
623.8949	Tide & current tables	VK600-794, VK602 (gen.), VK610-650 (Atl.: E.), VK628-644 (Brit. Isles & Eng. Ch.), VK653-674 (Medit.), VK702-711 (China, Japan, Asian coasts), VK715-756 (Pac.), VK727-733 (Australia & Oceania), VK741 (Am. W. Coast), VK759-792 (Atl: W., U.S., Carib.)

629.13	AERONAUTICS
629.1309	Flight (gen. hist.)
629.13092	Fliers (biog.)
629.132	Aeronautics (principles)
629.1323	Aerodynamics
629.1324	Meteorology, Aviation
629.1325	Flying
629.13251	Navigation, Aerial
629.13252	Piloting, Aerial
629.1325212	Takeoff (aviation)
629.1325213	Landing (aviation)
629.133+	Aircraft (types)
629.13324	Dirigibles
629.13334	Airplanes
629.133343	Propeller-driven airplanes
629.133347	Seaplanes
629.133348	Amphibious planes

629.134	Aircraft parts & components	
629.13432	Wings, Aircraft	
629.13434	Fuselages, Aircraft	
629.134351	Fuels, Aircraft	
629.134352-134354+	Engines, Aircraft	
629.1346	Maintenance & repair, Aircraft	
629.135	Instrumentation, Aircraft	
629.1351	Navigational instruments (air.)	
629.1352	Flight instruments	
629.136	Airports	
629.1363	Runways, Airport	
629.1368	Fire-fighting equipment, Airport	

900-999+	HISTORY & GEOGRAPHY	G (geog.), D-F
900-909	Geography & history (gen.)	G, C-D
910-919	Geography & travel	G, D-F
920-929	Biography (sometimes placed with country #s or topical #s in 930-999 or 000-999)	C-F
930-939	Ancient history	C-F
940-949	Europe	D-DR
940.3-.499	Great War (1914-18)	D501-680
940.53-5499	Second World War (1939-45)	D731-838
950-959	Asia	DS
960-969	Africa	DT
970-979	North America & America	E-F
980-989	South America	F
990-999	History (misc. areas: Oceania, Atlantic islands, Arctic, extraterr. worlds, etc.)	C-F, G, Q
993-996	Oceanica	DU

900-909	GEOGRAPHY & HISTORY (gen.)	G, C-D
903	Dictionaries & encyclopedias (history: gen.)	D9
909.8	World history (gen.: 1800-)	D299, D395
909.82	1900-1999 (20th c.: gen. hist.)	D421, D443
909.821	1900-1919 (gen. hist.)	D421, D521 (WWI: gen.)
909.822	1920-1929 (gen. hist.)	D653, D655-659, D720, D723-728 (1919-39)

910-919	TRAVEL & GEOGRAPHY	G (geog.), D-F (descr. & travel)
912	MAPS & ATLASES	G
912.4	Europe (maps & atlases)	G1796+
912.5	Asia (maps & atlases)	G2200+
912.73	United States (maps & atlases)	G1200+, G1201
912.9	Pacific Ocean area (maps & atlases)	G2860-3012
913-919	GEOGRAPHY & TRAVEL (by locale)	
914	EUROPE (geog. & travel)	D901-980, D907 (gen.), D921 (1901-50)
914.1	Great Britain & Ireland (geog. & travel)	DA11, DA600-668, DA969-987 (Ire.)
914.2	England (geog. & travel)	DA600-668, DA600 (gen.), DA630 (1901-45)

914.3	Central Europe & Germany (geog. & travel)	DD21-43, DB21-27, D901-980
914.31-35	Germany (geog. & travel)	DD21-43, DD41 (1871-1918)
914.36	Austria (geog. & travel)	DB21-27, DB26 (1901-45)
914.37	Czechoslovakia (geog. & travel)	DB191 (titles prior to 1979-80), DB2020
914.38	Poland (geog. & travel)	DK407 (1867-1945)
914.39	Hungary (geog. & travel)	DB916-917
914.4	France (geog. & travel)	DC28-45
914.5	Italy (geog. & travel)	DG428-429
914.581-582	Sicily (geog. & travel)	DG864
914.7	Soviet Union & Eur. Russia (geog. & travel)	DK27
914.76	White Russia & Western U.S.S.R. (geog. & travel)	
914.77	Black Sea area (geog. & travel)	DK511.C7
914.771	Ukraine (geog. & travel)	
914.79	Caucasus (geog. & travel)	
914.8	Scandinavia (geog. & travel)	DL10
914.92	Holland (geog. & travel)	DJ39
914.931-934	Belgium (geog. & travel)	DH433
914.94	Switzerland (geog. & travel)	DQ24
914.95	Greece (geog. & travel)	DF726
914.96	Balkan Peninsula (geog. & travel)	DR15, DR1221 (later works)
914.965	Albania (geog. & travel)	DR701.S5, DR917 (later books)
914.971-976	Yugoslavia (geog. & travel)	DR309, DR1221 (later books)
914.977	Bulgaria (geog. & travel)	DR60 (1879-1950)
914.98	Rumania (geog. & travel)	DR209 (1866-1950)
915	ASIA (geog. & travel)	DS9 (1901-50)
915.1	China (geog. & travel)	DS710 (1901-48)
915.2	Japan (geog. & travel)	DS810 (1901-45)
915.3	Arabian Peninsula (geog. & travel)	DS207
915.4	India, Pakistan, & Ceylon (geog. & travel)	DS335, DS413
915.6	Middle East (geog. & travel)	DS49-49.5
915.61-66	Turkey & Cyprus (geog. & travel)	DR428, DS54 (Cyprus)
915.67	Iraq (geog. & travel)	DS70.6, DS79+
915.69	Mediterranean, Eastern (geog. & travel)	DS44, DS49, D972-973
915.691	Syria (geog. & travel)	DS94
915.694	Palestine (geog. & travel)	DS107.3
915.7	Siberia & Asiatic Russia (geog. & travel)	DK755, DK584 (C.Asia)
916	AFRICA (geog. & travel)	DT55 (1901-50)
916.1	Tunisia & Libya (geog. & travel)	
916.2	Egypt & Sudan (geog. & travel)	DT55 (Egypt), DT124
916.3	Ethiopia (geog. & travel)	DT378
917	NORTH AMERICA (geog. & travel)	E41, E27
917.1	Canada (geog. & travel)	F1015
917.3	United States (geog. & travel: overall)	E169 (1914-45)
917.4-9	United States (geog. & travel: states, areas, & towns)	
917.4	New England & Middle Atlantic states (geog. & travel)	F2.3, F4, F9 (1865-1950), F106 (Mid.Atl.)
917.5	South Atlantic states & Florida (geog. & travel)	F106, F207.3 (S.Atl.), F309.3 (Fla.)
917.53	District of Columbia (geog. & travel)	F192.3, F194, F199
917.59	Florida (geog. & travel)	F309.3, F316
917.6	Gulf Coast & South Central states (geog. & travel)	F296 (Gulf), F396
917.64	Texas (geog. & travel)	F384.3, F391

| 917.7 | Great Lakes & North Central states (geog. & travel) F477.3 (Old NW.), |
| | F551 (Lakes area in gen.), F484.5 |

917.7 | Great Lakes & North Central states (geog. & travel)   F477.3 (Old NW.),
                                          F551 (Lakes area in gen.), F484.5
917.8 | Great Plains & American West (geog. & travel)   F591
917.9 | Pacific Coast & Far West (U.S.: geog. & travel)   F851
917.94 | California (geog. & travel)   F859.3, F861, F866 (hist.: 1869-1950)
918 | SOUTH AMERICA (geog. & travel)   F2211, F2223, F2236-2237
919 | PACIFIC OCEAN & MISC. (geog. & travel)   DU22
919.31 | New Zealand (geog. & travel)   DU411
919.4 | Australia (geog. & travel)   DU104
919.5 | New Guinea (geog. & travel)   DU740
919.6 | Pacific Ocean areas (misc.: geog. & travel)
919.69 | Hawaiian Islands (geog. & travel)   DU623

920-929 | BIOGRAPHY & GENEALOGY   CT (gen. or collec.), D-F, other
         specific classes for specialists or famous people in those areas
920 | BIOGRAPHY (gen.: SOMETIMES '92' or 'B' are used, followed by
         particular individuals in alphabetical order by last name. These may
         also be placed in specific discipline number areas followed by the
         standard subdivision, '092'. So, 355.0092 is for mil. biog.)
923 | BIOGRAPHY (social sciences: gov., law, commerce, etc.)
923.1 | HEADS OF STATE (biog.)
923.14 | Europe (biog.: heads of state)   D107
923.141-142 | Great Britain (biog.: heads of state)
923.143 | Germany (biog.: heads of state)
923.144 | France (biog.: heads of state)
923.145 | Italy (biog.: heads of state)
923.147 | Russia (biog.: heads of state)
923.15 | Asia (biog.: heads of state)   DS32 (collective)
923.151 | China (biog.: heads of state)
923.152 | Japan (biog.: heads of state)
923.173 | United States (biog.: heads of state)   E176.1 (Presidents: collective)
923.5 | MILITARY BIOGRAPHY (SEE ALSO 355.0092, 940.3+, .53+, etc.)
                                          U51-55
923.54 | Biography, Military (Eur.)
923.541-542 | Military biography (G.B.)   DA54 (collec.), DA69.3.A-Z (20th c.:
                 indiv.), DA89.1.A-Z (naval: 20th c.: indiv.), U55.G7
923.543 | Military biography (Ger.)   DD100 (group)
923.547 | Military biography (Rus.)   DK50.5-8
923.55 | Military biography (Asia)
923.551 | Military biography (China)   DS738 (group)
923.552 | Military biography (Japan)   DS838-839
923.573 | Military biography (U.S.)   E181 (mil.: collec.), E182 (naval:
                 collec.), U52-53
929 | GENEALOGY
929.7 | Royal houses (genealogy)
929.72 | Genealogy (royal houses: G.B.: hist. treatment poss. or in 941+)
                                          DA28.1-.35, CS418-424

940-949	EUROPE & THE WORLD WARS	D-DR, D501-651, D731-838
940	EUROPE & W. EUROPE (gen.)	D-DR
940.092	Biography (Eur.: group)	D106-110 (group)
940.2	Western Europe & Europe (1453+)	D208, D217
940.28	Europe (1789-1914)	D299, D359 (1801-1914)
940.287	Europe (1870-1899)	D395
940.288	Europe (1900-14)	D424, D443 (pol. & dipl.)
940.3-.499	WORLD WAR I (1914-18)	D501-680
940.3	European War (1914-18: gen.)	D521
940.31	First World War (econ., polit., social hist.)	D443, D453, D511-523, D610
940.311	Causes (WWI)	D511
940.3112	Causes (WWI: polit. & dipl.)	D610-621, D610
940.3113	Causes (WWI: econ.)	D635
940.3114	Causes (WWI: psychological & social)	
940.312	Peace efforts (WWI: preserve or restore)	D613, D641-644+ (armistice)
940.314	Results (WWI: dipl., econ., & polit.: SEE ALSO specific country #s)	D511-20, D511, D610-611, D643-644+
940.3141	Conferences & treaties (WWI)	D642-647
940.3142	Treaties (WWI: results)	D511-20
940.31422	Reparations (WWI)	D648-649
940.31424	Post-WWI territorial questions	D650, D651.A-Z
940.31425	New countries (post-WWI: formation)	D651
940.31426	Mandates (post-WWI)	D651
940.3144	Post-WWI reconstruction	D652-659, D653 (gen.), D657-658 (U.S.), D659.A-Z (other places)
940.315	Social groups (WWI)	D639.A-Z
940.31503	Ethnic or racial groups (WWI)	
940.315042	World War I & women	D639.W7, JX1965
940.3152	Religious groups & officials (WWI)	D639.R4, D622 (Cath. Church)
940.3155	Scientists (WWI)	D639.S2
940.3156	World War I & engineers	D529.7
940.3159	Refugees (WWI)	D637, D638.A-Z (by place)
940.316	Noncombatants, pacifists, sympathizers, etc. (WWI)	
940.3161	Orphans, children, similar noncombatants (WWI)	D639.C4
940.3162	Pacifists (WWI)	D613, UB342.A-Z (by place)
940.3163	Sympathizers, Enemy (WWI)	D570.8.A6 (U.S.), D636.A-Z (by locale)
940.32	Diplomatic history (WWI)	D610-621, D610 (gen.)
940.322	Allies & associates (WWI: dipl. hist.)	D511, D459 (Triple Entente)
940.32241-32242	Diplomacy (WWI: G.B.)	D621.G7, D610-611, D517
940.32244	Diplomacy (WWI: Fr.)	D621.F, D516
940.32273	Diplomacy (WWI: U.S.)	D619
940.32294	Diplomacy (WWI: Australia)	D621.A
940.324	Central Powers (WWI: dipl. hist.)	D511, D458 (Triple Alliance)
940.32443	Diplomacy (WWI: Ger. & Austria)	D621.G or .A, D515 (Ger.), D512 (Austria)
940.324561	Diplomacy (WWI: Turkey)	D621.T8, D520.T8, D463, D469.T8
940.325	Neutrals (WWI: dipl. hist.)	D611, D639.N
940.325494	Diplomacy (WWI: Switz.)	D621.S
940.332	Allies (WWI: gen. particip.)	D544
940.334	Central Powers (WWI: gen. particip.)	D531
940.335	Neutrals (WWI: gen. particip.)	D639.N, D615 (Belgium), D611

940.34-39	World War I (gen. particip.: by country: inclu. mobilization)	
940.341-342	World War I (gen. particip.: G.B.)	D546, DA577
940.343	World War I (gen. particip.: Ger.)	D531, DD228.8
940.3436	World War I (gen. particip.: Austria)	D539, DB86.7
940.3437	World War I (gen. particip.: Czech.)	D539.5.C8, DB215, DB2176
940.3438	World War I (gen. particip.: Poland)	D551, DK439
940.3439	World War I (gen. particip.: Hungary)	D540, DB953
940.344	World War I (gen. particip.: Fr.)	D548, DC387
940.345	World War I (gen. particip.: It.)	D569, DG570
940.346	World War I (gen. particip.: Sp.)	DP246
940.347	World War I (gen. particip.: Rus.)	D550, DK264.8
940.348	World War I (gen. particip.: Scan. countries)	D621.S3, DL85
940.3492	World War I (gen. particip.: Holland)	DJ285
940.3493	World War I (gen. particip.: Belgium)	D615, D541, DH682
940.3494	World War I (gen. particip.: Switz.)	DQ201
940.3496	World War I (gen. particip.: Balkan Penin.)	D560, DR47
940.3497	World War I (gen. particip.: Yug. & Bulg.)	D560, D561 (Serbia),
	D564 (Montenegro), D563 (Bulg.), DR47, DR363 (Yug.),	
	DR87.8 (Yug.), DR1280 (Yug.: newer titles)	
940.3498	World War I (gen. particip.: Rumania)	D565, DR263
940.354	World War I (gen. particip.: India)	D547.I5
940.3561	World War I (gen. particip.: Turkey)	D566, DR588
940.3676	World War I (gen. particip.: E. Africa)	D547.A, DT431
940.368	World War I (gen. particip.: S. Africa)	D547.A4, DT941
940.371	World War I (gen. particip.: Can.)	D547.C2
940.373-379	World War I (gen. particip.: U.S.)	D570
940.373	World War I (gen. particip.: U.S.: gen.)	D570, D619, E768, E780
940.374-379	World War I (gen. particip.: U.S.: by state)	
940.3747	World War I (gen. particip.: U.S.: N.Y.)	
940.3797	World War I (gen. particip.: U.S.: Calif.)	
940.3931	World War I (gen. particip.: New Z.: SEE ALSO 940.393 for titles	
	after 1988)	D547.N5
940.394	World War I (gen. particip.: Australia)	D547.A8
940.4	Military history (WWI)	D521 (gen.), D529-608
940.4003	Encyclopedias & dictionaries (WWI)	D510, D521, D523
940.4005	Magazines & serial pubns. (WWI)	D501
940.4006	Societies & associations (WWI)	D502, D504 (congresses)
940.4007	World War I (study & teaching)	D522.4, .7 (juv.)
940.40074	Exhibitions, museums, etc. (WWI)	D503
940.401	Strategy (WWI)	D521, D530, D550
940.4012	Strategy (WWI: Allies)	D544, D570
940.4013	Strategy (WWI: Central Powers)	D531
940.402	World War I (mobilization: SEE 940.34-39 for particular countries)	
940.403	Racial minorities (WWI: soldiers)	D547.N4 (blacks: G.B.),
	D570.8.I6 (Indians: U.S.), D639.N4 (blacks)	
940.405	Repression & atrocities (WWI)	D625 (gen.), D626.A-Z (by place)

940.409	Military history (WWI: by place)		
940.40941-40942	Great Britain (WWI: mil. hist.)	D546-547	
940.40943	Germany & Austria (WWI: mil. hist.)	D531-538 (Ger.),	
		D531 (gen.), D539 (Austria)	

940.40944 France (WWI: mil. hist.)   D548-549
940.40945 Italy (WWI: mil. hist.)   D569
940.40947 Russia (WWI: mil. hist.)   D550
940.409561 Turkey (WWI: mil. hist.)   D566
940.409571 Military history (WWI: Can.)   D547.C2
940.40968 Military history (WWI: S. Africa)   D547.A4
940.40973 Military history (WWI: U.S.)   D570
940.40993 Military history (WWI: New Z.: SEE ALSO 940.409931 for titles earlier
          than 1989)   D547.N5
940.40994 Military history (WWI: Australia)   D547.A8
940.41 World War I (mil. units & ops.: gen.)   D521
940.412-413+ Military history (WWI: units & ops.: by country: inclu. structure,
          hist., registers, etc.)   D532-578, D608
940.412+ World War I (Allies & associates: mil. units & ops.)   D544-550,
          D569-570
940.41241 Military history (WWI: units & ops.: G.B.)   D546-546.55+, D547
940.41244 Military history (WWI: units & ops.: Fr.)   D548-549
940.41247 Military history (WWI: units & ops.: Rus.)   D550
940.41271 Military history (WWI: units & ops.: Can.)   D547.C2
940.41273 Military history (WWI: units & ops.: U.S.)   D570-570.75
940.412931 Military history (WWI: units & ops.: New Z.)   D547.N5
940.41294 Military history (WWI: units & ops.: Australia)   D547.A8
940.413+ World War I (Central Powers: mil. units & ops.)   D531-540, D566
940.41343 Military history (WWI: units & ops.: Ger.)   D531-538
940.413436 Austria (WWI: mil. units & ops.)   D539
940.413561 Military history (WWI: units & ops.: Turkey)   D566
940.414 Fronts (WWI: Eur.)   D521, D530 (W.), D550 (E.)
940.4143 Fronts (WWI: Ger.)   D531, D551-552 (Russo-Ger.)
940.4144 Fronts (WWI: Fr. & W. in gen.)   D530, D544
940.4145 Fronts (WWI: It.)   D569
940.4147 Fronts (WWI: Rus. & E. in gen.)   D550, D551 (Rus.-Ger.-Austrian),
          D556 (Rus.-Austrian), D560 (Balkan)
940.415 Fronts (WWI: Asia)   D577-578
940.416 Fronts (WWI: Africa)   D575-576
940.42 Battles & campaigns, Land (WWI: 1914-16)
940.421 World War I (1914: W. Front)   D530, D541-542 (Bel.), D544-
          545 (Fr.), D545.A-Z (by battle, campaign, etc.)
940.422 World War I (1914: E. Front)   D550, D551-556
940.423 World War I (1914: misc. areas)
940.424 World War I (1915: W & Austro-It. fronts)   D530, D541-545,
          D569 (Italian)
940.425 World War I (1915: E. Europe)   D550, D551-557
940.426 World War I (1915: misc. areas)
940.427 World War I (1916: Eur. fronts)   D521, D530, D550
940.4272 World War I (1916: W. & Austro-It. fronts)   D530, D541-545,
          D569 (Italian)
940.4275 World War I (1916: E. Front)   D550, D551-557
940.429 World War I (1916: misc. areas)
940.4291 World War I (1916: Asia Minor, Gallipoli, etc.)   D566 (gen.), D566-
          568, D568.3 (Gallipoli)

940.43	Battles & campaigns, Land (WWI: 1917-18)	
940.431	World War I (1917: W. & Austro-It. fronts)	D530, D541-545, D569
940.432	World War I (1917: E. Front)	D550, D551-557
940.433	World War I (1917: misc. areas)	
940.434	World War I (1918: W. & Austro-It. fronts: inclu. last Ger. drives)	
		D530-531, D541-545
940.435	World War I (1918: W. Front: last Allied drives: 18 July-24 Sept.)	
		D530, D541-545
940.436	World War I (1918: W. Front: last Allied drives: 25 Sept.-11 Nov.)	
		D530, D541-545
940.437	World War I (1918: E. Front)	D550, D551-557
940.438	World War I (1918: misc. areas)	
940.439	World War I (Armistice)	D641
940.44	Battles & campaigns, Aerial (WWI)	D600-607
940.441	Aerial ops. (WWI: particular srvcs.: scouting, artill. spotting, bombing & naval support, coast patrol, anti-sub. work, etc.)	
940.442	Air raids (WWI)	D600-607
940.443	Air bases (WWI)	D532-538 (Ger.), D547-547.8 (G.B.), D548-549 (Fr.), D570.85+ (U.S.)
940.444	World War I (1914: aerial ops.)	
940.445	World War I (1915: aerial ops.)	
940.446	World War I (1916: aerial ops.)	
940.447	World War I (1917: aerial ops.)	
940.448	World War I (1918: aerial ops.)	
940.449	Aerial ops. (WWI: particular countries)	
940.44941	Aerial ops. (WWI: G.B.)	D602
940.44943	Aerial ops. (WWI: Ger.)	D604
940.44944	Aerial ops. (WWI: Fr.)	D603
940.44945	Aerial ops. (WWI: It.)	D607.I
940.44947	Aerial ops. (WWI: Rus.)	D605
940.44971	Aerial ops. (WWI: Can.)	D607.C
940.44973	Aerial ops. (WWI: U.S.)	D606, D570.6-7 (squadrons)
940.45	Battles & campaigns, Naval (WWI)	D580-595, D580 (gen.)
940.451	World War I (submarine ops.)	D590-595, D590 (gen.)
940.4512	Submarine ops. (WWI: Ger.)	D591 (gen.), D592.A-Z (by ship, battle, etc.)
940.4513	Submarine ops. (WWI: Allies)	D590
940.451341	Submarine ops. (WWI: G.B.)	D593 (gen.), D594.A-Z (by confrontation, ship, etc.)
940.451344	Submarine ops. (WWI: Fr.)	D595.F
940.451373	Submarine ops. (WWI: U.S.)	D595.U
940.4514	World War I (submarine ops.: specific events yr.-by-yr.)	
940.4516	World War I (antisub. ops.)	D580-589, D590
940.452	Blockades & blockade-running (WWI)	D581
940.453+	Naval bases (WWI)	D581-589
940.45341	Naval bases (WWI: in G.B.)	
940.45343	Naval bases (WWI: in Ger.)	
940.45347	Naval bases (WWI: in Rus.)	
940.45377	Naval bases (WWI: in U.S.)	
940.454	World War I (1914: naval ops.)	
940.455	World War I (1915: naval ops.)	
940.456	World War I (1916: naval ops.)	
940.457	World War I (1917: naval ops.)	
940.458	World War I (1918: naval ops.)	

940.459	World War I (naval ops.: particular countries)	D580-589
940.45941	Naval ops. (WWI: G.B.)	D581-582, VA458
940.45943	Naval ops. (WWI: Ger.)	D581-582
940.45944	Naval ops. (WWI: Fr.)	D583
940.45945	Naval ops. (WWI: It.)	D588
940.45947	Naval ops. (WWI: Rus.)	D585
940.459561	Naval ops. (WWI: Turkey)	D587
940.45971	Naval ops. (WWI: Can.)	D589.C
940.45973	Naval ops. (WWI: U.S.)	D589.U5-8
940.45994	Naval ops. (WWI: Australia)	D589.A
940.46	Commemorations, celebrations, & memorials (WWI: gen.)	
		D663-680, D663 (gen.)
940.465	Cemeteries & monuments (WWI)	D639.D4 (cem's.), D663-680 (mon's.), D675.W2
		(Tomb of Unkn. Soldier: Wash. D.C.)
940.46541-46542	Cemeteries & monuments (WWI: G.B. & Eng.)	
		D680.G7, D680.E
940.46543	Monuments & cemeteries (WWI: Ger.)	D680.G3
940.46544	Monuments & cemeteries (WWI: Fr.)	D680.F8
940.46545	Monuments & cemeteries (WWI: It.)	D680.I
940.46547	Monuments & cemeteries (WWI: Rus.)	D680.R
940.46571	Monuments & cemeteries (WWI: Can.)	D680.C
940.46573	Cemeteries & monuments (WWI: U.S.)	D670-675, D673.A-W (by state), D675.A-Z (by town)
940.46594	Monuments & cemeteries (WWI: Australia)	D680.A
940.467	Rolls of honored & dead (WWI)	D609, D609.A2 (gen.)
940.46741	Honored & dead (WWI: G.B.: rolls)	D609.G7
940.46743	Honored & dead (WWI: Ger.: rolls)	D609.G3
940.46744	Honored & dead (WWI: Fr.: rolls)	D609.F8-82
940.46773	Honored & dead (WWI: U.S.: rolls)	D609.U6-7
940.46794	Honored & dead (WWI: Australia: rolls)	D609.A8
940.47	Social services, prisons, & medical services (WWI)	
940.472	Prisoner-of-war camps & internment (WWI)	D627
940.47241-47242	P.O.W. camps & internment centers (WWI: in G.B.)	D627.G7
940.47243	P.O.W. camps & internment centers (WWI: in Ger.)	D627.G3
940.47247	P.O.W. camps & internment centers (WWI: in Rus.)	D627.R9
940.47273	Internment centers & P.O.W. camps (WWI: in U.S.)	D627.U6+
940.473	Prisoner exchanges	
940.475	World War I (medical srvcs.)	D628 (gen.), D629.A-Z (by country), D630.A-Z (biog.)
940.4752	Sanitary control (WWI: med. srvcs.)	
940.4753	Ambulance services (WWI)	D570.355 (U.S.)
940.4754-4759	Medical services (WWI: particular countries)	D629.A-Z
940.47541	British medical services (WWI)	D629.G7
940.47543	Medical services (WWI: Ger.)	D629.G3
940.47547	Medical services (WWI: Rus.)	D629.R9
940.47573	Medical services (WWI: U.S.)	D629.U6-8
940.476	Medical services (WWI: hospitals)	D628-629
940.4763+	Hospitals (WWI: in particular places)	D629.A-Z
940.476342	Hospitals (WWI: in Eng.)	D629.G7
940.476343	Hospitals (WWI: in Ger.)	D629.G3
940.476344	Hospitals (WWI: in Fr.)	D629.F8

940.4764-4769   Hospitals (WWI: operated by particular countries)
940.47641   Medical services (WWI: hospitals, British)   D629.G7
940.47643   Medical services (WWI: hospitals, German)   D629.G3
940.47644   Medical services (WWI: hospitals, French)   D629.F8
940.477   Welfare & relief services (WWI)   D637-638
940.4771   Welfare & relief services (WWI: Red Cross)   D628-630
940.4778+   Welfare & relief services (WWI: provided by specific countries)
                                                           D638.A-Z
940.477841 Welfare & relief services (WWI: by G.B.)   D638.G7
940.4778485   Welfare & relief services (WWI: by Swe.)   D638.S8
940.4778494   Welfare & relief services (WWI: by Switz.)   D638.S9
940.4779+   Welfare & relief services (WWI: in specific places)   D638.A-Z,
                 D657-658 (Reconstruc. in U.S.), D659.A-Z (by place)
940.477943   Relief & welfare services (WWI: in Ger.)   D638.G3, D659.G3
940.477944   Relief & welfare services (WWI: in Fr.)   D638.F8, D659.F8
940.477945   Relief & welfare services (WWI: in It.)   D638.I8, D659.I8
940.477947   Relief & welfare services (WWI: in Rus.)   D638.R9, D659.R9
940.478   Religious services (WWI)   D639.R4
940.48   World War I (misc. topics)
940.481+   Personal accounts, Allied (WWI)   D640, D570.9 (U.S.)
940.48141   Personal accounts, British (WWI)   D640, D546-547, D581-582 (naval)
940.48144   Personal accounts, French (WWI)
940.48173   Personal accounts, American (WWI: U.S.)   D570.9
940.48194   Personal accounts, Australian (WWI)
940.482+   Personal accounts, Central Power (WWI)   D640, D531-540
940.48243   Personal accounts, German (WWI)   D640, D531-538, D604 (aerial),
                                                           D591-592 (subs)
940.482436 Personal accounts, Austrian (WWI)   D640, D539)
940.483+   Allies (WWI: mil. & naval life & customs)   D544
940.48341   Naval & military life & customs (WWI: G.B.)   D546-547 (mil.),
                                           D581-582 (naval), D602 (aerial)
940.48344   Military & naval life & customs (WWI: Fr.)   D548-549
940.48373   Military & naval life & customs (WWI: U.S.)   D570, D589.U6-7 (naval),
                                                           D606 (aerial)
940.48394   Military & naval life & customs (WWI: Australia)   D547.A8
940.484   Central Powers (WWI: mil. & naval life & customs)
940.48443   Military & naval life & customs (WWI: Ger.)   D532-538, D581-
                                           582 (naval), D604 (aerial)
940.485   Unconventional warfare (WWI: espionage, intell., infilt., sabotage, etc.)
                                                           D639.S7-8
940.486   Unconventional warfare, Allied (WWI: espionage, intell., infilt.,
                 sabotage, etc.)
940.48641   Intelligence, espionage, & unconventional warfare (WWI: G.B.)
940.48644   Sabotage, intelligence, & unconventional warfare (WWI: Fr.)
940.48647   Infiltration, espionage, & unconventional warfare (WWI: Rus.)
940.48673   Espionage, sabotage, & unconventional warfare (WWI: U.S.)
940.487   Unconventional warfare, Central Power (WWI)
940.48743   Intelligence, espionage, & unconventional warfare (WWI: Ger.)
                                                           D619.3-5 (in U.S.)

940.488	News & propaganda (WWI)	D639.P6-7, D631-633, D619.3
940.4886	Propaganda, Allied (WWI)	
940.488641	Propaganda, British (WWI)	D639.P7.G7
940.488644	Propaganda, French (WWI)	D639.P7.F8
940.488647	Propaganda, Russian (WWI)	D639.P7.R9
940.488673	Propaganda, American (WWI: U.S.)	D632, D639.P7.U5+
940.4887	Propaganda, Central Power (WWI)	
940.488743	Propaganda, German (WWI)	D639.P7.G3, D619.3 (in U.S.)
940.4889+	News & propaganda (WWI: in specific countries)	
940.488941	News & propaganda (WWI: in G.B.)	
940.488943	News & propaganda (WWI: in Ger.)	
940.488947	News & propaganda (WWI: in Rus.)	
940.488973	News & propaganda (WWI: in U.S.)	
940.49	Humor, comics, pictorials, & miscellanea (WWI)	
940.494	Anecdotes (WWI)	
940.496-497	Comics, caricatures, humor (WWI)	
940.5	Europe (20th c. or 1918-)	D424-425, D720 (1919-39), D431-443, D551, D720-728
940.51	Europe (1918-29)	
940.53-5499	WORLD WAR II (1939-45)	D731-838
940.531	Second World War (econ., polit., social hist.)	D421, D443, , D720-728, D743, D748
940.5311	Causes (WWII: gen.)	D741 (gen.), D742.A-Z (by country), D720-728
940.53112	Causes (WWII: dipl. & polit.)	D741-742, D443, D727, D748
940.53113	Causes (WWII: econ.)	D741-742, D720-728, D421, D800
940.53114	Causes (WWII: psychological & social)	D741-742, D726, D421
940.5315+	Social groups (WWII)	
940.531503	Ethnic or racial groups (WWII)	
940.531503924	Jews (WWII: SEE ALSO 940.5315296)	D810.J4, D804.G4, D829.J4, DS135
940.53150396073	Afro-Americans (WWII)	E185, D810.N4
940.5315042	World War II & women	D810.W7
940.532	World War II (dipl. hist.)	D748-754, D748 (gen.)
940.532241	Diplomacy (WWII: G.B.)	D750
940.532244	Diplomacy (WWII: Fr.)	D752
940.532247	Russia (WWII: dipl. hist.)	D754.R9 or .S65 (Sov. U.)
940.532443	Diplomacy (WWII: Ger.)	D751
940.532445	Italy (WWII: dipl. hist.)	D754.I8
940.5341-5342	British Isles (WWII: gen. particip.)	
940.5343	World War II (gen. particip.: Ger.)	D751, D757, DD253-256.5
940.5347	World War II (gen. particip.: Rus.)	D764, D754.R9 or .S65, DK267-273, DK273
940.5373	World War II (gen. particip.: U.S.)	D769, E806-813, E806 (gen.)

940.54	Military history (WWII)	D743
940.5401	Strategy (WWII)	D743
940.54094-54099	Military history (WWII: by place)	D757-769
940.540941-540942	Military history (WWII: G.B.)	D759-760
940.540943	Military history (WWII: Ger.)	D757
940.540944	Military history (WWII: Fr.)	D761
940.540945	Military history (WWII: It.)	D763.I8-817
940.540947	Military history (WWII: Rus.)	D764
940.540971	Military history (WWII: Can.)	D768.15
940.540973	Military history (WWII: U.S.)	D769, D769.25-4 (armies,

div's., regt's.), D769.45-598 (naval particip., units, ops.)

940.5409931	Military history (WWII: New Z.: SEE ALSO 940.540993 for titles	
	prior to 1989)	D767.85
940.540994	Military history (WWII: Australia)	D767.8
940.541	World War II (mil. units & ops.: gen.)	D743
940.544	Battles & campaigns, Aerial (WWII: inclu. comb. air & naval ops. as	
	well as antiaircraft defenses)	D785-792, D785 (gen.)
940.5449+	Aerial ops. (WWII: by country: inclu. specific craft, units, fliers)	
940.545	Battles & campaigns, Naval (WWII: SEE ALSO 940.542 for ops. by	
	theatre)	D770-784, D770 (gen.), D773 (U.S.: gen.),

D774.A-Z (U.S.: by ship, battle, etc.), D769.45-598 (U.S.: by
fleet, squadron, base, etc.)

940.5451+	World War II (submarine ops.: SEE ALSO 940.542 for ops. by theatre)	
	D780- 784, D780 (gen.), D781-782 (Ger.), D783 (U.S.),	
	D784.A-Z (other lands)	
940.5451943	Submarine ops. (WWII: Ger.)	D781-782
940.5452	Blockades & blockade-running (WWII)	D770, D771 (Anglo-Grmn.),
		D773 (U.S.)
940.5453411	Scapa Flow Naval Base (G.B.: Scot.: WWI & II)	
940.5459+	World War II (naval ops.: particular countries)	D770-784
940.5472+	Prisoner-of-war camps & internment centers (WWII: SEE ALSO	
	940.5317+ for post-1988 titles on internment camps)	D805
940.5475	World War II (medical srvcs.)	D806-807, D806 (gen.)
940.5477	Welfare & relief services (WWII)	D808-809
940.5485	Unconventional warfare (WWII: inclu. espionage, infilt., intelligence,	
	subversion)	D810.S7 (gen.), .S8.A-Z (by spy), D802

(underground), D802.F8 (Fr. undergr.), UB250-274, UB273-274
(sabo.), UB251.A-Z (intell., by country), UB271.A-Z (espion., by
country respons.), VB230-250 (naval intell. & espionage)

940.5488	News & propaganda (WWII)	D810.P6 (gen.), .P7.A-Z (by country)
941	BRITAIN & BRITISH ISLES	DA
941.003	Encyclopedias & dictionaries (G.B.)	DA34
941.081	Britain (19th c. & Victorian era of 1837-1901)	DA550-566,
		DA550 (gen.)
941.082	Britain (20th c. & Edward VII era of 1901-1910)	DA567-570 (Ed.
	VII), DA570 (gen.), DA566 (20th c.: gen.)	
941.083	Britain (1910-36: George VI)	DA573-578, DA576 (gen.), DA577
	(WWI era), DA578 (1920-39)	
941.1	SCOTLAND	DA750-890, DA760 (gen.)
941.1083	Scotland (1910-36)	DA821
941.34	Edinburgh, Scot.	DA890.E2-4

941.5	IRELAND (overall)	DA900-995, DA910 (gen.)
941.508	Ireland (19th-20th c.)	DA950-965+
941.5082	Ireland (20th c.)	DA959-965
941.50821	Ireland (1900-20)	DA960
941.6	Northern Ireland	DA990.U45-46
941.7	Eire (Republic of Ireland)	DA963

942	ENGLAND & WALES	DA20-745, DA20-690 (Eng.), DA700-45 (Wales)
942.083	England (1910-36)	DA576
942.1	London, Eng.	DA675-689, DA677 (gen.)
942.9	Wales	

943   GERMANY & CENTRAL EUROPE   DD (Ger.), DB (Austria,
                Hung., Czech.), DK401-441 & DK4010-4800 (Pol.)
943.0004924   Jews (Central Eur.)
943.004924   Jews (Ger.)   DS135.G3-5
943.084   Germany (1888-1918: Fred. & William II eras)   DD224-232,
                DD228 (gen.), DD228.8 (WWI era), DD448 (Prussia)
943.085   Weimar Republic (Ger.: 1918-33)   DD233-251, DD237 (gen.),
                DD251 (Hindenb. era), DD453 (Prussia)
943.155   Berlin, Ger.   DD851-900, DD860 (gen.)
943.3   Bavaria   DD801.B31-55
943.4   Rhine River Valley   DD801.R7-76
943.42   Saar (Ger.)   DD801.S13
943.48   Black Forest (Ger.)   DD801.B63-65
943.6   AUSTRIA   DB1-170+
943.604   Austria (19th c. & 1815-1919)   DB80-93, DB80 (19th c.: gen.),
                DB85 (1848-1916: Franz Josef), DB86.7 (WWI time)
943.605   Austria (20th c. & 1919-)   DB91 (20th c.), DB96 (1918-)
943.613   Vienna, Austria   DB841-860, DB847 (gen.)
943.648   LIECHTENSTEIN   DB540.5
943.7   CZECHOSLOVAKIA   DB191-217 (older works), DB2000-3150 (newer)
943.702   Czechoslovakia (to 1918)
943.7024   Czechoslovakia (19th c.: 1815-1918)   DB214, DB2176
943.8   POLAND   DK401-441 (older titles), DK4010-4800 (titles 1970+?),
                DK414, DK4140
943.803   Poland (1795-1918: foreign rule)   DK434.9, DK4349, DK439
943.84   Warsaw, Pol. (area)   DK651.W2, DK4610-4645
943.9   HUNGARY   DB901-975+, DB906, DB925
943.9042   Hungary (1686-1918: Hapsburg rule)   DB933 (19th c.)
943.9043   Hungary (1867-1918) DB945 (1867-1900)
943.905   Hungary (20th c.: 1918-) DB947-950, DB947 (gen.), DB950.A-Z (biog.)

944   FRANCE   DC
944.07   France (1848-70: 2d Repub. & 2d Empire & Franco-Ger. War: SEE ALSO
                944.0812)   DC272-292, DC272, DC276
944.08   France (1870- & 20th c.: 3d, 4th, 5th Repub's.)   DC289+, DC335+
944.081   France (1870-1945: 3d Repub.)   DC335
944.0812   France (1870-1899: inclu. Franco-Ger. War)   DC330, DC281-
                326 (F-G War), DC289
944.0813   France (1900-14)   DC361 (20th c.), DC375-385
944.0814   France (1914-18: WWI era)   DC387
944.0815   France (1918-39)   DC389-396
944.36   Paris, Fr. (area)   DC701-790, DC707 (gen.), DC735 (1871-1914),
                DC737 (1914-)

945	ITALY DG
945.09	Italy (1870- & 20th c.) DG555-575+, DG555, DG570 (WWI era)
945.091	Italy (1918-46: SEE ALSO 963.056 for Italo-Eth. War of 1935-6)
	DG566-575, DG571, DG571-572 (Fascist period),
	DG572 (WWII era)
945.632	Rome, It. DG803-818, DG808, DG813 (1871-)
945.634	Vatican City DG800

946	IBERIAN PENINSULA & SPAIN DP, DP1-402+ (Sp.),
	DP501-900+ (Port.)
946.08	Spain (1868-) DP222 (1868-86), DP233 (1886- & 20th c.)
946.89	GIBRALTAR (Br. colony) DP302.G31-41
946.9	PORTUGAL DP501-900+
946.904	Portugal (1910-) DP675

947	UNION OF SOVIET SOCIALIST REPUBLICS (Russia)
	DK, DK1-275, DK501-973+
947.08	Russia (1855-) DK219+, DK220-221
947.081	Russia (1855-81: Alexander II: might SEE ALSO 956.101 for
	Russo-Turk. War) DK219-228,
	DK220-221, DR573 (R-T War)
947.082	Russia (1881-94: Alexander III) DK234-243, DK240-241
947.083	Russia (1894-1918: Nicholas II: perhaps SEE ALSO 952.031 for
	Russo-Jpn. War) DK251-264.3, DK258,
	DK260-262, DS516-517 (R-J War)
947.084	Russia (20th c. & 1917-: Communist period) DK246
947.0841	Soviet Union (1917-24: Rev. period & Lenin era) DK265 (Rev.),
	DK265-266.5+
947.1	FINLAND (SEE ALSO 948.97 for works after 1970 or so) DK445-465,
	DL1002-1180+ (pubns. 1970+)
947.31	Moscow, Rus. DK591-609, DK601 (hist. to 1950)
947.45	Leningrad, Rus. DK541-579, DK568 (1801-)
947.65	Belorussia DK511.W5 (White Russia)
947.7	Black Sea region (Rus.) DK509
947.71	Little Russia (Ukraine) DK508
947.717	Odessa & Crimea areas (Rus.) DK511.C7
947.85	Volgograd, Rus. (ALSO Tsaritsyn or Stalingrad) DK651.S7
947.87	Ural Mts. region (Rus.) DK511.U7
947.9	Caucasus area (Rus.) DK511.C1-35
947.95	Georgian Republic (U.S.S.R.) DK511.G3-47, .G47 (gen. hist., 1917-)

948	NORTHERN EUROPE & Scandinavia DL
948.07	Scandinavia & N. Europe (1814-1905) DL81 (1814-1900)
948.08	Scandinavia & N. Europe (20th c.: 1905-) DL83-87+
948.081	Scandinavia & N. Europe (1905-19) DL83
948.1	NORWAY DL401-596, DL448 (gen.)
948.104	Norway (20th c.: 1905-) DL527+
948.1041	Norway (1905-45) DL530-532
948.5	SWEDEN DL601-991+, DL648
948.505	Sweden (20th c.: 1905-) DL860+
948.5051	Sweden (1905-45) DL860-868

948.9   DENMARK & FINLAND
948.9   DENMARK (overall)   DL101-291+, DL148
948.905   Denmark (1906-)   DL250 (20th c.)
948.9051   Denmark (1906-45)   DL253-257
948.97   FINLAND   DK445-465 (mostly pre-1970 pubns.), DL1002-
                1180+ (1970+ titles)
948.9702   Finland (1809-1917)   DK458, DL1065
948.9703   Finland (1917-)   DK459, DL1066.5
948.97031   Finland (1917-39)   DK459, DL1084
948.971   Helsingfors, Fin. (Helsinki: area)   DK465.H5, DL1175,
                                                        DL1175.48 (1917-)

949   EUROPE (misc. areas: Iceland, Belg., Switz., Greece, etc.)
949.2   HOLLAND (NETHERLANDS)   DJ, DJ109 (gen.)
949.207   Holland (20th c.)   DJ216 (19th-20th c.)
949.2071   Holland (1890-1948: Q. Wilhelmina era)   DJ281-287, DJ281 (gen.),
                                        DJ285 (WWI time), DJ287 (WWII era)
949.3   BELGIUM   DH401-811+, DH521
949.304   Belgium (1909-)   DH677 (20th c.)
949.3041   Belgium (1909-34: Albert I)   DH681-685, DH681, DH682 (WWI)
949.35   LUXEMBOURG   DH901-925, DH916 (1815-)
949.4   SWITZERLAND   DQ, DQ54
949.407   Switzerland (20th c.)   DQ201
949.4071   Switzerland (1900-18)
949.5   GREECE   DF, DF757
949.506   Greece (1821-1924: Monarchy)   DF802
949.507   Greece (20th c.: 1924-)   DF833 (20th c.), DF838 (WWI)
949.6   BALKAN PENINSULA (inclu. Balkan Wars of 1912-13)   DR1-48,
                                        DR45 (20th c.), DR46 (Balkan Wars)
949.65   ALBANIA   DR701.S49-86 (known as Scutari for earlier works),
                DR701.S5, DR941-979+ (for later works), DR941 (gen.)
949.6501   Albania (to 1912)   DR701.S5, DR940-0941, DR962
949.6502   Albania (1912-46)   DR701.S6 (1914-17), .S85 (1939-43), DR971,
                                        DR972 (WWI), DR975 (WWII)
949.7   YUGOSLAVIA (overall)   DR301-396+ (earlier books), DR1202-1307+
949.7+   YUGOSLAVIA & BULGARIA
949.701   Yugoslavia (to 1918)   DR317, DR1274
949.702   Yugoslavia (20th c. & 1918-)   DR357, DR1274, DR1282
949.7021   Yugoslavia (1918-39: Kingdom)   DR366, DR1289
949.71   SERBIA (inclu. Belgrade)   DR301-396, DR1932-2125+
949.7101   Serbia (to 1918)   DR317, DR1965
949.71015   Serbia (1878-1918: Independence)   DR351-363, DR2006-2032
949.7102   Serbia (1918-)   DR366, DR2034
949.72   CROATIA (inclu. Dalmatia, Istria, Slavonia)   DB361-380, DR1502-1645
949.73   Slovenia   DR381.S6, DR1352-1485+
949.74   Yugoslavia (central republics: Bosnia, Herzegovina, Montenegro)
949.742   HERCEGOVINA (Herzegovina) & BOSNIA   DB231-250 (Bos.),
                                        DB521-540 (Her.), DR1652-1785
949.745   MONTENEGRO   DR101-196, DR1802-1928
949.76   MACEDONIA   DR701.M13-42, DR2152-2285+
949.77   BULGARIA   DR51-98
949.7702   Bulgaria (1878-1946)   DR85-93, DR89 (1918-43)
949.8   ROMANIA (Rumania)   DR201-296
949.802   Romania (1861-1947: Monarchy)   DR250-266, DR250,
                                        DR263 (1914-18), DR264 (1918-44)

950-959	Asia DS	
950	ASIA (gen.) DS, DS5, DS33	
950.3	Asia (1480-1905) DS33	
950.4	Asia (20th c.) DS35	
950.41	Asia (1905-45) DS35	

951	CHINA (plus surrounding areas) DS701-796+, DS706, DS735
951.03	China (1644-1912: inclu. Sino-Japanese War, 1894-5: SEE ALSO 952.03 for Sino-Jpn. War of 1894-5) DS764.4-767.7
951.04	China (1912-49) DS773.83-777.544, DS774
951.041	China (1912-27) DS776.4-777.462, DS776.4
951.156	Peking, China DS795
951.249	FORMOSA (Taiwan) DS895.F7-77 (books prior to about 1970), DS798.92-799.99+
951.25	HONG KONG DS796.H7
951.2504	Hong Kong (1843-1945) DS796.H757
951.7	MONGOLIA DS793.M7
951.8	MANCHURIA DS781-784+, DS784 (1932-45)
951.9	KOREA DS901-935, DS916 (20th c.)

952	JAPAN DS801-897+
952.03	Japan (1868-1945: Imperial power) DS881.9
952.031	Japan (1868-1912: Meiji or Matsuhito period: inclu. Sino-Jpn. War of 1894-5 & Russo-Jpn. War of 1904-5: SEE ALSO 951.03 for Sino-Jpn. War of 1894-5 & 947.083 for Russo- Jpn. War of 1904-5) DS881.98-885.5, DS882, DS885
952.032	Japan (1912-26: Taisho or Yoshihito era) DS885.8-888, DS886 (gen.)
952.135	Tokyo, Japan DS896, DS896.64 (1867-1945), DS897.T6 (for earlier works)

953	ARABIAN PENINSULA DS201-248+, DS244 (1914-)
954	Southern Asia & India DS335-498+
954	INDIA (overall) DS436
954.03	India (1785-1947: British rule) DS463-480, DS463 (gen.)
954.0356	India (1905-16) DS480.2-3
954.0357	India (1916-26) DS480.4-6

955	PERSIA (Iran) DS251-325, DS272
955.05	Iran (1906-) DS298, DS313-318+
955.051	Iran (1906-25) DS315-316
956	MIDDLE EAST (NEAR EAST) DS41-326
956.02	Near East (1900-18) DS62.4
956.1	TURKEY & CYPRUS DR401-741, DS47-53, DS54 (Cyp.)
956.1	TURKEY (overall) DR440
956.101	Turkey (ca. 640-1918: inclu. Russo-Turkish War, 1877-8: PREFER 947.081 for Russo-Turk. War of 1877-8) DR440, DR588 (1914-18), DR573 (R-T War)
956.102	Turkey (1918-45) DR589-590
956.45	CYPRUS DS54
956.4503	Cyprus (1878-1960: British rule) DS54.8
956.7	IRAQ DS67-79, DS70.9
956.703	Iraq (1553-1920: Ottoman rule) DS77

956.9	MEDITERRANEAN REGION (EASTERN)	DS80-151+, DS62
956.91	SYRIA	DS92-99, DS95.5
956.9103	Syria (1516-1920: time of Ottomans)	DS97.5-6
956.94	ISRAEL & PALESTINE	DS101-131+, DS116-117, DS123
956.9403	Palestine (640-1917)	DS124-125, DS125.5 (WWI yrs.)
956.9404	Israel (1917-48: Brit. rule)	DS126, DS126.3 (WWII era)

957	SIBERIA	DK751-781, DK761

959	SOUTHEAST ASIA	DS521-689+, DS518 (1904-45: Far E. ?), DS525, DS541
959.05	Asia, Southeast (20th c.)	DS526.6-7+
959.9	PHILIPPINE ISLANDS	DS651-689, DS655, DS668
959.902	Philippine Islands (1564-1898: Span. period)	
959.903	Philippine Islands (1898-1946: U.S. era)	DS679-686.4, DS685

960-969	Africa	DT
960	AFRICA (gen.)	DT, DT3 (gen.), DT20 (gen. hist.)
960.31	Africa (1900-45)	DT29

961	NORTH AFRICA	DT160-346
961.03	North Africa (1830-1950: Eur. era)	DT176
961.1	TUNISIA	DT241-269, DT254
961.104	Tunisia (1881-1956)	DT264
961.2	LIBYA	DT211-239, DT224
961.203	Libya (1911-52: Ital. rule)	DT235
962	EGYPT & SUDAN	DT43-159
962	EGYPT (overall)	DT43-107, DT115-154, DT77
962.04	Egypt (1882-1922: Brit. protec.)	DT107-107.8, DT107 (gen.)
962.4	SUDAN	DT108 (older works), DT154.1-159
963	ETHIOPIA (Abyssinia)	DT371-398, DT381
963.05	Ethiopia (1896-1941 & 20th c.)	DT386-387.9, DT386
964	MOROCCO (in sum)	DT301-330, DT305, DT314
965	ALGERIA	DT271-299, DT275, DT284
966	SAHARA DESERT & West Africa	
967.6	EAST AFRICA (Uganda & Kenya)	DT421-435+ (newer titles), DT431
967.62	KENYA	DT434.E2, DT433.5-434, DT433.522, DT433.557
967.6203	Kenya (1895-1963: Brit. rule)	DT433.57-577
967.8103	ZANZIBAR (1890-1963)	DT435, DT449.Z2-29 (newer works), DT449.Z28
967.82	TANGANYIKA (ALSO Ger. W. Africa)	DT436-449, DT444
967.8202	GERMAN WEST AFRICA (1884-1916)	DT444, DT447 (newer books)
967.8203	Tanganyika (1916-61: Brit. era)	DT444, DT447
968	AFRICA, SOUTHERN	DT730-990+, DT732-733
968	SOUTH AFRICA (overall)	DT751-944, DT766
968.048	Boer War (S. Africa: 1899-1902: SEE ALSO 941.081 or 968.204)	DT930-939
968.05	South Africa (1910-61: Union)	DT779
968.052	South Africa (1910-19: Louis Botha)	DT779.5
969.1	MADAGASCAR	DT469.M21-38

970-979	North America & America	E-F
970	NORTH AMERICA (gen.)	E-F1392+, E11-45, E31-45
970.05	North America (1900-)	E45, E18.85
970.051	North America (1900-18)	
971	CANADA	F1001-1140
971.05	Canada (1867-1911: Dominion)	F1033
971.06	Canada (20th c. & 1911-)	F1034
971.061	Canada (1911-21)	
971.4	Quebec	F1051-1055
971.6	Nova Scotia	F1036-1040, F1038 (gen.)
971.8	Newfoundland	F1121-1139

972 CARIBBEAN, MEXICO, & CENTRAL AMERICA F1201-1392 (Mex.), F1421-2175

972	MEXICO (overall)	F1201-1392, F1208, F1226
972.081	Mexico (1867-1917)	F1233.5-1234
972.082	Mexico (1917-64)	F1234-1235
972.8	CENTRAL AMERICA	F1421-1577, F1436
972.87	PANAMA	F1561-1577, F1566
972.87051	Panama (1904-45)	F1566.5
972.9	WEST INDIES	F1601-2175+, F1608, F1621
972.91	CUBA	F1751-1849, F1758, F1776
972.9106	Cuba (1899-)	F1787-1788

973	UNITED STATES	E-F975+, E178 (gen.)
973.03	Encyclopedias & dictionaries (U.S.)	E174
973.05	Serials & periodicals (U.S.)	E171
973.06	Clubs & societies (U.S.)	E172
973.8	United States (1865-1901)	E660-738, E661
973.89	United States (1898: Sp.-Am. War: SEE ALSO 946.08 for Sp.-Am. War, 1898)	E714-735, E715
973.9	United States (20th c.)	E740-749, E741
973.91	United States (1901-53)	E741, E740-816
973.911	United States (1901-1909: Theodore Roosevelt admin.)	E756-760, E756
973.912	United States (1909-13: Wm. Howard Taft era)	E760-765, E761
973.913	United States (1913-21: Woodrow Wilson)	E765-783, E766, E780 (WWI era)

974-979	UNITED STATES (local: regions, states, towns, etc.: note that Hawaii is placed at 996.9)	F1-900+
974	New England & Middle Atlantic states	F1-105 (New Eng.), F106-205 (Mid. At.), F1-15, F106
974.041	New England & Middle Atlantic states (1865-1918)	F9 (New Eng.), F106 (Mid. At.)
974.4	Massachusetts	F61-75, F64
974.7	New York	F116-130, F119
974.7041	New York (1865-1918)	F124 (1865-1950)
974.71	New York City, N.Y.	F128, F128.3
975	South Atlantic states	F206-295, F206-220, F209, F215 (1865-)
975.3	District of Columbia	F191-205, F194
975.303	Washington, D.C. (1865-1933)	F198-199
975.5	Virginia	F221-235, F226, F231 (1865-1950)
976	South Central states & Gulf Coast	F296-475, F296-395 (Gulf), F296-301, F396-475 (Old S.W.), F396

977	North Central states	F476-705, F476-590 (Old N.W.), F476-485, F591-705 (Trans-Miss.), F591-596
977.3	Illinois	F536-550, F541, F546 (1865-1950)
977.311	Chicago, Ill.	F548
978	Western states	F591-785, F591-596, F591
979.03	Pacific Coast & Great Basin (U.S.: 20th c.)	F786, F852
979.4	California	F856-870, F861 (gen.)
979.405	California (1900-)	F866 (1869-1950)
979.4051	California (1900-18)	F866
979.49	California, Southern	F867

980-989	South America	F
980	SOUTH AMERICA (overall: inclu. Latin Am. in gen.)	F2201-3799+, F2201-2239, F2231 (GEN.)
980.032	South America (1900-18)	F2236 (1830-)
981	BRAZIL	F2501-2659, F2521
982	ARGENTINA	F2801-3021+, F2831 (gen.)
982.06	Argentina (20th c.)	F2847-2849+
982.061	Argentina (1910-46)	F2848
983	CHILE	F3051-3285, F3081 (gen.)
985	PERU	F3401-3619, F3431
989.2	PARAGUAY	F2661-2699
989.5	URUGUAY	F2701-2799, F2721 (gen.)

990-999	History (misc. areas: Oceania, Atlantic islands, Arctic, extraterr. worlds, etc.)	C-F, G, Q
990	OCEANICA & other misc. areas (SEE ALSO 995 for gen. works after about 1988)	DU, DU28.3
993-996	OCEANIA	DU

993	NEW ZEALAND & MELANESIA (overall: SEE ALSO 993.1 for N.Z. works prior to 1989, 995 for Mel. with pubn. dates after about 1988)	DU400-490+
993.03	New Zealand (1908-: Dominion: SEE ALSO 993.103 for works before 1989)	
993.031	New Zealand (1908-18: SEE ALSO 993.1031 for works prior to about 1989)	
993.1	NEW ZEALAND (PREFER 993 after 1988)	DU400-430
993.102	New Zealand (1840-1908: SEE ALSO 993.02 for works after 1988)	DU420
993.1023	New Zealand (1876-1908: Centralized gov.)	DU420
993.103	New Zealand (1908-: Dominion: PREFER 993.03+ for titles after 1988)	DU420-421
993.1031	New Zealand (1908-18)	
993.122	Auckland, New Z. (area)	DU430.A79
993.155	Christchurch, New Z. (area)	DU430.C5
993.2-993.7	MELANESIA (PREFER 995 after 1988)	DU490 (gen.)

994	AUSTRALIA DU80-398, DU450-480, DU110 (gen.)	
994.03	Australia (1851-1901: Colonial era)	
994.032	Australia (1891-1901)	
994.04	Australia (1901-45) DU116	
994.041	Australia (1901-22)	
994.31	Brisbane, Australia DU278	
994.4	New South Wales (Australia) DU150-180, DU170	
994.41	Sydney, Australia (area) DU178	
994.5	Victoria (Australia) DU200-230, DU220	
994.51	Melbourne, Australia DU228	
995	MELANESIA, NEW GUINEA, & OCEANIA (SEE ALSO 993.2-7 for titles on Mel. & New G. before 1989; 990 for gen. titles on Oceania prior to 1989) DU739-746, DU739	
995	NEW GUINEA (overall)	
995.8	Bismarck Archipelago (SEE ALSO 993.6 for books before 1989)	
996	POLYNESIA & other Pacific areas DU510 (Poly.: gen.)	
996.13	SAMOA, AMERICAN DU819.A1, DU810-819, DU815	
996.14	SAMOA, WESTERN DU819.A2, DU810-819, DU815	
996.5	MICRONESIA DU500 (gen.)	
996.9	HAWAIIAN ISLANDS (overall) DU620-629, DU625	
996.903	Hawaiian Islands (1898-1959: U.S. Terr.) DU627.5	
997	ATLANTIC OCEAN ISLANDS	
997.1	Falkland Islands (S. Atl. Ocean: G.B.) F3031	
998.2	GREENLAND	

III. INDEX TO LIBRARY OF CONGRESS & DEWEY CLASSIFICATION

Following is a unified index to both of the preceding classification sections--
Library of Congress and Dewey. Words and phrases are followed by either
LC, Dewey, or sometimes both kinds of numbers. Since this listing was
generated by alphabetizing a combined LC/Dewey database, one might find
either form given first. Entries missing one or the other of the types do so
because exact translations could not be found or do not exist. A similar
warning as in other sections: do not use this part of the book alone for
complete knowledge of a topical area. Class index entries, class numbers and
ranges, and subject/corporate phrases from the different sections should all
be consulted for the most thorough group of control points.

INDEX WORDS/PHRASES: POSSIBLE CLASS NUMBERS (LC AND/OR DEWEY)

5 in. guns, Naval (U.S.: manuals)   VF393.A5.5
1900-1999 (20th c.: gen. hist.)   909.82 D421, D443
1900-1919 (gen. hist.)   909.821   D421, D521 (WWI: gen.)
1920-1929 (gen. hist.)   909.822   D653, D655-659, D720, D723-728 (1919-39)

AACHEN, Ger. (Aix-la-Chapelle)   DD901.A25-28
Abandoning ship (plus other misc. marine topics of disaster)   VK1259
Abdul Hamid II (Tur.: monarch, 1876-1909: ALSO works on era)   DR571
Abyssinia (19th -20th c.)   DT386   963.03-05+
Accidents, Marine   VK199
Accounting & accounts, Military (inclu. records, muster rolls, etc.)   UB160-165
Accounting & accounts, Naval (inclu. ships' records)   VC500-505   359.622
Addis Ababa, Eth.   DT390.A3
Aden   DS247.A2
Adjutant generals' offices   UB170-175
Administration (air forces: structure & personnel: gen.)   UG770-775   358.41,
                                                        .413, .416+
Administration (marines)   359.966   VB21-124
ADMINISTRATION, MILITARY   UB
Administration, Military (Asia: gen.)   UB99
Administration, Military (command, intelligence, law, etc.)   UB   355, .6
Administration, Military (Eur.: gen.)   UB55
Administration, Military (G.B.: gen.)   UB57   355.60941, 354.41066
Administration, Military (gen. hist.)   UB15
Administration, Military supply & finance   355.62   UC260-267, UA
Administration, Military (U.S.: gen.)   UB23
ADMINISTRATION, NAVAL   359.6   VB, VB15, VB21-124 (by place),
             VB23 (U.S.), VC (maint.), VC10, VC20-258 (by place), VC20-65 (U.S.)
Administration, Naval (Asia: gen.)   VB99   359.6095
Administration, Naval (command, personnel, law, etc.)   VB
Administration, Naval (Eur.: gen.)   VB55   359.6094
Administration, Naval (gen. hist.)   VB15   359.6, .1-3
Administration, Naval (misc. topics)   VB955
Administration, Naval supply & finance   359.62   VC10, VC20-258 (by
                                        place), VC20-65 (U.S.)
Admirals, commanders, etc. (admin.: inclu. duties)   VB190
Adriatic coast (Yug.)   DR1350.A35

Advanced guard   U167.5.A35
Aegean Sea   DR701.A5
Aerial observations (artillery)   UF805
AERIAL OPS. (Sp. Civil War, 1936-39)   DP269.4
Aerial ops. (WWI: Can.)   940.44971   D607.C
Aerial ops. (WWI: Fr.)   940.44944   D603
Aerial ops. (WWI: G.B.)   940.44941   D602
Aerial ops. (WWI: gen.)   D600
Aerial ops. (WWI: Ger.)   940.44943   D604
Aerial ops. (WWI: It.)   940.44945   D607.I
Aerial ops. (WWI: misc. countries)   D607.A-Z
Aerial ops. (WWI: particular countries)   940.449
Aerial ops. (WWI: particular srvcs.: scouting, artill. spotting, bombing & naval
                    support, coast patrol, anti-sub. work, etc.)   940.441
Aerial ops. (WWI: Rus.)   940.44947   D605
Aerial ops. (WWI: U.S.)   940.44973   D606, D570.6-7 (squadrons)
Aerial ops. (WWII: by country: inclu. specific craft, units, fliers)   940.5449+
Aerial ops. (WWII: gen.)   D785   940.544
Aerial reconnaisance (U.S.)   UG763
Aerial warfare & air forces   358.4 (inclu. naval av. for works prior to 1989--SEE
                    359.94 after 1988)   UG622-1425, UG630, UG633-634 (U.S.),
                    UG635.A-Z (places besides U.S.), VG90-95 (naval av.)
Aerodynamics   629.1323
Aeronautics   629.13
Aeronautics (principles)   629.132
AFRICA   960-969   DT
Africa (1884-1945: gen.)   DT29   960.23-31
Africa (1900-45)   960.31   DT29
Africa (gen.)   960   DT, DT3 (gen.), DT20 (gen. hist.)
Africa (geog. & travel)   916   DT55 (1901-50)
Africa (mil. status: gen.)   UA855   355.03306
Africa (naval status)   VA670-700
Africa (overall)   DT1-38   960
Africa (post-WWI territorial ?s)   D651.A4
Africa, Southern   968   DT730-990+, DT732-733
African colonies (WWI: Ger.: by place)   D576.A-Z
African colonies (WWI: Ger.: gen.)   D575   940.416
Afro-Americans (armed forces)   UB418.A47
Afro-Americans (U.S. Navy)   VB324.A47
Agricultural products (mil. raw materials)   355.245   UA929.95.A35
Agriculture (defense)   UA929.95.A35
Agriculture, forestry, hunting   S   630-639, 574, 581, 799
AIR bases & fields (U.S.: by name)   UG634.5.A-Z
Air bases (mil. design)   623.6613   UG633-634.5 (U.S.), UG635 (other lands)
Air bases (WWI)   940.443   D532-538 (Ger.), D547-547.8 (G.B.),
                    D548-549 (Fr.), D570.85+ (U.S.)
Air battles & campaigns (WWII)   940.5442   D785+
Air defenses (U.S.)   UG733   358.41450973
AIR FORCE administration   358.416   UG770-775, UG1100-1135, UG630-635
Air force bombs (by specific type)   UG1282.A-Z
Air force communications & ops.   358.46   UA940-945, UG611-612.5
Air force equipment (gen.: planes, bombs, etc.)   UG1200   358.418, .412
Air force facilities   623.66   UG633-635, UG21-124 (engnrg. by place),
                    UG360-390 (field engnrg.)
Air force history (G.B.)   DA89.5-6

Air force life & customs   358.411   U750-773, UG770-775, UG1130-1135
Air force manuals & regulations (places except U.S.) UG675.A-Z
Air force officers (countries except U.S.)   UG795.A-Z
Air force ops. (gen.)   358.414   UG630, UG633-635, UG700-765
Air force ops. (WWI)   D600-607   940.44
Air force ordnance (gen.: U.S.)   UG1273
Air force personnel   358.4161   UG1130-1135
Air force planes (countries besides U.S.)   UG1245.A-Z
Air force planes (Fr.)   UG1245.F8   358.400944
Air force planes (G.B.)   UG1245.G7   358.400941, .414741-414742,
            623.740941, .7460941
Air force planes (Ger.)   UG1245.G3   358.400943, .414743, 623.740943
Air force planes (It.)   UG1245.I8   358.400945
Air force planes (Rus.)   UG1245.R9   358.400947
Air force planes (U.S.: PREFER UG1242 for particular types)   UG1243
            358.40973, .4140973, .414773, 623.740973, .7460973
Air force regulations & manuals (Ger.)   UG675.G3
Air force tactics (gen.)   UG700
Air force training & education (U.S.)   UG638-638.8
Air force units (types)   358.4131
AIR FORCES & air warfare   UG622-1425   358.4, 623.74-746
Air forces & warfare (essays & lectures)   UG627
Air forces & warfare (hist.: gen.)   UG625   358.4009
Air forces (Australia)   UG635.A8
Air forces (Fr.)   UG635.F8
Air forces (G.B.)   UG635.G7
Air forces (Ger.)   UG635.G3
Air forces (It.)   UG635.I8
Air forces (places besides U.S.)   UG635.A-Z
Air forces (policy & status)   358.403   UG630-635, UA
Air forces (Rus.)   UG635.R9
Air forces (Sov.Un.)   UG635.S65
Air forces (U.S.: by state)   UG634.A-W
Air forces (U.S.: gen.)   UG633   358.400973
Air museums & exhibitions (by country or area)   UG623.3.A2-Z
Air-raid warning systems (design)   623.737 (SEE .37 for titles prior to 1989)
            UG730-735
Air raids (WWI)   940.442   D600-607
Air traffic control (mil. engineering)   623.666
Air transport, Military UC330-335 358.44
Air warfare   D437   358.41409, 358.41447
Air warfare & forces (collected works: gen.) UG624
Air warfare & forces (gen.)   UG630   358.4
Air warfare (gen.)   358.41
Air warfare (hist.: gen.)   358.41409   UG625
AIRCRAFT carriers (G.B.)   V874.5.G7   623.82550941
Aircraft carriers (gen.)   V874   623.8255, 359.3255
Aircraft (heavier-than-air: mil. engineering)   623.746   UG1240-1245,
            UG630-635, TL685.3, VG90-95
Aircraft (lighter-than-air: mil. design)   623.741   UG1310-1375
Aircraft components (cabins, engines, fuselages, instruments, wings, etc.)
            623.746049   TL672-683
Aircraft guns & small weapons (gen.)   UG1340
Aircraft instrumentation (flight)   629.1352
Aircraft instrumentation (navig.)   629.1351

Aircraft launching & recovery equipment (carriers)   V875.A36
Aircraft, Naval   359.94834
Aircraft parts & components   629.134
Aircraft (types: engineering)   629.133+
Airfields & bases (countries besides U.S.: by name of base)   UG635.x2.A-Z
Airmen & non-commissioned air officers   UG820-825   358.41338
Airplanes   629.13334 (engineering)
Airplanes (air force: by type)   UG1242.A-Z
Airplanes (air force: gen.)   UG1240
Airplanes, Military   UG1240-1245   623.746, 358.418
Airports (engineering)   629.136
Airships or dirigibles (gen.)   UG1220   623.743
Airships, Rigid (mil. engineering)   623.7435
Airships, Semirigid & nonrigid (mil. engineering)   623.7436-7437
Aisne, Fr. (WWI)   D545.A5
ALBANIA   949.65   DR701.S49-86 (known as Scutari for earlier works),
      DR701.S5, DR941-979+ (for later works), DR941 (gen.)
Albania (to 1912)   949.6501   DR701.S5, DR940-0941, DR962
Albania (1912-46)   949.6502   DR701.S6 (1914-17), .S85 (1939-43), DR971,
      DR972 (WWI), DR975 (WWII)
Albania (1912-44)   DR970-975
Albania (1912-44: gen.)   DR971
Albania (1912-18)   DR972, DR46+ (Balkan War etc.)
Albania (1914-17: Kingdom)   DR701.S6   949.6502
Albania (1917-25)   DR701.S7   949.6502
Albania (gen.)   DR941
Albania (geog. & travel)   914.965   DR701.S5, DR917 (later books)
Albania (post-WWI territorial ?s)   D651.A5
Albania (Scutari)   DR701.S49-86 (SEE ALSO DR941-979 for later titles)   949.65
Albania (WWI)   D569.5
Alfonso XIII (Sp.: King, 1886-1931)   DP238
Algeria   DT271-299, DT275, DT284   965
Algeria (1900-62: last of Fr. rule)   965.04   DT295 (older titles), DT294.5-295.3
Alien enemies (WWI)   D636
Alien enemies (WWI: by country)   D636.A3-Z
Alien enemies (WWI: G.B.)   D636.G7
Alien enemies (WWI: gen.)   D636.A2
Alien enemies (WWI: U.S.)   D570.8.A6
Allenby, Edmund Henry H. Allenby, 1st Viscount (G.B.: 20th c. mil. biog.)
      DA69.3.A6

Alliances, Military   355.031
Allied forces (air)   358.41356   UG625, UG630+
Allied forces (inclu. various multi-nat. & combined ops.)   355.356   UA12 (U.S.),
      UA15, U260 (comb. ops.)
Allied intervention (Rus. Rev.: by country)   DK265.42.A-Z
Allied naval forces (inclu. various coalition forces)   359.356   VA40-42, VA,
      U260
Allies & Allied military ops (WWI: gen.)   D544   940.412+, .414, .42-3, 944.0814
Allies & associates (WWI: dipl. hist.)   940.322   D511, D459 (Triple Entente)
Allies (WWI: gen. particip.)   940.332   D544
Allies (WWI: mil. & naval life & customs)   940.483+   D544
Allowances & pay (U.S. Navy: tables inclu. interest)   VC54

Almanacs & yearbooks, Nautical (American: inclu. abridged)   VK7
Almanacs, annuals, etc., Military (countries besides U.S.)   U10.A-Z
Almanacs, annuals, etc., Military (G.B.)   U10.G7
Almanacs, annuals, etc., Military (U.S.)   U9
Almanacs, Naval (official)   V9   359.00202
Alps   DQ820-829   949.47
Alsace, Fr. (WWI)   D545.A55 (SEE ALSO DD801.A57)
Alsace-Lorraine (Ger.)   DD801.A31-69
Ambulance companies (WWI: U.S.)   D570.355   940.4753
Ambulance services (WWI)   940.4753   D570.355 (U.S.)
Ambulances (mil. design)   623.74724   UH500-505
Ambulances, Military (plus transport)   UH500-505   623.74724
America (1901-)   E18.185   970.05
America & North America (gen.), United States   E   970, 973
America (gen.)   E1-143   970
America (mil. status: gen.)   UA21   355.03301812
AMERICAN Expeditionary Force Univ. (WWI)   D639.E35
American Legion (WWI)   D570.A1-14.Z9
American Legion (WWI: Auxiliary, publications, by state)   D570.A14-A14.A6-W
American Legion (WWI: by city)   D570.A13.A-Z
American Legion (WWI: by state)   D570.A12.A-Z
American Legion (WWI: France)   D570.A135
American Legion (WWI: gen.)   D570.A1
American literature in English   PS   810-819
American military ops. & U.S. (WWI: gen. unofficial)   D570.A5-Z   940.373,
41273, .40973, 327.73
American Red Cross   UH537.A
American Samoa   DU819.A1   996.13
American waters (gen.: pilot & sailing guides)   VK804   623.89297
Americanization, civilization, etc. (U.S.)   E169.1
Ammunition & other ruinous media (design)   623.45   UF700-770
Ammunition (navies)   359.825
Ammunition, Artillery   UF700   358.825, 623.45
Ammunition, Naval   VF460   359.825, 623.45
Ammunition, Small arms   355.8255
Amnesty (WWI)   D639.A6
Amphibious ops.   U261   359.83, .96
Amphibious planes   629.133348
Amsterdam, Neth.   DJ411.A5-59
Analysis, Air warfare (real & imagined)   358.4148   UG630-635
Analysis, Military (real & mock events)   355.48   UA719-740+, U161-167+
Analysis, Naval warfare (real & imagined battles, campaigns, etc.)   359.48
V25-55, V160-178
Anarchism & anarchists (WWI)   D639.A64
Anarchists (Rus. Rev., 1917-21)   DK265.9.A5
Anchors, cables, etc. (marine engin.)   VM791
Ancient history   930-939   C-F
Anecdotes (WWI)   940.494
Anglo-Egyptian Sudan (1899-1955)   DT108.6   962.403
Anglo-French & Allied military ops (WWI)   D544-549+
Anglo-German naval conflict & blockade (WWI: gen.)   D581
Anglo-Saxon supremacy   D446
Angola (Portuguese West Africa)   DT591-617   967.3

Animals (WWI: use of)   D639.A65
Animals, Military UH87-100
Animals, Use of (mil. sci.)   355.424
Annapolis (U.S. Naval Acad.: gen. hist's. & other titles)   V415.L1
Annapolis (U.S. Naval Acad.: life & conditions)   V415.P1
Annual registers (20th c.: politics and diplomacy)   D440
Anti-Semitism   DS145
Anti-Soviet propaganda (1925-53: gen.)   DK272.5
Anti-submarine & submarine ops. (WWI: gen.)   D590
Antisubmarine warfare   V214   359.3254, .42-43
Antitank guns   UF628   623.42, .44, .4518
Antwerp area (Bel.)   DH801.A6-69
Antwerp, Bel.   DH811.A55-68
Antwerp, Siege of (1914) D542.A6
Appliances, Ships' (engin.: gen.)   VM781   623.86
Arabia (WWI)   D568.4
Arabian Desert (Egypt)   DT137.A7
Arabian Penninsula   953   DS201-248+, DS244 (1914-)
Arabian Peninsula (gen.)   DS223
Arabian Peninsula (geog. & travel)   915.3   DS207
Archibald, James Frances J. (WWI: Ger. spy in U.S.)   D619.5.A7
Architecture, Military   UG460   623.1
Architecture, Naval (collected, nonperiodical works) VM7
Argentina   F2801-3021+, F2831 (gen.)   982
Argentina (1810-)   F2846   982.03+
Argentina (20th c.)   982.06 F2847-2849+
Argentina (WWI: dipl. hist.)   D621.A8
Argonne, Battle of the (1915)   D545.A6
Argonne, Battle of the (1918)   D545.A63
Arizona   979.1   F806-820
Arizona (battleship: U.S.)   VA65.A75
Arlington National Cemetery (Arlington, Va.) F234.A7
Armament (modern: Asia: by country)   U821.A-Z
Armament (modern: Eur.: by place)   U820.A-Z
Armament (modern: gen.)   U815
Armament (modern: U.S.)   U818
Armament, Naval (gen.)   V950   623.8251
Armenia   DK509 (gen. titles), DS161-199 (earlier titles), DK680-689 (later
                 works)   956.62
Armenia (1901-)   DS195   956.6202
Armenia (post-WWI territorial ?s)   D651.A7
ARMIES & navies (of the world)   UA15
Armies etc. (Sp.-Am. War, 1898)   E725   973.894, 946.08
Armies etc. (Sp.-Am. War, 1898: Sp.)   E725.9 973.894, 946.08
Armies etc. (Sp.-Am. War, 1898: U.S.)   E725.3-8   973.894
Armies etc. (WWI: G.B.: by #)   D546.5.1st-
Armies etc. (WWI: Ital.)   D569.A25
Armies etc. (WWI: U.S.)   D570.25-.358   940.412+, .44973, .45
Armies (organiz., descrip., & world status) UA   355
Armies (U.S.: by #/author)   UA27.3.1st-
Armies (WWI: Prus.)   D532.1
Armistice (WWI)   D641   940.439

ARMOR & CAVALRY   UE (SEE ALSO UA for specific armies) 357-358.1
Armor & cavalry (Asia)   UE99-113
Armor & cavalry (Australia & New Z.)   UE121-122.5   357.099+
Armor & cavalry (Austria)   UE65   357.109436
Armor & cavalry (essays & speeches)   UE149
Armor & cavalry (Eur.)   UE55-95
Armor & cavalry (Fr.)   UE71   357.0944
Armor & cavalry (G.B.)   UE57-64
Armor & cavalry (G.B.: by date)   UE58
Armor & cavalry (gen. hist.: inclu. several countries)   UE15   357.09, .109,
                                                                                                        358.1809
Armor & cavalry (Ger.)   UE73   357.0943
Armor & cavalry (It.)   UE79
Armor & cavalry manuals (U.S.)   UE153-154
Armor & cavalry (Rus.: Asia)   UE109
Armor & cavalry (Rus.: Eur.)   UE85   357.0947
Armor & cavalry (U.S.)   UE23   357.0973
Armor & weapons, Naval   359.8351
Armor plate (naval sci.)   V900-925
Armor plate (naval sci.: gen.)   V900   623.81821, .8251
Armor, Naval (U.S.)   V903   623.82510973
Armor-piercing shells & devices (design)   623.4518
ARMORED cars & other combat vehicles (land: design)   623.7475
Armored forces & warfare (tanks, armored cav., etc.)   358.18   UG446.5, UE147
Armored units & cavalry (Ger.)   UA714   357.10943, .50943, 358.180943
Armored units & cavalry (It.)   UA744
Armored units & cavalry (Rus.)   UA774
Armored units & cavalry (U.S.: inclu. mechanized: gen.)   UA30   357.10973
Armories, arsenals, magazines (gen.)   UF540
ARMS & armor (hist.)   U799-897
Arms & ordnance, Naval (gen.)   VF350-355   359.82, 623.418
Arms (gen.: pubn. dates 1801+)   U800.A3-Z   355.8, 623.4
Arms manuals (infantry)   UD320-325
Arms, Small (infantry: gen.)   UD380
Arms, Small (marines: gen.)   VE360   359.96824, 623.44
Arms, Small (navies: gen. & by place)   VD360-365   359.824, .8242
ARMY artillery (inclu. field & antitank)   358.12   UF400-405, UF15,
                        UF21-124 (by place), UF150-157+ (manuals & tactics)
Army corps (WWI: Fr.)   D548.1
Army corps (WWI: U.S.)   D570.27.A-Z
Army corps (WWI: U.S.: gen.: newer titles)   D570.27.A1.A-Z
Army corps (WWI: U.S.: specific units: newer titles)   D570.27.1st-
Army medical schools (U.S.: by region or state)   UH398.5.A-Z
Army posts (Fr.: by place)   UA702.32.A-Z
Army posts (Fr.: gen.)   UA702.3
Army posts (U.S.: by place)   UA26.A7-Z
Army posts (U.S.: gen.)   UA26.A1-6
Army reserves (U.S.)   UA42
Army staffs (U.S.)   UB223
Army War College (U.S.)   U413
Arnhem, Neth.   DJ411.A8
Arras, Fr. (WWI)   D545.A7
Arsenals, armories, etc. (U.S.: gen.)   UF543
Artificers, Military (U.S.: ALSO tech. troops)   UG503
Artificers, Naval (gen.: inclu. carpenters' mates etc.)   VG600

ARTILLERY   UA (for specific armies & units), UF   358.1+, 355.82+
Artillery & rifle ranges   U300-305
Artillery, Antiaircraft (land)   358.13   UF625
Artillery (Asia)   UF99-113
Artillery (Australia & New Z.)   UF121-122.5
Artillery batteries (U.S.: by #/author)   UA33.1st-
Artillery (by place)   UF21-121 (SEE ALSO UA for particular armies)
Artillery, Coast   355.8217, 358.16   UF450-455
Artillery (design)   623.41   UF, UF1-910+, UF15 (gen.), UF144-145 (gen.),
                        UF21-124 (by place), UF23 (U.S.), VF320-325 (naval)
Artillery equipment, Naval   VF320-325
Artillery, Field   355.8212   UF400-405
Artillery, Field (U.S.)   UF403-404
Artillery fire control (inclu. instruments: gen.)   UF848   623.558
Artillery (Fr.)   UF71   358.120944
Artillery (G.B.)   UA658   358.10941, .120941
Artillery (G.B.: by date periods)   UF58
Artillery (G.B.: gen.)   UF57   358.120941
Artillery (G.B.: WWI)   UF58.1914-18
Artillery (gen. hist.)   UF15   358.109, .1209, 355.82, .821
Artillery (Ger.)   UA715, UF73   358.120943
Artillery, Howitzer & mortar (places besides U.S.)   UF475.A-Z
Artillery installations (arsenals, depots, target ranges, schools, etc.)   355.73
                                                UF540-545
Artillery instruments (misc.)   UF856.A-Z
Artillery (lt.)   UA745, UF79
Artillery, Land missile forces & armored warfare   358.1   UF, UF15, UF21-124,
                                UE147, UA32-33 (U.S.), UA
Artillery manuals (U.S.)   UF153-154
Artillery (misc.: design)   623.419 (for space artil. after 1988)
Artillery, Mountain (U.S.)   UF443-444
Artillery museums & exhibitons (gen.)   UF6.A1.A-Z   358.12
Artillery, Naval   359.8218, 355.8218   VF320-325
Artillery projectiles (gen.)   UF750
Artillery (pubn. 1801+)   UF145   358.12
Artillery, Railway (U.S.: gen.)   UF493
Artillery range finders (particular types) UF850.A3-Z
Artillery (Rus.)   UA775
Artillery (Rus.: Eur.)   UF85
Artillery services, Naval   359.9812
Artillery shells & other projectiles (design)   623.4513   UF750-760, VF480 (naval)
Artillery, Siege (gen.)   UF460
Artillery (specific pieces)   355.822
Artillery (titles in collections)   UF7
Artillery (Turkey)   UF111
Artillery (U.S.)   UF23   358.120973, .10973, 355.820973
Artillery (U.S.: gen.)   UA32   358.10973, .120973
Artillery (U.S.: N.Y. reserves)   UA366-367.75
Artillery (WWI: Fr.)   D548.6
Artillery (WWI: G.B.)   D546.52
Artillery (WWI: official reports)   D529.5
Artillery (WWI: Prus.)   D532.5
Artisans, Naval (carpenters' mates, painters, etc.)   VG600-605
Arts & architecture (visual, decorative & applied)   N   700-709, 720-769
Arts, architecture, music, sports, & recreation   700-799   N, NB-NX, NA, M, GV

ASIA   DS   950-959, DS5, DS33
Asia (1480-1905)   950.3   DS33
Asia (20th c.)   DS35   950.4
Asia (1905-45)   950.41   DS35
Asia (biog.: heads of state)   923.15   DS32 (collective)
Asia (geog. & travel)   915   DS9 (1901-50)
Asia (maps & atlases)   912.5   G2200+
Asia (mil. status: gen.)   UA830   355.03305, .03325, .03355
Asia (naval status: gen.)   VA620   359.03095
Asia, Russian   DK750
Asia, Southeast (20th c.)   959.05   DS526.6-7+
Asia, Soviet Central   DK845-973   958
ASSOCIATIONS, periodicals, conferences (Russo-Fin. War, 1939-40)   DL1095
Associations, periodicals, societies (U.S.: 20th c.)   E740
Associations, periodicals, societies (U.S.: army reserves)   UA42.A6.A-Z
Associations, societies (U.S.)   E172
Associations, societies (WWI)   D502
Associations, societies (WWI: G.B.)   D546.A1-19
Associations, societies (WWI: misc. American military)   D570.A15.A-Z
Associations, societies (WWI: U.S.)   D570.A1-15
Assyria & Mesopotamia (WWI)   D568.5
Astor, Nancy W. Langhorne, Viscountess (G.B.: 1910-36 era)   DA574.A8
Astrology (WWI)   D639.A75
Athens, Gr.   DF915-936, DF925 (1901-)   949.512
ATLANTIC Coast (S.Am.)   F2214   980.009821, .009636
Atlantic Coast (U.S.: Maine to Flor.)   F106   974-975
Atlantic Fleet (U.S.)   VA63.A83
Atlantic Ocean (all & east: pilot & sailing guides)   VK810-880
Atlantic Ocean (all & east: tide & current tables)   VK610-680
Atlantic Ocean (West: pilot & sailing guides)   VK959-992
Atlantic Ocean Islands   997
Atrocities, war crimes, trials (WWI)   D625-626
Atrocities, war crimes, trials (WWI: Austria)   D626.A9
Atrocities, war crimes, trials (WWI: Ger. & Central Powers)   D626.G3
Attachés, Military   UB260
Attachés, Naval   VB240
Attack & defense plans (gen.)   UA920   355.0330+, .0332+, .0335+, .4+
Attack, defense, & siege   UG443-449
Auckland, N.Z.   DU430.A8   993.122
AUSTRALIA   DU80-398, DU450-480, DU110 (gen.)   994
Australia (1851-1901: Colonial era)   994.03
Australia (1891-1901)   994.032
Australia (1901-45: Commonwealth)   DU116   994.04
Australia (1901-22)   994.041
Australia & Anzacs (WWI)   D547.A8
Australia. Army (descrip. & hist.)   UA872   355.00994, .30994, .310994
Australia. Army (special branches by name)   UA873.A-Z
Australia (gen.)   DU110   994
Australia (mil. policy)   355.033594   UA870-874
Australia (mil. status)   UA870+   355.033094, .033294, .033594
Australia (mil. status: states, territories, localities)   UA874.A-Z
Australia (naval status: gen.)   VA713.A5-Z   359.030994, .00994, .4794
Australia, New Zealand, Tasmania   DU80-480

AUSTRIA   DB1-860   943.6
Austria (19th c. & 1815-1919)   943.604   DB80-93, DB80 (19th c.: gen.),
                                 DB85 (1848-1916: Franz Josef), DB86.7 (WWI time)
Austria (1801-)   DB38   943.604
Austria (1848-1916: Emp. Franz Joseph I)   DB85-90
Austria (1848-1916: gen.)   DB85
Austria (20th c.)   DB91-99+   943.605
Austria (20th c.: gen.)   DB91
Austria (20th c. & 1919-)   943.605   DB91 (20th c.), DB96 (1918-)
Austria (1914-18: WWI era)   DB86.7
Austria (1916-18: Emp. Karl I: gen.)   DB92
Austria (1918-: Republic)   DB96   943.6051
Austria & Austria-Hungary (mil. status)   UA670   355.0330436
Austria & Austro-Hungarian Empire (gen.)   DB17
Austria, Czechoslovakia, Hungary   DB 943.6-943.9
Austria (geog. & travel)   914.36   DB21-27, DB26 (1901-45)
Austria-Hungary. Army (gen.)   UA672   355.309436
Austria, Hungary, Czechoslovakia DB 943.6-9
Austria (naval status)   VA470-479   359.2809436
Austria (post-WWI territorial ?s)   D651.A95
Austria (WWI: causes, aims, results)   D512
Austria (WWI: mil. units & ops.)   940.413436 D539
Austrian & Austro-Hungarian military ops. (WWI) D539
Austrian & Austro-Hungarian military ops. (WWI: special divisions) D539.5.A-Z
Austrian-Franco naval conflict (WWI: by battle, ship, etc.)   D584.A-Z
Austrian question (20th c.)   DB48
Automatic firearms (rifles, machine guns, etc.)   355.82424   UF620
Automatic weapons (machine & submach. guns, auto. rifles, etc.: design)
                     623.4424   UD390-395, UF620 (mach. g's.)
Automobiles (WWI)   D639.A8
Auxiliaries, Army (U.S.)   UA565.A-Z
Azerbaijan (post-WWI territorial ?s)   D651.A98
Azerbaijan S.S.R.   DK690-699
Azerbaijan S.S.R. (1917+)   DK697.3-5
Azimuth instrument (artillery)   UF850.A9

BACTERIOLOGY, Military (inclu. vaccination)   UH450-455
Baden military ops. (WWI)   D533
Badges, brevets, medals of honor, rewards, etc. (navies) VB330-335
Badges, insignia, etc. (mil.: SEE ALSO UB430+ for decorations)   UC530-535
Badoglio, Pietro (It.: 1900-46 period)   DG575.B2
Bahrein   DS247.B2-28
Bakeries (mil.)   UC730-735
Baku (Rus.: prov.)   DK511.B2
Baku, Rus.   DK699.2-39
Baldwin, Stanley, 1st Earl (G.B.: 20th c.)   DA566.9.B15
Balfour, Arthur James Balfour, 1st Earl of (G.B.: 20th c.)   DA566.9.B2

BALKAN conflict (WWI)   D560-565
Balkan conflict (WWI: gen.)   D560   940.4147
Balkan Peninsula (inclu. Balkan Wars of 1912-13)   949.6   DR1-48,
                                    DR45 (20th c.), DR46 (Balkan Wars)
Balkan Peninsula (1913-19)   DR47
Balkan Peninsula & Eastern Europe (1901-: gen.)   DR45
Balkan Peninsula, Eastern Europe DR (titles written prior to about 1978-79)
                        949.6-949.8, 943.7-943.9, 947, 947.8, 956
Balkan Peninsula (geog. & travel)   914.96   DR15, DR1221 (later works)
Balkan States (mil. status: descrip. & hist.)   UA822
Balkan States (mil. status: gen.)   UA820   355.0330496
Balkan War (1912-13)   DR46   949.6
Ballistic instruments   UF830.A-Z
BALLISTICS   UF820-830   623.51+
Ballistics & gunnery (engineering)   623.5   UF800-830, UF820
Ballistics (engineering)   623.51   UF820-830
Ballistics, Exterior   UF825   623.514
Ballistics, Exterior (environmental)   623.514   UF825
Ballistics, Interior   UF823   623.513
Ballistics, Interior (within bore)   623.513   UF823
Ballistics, Terminal (effects on targets) 623.516
Balloons & kites, Air force   UG1370-1375   623.741-744
Balloons, Military (design)   623.742   UG1370-1375
Baltic provinces (post-WWI territorial ?s)   D651.B2
Baltic Sea (mil. status)   UA646.53   355.033016334, .4716334, 359.4716334
Baltic States   DK502.3-505
Baltic States (gen.)   DK502.7
Bands & music, Military   UH40-45
Bands & music, Naval (SEE ALSO ML1300-1354)   VG30-35
Banking services, Military   UH60-65
Barbary States   DT181-346   961.1-2, 964-965, 966
Barracks & camps, Military (gen.)   UC400   355.412, .7
Barracks & quarters, Air force UG1140-1145   358.4171
Barracks, quarters, housing (naval)   VC420-425
Barrage balloons & nets (design)   623.744   UG1370-1375, UG730-735, UF625
Bases & fields, Air force   358.417   UG634.5.A-Z (U.S.: by name),
                                UG635.A-Z (other countries)
Bases & stations, Naval   359.7   V220 (gen.), VA67-750 (by place),
                VA69-70 (U.S.), VA459-461 (G.B.), VA516-517 (Ger.),
            VA576-577 (Rus.), VA656-657 (Japan), VC412-425 (maint.: gen.)
Bases, ports, & docks (naval: gen.: SEE ALSO VA67-750 for specific countries)
                                    V220   359.7
Bases, ports, etc. (G.B. Royal Navy: by place)   VA459.A3-Z
Bases, ports, etc. (U.S. Navy: by place)   VA68.A-Z
Basic training (mil.: inclu. drills, survival exercises, etc.)   355.54   U400-717,
                                    U765-773, U320-325
Basic training (mil. living conditions: ALSO regular quarters)   355.1292
Basic training (naval)   359.54   V260-265
Batteries, Storage (submarine architec.)   VM367.S7

Battle conditions, Naval   359.1294
Battle of the Atlantic, freedom of the seas, general naval ops. (WWII)   D770
    940.545
Battlefield guides (WWI: gen.: SEE ALSO specific battles)   D528
Battlefield guides (WWII: gen.: particular battles at D756.5 etc.)   D747
BATTLES & CAMPAIGNS, Aerial (WWI)   940.44   D600-607
Battles & campaigns, Aerial (WWII: inclu. comb. air & naval ops. as well as
    antiaircraft defenses)   940.544   D785-792, D785 (gen.)
Battles & campaigns, Land (WWI: 1914-16)   940.42
Battles & campaigns, Land (WWI: 1917-18)   940.43
Battles & campaigns, Naval (WWI)   940.45   D580-595, D580 (gen.)
Battles & campaigns, Naval (WWII)   940.545 (SEE ALSO .542 for ops. by
    theatre)   D770-784, D770 (gen.), D773 (U.S.: gen.), D774.A-Z (U.S.: by
    ship, battle, etc.), D769.45-598 (U.S.: by fleet, squadron, base, etc.)
BATTLES, CAMPAIGNS, SIEGES (Rus.-Jpn. War, 1904-5: by name)   DS517.15-5
Battles, campaigns, sieges (Russo-Polish, other Polish conflicts, 1918-21: by
    name)   DK4407.A-Z
Battles, campaigns, sieges (WWI: Belgium: by place)   D542.A-Z
Battles, campaigns, sieges (WWI: Bulg.)   D563.A3-Z
Battles, campaigns, sieges (WWI: Fr.: by place)   D545.A-Z
Battles, campaigns, sieges (WWI: Greece)   D569.3.A-Z
Battles, campaigns, sieges (WWI: Italy)   D569.A3-Z
Battles, campaigns, sieges (WWI: Montenegro)   D564.A3-Z
Battles, campaigns, sieges (WWI: Rum.)   D565.A3-Z
Battles, campaigns, sieges (WWI: Russo-Austrian: by place)   D557.A-Z
Battles, campaigns, sieges (WWI: Russo-German)   D552.A-Z
Battles, campaigns, sieges (WWI: Serbia)   D562.A-Z
Battles, campaigns, sieges (WWI: Turco-Egyptian)   D568.A3-Z
Battles, campaigns, sieges (WWI: Turco-Russian: by place)   D567.A3-Z
Battles, sieges, etc. (WWI: Jp.)   D572.A-Z
BATTLESHIPS (as equip.)   359.8352
Battleships (besides U.S.: by place)   V815.5.A-Z
Battleships (engineering)   623.8252   V750
Battleships (G.B.)   V815.5.G7   623.82520941
Battleships (gen.: construc., armament, etc.: SEE V750 for earlier titles)   V815
    623.8252, .81252, 359.3252
Battleships (Ger.)   V815.5.G3   623.82520943
Battleships (handling)   623.88252   V750
Battleships (Japan)   V815.5.J3   623.82520952
Battleships (U.S.)   V815.3   623.82520973, 359.32520973
Battleships (units)   359.3252   V750, V765-767, V799-800, VA,
    VA65.A-Z (U.S.: by name)
Bavaria   DD801.B31-55   943.3
Bavarian military ops. (WWI: divided like Prussian #'s at D532)   D534-534.9
Bayonet drill   UD340-345
Bayonet drill (naval seamen)   VD340-345
Bayonets   UD400
Bayonets (marines)   VE380   623.441
Bayonets (navies)   VD380   359.8241
Beacons, buoys, etc. (marine navig.)   623.8944   VK1000-1249, VK1010,
    VK1021-1124, VK1023-1025 (U.S.)
Beacons, foghorns, lighthouses, etc. (gen.)   VK1010   623.8942, 387.155
Beacons, foghorns, lighthouses, etc. (lists: gen.: inclu. Br. Admiralty)   VK1150
    623.8944

Beatty, David Beatty, 1st Earl (G.B.: 20th c. naval biog.)   DA89.1.B4
Beaverbrook, William Maxwell Aitken, Baron (G.B.: 20th c.)   DA566.9.B37
Belgian Congo   DT641-665   967.5
Belgian military ops & battles in Belgium (WWI: gen.)   D541
BELGIUM   DH418-811+, DH521   949.3
Belgium (20th c.)   DH677   949.304
Belgium (1909-)   949.304   DH677 (20th c.)
Belgium (1909-34: Albert I)   949.3041   DH681-685, DH681, DH682 (WWI)
Belgium (1914-18: WWI)   DH682
Belgium & Belgian neutrality (WWI: dipl. history)   D615
Belgium & Luxembourg   DH401-925
Belgium (geog. & travel)   914.931-934   DH433
Belgium (mil. status)   UA680-689   355.0330493
Belgium (naval status)   VA480-489
Belgium (post-WWI territorial ?s)   D651.B3
Belgium (WWI: causes, aims, results)   D518
Belgium (WWI: occupation)   D623.B4
Belgrade, Serbia (Yug.)   DR2106-2124
Belgrade, Yug.   DR386
Belleau Wood, Fr. (WWI)   D545.B4
Belorussia   947.65   DK511.W5 (White Russia)
Benefits, pay, allowances (air forces: U.S.)   UG943
Bengal (E. Pak.)   DS485.B39-492
Bengal (W. Pak.)   DS485.B493   954.14
Berlin, Ger.   943.155   DD851-900, DD860 (gen.)
Berlin, Ger. (1914-21)   DD879
Bermuda & West Indies (geog. & travel)   917.29   F1611
Bern, Swit.   DQ401-420   949.45
Bessarabia (post-WWI territorial ?s)   D651.B4
BIBLIOGRAPHIES (inclu. partic. kinds, subjects, etc.)   010-019, 016 (SEE ALSO
     subject #'s like 359+, 940+, etc.)   Z
Bibliographies (G.B.: hist.)   Z2016-2020+   016.941-942, .94109
Bibliographies (Ger.: hist.)   Z2237   016.94309
Bibliographies (mil. hist.: Ger.)   Z2241.M5   016.3550943
Bibliographies (mil. hist.: U.S.)   Z1249.M5   016.3550973, .35500973,
Bibliographies (mil. sci. & hist.)   Z6724   016.355, .35509, 355.009, .0009
Bibliographies (naval hist.: G.B.)   Z2021.N3   016.3590941
Bibliographies (naval hist.: U.S.)   Z1249.N3   016.3590973, .35900973,
               35930973, .3593310924
Bibliographies (naval sci. & hist.)   Z6616   016.359, .35909, .35900722
Bibliographies (Rus.: hist.)   Z2506-2510+   016.94709
Bibliographies (specific subjects)   016   Z (sometimes D-F, U-V, or other
     subject classes)
Bibliographies (U.S.: hist.)   Z1236-1245+, Z1236   016.97309
Bibliographies (U.S.: hist.: 1900-45)   Z1244   016.9730904, .97309044 (WWII)
Bibliographies (WWI)   Z6207.E8 or .W7 016.9403
Bibliography & library science   Z (bibliog's. sometimes classed with A-Z subject #s)
               010-028+
Bicycle troops (mech. cav.)   357.52   UH30-35
Bicyclists, Military (gen.)   UH30   357.52
Billeting   UC410
Binoculars & telescopes, Military   UF845
Binoculars (naval clothing: inclu. other misc. accessories)   VC340

BIOGRAPHY & genealogy   920-929   CT (gen. or collec.), D-F, other specific
    classes for specialists or famous people in those areas
Biography & memoirs (WWI: medical: by name)   D630.A-Z
Biography (1832-1914: by name)   DK436.5.A-Z
Biography (1871-late 19th c.: collected)   D399-399.8
Biography (1871-late 19th c.: individual)   D400.A-Z
Biography (20th c.: collective: gen.)   D412   920.02
Biography (20th c.: individual or memoir by name)   D413.A-Z
Biography (20th c.: memoirs and collective)   D412-412.8
Biography, Air force (collective)   UG626   358.400922
Biography, Air force (G.B.: collective)   DA89.6.A1
Biography, Air force (G.B.: inclu. memoirs)   DA89.6.A-Z
Biography, Air force (individual)   UG626.2.A-Z   358.400924
Biography (Australia: 1901-45)   DU116.2 (SEE DU114 for earlier pubns.)
Biography (Australia: by name)   DU114.A3-Z (SEE ALSO DU116.2 for later works)
Biography (Australia: collective)   DU114.A2
Biography (Austria: 1848-1916)   DB90.A-Z
Biography (Austria: 20th c.: by name: inclu. memoirs)   DB98.A-Z
Biography (Austria: misc. royalty)   DB89.A-Z
Biography (Bel.: 1909-34)   DH685.A-Z
Biography (Bulg.: 1879-1943: inclu. memoirs)   DR85.5.A-Z
Biography (Bulg.: 1887-1918: by name)   DR88.A-Z
Biography (China: 1912-49 period: except Sun Yat Sen)   DS777.15.A-Z
Biography (Czech.: 1918-39)   DB2200-2201.A-Z
Biography (Eur.: group)   940.092   D106-110 (group)
Biography (Fin.: 20th c.)   DK461.A-Z
Biography (Fin.: 1918-39)   DL1088-1088.5
Biography (Fr.: 1871-1940: by name: inclu. memoirs & autobiog.)   DC342.8.A-Z
Biography (Fr.: 1871-1940: collective)   DC342
Biography (Fr.: 20th c.: by name)   DC373.A-Z
Biography (Fr.: 20th c.: collective)   DC371
Biography (G.B.: 1837-1901: except prime ministers: inclu. memoirs)   DA565.A-Z
                                                                        941.0810924
Biography (G.B.: 1850-1901: prime ministers besides Gladstone)   DA564.A-Z
Biography (G.B.: 20th c.: collective)   DA566.9.A1
Biography (G.B.: 20th c.: inclu. memoirs)   DA566.9.A-Z   941.0820922-24
Biography (G.B.: 1901-10)   DA568.A-Z
Biography (G.B.: 1910-36: collective)   DA574.A1
Biography (G.B.: 1910-36: inclu. memoirs)   DA574.A-Z
Biography (G.B.: 1910-36: various royalty)   DA574.A2-45
Biography (gen.)   920 (sometimes '92' or 'B' are used, followed by particular
                          individuals in alphabetical order by last name. These may
                          ALSO be placed in specific discipline number areas followed by
                          the standard subdivision, '092'. So, 355.0092 is for mil. biog.)
Biography (Ger.: 1888-1918+: by name)   DD231.A-Z
Biography (Ger.: 1888-1918+: collective)   DD231.A2
Biography (Ger.: mostly pre-WWI: by name)   DD219.A-Z
Biography (Hung.: 20th c.: by name, inclu. memoirs)   DB950.A-Z
Biography (India: thru 1900: by name)   DS479.1.A-Z
Biography (India: 1901-: inclu. memoirs)   DS481.A-Z
Biography (It.: 1871-1947: collec.)   DG574
Biography (It.: 1871-1941)   DG556.A-Z
Biography (It.: 1900-46: by name, inclu. memoirs)   DG575.A-Z
Biography (Japan: 20th c.: inclu. memoirs: SEE ALSO DS890)   DS885.5.A-Z
Biography (Japan: Imperial family & rulers)   DS834.1

Biography (merch. marine)   VK139-140
BIOGRAPHY, MILITARY   355, 355.0092, .00922-00924, .3310922-0924,
                            U51-55 (SEE ALSO D-F war & country #s)
Biography, Military engineering (collective)   UG127
Biography, Military engineering (indiv.)   UG128.A-Z (SEE ALSO UG21-124)
Biography, Military (Eur.)   923.54
Biography, Military (except U.S.: group by place)   U54.A-Z
Biography, Military (except U.S.: individual)   U55.A-Z
Biography, Military (G.B.: 1850-1900: collective)   DA68.32.A1
Biography, Military (G.B.: 1850-1900: inclu. memoirs: by name)   DA68.32.A-Z
Biography, Military (G.B.: 20th c.: collective)   DA69.3.A1
Biography, Military (G.B.: 20th c.: inclu. memoirs)   DA69.3.A-Z   355.3310922-24
Biography, Military (G.B.: collective)   DA54
Biography, Military (Ger.: collective: gen.)   DD100.A2
Biography, Military (Ger.: collective: officers)   DD100.A3-Z
Biography, Military (It.: collective)   DG481
Biography, Military medical (collective, inclu. nurses)   UH341   355.3450922
Biography, Military (Rus.: collective)   DK50.5-8
Biography, Military (U.S.: individual)   U53.A-Z   355.330973
Biography (Montenegro: 1918-45)   DR1890-1891
BIOGRAPHY, NAVAL   359.0092   V61-64 (SEE ALSO D-F #s for indiv.
                            biog's. from particular countries), V61-64,
                            V63.A-Z (U.S.: by name), V64.A-Z (other countries)
Biography (naval architec.)   VM139-140
Biography, Naval (G.B.: 20th c.: by name)   DA89.1.A-Z
Biography, Naval (G.B.: 20th c.: collective)   DA89.1.A1
Biography, Naval (G.B.: collective)   DA74
Biography, Naval medical (gen.)   VG226
Biography, Naval medical (places besides U.S.)   VG228.A-Z
Biography, Naval (places besides U.S.: by place)   V64.A-Z
Biography, Naval (U.S.: by name)   V63.A-Z   359.00924, .3310924,
                            940.410924, .450924, .540924, .5420924, .5450924
Biography, Naval (U.S.: by name)   VB314.A-Z   359.3310973, .3310924
Biography (Neth.: by name)   DJ283.A-Z
Biography (New Z.: inclu. memoirs: by name)   DU422.A-Z
Biography (Palestine: 19th-20th c.)   DS125.3.A-Z
Biography (Palestine: 19th-20th c.: collective)   DS125.3.A2
Biography (Pol.: 1832-1914: by name)   DK436.5.A-Z
Biography (Pol.: 1918-: inclu. memoirs)   DK440.5.A-Z
Biography (Pol.: 1918-45: by name, inclu. memoirs)   DK4420.A-Z
Biography (Royal Naval Coll., Dart.: by name)   V515.M1.A-Z
Biography (Rum.: 1881-1914)   DR253.A-Z
Biography (Rum.: 1914-27)   DR262.A-Z
Biography (Rus.: 1881-94)   DK235-236.A-Z
Biography (Rus.: 1894-1917: by name, inclu. memoirs)   DK254.A-Z
Biography (Rus.: 1894-1917: collective)   DK253
Biography (Serbia: 1804-1918)   DR2012
Biography (Serbia: 1903-18)   DR2031
Biography (social sciences: gov., law, commerce, etc.)   923
Biography   920-929 (sometimes placed with country #s or topical #s in 930-999
                            or 000-999)   C-F
Biography (Sp.: 1886-1931)   DP235-236
Biography (Swe.: 1907-50: by name)   DL870.A-Z
Biography (Swit.: 20th c.)   DQ206-207
Biography (Tur.: 1909-: inclu. memoirs)   DR592.A-Z

Biography (U.S.: 1865-1900: by name)   E664.A-Z
Biography (U.S.: 1865-1900: collective)   E663
Biography (U.S.: 20th c.: by name)   E748.A-Z
Biography (U.S.: 20th c.: collective)   E747
Biography (U.S. Marines)   VE25 (PREFER E #s)
Biography (U.S. Mil. Acad.: by name)   U410.M1.A1-Z
Biography (U.S. Naval Acad.: by name)   V415.M1.A-Z
Biography (WWI: collective)   D507   940.3092, .481-2. Also use country #'s
Biography (Yug.: 20th c.)   DR359.A-Z
Biography (Yug.: 20th c.: collective)   DR359.A2
Biological agents (ammunition: design)   623.4594
Biological agents (mil.)   355.82594
Biological warfare   358.38   UG447.8
Birkenhead, Frederick E. S., 1st Earl of (G.B.: 20th c.)   DA566.9.B5
Bismarck Archipelago (gen.)   DU550   993.6
Bismarck, Otto von (inclu. family)   DD218
Black Forest (Ger.)   943.48   DD801.B63-65
Black Sea area (geog. & travel)   914.77   DK511.C7
Black Sea region   DJK61-66
Black Sea region (Rus.)   947.7   DK509
Black Watch (WWI)   D547.B6
Blacks (in U.S.)   E185   973.0496
Blacks (Sp.-Am. War, 1898: U.S.: Negroes)   E725.5.N3
Blacks (WWI: Negroes)   D639.N4
Blacks (WWI: Negroes: G.B.)   D547.N4
Blacks as soldiers & seamen (U.S.)   E185.63
Blinkers & electrooptical signal devices (mil. engineering)   623.7314   UG580,
                UG614-614.5, VK387
Blockades & blockade-running (WWI)   940.452   D581
Blockades & blockade-running (WWII)   940.5452   D770,
                D771 (Anglo-Grmn.), D773 (U.S.)
Blockades, Naval   V180   355.44, 359.42-43, 940.452, .5452
Blueprints, drawings, designs (naval architec.: laying out)   VM297.5
Boat attack (naval tactics)   V178   359.32, .42
Boatswains   VG950-955
Boatswains' mates (U.S.)   VG953
Boatyards, Small craft (by name)   VM321.52.A-Z
Boatyards, Small craft (gen.)   VM321.5
Boer War (S. Africa: 1899-1902)   968.048 (SEE ALSO 941.081 or 968.204)
                DT930-939
Boilers, Marine   VM741-750   623.873
Bomb disposal & demolition (army engineers)   358.23   UG370, UG550-555
Bomb shelters (plus other special civil defense topics like psych. aspects)   UA926.5
Bombers (air force)   UG1242.B6   623.7463, 358.42
Bombing, dog fighting, other air tactics (U.S.)   UG703
Bombs, Air force   UG1280-1285   358.418251, 623.451
Bombs, ammunition, etc.   355.825
Bombs & projectiles, Aircraft (inclu. std. & nuclear)   UF767   623.451
Bosnia & Bosnia-Herzegovina (20th c.)   DB250
Bosnia & Hercegovina (1878-1918: Austrian control)   DR1722-1732
Bosnia & Hercegovina (1914-18: WWI)   DR1732
Bosnia & Hercegovina (Herzegovina)   DR1652-1785 (SEE ALSO DR357 etc.)
                949.742
Boston, Mass. (1865-1950)   F73.5
Boxer Rebellion (China: 1899-1901)   DS770-772   951.03

Boy Scouts (WWI)   D639.B6
Boys (armed forces)   UB418.B69
Brandenburg, Ger.   DD901.B65
Brazil   F2501-2659, F2521   981
Brazil (1889-)   F2537   981.05+
Breech-loading ordnance   UF560-565... .B.L.
Bremen, Ger.   DD901.B71-79
Bremen (pass. ship)   VM383.B7
Brest, Fr.   DC801.B83
Brest, Fr. (WWI: U.S. training camp)   D570.37.B7
Brest-Litovsk, Russia (WWI: treaty: 3 Mar. 1918)   D614.B6
Brest-Litovsk, Ukraine (WWI: treaty: 9 Feb. 1918)   D614.B5
Brevets, badges, medals, etc. (U.S. Navy: inclu. Navy Cross)   VB333
                                              359.13420973

Briand, Aristide (Fr.: 20th c.)   DC373.B7
Bridge troops & sappers (gen.)   UG510
Bridges (London, Eng.: inclu. London Bridge)   DA689.B8
Bridges (mil. engineering)   UG335   623.67
Bridges of the Rhine (WWI: peace topic)   D650.B7
Britain (19th c. & Victorian era of 1837-1901)   941.081   DA550-566, DA550 (gen.)
Britain (20th c. & Edward VII era of 1901-1910)   941.082   DA567-570 (Ed. VII),
                                              DA570 (gen.), DA566 (20th c.: gen.)
Britain (1910-36: George VI)   941.083   DA573-578, DA576 (gen.),
                                              DA577 (WWI era), DA578 (1920-39)
Britain & British Isles   941   DA
BRITISH aerial ops. (WWI)   D602   940.44941
British aerial ops. (WWII)   D786   940.544941
British air force history (gen.)   DA89.5   358.400941
British armament (modern)   U820.G3
British Central Africa (1901-52)   DT855   968.97
British East Africa & East Africa   DT421-435   967.6
British East Indies   DS648 (SEE DS646.3 for Borneo)
British Empire   DA10-18
British Empire & Britain (WWI: by place or name) D547.A-Z
British Empire (gen.)   DA16   909.824+
British espionage (gen.)   UB271.G7   327.120941
British (in U.S.)   E184.B7
British infantry (gen.)   UD57   356.10941
British Isles & English Channel (pilot & sailing guides)   VK827-844
                                              623.892916336, .8929422
British Isles (pilot guides)   623.892941-892942   VK827-838.5
British Isles (tide & current tables) VK627-638
British marines (gen.)   VE57   359.960941
British medical services (WWI)   940.47541   D629.G7
British military education (special time periods)   U511
British military history (gen.)   DA50   355.00941
British military ops. & British Empire (WWI: special)   D546.3-547.8+
British military ops. & Great Britain (WWII: gen.)   D759   940.54091, .5341-
                                              5342, 942.084
British military ops., British Empire, & England (WWI)   D546-547.8+, D547.A-Z+
British military ops. (WWI: gen.)   D546.A2-Z   354.42066, 940.48341, .412+,
                                              941.083
British mission to U.S. (WWI)   D570.8.M6.B5

174

British naval education (special topics)   V511-512
British naval history (gen.)   DA70   359.00941
British naval ops. & Anglo-German naval conflict (WWI: by battle, ship, etc.)
                                                      D582.A-Z

British Somaliland   DT406   967.73-7305+
British South Africa   DT751-848   968-968.7
British submarine ops. (WWI: by battle, ship, etc.)   D594.A-Z
British submarine ops. (WWI: gen.)   D593   940.451341
British West Africa   DT491-518   966, 966.4-51, .7, .81, .9
Browning machine guns   UF620.B6
Bruges, Bel. (WWI)   D542.B7
Brussels, Bel.   DH802-809
Brussels, Bel. (20th c.)   DH807.5
Bryan, William Jennings (U.S.: 1865-1900 era: works)   E660.B87-94
Bucharest, Rum.   DR286   949.82
Budapest, Hun. (20th c.)   DB872
Budgets, Naval (G.B.)   VA455
Budgets, Naval (gen.)   VA25   359.622
Budgets, Naval (Ger.)   VA511
Budgets, Naval (U.S.)   VA60   359.6220973
Buenos Aires, Arg.   F3001   982.11
Buildings (London, Eng.)   DA686-687
Buildings, Public (Berlin, Ger.)   DD896
Buildings (Washington, D.C.)   F204.A-Z
Bukowina (20th c.)   DB280
BULGARIA   DR51-98   949.77
Bulgaria (1878-1946)   949.7702   DR85-93, DR89 (1918-43)
Bulgaria (1879-1943)   DR85   949.7702
Bulgaria (1887-1918: reign of Ferdinand)   DR87
Bulgaria (1912-13: Balkan War period)   DR87.7
Bulgaria (1914-18: WWI)   DR87.8
Bulgaria (geog. & travel)   914.977   DR60 (1879-1950)
Bulgaria (mil. status)   UA824   355.03304977
Bulgaria (post-WWI territorial ?s)   D651.B8
Bulgaria (WWI: gen.)   D563.A2
Bulletins, misc. collections, serials (WWI: U.S.: official)   D570.A2
Bulletproof clothing, materials, etc.   UF910
Bullets   UF770   623.455
Bullets (navies)   VF500   359.8255, 623.455
Bunkers, caves, shelters (defense engineering: protective construc.)   623.38
Bunks & bedding (mil.)   UC550-555
Burial services, graves registration, & naval military mail   359.69
Burma   959.1   DS485.B79-892, DS527-530 (newer works), DS528.5
Buses (mil. design)   623.74723

CABLES (naval supplies)   VC279.C3
Caen, Fr.   DC801.C11
Cairo, Egypt   DT139-152   962.16
Caissons, gun carriages, etc. (U.S.: gen.)   UF643
CALIFORNIA   F856-870, F861 (gen.)   979.4
California (1869-1950)   F866 (SEE D570.85.C2-21 for 1914-18 war years &
                              D769.85.C2-21 for 1939-45)   979.404-4053
California (1900-)   979.405   F866 (1869-1950)
California (1900-18)   979.4051   F866
California (gen.)   F861   979.4

California National Guard (gen.)   UA90
California, Southern   979.49   F867
California (WWI: gen.)   D570.85.C2
California (WWI: Reconstruction)   D658.C2-21
Camel batteries   UF420
Camel troops & camelry   UE500
Camels, elephants, etc. (mil. transp.)   UC350
Cameroon (mil. status)   UA859
Cameroons (German West Africa) & Togoland DT561-584   966.6695, .81, 967.1
Cameroons (post-WWI territorial ?s)   D651.C3
Cameroons (WWI)   D576.C3
Camouflage   UG449, V215 (naval)   358.3, 623.77
Camouflage, Marine   V215   623.77
Camp-making (mil. sci.)   UG365   355.412, .544, .71
Camps & barracks, Military   UC400-440
Camps, Training (armor & cavalry: U.S.)   UE433-434
CANADA   F1001-1140+   971
Canada (1867+)   F1033   971.05+
Canada (1867-1911: Dominion)   971.05   F1033
Canada (20th c. & 1911-)   971.06   F1034
Canada (1911-21)   971.061
Canada (1914+)   F1034 (SEE ALSO D768.15 for 1939-45 war years)   971.061+
Canada (E. coast: pilot & sailing guides)   VK985
Canada (gen.)   F1026
Canada (geog. & travel)   917.1   F1015
Canada (mil. status: gen.)   UA600   355.033271, .033571, .033071
Canada (naval status: gen.)   VA400   359.030971, .4771
Canada (WWI)   D547.C2
Cannons, howitzers, mortars, small rockets, other specific artillery (design)   623.42
Canteens & post exchanges, Military (U.S.)   UC753
Canteens & ship exchanges   VC390-395
Canteens (mil. equip.)   UC529.C2
Canteens (off-post mil. recreation: U.S.)   UH905
Canton, China   DS796.C2
Carbines, rifles, etc. UD390
Career guidance (naval sci.)   VB259
Cargo & personnel transport planes (design)   623.7465   TL685.7
Cargo ships, freighters, & tankers (engineering)   623.8245   VM391-395,
                                          VM455-459, VM455 (tankers)
Caribbean, Mexico, & Central America   972   F1201-1392 (Mex.), F1421-2175
Caribbean Sea Area   F2161-2175   972.9, 909.096365
Caricatures, comics, humor (WWI)   940.496-497
Carol I (Bulg.: King, 1881-1914)   DR255
Carpathian Mts. region   DJK71-75
Carpathian Mts. (Uk.)   DK508.9.C37
Carpenters & other naval artisans (U.S.)   VG603
Carriers, Aircraft (as units: SEE 359.3255 for works before 1989)   359.9435
Carriers, Aircraft (design)   623.81255   V874-875
Cartridges   UF740-745   623.455
Cartridges, Naval   VF470   359.8255
Cases (courts of inquiry, naval: U.S.)   VB814.A-Z (PREFER KF #s)
Cases (courts of inquiry: by place: SEE KF7642 etc. for U.S.)   UB867.A-Z
Cases (courts-martial, mil.: by place)   UB857.A-Z (for U.S. SEE KF7642, 7652, etc.)
Cases (courts-martial, naval: besides U.S.: by place)   VB807.A-Z
Cases (courts-martial, naval: U.S.)   VB806 (PREFER KF7646-7650)

Catholic Church (WWI)   D622
Caucasus area (Rus.)   DK511.C1-35   947.9
Caucasus (geog. & travel)   914.79
CAUSES, aims, results (WWI)   D511-520   940.31-2
Causes, aims, results (WWI: gen.) D511   940.311, .314
Causes, aims, results (WWI: misc. countries)   D520.A-Z
Causes, aims, results (WWII: by country)   D742.A-Z   940.534-539
Causes, aims, results (WWII: gen.)   D741   940.5311, 327+
Causes (WWI)   940.311   D511
Causes (WWI: econ.)   940.3113   D635
Causes (WWI: polit. & dipl.)   940.3112   D610-621, D610
Causes (WWI: psychological & social)   940.3114
Causes (WWII: dipl. & polit.)   940.53112   D741-742, D443, D727, D748
Causes (WWII: econ.)   940.53113   D741-742, D720-728, D421, D800
Causes (WWII: gen.)   940.5311   D741 (gen.), D742.A-Z (by country), D720-728
Causes (WWII: psychological & social)   940.53114   D741-742, D726, D421
Causes of war (economic)   355.0273   HB195
Causes of war (political)   355.0272
Causes of war (psychological) 355.0275
Causes of war (sociological)   355.0274
CAVALRY & armor (Asia: gen.)   UE99   357.095
Cavalry & armor (by place)   UE21-124 (SEE ALSO UA for specific units)
Cavalry & armor (collections)   UE7
Cavalry & armor (Eur.: gen.)   UE55   357.094
Cavalry & armor (G.B.: gen.)   UE57   357.0941
Cavalry & armored regiments (U.S.: by #/author)   UA31.1st-
Cavalry (armored & mechanized)   UE
Cavalry (Austria & Austria-Hung.)   UA674
Cavalry (G.B.)   UA654-657   357.10941
Cavalry, Horse   357.1   UE15, UE21-124, UE150+, UA
Cavalry horses (gen.)   UE460
Cavalry installations (horse)   357.187   UE350, UE430-435, UC400-405, UA
Cavalry, Mechanized   357.5   UE147-149, UE150-155 (manuals), UE159,
                  UE160-302 (by place)
Cavalry regiments (Sp.-Am. War: U.S.: by #)   E725.45.1st-
Cavalry (U.S.: Calif. reserves)   UA95
Cavalry (U.S.: N.Y. reserves)   UA365
Cavalry (WWI: Fr.)   D548.4
Cavalry (WWI: G.B.)   D546.54
Cavalry (WWI: official reports)   D529.4
Cavalry (WWI: Prus.)   D532.4
Cavell, Edith (WWI: medical biog.)   D630.C3
Celebrations & commemorations, Military   355.16
Celebrations, memorials, monuments (WWI: misc.)   D665
CEMETERIES & graves, Military   UB390-397
Cemeteries & monuments (WWI)   940.465   D639.D4 (cem's.), D663-680
                  (mon's.), D675.W2 (Tomb of Unkn. Soldier: Wash. D.C.)
Cemeteries & monuments (WWI: G.B. & Eng.)   940.46541-46542   D680.G7, D680.E
Cemeteries & monuments (WWI: U.S.)   940.46573   D670-675,
                  D673.A-W (by state), D675.A-Z (by town)
Cemeteries (naval)   VB300-305   351.86, .866
Censorship, press, publicity (WWI: gen.)   D631 (SEE ALSO D639.P6-7 for
   propaganda)   940.315097

CENTRAL Africa   DT351-364   967
Central America   F1421-1577, F1436   972, 972.8+
Central Asia & Tibet (pubns. to 1950: gen.)   DS785.A5-Z   951.5, 958 (C. Asia)
Central Asia (Rus, Rev., 1917-21)   DK265.8.S63
Central Asian question (19th c.)   D378
Central Asian question (20th c.)   D471-72
Central Asian question (20th c.: by country)   D472.A-Z
Central Asian question (1914-)   D471
Central Europe & Germany (geog. & travel)   914.3   DD21-43, DB21-27, D901-980
Central Powers (WWI: dipl. hist.)   940.324   D511, D458 (Triple Alliance)
Central Powers (WWI: gen. particip.)   940.334   D531
Central Powers (WWI: mil. & naval life & customs)   940.484
Ceremonies, honors, & salutes (navies: gen.)   V310   359.17, .1349
Ceremonies, Military   355.17   U350-355
Chamberlain, Austen, Sir (G.B.: 20th c.)   DA566.9.C43
Chamberlain, Joseph (G.B.: 1837-1901 time period)   DA565.C4
Champagne, Fr. (WWI)   D545.C37
Chaplains, Military (U.S.)   UH23   355.3470973
Chaplains, Naval (U.S.)   VG23   359.3470973
Chaplains or religious officials, Military (gen.)   UH20   355.347
Chaplains or religious officials, Naval   VG20-25
Charges, Demolition (destructors, bangalore torpedoes, etc.: design)   623.4544
                                                                                                                                  UG370, UF860
Charities, refugees, relief work (WWI: gen.)   D637   940.477+
Charities, refugees, relief work (WWII: by country)   D809.A-Z   940.54778+
Charleroi, Bel. (WWI)   D542.C4
Chart use, Nautical (plus other misc. topics on naut. instruments)   VK587
Chasseurs (WWI: Fr.: includes Blue Devils & Chasseurs alpins)   D548.5
Château-Thierry, Battle of (1918)   D545.C4
Chemical & biological weapons (design)   623.4516   UG447-447.6 (chem.),
                                                  UG447 (gen.), UG447.5.A-Z (type gas), UG447.8 (bio.)
Chemical & biological weapons (projectiles etc.)   355.82516   UG447-447.8
Chemical industry (defense)   UA929.95.C5
Chemical warfare   358.34   UG447-447.6
Chemical warfare (inclu. flames)   UG447-447.6   623.4516
Chicago, Ill.   F548   977.311
Chicago, Ill. (1892-1950)   F548.5   977.31103-033
Children & orphans (WWI)   D639.C4   940.53161
Chile   F3051-3285, F3081 (gen.)   983
CHINA   DS701-796+   951
China (1644-1912: Ch'ing Dynasty: gen.: inclu. Sino-Japanese War, 1894-5)   951.03
        (SEE ALSO 952.03 for Sino-Jpn. War of 1894-5)   DS754, DS764.4-767.7
China (1861-1912)   DS761
China (1912-49)   951.04   DS773.83-777.544, DS774
China (1912-28: gen.)   DS776.4   951.041
China (1912-27)   951.041   DS776.4-777.462, DS776.4
China (1913: 2d Rev.)   DS777.2
China (biog.: heads of state)   923.151
China (gen.: pubn. 1801+)   DS735.A3-Z 951
China (mil. capabil.)   355.033251
China (mil. status)   UA835   355.033051, .033251, .033551
China (naval status) VA630-639   359.030951
Chinese-Japanese War (1894-5)   DS764.4-767.7   951.03, 952.031
Chinese Revolution (1911-12)   DS773.32-6   951.03
Chinese troops (WWI: Fr. ops.)   D549.C5

Christchurch, N.Z.   DU430.C5   993.155
Christian Science (WWI)   D639.C5
Christian X (Den.: 1912-47 period: also gen. histories of time) DL255
Chronologies, outlines, syllabi, tables, etc. (20th c.)   D427   909.82, 940.28
Chronologies (U.S.)   E174.5
Chronometers, Nautical (PREFER QB107)   VK575
Church of England (WWI)   D639.C54
Churchill, Randolph Henry Spencer, Lord (G.B.: 1837-1901 era)   DA565.C6
Churchill, Winston Leonard Spencer, Sir (G.B.: 20th c.)   DA566.9.C5
Civic programs (armed forces: U.S.)   UH723
CIVIL defense (countries besides U.S.)   UA929.A-Z
Civil defense (G.B.)   UA929.G7
Civil defense (gen.)   UA926.A3-Z
Civil defense (Sov.Un.)   UA929.S65
Civil defense (U.S.: gen.) UA927
Civil depts. (naval admin.: gen.)   VB170
Civil engineering (navies)   VG590-595 (SEE ALSO VA66.C6+)
Civil liberties (WWI: U.S.)   D570.8.C4
Civilian personnel (mil. admin.: gen.)   UB180   355.23
Civilian personnel (mil. resources) 355.23
Civilian personnel (naval admin.)   VB180-187
Civilian personnel (naval admin.: places besides U.S.)   VB185.A-Z
Civilian personnel (navies)   359.23   VB170-187
CIVILIZATION, customs, social life (20th c.)   D429 (SEE ALSO CB415, GT146)
                                            940.5,320.904,327.09
Civilization, customs, social life (Australia)   DU107
Civilization, customs, social life (Fr.: 20th c.)   DC365
Civilization, customs, social life (Fr.: 1901-)   DC33.7
Civilization, customs, social life (G.B.: 20th c.)   DA566.4
Civilization, customs, social life (Ger.)   DD67
Civilization, customs, social life (Ger.: 1888-1918)   DD228.3
Civilization, customs, social life (It.: 1816-1945)   DG450
Civilization, customs, social life (Japan: 1868+)   DS822.25
Civilization, customs, social life (Palestine & the Jews)   DS112-113
Civilization, customs, social life (Pol.)   DK411
Civilization, customs, social life (Rus.: gen.)   DK32
Civilization, customs, social life (Swit.)   DQ36
Civilization, customs, social life (U.S.: gen.)   E161
Class histories (Royal Naval Coll., Dart.: by date)   V515.K3
Class histories (U.S. Naval Acad.: by date) V415.K4
Classification, Military   UB337
Clemenceau, Georges (Fr.: 1871-1940 era) DC342.8.C6
Clerks & yeomen, Naval (U.S.)   VG903
CLOTHING & equipment, Military   UC460-535
Clothing & equipment, Military (places besides U.S.)   UC465.A-Z
Clothing, equipment, food, & office supplies (navies)   359.81 (SEE ALSO
           .65-66)   VC280-345 (clothing & equip.), VC350-410 (food etc.)
Clothing, food, & equipment (air forces)   358.4165-4166   UG1100-1105,
                           UG1160-1165, UC460-465, UC700-705
Clothing, food, & equipment (mil. admin.)   355.65-66 (PREFER .81)   UC460-535,
                           UC700-735
Clothing, food, camp equipment, etc.   355.81 (SEE ALSO .65-66)   UC460-465+,
                           UC700-705
Clothing, Naval (inclu. related items)   VC280-345

CLUBS & societies (U.S.)   973.06   E172
Clubs, Military (by place, except U.S. & G.B.)   U59.A-Z
Clubs, Military (G.B.)   U58
Clubs, Navy (Am. besides U.S.)   V67.A-Z
Clubs, Navy (besides U.S. & G.B.: by country)   V69.A-Z
Clubs, Navy (G.B.)   V68
Clubs, Officers' (mil.)   UC740-745
Coaling stations, Naval (gen.) V240 (SEE ALSO VA67-750)
Coaling stations, Naval (Ger.) VA517
Coaling stations, Naval (U.S.: by place)   VA74
COAST artillery (gen.)   UF450
Coast artillery (WWI: U.S.)   D570.325
Coast defense, Naval   V200 (SEE ALSO UG410-442) 359.45
Coast defenses   UG448, UG410-442 (specific places)   358.16, 355.45
Coast guard   359.97 (SEE ALSO 363.286 for U.S.C.G.)   VG50-55, VG53 (U.S.)
Coast guard & coast signal service   VG50-55   359.97
Coast guard & coast signal service (places besides U.S.)   VG55.A-Z
Coast guard craft (engineering: ALSO police boats, revenue cutters, etc.)
                                   623.8263   VM397
Coast guard vessels (naval architec.: by type) VM397   623.8245, 359.9732
Coast guard vessels (units)   359.3263   VM397
Coast guns (U.S.: handbooks)   UF563.A7
Coastal artillery (design)   623.417   UF450-455
Coasts, French (gen. & Eng. Ch.: pilot & sailing guides)   VK845
Coasts, French (gen. & Eng. Ch.: tide & current tables)   VK645
Coasts, United States (pilot & sailing guides)   VK993
Coasts, United States (tide & current tables)   VK793
Code signals (merch. marine)   VK391
Cold storage (naval architec. & engin.) VM485
Coldstream Guards (G.B.)   UA651.C6
Coldstream Guards (WWI)   D547.C6
College, school, etc. (WWI: U.S.: by name)   D639.E4.A-Z
Collision & grounding, Nautical (prevention)   623.8884   VK371-378
Collisions & avoidance, High seas   VK371-378
Colonial troops   UA14
Colonial troops (Fr.) UA709
Colonial troops (G.B.: inclu. natives: gen.)   UA668
Colonial troops (Ger.)   UA719
COLONIES, British   DA10-18 (SEE ALSO JV1000-1099 for other collective
                              works & D-F for specific colonies)
Colonies, Dutch   DJ500 (PREFER D-F #s for indiv. colonies or JV2500-2599 for
                              collective)
Colonies, French   DC890 (PREFER D-F for individual colonies or JV1800-1899 for
                              collective works)
Colonies, German   DD905 (PREFER D-F #s for specific colonies or JV2000-2099
                              for collective titles)
Colonies, Portuguese   DP802.A-Z (SEE ALSO D-F for indiv. places & JV4200-
                              4299 for collective)
Colonies (WWI)   D573-578
Colonies (WWI: Fr.) D548.9.C
Colonies (WWI: G.B.: gen.)   D547.A1
Colonies (WWI: gen.)   D573
Colonies (WWI: Ger.: Pacific, Asiatic, & other)   D577-8
Colored troops (WWI: Fr. ops.)   D549.C7

Colors & standards, Military   355.15   UC590-595, U360-365
Colors & standards (navies)   359.15   V300-305
Colors, flags, standards (mil.: U.S.)   UC593-594
Colt machine guns   UF620.C6
Combat & support aircraft   358.4183-4184   UG1240-1245, UG1242.A-Z (by
                type), UG1243 (U.S.), UG633-635, VG90-95 (naval), TL685+
Combat conditions (mil. life)   355.1294
Combat craft, Light (torpedo boats etc.: engineering)   623.8258
                V830-835 (p.t.'s), V880
Combat units (by service field)   355.35   UA
Combat vessels, Small (P.T.'s etc.: units)   359.3258   V830-840, V880-885
Combined ops. (joint: air, army, navy)   U260
Combined ops., Military (2 or more types of forces)   355.46
Combined ops., Naval (2 or more types of forces)   359.46
Command & control systems   UB212
Command control   UB200-245   355.41, .33, .6
Command of ships (naval admin.: gen.)   VB200   359.33, .6, 158.4, 350.00323
Commandeering, compensation, etc. (naval: by country or place)   VC268.A-Z
Commando tactics   U262   355.425
Commemorations & celebrations (navies)   359.16   V310
Commemorations, celebrations, & memorials (WWI: gen.)   940.46   D663-680,
                D663(gen.)
Commencement addresses (U.S. Naval Acad.: by speaker)   V415.F3.A-Z
Commerce, communications, & transport   380-389   HF, HE
Commissioned & warrant officers, Air force   358.41332   UG820-825
Commissioning, draft, examination, registration, other methods of naval personnel
    procurement   359.2236   VB260-275 (enlisted pers.), VB307-315 (officers)
Commissioning, registration, classification, exams, etc. (mil. manpower procure.)
                355.2236   UB330+, U400+
Commissions, Military (gen.)   UB870
Commissions, Peace (WWI: by country)   D647.A3-Z
Commissions, Peace (WWI: U.S.)   D647.U6
COMMUNICATION & transport (mil. resources)   355.27   UA940-945,
                UA929.95.T7, UC10+, UC270-275
Communication & transport (naval resources)   359.27   VC530-580 (trans.),
                VB255, VG70-85, V270
Communication equipment, Military   355.85   UG570-613, UA940-945
Communication equipment, Naval   359.85   VG70-85
Communication routes (except U.S.)   UA955.A-Z
Communication routes (mil. sci.)   UA950-979
Communication routes (U.S.)   UA953-954
Communication systems, Naval (blinkers & electrooptical: design)   623.85614
Communication systems, Naval (flag & semaphore: design)   623.85612
                V280-285, V300-305 (flags), VK385
Communication systems, Naval (pyrotechnical: design)   623.85613
Communication systems, Naval (radio telegraph: design)   623.85642   VG70-75
Communication systems, Naval (visual: design)   623.8561   V280-305

COMMUNICATIONS, Military (U.S.)   UA943-944
Communications, Naval (inclu. radio, radar, wireless telegraph: gen.)   VG76
                                                    623.8564, .734
Communications services, Naval   359.983   VG70-85
Communications, signaling, & cryptography forces (mil. engineers)   358.24
                            UG570-611.5, UA940-945, UB290 (cryp.)
Communications systems, Naval (engineering)   623.856   VG70-85, VB255
Communications technology (mil. engineering)   623.73   UG590-613.5, UG580,
                                            UG590, UG570-575
Compasses (sea, air, or land: inclu. gyro type)   VK577   623.82
Compi`egne, Fr. (WWI)   D545.C7
Compulsory service & exemption (mil.: besides U.S.)   UB345.A-Z
Comrades of the Great War (G.B.)   D546.A12
Conduct & rewards, Military   355.13   U765+
Conduct & rewards, Naval   359.13   VB840-845, VB843 (U.S.)
Conduct, discipline, & reward (air forces: etiquette, enforcement, punishments, etc.)
                            358.4113   UB790-795, UB430-435
Conferences (air forces)   UG623
Conferences & treaties (WWI)   940.3141   D642-647
Conferences (marine navig. & merch. marine)   VK5
Conferences (naval architec.)   VM5
Conferences (naval sci.)   V7   359.0060+, .0063
Conferences (WWI)   D504
Congresses, International (relief, sick, wounded, etc.: misc.: by date)   UH534
Conscientious objectors   355.224   UB341-342
Conscientious objectors (by country)   UB342.A-Z
Conscientious objectors (gen.)   UB341   355.224
Conscription & exemption (mil. service)   UB340-345
Conscription or draft (navies)   359.22363
CONSTRUCTION & maintenance (army engineers)   358.22   UG360-390+, UG15-124
Construction Battalions (U.S. Navy)   VA66.C6-65   359.33+, .90973
Construction Div. (U.S. Army)   UC45
Construction of warships (1860-1900: armored vessels)   V799
Construction of warships (1901+)   V800   623.825, 359.325+
Construction of warships (materials: besides U.S.)   V805.5.A-Z
Construction of warships (materials: gen.)   V805
Construction of warships (materials: U.S.)   V805.3
Construction, Road (mil. engineering)   623.62   UG330
Contract administration (mil.)   355.6211   UC267
Contract administration (navies)   359.6211   VC267
Contracts & claims, Naval (supplies: by place)   VC267.A-Z
Contracts & procurement, Air force (U.S.)   UG1123
Contracts & specifications (naval architec.)   VM295-296
Contracts, Military (supplies)   UC267
Convoy lanes (N. Atlantic: pilot & sailing guides)   VK813
Convoys, Naval   V182   359.4-43
Cookery & diet, Medical (mil.)   UH487
Cookery, Naval   VC370-375   359.81
Cooking (mil.: gen.)   UC720
Coolies (mil. transp.)   UC349
Cooling & heating (naut. craft: engineering)   623.853   VM481
Corporal punishment & flogging (mil. sci.: gen.)   UB810
Corporal punishment (naval)   VB910   364.67, 343.0146, 359.13325
Corvettes & frigates (besides U.S.)   V826.5.A-Z

Cossacks (Rus. Rev., 1917-21)   DK265.9.C62
Cossacks (Ukr.)   DK508.55
Costs, Military   UA17   355.622
Costs, Naval (budgets etc.)   VA20-25
Councils of Defense (WWI: U.S.: by state)   D570.8.C8.A-Z
Counterintelligence (mil.)   355.3433
Counterintelligence, Naval   359.3433
Countermining (defense engineering)   623.36 (SEE ALSO .3)   UG490
Course navigation (marine: inclu. celestial)   623.89   VK549-572+
COURTS-martial, Military   UB855.A-Z (besides U.S., for which SEE KF7625-7659)
Courts-martial, Military (gen.)   UB850   343.0146, 355.13325
Courts-martial, Naval (besides U.S.: by place)   VB805.A-Z
Courts-martial, Naval (gen.)   VB800   343.0146
Courts-martial, Naval (U.S.)   VB803 (PREFER KF7646-7650)
Courts of inquiry, Military (gen.)   UB860
Courts of inquiry, Naval   VB810-815   343.0143
Courts of inquiry, Naval (besides U.S.)   VB815.A-Z
Crimea (Rus.)   DK511.C7   947.717
Crimes, Military (gen.)   UB780   355.1334
Crimes, Naval (gen.)   VB850   359.1334
Crippled sailors, Employment of (PREFER UB360-366)   VB278
CROATIA (inclu. Dalmatia, Istria, Slavonia)   DB361-380, DR1502-1645   949.72
Croatia (1849-1918)   DR1579
Croatia (1914-18: WWI)   DR1582
Croatia & Slavonia (1848-1918)   DB378.5
Croatia (gen.)   DR1510, 1535
Croatia (post-WWI territorial ?s)   D651.C78
CRUISERS (as equip.)   359.8353
Cruisers (besides U.S.)   V820.5.A-Z
Cruisers (G.B.)   V820.5.G7
Cruisers (gen.: tech. info.)   V820   623.8253, .81253, 359.3253
Cruisers (handling)   623.88253   V820-820.5
Cruisers (in units)   359.3253   V820-820.5, VA65.A-Z (U.S.: by name)
Cruisers (naval engineering)   623.8253   V820-820.5
Cruisers (U.S.)   V820.3
Cryptography & ciphers   UB290   358.24
Cryptography (WWI)   D639.C75
Cuba   F1751-1849, F1758, F1776   972.91
Cuba (1899-)   972.9106   F1787-1788
Cuba (post-WWI territorial ?s)   D651.C8
Cuba (Sp.-Am. War, 1898)   E717.1
Cullum's Register (U.S. Mil. Acad.)   U410.H5
Cupolas, Revolving (& other portable gun shelters)   UF660
Curiosities, Military (inclu. collector's hdbks.)   U790
Curiosities, Naval   V745   359.00207, .002
Current & tide tables (Atlantic Ocean: west)   VK759-792
Current & tide tables (gen.: pubn. 1801+)   VK602   623.8949
Current events yrbks. (20th c.: nonserial: includes pictorial titles: by time then
    author)   D410.5
Curzon, George Nathaniel Curzon, 1st Marquis (G.B.: 1837-1901 biog.)
                                         DA565.C95
Customs & laws of war (inclu. treatment of prisoners)   UB485 (SEE ALSO JX)
Customs, Military (gen.)   U750
Customs, Naval (gen.)   V720   359.1
Cyclists, Military   UH30-35

Cylinders, valves, etc. (internal combustion engines: marine engineering)
623.87237   VM769
Cyprus   DS54   956.45
Cyprus (1878-1960: British rule)   956.4503   DS54.8
Czech military ops. (WWII: gen.)   D765.5
CZECHOSLOVAKIA (inclu. Bohemia, Moravia, Slovakia)   DB191-217 (earlier
     titles), DB2000-3150+ (for most titles cataloged after 1979)   943.7
Czechoslovakia   DB2000-2299   943.7+
Czechoslovakia (19th c.: 1815-1918)   943.7024   DB214, DB2176
Czechoslovakia (1801-1976 pubns.)   DB2062
Czechoslovakia (1815-1918: gen.)   DB2176   943.7024
Czechoslovakia (20th c.)   DB215   943.7024-703+
Czechoslovakia (to 1918)   943.702
Czechoslovakia (gen.)   DB2011
Czechoslovakia (geog. & travel)   914.37   DB191 (titles prior to 1979-80), DB2020
Czechoslovakia (mil. status)   UA829.C95   355.0330437
Czechoslovakia (post-WWI territorial ?s)   D651.C9
Czechoslovakian military ops. (WWI)   D539.5.C8
Czechs (in Pol.)   DK4121.5.C9

DALMATIA (20th c.)   DB420
Dalmatia (post-WWI territorial ?s)   D651.D3
Dalmatia (Yug.: local Croatia)   DR1620-1630   949.72
Damage control (warships)   V810   623.888
Danube River Valley (gen.)   DJK76
Danube River Valley (Yug.)   DR1350.D35
Danzig   DD901.D2-29
Danzig (19th-20th c.)   DD901.D28
Danzig, Pol. (1793-1919)   DK4672
Danzig, Pol. (Gdansk)   DK4650-4685
Dardanelles (Tur.)   DR701.D2
Dartmouth (Royal Naval College: Act of incorp.)   V515.A1
Dawes Plan (WWI)   D649.G3.A4-5
DEAD reckoning (naut. navig.)   623.8923   VK572
Dead reckoning (naut. navig.)   VK572   623.8923
Dead, Treatment of   UH570
Dead, wounded, decorated (WWI: lists: Fr.)   D609.F8-82
Dead, wounded, decorated (WWI: lists: G.B.)   D609.G7
Dead, wounded, decorated (WWI: lists: U.S.)   D609.U6-7
Dead (WWI: burial, cemeteries, etc.)   D639.D4
Decorations, Military (gen.)   UB430
DEFENSE & attack plans (U.S.)   UA923   355.033073, .4773
Defense, attack, & siege (gen.: pubn. 1789+)   UG444   355.4+
Defense, Industrial (U.S.)   UA929.6-8
Defenses, Air   UG730-735, UF625 (antiaircraft), UA926+ (civil defense)
     358.4145, .13
Defenses, Air (places besides U.S.)   UG735.A-Z
Defenses, Direct-invasion (barriers, flooding, traps, etc.)   623.31   UG375,
     UG403, UG407-409, UG448 (coast)
Defenses, Fortified (Eur.: gen.)   UG428   623.194, 355.474
Delivery or charge-holding devices (naval ammun.)   359.8251
Demobilization (by country)   UA917.A3-Z
Demobilization (gen.)   UA917.A2   355.29
Demobilization (mil. resources: gen.)   355.29   UA917
Demobilization, Naval (inclu. civil employ.)   VB277   359.29, .1154

Democracy (WWI)   D639.D45
Demolition (mil. engineering)   623.27   UG37
Demolition charges   355.82545
Demolitions (mil. engineering)   UG370   623.4545, 358.23
DENMARK   DL101-291+, DL148(gen.)   948.9
Denmark (20th c.)   DL250   948.905
Denmark (1912-47: time of Christian X)   DL255-257   948.9051
Denmark (1914-18: WWI)   DL256
Denmark & Finland   948.9
Denmark (mil. status)   UA690-699   355.0330489
Denmark (naval status)   VA490-499
Denmark (WWI: dipl. hist.)   D621.S4
Dentistry, Military   UH430-435
Dentistry, Naval   VG280-285
Depression range finder   UF850.D4
Depth charges   359.8254
Depth charges, Naval   VF509   623.45115, .4517
DESCRIPTION & travel (Arabian Penin.: 1801-1950)   DS207
Description & travel (Asia: 1901-50)   DS9   915.044
Description & travel (Australia: 1901-50)   DU104   919.4044
Description & travel (Austria: 1901-45)   DB26
Description & travel (Bel.: 1831-1945)   DH433
Description & travel (Bel. & Holl.: 1901-50)   DH39
Description & travel (Brit. Empire)   DA11
Description & travel (Bulg.: 1879-1950)   DR60
Description & travel (Can.: 1867-1950)   F1015   917.1045-1063
Description & travel (China: 1901-48)   DS710   915.1043-1044
Description & travel (Cuba: 1898-)   F1765   917.291046
Description & travel (Czech.: 1901-45)   DB2020
Description & travel (Den.: 1901-50)   DL118
Description & travel (E. Eur. & Balkan Penin.: 1901-50)   DR15
Description & travel (Eastern Europe: 1901-50)   DJK17
Description & travel (Egypt & Egyp. Sudan: 1901-50)   DT55   916.2044-2045
Description & travel (Ethiopia: 1901-50)   DT378
Description & travel (Europe: 1901-1950)   D921   914.045
Description & travel (Fin.: 1901-44)   DL1015.2
Description & travel (Fr.: 1871-1945)   DC28
Description & travel (G.B.: 1901-45)   DA630   914.1-2, 914.10482
Description & travel (Ger.: 1871-1918)   DD41
Description & travel (It.: 1901-18)   DG428   914.5009
Description & travel (Lux.: to 1945)   DH906
Description & travel (Mid. East, SW. Asia: 1901-50)   DS49   915.6044
Description & travel (Montenegro: 1860-1950)   DR109
Description & travel (N. Africa: 1901-50)   DT165   916.2043
Description & travel (New. Z.: 1840-1950)   DU411   919.31042-310435
Description & travel (Neth.: 1901-45)   DJ39
Description & travel (Palestine: 1901-50)   DS107.3
Description & travel (Paris, Fr.: ALSO gen. hist.)   DC707
Description & travel (Pol.: 1867-1945)   DK407
Description & travel (Pol.: 1867-1944)   DK4070
Description & travel (Rum.: 1866-1950)   DR209
Description & travel (Rus.: 1901-44)   DK27   914.70904
Description & travel (S.Am.: 1811-1950)   F2223
Description & travel (Scan., N. Eur., Fin.: 1901-50)   DL10
Description & travel (Siberia: 1801-1945)   DK755

Description & travel (Swe.: 1901-50)   DL618
Description & travel (Swit.: 1901-50)   DQ24
Description & travel (Tur.: 1901-50)   DR428
Description & travel (Yug.: 1860-1944)   DR309
Description & travel (Yug.: 1901-44)   DR1221   914.971+
Description (Rome, It.: 1861-1950) DG806
Description, travel, civilization, customs (U.S.: 1866-1913)   E168
Description, travel, civilization, customs (U.S.: 1914-45) E169   917.3049
Desert warfare   U167.5.D4
Desertion (mil.)   UB788
Desertion (naval)   VB870-875   359.1334
Designs, drawings, blueprints (naval architec.)   VM297   623.812
DESTROYER escorts (d.e.'s) & destroyers (naval engineering)   623.8254
                                                          V825-825.3
Destroyer escorts (d.e.'s) & destroyers (units)   359.3254   V825-825.5,
                                                          VA65 (U.S.)
Destroyers (as equip.)   359.8354
Destroyers (besides U.S.: by place)   V825.5.A-Z
Destroyers (gen.)   V825   623.8254, .81254, 359.3254
Destroyers (handling)   623.88254   V825-825.5
Destroyers (U.S.)   V825.3
Deterrence   U162.6
Detonators   355.82542
Detonators (design: fuses, percus. caps, primers, etc.)   623.4542   UF780, VF510
Deutschland (submarine: Ger.: WWI)   D592.D4
Dewey, George, Adm. (Sp.-Am. War era)   E714.6.D51
Dewey, Thomas (U.S.: 20th c.)   E748.D48
Dictionaries (20th c. history)   D419   909.8203, 320.03, 320.904
DICTIONARIES & ENCYCLOPEDIAS (air forces & warfare)   UG628   358.4003
Dictionaries & encyclopedias (artillery)   UF9   358.1203
Dictionaries & encyclopedias (history: gen.)   903   D9
Dictionaries & encyclopedias (mil. & naut. engineering)   623.003 (SEE ALSO 603)
                                                          UG144-147
Dictionaries & encyclopedias (mil. sci.)   U24-25   355.003
Dictionaries & encyclopedias (naval forces) 359.003   V23
Dictionaries & encyclopedias (naval sci.: gen.)   V23   359.003
Dictionaries & encyclopedias (U.S.)   E174   973.03
Dictionaries & encyclopedias (WWI: includes 'Times' index and chronology) D510
DICTIONARIES, CHRONOLOGIES, ETC. (Asia)   DS31
Dictionaries, chronologies, etc. (G.B.)   DA34
Dictionaries, chronologies, etc. (Japan)   DS833
Dictionaries, chronologies, etc. (military history: world)   D25.A2
Dictionaries, chronologies, etc. (Palestine, the Jews)   DS114
Dictionaries, chronologies, etc. (Rus.)   DK36
Dictionaries, Military (G.B.)   DA52
Dictionaries, Naval (G.B.)   DA72
Dictionaries (naval sci.: multi-ling.)   V24
Diesel engines (marine engineering)   623.87236   VM770
Diesel, oil, & gas engines (marine engin.)   VM770   623.8723
Dinant, Bel. (WWI)   D542.D4
Dinaric Alps (Yug.)   DR1350.D55

DIPLOMACY (20th c.)   D451-457
Diplomacy (20th c.: gen. special)   D455
Diplomacy (20th c.: gen.)   D453   909.82, 327.3-9, 320.9
DIPLOMACY & POLITICS (Africa: 19th-20th c.: gen.)   DT31.5
Diplomacy & politics (Bel.: gen.)   DH566
Diplomacy & politics (Bulg.)   DR72
Diplomacy & politics (Ger.: 1918-)   DD240-241
Diplomacy & politics (Ger.: gen.)   DD112   320.943, 327.43+
Diplomacy & politics (India, pre-1947 Pak.: 20th c.)   DS448
Diplomacy & politics (Iran)   DS274
Diplomacy & politics (Iraq: gen.)   DS70.95
Diplomacy & politics (It.)   DG491-499
Diplomacy & politics (Japan)   DS840-849   320.952, 327.52
Diplomacy & politics (Lux.)   DH908.5
Diplomacy & politics (Neth.: 1795-20th c.)   DJ147
Diplomacy & politics (Nor.: gen.)   DL458
Diplomacy & politics (Pacific: gen.: inclu. colonial rule)   DU29
Diplomacy & politics (Pol.)   DK418, DK4178.5-4185
Diplomacy & politics (Port.)   DP555-557   320.9469, 327.469+
Diplomacy & politics (Rum.)   DR226
Diplomacy & politics (Rus.-Jpn. War, 1904-5)   DS517.13
Diplomacy & politics (Saudi Arabia: gen.)   DS227
Diplomacy & politics (Serbia: gen.) DR1975
Diplomacy & politics (Sp.)   DP83-86
Diplomacy & politics (Swe.)   DL658-659
Diplomacy & politics (Swe.: 1907-50)   DL867.5   948.5051-2
Diplomacy & politics (Swit.)   DQ68-76   320.9494, 327.4940+
Diplomacy & politics (Swit.: 1798-20th c.)   DQ75
Diplomacy & politics (Syria: gen.)   DS95.5
Diplomacy & politics (Tur.: 1918-)   DR477   327.5610+, 320.9561
Diplomacy & politics (Yug.)   DR326
Diplomacy & politics (Yug.: 1918-45)   DR367.A-Z
DIPLOMACY (Australia: gen.)   DU113   327.94
Diplomacy (Brazil: gen.)   F2523   327.81
Diplomacy (Can.: gen.)   F1029   327.71
Diplomacy (Chile: gen.)   F3083
Diplomacy (China: gen.)   DS740.4   327.51
Diplomacy (Den.: gen.)   DL159
Diplomacy (Fin.: gen.)   DL1046   327.4897
Diplomacy (Fr.: gen.)   DC55
Diplomacy (G.B.: gen.)   DA45   327.41+
Diplomacy (Ger.: 1888-1918: gen.)   DD228.6   327.43+
Diplomacy (Greece: gen.)   DF785
Diplomacy (Hung.: gen.)   DB926
Diplomacy (Ire.: 20th c.)   DA964.A-Z
Diplomacy (Japan: gen.)   DS845   327.52
Diplomacy (Latin Am.: gen.)   F1415   327.8
Diplomacy (Liech.: gen.)   DB893
Diplomacy (Mex.: gen.)   F1228
Diplomacy (Rus.)   DK65-69
Diplomacy (Sp.: 1814-20th c.) DP85.8
Diplomacy (U.S.: gen.)   E183.7   327.73
Diplomacy (Ukr.: gen.)   DK508.56

DIPLOMACY (WWI)   D610-621   940.32
Diplomacy (WWI: Australia)   940.32294   D621.A
Diplomacy (WWI: Fr.)   940.32244   D621.F, D516
Diplomacy (WWI: G.B.)   940.32241-32242   D621.G7, D610-611, D517
Diplomacy (WWI: gen.)   D610
Diplomacy (WWI: Ger. & Austria)   940.32443   D621.G or .A, D515 (Ger.),
                                                   D512 (Austria)
Diplomacy (WWI: Switz.)   940.325494   D621.S
Diplomacy (WWI: Turkey)   940.324561   D621.T8, D520.T8, D463, D469.T8
Diplomacy (WWI: U.S.)   940.32273   D619
Diplomacy (WWII)   D748-754   940.532+, .5322-5325, 327.+
Diplomatic history (WWI)   940.32   D610-621, D610 (gen.)
Diplomatic history (WWI: misc. countries)   D621.A-Z
Directories (naval architec.)   VM12
Dirigibles   629.13324
Dirigibles (Ger.)   UG1225.G3
Dirigibles (mil. engineering)   623.743   TL659, UG1220-1225
Dirigibles (places outside U.S.)   UG1225.A-Z
Disability benefits, pensions, etc. (naval admin.: U.S.)   VB283
Disabled American Veterans of the World War (WWI)   D570.A15.D5
Disabled veterans (U.S.: rehab.)   UB363-364
Disarmament (WWI: Ger.)   D650.D5
Disasters, Submarine   VK1265
Discharge, promotion, recruitment, enlistment (mil. sci.: countries besides U.S.)
                                                   UB325.A-Z
Discharge, promotion, recruitment, enlistment (naval sci.: places besides U.S.)
                                                   VB265.A-Z
Discharge, retirement, other termination (mil.)   355.114   UB320+
Discipline & conduct, Military (regulation)   355.133
Discipline & enforcement (naval conduct)   359.1332   VB850-855, VB890-925
Discipline, Military (U.S.)   UB793 (SEE ALSO KF7590)
Discipline, Naval (besides U.S.)   VB845.A-Z
Discipline, Naval (G.B.)   VB845.G7
Discipline, Naval (U.S.)   VB843   359.130973
Disinfection & fumigation (naval engin.)   VM483
Dispensaries, Naval   VG270-275
Disraeli, Benjamin, 1st Earl of Beaconsfield (G.B.: 19th c.: Prime Min.)   DA564.B3
Distance finders (inclu. tables etc.)   VK579
District of Columbia   975.3   F191-205, F194
District of Columbia (geog. & travel)   917.53   F192.3, F194, F199
District of Columbia (WWI)   D570.85.D6
Diving (marine engin.)   VM975-989 (SEE GV840.S78 for skindiving),
                                   VM981 (gen.)   627.72 (gen.)
Diving (marine engin.: hist.)   VM977   627.7209, 623.8257 (subs.), 359.3257
                                   (subs.-naval ops.), 797.23 (scuba)
Diving (marine engin.: special types)   VM985-989
Divisions (U.S. Army: by place)   UA27.A-Z
Divisions (U.S.: by #/author)   UA27.5.1st-
Divisions (WWI: Fr.)   D548.2
Divisions (WWI: U.S.)   D570.3.A-Z (newer bks. may use A1 or #'s like D570.27)
Dnepropetrovsk (Uk.)   DK508.9.D64
Documentary films, slides, etc. (WWI: catalogs)   D522.22

Dog fighting, bombing, other air tactics (countries besides U.S.)   UG705.A-Z
Dogs, Military   UH100
Dogs (mil. transp.)   UC355 (SEE ALSO UH100)   355.424
Dogs (WWI)   D639.D6
Don River Valley (Rus.)   DK511.D7
Downing St. (London, Eng.: No. 10)   DA687.D7
Draft & exemption (mil.: Japan)   UB345.J3
Draft & exemption (mil.: U.S.)   UB343-344   355.2236306073
Draft, Military   355.22363   UB340-345, UB343 (U.S.)
Draftsmen & surveyors, Naval (gen.)   VG920
Dreams (WWI)   D639.D7
Dresden (cruiser: WWI)   D582.D8
Drill camps, instruction bases, maneuver grounds (gen.)   U290
Drill camps, maneuver grounds, etc. (U.S.: by name)   U294.5.A-Z
Drill regulations, Marine (U.S.)   VE160-162
Drill regulations, Naval (U.S. reserves)   VD161
DRILLS, maneuvers, & tactics (artillery: by place)   UF160-302
Drills, Marine (Eur.)   VE215-269
Drills, Marine (G.B.)   VE234
Drills, Marine (Ger.)   VE231
DRILLS, NAVAL (Asia)   VD270-280
Drills, Naval (Australia)   VD295   359.50994
Drills, Naval (Eur.)   VD215-269
Drills, Naval (G.B.)   VD234   359.50941
Drills, Naval (Ger.)   VD231   359.50943
Drills, Naval (New Z.)   VD298
DRILLS, NAVAL ORDNANCE (Asia)   VF270-280
Drills, Naval ordnance (Australia)   VF295
Drills, Naval ordnance (Eur.)   VF215-269
Drills, Naval ordnance (Fr.)   VF228
Drills, Naval ordnance (G.B.)   VF234
Drills, Naval ordnance (Ger.)   VF231
Drills, Naval ordnance (Rus.)   VF252
Drills, Naval ordnance (U.S.: gen.)   VF160
Drills, Naval (Rus.)   VD252
Drills, Naval (U.S.)   VD160-162
Drills, tactics, & maneuvers (armor & cavalry: Eur.)   UE215-269
Drills, tactics, & maneuvers (infantry: U.S.)   UD160-162
Dry docks, shipyards, etc. (naval engineering)   623.83   VM301
Dutch East Indies & Indonesia   DS611-649

EAST Africa   DT365-469   967.6, 963
East Africa (to 1960)   DT431
East Africa (1884-1960: gen.)   DT365.7   967.6
East Africa (Uganda & Kenya)   967.6   DT421-435+ (newer titles), DT431
East African islands   DT469.A-Z
East Anglia, Eng. (WWI)   D547.8.E3
East Coast (U.S.: pilot & sailing guides)   VK981
East Coast (U.S.: tide & current tables)   VK781   623.8949091634
EASTERN Europe (1815-1918)   DJK48
Eastern Europe & Balkan Peninsula   DR (SEE DJK for gen. bks. on E. Eur. after
                                                                        about 1977-78)   949.6-8
Eastern Europe   DR (pubns. prior to 1978 & specific countries), DJK (titles after
                                     about 1977-78)   943.7-943.9, 947, 947.8, 949.6-949.84
Eastern Front (WWI)   D550-569

Eastern question (1801-1914/20)   D371-379   949, 320.956, 327.41-42
Eastern question (20th c.)   D461-475   320.95, 956.03, 325.342
Eastern question (20th c.: by country)   D469.A-Z
Eastern question (20th c.: gen.)   D463
Eastern question (general: 19th c.)   D374
Economic aspects (Rus. Rev., 1917-21)   DK265.9.E2
Economic factors of war   355.023 (PREFER 355.02)   HB195, HC65, JX1953
Economic matters (WWI: commerce, finance, mail)   D635 (SEE ALSO HC56,
                                                      HF3030, HJ236, HJ8011)

Economics   330-339   HB-HJ
Edinburgh, Scot.   941.34   DA890.E2-4
Education   L   370-379
Education & employment of veterans (U.S.)   UB357-358   355.1150973
Education & training, Air force   UG637-639   358.415+
Education & training, Military (U.S.)   355.50973
EDUCATION, MILITARY   U400-714   355.07
Education, Military (Asia)   U635-660
Education, Military (Australia)   U700-704   355.0071094
Education, Military (Austria-Hung.: gen.)   U550
Education, Military (Balkan States)   U625
Education, Military (Eur.)   U505-630   355.007104+
Education, Military (Fr.)   U565-569
Education, Military (G.B.)   U510-549.3
Education, Military (gen.: pubns. 1801+)   U405
Education, Military (Ger.)   U570-574   355.0071043
Education, Military (It.)   U585-589
Education, Military (Japan)   U650-654   355.0071052
Education, Military (New Z.)   U705-709
Education, Military (Rus.)   U600-604   355.0071047
Education, Military (Tur.)   U620-624
Education, Military (U.S.)   U407-439
EDUCATION, NAVAL   V400-695
Education, Naval (Asia)   V625-650
Education, Naval (Australia)   V690-694   359.007094
Education, Naval (Can.)   V440-444
Education, Naval (Eur.)   V500-623
Education, Naval (Fr.)   V565-569
Education, Naval (G.B.)   V510-530
Education, Naval (Ger.)   V570-574
Education, Naval (hist.: 20th c.)   V409
Education, Naval (hist.: gen.)   V401
Education, Naval (It.)   V585-589
Education, Naval (Japan)   V640-644
Education, Naval (New Z.)   V694.1-5
Education, Naval (Rus.)   V600-604
Education, Naval (Turkey)   V650.T9
Education, Naval (U.S.)   V411-438
EDUCATION (WWI)   D639.E2-6
Education (WWI: G.B.)   D639.E5-53
Education (WWI: gen.)   D639.E2
Education (WWI: Ger.)   D639.E47
Education (WWI: U.S.)   D639.E3-42
Education (WWI: U.S.: gen.: inclu. Student Army Training Corps)   D639.E3
Edward VII (G.B.: King: 1901-1910)   DA567

EGYPT   UA865   355.033062
Egypt (1879-1952)   DT107   962.03-052
Egypt (1882-1922: Brit. protec.)   962.04   DT107-107.8, DT107 (gen.)
Egypt (1892-1914: Abbas II era)   DT107.6
Egypt (1914-17: Hussein Kamil)   DT107.7   962.04
Egypt (1917-36: Fuad I)   DT107.8   962.04-051
Egypt & Sudan   962   DT43-159
Egypt & Sudan (geog. & travel)   916.2   DT55 (Egypt), DT124
Egypt & the Egyptian Sudan   DT43-154   962
Egypt (gen.)   DT43-107, DT77, DT115-154   962
Egypt (naval status)   VA690   359.030962
Egypt (WWI)   D568.2
Egyptian naval ops. (WWI)   D586
Egyptian Sudan (inclu. Anglo-Egyptian)   DT108, DT154.1-159 (newer titles)   962.4
Eire (Republic of Ireland)   941.7   DA963
ELECTRIC engines (marine engineering)   623.8726   VM773
Electric lighting (naut. craft: engineering)   623.852   VM491-493
Electric plants (defense)   UA929.95.E4
Electric propulsion (marine engin.)   VM773   623.8726
Electrical engineering (mil.)   623.76   UG480, VM471-479
Electrical systems (naut. craft: engineering)   623.8503   VM471-475
Electricians, Military   UG560-565
Electricity (mil. uses)   UG480   623.76
Electricity (naval architec. & engin.)   VM471-479   623.8503, .852, .8726
Electricity (naval architec. & engin.: U.S. Navy)   VM473
Elephant batteries   UF430
Employees, Civilian (naval admin.: U.S.)   VB183
Employment & education of veterans (countries except U.S.)   UB359.A-Z
Employment for crippled soldiers & sailors   UB360-366 (PREFER), UH560
                                                    355.1154-1156
Encampment & field training (mil.)   355.544   U180-185, UG400-409+
Encampments   355.412   U180-185
Encampments   U180-185   355.412
Encyclopedias & dictionaries (G.B.)   941.003   DA34
Encyclopedias & dictionaries (U.S.)   973.03   E174
Encyclopedias & dictionaries (WWI)   940.4003   D510, D521, D523
Enforcement (naval conduct)   359.13323
Engine auxiliaries (marine engineering: boilers, blowers, pumps, propellers, etc.)
                623.873   VM753-757 (propellers), VM741-750 (boilers),
                VM821 (pumps), VM781+
Engine fuels, Marine   623.874   VM779
Engineer forces, Army   358.2   UG15, UG21-124 (by place), UG23 (U.S.),
                UG500-620
ENGINEERING   620   T
Engineering facilities, Naval   359.74   VM621-724, VM623 (U.S.), VC590-595
Engineering installations, Military   355.74
Engineering ops. (WWI)   D607.3
Engineering services (air forces)   358.47
Engineering services, Naval   359.982
Engineering systems (naut. craft: mech., electric, water, etc.)   623.85   VM471-505
Engineering, Camouflage (mil.)   623.77   UG449, UG1240-1245 (air forces),
                V215 (ships)
Engineering, Civil (navies: gen.)   VG590
Engineering, Defense   623.3   UG400-442

Engineering, Marine (gen.)   VM600-605   623.87
Engineering, Marine (hist.: by place)   VM621-724
ENGINEERING, MILITARY   UG1-620
Engineering, Military & nautical   623   UG, VM (naval), V, UG15 (mil.: gen.),
                    UG21-124 (mil.: by place), UG23 (U.S.), V750-895 (vessels)
Engineering, Military & nautical (construction)   623.047   UG460
Engineering, Military & nautical (mechanical)   623.045   UG450
Engineering, Military & nautical (optical)   623.042   UG476, UG487
Engineering, Military (Asia)   UG99-113
Engineering, Military (Australia + New Z.)   UG121-122.5
Engineering, Military (by country or area)   UG21-124
Engineering, Military (essays & lectures)   UG156
Engineering, Military (Eur.)   UG55-95   358.2094
Engineering, Military (Fr.)   UG71
Engineering, Military (G.B.)   UG57
Engineering, Military (gen. hist.)   UG15   358.2, .209
Engineering, Military (gen.: pubn. 1801+)   UG145
Engineering, Military (Ger.)   UG73
Engineering, Military (Japan)   UG105
Engineering, Military (Rus.: Eur.)   UG85
Engineering, Military (U.S.)   UG23-25   358.20973
Engineers (WWI: G.B.)   D546.55
Engineers (WWI: official reports)   D529.7
Engineers (WWI: Prus.)   D532.8
Engineers (WWI: U.S.)   D570.309-.31
Engines, Aircraft   629.134352-134354+
Engines, Marine (gen.)   VM731   623.872
Engines, Marine (types: design)   623.872   VM731-779, VM731
ENGLAND   DA20-690
England (1485-)   DA300
England (1702-)   DA470
England (19th. c.)   DA530
England (1837-1901: Queen Victoria)   DA550-565   941.08
England (20th c.: misc. overall)   DA566-566.9
England (1901-10: King Edward VII)   DA567-570   941.082
England (1910-36)   942.083   DA576
England (1910-36: King George V)   DA573-578   941.083
England & Wales   942   DA20-745, DA20-690 (Eng.), DA700-45 (Wales)
England (gen.)   DA30   941, 942
England (geog. & travel)   914.2   DA600-668, DA600 (gen.), DA630 (1901-45)
English Channel (tide & current tables)   VK639-644
English literature   PR 820-829
English poetry, satire, etc. (WWI)   D526.2 (PREFER PR, PS)
ENLISTED personnel & non-coms, Air force   358.41338   UG820-825
Enlisted personnel & non-coms, Naval   359.338   VB260-275
Enlisted personnel (inclu. non-coms)   355.338   UB320, U765+
Enlisted personnel, Naval (G.B.: by city or other div.)   VD64.A-Z
Enlisted personnel, Naval (gen.: nonperiodical collections)   VD7
Enlisted personnel (naval sci.: Ger.: inclu. enlistment, promotion, etc.) VB265.G3
                                                               359.2230943
Enlisted personnel (naval sci.: inclu. recruitment, enlistment, promotion, discharge,
    etc.)   VB260-275
Enlisted personnel, Naval (U.S.: by city)   VD25.A-Z

Enlistment, Military   355.22362   UB320-325, UB323 (U.S.)
Enlistment, recruiting, etc. (air forces: gen.)   UG880
Enlistment, recruitment, promotion, discharge (mil. sci.: U.S)   UB323   355.20973
Enlistment, recruitment, promotion, discharge (Naval sci.: U.S.: by region or state)
                                                                VB264.A-Z

Entanglements & misc. fortification   UG407
Entertainment & recreation for soldiers (WWI)   D639.E8
Envelopment (mil. sci.)   U167.5.E57
Enver Pasha (Tur.: 1909- period: ALSO '...Pasa')   DR592.E55
EQUIPMENT & clothing, Military (gen.)   UC460
Equipment, Air force (gen.: planes, bombs, etc.: U.S.)   UG1203   358.4180973
EQUIPMENT & SUPPLIES (air force)   UG1100-1425
Equipment & supplies (horse cavalry)   357.188   UE440-445, UC260-267
Equipment & supplies (infantry)   356.186   UD380+, UC260-267, UC460+
Equipment & supplies, Military   355.8   U800+, UC260-267
Equipment & supplies, Naval (develop., procure., issue, util., shipping, etc.)
            359.8   VC, VF, VC10, VC20-258, VC20 (U.S.: gen.),
            VC260-267, VF145,   VF21-124, VF23 (ordnance: U.S.),
            VF57 (G.B.), VF73 (Ger.), VF105 (Japan), VF71 (Fr.)
Equipment & supplies (naval submarines)   359.938
Equipment & supply procurement (air forces)   358.416212 UG1120-1125,
                                                        UG1123 (U.S.)
Equipment, fuel, supplies, etc. (ships)   VC270-279
Equipment, Infantry   UD370-375
Equipment, Lifesaving (marine navig.: gen.)   VK1460-1461   623.865
Equipment (marines)   VE350-355
Equipment, Medical corps   UH510-515
Equipment, Military (countries except U.S.)   UC525.A-Z
Equipment, Military (gen.)   UC520   355.8
Equipment, Military (special: by name)   UC529.A-Z
Equipment, Naval artillery (places other than U.S.)   VF325.A-Z
Equipment, Naval (misc.)   V980
Equipment (naval seamen)   VD350-355
Equipment (submarine boats: special)   VM367.A-Z
ESPIONAGE & spies (mil. admin.)   UB270-271
Espionage & spies (naval admin.)   VB250   359.3432-3433
Espionage & unconventional warfare (mil.)   355.343 (SEE ALSO 327.12)
                                                UB250-290
Espionage (by country responsible)   UB271.A-Z (SEE D-F #s for other cases
                                        in particular countries or particular wars)
Espionage, conspiracies, propaganda in U.S. (WWI: German)   D619.3
Espionage, conspiracy, propaganda in U.S. (WWII)   D753.3
Espionage in U.S. (WWI: Ger.: by case)   D619.5.A-Z
Espionage, secret service, spies (WWI)   D639.S7-8
Espionage (U.S.: gen.)   UB271.U6   327.120973
Estonia   DK511.E4-8, DK503 (later pubns.)   947.41
Estonia (1800-1918)   DK503.73   947.41
Estonia (post-WWI territorial ?s)   D651.E3 or 8
Ethics, prophecy, religious questions (WWI)   D524
Ethiopia (Abyssinia)   963   DT371-398, DT381
Ethiopia (1889-1928: inclu. 1895-6 conflict w. Italy)   DT387-387.6   963.043-054
Ethiopia (1896-1941 & 20th c.)   963.05   DT386-387.9, DT386
Ethiopia (geog. & travel)   916.3   DT378
Ethiopia (mil. status) UA860   355.033063
Ethnic or racial groups (WWI)   940.31503

193

FALKLAND Islands   F3031   997.11
Falkland Islands, Battle of (1914)   D582.F2
Falkland Islands (S. Atl. Ocean: G.B.)   997.1   F3031
Far East (1904-45: inclu. Far Eastern question)   DS518 (SEE ALSO DU29)
                                                 327.5, 950.41
FAR EASTERN question (China: 1861-1945)   DS740.63
Far Eastern question (France)   DS518.2
Far Eastern question (G.B.)   DS518.4
Far Eastern question (Ger.)   DS518.3
Far Eastern question (misc. countries)   DS518.9.A-Z (SEE DS845 for Japan,
                                                 DS740.63 for China)
Far Eastern question (Netherlands)   DS518.5
Far Eastern question (Port.)   DS518.6
Far Eastern question (Russia)   DS518.7
Far Eastern question (U.S.)   DS518.8
Fascism (1919-39)   D726.5 (SEE ALSO JC481 and 'D' numbers for Italy, Ger.)
                          320.533, 321.94094
Fashion (WWI)   D639.F3
Ferdinand (Rum.: King, 1914-27: also works on era)   DR261
Ferrying (mil. engineering)   UG385
FIELD & rail artillery (design)   623.412   UF400-405, UF490-495 (rail)
Field artillery (gen.)   UF400   358.12
Field artillery (places besides U.S.)   UF405.A-Z
Field artillery (U.S.: N.Y. reserves: also gen. artil.)   UA366
Field artillery (WWI: U.S.)   D570.32
Field engineering (mil.)   UG360-390
Field engineering (misc. topics)   UG390
Field fortification   UG403
Field kits & equip. (mil.)   UC540-585
Field kits & equip. (mil.: U.S.)   UC543-544
Field ovens (mil.)   UC730
Field service, Infantry   UD440-445
Field service (mil. sci.)   U170-175
Fighter planes   UG1242.F5   623.7464, 358.43
Figureheads, ornaments, decorations on ships   VM308
Films, lantern slides, etc.: (WWI)   D527.3
Finances & supplies (air force admin.)   358.4162   UG1100-1105, UG1100-1425
Financial administration (mil.)   355.622   UB150-155, UC263-267, UA21-876,
                                                 UA910-915
Financial administration (navies)   359.622   VC20-258, VC500-505, VA
FINLAND   DK445-465 (pre-1970 pubns.), DL1002-1180+ (pubns. from around
                 1970 on)   947.1, 948.97 (works after 1970 or so)
Finland (1809-1917: Russian control)   DK458, DL1065   948.9702
Finland (20th c.)   DL1066.5   948.9703
Finland (20th c.: inclu. Revolution, 1917-18)   DK459   948.9703
Finland (1917-)   948.9703   DK459, DL1066.5
Finland (1917-39)   948.97031   DK459, DL1084
Finland (gen.)   DL1032   948.97
Finland (geog. & travel)   914.897 (SEE ALSO .71 for earlier works)
                          DK450, DL1015.2 (books cataloged after 1969-70)

FIRE control, Artillery (inclu. instruments)   UF848-856
Fire control, Naval gunnery (inclu. instruments)   VF520-530
Fire drills, Naval (Fr.: also quarter, watch, station, etc.)   VD228
Fire-fighting equipment, Airport   629.1368
Fire-fighting (mil. airfields)   623.668
Fire-fighting, Nautical (technology) 623.8886   VK1258
Firearms, Portable (design)   623.442   UG520-525, UD380-385+
Fires & shipwrecks (gen.)   VK1250   910.453
Fires (mil. qtrs.)   UC425
Fires, Nautical (by name of ship)   VK1257.A-Z
FIRING & fire control (mil. engineering)   623.558   UF848-856, UF848 (gen.),
               UF850.A-Z (range finders), VF520-530 (naval)
Firing (armor & cavalry)   UE400-405
Firing devices (primers, percussion caps, etc.)   UF780
Firing instructions, Artillery   UF670-675
Firing instructions, Naval   VF450-455
Firing or sharpshooting (infantry: gen.)   UD330
Firing tests (artillery)   UF810
First-aid handbooks, Naval   VG466
First-aid manuals, Soldiers'   UH396 (SEE ALSO UH393-395)
First World War (econ., polit., social hist.)   940.31   D443, D453, D511-523, D610
Fisher, John Arbuthnot Fisher, Baron (G.B.: 20th c. naval biog.)   DA89.1.F5
Fiume & Italy (post-WWI territorial ?s: gen.)   D651.I6
Flag officers, Naval (above captain)   359.331   VB190, VB200-205, VB310-315
Flag signals (merch. marine)   VK385
Flags, colors, standards (mil.)   UC590-595
Flags, Naval & marine (besides U.S.)   V305.A-Z
Flags, Naval & marine (gen.)   V300 (SEE ALSO VK385)   359.15
Flame & chemical weapons (gen.)   UG447 358.34
Flame throwers, tear-gas devices, smoke mortars, other chemical weapons (design)
                           623.445   UG447-447.5
Flanders area (Bel.)   DH801.F4-49
Fleets, squadrons, etc. (G.B.: by name)   VA457.A-Z 359.310941
Fleets, squadrons, etc. (Ger.: by name)   VA514.A-Z 359.310943
Fleets, squadrons, etc. (U.S. Navy: by name)   VA63.A-Z   359.310973
Fliers (biog.)   629.13092
Flight (gen. hist.)   629.1309
Flight training, Air force (U.S.: gen.: inclu. other educ.)   UG638 358.4150973
Flights, groups, squadrons, wings, etc. (naval aviation)   359.9434
Floating batteries   V890
Flogging & corp. punish. (countries besides U.S.)   UB815.A-Z
Florence, It.   DG760
Florida   F306-320, F311   975.9
Florida (WWI)   D570.85.F5-51
Flying   629.1325
Foch, Ferdinand (Fr.: 1871-1940 era)   DC342.8.F6
Fog signals (merch. marine)   VK383
Foghorns, beacons, lighthouses, etc. (hist's.)   VK1015
Food, clothing, & equipment (naval admin.)   359.65-66 (SEE ALSO .81)
        VC280-285+, VC283 (clothing: U.S.), VC350-355 (food etc.), VC353 (U.S.)
Food, cooking, water, etc.   UC700-780   355.65-66, .81
Foot forces warfare   356   UD, U14-43, UA
Ford Peace Expedition (WWI)   D613.5
Forecaster, Weather (navies: U.S.)   VG613

Foreign legions   355.359
Foreign participation (Rus. Rev., 1917-21: by country)   DK265.9.F52.A-Z
FOREIGN RELNS. & politics (Fr.: 20th c.)   DC369   944.08
Foreign relns. & politics (G.B.: 20th c.)   DA566.7
Foreign relns. & politics (Ger.: 1871-1918)   DD221
Foreign relns. & politics (Scan., N. Eur., Fin.: gen.)   DL55
Foreign relns. (Africa-Fr.: 19th-20th c.)   DT33.5
Foreign relns. (Africa-G.B.: 19th-20th c.)   DT32.5   960.23-3, 325.3+
Foreign relns. (Africa-Ger.: 19th-20th c.)   DT34.5
Foreign relns. (Africa-It.: 19th-20th c.)   DT35.5
Foreign relns. (Asia-particular other areas or countries)   DS33.4.A-Z
Foreign relns. (Australia-G.B.)   DU113.5.G7   327.94041
Foreign relns. (Australia-Japan)   DU113.5.J3   327.94052
Foreign relns. (Australia-other specific lands)   DU113.5.A-Z   327.940+
Foreign relns. (Australia-U.S.)   DU113.5.U6-7   327.94073
Foreign relns. (Austria: by other country)   DB49.A-Z
Foreign relns. (Bel.-Fr.)   DH569.F8
Foreign relns. (Bel.-Ger.)   DH569.G3
Foreign relns. (Bel.: by country)   DH569.A-Z
Foreign relns. (Bulg.-Ger.)   DR73.G3   327.4977043
Foreign relns. (Bulg.-Rus.)   DR73.R9
Foreign relns. (Bulg.-specific countries)   DR73.A-Z
FOREIGN RELNS. (CAN.-Fr.)   F1029.5.F8   327.71044
Foreign relns. (Can.-G.B.)   F1029.5.G7 327.71041
Foreign relns. (Can.-Ger.) F1029.5.G3 327.71043
Foreign relns. (Can.-It.)   F1029.5.I8
Foreign relns. (Can.-other places) F1029.5.A-Z   327.710+
Foreign relns. (Can.-Rus.)   F1029.5.R9   327.71047
Foreign relns. (Can.-U.S.)   F1029.5.U6-7   327.71073
Foreign relns. (Chile-Japan)   F3083.5.J3
Foreign relns. (Chile-U.S.)   F3083.5.U6-7
FOREIGN RELNS. (CHINA: 20th c. & 1912-49)   DS775.8
Foreign relns. (China & other lands: by name)   DS740.5.A-Z   327.510+
Foreign relns. (China-G.B.)   DS740.5.G5-6
Foreign relns. (China-Ger.)   DS740.5.G2-3   327.51043
Foreign relns. (China-Hong Kong)   DS740.5.G6.H6
Foreign relns. (China-Japan)   DS740.5.G6.J3   327.51052
Foreign relns. (China-Sov. Un.)   DS740.5.S65   327.51047
Foreign relns. (China-U.S.)   DS740.5.U6-7 (PREFER E183.8.C5)   327.51073
Foreign relns. (Cuba-U.S.)   F1776.3.U6-7
Foreign relns. (Czech.: 1918-: gen.)   DB2189
Foreign relns. (Czech.: by country)   DB2078.A-Z
Foreign relns. (Den.-G.B.)   DL159.5.G7
Foreign relns. (Den.-Ger.)   DL159.5.G3
Foreign relns. (Den.-other lands)   DL159.5.A-Z
Foreign relns. (Eastern Europe)   DJK43-44
Foreign relns. (Egypt & various countries)   DT82.5.A-Z 327.620+
Foreign relns. (Egypt-G.B.)   DT82.5.G7   327.62041
Foreign relns. (Egypt-Ger.)   DT82.5.G3   327.62043
Foreign relns. (Fin. & other partic. lands)   DL1048.A-Z
Foreign relns. (Fin.-Ger.)   DL1048.G3
Foreign relns. (Fin.-Rus.)   DL1048.R9
Foreign relns. (Fin.-Sov. Un.)   DL1048.S65

```
FOREIGN RELNS. (FR.: 19th-20th c.)    DC58
Foreign relns. (Fr.-G.B.)          DC59.8.G7        327.44041
Foreign relns. (Fr.-Ger.)          DC59.8.G3        327.44043
Foreign relns. (Fr.-Rus.)          DC59.8.R9
Foreign relns. (Fr.-Sov.Un.)       DC59.8.S65
Foreign relns. (Fr.: by country)       DC59.8.A-Z  327.440+
Foreign relns. (G.B.-Fr.)          DA47.1          327.41044
Foreign relns. (G.B.-Ger.)         DA47.2          327.41043
Foreign relns. (G.B.-misc. countries: SEE E183.8 for U.S.)     DA47.9.A-Z
Foreign relns. (G.B.-other countries)     DA47     327.410+
Foreign relns. (G.B.-Rus.)         DA47.65         327.41047
FOREIGN RELNS. (GER.: 19th-20th c.)       DD117   327.43+
Foreign relns. (Ger.:1888-1918: by country) DD228.7.A-Z
Foreign relns. (Ger.: 1918-: by country) DD241.A-Z
Foreign relns. (Ger.: by country)    DD120.A-Z     327.430+
Foreign relns. (Ger.-Fr.)          DD120.F8        327.43044
Foreign relns. (Ger.-Fr.: 1888-1918)    DD228.7.F8
Foreign relns. (Ger.-Fr.: 1918-)     DD241.F8
Foreign relns. (Ger.-G.B.)         DD120.G7        327.43041
Foreign relns. (Ger.-G.B.: 1888-1918)   DD228.7.G7
Foreign relns. (Ger.-G.B.: 1918-)    DD241.G7
Foreign relns. (Ger.-Ire.)         DD120.I6
Foreign relns. (Ger.-Ire.: 1918-)    DD241.I6
Foreign relns. (Ger.-It.)          DD120.I8
Foreign relns. (Ger.-It.: 1918-)     DD241.I8
Foreign relns. (Ger.-Japan)        DD120.J3        327.43052
Foreign relns. (Ger.-Japan: 1918-)   DD241.J3
Foreign relns. (Ger.-Pol.: 1918-)    DD241.P7
Foreign relns. (Ger.-Rus.)         DD120.R9            327.43047
Foreign relns. (Ger.-Rus.: 1888-1918)   DD228.7.R8-9
Foreign relns. (Ger.-Rus.: 1918-)    DD241.R9
Foreign relns. (Ger.-Sov. Un.)     DD120.S65
Foreign relns. (Ger.-U.S.)         DD120.U6-7
Foreign relns. (Ger.-U.S.: 1888-1918)   DD228.7.U6-7
Foreign relns. (Ger.-U.S.: 1918-)   DD241.U6-69+
Foreign relns. (Greece: by country)      DF787.A-Z
Foreign relns. (Greece-G.B.)       DF787.G7
Foreign relns. (Greece-Ger.)       DF787.G3
Foreign relns. (Greece-It.)        DF787.I8
Foreign relns. (Hung.-Ger.)        DB926.3.G3
Foreign relns. (Hung.-other lands)    DB926.3.A-Z
Foreign relns. (Hung.-Sov. Un.)       DB926.3.S65
Foreign relns. (Iran-Ger.)         DS274.2.G3      327.55043
Foreign relns. (Iran-other countries)     DS274.2.A-Z      327.550+
Foreign relns. (Iran-Rus.)         DS274.2.R9      327.55047
Foreign relns. (Iran-U.S.)         DS274.2.U6-7    327.55073
Foreign relns. (Iraq-G.B.)         DS70.96.G7
Foreign relns. (Iraq-Ger.)         DS70.96.G3
Foreign relns. (Iraq-other specific places)    DS70.96.A-Z
Foreign relns. (Ire.: 20th c.: gen.)   DA964.A2
Foreign relns. (Ire.-G.B.: 20th c.)    DA964.G7
Foreign relns. (Ire.-Ger.: 20th c.)    DA964.G3
```

```
FOREIGN RELNS. (IT.: 1861-1945)       DG498
Foreign relns. (It.-Alb.)             DG499.A5
Foreign relns. (It.: by country) DG499.A-Z        327.450+
Foreign relns. (It.-Eth.)             DG499.E7
Foreign relns. (It.-Fr.)              DG499.F8
Foreign relns. (It.-G.B.)             DG499.G7
Foreign relns. (It.-Ger.)             DG499.G3
Foreign relns. (It.-Rus.)             DG499.R9
Foreign relns. (It.-Sov.Un.)          DG499.S65
Foreign relns. (It.-Swit.)            DG499.S9
Foreign relns. (It.-U.S.)             DG499.U6-7
Foreign relns. (It.-Yug.)             DG499.Y8
FOREIGN RELNS. (JAPAN: 1868-1912)      DS882.6
Foreign relns. (Japan-Asia)       DS849.A75       327.5205
Foreign relns. (Japan-China)      DS849.C5        327.52051
Foreign relns. (Japan-G.B.)       DS849.G7    327.52041
Foreign relns. (Japan-Ger.)       DS849.G3    327.52043
Foreign relns. (Japan-India)      DS849.I4
Foreign relns. (Japan-other places)    DS849.A-Z  327.520+
Foreign relns. (Japan-Rus.)           DS849.R9    327.52047
Foreign relns. (Japan-Sov. Un.)       DS849.S65 327.52047
Foreign relns. (Japan-U.S.)       DS849.U6-7 327.52073
FOREIGN RELNS. (LATIN AM. & other places except U.S.)    F1416.A-Z   327.80+
Foreign relns. (Latin Am.-Fr.)        F1416.F8
Foreign relns. (Latin Am.-G.B.)       F1416.G7
Foreign relns. (Latin Am.-Ger.)       F1416.G3        327.8043
Foreign relns. (Latin Am.-It.)        F1416.I8
Foreign relns. (Latin Am.-Japan)      F1416.J3        327.8052
Foreign relns. (Latin Am.-Rus.)       F1416.R9
Foreign relns. (Latin Am.-U.S.)       F1418    327.8073
Foreign relns. (Libya-It.)        DT227.5.I8
Foreign relns. (Liech.: by country)  DB894.A-Z
Foreign relns. (Liech.-Ger.)          DB894.G3
Foreign relns. (Lux.: by country)  DH908.6.A-Z
Foreign relns. (Lux.-Ger.)         DH908.6.G3
Foreign relns. (Mex.-Ger.)         F1228.5.G3 327.72043
Foreign relns. (Mex.-Rus.)         F1228.5.R9 327.72047
Foreign relns. (Mex.-Sov.Un.) F1228.5.S65       327.72047
Foreign relns. (Mex.-U.S.)         F1228.5.U6-7    327.72073
Foreign relns. (Mid. East, SW. Asia: by specific country)    DS63.2.A-Z       327.560+
Foreign relns. (N. Zea.-Japan) DU421.5.J3 327.931052
Foreign relns. (N. Zea.-other specific places)    DU421.5.A-Z      327.9310+
Foreign relns. (N. Zea.-U.S.)     DU421.5.U6-7    327.931073
Foreign relns. (Neth.: by country)  DJ149.A-Z
Foreign relns. (Neth.-Ger.)           DJ149.G3
Foreign relns. (Nor.-G.B.)            DL459.G7
Foreign relns. (Nor.-Ger.)            DL459.G3
Foreign relns. (Nor.-Swe.)            DL459.S8
Foreign relns. (Pacific-Fr.)          DU50
Foreign relns. (Pacific-G.B.)         DU40
Foreign relns. (Pacific-Ger.)         DU60
Foreign relns. (Pacific-Sp.)          DU65
Foreign relns. (Pacific-U.S.)         DU30
```

```
Foreign relns. (Peru-Ger.)          F3434.G3
Foreign relns. (Peru-Japan)         F3434.J3
Foreign relns. (Peru-U.S.)          F3434.U6-7
FOREIGN RELNS. (POL.: 1918-45)      DK4402.5
Foreign relns. (Pol.: by country)   DK418.5.A-Z
Foreign relns. (Pol.-Fr.)           DK418.5.F8, DK4185.F8 (newer titles)
Foreign relns. (Pol.-G.B.)      DK418.5.G7
Foreign relns. (Pol.: gen.)     DK4180
Foreign relns. (Pol.-Ger.)          DK418.5.G3 (earlier titles), DK4185.G3
Foreign relns. (Pol.-Rus.)          DK418.5.R9, DK4185.R9 (later works)
Foreign relns. (Pol.: with particular countries)    DK4185.A-Z
Foreign relns. (Port.-G.B.)     DP557.G7
Foreign relns. (Port.-Ger.)     DP557.G3
Foreign relns. (Rum. & partic. countries)    DR229.A-Z
Foreign relns. (Rum.-Ger.)      DR229.G3    327.498043
Foreign relns. (Rum.-Rus.)      DR229.R9
FOREIGN RELNS. (RUS. & non-U.S. Am. countries)   DK69.3.A-Z
Foreign relns. (Rus.-Asia: gen.: pubns. 1801-)    DK68.A3-Z
Foreign relns. (Rus.-Asian countries by name)     DK68.7.A-Z
Foreign relns. (Rus.-Balkan Penin.)    DK67.4
Foreign relns. (Rus.-Bulg.)         DK67.5.B8
Foreign relns. (Rus.-Can.)          DK69.3.C2-29
Foreign relns. (Rus.-Cath. Church) DK67.3
Foreign relns. (Rus.-China)    DK68.7.C5        327.47051
Foreign relns. (Rus.-Czech.)   DK67.5.C95
Foreign relns. (Rus.-Europe)   DK67
Foreign relns. (Rus.-Fin.)     DK67.5.F5
Foreign relns. (Rus.-Fr.)      DK67.5.F8
Foreign relns. (Rus.-G.B.)     DK67.5.G7
Foreign relns. (Rus.: gen.)    DK66         327.47
Foreign relns. (Rus.-Ger.)          DK67.5.G3
Foreign relns. (Rus.-Greece)        DK67.5.G8
Foreign relns. (Rus.-Hung.)    DK67.5.H9
Foreign relns. (Rus.-India)    DK68.7.I4
Foreign relns. (Rus.-Iran)     DK68.7.I55
Foreign relns. (Rus.-It.)           DK67.5.I8
Foreign relns. (Rus.-Japan)         DK68.7.J3         327.47052
Foreign relns. (Rus.-Mex.)     DK69.3.M6
Foreign relns. (Rus.: particular areas)   DK67-69    327.470+
Foreign relns. (Rus.-Pol.)     DK67.5.P7
Foreign relns. (Rus.-Rum.)     DK67.5.R8
Foreign relns. (Rus.-specific Eur. countries)     DK67.5.A-Z
Foreign relns. (Rus.-Swe.)     DK67.5.S8
Foreign relns. (Rus.-Tur.)     DK68.7.T8
Foreign relns. (Rus.-U.S.)     DK69 (PREFER E183.8.R9)    327.47073
Foreign relns. (Rus.-Yug.)     DK67.5.Y8
Foreign relns. (Saudi Arab. Penin.: G.B.)     DS228.G7
Foreign relns. (Saudi Arab. Penin.: Ger.)     DS228.G3
Foreign relns. (Saudi Arabia-specific countries)  DS228.A-Z
Foreign relns. (Serbia-other specific places)     DR1976.A-Z
Foreign relns. (Slovakia: 1918-)    DB2809
Foreign relns. (Slovakia: 1939-45)  DB2819
```

FOREIGN RELNS. (SP.-Fr.: 1931-39)   DP258.F8
Foreign relns. (Sp.-Ger.)   DP86.G3   327.46043
Foreign relns. (Sp.-Rus.)   DP86.R9   327.46047
Foreign relns. (Sp.-Sov. Un.)   DP86.S65
Foreign relns. (Sp.-specific lands: 1931-39)   DP258.A-Z
Foreign relns. (Sp.-U.S.: 1931-39)   DP258.U6-7
Foreign relns. (Sp.: with partic. countries)   DP86.A-Z   327.460+
FOREIGN RELNS. (SWE.-Fin.)   DL659.F5
Foreign relns. (Swe.-G.B.)   DL659.G7
Foreign relns. (Swe.-Ger.)   DL659.G3
Foreign relns. (Swe.-Nor.)   DL659.N8
Foreign relns. (Swe.-Rus.)   DL659.R9
Foreign relns. (Swe.-Sov. Un.) DL659.S65
Foreign relns. (Swe.-U.S.)   DL659.U6-7
Foreign relns. (Swe.: 1818-20th c.)   DL658.8
FOREIGN RELNS. (SWIT.-Fr.)   DQ76.F8
Foreign relns. (Swit.-G.B.)   DQ76.G7
Foreign relns. (Swit.-Ger.)   DQ76.G3   327.494043
Foreign relns. (Swit.-It.)   DQ76.I8   327.494045
Foreign relns. (Swit.-Rus.)   DQ76.R9
Foreign relns. (Swit.-specific countries)   DQ76.A-Z   327.4940+
Foreign relns. (Swit.-U.S.)   DQ76.U6-7   327.494073
Foreign relns. (Syria-Fr.)   DS95.6.F8
Foreign relns. (Syria-G.B.)   DS95.6.G7
Foreign relns. (Syria-Ger.)   DS95.6.G3
Foreign relns. (Tunisia-It.)   DT257.5.I8
Foreign relns. (Tur.-G.B.)   DR479.G7
Foreign relns. (Tur.-Ger.)   DR479.G3
Foreign relns. (Tur.-particular countries)   DR479.A-Z
Foreign relns. (Tur.-Rus.)   DR479.R9
Foreign relns. (Ukr.: by country)   DK508.57
FOREIGN RELNS. (U.S.: 1865-1900: gen.)   E661.7 (SEE ALSO E183.8.A-Z)
Foreign relns. (U.S.: 1897-1901: gen.)   E713
Foreign relns. (U.S.: 20th c.: gen.)   E744   327.73
Foreign relns. (U.S.: 1913-21)   E768
Foreign relns. (U.S.-China)   E183.8.C5   327.73051
Foreign relns. (U.S.-Fr.)   E183.8.F8   327.73044
Foreign relns. (U.S.-G.B.)   E183.8.G7   327.73041
Foreign relns. (U.S.-Ger.)   E183.8.G3   327.73043
Foreign relns. (U.S.-It.)   E183.8.I8   327.73045
Foreign relns. (U.S.-Japan)   E183.8.J3   327.73052
Foreign relns. (U.S.-other places)   E183.8.A-Z   327.730+
Foreign relns. (U.S.-Russia)   E183.8.R9   327.73047
Foreign relns. (U.S.-Sov.Un.)   E183.8.S65   327.73047
Foreign relns. (Urug.-It.)   F2722.5.I8
Foreign relns. (Venez.-Ger.)   F2321.3.G3
Foreign relns. (Viet.-Japan)   DS556.58.J3
Foreign relns. (W.Ind.-G.B.)   F1622.5.G7
Foreign relns. (W.Ind.-Ger.)   F1622.5.G3
Foreign relns. (W.Ind.-U.S.)   F1622

FOREIGN RELNS. (YUG.: 1918-45)   DR1292
Foreign relns. (Yug.-G.B.: 1918-45)   DR367.G7
Foreign relns. (Yug.: gen.)   DR1257-1258
Foreign relns. (Yug.-Ger.: 1918-45)   DR367.G3
Foreign relns. (Yug.-It.: 1918-45)   DR367.I8
Foreign relns. (Yug.-Rus.: 1918-45)   DR367.R9
Foreign relns. (Yug.-specific countries)   DR327.A-Z
Foreign relns. (Yug.-U.S.: 1918-45)   DR367.U6-7
Forest fighting   U167.5.F6
Formosa (Taiwan)   951.249   DS895.F7-77 (books prior to about 1970),
    DS798.92-799.99+ (many post-1969 pubns.)
Formosa (19th-20th c.)   DS895.F75   951.24903-24904
FORTIFICATION   UG400-442
Fortification (gen.: pubn. 1801+)   UG401   355.544, 623.1
Fortification, Permanent   UG405
Fortifications (by place)   UG410-442   623.19+, 355.45-47+
Fortifications (Eur.: by region or country)   UG429.A-Z
Fortifications (Eur.: by town or place)   UG430.A-Z
Fortifications (mil. engineering)   623.1   UG400-442
Fortifications (mil. engineering: by place)   623.19 (for works prior to 1989 SEE
    ALSO .109)   UG410-442
Fortified defenses (Asia)   UG431-433   623.195
Fortified defenses (Eur.)   UG428-430
Fortified defenses (Ger.)   UG429.G3
Fortified defenses (U.S.)   UG410-412   623.1973, 355.4773
Fortress & garrison artillery (U.S.: gen.)   UF483
Foul-weather gear, Naval (plus other special clothing)   VC307   359.81
Fouling, corrosion, etc. (marine engin.)   VM951
Fragmentation bombs (aerial)   UG1282.F7   623.4514
FRANCE   DC   944
France (1515-)   DC110
France (1848-70: 2d Repub. & 2d Empire & Franco-Ger. War)   944.07,
    944.0812   DC272-292, DC272, DC276
France (1870- & 20th c.: 3d, 4th, 5th Repub's.)   944.08   DC289+, DC335+
France (1870-1945: 3d Repub.)   944.081   DC335
France (1870-1899: inclu. Franco-Ger. War)   944.0812   DC330,
    DC281-326 (F-G War), DC289
France (1871-1940: 3rd Repub.)   DC334-354+
France (20th c.: overall)   DC361-373, DC361   944.081
France (1900-14)   944.0813   DC361 (20th c.), DC375-385
France (1906-13: time of Clément Fallières)   DC380   944.0813
France (1913-20: era of Pres. Raymond Poincaré)   DC385
France (1914-18: WWI era)   DC387   944.0814
France (1918-39)   944.0815   DC389-396
France (1919-40: Reconstruc.)   DC389-396
France & French military ops. (WWI: gen.)   D548   940.344, .412+
France. Army (gen.)   UA702   355.00944, .30944
France. Army (infantry, cavalry, armor, artillery)   UA703-705
France (biog.: heads of state)   923.144
France (gen. hist., culture)   DC17
France (gen. hist.: pubn. 1815-)   DC38
France (geog. & travel)   914.4   DC28-45
France (lighthouses, beacons, foghorns, etc.)   VK1071-1072
France (lighthouses, beacons, foghorns, etc.: lists)   VK1173   623.89440944

France (mil. capabil.)   355.033244
France (mil. status: gen.)   UA700   355.033044
France (naval geog.)   359.4744   VA500-509
France (naval status: gen.)   VA503.A5-Z 359.030944, .4744
France (post-WWI relns.: U.S.: inclu. defensive alliance bet. Fr., U.S., G.B.)
                                                    D651.F6.A2-Z

France (post-WWI territorial ?s)   D651.F5-7
France (post-WWI territorial ?s: gen.)   D651.F5
France (WWI: causes, aims, results)   D516
France (WWI: mil. hist.)   940.40944   D548-549
France (WWI: Reconstruction)   D659.F8
France (WWII: causes, aims, results)   D742.F8
France (WWII: dipl. history)   D752   940.532244
Franco-German War (1870-71: gen.)   DC289
Franco-Prussian War (1870-71)   DC281-326
Frankfurt, Ger.   DD901.F71-79
Franz Ferdinand (Austria: Archduke)   DB89.F7
Franz Joseph I (Austria: Emp.: 1848-1916)   DB87
Fraternities (WWI: U.S. educ.: by name)   D639.E42.A-Z
Freedom of the seas & naval ops. (gen.: WWI)   D580
Freemasons (WWI)   D639.F8
Freighters (naval architec.)   VM391-395   623.8245, 387.544
FRENCH aerial ops. (WWI)   D603   940.44944
French Canadians   F1027
French Foreign Legion (WWI)   D548.35
French Indochina   DS531-560   959.4, 959.6-7
French Indochina (1884-1945)   DS549   959.703
French military history (gen.)   DC45   355.00944, .033044
French military ops. & France (WWI)   D548-549
French military ops. (WWI: misc.: includes colonial)   D548.9.A-Z
French military ops. (WWI: special groups by name)   D549.A-Z
French mission to U.S. (WWI)   D570.8.M6.F4
French naval history (gen.)   DC50
French naval ops. & Franco-Austrian naval conflict (WWI)   D583
French poetry, satire, etc. (WWI)   D526.3
French West Africa   DT521-553   966, 966.1-3, .52, .68, .81
Friends, Society of (WWI)   D639.F9
Frigates & corvettes (gen.)   V826   623.8254
Frigates (U.S.)   V826.3
Frogmen (navies: gen.)   VG86   359.984
FRONTS (WWI: Africa)   940.416   D575-576
Fronts (WWI: Asia)   940.415   D577-578
Fronts (WWI: Eur.)   940.414   D521, D530 (W.), D550 (E.)
Fronts (WWI: Fr. & W. in gen.)   940.4144   D530, D544
Fronts (WWI: Ger.)   940.4143   D531, D551-552 (Russo-Ger.)
Fronts (WWI: It.)   940.4145   D569
Fronts (WWI: Rus. & E. in gen.)   940.4147   D550, D551 (Rus.-Ger.-Austrian),
                                                    D556 (Rus.-Austrian), D560 (Balkan)
FUEL & light (mil. qtrs.)   UC420
Fuel, Naval (other than U.S.)   VC276.A5-Z
Fuel, Naval (U.S.)   VC276.A3-49   359.83
Fuel supplies & costs, Naval   VC276
Fuel supplies (WWII)   D810.F83
Fuels, Aviation   629.134351
Fuels, Marine engine   VM779   623.874

Furloughs   UB420-425
Furloughs, leaves, etc. (air forces: U.S.)   UG973
Furloughs, leaves, other inactive periods (navies)   359.113   VB260-275,
        VB307-315

Furnishings (mil. qtrs.)   UC415
Furniture (naut. design)   623.866
Fuselages, Aircraft   629.13434

GALICIA (20th c.)   DB500
Galicia (Pol.)   DK4600.G34
Galicia (Pol.: Polish wars, 1918-21)   DK4407.G3
Galicia (post-WWI territorial ?s)   D651.G18
Galleys & equipment (naval sci.)   VC398
Gallipoli & the Dardanelles (WWI)   D568.3
Gallipoli (Tur.)   DR701.G3
Gambetta, Léon Michel (Fr.: 1871-1940 era)   DC342.8.G3
Garand rifle   UD395.G4
Garbage disposal (mil. engineering)   623.754
Garrison & fortress artillery (gen.)   UF480
GAS masks (mil.)   UG447.6
Gas regiments (WWI: Fr.)   D548.75
Gas regiments (WWI: Prus.)   D532.7
Gas regiments (WWI: U.S.)   D570.345
Gas-turbine engines (marine engineering)   623.87233   VM740, TJ778
Gas warfare (by chem. name)   UG447.5.A-Z   623.4516
Gas warfare (WWI)   D607.5 (PREFER UG447)
Gases, poisons, other chemical agents (design)   623.4592
Gatling machine guns   UF620.G3
Gdansk, Pol. (Danzig: gen.)   DK4670
Gear, equipment, & outfitting (nautical: engineering)   623.86
        VM781-861, VM781 (gen.)
Genealogy   929
Genealogy (royal houses: G.B.)   929.72 (hist. treatment poss. or in 941+)
        DA28.1-.35, CS418-424
GENERAL & flag officers (above army col. or navy capt.)   355.331   UB200, UB210
General officers (air forces)   358.41331   UG790-795
General orders (naval: U.S.)   VB365
General orders (Rus. military: collections)   UB657
General staff & headquarters (WWI: U.S.)   D570.25.A-Z
General works (gen. almanacs, encyclopediae, etc.)   A   000-099
Generals, marshals, commanders (admin.: duties etc.)   UB200   355.331
Geneva & Hague conventions UH531-533 (PREFER JX5136 & JX5243)
        341.6+, .65
Geneva, Swit.   DQ441-460   949.45
GEOGRAPHY, Air warfare   358.4147   UG633-635, UA
Geography & history   900-999   G, D-F
Geography & history (gen.)   900-909   G, C-D
Geography & travel   910-919   G, D-F
Geography & travel (by locale)   913-919
Geography, anthropology, sports, & recreation   G   910-919, 301, 790's
Geography, Marine military (strategic & tactical)   359.9647+   VE21-124, VA
Geography, Military (gen. inclu. Eur.)   UA990   355.47
Geography, Military (tactical & strategic)   355.47   UA985-997
Geography, Naval (strategic & tactical)   359.47   UA985-997, VA160-178,
        VA49-750 (by place)

Geology & seismology, Military   UG465-465.5
Geonavigation, Marine   623.892
Geonavigational aids, Marine (misc. non-electronic)   623.894
George V (G.B.: King: 1910-36)   DA573
Georgia (Rus.)   DK511.G3-47 (earlier pubns.), DK670-679
Georgia (Transcaucasia: post-WWI territorial ?s)   D651.G2
Georgia (WWI: Reconstruction)   D658.G4-41
Georgian Republic (U.S.S.R.)   947.95   DK511.G3-47, .G47 (gen. hist., 1917-)
Georgian S. S. R. (1801-1921)   DK677.4-6
Germ warfare (WWII: bacterial)   D810.B3
GERMAN aerial ops. (WWI)   D604   940.44943
German-Americans (WWI)   D620
German armament (modern)   U820.G7
German Austria & Bavaria   DD791-800
German colonies (WWI)   D574-576
German colonies (WWI: gen.)   D574
German culture (in other lands: gen.)   DD68
German East Africa (gen.: later Tanganyika)   DT444
German East Africa (post-WWI territorial ?s)   D651.A41
German East Africa (WWI)   D576.G3
German East Indies   DS649
German espionage (gen.)   UB271.G3   327.120943
German field artillery   UF405.G3
German marching (mil.)   UD315.G3
GERMAN MILITARY education (special times)   U571
German military history (gen.)   DD101   355.00943
German military ops. (WWI: by misc. place)   D538.A-Z
German military ops. (WWI: West & gen.: includes Hindenburg, Ludendorff memoirs)
          D531   940.343, .40943, .413+, 943.084-085
German military ops. (WWI: West & overall)   D531-538
German military ops. (WWI: West: special by area, type)   D532-538
German military ops. (WWII: gen.)   D757   940.5343, .54013, .5413, .5421, 943.086
German naval education (main school)   V574.A2-65
German New Guinea (N.E.)   DU742 (SEE ALSO DU550+ for Bismarck Arch.)
          993.6, 995
German poetry, satire, etc. (WWI)   D526.5
German Southwest Africa (post-WWI territorial ?s)   D651.A42
German Southwest Africa (WWI)   D576.G5
German submarine ops. (WWI: by ship, engagement, etc.)   D592.A-Z
German submarine ops. (WWI: gen.)   D591   940.4512
German West Africa (1884-1916)   967.8202   DT444, DT447 (newer books)
GERMANS (in Arg.)   F3021.G3
Germans (in Brazil)   F2659.G3
Germans (in Mex.)   F1392.G4
Germans (in N.Y.)   F130.G3
Germans (in other lands: gen.)   DD119.3
Germans (in Pol.)   DK4121.5.G4
Germans (in S.Am.)   F2239.G3
Germans (in U.S.)   E184.G3

GERMANY   DD   943
Germany (1519-)   DD175
Germany (1871-1918: New Empire)   DD217-231   943.08
Germany (1871-1918: New Empire: gen.)   DD220
Germany (1871-1888: Kaiser Wilhelm I era)   DD223
Germany (1888-1918: Fred. & William II eras)   943.084   DD224-232, DD228
                                          (gen.), DD228.8 (WWI era), DD448 (Prussia)
Germany (1888-1918: Kaiser Wilhelm II era)   DD228-231   943.084
Germany (1888-1918: Kaiser Wilhelm II era: gen.)   DD228
Germany (20th c.: gen.)   DD232
Germany (1914-1918: WWI period)   DD228.8   943.08
Germany (1918-: revolution & Republic)   DD233-251+   943.085
Germany (1918-: revolution & Republic: gen.)   DD237
Germany (1918: Revolution)   DD248
Germany (1919-25: Ebert period)   DD249
Germany (air war geog.)   358.414743   UG635.G3
Germany & Austria (WWI: mil. hist.)   940.40943   D531-538 (Ger.), D531 (gen.),
                                              D539 (Austria)
Germany & Central Europe   943   DD (Ger.), DB (Austria, Hung., Czech.),
                              DK401-441 & DK4010-4800 (Pol.)
Germany & Central Europe (mil. geog.)   355.4743   UA995.G3
Germany & Central Europe (mil. policy)   355.033543 UA710+, UA710-719
Germany & Prussia   DD   943
Germany. Army (gen.)   UA712   355.00943, .30943, .310943
Germany. Army (local)   UA718.A-Z
Germany. Army (special units: by name)   UA716.A-Z
Germany (biog.: heads of state)   923.143
Germany (gen. hist., culture, etc.) DD17
Germany (gen.: pubn. 1801-)   DD89
Germany (geog. & travel)   914.31-35   DD21-43, DD41 (1871-1918)
Germany (lighthouses, beacons, foghorns, etc.)   VK1073-1074
Germany (mil. status)   355.033043
Germany (mil. status: gen.)   UA710   355.033043, .033243, .033543
Germany (naval geog.)   359.4743   VA510-519, VA513 (gen.)
Germany (naval hist.)   359.00943   VA510-519
Germany (naval status: gen.)   VA513.A5-Z   359.030943, .00943, .30943, .4743
Germany (pilot guides)   623.892943   VK822, VK824
Germany (post-WWI territorial ?s)   D651.G3
Germany (WWI: causes, aims, results)   D515
Germany (WWI: Reconstruction)   D659.G3
Germany (WWII: causes, aims, results)   D742.G3
Germany (WWII: dipl. history)   D751   940.532443
Gibraltar (Br. colony)   946.89   DP302.G31-41
Gladstone (G.B.: 19th c.: Prime Min.)   DA563
Glasgow Highlanders (WWI)   D547.G5
Goeben & Breslau (cruisers: Ger.: WWI)   D582.G7
Gold Coast (Ghana: WWI)   D576.G7
Gordon, Charles Alexander, Sir (G.B.: 19th c. mil. biog.)   DA68.32.G6
Goriunov machine guns   UF620.G6
Gorizia, It. (WWI)   D569.G7
Grain industry (defense)   UA929.95.G7
Graves registration & burial services (navies)   359.699
Graves registration & military burial   355.699
Graydon aerial torpedo thrower   V855.G7

Great Basin & Pacific Coast states   979   F786-915, F786-850 (New S.W.),
                                                  F786-788, F851-915 (Pac. states), F851
GREAT BRITAIN   DA   941-942
Great Britain (1837-1901: gen.)   DA550   941.08
Great Britain (20th c.: gen.)   DA566   941.082
Great Britain (1901-10: gen.)   DA570
Great Britain (1910-36)   DA576
Great Britain (1914-19: WWI era)   DA577
Great Britain (1920-39)   DA578
Great Britain (air war geog.)   358.414741   UG635.G7
Great Britain & British military ops. (WWII)   D759-760
Great Britain & Ireland (geog. & travel)   914.1   DA11, DA600-668, DA969-987 (Ire.)
Great Britain & Ireland (lighthouses, beacons, foghorns, etc.: lists)
                                      VK1153-1159   623.89440941
Great Britain. Army   UA649-668
Great Britain. Army (gen.)   UA649   355.00941, .310941
Great Britain (biog.: heads of state)   923.141-142
Great Britain. Fifth Army (WWI)   D546.5.5th
Great Britain (lighthouses, beacons, foghorns, etc.) VK1057-1064
Great Britain (mil. geog.)   355.4741-4742   UA995.G7
Great Britain (mil. policy)   355.033541-033542   UA647+,UA647-668
Great Britain (mil. status)   UA647   355.033041
Great Britain (naval geog.)   359.4741-4742   VA452-467, VA454 (gen.)
Great Britain (naval hist.)   359.00941-00942   VA452-467, DA70-89
Great Britain (naval policy & status)   359.030941
Great Britain (post-WWI relns.: countries other than U.S.)   D651.G7
Great Britain (post-WWI relns.: U.S.: inclu. defensive alliance w. Fr., U.S.)   D651.G6
Great Britain (post-WWI territorial ?s)   D651.G5-7
Great Britain (post-WWI territorial ?s: gen.)   D651.G5
Great Britain. Royal Naval College, Dartmouth (admin.)   V515.C1-K3
Great Britain. Royal Navy (gen.)   VA454   359.0309441, .30941, .4741-
                                      4742, .00941
Great Britain (WWI: causes, aims, results)   D517
Great Britain (WWI: mil. hist.)   940.40941-40942   D546-547
Great Britain (WWI: Reconstruction)   D659.G7
Great Britain (WWII: causes, aims, results)   D742.G7
Great Britain (WWII: dipl. history)   D750   940.532241
Great circle routing (marine navig.)   VK571
Great Lakes & North Central states (geog. & travel)   917.7   F477.3 (Old NW.),
                                      F551 (Lakes area in gen.), F484.5
Great Plains & American West (geog. & travel)   917.8   F591
Great War (1914-18)   940.3-.499   D501-680
Greater Antilles (Cuba, Haiti, Puerto Rico, Jamaica, etc.) F1741-1991 972.9, .91-95
Greco-Turkish War (1897)   DR575
GREECE   949.5   DF, DF757
Greece (1821-1924: Monarchy)   949.506   DF802
Greece (20th c.: gen.)   DF833   949.507
Greece (20th c.: 1924-)   949.507   DF833 (20th c.), DF838 (WWI)
Greece (1914-18: WWI)   DF838   949.506
Greece & Macedonia (WWI)   D569.2
Greece & unredeemed Greeks (post-WWI territorial ?s)   D651.G8

Greece (gen.)   DF751   949.5
Greece (geog. & travel)   914.95   DF726
Greece (mil. status)   UA720-729   355.0330495
Greece (modern)   DF701-951+
Greece (naval status)   VA520-529
Greece (WWI: dipl. hist.)   D616
Greenland   998.2
Grenades   UF765   623.45114
Grenades, Hand & rifle   355.825114   UF765
Grenades, Hand or rifle (design)   623.45114   UF765
Grenades, mines, etc.   355.82511
Grenades, mines, nuclear weapons (design)   623.4511
Grenadier Guards (WWI)   D547.G7
Grey, Edward (G.B.: 20th c.)   DA566.9.G8
Guards Division (WWI: G.B.)   D547.G8
Guerrilla warfare & small wars   U240   355.02184, 356.15
Guiana (Brit., Dutch, & Fr.)   F2351-2471   988
Guidebooks (Berlin, Ger.)   DD859
Guidebooks (G.B.)   DA650
Guidebooks (Ger.)   DD16
Guidebooks (London, Eng.)   DA679   914.21
Guidebooks (Paris, Fr.)   DC708
Guides & marching (mil.)   UD313-314
Gulf states (U.S.: gen.)   F296   976
GUN carriages, caissons, limbers, etc. (gen.)   UF640   623.43
Gun carriages, Disappearing   UF650
Gun carriages, Naval   VF430   623.43
Gun carriages, Self-propelled (plus track-layer tractors & other self-contained)
                                                                                        UF652
Gun handbooks (U.S.: by mm. or cm. then date)   UF563.A4.1+
Gun mounts   355.823
Gun mounts (design)   623.43
Gun salutes & other military rewards (misc.)   355.1349 (use 355.134 with
                                                                                1989+ pubn.)
GUNNERY (engineering)   623.55   UF800-805, VF144-302
Gunnery practice, Naval (G.B.)   VF315.G7   623.5530941
Gunnery practice, Naval (U.S.)   VF313   623.5530973
Gunnery, Aircraft (engineering)   623.555
Gunnery, Artillery (gen.)   UF800   623.55
Gunnery, Land (engineering)   623.551   UF800-805
Gunnery, Naval (engineering)   623.553   VF144-302, VF145 (gen.), VF150-
                                                155 (hdbks.), VF160-302 (drill bks.), VF160 (U.S.)
Gunpowder, cordite, & other explosives (design: inclu. propellant types)   623.4526
                                                                                        UF870
Guns (gen.)   U880   623.4
Guns (misc. types: mil. sci.)   UF630
Guns, Aircraft   UG1340-1345   623.7461
Gustav V (Swe.: King, 1907-50)   DL867
Gynecology (WWI)   D639.G8
Gypsies   DX1-301
Gypsies in Czechoslovakia   DX222
Gypsies in Europe (gen. & elsewhere)   DX145
Gypsies in Germany   DX229
Gypsies in Russia (inclu. Poland & Lith.)   DX241

HAAKON VII (Nor.: King, 1905-57)   DL530
Hague & Geneva conventions (official works: by date)   UH531 (PREFER JX5136 &
                                                                    JX5243)
Haig, Douglas Haig, 1st earl (G.B.: 20th c. mil. biog.)   DA69.3.H3
Hammocks, berths, etc. (naval architec.)   VM511
Hampton Roads Naval Training Station (Va.)   V434.H2
Hand signaling (mil.)   UG582.H2
Hand-to-hand combat & self-defense (training: inclu. unarmed & knife fighting)
                                        355.548   U167.5.H3, U262
HANDBOOKS & manuals (marine navig. & merch. marine)   VK155   623.890202
Handbooks & manuals (marines: G.B.)   VE155.G7
Handbooks & manuals (mil. hygiene: Eng. & Am.)   UH623
Handbooks & manuals (naval ordnance)   VF150-155
Handbooks & manuals, Soldiers'   U110-145   355.00202
Handbooks & manuals, Soldiers' (by place except U.S.)   U115.A-Z
Handbooks & manuals (U.S. Navy: Pay & allowances)   VC60
Handbooks & tables (naval pay & allowances: U.S.)   VC54-60
Handbooks, Gun (U.S.: artillery)   UF563.A4-8
Handbooks, Gun (U.S.: by class or type)   UF563.A7-8 (sometimes use
                    UF563.A4-6 with measure. & alphab. symbol: e.g.
                    UF563.A5.12 in.M for 12 in. mortar or ... Mt. for mountain)
Handbooks, Gun (U.S.: by inches)   UF563.A5
Handbooks, Gun (U.S.: by pounds)   UF563.A6
Handbooks, Infantry (U.S.)   UD153
Handbooks, Medical & surgical (navies)   VG460-466
Handbooks, Naval   V110-145
Handbooks, Naval officers'   V130-135   359.3320202
Handbooks, Naval reserve   V140-145
Handbooks, Officers'   U130-135
Handbooks, Petty officers'   V120-125
Handbooks, Seamen's (gen.)   V110   359.00202
Handbooks, tables, etc. (marine engin.)   VM607   623.870202
Handbooks, tables, etc. (ship calculations: naval architec.)   VM151
                                        623.810202, .810212
Handling of nautical craft (gen.)   623.881   VK541
Handling of nautical craft (powered)   623.8814   VK541, VK145, VK205, VB200-205
Harbor piloting (inclu. approach)   623.8929   VK321-369.8
Harbors & ports   VK321-369+   387.1+
Harbors, canals, dams (mil. engineering)   UG350   623.64
Harvard Univ. (WWI)   D639.E4.H3
Hatchways, ladders, other special fittings (marine engin.)   VM851
Hawaii (1900-59: U.S. Territory)   DU627.5.A6-Z   996.903
Hawaii (WWI)   D570.87.H3
Hawaiian Islands (WWII)   D767.92, D769.87.H3   940.539969, 996.903
Hazing (U.S. Naval Acad.: Cong. docs.)   V415.E9
Headgear, Naval   VC320
Headquarters, Military   UB230-235
Headquarters, Naval (ops. inclu. aides) VB210
Heads of state (biog.)   923.1
Health, hygiene, & sanitation (navies)   VG470-475
Health, hygiene, & sanitation (navies: U.S.)   VG473
Heat or other radiations (ammunition: design)   623.4595
Heating, ventilation, & sanitation (naval architec. & engin.)   VM481-482
Heidelberg, Ger.   DD901.H55-59
Heliograph (mil. signal.)   UG582.H4

Helmets, hats, etc. (mil.)   UC500-505
Helsingfors, Fin. (Helsinki: area)   948.971   DK465.H5, DL1175, DL1175.48 (1917-)
Helsinki, Fin. (1917-)   DL1175.48
Hemp (naval supplies)   VC279.H45
Hercegovina & Bosnia (1878-1918: Austrian rule: gen.)   DR1723
Hercegovina (Herzegovina) & Bosnia   949.742   DB231-250 (Bos.), DB521-
540 (Her.), DR1652-1785
Herzegovina (20th c.)   DB540
Herzegovina (Hercegovina) & Bosnia (gen.)   DR1660, 1685
Hessian military ops. (WWI)   D535
Hierarchy, Air force   358.4133   UG770-775
Hierarchy (marines)   359.9633
Hierarchy, Military (mil. personnel)   355.33   UA, UB410-415, UB210
Hierarchy, Naval   359.33   V110-145, VA, VB21-124, VB23 (U.S.),
VB257-258.5, VB203
High-explosive devices (torpedoes, blockbusters, etc.: design)   623.4517
V850-855 (torpedoes), UF860-870
High explosives (design: inclu. dynamite, nitro, TNT)   623.4527   TP285,
TP270-295
Highways (U.S.)   UA963-964
Hindenburg, Paul von (Ger.: 1888-1918+ period)   DD231.H5
Hispanic-Americans (armed forces)   UB418.H57
Historic monuments (WWI)   D639.H5
Histories, Official (WWI: U.S.)   D570.A4
Historiography (WWI)   D522.42
History & geography   900-999+   G (geog.), D-F
History (auxiliary: civilization, gen. archaeology, heraldry, gen. biography)   C   900-
909, 920-929, 930-939+
History (gen., Eastern Hemisphere, Oceania)   D   909, 930-969, 990-996
History (gen., world wars, Eur. overall, etc.)   D1-1075+   909, 940, 950
History (misc. areas: Oceania, Atlantic islands, Arctic, extraterr. worlds, etc.)   990-
999   C-F, G, Q
Holland (Netherlands))   949.2   DJ, DJ109 (gen.)
Holland (1890-1948: Queen Wilhelmina era)   949.2071   DJ281-287,
DJ281 (gen.), DJ285 (WWI time), DJ287 (WWII era)
Holland (20th c.)   949.207   DJ216 (19th-20th c.)
Holland (geog. & travel)   914.92   DJ39
Holy See (1870-)   DG799
Home defense (coasts, frontiers, other valuable redoubts)   355.45   UA (gen.),
UG410-442 (fortific's.), UG410-412 (U.S.), UG428-430 (Eur.), UG429.G7 (G.B.)
Home defense, Air force   358.4145   UG730-735, UG630-635
Home defense, Naval   359.45   VA45, V200
Home guard naval forces   359.351   VA45
Home guards & frontier troops   355.351   UA42 (U.S. Nat. Guard)
Homes, Sailors'   VB290-295 (SEE ALSO UB380-385)
Hong Kong   DS796.H7   951.25
Hong Kong (1843-1945)   951.2504   DS796.H757
Honored & dead (WWI: Australia: rolls)   940.46794   D609.A8
Honored & dead (WWI: Fr.: rolls)   940.46744   D609.F8-82
Honored & dead (WWI: G.B.: rolls)   940.46741   D609.G7
Honored & dead (WWI: Ger.: rolls)   940.46743   D609.G3
Honored & dead (WWI: U.S.: rolls)   940.46773   D609.U6-7
Hood (battle cruiser: G.B.: WWII)   D772.H6, VA458.H6
Hoover, Herbert (U.S.: Pres., 1929-33)   E802
Hornchurch, Eng. (WWI)   D547.8.H6

HORSE artillery   UF410
Horse cavalry (gen. & ops.)   357.184   UE150-475, UE150+, UE157+
Horse cavalry (pubn. 1801+)   UE145   357.1
Horses & mules, Military   UC600-695
Horses & mules, Military (U.S.)   UC603-604
Horses, Artillery   UF370
Horses, Cavalry   UE460-475
Horthy, Miklós (Hung.: 20th c.)   DB950.H6
HOSPITAL corps, Naval   VG310-325
Hospital corps, Naval (places besides U.S.)   VG325.A-Z
Hospital corps, Naval (U.S.)   VG320
Hospital services & hospitals, Naval   VG410-450 (SEE ALSO D #s for
                                                                                particular wars)
Hospital services, Military   UH460-485
Hospital services, Naval (gen.)   VG410   359.72
Hospital services, Naval (U.S.)   VG420-425
Hospital ships   VG450   623.8264, 359.3264
HOSPITALS, medical services, Red Cross (WWI: gen.)   D628
Hospitals, Military (except U.S.)   UH475.A-Z
Hospitals, Military (gen.)   UH470   355.72
Hospitals, Naval (gen.)   VG420
Hospitals, Naval (U.S.: by town)   VG425.A-Z
Hospitals (WWI: in Eng.)   940.476342   D629.G7
Hospitals (WWI: in Fr.)   940.476344   D629.F8
Hospitals (WWI: in Ger.)   940.476343   D629.G3
Hospitals (WWI: in particular places)   940.4763+   D629.A-Z
Hospitals (WWI: operated by particular countries)   940.4764-4769
Hotchkiss machine guns   UF620.H8
Hotchkiss ordnance   UF560-565... .H.
Housing administration (air forces)   358.4167   UG1140-1145
Housing administration (mil.)   355.67 (SEE ALSO .71 & .12 [gen.])   UC400-440
Housing administration (navies)   359.67   VC420-425
Housing & barracks, Naval (places besides U.S.)   VC425.A-Z
Howitzers & mortars   UF470-475
Howitzers & mortars (Fr.)   UF475.F8
Howitzers & mortars (G.B.)   UF475.G7
Hudson River (N.Y.)   F127.H8
Hull design (naval architec.)   623.8144   VM156
Hulls (special construc.: anti-fire & -shock, corrosion-resistant, etc.)   623.848
Human resources (air forces: enlistment etc.)   358.4122   UG880-885
Human resources (mil.)   355.22   UA17.5, UB320+, UB340+
Human resources (navies)   359.22
Humor, comics, pictorials, & miscellanea (WWII)   940.549   D743.9, D745
Hungarian military ops (WWI)   D540
HUNGARY   943.9   DB901-975+, DB906, DB925
Hungary (1686-1918: Hapsburg rule)   943.9042   DB933 (19th c.)
Hungary (1867-1918)   943.9043   DB945 (1867-1900)
Hungary (20th c.)   DB947-957+   943.9043+
Hungary (20th c.: gen.)   DB947
Hungary (1914-18: WWI era)   DB953   943.9043
Hungary (20th c.: 1918-)   943.905   DB947-950, DB947 (gen.), DB950.A-Z (biog.)

Hungary (gen.)   DB906   943.9
Hungary (gen.: pubn. dates 1801+)   DB925
Hungary (geog. & travel)   914.39   DB916-917
Hungary, Liechtenstein   DB861-975+
Hungary (mil. status)   UA829.H9   355.0330439
Hungary (post-WWI territorial ?s)   D651.H7
Hydrography, Marine   VK588-597
Hydrology, Military   UG468
Hygiene & sanitation, Military   UH600-629
Hygiene & sanitation, Military (besides U.S.)   UH605.A-Z
Hygiene, health, & sanitation (navies: special: tropics, drinking water, alcohol
          problem, venereal diseases, diet, etc.)   VG471
Hygiene, Mental (besides U.S.)   UH629.5.A-Z

IBERIAN Peninsula & Spain   DP, DP1-402+ (Sp.), DP501-900+ (Port.)   946
Ice excavation, tunnels, rooms, etc. (mil. engineering)   UG343
Icebergs   VK1299
Icebreakers (naval architec.)   VM451   623.828
Iceland   949.12   DL301-398+, DL375 (1918-)
Iceland (1801-1918)   DL365
Idealism (WWI)   D639.I2
Illegitimate war babies (WWI)   D639.I5
Illinois (WWI)   D570.85.I3-31
Imaginary naval battles & wars   V253   359.47
Imperial War Museum (London, G.B.)   U13.G72.L69
Incendiary bombs (aerial)   UG1282.I6   623.4516
Incendiary weapons   UG447.65
Indemnity & reparations (WWI: gen.)   D648   940.31422
India   954   DS436, DS401-481
India (1862-1914)   DS479   954.035
India (1914-19)   DS480.4   954.0356-0357
India (WWI)   D547.I5
Indians as soldiers (WWI: U.S.)   D570.8.I6
Indians (N. Am.)   E77-99   970.00497, .1-5, 973.0497
Indians (U.S. Navy: native-Am's.)   VB324.I5
Indochina   DS521-560   959-959.7
Indonesia (1602-1945: Dutch period)   959.802   DS642-643
Indonesia (1798-1945)   959.8022   DS643
Indonesia & Malay Archipelago   959.8   DS611-649
Induction & exemption (mil.)   UB340   355,22363, .225
INDUSTRIAL defense (by specific industry)   UA929.95.A-Z (SEE ALSO H
          industry #s)
Industrial defense (gen.)   UA929.5   355.28, .26
Industrial defense (places besides U.S.)   UA929.9.A-Z
Industrial mobilization (by country)   UA18.A3-Z (SEE ALSO D-F for specific wars)
Industrial resources & raw materials (air forces)   358.4124-4126
          UG1100-1105, UG630+
Industrial resources (mil. use) 355.26   UA18, UA929.5+, HC106+
Industrial resources (navies)   359.26
Industry, Shipbuilding (gen.)   VM298.5   338.476238, 387.5+

INFANTRY   356.1   UD, UD15, UD21-124 (by place), UD144-145+, UA
Infantry arms (small: U.S.)   UD383-384
Infantry (Asia)   UD99-113
Infantry (Australia)   UD121   356.10994
Infantry (Austria)   UD65   356.109436
Infantry (Austria & Austria-Hung.)   UA673
Infantry (Can.)   UD26
Infantry (collections) UD7
Infantry (Eur.)   UD55-95
Infantry (Fr.)   UD71   356.10944
Infantry (G.B.)   UA650-653, UD57-64
Infantry (G.B.: by date)   UD58
Infantry (G.B.: gen.)   UA650   356.10941
Infantry (gen.)   356.18   UD160-302, UD160 (U.S.)
Infantry (gen. hist.)   UD15   356.09, 109, 355.009
Infantry (gen.: pubn. 1801+)   UD145   356.1
Infantry (Ger.)   UA713.A1-Z9.A-Z, UD73   356.10943
Infantry (Ger.: by group name)   UA713.Z9.A-Z
Infantry (Ger.: by regiment #)   UA713.Z6.1st-
Infantry (Ger.: gen.)   UA713.A6-Z4
Infantry (hist.: by area or country regardless of specific unit)   UD21-124 (SEE
                                                                       ALSO UA)

Infantry (It.)   UA743, UD79   356.10945
Infantry manuals (gen.)   UD150   356.10202
Infantry, Mounted (U.S.)   UD453-454
Infantry (New Z.)   UD122.5
Infantry regiments etc. (WWII: U.S.: by #)   D769.31.1st-
Infantry regiments (G.B.: by name)   UA651.A-Z
Infantry regiments (Sp.-Am. War: U.S.: by #)   E725.4.1st-
Infantry regiments (U.S.: by #/author)   UA29.1st-
Infantry (Rus.)   UA773.A1-Z9.A-Z
Infantry (Rus.: Asian)   UD109
Infantry (Rus.: by group name)   UA773.Z9.A-Z
Infantry (Rus.: by regiment #)   UA773.Z6.1st-
Infantry (Rus.: Eur.)   UD85   356.10947
Infantry (Rus.: gen.)   UA773.A6-Z4
Infantry tactics & maneuvers (Asia: gen.)   UD270
Infantry tactics & maneuvers (Eur.: gen.)   UD215
Infantry tactics & maneuvers (U.S.: gen.)   UD160
Infantry (tactics, use, gen. hist's.)   UD (SEE ALSO UA for specific armies)   356
Infantry (U.S.)   UD23   356.10973
Infantry (U.S.: Calif. reserves)   UA93-94
Infantry (U.S.: gen.)   UA28   356.10973
Infantry (U.S.: N.Y. reserves) UA363-364
Infantry (WWI: Fr.)   D548.3
Infantry (WWI: G.B.)   D546.53
Infantry (WWI: official reports)   D529.3
Infantry (WWI: Prus.)   D532.3
Infantry (WWI: U.S.)   D570.33 (newer bks. may use A1 or #'s as in D570.27)
Infiltration, espionage, & unconventional warfare (WWI: Rus.)   940.48647
Information & recreation, Military (U.S.: gen.)   UH805   355.3460973
Information & recreation services, Naval (U.S.: gen.) VG2025-2026   359.3460973
Information security (mil. data: gen.)   UB246
Inquiry, Courts of (mil.: by country)   UB865.A-Z
Inquiry, Courts of (naval: U.S.)   VB813 (PREFER KF7646-7650)

Insignia & badges (naval clothing) VC345   359.1342
Insignia, badges, etc. (air force)   UG1180-1185
Insignia, badges, etc. (mil.: U.S.)   UC533
Inspection, Military   UB240-245
Inspection, Naval (inclu. inspectors)   VB220-225
Inspection (small arms: infantry)   UD382
Installations, Infantry   356.187   UC400-405, U180-185
INSTRUCTION camps, maneuver grounds, etc. (U.S.)   U293
Instruction (marine engin.)   VM725-728   623.8707
Instruction (marine engin.: places except U.S.)   VM728.A-Z
Instruction (merch. marine)   VK401-529
Instruction (mil. engineering)   UG157
Instruction (naval architec.)   VM165-276
Instruction (naval architec.: by place)   VM171-274
Instruction (naval medicine)   VG230-235
Instruction (naval ordnance)   VF357
Instruction (ordnance & small arms)   UF527
Instruction (WWI)   D522.4
Instrumentation, Aircraft   629.135
Instrumentmen, Naval   VG1030-1035
Instruments, Artillery (specific types)   UF849-856
Instruments, Nautical   VK573-587
Instruments, Nautical (design)   623.863   VK573-587
Instruments, Nautical (special)   VK575-584
Instruments, Naval gunnery   VF520   623.558
INTELLIGENCE & military espionage (inclu. cryptanalysis, data analysis, etc.)
        355.3432   UB250-251, UB251.A-Z (by country), UB270-271,
        UB271.A-Z (by place), UB271.x2.A-Z (by spy), UB271.R92.S565 (R. Sorge)
Intelligence, espionage, & unconventional warfare (WWI: G.B.)   940.48641
Intelligence, espionage, & unconventional warfare (WWI: Ger.)   940.48743
                                              D619.3-5 (in U.S.)
Intelligence, Military   UB250-271
Intelligence, Military (by country)   UB251.A-Z
Intelligence, Naval   359.3432   VB230-254, VB230, UB250-271
Intelligence, Naval (by country)   VB231.A-Z   359.343209+
Inter-allied Military Commission of Control in Germany (WWI)   D650.I6
Inter-war period (1919-39: gen.)   D720   940.5-.52
Internal combustion engines (marine engineering)   623.8723   VM770
International forces   355.357 (perhaps PREFER 355.356)
International military law   UB481 (PREFER JX areas)   341.6
International naval law   VB353
Internment centers & P.O.W. camps (WWI: in U.S.)   940.47273   D627.U6+
Intrenching tools (mil.)   UG380
Iran (Persia)   DS251-325   955
Iran (1906-25)   955.051   DS315-316
Iran (1909-25: Ahmed era)   DS315   955.05-051
Iraq   956.7   DS67-79, DS70.9
Iraq (1517-1918: Turkish period)   DS77   956.703
Iraq (1553-1920: Ottoman rule)   956.703   DS77

214

IRELAND   941.5   DA900-995, DA910 (gen.)
Ireland (19th-20th c.)   941.508   DA950-965+
Ireland (20th c.)   DA959-965, DA959   941.5082
Ireland (1900-20)   941.50821   DA960
Ireland (1901-22)   DA960
Ireland (1914-21)   DA962
Ireland (WWI)   D547.I6
Irish troops (G.B.)   UA665
Irregular troops (guerrillas, brigands, etc.)   356.15   U240, U167.5.A-Z
Israel (inclu. Palestine)   956.94   DS101-131+, DS116-117, DS123
Israel (70 A.D.+)   DS123
Israel (1917-48: Brit. rule)   956.9404   DS126, DS126.3 (WWII era)
Istanbul, Tur. (Constantinople)   DR716-739   956.3
Istria (post-WWI territorial ?s)   D651.I5
ITALIAN East Africa & Northeast Africa   DT367   963
Italian military history (gen.)   DG482   355.00945
Italian military ops (WWI: gen.)   D569.A2   940.4145
Italian military ops. (WWII: gen.)   D763.I8
Italian mission to U.S. (WWI)   D570.8.M6.I8
Italian naval ops. (WWI)   D588
Italian poetry, satire, etc. (WWII)   D745.7.I8
Italian Somaliland   DT416   967.73-7305+
Italians (in N.Y.)   F130.I8
Italians (in U.S.)   E184.I8
ITALY   945   DG
Italy (476-)   DG401-579
Italy (1870- & 20th c.)   945.09   DG555-575+, DG555, DG570 (WWI era)
Italy (1871-1947: gen.)   DG555   945.09
Italy (1871-1947: United Italy: Monarchy)   DG555-575
Italy (1900-46: times of Vittorio Emanuele III, Umberto II)   DG566-575
Italy (1914-18: WWI)   DG570   945.0814
Italy (1918-46)   945.091 (SEE ALSO 963.056 for Italo-Eth. War of 1935-6)
              DG566-575, DG571, DG571-572 (Fascist period), DG572 (WWII time)
Italy & Italian neutrality (WWI: dipl. history)   D617
Italy. Army (gen.)   UA742   355.30945
Italy (biog.: heads of state)   923.145
Italy (gen. hist., culture, etc.)   DG417
Italy (gen.: titles dated after 1800)   DG467
Italy (geog. & travel)   914.5   DG428-429
Italy (lighthouses, beacons, foghorns, etc.) VK1079-1080
Italy (mil. status)   UA740   355.033045
Italy (naval geog.)   359.4745   VA540-549
Italy (naval status: gen.)   VA543.A5-Z 359.030945, .00945, .30945, .4745
Italy (post-WWI relns.: U.S.)   D651.I7
Italy (post-WWI territorial ?s: inclu. Fiume)   D651.I6-8
Italy, Sicily, Sardinia, Malta   DG 945
Italy (WWI)   D569   940.4145
Italy (WWI: causes, aims, results: includes Treaty of London, 1915)   D520.I7
Italy (WWI: mil. hist.)   940.40945   D569
Italy (WWI: Reconstruction)   D659.I8
Italy (WWII: dipl. hist.)   940.532445 D754.I8

JAMAICA (WWI)   D547.J3
JAPAN   DS801-897+   952
Japan (1868+: modern era)   DS881.85+   952.03
Japan (1868-1945: Imperial power)   952.03   DS881.9
Japan (1868-1912: Meiji or Matsuhito period: inclu. Sino-Jpn. War of 1894-5 & Russo-
                 Jpn. War of 1904-5)   952.031 (SEE ALSO 951.03 for
                 Sino-Jpn. War of 1894-5 & 947.083 for Russo-Jpn. War of
                 1904-5)   DS881.98-885.5, DS882-5, DS882
Japan (20th c.)   DS885   952.03-04
Japan (1912-26: Taisho or Yoshihito era)   952.032   DS885.8-888, DS886 (gen.)
Japan (1914-18: WWI era)   DS887   952.032
Japan & China (mil. policy)   355.033551 (China)-033552 (Japan)   UA830,
                              UA835+, UA845+
Japan. Army (gen.)   UA847   355.00952, .30952, .310952
Japan (biog.: heads of state)   923.152
Japan (gen. & cultural)   DS806
Japan (gen. history, descrip., culture)   DS835
Japan (mil. status)   355.033052   UA845+
Japan (naval hist.)   359.00952   VA650-659
Japan (naval status: gen.)   VA653.A5-Z   359.030952, .00952, .30952, .4752
Japan (post-WWI reins.: U.S.)   D651.J4
Japan (post-WWI territorial ?s)   D651.J3-5
Japan (WWI: causes, aims, results)   D519
Japan (WWII: causes, aims, results)   D742.J3
Japan (WWII: dipl. history)   D754.J3   940.532452
Japanese armament (modern)   U821.J3
Japanese (in U.S.)   E184.J3
Japanese military ops. & Japan (WWII: gen.)   D767.2   940.5352, .540952,
                                           .541352, 952.033
Japanese military ops. (WWI: gen.)   D571
Japanese mission to U.S. (WWI)   D570.8.M6.J4
Jellicoe, John Rushworth Jellicoe, 1st Earl (G.B.: 20th c. naval biog.)   DA89.1.J4
Jerusalem, Pal.   DS109
Jerusalem, Pal. (1917-)   DS109.93
Jewish question   DS141
JEWS (by country or area)   DS135.A-Z   Usually 004924 after Dewey place #s
Jews (Central Eur.)   943.0004924
Jews (Eng. and G.B.)   DS135.E5-6
Jews (Eur.)   DS135.E8-9   940.04924 (single '0' after decimal in this case)
Jews (Ger.)   DS135.G3-5   943.004924
Jews (in N.Y.)   F130.J5
Jews (in S.Am.)   F2239.J5
Jews (in U.S.)   E184.J5
Jews (It.)   DS135.I8-9   945.004924
Jews, Modern   DS143
Jews (outside Israel: economic, political, social conditions)   DS140-140.5
Jews, Palestine, & Israel (gen. histories)   DS117
Jews (Rus.)   DS135.R9-95   947.004924
Jews (S. Am.)   DS135.S8 (PREFER E #s in most cases)
Jews (Sp.-Am. War, 1898: U.S.)   E725.5.J4
Jews (U.S.)   DS135.U6-7 (PREFER E184.J5 in most cases)   973.004924
Jews (WWI: includes Ukrainian pogroms)   D639.J4 (SEE DS145.P5-7 for Protocols
                                         of the Wise Men of Zion)
Jews (WWI: peace topic)   D650.J4
Joffre, Joseph J. (Fr.: 1871-1940 era)   DC342.8.J6

Jordan   DS153-154   956.95
Jordan (1517-1918: Turkish rule)   DS154.4   956.9503
Judiciary, Military (by country except U.S.)   UB845.A-Z (for U.S. SEE KF7601-7679)
Judiciary, Naval (U.S.: inclu. overall naval justice)   VB793
Justice, Naval (gen.: inclu. judiciary)   VB790   343.014, .0146
Jutland, Battle of (1916)   D582.J8
Juvenile works (WWI)   D522.7

KEMAL, Mustafa (Tur.: 1909- era)   DR592.K4
Kenya   967.62   DT434.E2 (older titles), DT433.5-434 (newer books),
        DT433.522, DT433.557
Kenya (1895-1963: Brit. era)   DT433.57-433.577   967.6203
Kenya (mil. status)   UA860.5   355.03306762
Kerensky, Aleksandr (Rus.: 1894-1917: biog.)   DK254.K3
Khartoum, Egypt   DT154.K63
Kiel Naval Base (Ger.)   VA516.K4
Kiev, Rus.   DK651.K37
Kiev, Uk. (Kyiv)   DK508.92-939, DK508.95.K54
King's Liverpool Regiment (WWI)   D547.K43
King's Own Scottish Borderers (WWI)   D547.K47
Kitchener, Horatio Herbert K., 1st Earl (G.B.: 19th c. mil. biog.)   DA68.32.K6
Knapsacks (mil. equip.)   UC529.K6
Knives, bayonets, swords, etc. (design)   623.441   UD420-425, UD400 (bayonets)
Knots & splices (naut. ropes & cables)   623.8882   VM533
Konigsberg (cruiser: Ger.: WWI)   D582.K6
Korea   DS901-935+   951.9
Krakow, Pol. (Cracow)   DK4700-4735
Krupp armor plating (naval sci.)   V907.K7
Kurile Islands (Japan or Russia)   DS895.K9   957.7

LABOR (WWI)   D639.L2
Labrador   F1135-1139
Lake Baikal (Sib.)   DK771.B3
Lake Superior & Upper Peninsula (Mich.)   977.49   F572.N8 (N. Penin.),
        F552 (Lake Sup.)
Lanai (Haw. Is.)   DU628.L3   996.923
Land forces warfare   356-357   UD-UF
Land (mil. bases, reservations, etc.)   355.79
Land (naval bases etc.)   359.79 VC412-416
Land transport (mil. engineering)   623.61
Land vehicles, Motorized (mil. design)   623.747   UC270-275, UC340-345
Landing (aviation)   629.1325213
Landing craft (naval engineering)   623.8256   V895
Landing craft (navies: units)   359.3256   V895
Landing maneuvers & debarkation   U200
Landing ops. & field service tactics (naval: inclu. shore srvc., small arms instruc.,
        etc.)   V175   355.41, .422
Language   400-499   P
Languages & literatures   P   400-499, 800-899
Lapland (Fin.)   948.977   DL971.L2, DL1170.L2
Latin America & the West Indies   F1201-3799+   972, 980-989
Latin America (1898-)   F1414   980.032+
Latitude & longitude (marine navig.: inclu. tables)   VK565
Latrines & sewers (mil. qtrs.)   UC430
Lattre de Tassigny, Jean Joseph (Fr.: 20th c.)   DC373.L33

Light lists (marine navig.) 623.8945 VK1150-1246, VK1150, VK1151-1185 (Eur.),
  VK1203-1209 (Asia), VK1211-1223 (Australia & Pac.), VK1241-1246 (N.Am.)
Light signals (merch. marine) VK387
LIGHTHOUSES 623.8942 VK1000-1249 (gen. & by place), VK1010,
  VK1021-1124, VK1023-1025 (U.S.), VK1243 (U.S.: lists)
Lighthouses, beacons, foghorns, etc. (by area) VK1021-1124
Lighthouses, beacons, foghorns, etc. (Eur.: gen.) VK1055
Lighthouses, beacons, foghorns, etc. (Eur.: gen.: lists) VK1151 623.8944094
Lighthouses, beacons, foghorns, etc. (inclu. buoys & lightships) VK1000-1249
Lighthouses, beacons, foghorns, etc. (N. Am.: lists) VK1241-1246 623.8944097
Lighthouses, beacons, foghorns, etc. (U.S.: by area) VK1024
Lighting (naval architec. & engin.) VM491-493
Lights, Ships' (engin.) VM815
Lightships 623.8943 VK1010, VK1021-1124
Lightships, icebreakers, other misc. ships (engineering) 623.828
                                                          VM451 (icebreakers)

Lille, Fr. (WWI) D545.L5
Limited war 355.0215 (also older titles on total war) UA11+, U21+, UA11
Line functions (mil. organiz.) 355.33041
Line positions (naval hier.) 359.33041
Liners, Passenger (by name) VM383.A-Z
LISTS & registers (Calif. Nat. Guard) UA92
Lists & registers (N.Y. Nat. Guard) UA362
Lists & registers (U.S. Army: vets.) UA37
Lists & registers (WWI: decorated, dead, wounded) D609 940.467
Lists (beacons, foghorns, lighthouses, etc.) VK1150-1249
Lists, Naval (U.S.: also official yearbooks) V11.U6
Literature 800-899 P
Literature (gen. & gen. collections) PN 800-809
Lithuania DK511.L2-28 (earlier pubns.), DK505 947.5
Lithuania (1800-1918) DK505.73
Lithuania (1914-19) DK511.L26
Lithuania (post-WWI territorial ?s) D651.L5
Lithuania (WWI) D552.L5
Little Entente (1919) D460
Little Russia (Ukraine) 947.71 DK508
Litvinov, Maksim M. (Rus.: 1925-53 era) DK268.L5
Living conditions (air forces) 358.4112
Living conditions (marines) 359.9612 VE420-425
Living conditions, Military 355.12 U750-773, U750, U765
Living conditions (navies) 359.12 V720-743, V720 (gen.), V735 (modern),
                                   V736 (U.S.), V737 (G.B.)
Living conditions (navies: partic. situations) 359.129
Lloyd George, David (G.B.: 20th c.) DA566.9.L5
Loading & unloading nautical craft (plus cargo handling) 623.8881 VK235
LOCAL HISTORY (Arabian Penin.: cities) DS248.A-Z
Local history (Arabian Penin.: regions, sultanates, etc.: by place) DS247.A-Z
Local history (Arg.: towns etc.) F3011.A-Z
Local history (Armenian S. S. R.) DK689
Local history (Australia) DU145-398
Local history (Bel.: provinces, regions, etc.) DH801.A-Z
Local history (Bel.: towns except Brussels) DH811.A-Z
Local history (Brazil: regions, states, etc.) F2541-2636+
Local history (Bulg.) DR95-98
Local history (Calif.: towns etc.) F869.A-Z

Local history (China: cities & towns)   DS796.A-Z
Local history (Croatia)   DR1620-1636+
Local history (Den.: towns etc.)   DL291
Local history (Egypt: cities, towns, other)   DT154.A-Z
Local history (Egypt: provinces, regions, etc.)   DT137.A-Z
Local history (Eng.: towns besides London)   DA690.A-Z   942.2+
Local history (Ethiopia: kingdoms, regions, towns, etc.)   DT390.A-Z   963.056
Local history (Eur. Russia, Poland: provinces, governments, regions, etc.)
                                                            DK511.A-Z
Local history (Fin.: regions, provinces, etc.)   DL1170.A-Z
Local history (Fr.: north, east, Riviera, etc.)   DC601-609+
Local history (Fr.: regions, prov.'s, depts., etc.: by name)   DC611.A-Z
Local history (Fr.: towns besides Paris)   DC801.A-Z
Local history (G.B.: counties, regions, etc.: by name)   DA670.A-Z   942+
Local history (Ger.: areas, towns except Berlin)   DD901.A-Z
Local history (Ger.: large areas)   DD701-800
Local history (Ger.: provinces, regions, states, etc.)   DD801.A-Z
Local history (It.: large areas, cities)   DG600-980
Local history (It.: non-metro. towns, provinces, etc.)   DG975.A-Z
Local history (Japan: towns & cities)   DS897.A-Z
Local history (Libya)   DT238-239
Local history (London, Eng.)   DA675-689   942.1
Local history (N. Zea.: regions, towns, dependencies, etc. except Wellington)
                                                            DU430.A-Z
Local history (N.Y.: regions, counties, etc.)   F127.A-Z
Local history (Neth.: islands, provinces, regions, etc.)   DJ401.A-Z
Local history (Neth.: towns, cities, etc.)   DJ411.A-Z
Local history (Nor.: towns, villages, etc.)   DL596.A-Z
Local history (Palestine: regions, towns, etc.)   DS110.A-Z
Local history (Paris, Fr.)   DC701-790+   944.36
Local history (Pol.)   DK4600-4800
Local history (Pol.: provinces)   DK4600.A-Z
Local history (Prus.: provinces, regions, etc.)   DD491.A-Z
Local history (Rum.)   DR281-296
Local history (Rus. Rev., 1905-6: by place)   DK264.2.A-Z
Local history (Rus. Rev., 1917-21: by place)   DK265.8.A-Z
Local history (Rus.: towns other than Moscow in Eur., Pol. areas)   DK651.A-Z
Local history (Russia)   DK501-973+
Local history (S.Am.: regions)   F2212-2217
Local history (Samoan Is.: partic. islands, towns, etc.)   DU819.A3-Z
Local history (Scotland: counties, regions, etc.)   DA880.A-Z
Local history (Serbia)   DR2075-2125
Local history (Siberia: provinces, regions, etc.)   DK771.A-Z
Local history (Siberia: towns etc.)   DK781.A-Z
Local history (Swe.)   DL971-991
Local history (Swit.: cantons, cantonal capitals)   DQ301-800
Local history (Swit.: lakes, peaks, regions)   DQ841.A-Z (SEE ALSO DQ820+ for
                                                more Alps #s)
Local history (Swit.: towns except cantonal capitals)   DQ851.A-Z (SEE DQ301-
                                                800 for canton capitals)
Local history (Tur.: Eur. regions: by name)   DR701.A-Z
Local history (Ukraine: regions, oblasts, etc.)   DK508.9.A-Z
Local history (Ukraine: towns etc.)   DK508.95.A-Z
Local history (Washington, D.C.: cemeteries, churches, hotels, statues, parks,
                                                circles, streets, etc.)   F203

Local history (WWI: Austria: by place)   D539.7.A-Z
Local history (WWI: Calif.)   D570.85.C21.A-Z
Local history (WWI: England: by place) D547.8.A-Z
Local history (WWI: Ger.: by place)   D538.5.A-Z
Local history (WWI: Port.: by place)   D549.52.P82.A-Z
Local history (Yug.)   DR381-396
Local history (Yug.: provinces, regions, etc.)   DR381.A-Z
Local history (Yug.: regions not limited to partic. sections or old republics)
                                                    DR1350.A-Z
Local history (Yug.: sections & old republics: Slovenia, Bosnia, Montenegro, etc.)
                                                    DR1352-2285+

Lodge, Henry Cabot (U.S.: 1865-1900 era)   E664.L7
Lodz Voivodeship (Pol.)   DK4600.L63
Logistics & support, Air force   358.4141   UG1100-1105
Logistics & troop movement   355.411
Logistics (mil. sci.)   U168   355.411
Logistics, Naval   V179   359.411
Logs, Nautical   VK581
Lombardy & Milan, It.   DG651-662
LONDON, Eng.   942.1   DA675-689, DA677 (gen.)
London, Eng. (1901-50)   DA684   942.1082
London, Eng. (boroughs, streets, etc.) DA685.A-Z
London, Eng. (gen.)   DA677   942.1
London, Eng. (WWI)   D547.8.L7
London Regiment (WWI)   D547.L6
Longitude & time at sea (marine navig.: inclu. tables)   VK567
Looting & other mil. crimes   UB789
Looting & other naval crimes   VB880
Lorraine, Battle of (1914)   D545.L7
Los Angeles, Calif.   F869.L8   979.494
Los Angeles, Calif. (WWI)   D570.85.C21.L52
Louvain, Bel. (WWI)   D542.L7
Low Countries   DH-DJ
Lucerne, Lake (Swit.)   DQ841.L8
Lucerne, Swit.   DQ501-520   949.45
Ludendorff, Erich (Ger.: 1888-1918+ period)   DD231.L8
Lusitania (steamship: WWI)   D592.L8
Luxembourg   949.35   DH901-925, DH916 (1815-)
Luxemburg   DH901-925
Luxemburg (1815-)   DH916
Luxemburg (gen.)   DH908   949.35
Luxemburg (gen. hist., culture, etc.)   DH905
Luxemburg (post-WWI territorial ?s)   D651.L8
Lvov, Siege of (Polish wars, 1918-21)   DK4407.L9
Lyons, Fr.   DC801.L96-988
Lytton, Edward George E. Lytton Bulwer-Lytton, Baron (G.B.: 1837-1901 time)
                                                    DA565.L9

M1 rifle   UD395.M17
MacDonald, James Ramsay (G.B.: 20th c.)   DA566.9.M25
MACEDONIA   DR701.M13-42, DR2152-2285+   949.76
Macedonia (1878-1912)   DR2214
Macedonia (1912-45)   DR2230
Macedonia (1912-19)   DR2237
Macedonia (gen., descrip., culture, hist.)   DR2160, 2185
Macedonia (post-WWI territorial ?s)   D651.M3
MACHINE-GUN battalions (WWI: U.S.)   D570.34
Machine-gun regiments (WWI: Prus.)   D532.6
Machine-gun warfare   U167.5.M3
Machine guns (gen.)   UF620.A2   623.4424
Machine guns, Naval (gen.)   VF410.A2   623.4424
Machine guns (specific types)   UF620.A3-Z
Machinists, Naval   VG800-805
Madagascar   DT469.M21-38   969.1
Madrid, Sp. (1801-1950)   DP361
Magazines & serial pubns. (WWI)   940.4005   D501
Magazines, armories, etc. (countries except U.S.)   UF545.A-Z
Magazines, Ordnance (navies: gen.)   VF380   359.75
Mail, Military   355.693
Mail, Military (navies)   359.693
Maine (battleship: U.S.)   VA65.M2
MAINTENANCE & building devices & procedures, Marine (engin.)   VM901-965
Maintenance & repair (aircraft)   629.1346
Maintenance & repair (naut. engineering)   623.8208 (SEE ALSO .00288 after
                                1988)   VM763 (engines)
Maintenance & repair, Naval (yards etc.)   VC417
Maintenance & repair (ordnance)   623.48   UF350-355, UF550-560
Maintenance & repair (small craft)   VM322
MAINTENANCE & TRANSPORT (mil.: Asia)   UC234-245
Maintenance & transport (mil.: Australia)   UC255
Maintenance & transport (mil.: Can.)   UC90-93
Maintenance & transport (mil.: Eur.)   UC158-233
Maintenance & transport (mil.: G.B.)   UC184-187
Maintenance & transport (mil.: Ger.)   UC180-183
Maintenance & transport (mil.: New Z.)   UC256.5
Maintenance & transport (mil.: Rus.)   UC208-211
Maintenance & transport (mil.: U.S.)   UC20-88
Maintenance & transport (mil.: U.S.: by time period)   UC23
Maintenance & transport, Military   UC
MAINTENENCE, NAVAL   VC   359.6-8
Maintenance, Naval (Asia)   VC230-245
Maintenance, Naval (Australia)   VC255-256   359.60944
Maintenance, Naval (Can.)   VC90-93
Maintenance, Naval (Eur.)   VC160-229
Maintenance, Naval (Fr.)   VC176-179
Maintenance, Naval (G.B.)   VC184-187   359.60941
Maintenance, Naval (Ger.)   VC180-183   359.60943
Maintenance, Naval (Ger.: by region or area)   VC183.A-Z
Maintenance, Naval (It.)   VC196-199
Maintenance, Naval (New Z.)   VC256.5
Maintenance, Naval (Rus.)   VC208-211
Maintenance, Naval (U.S.)   VC20-65

Malay Archipelago & Indonesia   DS600-605   959.8
Malaysia   959.5   DS591-599, DS592, DS596
Malta   945.85   DG994
Manchuria   951.803-804   DS781-784.2+, DS784 (1932-45)
Manchuria (19th-20th c.)   DS783.7
Mandates (post-WWI)   940.31426   D651
MANEUVERS, Air force (training)   358.4152
Maneuvers & tactics (armor & cavalry: by place)   UE160-302
Maneuvers & tactics (artillery: Eur.)   UF215-269
Maneuvers & tactics (horse cavalry & artillery)   UE158
Maneuvers, drills, & tactics (artillery: gen.)   UF157
Maneuvers, drills, & tactics (infantry: gen.)   UD157   356.18, 355.42
Maneuvers (mil. engineering)   UG320-325
Maneuvers (mil. sci.)   U250-255
Maneuvers (mil. sci.: gen.)   U250   355.52
Maneuvers (mil. sci.: places besides U.S.)   U255.A-Z
Maneuvers (mil. sci.: U.S.)   U253
Maneuvers, Naval   V245, U260-262 (combined — army, navy, air forces — or
                         amphibious warfare ops.)   359.52
Maneuvers, Naval (training)   359.52   V245
Mannerheim, Carl (Fin.: 20th c.)   DK461.M32
Manning of vessels (merch. marine)   VK221
Manpower (by country)   UA17.5.A3-Z
Manpower (gen.)   UA17.5.A2   355.22, .61
Manual of arms (infantry: U.S.)   UD323-324
Manual of arms (naval seamen)   VD320   359.5470202, .8240202
MANUALS & handbooks (marines: gen.)   VE150   359.960202
Manuals & handbooks (mil. hygiene: not Eng. or Am.)   UH625
Manuals & handbooks (naval ordnance: places besides U.S.) VF155.A-Z
Manuals & handbooks (naval ordnance: U.S.)   VF153
Manuals & handbooks, Soldiers' (U.S.)   U113
Manuals & regulations, Air force (gen.)   UG670
Manuals, Armor & Cavalry   UE150-155
Manuals (artillery)   UF150-155   358.120202
Manuals, Infantry   UD150-155
Manuals, Infantry (places besides U.S.)   UD155.A-Z
Manuals, medical & surgical (navies: besides U.S.)   VG465.A-Z
Manuals (mil. engineering)   UG150-155
Manuals, Naval ordnance (U.S.: by mm., cm., inches, or lbs.) VF393.A4-6
Manuals (naval seamen: gen.)   VD150, V110+, V120+ (SEE ALSO V110+ &
                       V120+)   359.00202, .40202
Manuals (naval seamen: places except U.S.)   VD155.A-Z
Manuals (naval seamen: U.S.)   VD153   359.402020973
Manuals (U.S. Marines)   VE23.A48
Manufacture (naval ordnance & arms: gen.)   VF370
Manufacture (ordnance & small arms: gen.)   UF530   623.4+, 338.476234
Manufacture (small arms & ordnance: U.S.: by state)   UF534.A-W
Manufacturers (small arms & ordnance)   UF537.A-Z
Map maneuvers & problems   U312
Mapping & surveying, Military (U.S.)   UG472
Maps & atlases   912   G
Maps & atlases (WWI)   D522.3, G1037 (PREFER)
Maps & atlases (WWII)   D743.3, G1038 (PREFER)
Marching & guides (countries except U.S.)   UD315.A-Z
Marching & guides (mil.: gen.)   UD310

Mariana Islands (Ladrones: inclu. Guam)   DU640-648, DU643-5 996.7
Marine barracks & quarters (gen.) VE420   359.961292, .9671
Marine drills (by place)   VE160-302
Marine drills (Eur.: gen.)   VE215
MARINE ENGINEERING   VM600-989
Marine engineering (hist.: Australia)   VM721
Marine engineering (hist.: Eur.)   VM655
Marine engineering (hist.: Fr.)   VM671
Marine engineering (hist.: G.B.)   VM657   623.870941-870942
Marine engineering (hist.: gen.)   VM615
Marine engineering (hist.: Ger.)   VM673   623.870943
Marine engineering (hist.: It.)   VM679
Marine engineering (hist.: Japan)   VM699   623.870952
Marine engineering (hist.: Rus.)   VM685
Marine engineering (hist.: U.S.)   VM623-625
Marine engineering (instruction: U.S.)   VM727
Marine engines   VM731-779
Marine hydrography & surveying (gen.) VK591
Marine lifesaving (hist's.)   VK1315
Marine military ops.   359.964   VE21-124 (by place)
Marine navigation & merchant marine   VK
Marine navigation & merchant marine (gen.: pubn. 1801+) VK145   623.89
Marine navigation (instruction: by locale: inclu. merch. marine)   VK421-524
Marine navigation science   VK549-572
Marine regiments (U.S.: by #)   VE23.25.1st+
Marine training camps (U.S.: gen.) VE432   359.9670973
Marine uniforms (U.S.)   VE403   359.96140973
MARINES   VE   359.96
Marines & marine warfare   359.96 (add to .96 those #s after 355 in 355.1-.8)
                                VE, VE7-500+, VE15 (gen.), VE21-124 (by place),
                                VE23 (U.S.), VE57 (G.B.), VE145-146
Marines (Australia & New Z.)   VE121-122.5
Marines (by geographic area)   VE21-124
Marines (Can.)   VE26
Marines (collected, nonserial titles)   VE7
Marines (Eur.)   VE55-96
Marines (G.B.)   VE57-64
Marines (gen. hist.)   VE15   359.96, .9609
Marines (Ger.)   VE73
Marines (It.)   VE79
Marines (Rus.)   VE85
Marines (WWI: U.S.: inland ops.)   D570.348
Maritime Provinces (Can.: Atlantic coast)   F1035.8   971.5-8
Marksmanship (naval seamen: U.S.)   VD333
Marne, Battle of the (1914)   D545.M3
Marshall Islands (inclu. Kwajalein Atoll) DU710   996.83
Martens, Ludwig (WWI: Ger. spy in U.S.)   D619.5.M3
Masaryk, Tomas G. (Czech.: era of 1918-)   DB2191.M38
Massachusetts   974.4   F61-75, F64
Massachusetts (1865-1950)   F70 (SEE D570.85.M4-41 for war years, 1914-18
                                & D769.85.M4-41 for 1939-45)   974.404-043
Massachusetts (WWI)   D570.85.M4-41
Masters' manuals (merch. marine: inclu. command of ships)   VK205
Mata Hari (WWI: spy: Zelle)   D639.S8.Z4

224

Material, Naval (U.S. Navy. Office of: reports)   VA52.A68-69
Matériel & equipment (marines)   359.968   VE350-390, VF (ordnance)
Matériel & equipment, Air force   358.418   UG1100-1425+, UG1100-1105
Maui (Haw. Is.)   DU628.M3   996.921
Maurras, Charles M. (Fr.: 20th c.)   DC373.M3
Mauser rifle   UD395.M3
Maxim machine guns   UF620.M4
McKinley, William (U.S.: 1865-1900 era: works)   E660.M14
Measurement of ships (naval architec.)   VM155
Mecca, Saudi Arabia   DS248.M4
Mechanical engineering (mil. applications)   UG450
Mechanical systems (naut. craft: engineering)   623.8501
Mechanized cavalry (gen. & ops.)   357.58   UE147-155, UE159,
        UE160-302 (by place)
Medals, badges, brevets, etc. (navies: gen.)   VB330   359.1342
Medals, decorations, badges, etc. (mil. rewards)   355.1342
Medals, decorations, etc. (mil.: U.S.)   UB433
Medals, decorations, other reward insignia (navies)   359.1342
Medals (WWI: U.S. naval)   D589.U8
Media & public relns. (mil.: gen.)   UH700   070.433, .449, 355.342
Media & public relns. (navies: gen.)   VG500   359.342, 070.433, .439
MEDICAL & health services, Air force   358.41345   UH201-655
Medical & health services, Military   355.345   UH201-629, UH215, UH223-225 (U.S.)
Medical & mental examinations (mil. recruits)   UB330-336
Medical & nursing services (navies)   359.345   VG100-475, VG115, VG121-
        224 (overall by place), VG123 (U.S.), VG350-355 (nurse corps)
Medical & relief services, Military   UH201-570
Medical & surgical handbooks (navies: gen.)   VG460   359.3450202,
        610.0202, 617.0260202
Medical biography, Military (indiv.: by name)   UH347.A-Z   355.3450924
Medical biography, Naval (U.S.: collective)   VG227.A1
Medical care for retired military   UB448-449
Medical care of veterans   UB368-369   355.115
Medical corps equipment (gen.)   UH510
Medical facilities, Naval   359.72   VG410-450, VG420 (U.S.), VG430 (G.B.)
Medical installations, Military   355.72   UH470-475
Medical schools, Army (places besides U.S.)   UH399.A-Z
Medical schools, Army (U.S.: gen.)   UH398
MEDICAL SERVICES (air forces)   UG980-985   358.41345
Medical services & Red Cross (WWI: G.B.)   D629.G7
Medical services & Red Cross (WWI: U.S.: gen.)   D629.U6
Medical services, hospitals, Red Cross (WWI)   D628-630   940.475+, .477+
MEDICAL SERVICES, MILITARY (Australia)   UH321-322
Medical services, Military (Can.)   UH226-227
Medical services, Military (Eur.)   UH255-295
Medical services, Military (Eur.: gen.)   UH255   355.345094
Medical services, Military (Eur.: WWI)   UH256.1914-18
Medical services, Military (Fr.)   UH271-272
Medical services, Military (G.B.: gen.)   UH257   355.3450941
Medical services, Military (Ger.)   UH273-274   355.3450943
Medical services, Military (hist., statistics, etc.: gen. & by place)   UH215-324
Medical services, Military (New Z.)   UH322.5
Medical services, Military (Rus.)   UH285-286
Medical services, Military (Rus.: Asia)   UH309-310
Medical services, Military (Tur.)   UH311-312

Medical services, Military (U.S.)   UH223-225   355.3450973
Medical services, Military (U.S.: official reports) UH223.A1-49
Medical services, Military (U.S.: unofficial) UH223.A6-Z
Medical services, Military (U.S.: WWI)   UH224.1917-18
MEDICAL SERVICES, NAVAL   VG100-475 (SEE ALSO UH201-515)
Medical services, Naval (Asia)   VG199-213
Medical services, Naval (Australia)   VG221
Medical services, Naval (Eur.)   VG155-196
Medical services, Naval (G.B.)   VG157
Medical services, Naval (Ger.)   VG173
Medical services, Naval (Rus.)   VG185
Medical services, Naval (U.S.)   VG123   359.3450973
MEDICAL SERVICES (WWI: Ger.)   940.47543   D629.G3
Medical services (WWI: hospitals)   940.476   D628-629
Medical services (WWI: hospitals, British)   940.47641   D629.G7
Medical services (WWI: hospitals, French)   940.47644   D629.F8
Medical services (WWI: hospitals, German) 940.47643   D629.G3
Medical services (WWI: particular countries)   940.4754-4759   D629.A-Z
Medical services (WWI: Rus.)   940.47547   D629.R9
Medical services (WWI: U.S.)   940.47573   D629.U6-8
Medical supplies   355.88   UH440-445
Medical supplies, Naval   359.88   VG290-295
MEDICINE   610-619   R
Medicine, Military (gen., hdbks., etc.)   UH390-396
Medicine, Military (places besides U.S.: manuals etc.)   UH395.A-Z
Medicine, Military (U.S.: official manuals etc.)   UH393
Medicine, Military (U.S.: unofficial manuals etc.) UH394
Medicine, psychiatry, & nursing   R   610-619, 649
MEDITERRANEAN Region (Eastern)   956.9   DS80-151+, DS62
Mediterranean Sea (lighthouses, beacons, foghorns, etc.: lists)   VK1176
    623.8944091638
Mediterranean Sea (mil. status)   UA646.55   355.03301638, 359.471638
Mediterranean Sea (pilot & sailing guides)   VK853-874   623.89291638, .8929448
Mediterranean Sea (tide & current tables)   VK653-674
Mediterranean, Eastern (geog. & travel)   915.69   DS44, DS49, D972-973
Melanesia   993.2-993.7 (PREFER 995 after 1988)   DU490 (gen.)
Melbourne, Australia   DU228   994.51
Memorials, monuments, celebrations (WWI: gen.)   D663 (SEE ALSO D503 for
    museums & NA9325 for fine arts)
Mennonites (WWI)   D639.M37
Mental & medical examinations (mil. recruits: gen.)   UB330   355.2236
Mental health, psychiatry, etc. (mil.: gen.)   UH629
MERCHANT MARINE & navigation (20th c.: hist. & conditions) VK20
Merchant marine & navigation (gen. hist's.)   VK15
Merchant marine & navigation (gen. special)   VK147
Merchant marine & navigation (hist. & conditions: by area or country) VK21-124
Merchant marine & navigation (instruction: U.S.)   VK423
Merchant marine & navigation (study & teaching: gen.)   VK401
Merchant marine (occupation)   VK160   387.0023
Merchant marine (WWI)   D639.M4-5
Merchant ships, Powered (engineering) 623.824
Mesopotamia (post-WWI territorial ?s) D651.M4
Messes & clubs, Naval officers' (gen.)   VC380   359.346
Messing (mil.: cooking: U.S.)   UC723

Metal ships (naval architec.)   VM146-147   623.8182
Metals (mil. raw materials)   355.242
Meteorology, Aviation   629.1324
Meteorology, Military   UG467
Mexico   F1201-1392   972-972.7
Mexico (1867-1917)   972.081   F1233.5-1234
Mexico (1910-46)   F1234   972.081-082
Michigan (inclu. Lakes Mich. & Huron)   F561-575, F566   977.4
Michigan (WWI: Reconstruction)   D658.M5
Micronesia   996.5   DU500 (gen.)
Middle Atlantic states & District of Columbia   F116-205
Middle East (Near East)   956   DS41-326
Middle East & Southwestern Asia   DS41-329   953, 955, 956
Middle East (geog. & travel)   915.6   DS49-49.5
Middle West & Mississippi River Valley (1865-1950)   F354   977.03
Mihailovi´c, Draza (Yug.: 20th c.)   DR359.M5
Milan, It.   DG660-662
Militarism & antimilitarism (inclu. mil.-indus. complex)   355.0213   JX1952,
                JX1963, UA23, U21.5, JF195.C5

MILITARY ADMINISTRATION   355.6   UB-UC
Military administration (Asia)   UB99-113
Military administration (Australia)   UB121-122   354.94066
Military administration (Austria)   UB65-66
Military administration (Belg.)   UB67-68
Military administration (by country)   UB21-124
Military administration (Can.)   UB26-27
Military administration (civil sections)   UB180-197
Military administration (Eur.)   UB55-95
Military administration (Fr.)   UB71-72   354.44066
Military administration (G.B.)   UB57-64
Military administration (G.B.: by time period)   UB58.1900+
Military administration (G.B.: Eng. & Wales)   UB59
Military administration (G.B.: Scot.)   UB61
Military administration (gen.: pubn. 1801-1970)   UB145   355.6
Military administration (gen.: pubn. 1971+)   UB146   355.6
Military administration (Ger.)   UB73-74   354.43066, 355.60943
Military administration (It.)   UB79-80
Military administration (misc. Eur. lands)   UB95.A-Z
Military administration (New Z.)   UB122.5
Military administration (Pol.)   UB95.P7
Military administration (Rus.: Asia & Sib.)   UB109-110
Military administration (Rus.: Eur.)   UB85-86   354.47066
Military administration (Scan.: gen.)   UB86.5
Military administration (Tur.)   UB111-112
Military administration (U.S.)   UB23-25   353.6, 355.60973
Military administration (U.S.: by state)   UB24.A-W
Military air transport (U.S.)   UC333-334   358.440973
Military & marine engineering   623   UG; VM
Military & nautical engineering (hist. & biog. works: overall)   623.009+   UG400-401
Military & nautical engineering (overall topics)   623.04
Military & naval history (G.B.: 20th c.)   DA566.5

Military & naval life & customs (WWI: Australia)   940.48394   D547.A8
Military & naval life & customs (WWI: Fr.)   940.48344   D548-549
Military & naval life & customs (WWI: Ger.)   940.48443   D532-538, D581-
                                                    582 (naval), D604 (aerial)
Military & naval life & customs (WWI: U.S.)   940.48373   D570, D589.U6-7 (naval),
                                                    D606 (aerial)
Military & naval science   355-359   U, V
Military animals (gen.)   UH87   355.24
Military artificers & technical troops (places besides U.S.)   UG505.A-Z
Military barracks & camps (U.S.)   UC403-404   355.70973
Military bases, camps, forts, reservations, etc. (geog. & hist. applic.)   355.709
MILITARY BIOGRAPHY   923.5 (SEE ALSO 355.0092, 940.3+, .53+, etc.)   U51-55
Military biography (Asia)   923.55
Military biography (G.B.)   923.541-542   DA54 (collec.), DA69.3.A-Z (20th c.:
                                            indiv.), DA89.1.A-Z (naval: 20th c.: indiv.), U55.G7
Military biography (Ger.)   923.543   DD100 (group)
Military biography (Rus.)   923.547   DK50.5-8
Military biography (U.S.)   923.573   E181 (mil.: collec.), E182 (naval: collec.),
                                            U52-53
Military biography (U.S.: collective)   U52
Military bridges (design)   623.67   UG335, UC320-325
Military capability   355.0332+
Military clothing & equipment (U.S.)   UC463-464
Military clubs (U.S.)   U56
Military commissions (by country except U.S., for which SEE KF7661)   UB875.A-Z
Military communications (except U.S.: by country)   UA945.A-Z
Military communications (gen.)   UA940   355.27, .41, .6
Military construction (U.S.: gen.)   UC46 (SEE ALSO UG for engineer., VC420+ &
                                            VG590+ for naval)   358.22
Military crimes (countries outside U.S.)   UB785.A-Z
Military crimes (U.S.)   UB783 (SEE ALSO KF7615-7618)
Military decorations, medals, rewards, etc.   UB430-435   355.1342
Military discipline   UB790-795   343.014, .13325
MILITARY EDUCATION & training (gen.)   U400   355.07
Military education (Asia: gen.)   U635
Military education (Austria-Hung.: special eras)   U551
Military education (Can.)   U440-444
Military education (Eur.: gen.)   U505
Military education (G.B.: gen.)   U510
Military education (Ger.: gen.)   U570
Military education (Ger.: special topics)   U572.A-Z
Military education (Japan: gen.)   U650
Military education (U.S.: Command & Gen. Staff Coll.)   U415
Military education (U.S.: gen.)   U408   355.0071073
MILITARY ENGINEERING   623.1-7   UG
Military engineering, air forces, & air warfare   UG   358.2, 623, 358.4 (air forces etc.)
Military engineering & air forces   UG
Military engineering (Asia: gen.)   UG99
Military engineering (collections)   UG7
Military engineering (Eur.: gen.)   UG55
Military engineering (field: gen.)   UG360
Military engineering (G.B.: by #'d regiment)   UG57.Z6.1st+
Military engineering (misc.)   623.7

Military engineering (U.S.: by #'d regiment)   UG125.1st+
Military engineering (U.S.: gen.)   UG23
Military engineering maneuvers (U.S.)   UG323
Military engineering manuals (U.S.)   UG153
Military enginering (Ger.: by #'d regiment)   UG73.Z6.1st+
Military equipment (U.S.)   UC523-524   355.80973
Military expeditions   U265
Military explosives, unguided rockets, etc.   UF860-880
Military flags, colors, standards (gen.)   UC590   355.15
Military footwear (U.S.)   UC493
Military forces & science   355-358   U
Military fortifications, Permanent (engineering)   623.12 (for titles after 1988
                                                     SEE ALSO .1)   UG405
Military fortifications, Temporary (engineering)   623.15   UG403
Military geography   UA985-997   355.47+, .0330+, 359.47+
Military geography (except U.S.)   UA995.A-Z
Military geography (U.S.)   UA993   355.4773, 359.4773
Military headgear   UC500
Military headquarters ops. (gen.: inclu. aides, adjutants, etc.)   UB230
MILITARY HISTORY (1801-1914/20)   D361   355.033003+
Military history (1871-late 19th c.)   D396   359.009
Military history (20th c.)   D431   355.020904, 355.009, 355.033+
Military history (Australia)   DU112.3   355.00994, .033094
Military history (Bel.: 1815-)   DH545
Military history (Bel.: gen.)   DH540
Military history (Bulg.)   DR70
Military history (Can.)   F1028   355.00971
Military history (China: 20th c. & 1912-49)   DS775.4
Military history (Egypt)   DT81
Military history (Fin.)   DL1036-1037   355.0094897
Military history (Fr.)   DC44-47
Military history (Fr.: 1871-1940)   DC339
Military history (Fr.: 19th-20th c.)   DC47
Military history (Fr.: 20th c.)   DC367
Military history (G.B.)   DA50-69.3
Military history (G.B.: 19th c.)   DA68
Military history (G.B.: 20th. c.: gen.)   DA69   355.00941, .033041, .033241, .033541
Military history (Ger.)   DD99-105
Military history (Ger.: 20th c.)   DD104   355.00943, .033043, .033242, .033543
Military history (Greece)   DF765
Military history (India: 1901-)   DS442.6
Military history (It.)   DG48-84
Military history (It.: 1792-20th c.)   DG484
Military history (Japan: 1868+)   DS838.7   355.00952, .033052, .033252, .033552
Military history (N. Zea.)   DU420.5   355.009931
Military history (Neth.)   DJ124
Military history (Nor.)   DL454   355.009481
Military history (Pol.)   DK417 (older titles), DK4170-4178
Military history (Pol.: 1795-1918)   DK4173
Military history (Pol.: 1919-)   DK4174
Military history (Rum.)   DR219
Military history (Rus.: 1801-1917)   DK53   355.00947
Military history (Rus.: 1917-)   DK54   355.00947, .033+

Military history (S. Afr.)   DT769   355.00968
Military history (Scan., N. Eur., Fin.)   DL52
Military history (Serbia)   DR1970
Military history (Swe.)   DL654
Military history (Swit.)   DQ59
Military history (Tur.)   DR448   355.009561
Military history (U.S.)   E181   355.00973, .033073
Military history (U.S.: 20th c.: inclu. biog.: more than 1 war)   E745   355.00973,
                                                                .033073, .033273, .033573
Military history (Ukr.)   DK508.54
Military history (world)   D25   355.48, 904.7, 909
MILITARY HISTORY (WWI)   940.4   D521 (gen.), D529-608
Military history (WWI: Australia)   940.40994   D547.A8
Military history (WWI: by place)   940.409
Military history (WWI: Can.)   940.409571   D547.C2
Military history (WWI: New Z.)   940.40993 (SEE ALSO .409931 for titles earlier than
                                    1989)   D547.N5
Military history (WWI: S. Africa)   940.40968   D547.A4
Military history (WWI: U.S.)   940.40973   D570
Military history (WWI: units & ops.: Australia)   940.41294   D547.A8
Military history (WWI: units & ops.: by country: inclu. structure, hist., registers, etc.)
                                    940.412-413+   D532-578, D608
Military history (WWI: units & ops.: Can.)   940.41271   D547.C2
Military history (WWI: units & ops.: Fr.)   940.41244   D548-549
Military history (WWI: units & ops.: G.B.)   940.41241   D546-546.55+, D547
Military history (WWI: units & ops.: Ger.)   940.41343   D531-538
Military history (WWI: units & ops.: New Z.)   940.412931   D547.N5
Military history (WWI: units & ops.: Rus.)   940.41247   D550
Military history (WWI: units & ops.: Turkey)   940.413561   D566
Military history (WWI: units & ops.: U.S.)   940.41273   D570-570.75
MILITARY HISTORY (WWII)   940.54   D743
Military history (WWII: Australia)   940.540994   D767.8
Military history (WWII: Fr.)   940.540944   D761
Military history (WWII: G.B.)   940.540941-540942   D759-760
Military history (WWII: Ger.)   940.540943   D757
Military history (WWII: It.)   940.540945   D763.I8-817
Military history (WWII: New Z.)   940.5409931 (SEE ALSO .540993 for titles prior
                                    to 1989)   D767.85
Military history (WWII: Rus.)   940.540947   D764
Military history (WWII: U.S.)   940.540973   D769, D769.25-4 (armies, div's.,
                                    regt's.), D769.45-598 (naval particip., units, ops.)
Military history (Yug.)   DR319
Military history (Yug.: gen.)   DR1251
Military horses & mules (gen.)   UC600
Military hospitals (U.S.)   UH473-474 (SEE ALSO D629.U6-8 & D807.U6-87 for
                              WWI & II)
Military hygiene & sanitation (U.S.)   UH603
Military information (security: besides U.S.)   UB248.A-Z
Military information (security: U.S.)   UB247
Military inspection   355.63   UB240-245
Military installations & land (inclu. bases, forts, camps, posts, etc.)   355.7
                              UA26+ (U.S.), UC400-405, UA600-876
Military intelligence (G.B.)   UB251.G7
Military intelligence (gen.)   UB250   355.3432
Military intelligence (Ger.)   UB251.G3   355.34320943

Military justice (admin.: gen.)   UB840   343.0143, .133
Military kits & field equip. (gen.)   UC540   355.81
MILITARY LAW   UB461-736
Military law (Asia)   UB685
Military law (Australia)   UB730-734
Military law (Austria)   UB600-604
Military law (Balkan states)   UB680-683
Military law (Can.)   UB505-509
Military law (Eur.: gen.)   UB590
Military law (Fr.)   UB615-619
Military law (G.B.)   UB625-629 (PREFER KD6000-6355)   343.010941
Military law (Ger.)   UB620-624   343.010943
Military law (New Z.)   UB734.5
Military law (Rus.: gen.)   UB655   343.010947
Military law (Rus.: statutes & compil's.)   UB655.A2
Military law (Tur.)   UB675-679
Military law (U.S.)   UB500-504 (PREFER KF7201-7755)   343.010973, .0106073
MILITARY LIFE & CUSTOMS   U750-773   355.1
Military life & customs (modern: Fr.)   U768
Military life & customs (modern: G.B.)   U767   355.10941
Military life & customs (modern: Ger.)   U769   355.10943
Military life & customs (modern: It.)   U770
Military life & customs (modern: misc. countries besides U766-771)   U773
Military life & customs (modern: Rus.)   U771   355.10947
Military life & customs (modern: U.S.)   U766   355.10973
Military life, customs, & postmilitary benefits   355.1   U750, U22
Military life (service periods, promotion, vet. benefits, etc.)   355.11
Military living conditions (partic. situations)   355.129   U765+
Military maintenance & transport (Asia: gen.)   UC234
Military maintenance & transport (Eur.: gen.)   UC158
Military maintenance & transport (gen.) UC10   355.6-8
Military maintenance & transport (U.S.: gen.)   UC20
Military maintenance & transport (U.S.: WWI era)   UC23.1917-1918
Military maneuvers   355.52   U250-255
MILITARY MEDICAL SERVICES (Asia: gen.)   UH299
Military medical services (G.B.: by period or date)   UH258
Military medical services (gen.: inclu. organization, surgeons, etc.)   UH400
Military medical services (hist., statistics, etc.: includes sanitary services: gen.)
                                                      UH215   355.345
Military medical services (U.S.: by time period or date: SEE ALSO particular wars)
                                                                              UH224
Military medical services, Military (Eur.: by date or period)   UH256
Military medicine (gen.: inclu. hdbks., manuals, etc.)   UH390   616.98023
Military missions   UA16
Military missions & attachés   355.032
Military motor vehicles (places besides U.S.)   UG620.A-Z
Military museums & exhibitions (gen.)   U13.A1
Military nursing (U.S.)   UH493
Military observations (collected: 2 or more wars)   U719
Military oceanography (U.S.)   V396.3-4
Military officers (except U.S.: by country)   UB415.A-Z
Military ops. (hist's. & types of persons)   355.409 (SEE ALSO 355.47 for geog.
                                                      treat.)   U27-43
Military ops. (Sp.-Am. War, 1898: gen.)   E717   973.89, .893, .895
Military ops. (WWI: West: gen.)   D530   940.41+, .421, .424, .4272, .431, .434

Military personnel (inclu. organization; readiness of partic. groups)   355.3
                                        UA15+, UA23-39+ (U.S.)
Military pistols & revolvers (design)   623.443   UD410-415
Military planning   U150-155
Military police & conduct enforcement   355.13323
Military police (gen.)   UB820   355.13323
Military police (WWI: U.S.)   D570.35
Military prison life   355.1295 (SEE ALSO 365.48)
Military prisons   355.13325 (SEE ALSO 365.48)   UB800-805
Military prisons & prisoners (gen.)   UB800   365.48, 355.13325, 344.03548
Military prisons (outside U.S.)   UB805.A-Z
Military quarters & camps (besides U.S.)   UC405.A-Z
Military railroads & rolling stock (engineering)   623.63   UC310-315,
                                        UF490-495 (r.r. artil.), UG345 (engnrg.)
Military railroads (U.S.: gen.)   UC313   355.830973
Military recreation & information services (gen.)   UH800   355.346
Military research, Aeronautical (U.S.: by state of origin)   UG643.5.A-W
Military research (U.S.)   U393
Military resources (prep., review, preserv.)   355.21
MILITARY SCIENCE   355-358   U
Military science (19th c.)   U41
Military science (20th c.)   U42   355.00904
Military science & engineering   U   355-358, 623
Military science & organization (ALSO armed forces, ground forces, etc.)
                                        355 (officers' hdbks. here)   U, U21+
Military science (gen.)   U1-900+   355
Military science (gen.: pubn. date 1789-)   U102   355, .43
Military science (history)   U27-45
Military science (history: by country or area)   U43.A-Z
Military science (history: gen.)   U27   355.009
Military science, military engineering, & air forces   U-UH   355-359, 623
Military science (misc. services: medical etc.)   UH
Military science (modern: 1800-)   U39
Military service as a profession   UB147
Military services (misc.)   UH
Military signaling (gen.)   UG580
Military skill (Indians of N. Am.)   E98.M5
Military social & welfare services (countries besides U.S.)   UH769.A-Z
Military sports (by place)   U328.A-Z
Military staffs (countries besides U.S.)   UB225.A-Z
MILITARY STATUS (20th c.)   355.033004   U42
Military status (1900-1919)   355.0330041
Military status (Africa)   UA855-868
Military status (Asia)   UA830-853
Military status (Asia: by country except India, China, Japan)   UA853.A-Z
Military status (Australia)   UA870-874
Military status (Austria & Austria-Hung.)   UA670-679
Military status (Balkan States)   UA820-827
Military status (by area or country)   355.03301-03309
Military status (Can.)   UA600-602
Military status (China)   UA835-839

Military status (Eur.) UA646-829
Military status (Fr.) UA700-709
Military status (G.B.) UA647-668 355.033041-033042, .033241, .033541
Military status (gen. hist.) 355.033 D25, U21+, U27, UA15
Military status (gen.: inclu. policy) 355.03
Military status (Ger.) UA710-719
Military status (hist. periods) 355.033001-033005
Military status (It.) UA740-749
Military status (Japan) UA845-849
Military status (misc. Eur. countries) UA829.A-Z
Military status (N. Am.) UA22-602
Military status (New Z.) UA874.3-7
Military status (Norway) UA750-759
Military status (Pacific islands) UA875-876
Military status (Rus. or Sov.Un.) UA770-779
Military status (S.Am.) UA612-645
Military status (Tur.) UA810-819
Military status (U.S.) UA23-585 355.033273
Military staus (W. Hemis.) UA21-645
Military status (world: gen.) UA10 355.03
Military status (worldwide: place by place) UA21-876+ 355.0330+
Military supplies & stores (gen.) UC260
Military supply ships (freighters, tankers, etc.: units) 359.3265 (SEE ALSO
.9853 after 1988) VA79
Military surveying, mapping, & topography UG470-474
Military tactics (partic. kinds: commando, retreats, blitz, landings, attacks &
counters, etc.) 355.422
Military tactics (special topics: by name) U167.5.A-Z
Military telegraph & troops (U.S.) UG603
Military transport engineering 623.6 UC, UC10, UC270-360, UC270-275 (gen.)
Military transport (U.S.) UC273-274
Military transport vessels & hospital ships (units) 359.3264 (SEE ALSO .9853 for
transp. ships on pubns. after 1988) VA79 (transports), VG450 (hosp. ships)
Military tunnels (design) 623.68 UG340
Military uniforms (U.S.) UC483-484 355.140973
Military units (marines) 359.9631
Military units (types: armies, div's., regiments, co's., mil. districts, etc.) 355.31
UA, UA23-39+ (U.S.), UA646-829 (Eur.),
UA830-853 (Asia), UA870-876 (Australia-Pac.)
Militia (Ger.) UA717
Militia, Naval (U.S.: state by state) VA90-387
Militia (U.S.: inclu. Nat. Guard etc.: state by state) UA50-549
MINE laying & sweeping (mil. engnrg.: land) 623.262 UG490
Mine sweeping & laying (mil. engineering: marine) 623.263 V856-856.5
Minelayers & minesweepers (naval engineering) 623.8262 V885 (sweepers),
V856-856.5 (both)
Minelaying, minesweeping, submarine mines, etc. (gen.) V856 623.2, .26, .263,
.36, .45115, .8262, 359.825115, .3262
Minerals (non-metal: mil. raw materials) 355.243

Mines (design)   623.45115   UG490, V856-856.5 (naval)
Mines (mil. equip.)   355.825115   UG490
Mines (naval ammun.)   359.825115
Mines, Land (inclu. countermeasures)   UG490   623.45115
Minesweepers   V885 (SEE ALSO V856)   623.8262
Minesweepers & minelayers (navies: units)   359.3262   V885, V856+
Minesweeping, minelaying, sub. mines, etc. (by place)   V856.5.A-Z
Mining & torpedo troops   UG550-555
Minorities & women in the armed forces (gen.)   UB416   355.22 (women), .3
Minorities & women in the armed forces (places besides U.S.)   UB419
Minorities & women in the armed forces (U.S.: by group name)   UB418.A-Z
Minorities & women (navies)   VB320-325
Minorities (U.S. Navy: by group)   VB324.A-Z
Missions to the U.S. (WWI: by country)   D570.8.M6.A-Z
Missions to the U.S. (WWI: overall)   D570.8.M5
Mississippi   F336-350   976.2
Missouri   977.8   F461-475, F466
Missouri (WWI)   D570.85.M8-81
MOBILIZATION   UA910-915
Mobilization and beginnings (WWI)   D528.5
Mobilization (except U.S.: by name of place)   UA915.A-Z
Mobilization (G.B.)   UA915.G7   355.280941
Mobilization (gen.)   UA910   355.28
Mobilization, Industrial (gen.)   UA18.A2   355.28
Mobilization (mil. resources: inclu. requisition, commandeering, voluntary, etc.)
                         355.28   UA910-915, UA913 (U.S.)
Mobilization, Naval (G.B.)   VA463   359.280941
Mobilization, Naval (Ger.)   VA518   359.290943
Mobilizaton, Naval (gen.)   VA48   359.28
Mobilization (U.S.)   UA913   355.280973
Mobilization (U.S. Navy)   VA77   359.280973
Model ships   623.8201
Models, Military   U311
Models, Ship   VM298   623.8201, 745.5928
Modern history (1453-)   D208   901.93, 909.8+, 940
Modern history (1789-)   D299   909.8+
Modern history (1801-1914/20)   D358   909.81
Modern history (1871-late 19th c.)   D395
Mohammed V (Tur.: ruler, 1909-18: also titles on era) DR583
Moltke, Helmuth (Ger.: 1871-1918 era)   DD219.M7
Mongolia   DS793.M7 (SEE ALSO DS19-23.1 for Mongols)   951.7
Mons, Bel. (WWI)   D542.M7
MONTENEGRO   DR101-196+, DR1802-1928 (SEE ALSO DR357+, DR1214)
                         949.745, .76
Montenegro (1860-1918: Nicholas I era)   DR154
Montenegro (1878-1918: Nicholas I)   DR1878-1883
Montenegro (1878-1918: Nicholas I: gen.)   DR1878
Montenegro (1912-18: Balkan wars & WWI)   DR1883
Montenegro (1914-18: WWI)   DR158
Montenegro (1918-45: gen.)   DR1885
Montenegro (gen.)   DR117, DR1810, 1835
Montenegro (post-WWI territorial ?s)   D651.M7
Montenegro (WWI: gen.)   D564.A2

MONUMENTS & cemeteries (WWI: Australia)   940.46594   D680.A
Monuments & cemeteries (WWI: Can.)   940.46571   D680.C
Monuments & cemeteries (WWI: Fr.)   940.46544   D680.F8
Monuments & cemeteries (WWI: Ger.)   940.46543   D680.G3
Monuments & cemeteries (WWI: It.)   940.46545   D680.I
Monuments & cemeteries (WWI: Rus.)   940.46547   D680.R
Monuments, memorials, celebrations (WWI)   D663-680   940.46+
Monuments, memorials, celebrations (WWI: countries other than U.S.) D680.A-Z
Monuments, memorials, celebrations (WWI: G.B.)   D680.G7
Monuments, memorials, celebrations (WWI: U.S.: by city)   D675.A-Z
Monuments, memorials, celebrations (WWI: U.S.: by state)   D673.A-W
Monuments, statues, memorials (London, Eng.)   DA689.M7
Monuments, statues, memorials (Washington, D.C.)   F203.4.A-Z
Moral & health protection (mil.: alcoholism, drug abuse, prostitution, venereal
     diseases, etc. & work vs.)   UH630
Morale, Military   355.123   U22
Morale (navies)   359.123
Moravia (20th c.)   DB2415-2421
Moravia (20th c.: gen.)   DB2416
Moroccan question (20th c.)   D475 (PREFER DT317)
Morocco   DT301-330   964
Morocco (1900-56)   964.04   DT324
Mortars & howitzers (U.S.: gen.)   UF473
Mortars (U.S.: handbooks)   UF563.A75
Moscow area (Rus.)   DK511.M6
Moscow, Rus.   DK591-609, DK601 (hist. to 1950)   947.31
Moscow, Rus. (to 1950)   DK601
Moscow, Rus. (Rev., 1917-21)   DK265.8.M6
Mosley, Oswald, Sir, Baronet (G.B.: 1910-36 biog.)   DA574.M6
MOTOR transport, Artillery   UF390
Motor transport (mil. sci.)   UC340-345   355.83
Motor transport (naval sci.)   VC570-575
Motor vehicles, Military (gen.) UG615   623.747, 355.83, 357.5+
Motorboats & launches (small craft: gen.)   VM341
Motorcycle troops (mech. cav.)   357.53   UC347
Motorcycles (mil. transp.)   UC347   623.7472
Motorized infantry   356.11 (pubns. before 1989 may inclu. regular infan. ALSO)
                    U167.5.M6, UD15, UD21-124+, UA
Motorized units (mil. sci.)   U167.5.M6
Mountain artillery   UF440-445
Mountain guns (U.S.: handbooks) UF563.A5.2.95in.Mt. (2.95)
Mountain warfare & troops   UD460-465   356.164
Mounted forces & warfare   357   UE, UE15, UE21-124, UE23 (U.S.),
                    UE57 (G.B.), UE65 (Austria), UD450-455
Mounted infantry (gen.)   UD450
Movie services, Military (gen.)   UH820
Movies (WWI)   D522.23
Mozambique (Portuguese East Africa)   DT451-465   967.9
Mukden, Battle of (Rus.-Jpn. War, 1904-5)   DS517.4
Mules & horses, Military (places besides U.S.)   UC605.A-Z
Munich, Ger.   DD901.M71-95

MUSEUMS, Air force (inclu. exhibitions: gen.)   UG623.3.A1   623.74074,
                                                                    358.40074
Museums & exhibitions (marine navig. & merch. marine)   VK6
Museums & exhibitions (mil. engineering)   UG6
Museums & exhibitions (naval architec.)   VM6
Museums & exhibitions (naval ordnance: gen.)   VF6.A1
Museums, Artillery (by city within area, whose 1st letter & shelf # are shown by
    'x' in 'x2')   UF6.x2.A-Z
Museums, Artillery (by country or region)   UF6.A2-Z
Museums, Artillery (inclu. exhibitions)   UF6
Museums, exhibitions, etc. (arms)   U804
Museums, exhibitions, etc. (arms: by country)   U804.A2-Z
Museums, exhibitions, etc. (WWI)   D503
Museums, Military (Fr.)   U13.F8
Museums, Military (G.B.)   U13.G7
Museums, Military (inclu. exhibitions)   U13.A-Z   355.0074
Museums, Military (U.S.)   U13.U6-7   355.0074073
Museums, Naval (gen.: inclu. exhibitions)   V13.A1 359.0074
Music   M   780-789
Music & bands, Military (gen.)   UH40
Music & bands, Naval (U.S.)   VG33   359.340973, .170973
Mustard gas   UG447.5.M8   623.4516
Muster rolls & accounts, Military (gen.: inclu. gen. corresp.: admin.)   UB160
Mutinies & military offenses   355.1334 (SEE 364.138 for war crimes)   UB780+
Mutinies (WWI)   D639.M8
Mutinies (WWI: by country)   D639.M82.A-Z
Mutiny & other naval offenses   359.1334   VB850-880
Mutiny (mil.)   UB787
Mutiny (naval: except U.S.)   VB865.A-Z
Mutiny (naval: gen.)   VB860   359.1334
Mutiny (naval: U.S.)   VB863
Mutual-aid agreements (WWII: U.S.: by country)   D753.2.A-Z
Muzzle-loading ordnance   UF560-565... .M.L.

NAMUR area (Bel.)   DH801.N2-29
Naples, It. (kingdom & later)   DG840-855
National characteristics (Ger.)   DD76
National Home & Vets' Admin. (U.S.: gen.)   UB383
National security (gen.)   UA10.5
National War College (U.S.: Wash., D.C.)   U412
Nationalities (WWI: U.S.)   D570.88.A-Z
Naturalized subjects in belligerent lands (WWI)   D639.N2-3
Nauru (Pleasant Island)   996.85
Nauru (post-WWI territorial ?s)   D651.N3
NAUTICAL almanacs & yearbooks   VK7-8
Nautical craft & types   623.82 VM, VM145
Nautical engineering & seamanship   623.8   VM (architec.), VK (navig.)
Nautical instruments (gen.)   VK573   623.894, .863
Nautical instruments (misc.)   VK584.A-Z
Nautical life (merchant marine: pop. titles)   VK149
Nautical lifesaving (by area)   VK1321-1424
Nautical pilots & piloting (gen. hist's.)   VK1515   623.8922, .892209
Nautical tables (gen.: inclu. azimuth)   VK563

Naval biography (collective)   V61   359.00922
Naval biography (places except U.S.: by person's name after country name)
V64.x2.A-Z

Naval biography (U.S.: collective)   V62   359.00922
Naval cemeteries (U.S.)   VB303-304
Naval ceremonies   359.17   V310
Naval chaplains (gen.)   VG20   359.347
Naval clothing & personal equipment (overall)   VC280-285
Naval coaling stations (U.S.: gen.)   VA73   359.70973, .750973
Naval command and leadership   VB200-205
Naval contracts (supplies: U.S.)   VC267.U6-7
Naval crimes (except U.S.)   VB855.A-Z
Naval crimes (G.B.)   VB855.G7
Naval crimes (Ger.)   VB855.G3
Naval crimes (U.S.)   VB853
Naval demobilization   359.29   VB277, UA917
Naval desertion (U.S.)   VB873
Naval design   623.81   VM, V750-995 (warships), VM15-20 (hist.),
VM21-124 (by place), VM23 (U.S.), VM57 (G.B.),
VM146 (metal ships), VM156 (theory), V750, V765, V800
Naval design (components & details)   623.814   VM, VM156
Naval discipline   VB840-845   359.13
Naval districts (U.S.: by #)   VA62.7.1st+
Naval districts (U.S.: gen.)   VA62.5   359.70973
Naval drills (seamen: by country or area: includes watch, station, quarter, fire)
VD160-302
NAVAL EDUCATION & training (gen.)   V400   359.007
Naval education (Asia: gen.)   V625
Naval education (Eur.: gen.)   V500
Naval education (G.B.: gen.)   V510   359.0071141, .50941, .550941, .007041
Naval education (Ger.: gen.)   V570   359.007043, .50943
Naval education (Japan: gen.)   V640   359.007052, .0071152, .50952, .550952
Naval education (U.S.: gen.)   V411   359.0071073, .0071173, .50973, .550973
Naval engineering & seamanship   623.8   VM, VK
Naval engineering (civil: U.S.)   VG593
Naval equipment & supplies (gen.: for ships)   VC270   359.8
Naval facilities (bases, docks, artificial harbors, etc.: design)   623.64   V220-230,
VA69-750 (by place), VA67-70 (U.S.), VM301
Naval flags (G.B.)   V305.G7
Naval flags (Japan)   V305.J3
Naval flags (U.S.: inclu. marine)   V303
Naval forces & divisions (WWII: U.S.: by name)   D769.52.A-Z
Naval forces & warfare   359   V-VM, V27-55, V101-109
Naval fuel (gen.: ALSO costs etc.)   VC276.A1   359.83, 623.874, .415
Naval gunnery practice (places except U.S.)   VF315.A-Z
Naval handbooks (seamen's: places besides U.S.)   V115.A-Z
Naval health, hygiene, & sanitation (gen.)   VG470

NAVAL HISTORY (1453-)   D215
Naval history (1801-1914/20)   D362
Naval history (20th c.)   D436   359.409, 904.7, 359.47
Naval history (Australia)   DU112.4   359.00994
Naval history (Can.)   F1028.5   359.00971
Naval history (Den.: 19th-20th c.)   DL154.7
Naval history (Dutch E. Ind.)   DS637
Naval history (Fin.)   DL1040-1042
Naval history (Fr.)   DC49-53
Naval history (Fr.: 19th-20th c.)   DC53
Naval history (Fr.: 20th c.)   DC368
Naval history (Fr. Indoch.)   DS545
Naval history (G.B.)   DA70-89
Naval history (G.B.: 20th c.)   DA89   359.00941, .4741
Naval history (Ger.)   DD106   359.00943, .4743
Naval history (It.: gen.)   DG486   359.00945
Naval history (Japan: 1868+)   DS839.7   359.00952, .4752
Naval history (Pol.)   DK417.7
Naval history (Pol.)   DK4177-4178
Naval history (Rum.)   DR225
Naval history (Rus.-Jpn. War, 1904-5)   DS517.1
Naval history (Rus.: 1917-)   DK59   359.00947
Naval history (Scan., N. Eur., Fin.)   DL53
Naval history (Swe.)   DL656
Naval history (Tur.)   DR451
Naval history (U.S.)   E182   359.00973, .4773
Naval history (U.S.: 20th c.)   E746   359.00973, .4773
Naval history (world)   D27   359, 904.7
Naval hospital corps (gen.)   VG310
Naval hospitals (places except U.S.)   VG430.A-Z
Naval hospitals (U.S.: by area or state)   VG424.A-Z
Naval inspection   359.63   VB220-225
Naval installations (hist. & geog. works)   359.709+
Naval intelligence (G.B.)   VB231.G7   359.34320941
Naval intelligence (gen.)   VB230   359.3432
Naval intelligence (Ger.)   VB231.G3   359.34320943
Naval intelligence (U.S.)   VB231.U6-7 359.34320973
Naval justice (admin. of)   VB790-925
Naval justice (places besides U.S.)   VB795.A-Z
NAVAL LAW   VB350-785
Naval law (Asia: gen.)   VB700
Naval law (Australia)   VB775
Naval law (by area or country)   VB360-785
Naval law (Can.)   VB370-379
Naval Law (Eur.: gen.)   VB530
Naval Law (FR.)   VB570-579
Naval Law (G.B.)   VB590-599 (PREFER KD6128-6158)   343.4101
Naval Law (Ger.)   VB580-589
Naval law (New Z.)   VB777
Naval law (Rus.)   VB650-659
Naval law (U.S.)   VB360-369 (PREFER KF7345-7375)

NAVAL LIFE & CUSTOMS   V720-743
Naval life & customs (modern)   V735-743
Naval life & customs (modern: G.B.)   V737   359.10941
Naval life & customs (modern: Ger.)   V739   359.10943
Naval life & customs (modern: Japan)   V743.J3
Naval life & customs (modern: misc. countries)   V743.A-Z
Naval life & customs (modern: Rus.)   V741   359.10947
Naval life & customs (modern: U.S.)   V736   359.10973
Naval living conditions (training or perm. bases)   359.1292
Naval machine guns (special by name)   VF410.A3-Z
Naval maintenance (Asia: gen.)   VC230
Naval maintenance (Eur.: gen.)   VC160
Naval maintenance (gen.)   VC10   359.6
Naval maintenance (U.S.: gen.)   VC20   359.60973
Naval medical biography (U.S.: indiv.)   VG227.A2-Z
Naval medical services (by place)   VG121-224
Naval medical services (gen.)   VG115   359.345, .72, 616.98024
Naval mobilization   359.28   VA48, VA77-750, VA77 (U.S.)
Naval museums & exhibitions (by country)   V13.A2-Z   359.00740+
Naval mutiny (by ship)   VB867.A-Z
Naval nurse corps (gen.)   VG350   359.345, 610.7349, .7361, 616.98024
Naval observations (wartime)   V701-716 (PREFER D-F areas)
Naval officers (except U.S.)   VB315.A-Z
Naval officers' clubs (U.S.)   VC383   359.3460973
Naval officers' clubs (U.S.: by state)   VC384.A-W
Naval officers' handbooks (U.S.)   V133
NAVAL OPS. (hist's.: gen.)   359.409   V27-55
Naval ops. (Sp.-Am. War, 1898)   E727-729   973.895
Naval ops. (Sp. Civil War, 1936-39)   DP269.3-35
Naval ops. (U.S. Navy. Office of: reports)   VA52.A7-79
Naval ops. (WWI)   D580-595   940.45
Naval ops. (WWI: Australia)   940.45994   D589.A
Naval ops. (WWI: Can.)   940.45971   D589.C
Naval ops. (WWI: Fr.)   940.45944   D583
Naval ops. (WWI: G.B.)   940.45941   D581-582, VA458
Naval ops. (WWI: Ger.)   940.45943   D581-582
Naval ops. (WWI: It.)   940.45945   D588
Naval ops. (WWI: misc. countries: by place)   D589.A-Z
Naval ops. (WWI: Rus.)   940.45947   D585
Naval ops. (WWI: Turkey)   940.459561   D587
Naval ops. (WWI: U.S.)   940.45973   D589.U5-8
Naval ops. (WWII)   D770-784
NAVAL ORDNANCE & arms (gen.)   VF350
Naval ordnance & arms (manufacture: U.S.)   VF373
Naval ordnance (Asia: gen.)   VF99
Naval ordnance (by country or place)   VF21-124
Naval ordnance drills (by place)   VF160-302
Naval ordnance (engineering)   623.8251   VF, VF21-124 (by place), VF23 (U.S.),
                                                            VF350-355
Naval ordnance (Eur.: gen.)   VF55
Naval ordnance material (besides U.S.)   VF395.A-Z
Naval ordnance material (gen.)   VF390   623.418
Naval ordnance (nonperiodical collections)   VF7
Naval ordnance (special overall)   VF147
Naval personnel (admin.: U.S.)   VB258   359.610973

Naval petty officers' handbooks (U.S.)   V123
Naval prisons & prisoners (gen.)   VB890   344.03548
Naval projectiles (gen.)   VF480   359.8251, 623.451
Naval propaganda & psychological warfare   359.3434   UB275-277
Naval provisions & subsistence (countries besides U.S.)   VC355.A-Z
Naval provisions & subsistence (U.S.)   VC353-354   359.810973
Naval quarters & barracks (U.S.)   VC423-424
Naval recreation & information services (gen.)   VG2020   359.346
Naval research (ordnance: places besides U.S.)   VF360.5.A-Z
Naval research (U.S.: by special establishment locale)   V394.A-Z
Naval research (U.S.: by state)   V393.5.A-W
Naval Reserve Officers' Training Corps (U.S.: N.R.O.T.C.)   V426   359.2232
Naval reserves (U.S.: gen.)   VA80   359.370973
Naval resources (preparation, eval., preserv.)   359.21
Naval schools (Ger.: by name or place)   V574.A7-Z
NAVAL SCIENCE   359   V
Naval science (19th c.)   V51   359.009034
Naval science (20th c.)   V53   359.00904, .40904
Naval science (ancient hist.)   V29-41   359.00901
Naval science (by region or country)   V55.A-Z   359.47+
Naval science (collected works: monographic)   V15-17
Naval science (gen.)   V, V1-995+   359, 623.8
Naval science (gen.: pubn. thru 1800)   V101
Naval science (gen.: pubn. 1801+)   V103
Naval science (history, antiquities, & biog.: gen., during peace & war)   V25-64 (SEE
                              ALSO D-F #s for specific countries, wars, etc.)
Naval science (medieval hist.)   V43-46   359.00902
Naval science (misc. services: medical etc.)   VG
Naval science (modern hist.: 17th-20th c.)   V47-53+   359.00903
Naval science, navigation, & naval architecture   V   359, 623, 629
Naval science, navigation, & shipbuilding   V-VM
Naval science (pop. works)   V107   359
NAVAL SEAMEN (by area or country)   VD21-124
Naval seamen (G.B.: Eng. & Wales)   VD59
Naval seamen (G.B.: N. Ire.)   VD63
Naval seamen (G.B.: Scot.)   VD61
Naval seamen (gen. hist.: enlisted way of life etc.)   VD15   359.338, .12
Naval seamen (Ger.: by locality)   VD74.A-Z
Naval seamen (U.S.: by state)   VD24.A-W
Naval services (misc.)   VG
Naval shipbuilding (hist.: Asia: gen.)   VM99   623.8095
Naval shipbuilding (hist.: by area or country)   VM21-124
Naval shipbuilding (hist.: Eur.: gen.)   VM55   623.8094
Naval shipbuilding (instruc.: gen.)   VM165   623.8107
Naval signaling (U.S.)   V283
Naval small arms (U.S.)   VD363   359.8240973
Naval stations & shore facilities (countries besides U.S.) VC416.A-Z
Naval stations & shore facilities (Ger.)   VC416.G3
Naval stations & shore facilities (U.S.: Calif.)   VC415.C2
Naval stations & shore facilities (U.S.: Fl.) VC415.F5
Naval stations & shore facilities (U.S.: Haw.)   VC415.H2

Navigation Aerial   629.13251
Navigation & merchant marine   VK
Navigation, Marine (gen. hist's.: modern: inclu. merch. marine)   VK18
Navigation, Marine (instruction: G.B.: inclu. merch. marine)   VK457
Navigation, Marine (science: hist.)   VK549   527.094, 387.155
Navy clubs (U.S.)   V66
Navy yards, shore facilities, stations, etc.   VC412-425
Near East (1900-18)   956.02   DS62.4
Near East & Southwestern Asia (modern)   DS62.4
Near East, Turkey, Italy, Greece (WWI)   D566-569
Netherlands (Holland)   DJ   949.2
Netherlands (1890-1948: gen. & biogs. of Queen Wilhelmina)   DJ281   949.2071
Netherlands (1914-18: WWI)   DJ285   949.2071
Netherlands (mil. status)   UA730-739   355.0330492
Netherlands (naval status)   VA530-539
Neutrality, other special diplomatic history (WWI)   D611
Neutrals (WWI: dipl. hist.)   940.325   D611, D639.N
Neutrals (WWI: gen. particip.)   940.335   D639.N, D615 (Belgium), D611
Neutrals (WWII: dipl. hist.)   940.5325
New Britain (Bismarck Arch.: inclu. Rabaul)   DU553.N35
New Brunswick   F1041-1045   971.5
New countries (post-WWI: formation)   940.31425   D651
New England (1865-1950)   F9   974.04-042
New England & Middle Atlantic states   974   F1-105 (New Eng.),
                                                                F106-205 (Mid. At.), F1-15, F106
New England & Middle Atlantic states (1865-1918)   974.041   F9 (New Eng.),
                                                                F106 (Mid. At.)
New Guinea   DU740-746   995.1-7, 995
New Guinea (mil. geog.)   355.4795
New Guinea (Papua: naval geog.)   359.4795   VA750.N, VA667.N
New Guinea (WWI)   D578.N4
New Jersey   F131-145   974.9
New London Naval Station (U.S.: Conn.)   VA70.N5
New South Wales (Australia: 1837-1950: gen.)   DU161
NEW YORK   F116-130, F119   974.7
New York (1865-1950)   F124 (SEE D570.85.N4-5 for 1914-18 war years &
                                                D769.85.N4-5 for 1939-45)   974.704
New York (1865-1918)   974.7041   F124 (1865-1950)
New York City area (N.Y.: 1901-50)   F128.5   974.7104-043
New York City, N.Y.   F128, F128.3   974.71
New York City, N.Y. (streets, bridges, railroads)   F128.67.A-Z
New York National Guard (gen.)   UA360
New York (WWI)   D570.85.N4-5
NEW ZEALAND   DU400-430   993.1 (PREFER 993 after 1988)
New Zealand (1840-1908)   993.102 (SEE ALSO 993.02 for works after 1988)   DU420
New Zealand (1876-1908: Centralized gov.)   993.1023   DU420
New Zealand (1908-: Dominion)   993.103 (works before 1989), 993.03+ (for titles
                                                after 1988)   DU420-421
New Zealand (1908-18)   993.031, 993.1031 (works prior to about 1989)
New Zealand & Melanesia (overall)   993 (SEE ALSO 995 for Mel. with pubn.
                                                dates after about 1988)   DU400-490+
New Zealand. Army (descrip. & hist.)   UA874.5   355.309931
New Zealand. Army (special sections)   UA874.6.A-Z
New Zealand (gen.)   DU420   993.1-1037+
New Zealand (geog. & travel)   919.31   DU411

243

New Zealand (mil. status: gen.)   UA874.3   355.0330931
New Zealand (naval status: gen.)   VA723.A5-Z   359.0309931, .009931, .47931
New Zealand (WWI)   D547.N5
Newfoundland   F1121-1139   971.8, .803 (1934-49)
NEWS & PROPAGANDA (WWI)   940.488   D639.P6-7, D631-633, D619.3
News & propaganda (WWI: in G.B.)   940.488941
News & propaganda (WWI: in Ger.)   940.488943
News & propaganda (WWI: in Rus.)   940.488947
News & propaganda (WWI: in specific countries) 940.4889+
News & propaganda (WWI: in U.S.)   940.488973
News & propaganda (WWII)   940.5488   D810.P6 (gen.), .P7.A-Z (by country)
Newspapers, media, & public relns. (navies: besides U.S.)   VG505.A-Z
Nicaragua (post-WWI territorial ?s)   D651.N5
Nicholas II (Rus.: Czar, 1894-1917)   DK258
Night fighting   U167.5.N5
Nile River (20th c.: descrip. & travel)   DT124   962.044-045
Nitti, Francesco (It. 1900-46 period)   DG575.N5
Non-combat services, Naval   359.34   VG1-2029+, VC10-580+
Non-commissioned officers, Air force (countries besides U.S.)   UG825.A-Z
Noncombat services (air forces)   358.4134
Noncombat services (mil.: inclu. soc. srvcs., dependent srvcs., civil activ's., etc.)
                                                                              355.34
Noncombatants, pacifists, sympathizers, etc. (WWI)   940.316
Nonexplosive agents (tear gas etc.: design)   623.459   UF780
Nonmilitary use of armed forces   UH720-725
Nordenfelt machine guns   UF620.N8
Nordenfelt ordnance   UF560-565... .N.
Norfolk Navy Yard (U.S.: Va.)   VA70.N7
Norfolk, Va.   F234.N8
Normandie (pass. ship)   VM383.N6
Normandy area (Fr.)   944.2   DC611.N841-899
North Africa   961   DT160-346
North Africa (1830-1950: Eur. era) 961.03 DT176
NORTH AMERICA   E-F1392+, E11-45, E31-45   970
North America (1900-)   970.05 E45, E18.85
North America (1900-18)   970.051
North America (1918-45)   970.052
North America (gen.)   E45
North America (geog. & travel)   917   E41, E27
North America (mil. status: gen.)   UA22   355.03307
North Atlantic Fleet (U.S.)   VA63.N8
North Atlantic (pilot & sailing guides)   VK811-814.5
North Atlantic (tide & current tables)   VK611   623.8949091631
North Central states   977   F476-705, F476-590 (Old N.W.), F476-485,
                                           F591-705 (Trans-Miss.), F591-596
North Sea & Baltic (pilot & sailing guides)   VK815-826
North Sea & Baltic (tide & current tables)   VK615-626
North Sea (mil. status)   UA646.6   355.033016336
Northcliffe, Alfred C. W. Harmsworth, 1st Viscount (G.B.: 20th c.) DA566.9.N7
Northeast Africa (1900-74)   DT367.75   963.05+

Northern Europe & Scandinavia   948   DL
Northern Europe (mil. status)   UA646.85   355.033048
Northern Europe, Scandinavia, Finland (1901-45)   DL83   948.08
Northern Ireland   941.6   DA990.U45-46
Northern Rhodesia (Zambia), Rhodesia (Zimbabwe), & Nyasaland (Malawi)   968.9
                    DT858-865 (Malawi, Nyasaland, Br. Central Afr. Protec.),
                    DT946-965 (Rhodesia), DT963 (Zambia)
Northumberland Fusiliers (WWI)   D547.N7
Northwest (U.S.: Old)   F476-590   977
Norway   DL401-596+, DL448 (gen.)   948.1
Norway (20th c.)   DL527   948.104
Norway (1914-18)   DL531
Norway (mil. status)   UA750   355.0330481
Norway (WWI: dipl. hist.)   D621.S45
Norwegian military ops. (WWII)   D763.N6
Nova Scotia   F1036-1040, F1038 (gen.)   971.6
Nuremberg, Ger.   DD901.N91-97
Nurse corps, Naval   VG350-355
Nurse corps, Naval (U.S.)   VG353
Nurses & nursing, Military (gen.)   UH490   355.345
Nursing & nurses, Military (besides U.S.)   UH495.A-Z
Nyasaland (Malawi, Brit. Cent. Afr. Protec.)   DT858-865

OBSERVATIONS, MILITARY   U719-740+
Observations, Military (Franco-Prussian War, 1870-1)   U729
Observations, Military (Russo-Jpn. War, 1904-5)   U735
Observations, Military (Russo-Turkish Conflict, 1877-8)   U730
Observations, Military (S.Afr. Conflict, 1899-1902)   U733
Observations, Military (Sp.-Am. War, 1898-9)   U731
Observations, Military (WWI)   U738
Observations, Naval (Franco-German War, 1870-1)   V707
Observations, Naval (Russo-Japanese War, 1904-5)   V713   952.031,
                                                                                     359.4752, .4747

Observations, Naval (Span.-Am. War, 1898)   V709
Observations, Naval (U.S. Civil War, 1861-5)   V705
Observations, Naval (WWI)   V715   940.45-453
Obstacles (mil. engineering)   UG375   355.544
Occupation & government, Military   355.49   D802 (WWII)
Occupation, Military (WWI: Rhineland)   D650.M5
Occupational rehabilitation of veterans (by occup.)   UB366.A-Z
Occupied territories (WWI: by country)   D623.A3-Z
Occupied territories (WWI: gen.: includes laws)   D623.A2
Oceania   993-996   DU
Oceania, Australia, New Zealand   DU   990-996
Oceania (mil. status)   UA875   355.03309
Oceanography, Military (gen.) V396   359.982, 551.46, 620.4162
Oceanography, Military (places besides U.S.)   V396.5.A-Z
Odessa & Crimea areas (Rus.)   947.717   DK511.C7
Odessa, Rus.   DK651.O2
Odessa, Uk.   DK508.95.O33
Offenses & crimes, Military   UB780-789
Offenses & crimes, Naval   VB850-880

OFFICERS, Air force (gen.)   UG790   358.41331-41332
Officers, Air force (Ger.)   UG795.G3
Officers, Air force (U.S.)   UG793
Officers' clubs & messes, Military (U.S.)   UC743
Officers' clubs & messes, Naval   VC380-385
Officers, Commissioned & warrant 355.332   UB407-415
Officers, Commissioned & warrant (navies)   359.332   VB307-315
Officers' handbooks, Naval (places besides U.S.)   V135.A-Z
Officers, Military (G.B.)   UB415.G7   355.3320941
Officers, Military (Ger.)   UB415.G3   355.3320943
Officers, Military (inclu. appt., promo., retire.)   UB410-415
Officers, Military (U.S.)   UB412-414   355.3320973
Officers, Naval (G.B.)   VB315.G7   359.3320941
Officers, Naval (inclu. appt., promo., rank, retire., etc.)   VB310-315
Officers, Naval (Rus.)   VB315.R9
Officers, Naval (U.S.: gen.)   VB313   359.3320973, .3310973
Officers, Non-commissioned (air: U.S.: inclu. airmen)   UG823
Officers Training Corps (WWI: G.B.)   D546.3
Officers, Warrant (mil.: gen.)   UB407
Officers, Warrant (naval: U.S.)   VB308   359.3320973
Oman   DS247.O6-68
Operational equipment, Air force (airplanes, bombs, guns, vehicles)   UG1200-1405
Optical instruments & tools, Artillery   UF849
Optimum ship routing   VK570
Orders, General (Rus. military: offic. compil's.)   UB657.A5
Orders, passes, field correspondence (mil. sci.)   UB280-285
Orders, passes, field correspondence (naval admin.)   VB255
Orders, Special (Rus. military: collec's. & compil's.)   UB657.A6-7
Orders, Transmission of (navies)   V270   359.27, .85
ORDNANCE   355.82   UF520-780, U800-823+
Ordnance, Air force   358.4182   UG1270-1275
Ordnance, Air force (gen.)   UG1270-1275   358.4182, 623.45+
Ordnance, Aircraft (design)   623.7461   UG1270-1275, UF530-537
Ordnance & arms, Naval (in sum)   VF350-375
Ordnance & arms, Naval (manufacture) VF370-375
Ordnance & small arms   UF520-537   355.82, 623.4+, .44
Ordnance & small-arms research (U.S.)   UF526.3
Ordnance & small arms (U.S.)   UF523   355.820973
Ordnance drills, Naval (Eur.: gen.)   VF215
Ordnance (engineering & design)   623.4   UF520-910+, UF520-
     525 (gen.), UF523 (U.S.), VF (naval), VF1-580, VF21-124 (by place), VF23 (U.S.)
Ordnance facilities, Naval   359.73   VF380-385
Ordnance laws (U.S.)   UF133 (PREFER KF7335)
Ordnance magazines & facilities (navies)   VF380-385
ORDNANCE MATERIAL (by type, mark #, ed. date, etc.)
                              UF560-565.A-Z.A-Z(II-IV) etc.
Ordnance material (countries besides U.S.)   UF565.A-Z
Ordnance material (Fr.)   UF565.F8
Ordnance material (G.B.) UF565.G7
Ordnance material (gen.)   UF560   355.82+, 623.4+
Ordnance material (Ger.) UF565.G3
Ordnance material (misc.)   VF420
Ordnance material (navies: U.S.)   VF393
Ordnance material (Rus.)   UF565.R9
Ordnance material (U.S.: gen.)   UF563   355.820973, 623.40973

ORDNANCE, NAVAL   VF   359.82, 623.8251
Ordnance, Naval (Asia)   VF99-113
Ordnance, Naval (Australia)   VF121
Ordnance, Naval (Eur.)   VF55-96   359.82094
Ordnance, Naval (Fr.)   VF71
Ordnance, Naval (G.B.)   VF57   359.820941
Ordnance, Naval (gen. hist's.)   VF15   359.8209
Ordnance, Naval (gen. pubns. 1801+)   VF145   359.82
Ordnance, Naval (Ger.)   VF73   359.820943
Ordnance, Naval (handbooks & manuals: gen.)   VF150
Ordnance, Naval (It.)   VF79
Ordnance, Naval (misc. topics)   VF580
Ordnance, Naval (Rus.)   VF85
Ordnance, Naval (U.S.)   VF23   359.820973, 623.82510973
Ordnance proper   UF560-780
Ordnance proper (navies)   VF390-395
Ordnance proper (navies: U.S.: documents)   VF393.A1-3
Ordnance proper (navies: U.S.: gen.)   VF393.A7-Z
Ordnance research, Naval (U.S.)   VF360.3
Ordnance stores, accounts, etc. (gen.)   UF550
Ore carriers   VM457   623.8245, 387.544
ORGANIZATION (air forces)   UG770-1045
Organization & personnel (cavalry: inclu. specific units)   357.043
Organization & personnel (infantry)   356.189
Organization & personnel (marines)   359.963   VB21-124
Organization & personnel, Naval   359.3   VA, VA50 (U.S.), VB21-124
Organization (armor & cavalry: gen.)   UE10
Organization (artillery forces)   UF10
Organization (infantry: gen.)   UD10
Organization (mil. maint. & transport: by country)   UC20-258
Organization (mil. medical: inclu. services)   UH400-485
Organization (mil. personnel: hist. & geog. treatment)   355.309
Organization (naval maintenance: by place)   VC20-258
Orientals (in Calif.)   F870.O6
Orientals (in U.S.)   E184.O6
Orkney Islands (Scot.)   DA880.O5-6
Orphans, children, similar noncombatants (WWI)   940.3161   D639.C4
Oslo, Nor. (Christiana)   DL581   948.2
Oxford and Asquith, Herbert Henry Asquith, 1st Earl of (G.B.: 20th c.)   DA566.9.O7
Oxford University (WWI)   D547.O7

P.O.W. camps & internment centers (WWI: in G.B.)   940.47241-47242   D627.G7
P.O.W. camps & internment centers (WWI: in Ger.)   940.47243   D627.G3
P.O.W. camps & internment centers (WWI: in Rus.)   940.47247   D627.R9
PACIFIC, Asiatic, & other colonies (WWI: Ger.: by place)   D578
Pacific, Asiatic, & other colonies (WWI: Ger.: gen.)   D577
Pacific Coast & Far West (U.S.: geog. & travel)   917.9   F851
Pacific Coast (U.S.: fortifications)   UG411.P2
Pacific Fleet (U.S.)   VA63.P2
Pacific Islands, German (post-WWI territorial ?s)   D651.P2
Pacific Islands (mil. status: by island or group name)   UA876.A-Z
Pacific Islands (smaller misc.: by name)   DU950.A-Z
Pacific (marine mil. geog.)   359.96479+   VE123, VA730
Pacific (naval geog.)   359.479   VA710-750, VA730
Pacific Northwest (1859-1950)   F852   979.5

Pacific Ocean (Oceania: gen.)   DU28.3   990, 990.09, 909.0964
Pacific States & Alaska   F851-915+   979
Pacifists (WWI)   940.3162   D613, UB342.A-Z (by place)
Packing & shipment (mil. supplies) UC277
Paderewski, Ignacy Jan (Pol.: 1918-45 era) DK4420.P3
Page, Walter Hines (U.S.: 1865-1900 era)   E664.P15
Pago Pago, Samoa   DU819.P3
Pakistan (Bengal: East & West)   DS485.B39-493 954.14
Palaces (London, Eng.)   DA689.P17
PALESTINE (640-1917)   956.9403   DS124-125, DS125.5 (WWI yrs.)
Palestine (19th-20th c.)   DS125   956.9403-9404
Palestine (1914-18: WWI)   DS125.5   956.9403-9404
Palestine (geog. & travel)   915.694   DS107.3
Palestine, Israel, & the Jews   DS101-151   956.94, 909.04924
Palestine (post-WWI territorial ?s) D651.P3
Palestine (WWI)   D568.7
PAMPHLETS, MINOR WORKS (20th c.)   D416
Pamphlets, minor works (20th c.: diplomacy)   D457
Pamphlets, minor works (20th c.: politics and diplomacy)   D450
Pamphlets, minor works (Rus.-Jpn. War, 1904-5)   DS517.8
Pamphlets, minor works, sermons (Rus. Rev., 1917-21)   DK265.17
Pamphlets, minor works, sermons (WWI)   D525
Pamphlets, minor works (WWI: American Legion)   D570.A14.Z9
Pamphlets, minor works (WWI: peace)   D646
Pamphlets, minor works (WWI: U.S.)   D570.15
Panama   F1561-1577, F1566   972.87
Panama (1903-52)   F1566.5   972.8705-052
Panceltism   D448.5
Pangermanism   D447
Panlatinism   D448
Pannonia   DJK77
Panslavism   D449
Panslavism (Eastern question: 19th c.)   D377.3-5
Papal States   DG791-800+
Papal States (modern)   DG796
Papen, Franz von (WWI: Ger. spy in U.S.)   D619.5.P2
Papua & New Guinea (gen.: inclu. Brit. terr. & Port Moresby, Owen Stanley Mts.,
Papua New   Guinea & New Guinea region)   995.3
Paraguay   F2661-2699   989.2
Paris, Fr. (1871-1914)   DC735
Paris, Fr. (1914-21)   DC736
Paris, Fr. (area)   944.36   DC701-790, DC707 (gen.), DC735 (1871-1914),
                    DC737 (1914-)
Passenger ships (engineering)   623.8243   VM381-385, VM383.A-Z (by ship
                    name), VM385.A-Z (by co.)
Passenger ships (naval architec.)   VM381-383
Passes, orders, field correspondence (mil. sci.: gen.)   UB280
Patrols & reconnaisance, Naval   V190   359.413
Pay & allowances (Ger. Navy)   VC181
Pay & allowances (marines)   VE490   359.9664
Pay & allowances (mil.: G.B.)   UC185
Pay & allowances (U.S. Navy)   VC50-65   359.135, .640973
Pay & benefits (air forces)   UG940-945   358.41135, .4164
Paymaster's Dept. (U.S. Army)   UC70-75

PEACE commissions (WWI: gen.)   D647.A2
Peace efforts (WWI: ongoing: gen.)   D613
Peace efforts (WWI: preserve or restore)   940.312   D613,
                                                        D641-644+ (armistice)
Peace (WWI)   D642-651   940.312, .3141
Peace (WWI: other special topics)   D650.A-Z
Peace (WWI: gen.)   D644   940.312
Peace (WWI: special topics)   D645
Peiping, China (Peking)   DS795   951.156
Peking, China   951.156   DS795
Pennsylvania Ave. (Washington, D.C.)   F203.7.P4
Pennsylvania (WWI)   D570.85.P4-41
Pensions, disability benefits, etc. (naval admin.)   VB280-285   359.115-1156
Pensions, Survivors' (mil.)   UB400-405
Pensions, Survivors' (naval)   VB340-345
Pensions, Veterans'   UB370-375   331.25291355 (PREFER), 355.1151, .64
PERIODICALS & ASSOCIATIONS (air forces)   UG622   358.005-006
Periodicals & associations (armor & cavalry)   UE1
Periodicals & associations (arms & armor: hist.)   U799
Periodicals & associations (artillery)   UF1
Periodicals & associations (Ger.: 1918-)   DD233
Periodicals & associations (infantry)   UD1
Periodicals & associations (marine navig. & merch. marine)   VK1
Periodicals & associations (mil. engineering)   UG1
Periodicals & associations (military: in English)   U1   355.005-006
Periodicals & associations (military medical services)   UH201
Periodicals & associations (military: U.S.)   UA23.A1.A-Z
PERIODICALS & ASSOCIATIONS (NAVAL architec.: Eng.)   VM1
Periodicals & associations (naval medical services)   VG100
Periodicals & associations (naval ordnance)   VF1
Periodicals & associations (naval: G.B.)   VA452
Periodicals & associations (naval: Ger.)   VA510
Periodicals & associations (naval: in English)   V1   359.005, .006+
Periodicals & associations (naval: U.S.)   VA49   359.005-007+
Periodicals & associations (WWI: prisons)   D627.A1   940.472+
Periodicals & yearbooks (U.S.)   E171
Periodicals, associations, yearbooks (20th c.)   D410
Periodicals, collected serials (WWI)   D501
Periodicals (mil. admin.)   UB1
Periodicals, serials, collections (WWII)   D731
Periscopes (submarine architec.)   VM367.P4
Persia (Iran)   955   DS251-325, DS272
Persia (1794-1925: Kajar dynasty)   DS298-316   955.04-051
Persia (geog. & travel)   915.5   DS258
Persia (post-WWI territorial ?s)   D651.P4
Persia (WWI)   D568.8

PERSONAL ACCOUNTS, Allied (WWI)   940.481+   D640, D570.9 (U.S.)
Personal accounts, American (WWI: U.S.)   940.48173   D570.9
Personal accounts, Australian (WWI)   940.48194
Personal accounts, Austrian (WWI)   940.482436   D640, D539)
Personal accounts, British (WWI)   940.48141   D640, D546-547, D581-582 (naval)
Personal accounts, Central Power (WWI)   940.482+   D640, D531-540
Personal accounts (Ch. Rev., 1911-12)   DS773.5-52
Personal accounts, expeditionary experiences (WWI: U.S.)   D570.9.A-Z (SEE
                     ALSO E745 for military biog.)
Personal accounts, French (WWI)   940.48144
Personal accounts, German (WWI)   940.48243   D640, D531-538, D604 (aerial),
                     D591-592 (subs)
Personal accounts (WWI)   D640 (SEE ALSO D570.9 for U.S. soldiers)   940.481+
Personal accounts (WWI: collective)   D640.A2
PERSONNEL administration, Military (civilian & mil.) 355.61   UB160-165,
                     UB180-197, UB410-415 (officers), UB320-338
Personnel administration, Naval (civilian & mil.)   359.61   VB257-258.5
Personnel administration (naval sci.: gen.)   VB257   359.61
Personnel, Air force   UG1130-1185
Personnel & administration (air forces: U.S.)   UG773
Personnel, Civilian (mil. admin.: U.S.)   UB193
Personnel, Civilian (naval admin.: gen.)   VB180
Personnel transport (navies)   VC550-555
Personnel transport vehicles (land: mil. design)   623.7472
Peru   F3401-3619, F3431   985
Pétain, Henri Philippe (Fr.: 1871-1940 era)   DC342.8.P4
Peter I Karadordevic (Serbia: ruler, 1903-18: ALSO gen. works on period)   DR2030
Peter I (Yug.: King, 1903-21: ALSO covers era)   DR360
Petrograd, Rus. (1801-)   DK568
Petroleum industry (defense)   UA929.95.P4
Petty officers' handbooks (gen.)   V120
Pharmacy services, Military   UH420-425
Philadelphia Navy Yard (U.S.: Penn.)   VA70.P5
Philadelphia, Penn.   F158   974.811
PHILIPPINE ISLANDS   DS651-689, DS655, DS668   959.9
Philippine Islands (1894-1901)   DS676-684   959.902-9031
Philippine Islands (1898-1946: U.S. era)   959.903   DS679-686.4, DS685
Philippine Islands (1898-1901: Rebellion)   DS679 (SEE ALSO E712-735 for
                     Span.-Am. War)   959.9031
Philippine Islands (gen.: pubn. 1801+)   DS668.A3-Z   959.9
Philippine Islands (Sp.-Am. War, 1898: ALSO Battle of Manila Bay)   E717.7
                     973.8937
Philippines (mil. status)   UA853.P5   355.0330599
Philosophy & psychology   100-199   B-BD, BH-BJ, BF
Philosophy, Naval (e.g. theory of naval sea power)   V25
Philosophy, psychology, religion   B   100-299
Photographers, Naval   VG1010-1015
Photographic interpretation (navies)   VG1020
Photography, Ballistic (inclu. photochronography)   UF840
Photography, Military   UG476   623.72
Photography, Military (mil. engineering)   623.72   UG476
Physical training (mil. sci.)   U320-325   355.54+
Physical training (navies: U.S.)   V263-264
Piave, 1st Battle of the (1917)   D569.P4
Piave, 2d Battle of the (1918)   D569.P5

Picardy, Fr. (WWI)   D545.P5
Pictorial and graphic histories (20th c.)   D426   779.990194, 909.82
PICTORIALS (naval: U.S.)   VA59   359.3250973
Pictorials, satires, etc. (Rus. Rev., 1917-21)   DK265.15
Pictorials (ships)   VM307   387.2+
Pictorials (U.S. Mil. Acad.)   U410.L3
Pictorials (U.S. Naval Acad.)   V415.L3
Pictorials (world navies)   VA42
Pictorials (WWI)   D522 (SEE ALSO D527)   940.49
Pigeons (WWI)   D639.P45
PILOT & sailing guides (Atl. Ocean: all & east: gen.)   VK810   623.8929163
Pilot & sailing guides (by area)   VK804-997
Pilot & sailing guides (E. Pac. & Am. W. Coast: gen.)   VK941
Pilot & sailing guides (Pac. Ocean & islands: gen.)   VK915   623.8929164
Pilot & sailing guides (W. Atlantic: gen.)   VK959
Pilot guides & sailing directions (gen.: pubn. 1801+)   VK802   623.8922, .8929+
Pilot guides (geog. treatment)   623.89291-89299   VK804-997
PILOTING, Aerial   629.13252
Piloting & pilot guides, Nautical   623.8922   VK1500-1661, VK1523-1525 (U.S.),
                                        VK1645 (gen.), VK798-803
Piloting & pilots, Nautical (by area)   VK1521-1624   623.291-89299
Piloting (gen.: mil. engineering)   623.746048 (SEE ALSO .7463 [bombers] or
     other types)   TL710+, UG670-675 (manuals), UG700-705 (tactics)
Piloting, Nautical (Eur.)   VK1555-1596   623.294
Piloting, Nautical (U.S.)   VK1523-1525   623.2973
Pilots & piloting, Nautical   VK1500-1661
Pilots & piloting, Nautical (gen.)   VK1645-1661
Pilsudski, Joseph (Pol.: 1918+ biog.)   DK440.5.P5, DK4420.P5
Pioneer troops   UG530-535
Pistols & revolvers (gen.)   UD410   355.8243, 623.443
Pistols & revolvers (marines)   VE390   359.968243
Piston & turboprop airplanes   629.133343
Planes, Fighter (design)   623.7464   TL685.3, TL686.A-Z (by manufac. or model),
                                        UG1242.F5
Planes, Reconnaisance (mil. design)   623.7467   UG1242.R4
Planning, Military (U.S.)   U153
Plans, Attack & defense (countries except U.S.)   UA925.A-Z
Plating, Armor (naval sci.: special type)   V907.A-Z
Plumbing (naval architec. & engin.)   VM501
Poetry, satire, etc. (WWI)   D526-526.7 (PREFER PQ-PT)
Poetry, satire, etc. (WWI: languages besides Eng., Fr., Ger.)   D526.7.A-Z
POLAND   DK401-441+ (older titles prior to 1976-77), DK414, DK4010-4800 (titles
                 1970+?), DK4140   943.8
Poland (1795-1918)   DK434.9 (older), DK4349-4395   943.803
Poland (1795-1918: foreign rule)   943.803   DK434.9, DK4349, DK439
Poland (1795-1918: gen.)   DK4349   943.803
Poland (1832-1914: gen.)   DK436.4
Poland (1864-1918)   DK4380   943.803
Poland (1867-1914)   DK438   943.803
Poland (20th c.)   DK4382
Poland (1914-18: WWI)   DK439 (older works), DK4390   943.803
Poland (1915-18: Austrian occupation)   DK4392
Poland (1918-: Republic: inclu. wars of 1918-21)   DK440   943.804
Poland (1918-45)   DK4397-4420   943.804

Poland (gen.)   DK4040
Poland (gen. history, culture, etc.)   DK404
Poland (gen.: pubns. 1801+)   DK414.A3-Z, DK4140 (newer works)
Poland (geog. & travel)   914.38   DK407 (1867-1945)
Poland (mil. status)   UA829.P7   355.0330438
Poland (post-WWI territorial ?s)   D651.P7
Poland (Revolution of 1905)   DK4383-4389
Poland (Revolution of 1905: gen.)   DK4385
Poles (in other lands)   DK4122
Police, Military (by country)   UB825.A-Z
Police, Naval (besides U.S.)   VB925.A-Z
Policy & status, Naval   359.03+ (country #s follow)   VA
Policy, Military   355.0335+
Policy, Military (gen.)   UA11
POLISH military history (gen.)   DK4170
Polish military ops. (1918-21, inclu. Russo-Polish conflict)   DK4406
Polish question   DK4182
Polish Republic (1918-39)   943.804   DK440, DK4400
Political prisoners (WWI: U.S.)   D570.8.P7
Political science   320-329   J
Political science, international law   J   320-329, 341
POLITICS & DIPLOMACY (1871-late 19th c.)   D397
Politics & diplomacy (20th c.)   D440-460
Politics & diplomacy (20th c.: collected works)   D442
Politics & diplomacy (20th c.: gen. special: projected, possible wars, other polit.
      events)   D445
Politics and diplomacy (20th c.: gen.: world pol., Triple Alliance & Entente, etc.)
        D443   940.5, 320.904, 327.09
Politics & diplomacy (1919-39)   D727   327.0904, .4, 909.822-23, 940.51-52
Politics & diplomacy (Africa: inclu. colonialism)   DT31-38   320.96, 327.6
Politics & diplomacy (Asia: gen.)   DS33.3   320.95, 327.5+
Politics & diplomacy (Austria)   DB46-49
Politics & diplomacy (Bosnia & Herceg.: 1878-1918)   DR1725
Politics & diplomacy (Egypt: gen.)   DT82
Politics & diplomacy (Fr.)   DC55-59
Politics & diplomacy (Ger.)   DD110-120
Politics & diplomacy (It.: gen.)   DG491   320.945, 327.45+
Politics & diplomacy (Japan: gen.)   DS841
Politics & diplomacy (Libya: gen.)   DT227
Politics & diplomacy (Middle East, SW. Asia)   DS63   320.956, 327.56+
Politics & diplomacy (Montenegro: 1918-45)   DR1887
Politics & diplomacy (N. Zea.: gen.)   DU421
Politics & diplomacy (Neth.: gen.)   DJ142
Politics & diplomacy (Palestine, Jews)   DS119-119.8
Politics & diplomacy (Port.: gen.)   DP556
Politics & diplomacy (Rus.)   DK60-63
Politics & diplomacy (Rus.: 1894-1939)   DK63
Politics & diplomacy (Rus.: gen.)   DK61   320.947
Politics & diplomacy (Sp.)   DP84
Politics & diplomacy (Swe.: gen.)   DL658.A3-Z 320.9485, 327.485
Politics & diplomacy (Swit.: gen.)   DQ69
Politics & diplomacy (Tunisia: gen.)   DT257
Politics & diplomacy (Tur.: 1876-1918: inclu. Panislamism)   DR476

POLITICS (China: 20th c. & 1912-49) DS775.7
Politics (Eastern Europe: gen.) DJK42
Politics (Eng.: gen.) DA40
Politics (Eng.: modern) DA42
Politics (Georgian S. S. R.: gen.) DK676.5-6
Politics (Ger.: 1888-1918) DD228.5
Politics (Pol.) DK4179
Politics (Rus. armed forces, 1917-21) DK265.9.A6
Politics (Serbia: gen.) DR1972
Politics (U.S.: 20th c.) E743 320.973, .904
Politics (U.S.: 1912 Pres. campaign) E765
Politics (U.S.: 1916 Pres. campaign) E769
Politics (U.S.: gen.) E183 320.973
Politics (Ukr.: gen.) DK508.554
Polynesia & other Pacific areas 996 DU510 (Poly.: gen.)
Polynesia (gen.) DU510 (SEE DU520-950 for specific island groups, individual
        islands, atolls, etc.) 996, 996.1-4, .9
Pomerania (Pol.) DK4600.P67
Pontoons & pontoon gear (naval architec.) VM469.5
Popular histories (20th c.) D422
Popular histories (20th c.: Europe) D425
Population (WWI) D639.P5
Port Arthur, Siege of (Rus.-Jpn. War, 1904-5) DS517.3
Port of London (Eng.) DA689.P6
Ports, bases, docks, etc. (G.B. Royal Navy: gen.) VA459.A1 359.70941,
        940.4530941 (WWI), .54530941 (WWII)
Ports, bases, docks, etc. (Ger. Navy: by name) VA516.A3-Z
Ports, bases, docks, etc. (U.S. Navy: gen.) VA67 359.70973, 940.4530973 (WWI)
Portsmouth Navy Yard (U.S.: N.H.) VA70.P8
Portsmouth, Eng. (Royal Naval Barracks) V522.5.P6
PORTUGAL DP501-900+ 946.9
Portugal (20th c.: gen.) DP672 946.904
Portugal (1910-: Republic) DP675 946.904
Portugal (1914-18: WWI) DP677 946.9041
Portugal (post-WWI territorial ?s) D651.P75
Portugal (WWI) D549.52.P8
Posen (post-WWI territorial ?s) D651.P8
Position finders (artillery) UF853 623.46
Possessions of the U.S. (WWI) D570.87.A-Z
Post exchanges & canteens, Military UC750-755
Post-war era & Reconstruction (WWI) D652-659 940.3144, .34-39
Post-WWI reconstruction 940.3144 D652-659, D653 (gen.),
        D657-658 (U.S.), D659.A-Z (other places)
Post-WWI territorial questions 940.31424 D650, D651.A-Z
Postal service, Military UH80-85 355.69
Postal service, Naval VG60-65 359.341
Posters (WWI) D522.25, D527.5
Power-driven craft (naut. engineering) 623.823 VM315
Power plants (marine engineering) 623.87 VM600-779, VM600,
        VM623 (U.S.), VM657 (G.B.), VM673 (Ger.), VM705 (Japan)
Power systems, Electric (naval sci.) VC418
Powerplants (naval design) 623.8147 VM731+
Prague, Cz. (20th c.) DB2629
Preservation of maps & charts UA997

Press & public relns. (mil.)   UH700-705
Press & public relns. (navies)   VG500-505
Press, publicity, censorship (WWI: U.S.)   D632
PRIMARY SOURCES (1871-late 19th c.)   D394
Primary sources (20th c.: collections)   D411
Primary sources (20th c.: diplomacy)   D451
Primary sources (20th c.: politics and diplomacy)   D441
PRIMARY SOURCES, DOCUMENTS (Australia)   DU80
Primary sources, documents (Australia: military status)   UA871
Primary sources, documents (Bulg.)   DR52
Primary sources, documents (Calif. army reserves)   UA91
Primary sources, documents (China: 20th c. & 1912-49)   DS773.83
Primary sources, documents(WWI: Reconstruction: collec's.)   D652
Primary sources, documents (Den.)   DL103
Primary sources, documents (Eastern Europe: politics)   DJK41
Primary sources, documents (Egypt)   DT43
Primary sources, documents (Eng.)   DA25
Primary sources, documents (Far East, E. & SE.Asia)   DS503
Primary sources, documents (Fin.)   DL1005
Primary sources, documents (Fin.: 20th c.)   DL1066
Primary sources, documents (Fr.)   DC3
Primary sources, documents (Fr.: 1871-1940)   DC334
Primary sources, documents (G.B.: War Dept., Parliament, other re military)
                                     UA648
Primary sources, documents (Ger. infantry)   UA713.A1-5
Primary sources, documents (Ger.: 1871-1918)   DD217
Primary sources, documents (Ger.: for. relns. & politics)   DD110
Primary sources, documents (India, pre-1947 Pak.)   DS403
Primary sources, documents (It.)   DG403
Primary sources, documents (Italo-Eth. War, 1935-6)   DT387.8.A1-7
Primary sources, documents (Japan)   DS803, DS840 (dipl. & polit. hist.)
Primary sources, documents (Jpn. military)   UA846
Primary sources, documents (N.Y. army reserves)   UA361
Primary sources, documents (naval: G.B.)   VA453
Primary sources, documents (naval: Ger.)   VA512
Primary sources, documents (Nor.)   DL403
Primary sources, documents (Palestine & the Jews)   DS102
Primary sources, documents (Pol.)   DK402
Primary sources, documents (Port.: 20th c.)   DP670
Primary sources, documents (Port.: dipl. & polit. hist.)   DP555
Primary sources, documents (Rum.)   DR203
Primary sources, documents (Rum.: 1881-1914)   DR252
Primary sources, documents (Rum.: 1914-27)   DR260
PRIMARY SOURCES, DOCUMENTS (RUS. military)   UA771
Primary sources, documents (Rus.)   DK3, UA773.A1-5
Primary sources, documents (Rus.: 1894-1917)   DK251
Primary sources, documents (Rus.: for. relns.)   DK65
Primary sources, documents (Rus.: politics & diplomacy)   DK60
Primary sources, documents (Rus.-Jpn. War, 1904-5)   DS516.A-Z
Primary sources, documents (Sp.: dipl. & polit. hist.)   DP83
Primary sources, documents (Swe.)   DL658.A2
Primary sources, documents (Swit.)   DQ3
Primary sources, documents (Swit.: dipl. & polit. hist.)   DQ68
Primary sources, documents (Tur.)   DR403

Primary sources, documents (U.S.)   E173
Primary sources, documents (U.S.: 20th c.) E740.5
Primary sources, documents (WWI)   D505
Primary sources, documents (WWI: peace: collections)   D642
Primary sources, documents (WWI: U.S. naval)   D589.U5
Primary sources, documents (Yug.)   DR1288
Prince of Wales (battleship: G.B.)   VA458.P75
Prisoner exchanges   940.473
Prisoner-of-war camps & internment (WWI) 940.472   D627
Prisoner-of-war camps (mil. life)   355.1296 (SEE ALSO 365.45) UB800-805
Prisoners, prisons, punishments (naval)   VB890-910
PRISONS & prisoners, Naval (except U.S.: by place)   VB895.A-Z
Prisons & prisoners, Naval (G.B.)   VB895.G7
Prisons & prisoners, Naval (Rus.)   VB895.R9
Prisons & prisoners, Naval (U.S.)   VB893   344.035480973
Prisons & prisoners (WWI: by country)   D627.A3-Z
Prisons & prisoners (WWI: gen.)   D627.A2
Prisons, Military (U.S.)   UB803 (SEE ALSO KF7675)
Procurement & contracts, Air force (gen.)   UG1120   358.41621
Procurement (mil. supplies)   355.6212   UC263-267, HD3858-3860
Procurement (mil. supplies: countries besides U.S.)   UC265.A-Z
Procurement (naval supples &equip.)   359.6212
Procurement (naval supplies: except U.S.)   VC265.A-Z
Projectile velocities & motions (gen.)   UF820   623.51
Projectiles, Artillery   UF750-770   623.451
Projectiles, Artillery (U.S.)   UF753
Projectiles, Naval   VF480-500
Promotion & demotion (air forces)   358.41112   UB320-325, UB410-415
Promotion & demotion (mil.)   355.112   UB320+
Promotion & demotion (navies)   359.112   VB260-275, VB307-315
Promotion, discharge, recruitment, enlistment (mil. sci.: gen.) UB320   355.2, .61
Promotion, discharge, recruitment, enlistment (naval sci.: enlisted personnel: U.S.)
                    VB263   359.2230973, .3380973
Prop-driven aircraft (mil. design)   623.746042
PROPAGANDA, Allied (WWI)   940.4886
Propaganda, American (WWI: U.S.)   940.488673   D632, D639.P7.U5+
PROPAGANDA & PSYCH. WARFARE (Ger.)   UB277.G3   355.34340943
Propaganda & psych. warfare (mil. sci.: gen.: SEE ALSO BF1045.M55 & HM263 for
    indiv. & social aspects)   UB275   355.3434
Propaganda & psych. warfare (naval sci.: gen.)   VB252   359.3434
Propaganda & psych. warfare (naval sci.: U.S.)   VB253   359.34340973
Propaganda & psych. warfare (Rus.)   UB277.R9   355.34340947
Propaganda & psych. warfare (Sov.Un.)   UB277.S65   355.34340947
Propaganda & psych. warfare (U.S.)   UB276   355.34340973
Propaganda, British (WWI)   940.488641 D639.P7.G7
Propaganda, Central Power (WWI) 940.4887
Propaganda, French (WWI)   940.488644 D639.P7.F8
Propaganda, German   DD119.5
Propaganda, German (WWI)   940.488743   D639.P7.G3, D619.3 (in U.S.)
Propaganda, Russian (WWI)   940.488647 D639.P7.R9
Propaganda (WWI: by country)   D639.P7.A-Z
Propaganda (WWI: gen.)   D639.P6 (SEE ALSO D631-633 for press)   940.488+
Propellers (marine engin.) VM753-757   623.81473
Propulsion & resistance (marine engin.)   VM751-759
Propulsion (naval architec. & engin.: gen.)   VM521   623.87

Protest movements (WWI)   D639.P77
Protocols of the Wise Men of Zion (WWI: anti-Semitism)   DS145.P49-7
Provisions & subsistence, Naval (gen.) VC350   359.81
Provisions & subsistence, Naval (Ger.) VC355.G3
Provisions & subsistence, Naval (Rus.)   VC355.R9
PRUSSIA (1871-1918: gen.)   DD448
Prussia, East & West (post-WWI territorial ?s)   D651.P89-9
Prussia, East (Pol.)   DK4600.P77
Prussian military ops. (WWI)   D532-532.9
Prussian military ops. (WWI: gen.) D532
Prussian military ops. (WWI: misc. regiments)   D532.9
Przemysl, Siege of (1914)   D557.P7
Psychiatry, Military (U.S.: inclu. mental health)   UH629.3
Psychical phenomena (WWI)   D639.P8
Psychological warfare & propaganda (countries except U.S.) UB277.A-Z
Psychological warfare & propaganda (mil.)   355.3434 (ALSO use 355.34 for
       propag.)   UB275-277, UB276 (U.S.), UB277.A-Z (except U.S.)
Psychological warfare & propaganda (naval sci.: places besides U.S.) VB254.A-Z
PUBLIC administration   350-359   H-J
Public figures (20th c.: collective biog.: men)   D412.6   920.02, 909.82, 940.50922
Public figures (Ger.: 1918-48: men)   DD244
Public information & relations (mil.)   355.342   UH700-705, UH703 (U.S.)
Public opinion (WWI: by place)   D639.P88.A-Z
Public opinion (WWI: gen.)   D639.P87
Public relations & information (navies) 359.342   VG500-505
Public relations & press (mil.: places besides U.S.)   UH705.A-Z
Public utilities (defense)   UA929.95.P93
Publications, Graduate (U.S. Naval Acad.)   V415.K1-4
Publicity, press, censorship (WWI: special topics)   D633
Puerto Rico   F1951-1983, F1971   972.95
Puget Sound (Wash.)   F897.P9
Pumps, Marine (engin.)   VM821
Punishment & enforcement, Military   355.1332
Punishment, Corporal (U.S.)   UB813
Punishments (naval conduct)   359.13325
Pursuit & fighter forces & ops. (air)   358.43   UG1242.F5, UG633 (U.S.),
          UG635.A-Z (places except U.S.), TL685.3, TL686.A-Z (by co. or name)
Pyrotechnic signal devices (mil. engineering)   623.7313   UG580, UF860

QUALIFICATIONS (naval personnel)   359.2234
Qualifications, Service (mil.)   355.2234
Quarter drills, Naval (Can.: also watch, station, other)   VD163
Quartermaster's Dept. (U.S.)   UC30-34   355.8
Quarters & barracks, Air force (U.S.)   UG1143
Quarters & barracks, Naval (gen.)   VC420-425, VC420   359.71
Quarters, Military (barracks, p.o.w. camps etc. on-site)   355.71   UC400-405
Quebec   971.4   F1051-1055
Queen's Westminster and Civil Service Rifles (WWI)   D547.Q3
Queens, princesses, etc. (20th c.: collective biography) D412.8
Quick-firing ordnance   UF560-565... .Q.F.

RACES & ethnography (Australia)   DU120-122
Races & ethnography (Ger.)   DD74
Races & ethnography (N. Zea.)   DU423
Races & ethnography (Pol.: by specific element)   DK4121.5.A-Z
Races & ethnography (Pol.: gen.)   DK4120
Races & ethnography (Rus.)   DK33
RACES, ETHNOGRAPHY, RELIGIOUS GROUPS (Calif.)   F870.A-Z
Races, ethnography, religious groups (Can.)   F1035.A-Z
Races, ethnography, religious groups (N.Y.)   F130.A-Z
Races, ethnography, religious groups (S.Am.)   F2239.A-Z
Races, ethnography, religious groups (U.S.: gen.)   E184.A1
Races, ethnography, religious groups (U.S.)   E184.A-Z   973.04+
Racial minorities (WWI: soldiers)   940.403   D547.N4 (blacks: G.B.),
          D570.8.I6 (Indians: U.S.), D639.N4 (blacks)
Racial problems, ethnology, anthropology (WWI)   D639.A7
Radio & radar (mil. engineering)   623.734   UG611-612.5
Radio, Military (gen.)   UG611
Radiotelegraphy (mil. engineering)   623.7342   UG600-607, VG76-78
Raids (mil. sci.)   U167.5.R34
RAILROAD artillery (gen.)   UF490
Railroad troops   UG520-525
Railroads, armored trains, etc. (mil. engineering)   UG345   623.63
Railroads (defense)   UA929.95.R3
Railroads (mil. transp.: gen.)   UC310   623.63, 355.83
Railroads (mil. transp.: U.S. regions or states)   UC314.A-Z
Railroads (naval transp.)   VC580
Railway artillery (countries besides U.S.)   UF495.A-Z
Railway artillery (Fr.)   UF495.F8
Railway artillery (Ger.)   UF495.G3
Railway gun cars   UF655 (SEE ALSO UF563.A76, UF565)   358.22
Railway gun matériel (U.S.: handbooks)   UF563.A76
Rainbow Division (WWI: U.S.)   D570.3.R3
Range finders, Artillery (gen.)   UF850.A2   623.46
Range tables, Artillery   UF857
Range tables, Naval ordnance VF550   623.5530212
Rangers & commandos   356.167   U262
Ranging & sighting apparatus (ordnance: design)   623.46   UF848-856, VF520
Rank, appointment, promotion, retirement, etc. (mil. officers: gen.)   UB410
          355.332
Rank, appointment, promotion, retirement, etc. (naval officers: gen.)   VB310
          359.332, .331
Rasputin, Grigory (Rus.: 1894-1917: biog.)   DK254.R3
Rathenau, Walther (Ger.: 1888-1918+ period)   DD231.R3
Rations (mil.)   UC710-715
Rations, Naval   VC360-365
Raw materials (mil. resources)   355.24   HC110.A-Z, UA18, UA929.5+
Raw materials (naval resources)   359.24   VC260-267, VF390+
Rearguard action   U215
Recoil (mil. engineering)   623.57

RECONNAISANCE & intelligence topography (mil. engineering)   623.71   UG470-474
Reconnaisance & patrols   U220   355.413, 358.45
Reconnaisance, Aerial   UG760-765   358.45
Reconnaisance, Cavalry   UE360   355.413, 358.45
Reconnaissance forces, Air (inclu. antisub. work)   358.45   UG760-765, UG1242.R4
Reconnaissance, Naval   359.413   V190
Reconnaisance planes   UG1242.R4   623.7467, 358.45
Reconstruction & post-war era (WWI: gen.)   D653
Reconstruction (Fr.: 1919-40)   DC389   944.0815
Reconstruction (WWI: countries outside U.S.)   D659.A-Z
Records & accounting (marines)   VE480
RECREATION & information services, Military   UH800-910
Recreation & information services, Military (besides U.S.)   UH819.A-Z
Recreation & information services, Military (U.S. Army)   UH810-815
Recreation & information services, Naval   VG2020-2029
Recreation & information services, Naval (places besides U.S.)   VG2029
Recreation, Military (off-post)   UH900-910
Recreation services, Military (inclu. sports, arts, music, libraries, clubs, etc.)
                         355.346   UH800-910, UH800, UH805 (U.S.)
Recreation services, Naval (sports, arts, music, dancing, libraries, etc.)   359.346
                         VG2020-2029, UH800-910
Recreation, social work, etc. (air forces)   UG990-995
Recruiting, enlistment, etc. (air forces)   UG880-885
Recruitment & enlistment, Military   355.223
Recruitment & enlistment (navies)   359.223   VB260-315
Recruitment, enlistment, promotion, discharge (mil. sci.)   UB320-325
Recruitment, enlistment, promotion, discharge (naval sci.: enlisted personnel: gen.)
                         VB260   359.223, .338, .11+
Recruits, Naval (inclu. medical & mental examinations)   VB270-275   359.2236
Red Cross & medical services (WWI: by country)   D629.A-Z
Red Cross (by country or region)   UH537.A-Z
Red Cross (gen.: wartime)   UH535   940.4771, .54771
Red Cross at sea   VG457
Red Guard (Rus. Rev., 1917-21: K̲rasnaia Gvardiia)   DK265.9.K73
Reed, Thomas Brackett (U.S.: 1865-1900 era)   E664.R3
Refrigeration (naval sci.)   VC400   623.8535
Refrigerators, Military   UC760
Refugees (WWI)   940.3159   D637, D638.A-Z (by place)
Refugees, relief work, charities (WWI: by country or area)   D638.A-Z
Refugees, relief work, charities (WWII: gen.)   D808   940.5477
Registers & lists (WWI: decorated, dead, wounded: by country)   D609.A3-Z
Registers & lists (WWI: decorated, dead, wounded: gen.) D609.A2
Registers, Official & unoff. (Royal Naval Coll., Dart.)   V515.H1-5
Registers, Official (U.S. Mil. Acad.)   U410.H3-4
Registers, Official (U.S. Naval Acad.: annual)   V415.H3-39
Registration (WWI: U.S.)   D570.8.R4
Regulation of conduct, Naval   359.133
REGULATIONS & manuals, Air force (U.S.)   UG673
Regulations & tactics (mil. engineering: Asia: gen.)   UG270
Regulations & tactics (mil. engineering: Eur.: gen.)   UG215
Regulations, Army (Rus.)   UB655.9-656.5
Regulations, Marine (U.S.)   VE23.A25
Regulations, Naval (U.S.)   VB363
Regulations (U.S. Naval Acad.)   V415.C3-6

Rehabilitation of disabled sailors VG478 (PREFER UB360+)
Rehabilitation of disabled veterans (gen.) UB360 355.1156, .1154
Reims, Fr. (WWI) D545.R4
RELIEF & welfare services (WWI: in Fr.) 940.477944 D638.F8, D659.F8
Relief & welfare services (WWI: in Ger.) 940.477943 D638.G3, D659.G3
Relief & welfare services (WWI: in It.) 940.477945 D638.I8, D659.I8
Relief & welfare services (WWI: in Rus.) 940.477947 D638.R9, D659.R9
Relief associations (besides U.S.) UH543-545
Relief societies (mil.: inclu. care of sick & wounded) UH520-560 361.05, .77
Relief societies (mil.: besides U.S.: by place) UH525.A-Z
Relief societies (mil.: U.S. by state or region) UH524.A-Z
Relief work, refugees, etc. (WWI: Armenia) D638.A7
Relief work, refugees, etc. (WWI: Near East) D638.E2
Relief work, refugees, etc. (WWI: U.S.) D638.U5
Religion 200-299 BL-BX
Religion (Sp. Civil War, 1936-39) DP269.8.R4
Religion, Christianity (WWI) D639.R4 940.478
RELIGIOUS & counseling services, Military 355.347 UH20-25
Religious & counseling services, Naval 359.347 VG20-25, VG2000
Religious groups & officials (WWI) 940.3152 D639.R4, D622 (Cath. Church)
Religious officials, Military (countries except U.S.) UH25.A-Z
Religious officials, Naval (places besides U.S.) VG25.A-Z
Religious services (WWI) 940.478 D639.R4
Remount & training services (cavalry: horse training, remount depots, care &
    breeding, etc.) 357.2 UE460-475, UC600-695
Remount Service (WWI: G.B.) D547.R4
Reparations & indemnity (WWI: by country) D649.A-Z
Reparations (WWI) 940.31422 D648-649
Reparations (WWI: Ger.) D649.G3
REPORTS, Congressional (U.S. Military Academy: by date) U410.E5
Reports, Congressional (U.S. Navy: official & others) VA53
REPORTS, OFFICIAL & unoff. (U.S. Naval Acad.) V415.F7
Reports, Official (army reserves: U.S.) UA42.A1-59
Reports, Official (military medical: U.S.: monographic) UH223.A3-39
Reports, Official (military medical: U.S.: serial) UH223.A1-29
Reports, Official (naval maint.: U.S.) VC25-38
Reports, Official (naval reserves: U.S.: Calif.) VA101
Reports, Official (Royal Naval Coll., Dart.: annual) V515.E1-49
Reports, Official (U.S. Army: War Dept., Dept. o/t Army, Adj. Gen., Inspec. Gen.,
    etc.: annual) UA24.A1-7
Reports, Official (U.S. Dept. Defense: formerly War Dept.) UA23.2
Reports, Official (U.S. Marines) VE23.A2-79
Reports, Official (U.S. Mil. Acad. Superinten.: annual) U410.E1
Reports, Official (U.S. Naval Acad. Superinten.: annual) V415.E1-4
Reports, Official (U.S. Navy Bur's. of Navigation, Personnel) VA52.A6-67
Reports, Official (U.S. Navy Dept.) VA52.A1-89
Reports, Official (WWI: military) D529
Reports, Official (WWI: military: misc. branches or modes) D529.9.A-Z
Reports, Official (WWI: military: special branches or modes) D529.3-9
Reports, Unofficial (naval maint.: U.S.) VC39
Reports, Unofficial (naval pay etc.: U.S.) VC64
Repression & atrocities (WWI) 940.405 D625 (gen.), D626.A-Z (by place)
Requisitions, Military UC15
Rescue aircraft (mil. engineering) 623.7466
Rescue ops., Nautical 623.8887 VK1321-1424, VK1323 (U.S.), VK1445 (gen.)

RESEARCH, Aeronautical (mil.: by company or establishment)   UG644.A-Z
Research, Aeronautical (mil.: gen.)   UG640   358.407, .40072+
Research, Aeronautical (mil.: places besides U.S.)   UG645.A-Z
Research & development (air forces equip. & supplies)   358.407
Research & development, Military   355.07
Research & development (naval equip. & supplies)   359.07   V390-395
Research & laboratories, Medical (mil.)   UH399.5-7
Research & laboratories, Naval medical   VG240-245
Research, Military   U390-395   355.07
Research, Naval (countries besides U.S.)   V395.A-Z
Research, Naval (gen.)   V390   359.07
Research (naval ordnance: gen.)   VF360   359.82072
Research, Naval (U.S.: gen.)   V393   359.070973
Research, Ordnance & small-arms   UF526
Research, Physiological (mil. hygiene)   UH627
Reserve Officers' Training Corps (U.S.: R.O.T.C.)   U428.5
RESERVES & militia, Infantry   UD430
Reserves, Army   355.37   UA, UA42 (U.S.), UA50-549 (U.S.: by state),
    UA661 (G.B.)
Reserves, Army (U.S.: Missouri)   UA290-299
Reserves, Army (U.S.: N.Y.: militia, volunteers, Nat. Guard, etc.)   UA360-369
Reserves, Army (U.S.: Nat. Guard, militia, volunteers, etc.)   UA42-560
Reserves, Army (U.S.: Penn.)   UA420-429
Reserves, Artillery   UF356
RESERVES, NAVAL   359.37   VA45, VA, VA80+
Reserves, Naval (G.B.)   VA464
Reserves, Naval (gen.)   VA45   359.37+
Reserves, Naval (Ger.)   VA519   359.370943
Reserves, Naval (Ger.: maint. & organ.)   VC182   359.370943
Reserves, Naval (U.S.)   VA80-390
Reserves, Naval (U.S.: Calif.)   VA100-107
Reserves, Naval (U.S.: Ill.)   VA160-167
Reserves, Naval (U.S.: maint. & organ.)   VC40-41   359.370973
Resistance & propulsion (marine engin.: gen.)   VM751
Resistance to projectiles (artillery)   UF900
Resolution of peace (WWI: U.S. Congress by date)   D643.A67
Resources (marines)   359.962   VA-VC
Resources, Air force   358.412   UG630+, UG1100+
Resources, Military   355.2   UA18, UA10
Resources, Naval   359.2   VB, VB21-124 (by place), VB23 (U.S.), VB144-146,
    VA49-750 (by place), VA50-80+ (U.S.)
Results (WWI: dipl., econ., & polit.)   940.314 (SEE ALSO specific country #s)
    D511-20, D511, D610-611, D643-644+
Retired military   UB440-445   355.1342
Retirement, resignation, other service termination (navies)   359.114
Revolvers & pistols   355.8243   UD410-415
Revolvers & pistols, Infantry (U.S. models)   UD413-414
Revolvers & pistols (navies)   VD390   359.8243
Rewards & privileges, Military   355.134   UB430-435
Rewards, badges, brevets, medals (navies: except U.S.)   VB335.A-Z
Rewards (navies: inclu. privileges, citations, medals, etc.)   359.134   VB330-335
Rhine Province (Prus.)   DD491.R4-52
Rhine River (Ger.)   DD801.R7-76   943.4
Rhine River Valley   943.4   DD801.R7-76
Rhodesia   DT946-965

Ribbons (WWI: commemorative)   D527.8
Rifle & artillery ranges (U.S.)   U303
Rifles   355.82425   UD390-395
Rifles & carbines (design)   623.4425   UD390-395
Rifles, carbines, etc. (infantry)   UD390-395   355.82425, 623.4425
Rifles, carbines, etc. (navies)   VD370   359.82425
Rifles (infantry: by type)   UD395.A-Z
Riga, Rus.   DK651.R5
Rigging & gear, Nautical (anchors, masts, rope, rudders, sails, etc.: design)
                    623.862   VM791 (anchors), VC279.R6 (rope)
Rio de Janeiro, Br.   F2646   981.53
River & stream crossing (infantry)   UD317
Roads & highways (gen.)   UA960
Roads (mil. engineering)   UG330   623.62
Roads (places outside U.S.)   UA965.A-Z
Roberts, Frederick Sleigh Roberts, 1st Earl (G.B.: 19th c. mil. biog.)   DA68.32.R6
Rocky Mts. area (Mont., Idaho, Wyo., Colo.)   F721-785   978
Rolls of honored & dead (WWI)   940.467   D609, D609.A2 (gen.)
Romania (Rumania)   949.8   DR201-296
Romania (1861-1947: Monarchy)   949.802   DR250-266, DR250,
                    DR263 (1914-18), DR264 (1918-44)
Rome, It.   .   945.632   DG803-818, DG808, DG813 (1871-)
Rome, It. (1871-)   DG813
Rome, It. (modern era)   DG803-818
Roosevelt, Franklin D. (U.S.: 20th c.: works)   E742.5.R5-7
Roosevelt, Theodore (U.S.: 1865-1900 era: works)   E660.R75-89
Roosevelt, Theodore (U.S.: Pres., 1901-9)   E757
Root, Elihu (U.S.: 1865-1900 era)   E664.R7
Rope (naval supplies)   VC279.R6
Rosters, Officers' (U.S. Mil. Acad.)   U410.H2
Rostov, Rus.   DK651.R7
Rough Riders (Sp.-Am. War: U.S. cavalry)   E725.45.1st
Rowboats, small sailboats, etc.   VM351
ROYAL Artillery Regiment (WWI)   D547.R5
Royal Fusiliers (WWI)   D547.R6
Royal Highlanders of Canada (WWI)   D547.R63
Royal houses (genealogy)   929.7
Royal Military Academy (Woolwich: div'd like U410.A-Z)   U518.A-Z
Royal Military Academy (Woolwich: gen. hist's.)   U518.L1
Royal Military College (Sandhurst)   U520.A-Z
Royal Naval College (Dartmouth)   V515.A1-R1+
Royal Naval College (Dartmouth: hist.)   V515.L1
Royal Naval College (Dartmouth: life, pictorials, etc.)   V515.P1
Royal Naval College (Greenwich: set up like V515)   V520.A1-R1+
Royal Naval Division (WWI)   D547.R7
Royal Scots (WWI)   D547.R8
Rubber (naval supplies)   VC279.R8
Rudolf (Austria:1848-1916 era: Crown Prince)   DB89.R8
Ruhr Valley (WWI: peace topic)   D650.R8
Rulers, kings, etc. (20th c.: collective biography)   D412.7   929.7

RUMANIA (Romania)   DR201-296   949.8
Rumania (1866-1944)   DR250-266
Rumania (1866-1944: gen.)   DR250
Rumania (1881-1914: Carol I) DR252-258   949.802
Rumania (1881-1914: gen.)   DR256
Rumania (1912-13: Balkan War era)   DR258
Rumania (1914-27: Ferdinand) DR260-263   949.802
Rumania (1914-18: WWI)   DR263
Rumania (geog. & travel)   914.98   DR209 (1866-1950)
Rumania (mil. status)   UA826   355.0330498
Rumania (post-WWI territorial ?s)   D651.R6
Rumania (WWI)   D565.A2
Runways, Airport   629.1363
Runways (mil. airfields: design)   623.663
RUSSIA   947 (SEE ALSO DK1-275+)
Russia (1855-)   947.08   DK219+, DK220-221
Russia (1855-81: Alexander II)   947.081 (might SEE ALSO 956.101 for Russo-
                    Turk. War)   DK219-228, DK220-221, DR573 (R-T War)
Russia (1881-94: Alexander III)   947.082   DK234-243, DK240-241
Russia (1881-94: gen.)   DK240
Russia (1894-1918: Nicholas II)   947.083 (perhaps SEE ALSO 952.031 for Russo-
          Jpn. War)   DK251-264.3, DK258, DK260-262, DS516-517 (R-J War)
Russia (1894-1917)   DK258-260   947.083
Russia (20th c.: gen.)   DK246   947.084
Russia (20th c. & 1917-: Communist period)   947.084   DK246
Russia (1904-17: empire status)   DK262
Russia (1905-6: Revolution: gen.)   DK263
Russia (1914-18: WWI era)   DK264.8   947.083
Russia (1918-: gen.)   DK266.A4-Z
Russia (air war geog.)   358.414747
Russia. Army (gen.)   UA772   355.30947, .00947
Russia (Asia: lighthouses, beacons, foghorns, etc.) VK1109-1110
Russia (biog.: heads of state)   923.147
Russia, Eastern & Estonia   DK503 (SEE DK511.E4 for earlier pubns. on Estonia)
                    947.41
Russia (Eur.: lighthouses, beacons, foghorns, etc.) VK1085-1086
Russia, Finland, Poland   DK
Russia (gen.)   DK17
Russia (mil. geog.)   355.4747   UA995.R9
Russia (mil. policy)   355.033547   UA770+
Russia (mil. status)   UA770   355.033047, .033247, .033547
Russia (naval geog.)   359.4747   VA570-579
Russia (naval status: gen.)   VA573.A5-Z   359.030947, .00947, .4747
Russia, Northern   DK501
Russia (pilot guides)   623.892947   VK809, VK821, VK870, VK910 (Siberia)
Russia, Poland, Finland, Soviet Asia   DK
Russia (post-WWI territorial ?s)   D651.R8
Russia, Southern (Black Sea, Caucasus, Armenia, etc.)   DK509
Russia (WWI: causes, aims, results: includes Panslavism)   D514
Russia (WWI: mil. hist.)   940.40947   D550
Russia (WWII: causes, aims, results)   D742.R9
Russia (WWII: dipl. hist.)   940.532247   D754.R9 or .S65 (Sov. U.)

RUSSIAN aerial ops. (WWI)   D605
Russian Asia   DK750-973+   957-958
Russian Central Asia (to 1920)   DK858
Russian espionage (gen.)   UB271.R9   327.120947
Russian military history   DK50-54
Russian military ops. and Eastern Front (WWI: gen.)   D550   940.4147, .40947
Russian military ops. (Rev., 1917-21)   DK265.2
Russian mission to U.S. (WWI)   D570.8.M6.R7
Russian naval history (1801-1917)   DK58
Russian naval ops. (Rev., 1917-21)   DK265.3
Russian naval ops. (WWI)   D585
RUSSIAN REVOLUTION (1905-6)   DK263-264.3
Russian Revolution (1905-6: reaction)   DK264.3
Russian Revolution (1905-6: special events)   DK264
Russian Revolution (1917-21)   DK265-265.9+
Russian Revolution (1917-21: Allied intervention, 1918-20)   DK265.4
Russian Revolution (1917-21: foreign particip.: gen.)   DK265.9.F5
Russian Revolution (1917-21: gen.)   DK265.A56-Z
Russian Revolution (1917-21: special topics)   DK265.9.A-Z
Russian S.F.S.R. (1917-45)   DK510.7-72
Russian S.F.S.R. (Russia)   DK510
Russians (in U.S.)   E184.R9
RUSSO-Austrian conflict (WWI)   D556-557
Russo-Austrian conflict (WWI: gen.)   D556
Russo-German conflict (WWI: gen.)   D551
Russo-Japanese War (1904-5)   DS516-517   952.031, 947.083
Russo-Japanese War (1904-5: gen.)   DS517
Russo-Japanese War (1904-5: reminiscences & misc.)   DS517.9
Russo-Polish War (1919-20: plus other Polish conflicts of the time)   DK4405
Ruthenia (post-WWI territorial ?s)   D651.R9

SAAR (Ger.)   943.42   DD801.S13
Saar Valley (post-WWI territorial ?s)   D651.S13
Sabotage equipment (mil. sci.)   UB274
Sabotage, intelligence, & unconventional warfare (WWI: Fr.)   940.48644
Sabotage (mil. sci.: gen.)   UB273   355.3437
Sabotage, Naval   359.3437   VG86-88 (underwater demolition), UB273-274
Safety & sanitation (mil. engineering)   623.75   UH600-629.5, U380-385,
                              VC417.5, VG470-475, VM481-482, V380-386
Safety equipment, Nautical (fire-fighting, life-saving, etc.: design)   623.865
                              VK1258, VK1460-1481
Safety, Marine   VK200
Safety measures, Naval (inclu. educ.)   V380-385
Safety technology, Marine (plus other misc. topics)   623.888
Sahara Desert   DT331-346   966
Sailing & pilot guides (official: British)   VK803
Sailing directions & pilot guides   VK798-997
Sailing ships, Modern (engineering)   623.822   VM321, VM351
Sailing vessels (handling)   623.8813   VK543
Sailing vessels (naut. engineering)   623.8203   VM156, VM142-145 (wooden),
                              VM331, VM351

SAILORS, NAVY (Asia)   VD99-113
Sailors, Navy (Australia)   VD121-122   359.3380994
Sailors, Navy (Can.)   VD26-27
Sailors, Navy (Eur.)   VD55-96
Sailors, Navy (Fr.)   VD71-72   359.3380944
Sailors, Navy (G.B.)   VD57-64
Sailors, Navy (gen.: pubn. 1970+)   VD146
Sailors, Navy (Ger.)   VD73-74
Sailors, Navy (Ire.)   VD76.5
Sailors, Navy (New Z.)   VD122.5
Sailors, Navy (Rus.)   VD85-86   359.3380947
Sailors, Navy (U.S.)   VD23-25
Sakhalin (Siberia)   DK771.S2
Salaries & wages, Military (admin.)   355.64 (SEE ALSO .135)   UC70-75
Salaries, Military   355.135 (SEE ALSO 355.64)   UC70-75 (U.S.),
    UC91-258 (other places), UC180-183 (Ger.), UC184-187 (G.B.), UC241 (Japan)
Salary & wage administration, Naval   359.64   VC50-258, VC50-65 (U.S.)
Salvage, Marine   VK1491
Salvation Army (WWI)   D639.S15
SAMOA, American   996.13   DU819.A1, DU810-819, DU815
Samoa (modern hist.)   DU817.A6-Z
Samoa, Western   996.14   DU819.A2, DU810-819, DU815
Samoa, Western (post-WWI territorial ?s)   D651.S3
Samoa, Western (WWI)   D578.S2
Samoan Islands   DU810-819   996.13-14
San Diego, Calif.   F869.S22   979.498
San Francisco Bay area (Calif.)   F868.S156   979.46
San Francisco, Calif.   F869.S3   979.461
San Marino (Republic)   DG975.S2
Sandhurst (Royal Mil. Coll.: descrip. & life)   U520.L1
Sanitary & medical services, Military   UH201-515
Sanitary control (WWI: med. srvcs.)   940.4752
Sanitation & hygiene, Military   UH600
Sanitation & refuse (naval sci.)   VC417.5
Sanitation, health, & hygiene (navies: places besides U.S.)   VG475.A-Z
Sanitation, heating, & ventilation (naval architec. & engin.)   VM481   623.853-854
Sanitation (naut. craft: engineering)   623.8546   VM481-483
Sappers & bridge troops (U.S.)   UG503
Satire, caricature (G.B.: 20th c.)   DA566.8
Satire, poetry, etc. (WWI: gen.)   D526
Saudi Arabia (1873-1914)   DS243   953.04
Saudi Arabia (1914-: gen.)   DS244   953.04-05
Saudi Arabia & Arabian Peninsula   DS201-248   953
Saving life & property (marine navig.)   VK1300-1491
Saxon military ops. (WWI)   D536
Saxony (Prus.)   DD491.S3-39

SCANDINAVIA   DL
Scandinavia & N. Europe (1814-1905)   948.07   DL81 (1814-1900)
Scandinavia & N. Europe (20th c.: 1905-)   948.08   DL83-87+
Scandinavia & N. Europe (1905-19)   948.081   DL83
Scandinavia (geog. & travel)   914.8   DL10
Scandinavia (lighthouses, beacons, foghorns, etc.)   VK1086.5   623.89420948
Scandinavia (mil. status)   UA646.7   355.033048, .033248, .033548
Scandinavia (naval geog.)   359.4748   VA619.S, VA590599 (Sweden)
Scandinavia, Northern Europe, Finland   DL
Scandinavia (WWI: dipl. hist.)   D621.S3
Scapa Flow Naval Base (G.B.: Scot.: WWI & II)   940.5453411
Scenic places (London, Eng.: bridges, parks, etc.)   DA689.A-Z
Scharnhorst (armored [WWI], battle [WWII] cruiser: Ger.)   VA515.S
Schleswig (post-WWI territorial ?s)   D651.S4
Schools (naval architec.: special)   VM275-276
Schools, Naval (Ger.)   V574.A-Z
Schools, Private naval (U.S.)   V430
SCIENCE & technology (WWI)   D639.S2
Science of marine navigation (gen.: pubn. 1801+)   VK555   623.81
Sciences (pure) & math   500-599   Q
Sciences (pure), math, & computer science   Q   500-599, 611-612
Scientists (WWI)   940.3155   D639.S2
Scotland   941.1   DA750-890, DA760 (gen.)
Scotland (20th c.)   DA821   941.1082
Scotland (1910-36)   941.1083   DA821
Scots Guard (WWI)   D547.S4
Scottish troops (G.B.)   UA664
Scraping, painting, etc. (marine engin.)   VM961
Scutari (Albania: gen.)   DR701.S5
Sea forces & warfare (hist.)   359.009+   VA, D-F, VA10, VA25-55
Seabees or naval construction battalions (WWII: U.S.: gen.)   D769.55
Seacoast artillery   UF450-455
Seacraft, Modern (specific types: engineering)   623.821-829
Seamanship   623.88   VK1-587+, VK541-547
Seamanship (marine navig. & merch. marine)   VK541-547   623.88
SEAMEN, NAVAL   VD
Seamen, Naval (Asia: gen.)   VD99   359.338095, .12095
Seamen, Naval (enlisted personnel in gen.: drill, way of life, etc.)   VD
Seamen, Naval (Eur.: gen.)   VD55   359.338094, .12094
Seamen, Naval (G.B.: gen.)   VD57   359.3380941, .120941
Seamen, Naval (gen.: pubn. 1801-1970)   VD145
Seamen, Naval (Ger.: gen.)   VD73   359.3380943, .120943
Seamen, Naval (misc. subjects)   VD430
Seamen, Naval (U.S.: gen.)   VD23   359.3380973, .120973
Seamen's handbooks (G.B.)   V115.G7
Seamen's handbooks (Ger.)   V115.G3
Seamen's handbooks (Rus.)   V115.R9
Seamen's handbooks (U.S. Navy)   V113
Seaplanes   629.133347
Seaplanes (air force)   UG1242.S3   629.133347, 623.7466-7467
Seattle, Wash.   F899.S4   979.777
Second World War (econ., polit., social hist.)   940.531   D421, D443, D720-728,
                                                                                              D743, D748

Secret service, espionage, military intelligence (WWII: spies)   D810.S7-8
                                                                  940.5485-5487+
Secret service, spies (WWI: gen.) D639.S7
Secretary of the Navy (U.S.: official docs.) VA52.A2-29
Security (defense info.)   UB246-249
Security, Industrial (defense purposes)   UB249
Security, Naval   V185
Seizure & disposition of German ships (WWI: U.S.)   D570.8.S4
Semaphore, flag signals, & heliograph (mil. engineering) 623.7312   UG582.S4,
                                                  UG580, UG582, VK385, V300-305
Semaphores (mil.)   UG582.S4
SERBIA (inclu. Belgrade)   DR1932-2125+ (SEE ALSO DR301+ & DR1202 areas)
                              949.71-71022
Serbia (to 1918)   949.7101   DR317, DR1965
Serbia (1804-1918)   DR2006-2032   949.71
Serbia (1804-1918: gen.) DR2007
Serbia (1878-1918: Independence)   949.71015   DR351-363, DR2006-2032
Serbia (1903-18: Peter I Karadordevic) DR2030-2032
Serbia (1914-18: WWI)   DR2032
Serbia (1918-45: gen.)   DR2034
Serbia (gen. histories)   DR1965
Serbia (gen., descrip., culture, history) DR1940
Serbia (WWI)   D561
Serbia (WWI: causes, aims, results)   D513
Serials & periodicals (U.S.)   973.05   E171
Sermons, minor works, pamphlets (WWI)   D525
Service flags (WWI: U.S.)   D570.8.S5
Service periods (navies)   359.11
Services, memorials, monuments, celebrations (WWI: U.S.)   D670-675
Sevastopol, Rus.   DK651.S45
Sevastopol, Uk.   DK508.95.S49
Seville, Sp.   DP402.S36-48
Sewage disposal (mil. design)   623.753   UC430, VM481, VM503
Sex (WWI)   D639.S3
Sextants & quadrants   VK583   527.028, 623.894
Shanghai, China   DS796.S2   951.132
Sharpshooting (infantry: U.S.)   UD333-334
Shells & shrapnel   UF760   623.4513-4518
Shells & shrapnel, Naval   VF490
Shells, bombs, missiles, other delivery units with charges (design)   623.451
                                                                        UF750-755

Shells, Naval artillery   359.82513
Sherwood Foresters (WWI)   D547.S5
Shetland Islands (Scot.)   DA880.S5
Ship exchanges & canteens (gen.)   VC390   359.341
Ship hulls (naut. engineering)   623.84   VM156
Ship trials (gen.)   VM880

SHIPBUILDING & maintenance appliances & activities (engin.: gen.)
                    VM901(SEE TC361 & 363 for dry & floating docks)
Shipbuilding industry   VM298.5-301
Shipbuilding industry (G.B.)   VM298.7.G7
Shipbuilding industry (places besides U.S.) VM298.7.A-Z
Shipbuilding industry (U.S.)   VM298.6   387.50973
Shipbuilding, Naval (gen. hist.)   VM15
SHIPBUILDING, NAVAL (HIST.: Asia)   VM99-113
Shipbuilding, Naval (hist.: Australia)   VM121-122   623.80994
Shipbuilding, Naval (hist.: Eur.)   VM55-96
Shipbuilding, Naval (hist.: Fr.)   VM71-72   623.80944
Shipbuilding, Naval (hist.: G.B.)   VM57-64   623.80941
Shipbuilding, Naval (hist.: Ger.)   VM73-74   623.80943
Shipbuilding, Naval (hist.: It.)   VM79-80   623.80945
Shipbuilding, Naval (hist.: Japan)   VM105-106   623.80952
Shipbuilding, Naval (hist.: New Z.)   VM122.5
Shipbuilding, Naval (hist.: Rus.)   VM85-86   623.80947
Shipbuilding, Naval (hist.: U.S.)   VM23-25   623.80973
Shipbuilding, Naval (instruc.: Australia) VM271
Shipbuilding, Naval (instruc.: Eur.: gen.)   VM205
Shipbuilding, Naval (instruc.: G.B.)   VM207
Shipbuilding, Naval (instruc.: Ger.)   VM223
Shipbuilding, Naval (instruc.: U.S.)   VM173
Shipment & packing (naval sci.)   VC537
SHIPS & crews (naval forces)   359.32   V750-895, V750, VA (indiv. ships)
Ships' appliances (engin.)   VM781-861
Ships (Australia. Navy: by name)   VA715.A-Z   359.32520994-.3260994
Ships (Australia. Navy: lists)   VA713.A1-49   359.30994, .320994, .3250994
Ships (design)   623.812   VM297, V765
Ships (Fr. Navy: lists)   VA503.A1-49   359.320944, .3250944
Ships (G.B. Royal Navy: by name)   VA458.A-Z   359.320941, .3252+-.326+
Ships (G.B. Royal Navy: lists)   VA456   359.325+, .320941
Ships (Ger. Navy: by name)   VA515.A-Z   359.320943, .3252+-.326+
Ships (Ger. Navy: lists)   VA513.A1-49   359.320943, .3250943
Ships (Japan. Imper. Navy: by name)   VA655.A-Z   359.320952, .3252+-.326+
Ships, Naval   V750 (gen.: SEE here for earlier works on battleships &
                    V815 for later works)
Ships (New Z. Navy: lists)   VA723.A1-49   359.309931
Ships, Powered (as units: group op. in squadrons etc., crew duties & life, hist's. of
                    indiv. ships   in most cases)   359.325 (SEE ALSO .83 &
                    .835-836 for ships as equip.: PREFER .325+ when in doubt)
                    V750, V765-767, V799-800
Ships' records & accounts (U.S.)   VC503-504
Ships' stores & equipment (except U.S.)   VC275.A-Z
Ships' stores & equipment (U.S.)   VC273-274
Ships (U.S. Navy: by name)   VA65.A-Z   359.32520973-.32560973
Ships (U.S. Navy: lists)   VA61   359.32, .320222
SHIPWRECKS & fires   VK1250-1299 (PREFER D-F 3 #s for specific wars)
Shipwrecks (Asia)   VK1286
Shipwrecks (Australia & Oceania)   VK1289-1294
Shipwrecks (by area)   VK1270-1294
Shipwrecks (by name)   VK1255.A-Z
Shipwrecks (Eur.)   VK1280-1282
Shipwrecks (U.S.)   VK1270-1273
Shipyards & shipbuilding companies (by name)   VM301.A-Z

Shoes & footwear, Naval   VC310
Shoes, footwear, gloves (mil.) UC490-495
Shooting (marines: inclu. marksmanship, training, etc.) VE330-335
Shooting (naval seamen: inclu. marksmanship, regs., etc.) VD330-335
SHORE facilities, yards, stations (navies: gen.)   VC412 359.7, 623.83
Shore patrol (G.B.)   VB925.G7
Shore patrol (gen.)   VB920 359.13323, .34
Shore patrol (Ger.)   VB925.G3
Shore patrol (U.S.)   VB923
Shore service   VF330-335
Shore service (marines) VE410
Shortwave radio (mil. engineering) 623.7341
Shotguns   UD396
Shrapnel & other antipersonnel devices (design) 623.4514   UF760-765, VF490
Siam (20th c.)   959.304   DS578
SIBERIA   DK751-781, DK761   957
Siberia (19th-20th c.)   DK766   957.08
Siberia (Rev., 1917-21)   DK265.8.S5
Siberia & Asiatic Russia (geog. & travel)   915.7   DK755, DK584 (C.Asia)
Siberia (gen.)   DK761
Siberia (gen. hist., exploration, culture, etc.)   DK753   957
Siberia (WWI)   D558
Sicily   945.8   DG869
Sicily (20th c.)   DG869
Sick & wounded, Care of (mil.: relief societies, etc.: U.S.: gen.)   UH523
Side arms & misc. weapons (design)   623.44 UD380-425
Sidearms, Modern (design)   623.444 (SEE ALSO .441 or .44)   UD420-425, UD400
Siege artillery   UF460-465
Siege warfare   355.44   UG443-449
Sighting & range apparatus (naval ordnance)   359.826
Sighting apparatus & other ordnance access.   355.826   UF848-856
Sights, Firearm   UF854
Sigma Alpha Epsilon (WWI: U.S. educ.: fraternity)   D639.E42.S5
SIGNAL corps & troops   UG570-575
Signal corps & troops (U.S.)   UG573
Signal service, Coast (plus coast guard: gen.)   VG50
Signaling, Merchant marine (flags, lights, codes, radio, etc.)   VK381-397
Signaling, Military   UG570-582   358.24, 623.73+, 355.85
Signaling, Military (particular types)   UG582.A-Z
Signaling, Naval (gen.)   V280-285   359.27, .983
Signals, Visual (mil. engineering)   623.731   UG582.V5
Silesia (20th c.)   DB660
Silesia Voivodeship (Pol.)   DK4600.S48
Silesia, Upper (post-WWI territorial ?s) D651.S5
Singapore   DS598.S7   959.52
Sino-Japanese War (1894-5: gen.)   DS765
Slaughterhouses, Military   UC770

Slavonia (Yug.: local Croatia) DR1633-1636   949.72
Slavs (Eastern question: 19th c.) D377
Slavs (WWI)   D639.S4
Slovakia (1800-1918)   DB678 (PREFER DB2000+), DB2796
Slovakia (1800-1945)   DB2795-2822+
Slovakia (1918-45) DB679-679.3 (PREFER DB2000+)
SLOVENIA   DR381.S6, DR1352-1485+   949.73
Slovenia (1814-1918: gen.)   DR1423
Slovenia (1849-1918: gen.)   DR1431
Slovenia (1914-18: WWI)   DR1434
Slovenia (gen.)   DR1370, 1376
Slovenia (post-WWI territorial ?s) D651.S53
SMALL ARMS   355.824   UF520-537+
Small arms (19th-20th c.)   U889
Small-arms ammunition (bullets, bazooka rockets, etc.: design)   623.455
                          UF700, UF740-745, UF770, TS538, VF500
Small arms & bayonet training   355.547   UD380-415, U169
Small arms & ordnance (besides U.S.: by place) UF525.A-Z
Small arms & ordnance (gen.) UF520   355.82
Small arms & ordnance (manufacture: U.S.: gen.)   UF533   338.4762340973
Small-arms & ordnance research (places besides U.S.)   UF526.5.A-Z
Small arms (by region or country) U897.A-Z
Small arms (gen.)   U884
Small arms (infantry) UD380-425   355.824+, 623.44
Small arms (infantry: countries besides U.S.)   UD385.A-Z
Small arms (marines) VE360-390
Small arms (navies) VD360-390
Small boat service (inclu. armament)   VD400-405   359.3258
Small craft   VM321-349
Small craft (gen.)   VM321
Small craft (naut. engineering) 623.8202   VM320-361, VM321, VM331, VM341
Small craft (naut. handling)   623.8812   VK543, GV811
Smoke screens & tactics UG447.7
Snipers, bazookamen, machine-gunners, & other special-weapon troops   356.162
                          U167.5.A-Z, UD390+, UF620
Snowshoeing (WWI)   D639.S5
Snowshoes, skis, skates, etc. (mil. transp.)   UC360
SOCIAL LIFE & politics (Washington, D.C.) F196
Social life, culture, customs (Berlin, Ger.)   DD866
Social life, culture, customs (London, Eng.) DA688
Social life, culture, customs (Moscow, Rus.)   DK600
Social life, culture, customs (Paris, Fr.)   DC715
Social life, culture, customs (Pol.) DK4110
Social sciences   300-399   G-H, J-L, U-V
Social sciences (economics, commerce, sociology, communism)   H   300-319,
                          330-389
Social sciences (gen.)   300-309   H1-99
Social services, prisons, & medical services (WWI)   940.47
Social services, prisons, & medical services (WWII)   940.547   D805-809
Social welfare services, Military (U.S. Army)   UH760
Social welfare services, Naval   VG2000-2005
Social work, Military (gen.)   UH750   355.34, .346-347
Social work, Naval (gen.)   VG2000
Social work, recreation, etc. (air forces: U.S.)   UG990
Socialism (WWI)   D639.S6

Societies & associations (WWI)   940.4006   D502, D504 (congresses)
Society Islands (inclu. Tahiti, Bora Bora, etc.)   DU870   996.21
Sociological factors of war   355.022 (SEE ALSO 303.66 & 306.2)
Sofia, Bulg.   DR97
Soignes Forest (Bel.)   DH801.S6
Soldiers' & sailors' homes   UB380
Soldiers' & sailors' homes (U.S.: state)   UB384.A-W
Soldiers' handbooks & manuals (gen.)   U110
Somaliland   DT401-420   967.7
Somme, Battle of the (1916)   D545.S7
Somme, 2d Battle of the (1918)   D545.S75
Sounding apparatus   VK584.S6
SOUTH AFRICA (1909-: Union)   DT779   968.05+
South Africa (1910-61: Union)   968.05   DT779
South Africa (1910-19: Louis Botha)   968.052   DT779.5
South Africa (1914-18: WWI period)   DT779.5
South Africa (mil. status)   UA856   355.00968, .033068
South Africa (naval status)   VA700.S52   359.030968
South Africa (overall)   968   DT751-944, DT766
South Africa (WWI)   D547.A4
SOUTH AMERICA   F, F2201-3799+   980-989
South America (1830-)   F2236   980.03
South America (1900-18)   980.032   F2236 (1830-)
South America & Latin Am. (in gen.)   980   F2201-3799+, F2201-2239,
                                                F2231 (GEN.)
South America & Latin America (WWI: causes, aims, results)   D520.S8
South America (gen.)   F2231   980
South America (mil. geog.)   355.478
South America (mil. status: gen.)   UA612   355.03308, .03328
South America (naval status: gen.)   VA415   359.03098
South America (northern: Brazil, Ven., Peru, etc.)   F2216
South America (southern: Arg., Chile, Uru., etc.)   F2217
South America (WWI: dipl. hist.)   D618
South American coasts (gen. & east: pilot & sailing guides)   VK961-968
South & South Atlantic states (1865-1950)   F215   975.04, 976.04
South Atlantic states   975   F206-295, F206-220, F209, F215 (1865-)
South Atlantic states & the South (U.S.: covers south of Mason-Dixon Line)
                                    F206-220   975-976
South Australia   DU300-330   994.23
South Central states & Gulf Coast   976   F296-475, F296-395 (Gulf), F296-
                                          301, F396-475 (Old S.W.), F396
South Seas (Oceanica: islands, chains, groups, etc.)   DU520-950
Southeast Asia   DS521-689+, DS518 (1904-45: Far E. ?), DS521-605, DS525,
                   DS541   959
Southeast Asia (1900-41)   959.051   DS518, DS526.6 (newer titles), DS549
Southeast Asia, Dutch East Indies, Philippines   DS521-689   959
Southern Africa   DT730-995   968
Southern Asia & India   954   DS335-498+
Southern California   F867   979.49
Southwest Africa (German Southwest Africa)   DT701-720   967.1, 968.8
Southwestern Asia & Middle East (gen. histories)   DS62

Soviet Union (1917-24: Rev. period & Lenin era)   947.0841   DK265 (Rev.),
                                                                  DK265-266.5+
Soviet Union (1918-)   DK266   947.084
Soviet Union (1918-: special inclu. espionage, sabotage) DK266.3
Soviet Union (1918-24: Lenin era)   DK266.5   947.0841
Soviets (Rus. Rev., 1917-21: councils)   DK265.9.S6
Spain   DP1-402+   946
Spain (1886-1931: period of Alfonso XIII)   DP234-247
Spain (1914-18: WWI)   DP246
Spain & Portugal (geog. & travel)   914.6   DP42, DP525 (Port.)
Spain (mil. status)   UA780-789   355.033046
Spanish-American War (1898)   E714-735   973.89-898
Spanish-American War (1898: gen.)   E715   973.89
Spanish Morocco   DT330   964.2
Spanish West Africa   964.8
Spark-ignition engines (marine engineering)   623.87234
Spaventa, Silvio (It.: 1871-1945 era)   DG556.S6
Specialist forces & warfare (armored land, technical land, & air)   358   UE-UG
Specialist forces, Naval   359.9
Specifications & contracts (naval architec.: gen.)   VM295
Speeches & essays (naval sci.: gen.)   V19
Speeches (Royal Naval Coll., Dart.: by speaker)   V515.F3.A-Z
Speeches (U.S. Naval Acad.: misc.: by speaker)   V415.F5.A-Z
Speeches (U.S. Navy)   VA54
SPIES, espionage (WWI: by name)   D639.S8.A-Z
Spies, German (by name)   UB271.G32.A-Z
Spies (mil. admin.)   UB270   327.12
Spies, Russian (by name)   UB271.R92.A-Z
Spies, secret service, etc. (Rus. Rev., 1917-21) DK265.9.S4
Spies, United States (by name)   UB271.U62.A-Z
Sports in navies   V267-268
Sports, Military (gen.)   U327
Springfield rifle   UD395.S8
Squadrons, fleets, flotillas, etc. (naval units)   359.31   VA, VA63.A-Z (U.S.),
                                                                  VB200-205
Squadrons (WWI: U.S. aerial)   D570.7
St. Louis public schools (WWI)   D639.E4.S3
St. Petersburg, Rus. (gen.)   DK561
Staff functions (mil. organiz.)   355.33042
Staff positions (naval hier.)   359.33042
Staffs, Army   UB220-225
Staffs, Military (gen.)   UB220
Stalin, Joseph (Rus.: biogs.)   DK268.S8
Stamboliski, Alexander (Bulg.: 1887-1918 time)   DR88.S77
Standards, colors, flags (mil.: places besides U.S.)   UC595.A-Z
Standards (naval architec.)   VM293
States of the U.S. (WWI)   D570.85.A-W   974-979
Statesmen (U.S.: collected works: 20th c.)   E742.5.A-Z (SEE E660 for up to 1921)
Statesmen (U.S.: collected works: inclu. some working through 1921)
                                      E660.A-Z (SEE E742.5 for rest of 20th c.)
Station drills, Naval (Eur.: gen.: ALSO quarter, watch, etc.)   VD215
Stations, shore facilities, yards (navies: U.S.: by state)   VC415.A-W
Statistics (militray medical: U.S.: unofficial)   UH223.A5
Statistics, Official (military medical: U.S.)   UH223.A4-49

Steam engines (marine engineering)   623.8722   VM741-749, TJ735-740
Steamship lines (by co. name)   VM385.A-Z
Steel & iron land defenses   UG408-409
Steerage, Nautical   VM565
Steering gear, Marine (engin.) VM841-845
Sten machine guns   UF620.S8
Stockholm, Swe.   DL976
Stores & supplies, Military (U.S.)   UC263-264
Stores & supplies, Naval (U.S.)   VC263-264   359.80973
Stores, Ordnance (U.S.: gen.)   UF553
Strassburg, Ger.   DD901.S81-89
Strategic lines, bases, etc.   UA930   355.43
STRATEGY, Air force   358.4143   U162-163, UG633-635
Strategy & military ops. (plans, attack, defense, etc.)   355.4   UA11,
          UA23 (U.S.), U27, U42-43, U102, U161-167
Strategy & naval ops.   359.4 (SEE ALSO .43 for strategic works prior to 1989)
          V27-55, V101-107, VA, VA10, VA50-750
Strategy (mil. sci.: pubn. 1789-)   U162   355.43
Strategy, Naval   359.43 (PREFER .4 with titles after 1988)   V160-165
Strategy, Naval (gen.: pubn. thru 1800) V160
Strategy (WWI)   940.401   D521, D530, D550
Strategy (WWI: Allies)   940.4012   D544, D570
Strategy (WWI: Central Powers)   940.4013   D531
Strategy (WWII)   940.5401   D743
Straubing, Ger. (WWI)   D538.5.S76
Stream & river crossing (artillery)   UF320
Street fighting   U167.5.S7
Streets, bridges, etc. (Berlin, Ger.)   DD887
Stresemann, Gustav (Ger.: 1888-1918+ period)   DD231.S83
Structural design (naval architec.: specific materials)   623.818
Structural design (naval architec.: steel)   623.81821   VM146
Structural theory & design (naval architec.) 623.817   VM156-163
Structure & personnel, Air force   358.413   UG770-775, UG1130-1135
Student publications (U.S. Naval Acad.)   V415.J1-7
Stuttgart, Ger.   DD901.S95-97
Subcaliber guns (U.S.: handbooks)   UF563.A8
SUBMARINE & anti-submarine ops (WWII)   D780-784   940.5451
Submarine boats   VM365-367
Submarine boats (gen.)   VM365   359.3257, 623.8257
Submarine cables (mil.)   UG607
Submarine forces & warfare   359.93
Submarine mines, minelaying, minesweeping, etc. (U.S.) V856.5.U6-7
SUBMARINE OPS. & submarine chasers (WWI)   D590-595   940.451+
Submarine ops. (WWI: Allies)   940.4513   D590
Submarine ops. (WWI: Fr.)   940.451344   D595.F
Submarine ops. (WWI: G.B.)   940.451341   D593 (gen.), D594.A-Z (by
          confrontation, ship, etc.)
Submarine ops. (WWI: Ger.)   940.4512   D591 (gen.), D592.A-Z (by ship,
          battle, etc.)
Submarine ops. (WWI: misc. countries besides Ger., G.B.)   D595.A-Z
Submarine ops. (WWI: U.S.)   940.451373   D595.U
Submarine warfare (gen.)   V210   359.3257, .42-43

SUBMARINES (besides U.S.)   V859.A-Z
Submarines, Conventionally-powered (navies: as equip.)   359.93832 (SEE .8357 for
                                                    works before 1989)
Submarines, Diesel & electric (navies: units)   359.32572
Submarines (gen.)   V857 (SEE ALSO V210-14 for sub warfare & VM365-7 for
                  construc.)   623.8257, .82572, .81257, 359.3257
Submarines (Ger.)   V859.G3   623.82570943
Submarines, Naval (as equip.) 359.8357 (SEE ALSO .93832 for titles after 1988)
Submarines, Naval (as units)   359.933 (SEE .3257 for titles prior to 1989)
Submarines, Naval (design)   623.81257   V858-859, VM365-367
Submarines, Naval (engineering) 623.8257   VM365-367, V857-859
Submarines (navies: handling)   623.88257   V857-859, V210-214
Submarines (U.S.)   V858   623.82570973, 359.32570973
Submersibles (naut. engineering) 623.8205   VM365-367
Submersibles (naval design)   623.812045
Subsistence & provisions, Naval (inclu. rations, galleys, water, etc.)   VC350-410
Subsistence Dept. (U.S. Army)   UC40-44
Subsistence (mil.: countries besides U.S.)   UC705.A-Z
Subsistence (mil.: gen.)   UC700
Subsistence (mil.: U.S.)   UC703-704
Subversion & sabotage (mil.) 355.3437   UB273-274UB275-277, UB276 (U.S.),
                                         UB277.A-Z (except U.S.)
Subversive activities (in U.S.: propaganda, espionage, 5th column, etc.)   E743.5
Sudan (1900-1955)   DT156.7
Sudan & Anglo-Egyptian Sudan   DT108, (older works), DT154.1-159   962.4
Sudan (gen.)   DT155.6
Suez Canal (Egypt: inclu. Isthmus)   DT154.S9   962.15
Sultan Muhammad Shah, Sir, Agha Khan (India: 1901+ era)   DS481.S8
Sun Yat Sen (China: 1912-49 era: biograpy & criticism)   DS777.A597.A-Z89
SUPPLIES & equipment (air force: gen.)   UG1100-1105   358.418
Supplies & stores, Military (inclu. procure., storage, specs., surplus, etc.)
                                                    UC260-267
Supplies & stores, Naval (inclu. stds., procure., storage, etc.)   VC260-268
Supplies & stores, Naval (management methods)   VC266   359.62
Supplies & stores, Naval (misc.)   VC279.A-Z
Supplies, Medical & surgical (mil.)   UH440-445   355.88
Supplies, Medical & surgical (navies)   VG290-295
Supplies, Military (use & disposal)   355.6213
Supplies, Naval (Ger.)   VC180   359.80943
Supplies (WWI)   D639.S9
SUPPLY administration (mil.) 355.621   UC260-267
Supply administration (navies)   359.621   VC260-267, VC263 (U.S.)
Supply & administrative services, Military (canteens, post-ex's., messes, etc.)
            355.341 (SEE ALSO 355.6 & .71)   UC, UC750-755, UH80-85
Supply & transport depts. (mil.: G.B.)   UC184
Supply depots, Military   355.75   UC260-269
Supply depots, Naval   359.75   VC260-265
Supply services, Naval (canteens, post exch's, messes, etc.)   359.341   VC,
            VC10, VC20-258 (overall by place), VC20-65 (U.S.), VC260-410
Supply ships (naval engineering)   623.8265   V865
Supply transport vehicles (land: mil. design)   623.7474
Supply vessels, transports, service craft, etc. (U.S. Naval Auxiliary Service)
                                                    VA79

Support & logistics, Military (logistics, camouflage, p.o.w. care, etc.)   355.41
U168, UC260-270

Support & logistics, Naval   359.41   V179, VC10
Support ships (naval engineering)   623.826   V865
Support vessels, Naval (units)   359.326   V865
Surgeons, Naval   VG260-265   359.345, 616.98024, 617.99
Surgical & medical handbooks (navies: U.S.)   VG463
Surveillance, Military   UG475   355.413, 358.45
Surveying, Hydrographic (gen. special)   VK593
Surveying, mapping, & topography (military: gen.)   UG470   623.71
Surveyors, draftsmen, & engineering aids (navies)   VG920-925
Survival (combat: escape & evasion)   U225
Survival after shipwrecks (plus other misc. lifesaving topics)   VK1445-1447
623.865

SWEDEN   DL601-991+, DL648   948.5
Sweden (20th c.)   DL860   948.505
Sweden (1907-50: Gustav V)   DL867-870
Sweden (1914-18: WWI era)   DL868
Sweden (mil. status)   UA790-799   355.0330485
Sweden (WWI: dipl. hist.)   D621.S5
Swiss Guards (Papal Guards)   UA745.5
Switzerland   DQ, DQ54   949.4
Switzerland (20th c.)   DQ201   949.407
Switzerland (1900-18)   949.4071
Switzerland (geog. & travel)   914.94   DQ24
Switzerland (mil. status)   UA800-809   355.0330494
Sword exercises (cavalry)   UE420-425
Swords   UD420-425
Sydney, Australia   DU178   994.41
Sympathizers, Enemy (WWI)   940.3163   D570.8.A6 (U.S.), D636.A-Z (by locale)
SYRIA   DS92-99, DS95.5   956.91
Syria (1516-1920: time of Ottomans)   956.9103   DS97.5-6
Syria (1517-1918: Turkish period)   DS97.5   956.9103
Syria (gen.)   DS95
Syria (geog. & travel)   915.691   DS94
Syria (post-WWI territorial ?s)   D651.S9
Syria (WWI)   D568.6

TABLES, formulae, statistics (marine geonavigation)   623.8920212
Tables, Nautical   VK563-567+   623.8920212
Tables, Nautical navigation (distances etc.)   VK799   623.8920212
Tables, outlines, etc, (WWI)   D522.5
Tables, Tide & current (collections)   VK603
TACTICS, Air force   358.4142   UG700-705
Tactics, Air warfare (bombing, strafing, dog fighting, air mining, etc.)   UG700-705
358.4142, .43
Tactics & maneuvers, Naval   VD157 (PREFER V167-178 & V245)
359.415, .4152
Tactics & operations, Infantry   356.183

TACTICS & REGULATIONS (MIL. ENGINEERING: Asia)   UG270-280
Tactics & regulations (mil. engineering: Australia & New Z.)   UG295-298
Tactics & regulations (mil. engineering: by place)   UG160-302
Tactics & regulations (mil. engineering: Can.)   UG163
Tactics & regulations (mil. engineering: Eur.)   UG215-269
Tactics & regulations (mil. engineering: Fr.)   UG228
Tactics & regulations (mil. engineering: G.B.)   UG234
Tactics & regulations (mil. engineering: Ger.)   UG231
Tactics & regulations (mil. engineering: Rus.)   UG252
Tactics & regulations (mil. engineering: U.S.)   UG160
TACTICS, MANEUVERS, & DRILLS (ARMOR & CAVALRY)   UE157-302
Tactics, maneuvers, & drills (armor & cavalry: Asia: gen.) UE270
Tactics, maneuvers, & drills (armor & cavalry: Australia)   UE295
Tactics, maneuvers, & drills (armor & cavalry: Austria)   UE219
Tactics, maneuvers, & drills (armor & cavalry: Eur.: gen.) UE215
Tactics, maneuvers, & drills (armor & cavalry: Fr.)   UE228
Tactics, maneuvers, & drills (armor & cavalry: Ger.)   UE231
Tactics, maneuvers, & drills (armor & cavalry: Rus.)   UE252
Tactics, maneuvers, & drills (armor & cavalry: U.S.: gen.)   UE160
Tactics, maneuvers, & drills (armored & mechanized cavalry)   UE159
TACTICS, MANEUVERS, & DRILLS (ARTILLERY)   UF157-302
Tactics, maneuvers, & drills (artillery: Asia: gen.)   UF270
Tactics, maneuvers, & drills (artillery: Australia & New Z.)   UF295-298
Tactics, maneuvers, & drills (artillery: Can.)   UF163
Tactics, maneuvers, & drills (artillery: Eur.: gen.)   UF215
Tactics, maneuvers, & drills (artillery: Fr.)   UF228
Tactics, maneuvers, & drills (artillery: G.B.)   UF234
Tactics, maneuvers, & drills (artillery: Ger.)   UF231
Tactics, maneuvers, & drills (artillery: It.)   UF243
Tactics, maneuvers, & drills (artillery: Rus.)   UF252
Tactics, maneuvers, & drills (artillery: Tur.)   UF264
Tactics, maneuvers, & drills (artillery: U.S.: gen.)   UF160
Tactics, maneuvers, & drills (horse cavalry: gen.)   UE157
TACTICS, MANEUVERS, & DRILLS (INFANTRY)   UD157-302
Tactics, maneuvers, & drills (infantry: Asia)   UD270-280
Tactics, maneuvers, & drills (infantry: Australia & New Z.) UD295-298
Tactics, maneuvers, & drills (infantry: Austria)   UD219-221
Tactics, maneuvers, & drills (infantry: Eur.) UD215-269
Tactics, maneuvers, & drills (infantry: Fr.)   UD228-230
Tactics, maneuvers, & drills (infantry: G.B.) UD234-236
Tactics, maneuvers, & drills (infantry: Ger.) UD231-233
Tactics, maneuvers, & drills (infantry: It.)   UD243-245
Tactics, maneuvers, & drills (infantry: Rus.) UD252-254
Tactics (marines)   359.9642   VE157
Tactics, Military   355.42   U164-167.5, U165
Tactics, Military (in different terrains, climates, weathers)   355.423
     U167.D4 (desert), .F6 (forest), .W5 (winter)
Tactics, Military (pubn. 1811-)   U165   355.42
Tactics, Naval   359.42   V167-178
Tactics, Naval (gen.)   V167   359.42
Taft, William Howard (U.S.: 1865-1900 era: works)   E660.T11-12
Tailoring (naval clothing)   VC330
Taiwan (1895-1945: gen.)   DS799.7
Takeoff (aviation)   629.1325212
Tallinn, Rus. (Reval)   DK651.T28

Tanganyika (German East Africa)   DT436-449, DT444   967.82
Tanganyika (to 1960: newer titles)   DT447
Tanganyika (1916-61: Brit. era)   967.8203   DT444, DT447
Tank warfare (WWI)   D608   358.18, 940.4+
Tankers (naval architec.)   VM455   623.8245, 387.544
Tanks, armored cars, etc. (attack, defense, & siege: SEE ALSO UE159-302 for
          armored cavalry)   UG446.5   355.422, 357.5, 358.18
Tanks (design)   623.74752   UG446.5
Tannenberg, Battle of (1914)   D552.T3
Target detection & selection (inclu. radar & other methods: engineering)
          623.557 (use .46 for ranging & siting apparatae)
Target practice   UF340-345
Target practice, Naval   VF310-315
Tasmania (Van Diemen's Land)   DU450-480, DU470   994.6
Tasmania (WWI)   D547.T3
Tatars (in Pol.)   DK4121.5.T3
Technical forces (chem., biol., & radiation warfare: pre-1989 titles may cover
          camouflage construc. & war matériel manufac.)   358.3
Technical forces, Naval (engineering, communic's., etc.)   359.98
Technical troops & artificers (gen.)   UG500   358.2-3
Technical troops & other special corps   UG500-565
Technology, medicine, engineering, agriculture, management   600-699
          T, R, QA76, S, H
Technology, photography, manufacturing, handicrafts, home economics   T   600-
          609, 620-629, 640-650, 660-699, 770-779
Telecommunication (defense)   UA929.95.T4
Telecommunications, Military   UG590-613.5
Telecommunications, Naval   VG70-85   359.415, .85, 623.856, .73
Telegraph & radio (WWI)   D639.T35
Telegraph, Military (inclu. telegraph troops)   UG600-605
Telegraph, Naval   VG70-75
Telegraph, radar, & radio communications (navies: wireless)   VG76-78
Telegraphy, Wire (mil. engineering)   623.732   UG600-607
TELEPHONE, Military (gen.)   UG610
Telephone, Military (places besides U.S.)   UG610.5.A-Z
Telephone, Naval   VG80-85   623.85645
Telephone, radio, & telegraph (military: gen.)   UG590   623.732-7345
Telephone (WWI)   D639.T4
Telephones, Radio (mil. engineering)   623.7345   UG611 (gen.), UG611.3 (U.S.),
          UG611.5.A-Z (other lands), VG76-85
Telephony, Wire (mil. engineering)   623.733   UG610-610.5
Telescopic sights (artillery)   UF855
Tents, Military   UC570-585
Terminals, Marine (bunkers, coal supplies, repairs, etc.)   VK358
Territorial questions (post-WWI: by place)   D651.A-Z
Territorial questions (post-WWI: gen.)   D650.T4 (SEE D651 for specific places)
          940.31424
Territories (U.S.: inclu. Alaska & Hawaii)   F965 (SEE ALSO DU620-629 for Haw.)
Testing (naval armor)   V910-915 (SEE ALSO VF540)
Tests (naval architec.)   623.819
Tests, Ordnance   UF890
Tests, Ordnance & firing (navies)   VF540
Texas (1918-45)   976.4062   F391
Thailand (19th-20th c.)   DS578   959.303-304

Theory & philosophy (nautical craft)   623.82001   VM156
Theory & philosophy (naval warfare)   359.001
Theory & principles (naval architec.)   VM156-163
Third Republic (Fr.: 1871-1940)   DC335
Thompson machine guns   UF620.T5
Thrace (post-WWI territorial ?s)   D651.T5
Tibet   951.5   DS785
Tibet & Central Asia (1951+ pubns.: gen.)   DS786
Tide & current tables   VK600-794, VK602 (gen.), VK610-650 (Atl.: E.),
    VK628-644 (Brit. Isles & Eng. Ch.), VK653-674 (Medit.),
    VK759-792 (Atl: W., U.S., Carib.)   623.8949
Tide & current tables (Atlantic Ocean: all & east: gen.)   VK610   623.894909163
Tide & current tables (by area)   VK607-794
Timber (naval supplies)   VC279.T5
Tirpitz, Alfred von (Ger.: 1888-1918+ period)   DD231.T5
Tiso, Jozef (Czech.: 1939-45 era)   DB2821.T57
TocH (WWI)   D639.T6
Togoland (post-WWI territorial ?s)   D651.T7
Togoland (WWI)   D576.T7
Tokyo, Japan (1867-1945)   DS896.64   952.13503
Tokyo, Japan (gen.)   DS896.6
Tomb of the Unknown Soldier (WWI: U.S.: Arlington, Va. or Washington, D.C.)
    D675.A74 or .W2

Tonnage tables (naval architec.)   VM153
Tools (naval supplies)   VC279.T6
Topography & mapping, Military (places except U.S.)   UG473.A-Z
TORPEDO & mining troops   UG550
Torpedo boat destroyers   V840   623.8254
Torpedo boat service   V837-838
Torpedo boats   V830-838   623.8258, 359.3258
Torpedo boats (Ger.)   V835.G3
Torpedo boats (places besides U.S.)   V835.A-Z
Torpedo boats (U.S.)   V833
Torpedoes (gen.: inclu. propelling or launching devices) V850   623.4517, 359.82517
Torpedoes (types or devices: by name)   V855.A-Z
Traffic control systems, Air   629.1366
TRAINING & EDUCATION, Air force   358.415   UG637-639
Training & education, Air force (gen.)   UG637
Training & education, Air force (places besides U.S.) UG639.A-Z
Training & education, Military   355.5   U400-717, U400 (gen.), U403 (modern),
    U408 (U.S.), U410 (West Pt.), U510-549 (G.B.)
Training & education, Military (modern hist.)   U403
Training & education, Naval   359.5 V400-695 (by place), V411-438 (U.S.), V260-265
Training & education, Naval (G.B.: stations, ships, engin. schools, etc.)   V522-525
Training & education, Naval (modern hist.: gen.)   V404
Training & education, Naval (U.S. Coast Guard)   V437   359.9707
Training camps (armor & cavalry: gen.)   UE430
Training camps (armor & cavalry: places besides U.S.)   UE435.A-Z
Training camps, Marine   VE430-435   359.967+
Training camps (WWI: U.S.: gen.)   D570.36
Training camps (WWI: U.S. in Europe)   D570.37.A-Z (SEE U294.5 for those in U.S.)
Training (cavalry horses)   UE470-475
Training, Horse cavalry   357.185   UE430-435, UE160-302 (by place)
Training (infantry)   356.184   U400-714 (educ.), U320-325

Training (marine navig. & merch. marine)   VK531-537
Training (marines)   359.965   VE430-435, V411-695, VE422 (U.S.)
Training, Military (Ger.: by school location)   U574.A-Z
Training, Naval reserve   359.2232   V400-695
Training, Officer (air forces)   358.4155
Training, Officer (mil. sci.)   355.55   U400-717 (educ.)
Training, Officer (navies)   359.55   V400-695, V411-438 (U.S.: Annapolis
                                                etc.), VB307-315
Training, Physical (mil. sci.: U.S.)   U323
Training, Physical (navies: countries besides U.S.)   V265.A-Z
Training, Physical (navies: gen.)   V260   359.54
Training planes (design)   623.7462
Training, Reserve   355.2232
Training schools, Naval (misc.)   V425.A-Z
Training ships (U.S. Navy: gen.)   V435
Training (shooting: marines: gen.)   VE330   359.96547
Training, Simulated (navies)   V252
Training stations, Naval (G.B.: by place)   V522.5.A-Z
Training stations, Naval (U.S.: gen.)   V433   359.50973, .70973
Training, Technical (air forces)   358.4156
Training, Technical (mil. sci.)   355.56
Training, Technical (navies)   359.56
TRANSPORT & maintenance (mil. sci.: gen. spec.)   UC12
Transport & maneuvers (mil. living conditions)   355.1293
Transport equipment & supplies, Military (vehicles, fuel, trains, etc.)   355.83
               UC270-360, UC270-275, UC340-345, UC260-267, UG615-620
Transport equipment & supplies, Naval (inclu. fuel, vehicles, ships [gen.], etc.)
               359.83   VC530-580, VC270-279, VC276, V750-895, UC320-325
Transport planes (air force)   UG1242.T7
Transport service (WWI: U.S.)   D570.72-.73
Transport ships & hospital ships (naval engineering) 623.8264   UC320-325,
                                                VG450 (hosp. ships)
Transport, Medical (mil.: gen.)   UH500
Transport, Military   UC270-360   358.25, .44, 355.27
Transport, Military (besides U.S.: by place)   UC275.A-Z
Transport, Motor (mil. sci.: U.S.)   UC343
Transport, Motor (navies: U.S.)   VC573
Transport, Naval   VC530-580
Transport, Personnel (navies: U.S.)   VC553
Transport, Railroad (mil.: places besides U.S.)   UC315.A-Z
Transportation (defense)   UA929.95.T7
Transportation, Military (gen.)   UC270   358.25
Transportation, Naval (gen.)   VC530-535   359.83, .27
Transportation services (mil. engineers)   358.25   UC270-275, UG345 (rail)
Transportation (WWI)   D639.T8
Transylvania (1801-1918)   DB740 (SEE DR281.T7 for 1918-)
Transylvania (post-WWI territorial ?s)   D651.T8
Travel & geography   910-919   G (geog.), D-F (descr. & travel)
Travel routes (mil. sci.: gen.)   UA950
Travel routes (misc.)   UA979

TREATIES (Fin.: 1918)   DK459.3
Treaties (Fin.-Rus.: 1920)   DK459.4
Treaties (Pol., 1921: Riga)   DK440.3
Treaties (Rus. Rev., 1905-6: Björkö)   DK264.1905
Treaties (Russo-Polish, other Polish conflicts: Riga: 1921)   DK4407.3
Treaties (Sp.-Am. War, 1898)   E723   973.892
TREATIES (WWI: Allies-Central powers)   D643   940.3141
Treaties (WWI: Austria: 10 Sept. 1919)   D643.A8-9
Treaties (WWI: Bulg.: 27 Nov. 1919)   D643.B5
Treaties (WWI: countries other than Ger.)   D643.A8-Z
Treaties (WWI: Ger.: 28 June 1919)   D643.A2-A7
Treaties (WWI: Hungary: 4 June 1920)   D643.H7-9
Treaties (WWI: misc. separate)   D614.A-Z
Treaties (WWI: misc. separate: collections)   D614.A2
Treaties (WWI: results)   940.3142   D511-20
Treaties (WWI: Turkey: S`evres: 10 Aug. 1920)   D643.T8
Treaties (WWI: U.S.-Austria)   D643.A83
Treaties (WWI: U.S.-Ger.)   D643.A68
Treaties (WWI: U.S.-Hung.)   D643.H8
Treatment of prisoners (Geneva & Hague conven.: unofficial)   UH533 (PREFER
                                                                                         JX5136 & JX5243)

TREATY of Neuilly-sur-Seine (WWI: texts)   D643.B6
Treaty of Portsmouth (Rus.-Jpn. War, 1904-5)   DS517.7
Treaty of St. Germain (WWI: texts by date)   D643.A8
Treaty of Trianon (WWI: non-U.S. texts)   D643.H7
TREATY OF VERSAILLES (WWI: 28 June 1919: collected texts)   D643.A2
Treaty of Versailles (WWI: official discussions by date)   D643.A6
Treaty of Versailles (WWI: other official by date)   D643.A65
Treaty of Versailles (WWI: preliminary discussions)   D643.A3-4
Treaty of Versailles (WWI: protocol)   D643.A51
Treaty of Versailles (WWI: reservations by date)   D643.A55
Treaty of Versailles (WWI: texts by date)   D643.A5.1919+
Treaty of Versailles (WWI: unofficial talks)   D643.A7.A-Z
Trench artillery (WWI: U.S.)   D570.327
Trench warfare   UG446   355.44
Trench warfare matériel (U.S.: handbooks)   UF563.A77
Trepper, Leopold (WWII: spy)   D810.S8.T65
Trials (Leipzig: 1921)   D626.G4
Trials, Ship (by name of vessel)   VM881.A-Z
Trials (WWI: atrocities, war crimes: by country accused)   D626.A-Z
Trieste (post-WWI territorial ?s)   D651.T85
Triple Alliance (1882)   D458 (SEE ALSO D397, D443, D511)
Triple Entente (1907)   D459 (SEE ALSO D443, D511)
Tripoli, Libya   DT239.T7
Troop support (air forces)   358.41415   UG700-705, UG260
Troop support (communication, supply, medical, p.o.w.'s, etc.)   355.415 (ALSO
                                                                    use 355.41 for newer titles on p.o.w. care)
                                                                    UC260-27, UA940-945

Troop support, Naval   359.415
Troops, Ski & mountain   356.164   UD470-475, U167.5.W5
Troops, Special-purpose   356.16   U167.5.A-Z
Troopships & waterways (mil. transp.: gen.)   UC320
Tropical hygiene (mil. sci.)   UH611
Trotsky, Leon (Rus.: 1894-1917: biog.)   DK254.T6
Tsingtao, China   DS796.T7

Tsushima, Battle of (Rus.-Jpn. War, 1904-5)   DS517.5
Tunisia   DT241-269, DT254   961.1
Tunisia (1881-1957: Fr. Protectorate)   DT264   961.104
Tunisia & Egypt (mil. geog.)   355.4761-4762
Tunisia (mil. status)   UA867.5   355.0330611
Tunnels (mil. engineering) UG340   623.68
Turbines, Marine   VM740   623.87233
Turco-Egyptian conflict (WWI)   D568.A2
Turco-Italian War (1911-12: Libya)   DT234
Turco-Russian conflict (WWI)   D567.A2
TURKEY (ca. 640-1918: inclu. Russo-Turkish War, 1877-8)   956.101 (PREFER
                  947.081 for   Russo-Turk. War of 1877-8)   DR440,
                  DR588 (1914-18), DR573 (R-T War)
Turkey (1876-1909: Abdul Hamid II)   DR571-579
Turkey (20th c.)   DR577   956.102
Turkey (1909-18: Mohammed V)   DR583-588   956.101
Turkey (1911-12: Turco-Italian War era)   DR586
Turkey (1912-13: Balkan War period)   DR587
Turkey (1914-18: WWI era)   DR588
Turkey (1918-45)   956.102   DR589-590
Turkey (1918-22: Mohammed VI)   DR589
Turkey & Albania (primarily Tur.)   DR401-741
Turkey & Asia Minor (lighthouses, beacons, foghorns, etc.)   VK1111-1112
Turkey & Cyprus   956.1   DR401-741, DS47-53, DS54 (Cyp.)
Turkey & Cyprus (geog. & travel)   915.61-66   DR428, DS54 (Cyprus)
Turkey & Islam (WWI: causes, aims, results)   D520.T8
Turkey & Near East (WWI: gen.)   D566   940.415, .4145
Turkey (mil. status)   UA810   355.0330561
Turkey (naval geog.)   359.4756   VA667.T9
Turkey (naval status)   VA667.T9   359.0309561
Turkey (overall)   956.1   DR440
Turkey (post-WWI territorial ?s)   D651.T9
Turkey (WWI: mil. hist.)   940.409561   D566
Turkish naval ops. (WWI)   D587
Turrets & cupolas, Naval   VF440
Turrets, Revolving (naval sci.: inclu. monitors)   V860
Tyrol & Vorarlberg (20th c.)   DB780
Tyrol (post-WWI territorial ?s)   D651.T95

U.S.   [SEE ALSO 'United States']
U.S. Army   UA24-39
U.S. Army (gen.)   UA25   355.00973, .30973, .310973
U.S. Army (special troops: by name)   UA34.A-Z
U.S. Coast Guard   VG53   359.970973
U.S. Dept. of Defense   UA23.2-6   353.6-7
U.S. Dept. of Defense (gen. hist.)   UA23.6
U.S. Marine Corps   VE23   359.960973
U.S. Marine Corps (official hist's.)   VE23.A3-32
U.S. Marine Corps (official monographs)   VE23.A5
U.S. Military Academy (West Point)   U410.A-R3+ 355.0071173
U.S. Military Academy (admin.)   U410.C3-H8
U.S. Military Academy (gen. hist.)   U410.L1
U.S. Military Academy (registers, unoff.)   U410.H5-8
U.S. military education (gen. special)   U408.3
U.S. National Guard (gen.)   UA42.A7-Z

U.S. NAVAL ACADEMY (Annapolis)   V415.A1-R4+   359.0071173
U.S. Naval Academy (Act of incorp.: PREFER KF7353.55)   V415.A1
U.S. Naval Academy (admin.)   V415.C3-H5
U.S. Naval Academy (Cong. docs.: gen.: by date)   V415.E5
U.S. Naval Academy (hist. & descrip.)   V415.L1-P1
U.S. Naval Academy (registers, unoff.)   V415.H5
U.S. NAVY   VA52-79 (SEE ALSO E182)
U.S. Navy (distribution: gen.)   VA62   359.4773, .31
U.S. Navy (gen.)   VA55   359.00973, .30973, .4773
U.S. Navy (gen.: 1881-1970 coverage)   VA58   359.00973
U.S. Navy (misc. units: by name)   VA66.A-Z
U.S. Navy (placement & stations)   VA62-74
U.S. Navy Dept. (official docs.: gen.)   VA52.A1-19
U.S. Veterans' Administration   UB382-384
U.S. War Dept. (ann. reports)   UA24.A1-149
UKRAINE   DK508-508.9+
Ukraine (1775-1917: gen.)   DK508.772
Ukraine (1917+: earlier pubns.)   DK508.8
Ukraine (1917-44)   DK508.79-835
Ukraine (1917-44: gen.)   DK508.812
Ukraine (Rev., 1917-21)   DK265.8.U4
Ukraine (geog. & travel)   914.771
Ukraine (post-WWI territorial ?s)   D651.U6
Ukrainians (in Pol.)   DK4121.5.U4
UNCONVENTIONAL WARFARE (air forces: intelligence, propaganda, etc.)
                                          358.41343
Unconventional warfare, Allied (WWI: espionage, intell., infilt., sabotage, etc.)
                                          940.486
Unconventional warfare, Central Power (WWI)   940.487
Unconventional warfare (navies)   359.343   VB230-250
Unconventional warfare (WWI: espionage, intell., infilt., sabotage, etc.)
                                          940.485   D639.S7-8
Unconventional warfare (WWII: inclu. espionage, infilt., intelligence, subversion)
          940.5485   D810.S7 (gen.), .S8.A-Z (by spy),D802(underground),
          D802.F8 (Fr. undergr.), UB250-274, UB273-274 (sabo.),
          UB251.A-Z (intell., by country), UB271.A-Z (espion., by country
          respons.), VB230-250 (naval intell. & espionage)
UNIFORMS, Air force   358.4114   UG1160-1165
Uniforms, Air force   UG1160-1165   358.4114
Uniforms, Infantry   356.1814
Uniforms, Marine   VE400-405   359.9614
Uniforms, Military (besides U.S.)   UC485.A-Z
Uniforms, Military (gen.)   UC480   355.14
Uniforms, Military (inclu. insignia, etiquette of, etc.)   355.14   UC480-535,
                                          UC483 (U.S.)
Uniforms, Naval (besides U.S.)   VC305.A-Z
Uniforms, Naval (gen.)   VC300   359.14, .81
Union of Soviet Socialist Republics (Russia)   [SEE ALSO 'Russia' or 'Soviet
    Union']   947   DK, DK1-275, DK501-973+

UNITED STATES   [SEE ALSO 'U.S.']   E-F975+, E151-860+, E178 (gen.)
                                         973-979.9+
United States (1865-1901)   973.8   E660-738, E661
United States (1865-1900+)   E660-738   973.8-89
United States (1865-1900: gen.)   E661   973.8
United States (1893-97: Pres. Grover Cleveland)   E706   973.85
United States (1897-1901: gen.)   E711
United States (1897-1901: Pres. Wm. McKinley)   E710-751   973.88
United States (1898: Sp.-Am. War)   973.89 (SEE ALSO 946.08 for Sp.-Am. War,
                                      1898)   E714-735, E715
United States (20th c.)   973.9+   E740-749, E741
United States (20th c.: gen.)   E741   973.9
United States (1901-09: gen.)   E756
United States (1901-09: Pres. Theodore Roosevelt)   E756-760, E756   973.911
United States (1909-13: Pres. Wm. Howard Taft: gen.)   E761   973.912
United States (1909-13: Wm. Howard Taft era)   973.912   E760-765, E761
United States (1913-21: gen.)   E766
United States (1913-21: Woodrow Wilson period)   E765-783, E766, E780 (WWI
                                                   era)   973.913
United States (1914-18: WWI era: internal)   E780   973.913
United States (1919-33: inclu. Roaring Twenties)   E784   973.913-916
United States aerial ops. (WWI)   D570.6, D606 (gen.)   940.44973
United States & U.S. military ops. (WWII: gen.)   D769.A5-Z (SEE ALSO E806
                                        for internal, general U.S. history, 1939-45)
                                        940.5373, .540973, .532273, 973.917
United States automatic machine guns   UF620.U6
United States (biog.: heads of state)   923.173   E176.1 (Presidents: collective)
United States (gen. & cultural, serials, societies, etc.)   E151
United States (gen. hist.)   E178   973
United States (geog. & travel: overall)   917.3   E169 (1914-45)
United States (geog. & travel: states, areas, & towns)   917.4-9
United States (lighthouses, beacons, foghorns, etc.)   VK1023-1025
United States (local), Canada, Newfoundland, Mexico, Central & South America
                                        F   974-79+, 971-2, 980-89
United States (local: regions, states, towns, etc.)   F1-975+   974-979 (note
                                                   that Hawaii is placed at 996.9)
United States magazine rifle   UD395.U6
United States (maps & atlases)   912.73   G1200+, G1201
United States medical services (WWI: by overseas locale)   D629.U8.A-Z
United States medical services (WWI: by place in U.S.)   D629.U7.A-Z
United States medical services (WWI: by state)   D629.U62.A-W
United States medical services (WWI: in Fr.)   D629.U8.F5-9
UNITED STATES (MIL. capabil.)   355.033273
United States (mil. geog.)   355.473   UA993
United States military ops. & U.S. (WWI)   D570-570.9+   940.373, 41273,
                                              40973, 327.73
United States military ops. & U.S. (WWII)   D769-769.99   940.532273, .5373,
                                              .540973, .541273, .5428
United States military ops. (WWI: gen. special)   D570.2
United States military ops. (WWI: organiz. units: land, sea, air)   D570.2-.79 (SEE
                     D570.A4-Z, D545 etc. for overall participation, battles, etc.)
United States (mil. policy)   355.033573
United States (mil. status)   355.033073   UA23
United States (mil. status: gen.)   UA23.A2-Z

UNITED STATES (NAVAL geog.)   359.4773   VA49-395, VA50 (gen.)
United States (naval geog.: partic. states)   359.4774-4779   VA90-387
United States (naval hist.)   359.00973   VA49-395, VA50-70, E182, E746 (20th c.)
UNITED STATES NAVAL OPS. & Coast Guard ops. (WWII: fleets, squadrons, bases,
     etc.)   D769.45-599 (SEE D773-4, D783 for overall works,
          specific ships & engagements, submarines)   940.545973
United States naval ops. (Sp.-Am. War, 1898: also gen. works on naval ops. of war)
          E727 (Manila Bay battle at E717.7)   973.895
United States naval ops. (WWI)   D570.4-.5   940.45+, .41273
United States naval ops. (WWI: by battle, ship, etc.)   D589.U7.A-Z
United States naval ops. (WWI: by battle, ship, etc.)   D570.5.A-Z (PREFER
          D589.U6-7)
United States naval ops. (WWI: gen.)   D570.4-5, D589.U5-8 (PREFER)
United States naval ops. (WWI: special: land batteries, Marine Corps landings, etc.)
          D570.45

United States (naval policy & status)   359.030973
United States ordnance (gen.)   UF563.A9-Z
United States (pilot guides: gen.)   623.892973 VK993
United States submarine ops. (WWI)   D595.U6-7
UNITED STATES (WWI: causes, aims, results)   D520.U6-7
United States (WWI: gen.)   D570   940.373
United States (WWI: neutrality & dipl. history)   D619   940.32273, .373
United States (WWI: Reconstruction: by state)   D658.A-Z
United States (WWI: Reconstruction: gen.)   D657
United States (WWI: special topics)   D570.8.A-Z (SEE D639 for outside U.S.)
United States (WWII: causes, aims, results)   D742.U5-6
United States (WWII: dipl. hist., inclu. neutral years)   D753-753.8
          940.532573, .532273, 973.917
United States (WWII: gen.)   D769   940.532273, .5373, .540973, .541273, .5428
Universal service   UB350-355
Universal service & training (mil. resources) 355.225   UB350-355
Ural Mts. (Rus.)   DK511.U7   947.87
Urban warfare tactics   355.426   U167.5.S7
Uruguay   F2701-2799, F2721 (gen.)   989.5

VATICAN City   945.634   DG800
Vedettes, scout & dispatch boats, other minor craft (gen.)   V880
Vehicles, Military (design: inclu. combat & support v's. & neces. ordnance) 623.74
          UC270-275+

Vehicles, Motor (air force: ground)   UG1400-1405
Vehicles, Motor (mil.: U.S.)   UG618
Venezuela   F2301-2349, F2321   987
Venice, Defense of (WWI)   D569.V4
Venice, It. (city state & modern)   DG670-679
Verdun, Battle of (WWI: 1914)   D545.V25
Verdun, 2d Battle of (WWI: 1916)   D545.V3
Verdun, Fr.   DC801.V45
Versailles, Fr. (also Trianon)   DC801.V55-57
Vessels (naval architec.: by use)   VM378-466
Vessels, Naval war (modern period)   V765-767   623.80904

VETERANS' benefits   355.115   UB356-405, UB356-358
Veterans' benefits & services   UB356-405   355.115
Veterans' education, employment, etc. (gen.)   UB356   355.1152, .1154
Veterans' homes & hospitals   UB380-385
Veterans' homes & hospitals (besides U.S.)   UB385.A-Z
Veteran's or Armistice Day addresses, services (WWI: U.S.)   D671
Veterans' rehabilitation (places besides U.S.)   UB365.A-Z
Veterinary services (mil.)   UH650-655   355.345
Vickers machine guns   UF620.V4
Victoria (G.B.: Queen: 1837-1901)   DA554
Vienna, Austria   943.613   DB841-860, DB847 (gen.)
Vienna, Austria (20th c.)   DB855
Vienna, Austria (gen. hist. & descr.)   DB847
Vietnam (Annam)   DS556   959.7
Vietnam (1802-1954)   DS558.8
Views (Russo-Japanese War, 1904-5)   DS516.5
Views (WWI)   D527 (SEE ALSO D522)
Views (WWII)   D746 (SEE ALSO D743.2+)
Virginia   F221-235, F226, F231 (1865-1950)   975.5
Vistula River & Valley (Pol.: Wisla)   DK4600.V5
Visual signaling (mil.)   UG582.V5
Vittorio Emanuele III (It.: King, 1900-46: gen. inclu. times)   DG566
Vittorio Veneto, Battle of (1918)   D569.V5
Vladivostok, Rus.   DK781.V5
Volga River Valley (Rus.)   DK511.V65
Volgograd, Rus. (also Tsaritsyn or Stalingrad)   947.85   DK651.S7
Voluntary enlistment (navies)   359.22362
Volunteers (Nat. Guard, militia, etc.: Illinois)   UA170-179

WAGES & salaries, Air force   358.4164   UG940-945, UC74 (U.S.), UC90+
Wagons & carts, Artillery   UF380-385
Wales   942.9
Wales (19th & 20th c.)   DA722   942.908+
Wales (WWI)   D547.W4
WAR (aftermath: occupation, reconstruc., etc.)   355.028
War & warfare   355.02   U21, U21.2, U102
War (causes)   355.027   U21.2, HB195, JX1952
War correspondents & public relns. (mil.: U.S.)   UH703
War correspondents & public relns. (navies: U.S.)   VG503
War crimes, atrocities, trials (WWI: gen.)   D625   940.405, .472
War crimes, atrocities, trials (WWII: gen.)   D803
War games   U310   355.5
War games, Naval   V250   359.52
Warfare & military forces (types)   356-359   UD-UG, V
Warfare (summary topics)   355.021   U161-162, UA10
Warning systems (defense engineering)   623.37 (SEE .737 for titles after 1988)
Warrant officers (mil.)   UB407-409
Warrant officers (naval: gen.)   VB307   359.332
Warsaw, Pol.   DK651.W2 (earlier works), DK4610-4645
Warsaw, Pol. (1795-1918)   DK4632

Warship handling (plus other seamanship topics)   VK545   623.8825
WARSHIPS (as equip.: develop., operation, tech. effectiveness)   359.835-836
                      (SEE ALSO .32+ for ships as units or indiv. ships)
Warships (construction, armament, types, etc.)   V750-995+ (SEE VA for status
                      & organiz. of specific navies around the world)
Warships, Fuel-powered (engineering)   623.825   V750, V765, V797-799
Warships, Fuel-powered (handling)   623.8825   VB200-205
Warships (naval architec.)   VM380 (PREFER V750-995+)   623.825, 359.32
Warships (powered: design)   623.8125   V750, V765-767, V799-800
Warships, Sail-driven (engineering)   623.8225   V750-797, V750, V795
Warships (types)   V815-895   623.825-826, 359.83, .325-326
WASHINGTON (state)   F886-900, F891   979.7
Washington, D.C. (1865-1933)   975.303   F198-199
Washington, D.C. area (1878-1950)   F199   975.303-304
Washington, D.C. (gen.)   F194
Washington, D.C. (streets, bridges, railroads)   F203.7.A-Z
Washington, D.C. (District of Columbia: WWII)   D769.85.D6
Watch drills, Naval (U.S.: gen.: ALSO quarter, station, other)   VD160   359.50973,
                              .1330973, .133220973
Watch duty (merch. duty)   VK233
WATER & sanitation (naut. craft: engineering)   623.854   VM503-505 (water),
                      VM481-483 (san.)
Water, Potable (naut. craft: engineering)   623.8542
Water, Sea (naut. craft: engineering)   623.8543
Water supplies, Military   UC780
Water supplies, Naval (inclu. preservation, purification, etc.)   VC410 (SEE VM503
                      for onboard storage)   623.854
Water supply (mil. engineering)   623.751   UC780, VC410, VM503-505
Water supply (naval architec. & engin.)   VM503-505   623.854
Waterways   UA970-975
Waterways & troopships (mil. transp.)   UC320-325   359.3264
Waterways (Ger.)   UA975.G3
Waterways (outside U.S.)   UA975.A-Z
Waterworks (defense)   UA929.95.W3
Watkin range finder   UF850.W3
Weapons systems (artillery)   UF500-505
Weapons systems, Naval   VF346-348
Weather forecaster, Naval (gen.)   VG610
Weights & measures (mil. metrology)   UG455
Weimar Republic (Ger.: 1918-33)   943.085   DD233-251, DD237 (gen.),
                      DD251 (Hindenb. era), DD453 (Prussia)
Welding & cutting, Underwater (marine engin.)   VM965
WELFARE & RELIEF SERVICES (WWI)   940.477   D637-638
Welfare & relief services (WWI: by G.B.)   940.477841   D638.G7
Welfare & relief services (WWI: by Swe.)   940.4778485   D638.S8
Welfare & relief services (WWI: by Switz.)   940.4778494   D638.S9
Welfare & relief services (WWI: in specific places)   940.4779+   D638.A-Z, D657-
                      658 (Reconstruc. in U.S.), D659.A-Z (by place)
Welfare & relief services (WWI: provided by specific countries)   940.4778+
                      D638.A-Z
Welfare & relief services (WWI: Red Cross)   940.4771   D628-630
Welfare & relief services (WWII)   940.5477   D808-809
Welfare services, Military (U.S.: gen.)   UH755
Welfare services, Naval (U.S.)   VG2003
Wellington, N.Z.   DU428   993.127

Welsh troops (G.B.)   UA663
WEST Africa   DT471-720   966-967, 968.8
West Africa (WWI)   D547.A5
West Coast (Am.: plus E. Pac.: pilot & sailing guides)   VK941-956
West Indies   972.9   F1601-2175+, F1608, F1621
West Indies (1902-45)   972.9051   F1623
West Indies (gen. hist.)   F1621
West Point (descrip. & life)   U410.M1.P1
West Point (U.S. Mil. Acad.: official hist's.)   U410.L1.A1-5
West Riding Territorials (WWI: G.B.)   D547.W5
West Turkestan & Khurasan (WWI)   D568.9
West (U.S.) & Trans-Mississippi   F591-705   978
WESTERN Australia   DU350-380   994.1
Western Europe & Europe (1453+)   940.2   D208, D217
Western Front (WWI)   D530-549
Western front (WWI: misc. countries: by place)   D549.52.A-Z
Western front (WWI: misc. countries: gen.)   D549.5
Western Hemisphere (gen.) & United States   E   970
Western Samoa (was Ger. Samoa)   DU819.A2   996.14
Western states   978   F591-785, F591-596, F591
Westphalia (Prus.)   DD491.W4-52
White House (Washington, D.C.)   F204.W5
White Russia & Western U.S.S.R. (geog. & travel)   914.76
White Russia (Belorussia)   DK511.W5   947.65
White Russia (Western Russia)   DK507
White Russians (in Pol.)   DK4121.5.W5
Whitehead torpedo   V855.W5
Wilhelm II (Ger.: Kaiser, 1888-1918: abdication & flight)   DD228.9
Wilhelm II (Ger.: Kaiser, 1888-1918: biog. inclu. family)   DD229
Wilson, Woodrow (U.S.: Pres., 1913-21)   E767
Wilson, Woodrow (U.S.: 1865-1900 era: works)   E660.W7-75
Wings, Aircraft   629.13432
Winter warfare   U167.5.W5
Wireless signals (merch. marine)   VK397
WOMEN (20th c.: collective biography) D412.5
Women & minorities (navies: gen.)   VB320   359.22
Women & minorities (U.S. Navy: gen.)   VB323
Women & minorities in the armed forces (U.S.: gen.)   UB417
Women & the military (sociology)   U21.75
Women & women's work (WWI)   D639.W7   940.315042
Women & women's work (WWII)   D810.W7
Women (armed forces: U.S.)   UB418.W65
Women (Ger.: 1918-48)   DD245
Women in armed forces   355.0082
Women in naval forces   359.229   VA49-750, VA390.W (U.S. Waves)
Women (Rus. Rev., 1917-21)   DK265.9.W57
Women (U.S. Navy)   VB324.W65
Women's military units   355.348   UA565.W6 (U.S. Wac's)
Women's naval units (gen.)   359.348   VA
Women's reserves (U.S.)   UA45
Wooden ships (naval architec.)   VM142-145   623.81
Woodrow Wilson Foundation   E772

WORLD HISTORY (1871-late 19th c.)   D394-400   909.81, 327.0904
World history (20th c.: collected)   D414-415
World history (20th c.: gen.)   D410-460+, D421-5, D421   909.82
World history (20th c.: several authors)   D414
World history (20th c.: single-author collections) D415
World history (1919-39)   D720-728
World history, Europe, Africa, Asia, Oceania   D-DX   900-949, 990's
World history (gen.: 1800-)   909.8   D299, D395
World navies (pop. works)   VA41
WORLD WAR I (1914-18)   D501-680   940.3-940.499
World War I (1914: aerial ops.) 940.444
World War I (1914: E. Front)   940.422   D550, D551-556
World War I (1914: misc. areas)   940.423
World War I (1914: naval ops.)   940.454
World War I (1914: W. Front)   940.421   D530, D541-542 (Bel.),
             D544-545 (Fr.), D545.A-Z (by battle, campaign, etc.)
World War I (1915: aerial ops.)   940.445
World War I (1915: E. Europe)   940.425   D550, D551-557
World War I (1915: misc. areas)   940.426
World War I (1915: naval ops.)   940.455
World War I (1915: W & Austro-It. fronts)   940.424   D530, D541-545, D569 (Italian)
World War I (1916: aerial ops.)   940.446
World War I (1916: Asia Minor, Gallipoli, etc.)   940.4291   D566 (gen.), D566-
             568, D568.3 (Gallipoli)
World War I (1916: E. Front)   940.4275   D550, D551-557
World War I (1916: Eur. fronts)   940.427   D521, D530, D550
World War I (1916: misc. areas)   940.429
World War I (1916: naval ops.)   940.456
World War I (1916: W. & Austro-It. fronts)   940.4272   D530, D541-545,
             D569 (Italian)
World War I (1917: aerial ops.)   940.447
World War I (1917: E. Front)   940.432   D550, D551-557
World War I (1917: misc. areas)   940.433
World War I (1917: naval ops.)   940.457
World War I (1917: W. & Austro-It. fronts)   940.431   D530, D541-545, D569
World War I (1918: aerial ops.)   940.448
World War I (1918: E. Front)   940.437   D550, D551-557
World War I (1918: misc. areas)   940.438
World War I (1918: naval ops.)   940.458
World War I (1918: W. & Austro-It. fronts: inclu. last Ger. drives)   940.434
             D530-531, D541-545
World War I (1918: W. Front: last Allied drives: 18 July-24 Sept.)   940.435
             D530, D541-545
World War I (1918: W. Front: last Allied drives: 25 Sept.-11 Nov.)   940.436
             D530, D541-545
World War I (Allies & associates: mil. units & ops.)   940.412+   D544-550,
             D569-570
World War I & Aftermath   D501-680   940.3-940.4889+
World War I & engineers   940.3156   D529.7
World War I & women   940.315042 D639.W7, JX1965
World War I (antisub. ops.)   940.4516   D580-589, D590
World War I (Armistice)   940.439   D641
World War I (Central Powers: mil. units & ops.)   940.413+   D531-540, D566
World War I (collected works)   D509
World War I (gen.)   D521   940.3, 940.4

WORLD WAR I (GEN. PARTICIP.: Australia)   940.394   D547.A8
World War I (gen. particip.: Austria)   940.3436   D539, DB86.7
World War I (gen. particip.: Balkan Penin.)   940.3496   D560, DR47
World War I (gen. particip.: Belgium)   940.3493   D615, D541, DH682
World War I (gen. particip.: by country: inclu. mobilization)   940.34-39
World War I (gen. particip.: Can.)   940.371   D547.C2
World War I (gen. particip.: Czech.)   940.3437   D539.5.C8, DB215, DB2176
World War I (gen. particip.: E. Africa)   940.3676   D547.A, DT431
World War I (gen. particip.: Fr.)   940.344   D548, DC387
World War I (gen. particip.: G.B.)   940.341-342   D546, DA577
World War I (gen. particip.: Ger.)   940.343   D531, DD228.8
World War I (gen. particip.: Holland)   940.3492   DJ285
World War I (gen. particip.: Hungary)   940.3439   D540, DB953
World War I (gen. particip.: India)   940.354   D547.I5
World War I (gen. particip.: It.)   940.345   D569, DG570
World War I (gen. particip.: New Z.)   940.3931 (SEE ALSO .393 for titles after
                                           1988)   D547.N5
World War I (gen. particip.: Poland)   940.3438   D551, DK439
World War I (gen. particip.: Rumania)   940.3498   D565, DR263
World War I (gen. particip.: Rus.)   940.347   D550, DK264.8
World War I (gen. particip.: S. Africa)   940.368   D547.A4, DT941
World War I (gen. particip.: Scan. countries)   940.348   D621.S3, DL85
World War I (gen. particip.: Sp.)   940.346   DP246
World War I (gen. particip.: Switz.) 940.3494   DQ201
World War I (gen. particip.: Turkey)   940.3561   D566, DR588
World War I (gen. particip.: U.S.)   940.373-379   D570
World War I (gen. particip.: U.S.: by state)   940.374-379
World War I (gen. particip.: U.S.: Calif.)   940.3797
World War I (gen. particip.: U.S.: gen.)   940.373   D570, D619, E768, E780
World War I (gen. particip.: U.S.: N.Y.)   940.3747
World War I (gen. particip.: Yug. & Bulg.)   940.3497   D560, D561 (Serbia),
                              D564 (Montenegro), D563 (Bulg.), DR47, DR363 (Yug.),
                              DR87.8 (Yug.), DR1280 (Yug.: newer titles)
World War I (gen. special)   D523
World War I (medical srvcs.)   940.475   D628 (gen.), D629.A-Z (by country),
                              D630.A-Z (biog.)
World War I (mil. units & ops.: gen.)   940.41   D521
World War I (misc. special)   D639.A-Z (SEE D570.8 for U.S.)
World War I (misc. topics)   940.48
World War I (mobilization)   940.402 (SEE .34-39 for particular countries)
World War I (naval ops.: particular countries)   940.459   D580-589
World War I (special topics)   D622-639
World War I (study & teaching)   940.4007   D522.4, .7 (juv.)
World War I (submarine ops.)   940.451   D590-595, D590 (gen.)
World War I (submarine ops.: specific events yr.-by-yr.)   940.4514
WORLD WAR II (1939-45)   D731-838   940.53-940.5499
World War II (dipl. hist.)   940.532   D748-754, D748 (gen.)
World War II (gen.)   D743   940.53, .54
WORLD WAR II (GEN. PARTICIP.: Australia)   940.5394   D767.8-82, DU116
World War II (gen. particip.: by country: inclu. exile govs., undergr. move's., pro- &
                              anti-Axis nat. groups, mobilization, etc.)   940.534-539
World War II (gen. particip.: Fr. & Monaco)   940.5344   D752, D761, DC397
World War II (gen. particip.: G.B.)   940.5341   D750, D759, DA587
World War II (gen. particip.: Ger.)   940.5343   D751, D757, DD253-256.5
World War II (gen. particip.: It.)   940.5345   D763.I8, DG571-572

World War II (gen. particip.: London, Eng.)   940.53421   D760.8.L7, DA684
World War II (gen. particip.: New Z.)   940.53931 (SEE ALSO .5393 for works after
        1988)   D767.85-852, DU411
World War II (gen. particip.: Paris, Fr. area)   940.534436   D762.P3, DC737+
World War II (gen. particip.: Rus.)   940.5347   D764, D754.R9 or .S65,
        DK267-273, DK273
World War II (gen. particip.: U.S.)   940.5373   D769, E806-813, E806 (gen.)
World War II (gen. particip.: U.S.: by area or state)   D769.85.A-Z, D769.85.A-Z,
        D769.87-88, F1-951+
World War II (mil. units & ops.: gen.)   940.541   D743
World War II (mobilization)   940.5402 (SEE .534-539 for particular countries)
        D800, HC, HF, HJ
World War II (naval ops.: particular countries)   940.5459+   D770-784
World War II (submarine ops.)   940.5451+ (SEE ALSO .542 for ops. by theatre)
        D780-784, D780 (gen.), D781-782 (Ger.),
        D783 (U.S.), D784.A-Z (other lands)
Wounded, Care of (mil.: inclu. relief societies: gen.)   UH520   361.05, .77, .9,
        940.477+
Wrecks, Nautical (research)   623.8885   VK1250+
Wroclaw, Breslau, Pol. (WWII)   D765.2.W7
Württemberg military ops. (WWI)   D537

Y.M.C.A., Y.W.C.A. (WWI)   D639.Y7
Yachts (small craft: gen.)   VM331
Yalta, Uk. (Jalta)   DK508.95.I24
Yalu, Battle of (Rus.-Jpn. War, 1904-5)   DS517.15
Yangtze River (China)   DS793.Y25   951.2
Yards & stations, Naval (U.S.: by place)   VA70.A-Z
Yards, Navy (gen.)   V230 (SEE ALSO VA67-750 for particular places)   359.7
Yards, stations, shore facilities (navies: U.S.: gen.)   VC414   359.70973
Yearbooks & almanacs, Nautical (non-American)   VK8
Yearbooks, Naval (official: also lists: by country: SEE ALSO VA #s if dept. reports
     involved)   V11.A-Z   359.0025+, .005
Yearbooks, Naval (unofficial)   V10
Yellow Peril   DS519
Yemen   DS247.Y4-48
Yeomen & clerks, Naval   VG900-905
Young Plan (WWI)   D649.G3.A6-7
Ypres, 1st Battle of (1914)   D542.Y6
Ypres, 2d Battle of (1915)   D542.Y7
Ypres, 3d Battle of (1917)   D542.Y72
Ypres, Bel. (WWI: gen.)   D542.Y5
Ypres, John Denton P. F., 1st Earl of (G.B.: 19th c. mil. biog.)   DA68.32.Y8
Yser, Battle of the (WWI)   D542.Y8

YUGOSLAVIA (Serbia)   DR301-396 (earlier pubns.), DR1214-1307+   949.7-71
Yugoslavia (to 1918)   949.701   DR317, DR1274
Yugoslavia (1800-1918)   DR1274   949.701
Yugoslavia (20th c.)   DR357   949.702, .7102
Yugoslavia (20th c. & 1918-)   949.702   DR357, DR1274, DR1282
Yugoslavia (1903-21: Peter I)   DR360-363   949.701-702
Yugoslavia (1914-18: WWI era)   DR363 (earlier pubns.), DR1280   949.7, .701
Yugoslavia (1918-45)   DR1288-1298   949.702
Yugoslavia (1918-45: gen.)   DR366, DR1289   949.702-7022
Yugoslavia (1918-45: inclu. Croatia, Serbia, Slovenia)   DR364-369
                           949.7021-7022, 949.7102 (Serbia)
Yugoslavia (1918-21: reign of Peter I)   DR1295
Yugoslavia & Bulgaria   949.7+
Yugoslavia (central republics: Bosnia, Herzegovina, Montenegro) 949.74
Yugoslavia (gen., descrip., culture, hist.)   DR301-396+ (earlier books),
                           DR1202-1307+, DR1214   949.7
Yugoslavia (gen. hist.)   DR317, DR1245-1246   949.7
Yugoslavia (geog. & travel)   914.971-976   DR309, DR1221 (later books)
Yugoslavia (mil. status)   UA827   355.0330497
Yugoslavia (post-WWI territorial ?s)   D651.Y8-9

ZANZIBAR (inclu. time as Brit. colony)   DT434.Z3, DT435,
                           DT449.Z2-Z29 (newer titles)
Zanzibar (island & coast)   DT435
Zanzibar (1890-1963)   967.8103   DT435, DT449.Z2-29 (newer works),
                           DT449.Z28
Zeebruge-Ostend raids (WWI: 1918)   D594.Z4
Zionism, Restoration, Judenstaat   DS149-151
Zurich, Swit.   DQ781-800   949.45

IV. LIBRARY OF CONGRESS SUBJECT & OTHER HEADINGS

The Library of Congress has constructed a controlled vocabulary system of LC subject, biographical, corporate, and other headings and phrases in order to provide consistent and thorough catalog access to its huge collection. Most academic and public libraries in the United States have adopted LC Subject Headings as the standard for catalog indexing, although some smaller public libraries may use the Sears group of headings. These are based on LC and represent a compact version.

As with the classification systems, change is inevitable in the ongoing subject vocabulary shown in this guide. The Library of Congress deliberately but regularly adds, amends, and drops headings and sub-headings in an attempt to keep pace with a changing world and language. Even corporate and other headings change as, for example, government agencies come into existence and then change names or as people's names finally require death dates. Rather than list only the latest approved descriptors, I have opted to include new and old so as to allow for better entrée in modernized or older catalogs. A richer vocabulary should also help with keyword-searching of entire records for buried terms when using online, optical-disk, or other electronic rosters of the future.

In using the LC subject headings, researchers should note that the network is predominantly alphabetic and specialized in nature rather than overarching as with some database thesaurus systems. The latter depend heavily upon cross-references within a controlled framework of broader, narrower, and parallel terms and phrases trying to describe their universe. While LC started in the late 1980's to employ scoped cross-references, the prime character remains particularly alphabetic and diverse rather than attached to any classified verbal skeleton.

Some effort is made to incorporate hierarchical concepts within the alphabetic sequence. Hence, under the many headings that begin with 'European War, 1914-1918' or World War, 1914-1918', LC has placed assorted subheadings and sub-subheadings in alphabetic suborder. Under 'World War, 1914-1918' may be found '—Aerial operations', '—Campaigns', '—Economic aspects', —France', '—Naval operations', and numerous other subtopics. Under or after 'World War, 1914-1918—Campaigns' may be found many geographical subdivisions such as '—Belgium', '—Black Sea region', '—German East Africa', '—Turkey and the Near East', '—Western', and others in alphabetical order. Under some topics one can see historical subdivisions in chronological arrangement. Therefore, under the main heading of 'Germany—History' will be seen the subheadings '—20th century', '—Revolution, 1918', '—1918-1933', and 'Allied occupation, 1918-1930' in that sequence.

The use of subdivisions allows for some gathering of similar subject groups within proximate alphabetic sets. Since the system simultaneously allows specialized descriptors and phrases in isolated positions throughout the alphabet, some confusion as to the best search method is natural. A combination of broader terms and subdivisions along with isolated or pinpoint headings is probably best, given the normal LC policy of assigning several terms of subject access to each cataloged title if warranted.

This division of the guide is organized in alphabetic array by LC term or proper-word heading or subject. Thus, mixed together as in many catalogs may be found historical events, tactical concepts, specific weapons, particular ships, airplane types and models, biographical names, government agencies, etc.

Please note that some electronic library catalogs place proper names of people and organizations into a separate file that encompasses these names as both subjects and authors, while many catalogs of whatever format would place such proper names into either subject or author catalogs depending on specific usage of each term. Also valuable to remember is the idea of searching corporate or government-agency authors as a means of quasi-subject searching. One could, for instance, find pertinent materials under 'United States. War Department' as an author that might not be listed under the subject terms considered for a particular search. I have chosen to keep all headings together so that readers need check only one listing and so as to avoid the separation of terms such as 'United States—History' from 'United States. Army'.

Following some of the headings are Library of Congress and/or Dewey Decimal Classification numbers that might be considered for browsing purposes in the stacks or shelflist. When two or more class numbers are given that begin with the same root, certain abbreviated forms may be seen. For example, LC numbers UG630 through UG670 might appear as 'UG630-70'. In the Dewey system, 358.4183 and 358.440973 could be listed as '358.4183, .440973'.

I have tried to include a large sampling of call numbers. Some of them represent typical range areas, but I have also presented a variety of numbers taken from outside the main historical and military spans that otherwise predominate. I did not discover nor devise numbers in every case. Many terms could be placed in a diverse number of classifications depending on individual library needs, and listing class examples would prove somewhat meaningless in these instances. I have attempted, nevertheless, to include at least representative numbers or ranges for the most important topics or topical groups.

Hopefully, the controlled-term section will help researchers to find more materials through knowledge of more headings and of related subdivision patterns and of classification possibilities. As stated in the class introductions, however, a thorough hunt will utilize both call numbers and regulated headings.

Adler, Viktor, 1852-1918 [Aust.-Hung.: For. Min.]   DB80, DB90.A34   943.604
Admirals—Portraits
Adriatic question   D650.T4, D651   940.322497
Aerial gunnery
Aerial reconnaisance   UG760-5   623.72
Aeronautical instruments TL587   629.135, .15
Aeronautics   TL500-830 (technology)   629.1-13+
    —Biography   TL539-40   926.2913, 629.130922, .1300922
    —History   TL512-32   629.109, .1309, .13009
Aeronautics, Military   UG630-70, JX5124 (int'nal. law), VG90 (naval)
                        623.746, 358.4
        —Germany UC535, UG635   358.410943, .411094
        —Great Britain   UG653 358.4135
        —History   UG623   358.40074
        —Observations   UG630-70   355.413, 358.45
        —Psychology   RC550, UG632   616.85, 623.746
        —Research   UG633   353.63
        —Russia   UG635   358.400947
        —United States E746, UG633, VG93 (naval), UC333   355.83,
                        358.400973, .413320924, .4183, .440973, 629.13
            —History   UG633 358.40973, .4130973
            —Statistics HE9803   387.74
Aeroplane carriers   V895   359.32
Aeroplanes, Military   [This spelling used mostly before 1980, after which SEE
        'Airplanes...']   TL685-6, UG633-5, VG93-5 (naval)   355.6213,
                        358.407, .4183, 623.740937, .746+, 629.133-134
Africa, North—History—1882-   DT204   916.103, 961.02+
Afro-American seamen
Afro-American soldiers   [For titles before around 1970 SEE 'Negro soldiers—
        U.S.']   E185   355.00917496, .330973, 973.0496073
Afro-American veterans
Agents provocateurs—Germany
Agriculture and state   HD1415, HD1773   338.1091724, .13
Air bases
Air bases, American [British, German, etc.]
Air bases, American
Air bases, British
Air bases, German
Air bases—United States UG634 358.417058
Air defenses
Air defenses, Military   UF625 (antiaircraft guns), UG630-5 (mil. aeronautics),
                U408   358.13, .39
Air forces—History
Air interdiction   UG700
Air pilots—Correspondence, reminiscences, etc.   TL510, TL540, TL721
                629.125-126, .1308-1309+, .1325243, .13453, 926.2913
Air pilots, Military   UG626-626.2 (biog.)
    —[country]
Air pilots—United States—Biography TL539-540 358.400922, 629.130924
Air power   JX1391, UG630, VG93   358.41+
    —History   UG630   358.4009
    —United States UG633, VG93 (naval)   358.40973, 623.4519

Air raid shelters   TH1097   623.388, 693.8
Air raid warning systems
Air-ships   TL650-68   629.133
Air warfare   UG630-5   358.30904, 358.414, 629.1339
   —History   D437, UG625, UG700   358.400904, .414+
   —Psychological aspects   UG630   355.23
Airborne troops   UD480   356.166
Aircraft carriers   [SEE ALSO 'Aerocraft carriers' for many works before 1980]
                  V874-5, D770, V895   359.3255+, .83, 623.8255, 940.545
   —Aircraft launching and recovery
Aircraft industry   HD9711 (economics), TL724-724.5 (technology)   338.47629+
   —Military aspects
   —United States   HD9711   382.45629+
Aircraft spotting
Aircraft survival equipment   UG633, VG93, TL697   629.134386
Airdrop
Airlift, Military   UC330-5
Airplane factories
Airplanes   [SEE ALSO 'Aeroplanes' for works before about 1981]   TL670-723,
            TL547   629.133+
   —Control systems   TL678
   —Design and construction   TL671   629.133-4+
   —Ditching   TL711.D5
Airplanes, Military   TL685.3, HD9711, UG633, UG1123, UG1240, UG1245,
                  VG93   338.4768, 358.4183, 623.746+, 629.133
      —Armament
      —Camouflage   UG1245, VG95   358.4183, 940.544943
      —History   UG1243-5   358.4183
      —Maintenance and repair
      —Motors   TL701, VG93   358.4183, .41621, 338.47623746
      —Parts
      —Registers
      —Turrets   UG630-5 (army), VG90-5 (navy)
Airplanes
   —Piloting   TL710-13   621.13252, 629.132
      —Handbooks, manuals, etc.
   —Radar equipment
   —Radio equipment   TL693-6
   —Recognition   TL670   629.1333
   —Registers   HE9769   629.133349
Airports   TL521, TL725   387.736, 629.1363
   —Defense measures   TL725   363.35
Aisne, Battle of the, 1914   D544, D545.A5
Aisne, Battle of the, 1917   D544, D545.A5
Aisne, Battle of the, 1918   D544, D545.A5
Aitken, William Maxwell   [SEE 'Beaverbrook, William...']
Albania
   —History   DR701   949.65
      —1912-1944
   —Politics and government
Albert I, 1875-1934   [Belg.: King]   DH514, DH681-2, D615   949.3040924,
                  940.3493, 923.1493, .1403, 929.793
Albrecht, 1865-1939 [Ger.: Duke of Württemberg, Field Marshal]   DD231.A42,
                  D521   943.0840924, 940.4

294

Alekseev, Mikhail Vasilevich, 1857-1918   [Rus.: Gen. of Infan.]
                                           DK265.19, .2, .9   947.0841
Alexander, Karadjordjevic, 1888-1934   [Serbia: Prince Reg.] DR341, DR359, D511
                                           949.7101, 940.311
Alexandra, 1872-1918   [Rus.: Empress]   DK254, DK258.A4, DK260
                                           947.080924, 923.147
Algeria—History—1830-1962   DT284, DT294   965, 965.03
Allenby, Edmund Henry Hynman, 1861-1936   [G.B.: Field Marshal]
          DA69.3.A6, D507   940.410922, .4331, .500924, 923.542
Alliances   JX4005, JX1907   341.2, .72, 327.08
Allied and Associated Powers (1914-1920). Treaties, etc.
     .Austria, 1919 Sept. 10   D643.A9
Allied Powers (1919-). Reparation Commission   DC59.8.G3, D648-9
Alsace-Lorraine question   DD801   923.544, 944.38308, 320.944383+
American Friends Service Committee
     . Foreign Service Section
American National Red Cross
American Protective League   D619.3
Amiens, Battle of, 1918   D544-545
Ammunition   TS538, UF543, UF700   355.415, .621, .82, 623.455,
                                           658.57, 688.7
—Transportation   UC323   359.982
Amphibian planes   TL684   629.133348+
Amphibious warfare   U261, U439, D25   359.83, 355.48
Anarchism and anarchists   HX821-970   320.570922, 335.83+, 923.347, 321.07
Angary, Right of
Anschluss movement, 1918-1938   DB48, DB97   320.943085, 943.605
Antiairborne warfare
Anti-aircraft artillery
Anti-aircraft guns   UF625   358.13, 623.41
Antisemitism   BM535, D5145, DS135, DS145, E184   301.451924, .452+,
                      296.387834+, 909.04924081
     —Germany   DS135, DS145-146   261.8345+, 301.451924+,
                      323.11924043, 956.94001
     —History   DS145-147   301.451924, 909.0974+, .04924
     —Russia
     —United States
Anti-submarine warfare
Antitank guns   UF628   358.18, 623.412
Antitank weapons
Arab countries—History-Arab Revolt, 1916-1918   DS223, DS36-39, DS63,
                      D568.4   953.02, 909.04927, .0974927
Arandora Star (Ship)   D801.G7
Archives—United States   CD3021-3022, CD3065, CD6028   025.171
     —Inventories, calendars, etc.   CD3026-3027, CD3041, HE565, Z6027,
                      Z6366   016.32773, .3312973, .910973,
                      .9405488673, 330.973, 350.0914, 387.2097471
Argentine Republic—History—1852-1933   F2848
Argonne, Battle of the, 1915   D544, D545.A6
Argonne, Battle of the, 1918   D544, D545.A63

Armaments   UA10   355.021, .03300+, .0335, 341.6705
  —Yearbooks
Armed forces   U21, U162, UA10, UA15   355.0330+, .0332
  —Appropriations and expenditures   UA17, JX1977   338.47355
  —History
Armed forces in foreign countries
Armed forces
  —Mobilization   UA910
  —Political activity   U21, UH720, JF1820 322.42, .5091724,   355.123094
  —Prayer-books and devotions   BV4588, BV273, BX2170, BM667
                                      242.68, .88, 264.093, 296.4
Armed merchant ships
Armenia—History—1917-1921   DS195   956.62
Armenian massacres, 1915-1923   DS195.5, DS51   361.530924, 947.92080924,
                                      956.62, .102
Armenian question   DS194-5, H31   364.15109561, 956.64
Armies   UA10, UA15, UA646   350.895, 355.30944, .3509
  —Equipment   UC460-5   356.186
  —History   U37, UA15   355.0094, .0097
  —Insignia   UC530-5   355.134, .14
  —Officers   UB410-15
  —Organization   UA10, UA15   355.022, 355
  —Staffs   UB220-5   355.33+
Armistices   JX1907   343.31
Armored personnel carriers   UG446.5
Armored trains   UG345
Armored vehicles, Military   UG446   355.83, 623.438, .7475
Armored vessels   V799-800   359.3252, 623.825
Arms and armor   U800-825 (mil.), HD9743 (industry), NK6600-6699 (art) 355.82,
                                      623.44, 739.75
Arms and armor, American   U818   355.820973, 623.444
Arms and armor—Bibliography—Catalogs   Z5693 018.1
Army War College (U.S.)   [SEE ALSO 'U.S. Army War College']
Arras, Battle of, 1917   D544-5
Art and war
Art treasures in war   N8750   733.3
Artillery   UF145, UF400, UF560-1   358.109, .12, 623.41, .412
  —Bibliography   Z6724 016.35996
Artillery, Coast   UF450-5
Artillery drill and tactics   UF157-302
Artillery, Field and mountain   UF400-45
Artillery—Great Britain   UF57   358.10942, .120941-120942
Artillery, Self-propelled
Artists for Victory, Inc.   NE508.A
Arz von Straussenburg, Arthur Albert, 1857-1935   [Aust.-Hung.: Baron, Gen.]
                                      UA672   355.309436
Aschaffenburg—Siege, 1945
Asia—Foreign relations   DS33, DS35, JX1569   327.5+
  —History—20th century   DS35
Asia, Southeastern—History   DS511, DS513, DS527, E744   325.5, 915.903,
                                      959.008
Asquith, Herbert Henry, 1852-1928   [G.B.: Prime Min.   DA566.9.O7
                                      941.0830924, 923.242
Atatürk, Kemal   [SEE 'Kemal Atatürk']
Attack and defense (Military science)   UG443-9   355.4

Australia
. Army
. Royal Australian Regiment. 8th Battalion   DS557   959.704342
. Australian Army
. A.I.F. 5th Light Horse Regiment
. A.I.F., 1914-1918   D547.A8
. A.I.F. Camel Corps
. Australian Imperial Force (1914-1921)   D520.A9
. 8th Battalion   D547.A8
. 28th Battalion
—Biography   DU116.2, U55   923.594
. Flying corps. 1 squadron   D607.A8, UG635.A8
—History—20th century   DU110, DU116   994.04
—History, Military   DU112   355.00994, .310994, 940.5394
—History, Naval   VB121   359.00994
. Navy   [SEE ALSO 'Australia. Royal Australian Navy']
—History   VA713, VB121   359.00994
—Politics and government—1901-1945   DU112, DU116   320.994042,
994.032
. Royal Australian Air Force   D792.A8, UG635, UG1242   940.544994,
358.400994, .4183
. Royal Australian Army Nursing Corps
. Royal Australian Navy
Australian Comforts Fund
Austria
—Foreign relations—Germany
—History
—1867-1918
—1918-1938   DB96   943.605
—Politics and government—1867-1918   DB90, DB92   320.540924,
943.604, 320.943604
—1918-1938   DB96-7   943.605
Austro-Hungarian Monarchy
. Heer   D539.5
—History   UA672   355.309436
. Heer. Tiroler Kaiserjaeger   D539.5.T57
. Kriegsmarine   VA473   359.8309436
Automobiles, Military   UG680-5
Averescu, Alexandru, 1859-1938   [Rum.: Lt. Gen., Prime Min.]   DR217, D565.A2,
D651.R6 949.8

Badoglio, Pietro, 1871-1956   [It.: Field Marshal]   D754.I8, D763   940.5345
Baker, Newton Diehl, 1871-1937   [U.S.: Sec. of War]   E748.B265, D570, D619
973.9130924, 940.373, 923.273
Balfour, Arthur James, 1848-1930   [G.B.: 1st Lord o/t Adm'ty, Sec. of State for For.
Aff.]   DA566.9.B2, D412.6, D570, VA454   942.080924, .0820924,
359.00941, .0942, 920.02, 923.242
Balkan Peninsula
—History
—20th century   DR48, DR36, D562.M32, D562   949.6, 914.9603
—War of 1912-1913   DR46 949.6
—Politics and government   D463, DJK4, DR10   309.1496, 320.9496
Ballistics   UF820   623.51, .50903
Balloons   TL609-39   629.13322

Battle casualties
Battle cruisers
Battles   D25, D210, D431   355.48
   —Europe
   —Germany
Battleships   V765-7, V800, VA58, VA454   359.32+, .3252,
                     .32520973, .83, 623.82530973, .8252
Bauer, Max Hermann, 1869-1929   [Ger.: Col.; polit. intriguer]   DD231.B38,
   DD228.8, D531, HC286.2   943.0840924, 940.31, .343, 929.1
Bavaria—Politics and government   DD801.B41
Beatty, David, 1871-1936 [G.B.: Adm. o/t Fleet]   D580-1, D582.J8, VA454
                                                         359.00941, .0942
Beaverbrook, William Maxwell Aitken, Lord, 1879-1964   [G.B.: Min. of Info. (WWI);
          Min. of Aircraft Produc., Min. of Supply, Lord Privy Seal, Lend-Lease
          admin. (WWII); Press empire lord]   DA566.9.B3, .B37,
          .C4 (Churchill), DA577.B35, UG635.G7   942.083-084,
          .0840924, 940.544,   070.50924, 090.50924, 910.544, 923.242
Belgian American Educational Foundation
Belgium
Belleau Wood, Battle of, 1918   D544-5   940.434
Below, Otto von, 1857-1944   [Ger.: Gen.]   DD231.B38, D569.C3, CR5327
                                                    940.431, 929.71
Benedict XV, 1854-1922   [Vatican: Pope: a.k.a. Benedictus]   DG555,
                              DG570, BX1376   945.09, 922.21
Benes, Eduard, 1884-1948   [Aust.-Hung.: Politician, Pres.]   DB217.B3-4, .M3,
          DB2191.B45   943.7020924, 923.1437, .2437, 940.3, .53
Benson, William Shepherd, 1855-1932   [U.S.: Adm.]   E766.D29, D611
                                                          973.913, 940.45
Beretta submachine gun   UF620.B45
Berezhany, Battle of, 1916-1917   D550-7
Bernstorff, Johann Heinrich, Count von, 1861-1939   [Ger.: Ambass. to U.S.]
                                                     D619   940.32
Beseler, Hans hartwig von, 1850-1921 [Ger.: Gen.]   D515, DK439, CR5327
                                                     940.311, .4, 929.71
Bethmann Hollweg, Theobold von, 1856-1921   [Ger.: Chanc.]   DD231.B5,
          DD228.5, D515   943.0840924, .84, 940.3112, 327.43
Bible—Prophecies
          —Great Britain
          —Russia
          —U.S.
Biography—20th century   CT119-120, D412   070.924, 364.1524, 920.00904,
                              923.2, 920.02
Bissolati, Leonida, 1857-1920 [It.: Politician]   DG555, DG570, D640, D643.A7,
                    HX288.B54, UA742   945.08-09, 940.3141
Black market
   —Europe
   —United States   HF5415   338.526
Blackouts in war
Bliss, Tasker Howard, 1853-1930   [U.S.: Gen.] E181   940.510924, 355.3310924
Boatyards

Boeing airplanes   TL686   629.133340973, 387.7334
Boeing bombers
Bomb reconnaisance   D787   658.47, 940.5412+
Bombardiers   D792.A-Z (by country)
—[country]
Bombardment   JX5117
Bombers   TL685, UG635, UG1242, VG95   358.4183, .420941,
                623.7463, 940.5449+
—Pictorial works   UG635   358.4209+
Bombing, Aerial   UG635   358.409
—Psychological aspects   UG632   363.352
Bombing and gunnery ranges   U300-305
Bombs   TP270, VF373   353.00711, 628.9
Bombsights
Bonar Law, Andrew, 1858-1923   [G.B.: Sec. of State for Colonial Aff., Chanc. o/t
    Excheq., later Prime Min.]   DA566.9.L3, DA577   942.083, 320.942
Boroevic von Bojna, Svetozar, 1856-1920   [Aust.-Hung.: Field Marshal]   D556,
                UA672   940.464436, 355.309436
Boselli, Paolo, 1838-1932 [It.: Prime Min.]   DG555, DG569.A2, .I8, DG570
                945.09, 929.1
Bothmer, Felix Graf von, 1852-1937   [Ger.: Gen.] D521, UA672   940.3-4,
                                                    355.309436
Boué de Lapeyr`ere, Auguste Emmanuel, 1852-1924 [Fr.: Vice Adm.]
            D568.3, D580, D583, DE98   940.425, 359.0091822
Bratianu, Ion, 1864-1927 [Rum.: Prime Min.]   D651.R6, DD120.G7
                                            327.430436, .498
Bren machine-gun   UF620.B57
Breslau (Cruiser)
Briand, Aristide, 1862-1932   [Fr.: Prem.] DC373.B7, DC385, DC387, D548,
                                D568.3   944.08, 940.425
British in Asia   DS35   954, 325.342095
British in foreign countries
Broqueville, Charles Marie, Baron de, 1860-1940   [Belg.: Prem.]   DH566   327.493
Browning automatic rifle
Browning firearms   TS533   683.4
Brusilov, Aleksei Alekseevish, 1853-1926   [Rus.: Gen. of Cav.]   D550, U55
                                            940.4147, .425
Brzeziny, Battle of, 1914   D551-2
Bulgaria—Politics and government—1878-1944   DR85, JN9609   320.9497703
Bullard, Robert Lee, 1861-1947   [U.S.: Gen.]   U53.B78, D570   355.3310924,
                                                940.41273
Bullets
Bülow, Karl von, 1846-1921 [Ger.: Field Marshal]   D507, D530, D545.M3
                                                940.30922, .4140922
Bund Deutscher Offiziere   DD256.5
Byng, Julian Hedworth George, 1861-1935   [G.B.: Gen.]

Cables, Submarines   TK5661
Cadorna, Luigi, 1850-1928   [It.: Gen.] D569.C3, D520.I7, UA742   945.08,
                                940.431, 929.1
California
    —History—1850-1950   F864   979.404
    . National Guard   UA99   355.3510973
California, Southern
        —History—1850-1950   F867-9   979.47-498 917.949035

Cambrai, Battle of, 1917   D544-5   940.431
Camouflage (Military science) UG449, V215 (naval)   358.18, .414
Camps (Military)   U180-5, UC400-5, UG635 (camp-making)
Canada
    . Army
        . Princess Patricia's Canadian Light Infantry   D547   940.41271
    . Canadian Army. Canadian Expeditonary Force
    —Claims vs. Italy   JX5486.C16
    —Foreign relations—1914-1945   F1034
    —History—1914-1945   F1033-4   971.06, .063
    —Politics and government—1914-1945   F1034 JL197   320.971, 923.271,
                                            940.540971

Canteen (British Navy)   VC395.G7
Canteen (United States Army)   UC753
Canteens (War-time, emergency, etc.)
Cantigny, Battle of, 1918   D544-5
Capelle, Eduard von, 1855-1931   [Ger.: Adm.]   DD231.T5, VA513 359.030943
Capello, Luigi Attilo, 1859-1941   [It.: Gen.]   D569.A2, .C3, DG570, UA742
                                            940.431, 945.08, 929.1
Capitulations, Military   D815-16   940.54012, .5314
Caporetto, Battle of, 1917   D560-4, D569   940.431
Capture at sea   JX5228
Carden, Sackville Hamilton, Sir, 1857-1930 [G.B.: Adm.]   D568.3, VA454
                                            940.425, 359.00941-00942
Carol I, 1839-1914   [Rum.: King]   D511, D741   940.311
Carol II, 1893-1957   [Rum.: King]   DR266
Carson, Edward Henry, 1854-1935 [G.B.: 1st Lord o/t Adm'ty.]   DA965.C25,
                    D591, VA454   359.00941-00942, 340.0924, 923.242
Cartridges   TS538, UF740-5   355.82, 623.455, .4553, 683.406
Carzano, Battle of, 1917   D569.C
Castelnau, Noel Joseph Edouard, 1851-1944   [Fr.: Gen.]   D511, D530,
                    D545.M3, .V3   940.41, .421, .427, 327.42044
Catholic Church
    —Charities   HV530, BX2351   249, 261.83
    —Diplomatic service   JX1801-2
    —History—Modern period, 1500-   BX1330, BX1396, BV601
                                            270-82, 282.0903
        —20th century   BX1389, BX1746   262.001, 282.0904, .73
    —Political activity
    —Relations (diplomatic)   BX1790-3, BX850-1691 (hist.), BX1908 (legates &
                    nuncios), JX1552 (int'nal. law)   261.87, 262.13, 341.33, 261.7
        —Germany   D810.C6, BX1378   262.130924
    —Relations (diplomatic) with Germany   BX1378 262.130924
    —Relations (diplomatic) with Great Britain   BR750, BX1493, BX2470, DA356
                                            248.894094, 261.7, .87, 282.42
Cavalry   UE
    —History   UE15   357.109
Cavid Bey, Mehmed, 1875-1926   [Tur.: Min. of Fin.]   DR584, D566, DD120.G3
                                            956.101, 327.430561
Cemal Pasa, Ahmed, 1872-1922   [Tur.: Gen., Navy Min., Mil. Gov. of Syria
        DR584, DR588, DD120.G3   956.1010924, 327.430561
Central Europe—History   DR36-48   940.55
Cer, Battle of, 1914   D564-5
Champagne, Battles of, 1914-1917   D544, D545.C37
Charities—History   HV16 361.0209, .73

Charles I, 1887-1922   [Aust.-Hung.: Emperor, King] DB92, CT903, CT1053,
        UA672   920.043, 355.3090436
Château-Thierry, Battle of, 1918   D544-5
Chauvel, Henry George, Sir, 1865-1945   [Australia: Gen.]   DU116.2.C47
Chemical warfare   JX1974-7, JX5135, UG447   341.63, .67, .73, 350.895,
        358.34, 363.352
   —History—20th century   UG447
China
   —Description and travel—1901-1948   DS710   915.103-104
   —Foreign relations   DS740   301.291821051, 327.51
      —Japan   DS740, DS777   327.51052, .52051
      —Russia   DK68, DS740   327.47051, .51047
      —United States   E183, DS740   327.51073, .73051
   —History—Republic, 1912-1949   DS773-7   951.04
Church work with military personnel   BV4457 253.5
Churchill, Winston Leonard Spencer, 1874-1965 [G.B.: 1st Lord o/t Adm'ty., Min. of
     Munitions (WWI), Pr. Min. (WWII)]   DA566.9.C4-5, D521, D568, D734,
     D743-4, D750, D753, D842, DA69, DA587   941.0820924, 942.084-
     085, 940.425, .45, .5322, .54012, .540942, 359.3310924, 968.040922
   —Addresses, essays, lectures
   —Anecdotes, facetiae, satire, etc.
   —Bibliography
   —Correspondence
   —Fiction
   —Funeral and memorial services
   —Language   PE1421
   —Oratory
   —Poetry
   —Portarits, caricatures, etc.
   —Quotations
   —Views on international relations
Ciphers   UB290   652.809
Civil defense   UA926-9, JX1907   355.4307, 363.34-35, 353.007-008
   —Warning systems
Civil supremacy over the military   JF195, JF256, DS919, E835 (U.S. hist.), JK558,
     KF27, U410   353.00895, .032, 355.0213+, 322.50904, .5091724
Clemenceau, Georges Eugene Benjamin, 1841-1929 [Fr.: Prem.] DC342.8.C6,
     DC335, D412.6, D521, D650.M5   944.081, 940.3, 920.02, 923.244
Coast defenses   UG410-48   355.45
Col di Lana, Battle of, 1916   D569.C
Colmar, Battle of, 1915
Colt firearms   TS533-7   683.43, 623.443
Combat patrols
Combat
   —Physiological aspects
   —Psychological aspects
Combat survival
Combatants and noncombatants (International law)
Combined operations (Military science)   U260 (allied nations)
Command and control systems   TK5102 621.38
Command of troops   UB210
Commission to Study the Oragnization of Peace
Communications, Military   UA940-5, U408, UG590   355.6, .85, 358.24

Communism　　　　HX626-795, HX36, HX44, HX56, HX134, DK254, DK274
　　　　　　　　　　320.91717, 321.642, 335.008, .408-409, .413, .42-43
　—China　　　　　DS77, DS711, DS740, DS774-8, HX387-8, JQ1519　　320.951,
　　　　　　　　　　335.430951, .4340951, 355.0951, 951.041-05
　—Germany　　　　HX273　　　335.40943
　—History　　　　　DK254, HC101, HX36-56, HX276, HX312, HX628
　　　　　　　　　　320.5322, 322.42, 330.904, 335.009, .401, .409, .41-43,
　　　　　　　　　　.438145, 947.0841
　—Russia　　　　B2430, DK254, DK265-8, DK273-6, HC335, HN523, HX312-14,
　　　　　　　　JN6598　　　142.7, 301.1520947, 320.53220947, .947084,
　　　　　　　　321.642, 329.947, 330.947, 335.413, .430947, 947.083-085
　　—History
　　—Sources
Communist International　　　HX11, HX112, HX237, HX387　　　329.072, .078,
　　　　　　　　　　335.0094, .4309597, .44, .441
Conrad von Hötzendorf, Franz Count, 1852-1925　　[Aust.-Hung.]　　DB90.C7,
　　　　　　　　　　　　　　　　　　　　　　　　　UA672　　355.309436
Conscientious objectors　UB341-2, BX8128, BX8643　　267.23, 289.33, 355.22
　—United States　　UB342.U5　　　343.73012, 355.1334, .2240973
Constantine I, 1868-1923 [Greece: King]　DF837-8, DF757, D569.2　　949.506,
　　　　　　　　　　940.414, 327.495
Consular reports—United States
Consular service
Contraband of war　　　JX5231-2, D581　　　940.452
Convoy　　　JX5268
Cookery, Marine　　　VC373　　　359.81, 641.5753
Cooperative for American Remittances to Europe, Inc.
Corfu, Declaration of, 1917　　　D651.Y8
Coronel, Battle of, 1914　　　D580-9　　　940.421, .454
Corporate state　　　HD3611-16 (econ. hist.), JC478, JC481 (fascism)
　　　　　　　　　　301.1832, 330.15, 335.609, .60943
　—Italy
Cossacks—History　　　D810.C9, DK35　　　940.5473, 914.70691714
Courts-martial and courts of inquiry　　　UB850-67 (mil.), VB800-15 (naval)　　355.9,
　　　　　　　　　　.133, .1332, 358.411332, 359.1332
　—United States　KF26, KF7620, UG633　　　355.133, .9, 358.41, 359.1
Courts of honor　　　UB880
Crimes against humanity
Cruisers (Warships)　　　V820　　　359.3253+
Cryptographers　　　UB290　　358.24
Cryptography　　　Z103-4　　001.5436, .543609, 358.24, 652.8
Ctesiphon, Battle of, 1915　　　D568.5
Curtis Hawk (Fighter planes)　　　TL685　　　623.7464
Curzon, George Nathaniel, 1859-1925　　[G.B.: Lord Privy Seal, For. Aff. Sec.]
　　　　DA565.C95, DS480　　　942.0810924, 327.20924, 923.242, 954.0350924
Czechoslovakia
　—Foreign relations—Germany　　　DB205 327.437043
　—History—1918-1938　　　DB215　943.703 (For. relns.)

Dalmatia (Croatia)—History
Damage control (Warships)   V810   623.888
Daniels, Josephus, 1862-1948   [U.S.: Sec. o/t Navy] E766.D29+, E748,
        D589.U6, D611   973.90924, .913, 070.40924,
        327.73072, 359.04, 923.273, 940.373, .45
Danilov, Yury Nikiforovich, 1866-1937   [Rus.: Lt. Gen.]   D550, D551
        940.4147, .91
D'Annunzio, Gabrielle, 1863-1938   [It.: writer, general troublemaker]   DA879.F5,
        DG555, PQ4804.R5   945.09, 949.72, 928.5
Danube Swabian Association of the U.S.A.
Danube Valley—History   DB446   914.9603, 943.48, 949.6
De Robeck, John Michael, Sir   [G.B.: Adm. o/t Fleet]   D568.3, VA454
        940.425, 359.00941, .0942
Defense contracts   UC267, UG633, VC267, HC79   338.091724, 353.00713
    —United States   U393, UC263-7, UG633, VC267 (naval), HC110, HD9743
        338.4735500973, .476234, 343.73013, 346.73023, 351.711-712,
        355.6210973, .70973, 358.4162110973
Defense information, Classified
Delcassé, Théophile, 1857-1923   [Fr.: For. Aff. Min.]   DC342.8.D36-38, DC387,
        D511   944.0810924, 327.42044, 923.244
Demolition, Military
Denmark
    —Foreign relations—1906-1945
    —History—Christian X, 1912-1947   DL148, DL160   948.9
    —Politics and government—1912-1945   JN7013, JN7111, JN7295
        301.449209489, 320.09489, .448
Deployment (Strategy)
Depth charges
Desert warfare
Desertion, Military—United States   UB788, KF7618, KF7652   355.1334,
        .1330924, .1334
Desertion, Naval—United States
Destroyer escorts
Destroyers (Warships)   V825, VA53, VA454   359.32, .3254+, .6213, 359.83,
        623.8254
Deterrence (Military strategy)   U162   355.43
Deterrence (Strategy)   U162.6   355.0217, .033+, .033509, .43, .4307
    —Mathematical models   U162   355.03350184
Dimitrijevi´c-Apis, Dragutin, 1876-1917   [Serbia: Col.: mil. intell.]   D741, DB89.F7,
        DJK4.S93, DR341   940.311, 943.604, 949.6, .7101
Diving, Submarine   D784.G3 (Ger.), D780, GV340, GV840, VM965, VM977,
        VM981+   359.98, 387.55, 623.82+, 627.7, .703, .72+, .7209
Dogger Bank, Battle of the, 1915   D580-2
Dogs, War use of   UH100
Douglas airplanes   TL686.D   338.476291
Douglas transport planes   TL686.D65, HE9769   387.7334, 629.1333+
Dresden (Cruiser)   D582.D8
Drina, Battles of the, 1914   D560-4
Dry-docks   TC361   627.35
Dubail, Auguste Yvon Edmond, 1851-1934   [Fr.: Gen.]   D544, D545.V3,
    DC373.S3, JN2562, UA700   320.944081, 940.427, 944.081
Dukhonin, Nikolai Nikolaevich, 1876-1917   [Rus.: Lt. Gen.]   DK265.2, DK265.9.A6
        947.0841
Dummy warships
Durazzo, Battle of, 1918   D580-9

Eastern question (Balkan)
Eberhardt, Andrei Augustovich, 1856-1919 [Rus.: Adm.]   D585, DE98, DK56
                                        359.00947, .0091822, 940.45947
Ebert, Friedrich, 1871-1925   [Ger.: Politician] DD247.E2, DD221, DD248
Economic assistance   D839, E744, HC59-60, HC101, HC106, HC240,
        HC435, HG136, JX1977, HG4517, KF4668   309.2233,
    338.4730154, .90091724, 343.73+, 353.00722, .00825, 358.00892, 387.1
Economic assistance, American
Eichhorn, Hermann von, 1848-1918   [Ger.: Field Marshal] DD120.R8, DD228.8,
                                CR5327   940.3243, .343, 929.71
Elections—United States—History   JK97, JK1965, JK171   324.73,
                                329.0237302-0237303
Electronic intelligence
Emergency communication systems
Emergency medical services RA645.5-7, RA975, RD81   361.5, 362.11,
                        614.875, 940.5475, 344.73041, 362.18
Emergency water supply
Emigration and immigration law—United States   JV6424, JV6507, JV6874, JX1977,
            KF4800, KF4807, KF4819, KF8925   323.60973, .6310973,
        325.240973, .24580973, 342.73082, 362.8
Émigrés   DC158.1-17   325.244, 942.00441
Enemy property
Enfield rifle
England   [SEE ALSO 'Great Britain']
    —Civilization—20th century   DA566   914.20382-20384
    —Social life and customs—20th century   DA566   914.2820385, 941.083,
                                942.0823

Englandspiel
Enver Pasa, 1881-1922   [Tur.: Gen., Min. of War] DT234.E48, D566, DD120.G7,
    DK511.C2, DR440, DR584   956.101, 327.430436, .430561, .5610+, 947.9
Erzberger, Matthias, 1875-1921 [Ger.: State Sec. without Portfolio]   DD231.E7
                                        943.0840924
Espionage   UB270-1   327.120904, 351.74, 355.343, 364.131, 940.548673
Espionage, American [British, German, etc.]
Espionage, American   UB271   327.120973
Espionage, British
Espionage, German   UB271, D810   327.120943
    —United States   D810   940.548743
Espionage, Russian   DK61, DK266, UB271   327.120947, 355.3432+,
                        364.13
Estonia—History—1918-1940   DK511   947.41
Étaples (France), Mutiny, 1917
Europe
        —Civilization—20th century   CB53, CB417, D102, D429, D1055
                            910.03924, 914.031-032, 940.2+
        —Description and travel—1800-1918   D919, D974, D907, D921   914+, .0428
Europe, Eastern
        —History   DK440, DR36-8, DR43, DR48   943.804+
            —Autonomy and independence movements   DJK48
Europe
        —History—20th century   D104, D421, D424, D411   909.82, 940.5
        —Politics—1871-1918   D397, D453   940.28, .3112
        —Relations (military) with the United States   D1065   327.4073

European War, 1914-   [SEE 'European War, 1914-1918' for titles cataloged after
     the conflict. Subdivisions may be found under either]
European War, 1914-1919
European War, 1914-1918   [Newer term for publications after 1981 or so is 'World
                    War, 1914-1918'. Subdivisions may be found under either]
                    D501-680+, D511, D521, D523, D639, D644
                    940.3-940.499, 940.3+, 940.4+
—Addresses, essays, lectures   D509, D523   940.308, .31
—Addresses, sermons, etc.   D443, D509, D517, D525, B945   301.593,
                    .953, 940.3081, .314, .34208, .4008
—Aerial operations   D600-607, DA89, TL540, UG633   358.43, 623.746,
                    923.542, 940.44, .54
—Aerial operations, American   D437, D606   904.7, 940.44973
—Aerial operations, British   D602, UG635   940.44942, .544941
     —Pictorial works   UG635   358.400941
—Aerial operations, French   D603   940.44944
—Aerial operations, German   D604   940.44943
—Africa, German Southwest   DT779, D576   940.48243
—Air-fleet bases, Naval—Germany   D580
—Alsace   D640
—Anecdotes   D509, D521, D523, D640, D525   940.3, .4, .548
—Arabia   D568   923.542, 940.415
—Armenia   D638, DS195
—Armistices   D641-2   940.434, .439
—Art and the war   N9150, N6491   745.09041
—Asia, Western   D566
—Atrocities   D541, D626
—Australia   D547.A8   940.394
—Austria
—Automobiles   D639
—Balkan Peninsula   D560
—Battlefields   D528   940.46
—Belgium   D541-2, DH681-2   940.4313, 949.3040924
     —Louvain   D542
—Bibliography   Z674, Z1035, Z6207   016.9403
—Biography   D507, D570   940.30922, .4, .410922, .46
—Blockades   D581, D619   940.452
—Bohemia   DB217   943.702
—California—Los Angeles County
—Campaigns   D521, D530   940.3, .401, .414, .421
     —Africa   D568, D573   940.4
          —German East   D576   940.41676
          —Tanganyika   D576   940.416, .5423
     —Africa, German Southwest
     —Balkan Peninsula   D561, D569   940.414
     —Belgium   D541   940.4144
     —Eastern   D550-2   940.4326
     —France   D544, D548, DC342, D608   940.4144, .42, .43, .457, .5421
     —Italo-Austrian   D569
     —Maps   G1037   911.09403
     —Mesopotamia and the Persian Gulf
     —Poland
     —Serbia   D561   940.4256

European War, 1914-1918
  —Campaigns
    —Turkey and the Near East   D566-8, D588   940.415, .4153
      —Egypt   D568
      —Gallipoli   D568   940.4143, .425, .4259, .455
    —Turkey and the Near East
      —Mesopotamia D568   956.7, 940.41567
      —Palestine   D568   940.415, .4291, .438
      —Persia   D568   923.843
    —Western   D509, D530-1, D544-6, DC342   940.4+, .4144,
                                       .421,.4216, .436
  —Canada   D520, D547, D640
  —Catholic Church   D622
  —Causes   CB245, D511, D515, JX1907   940.311, .341
  —Censorship   D631-2   940.405
    —United States   D632   940.405
  —Children   HV640   362.7
  —China   D621, D549, DS775   940.351, 951+
  —Chronology   D522
  —Church of England   D639   261.873
  —Confiscations and contributions—United States   JX5313   341.67
  —Congresses, conferences, etc.   JX1908
  —Conscientious objectors
    —Great Britain   UB342, UB345   355.224, 940.316
    —United States   UB342   355.224, 940.3162
  —Czechoslovak Republic   D558, DB217   940.322, .4147, 943.7030924
  —Deportations from France   D639
  —Diplomatic history D505, D610-11, D619, JX1906-7   940.3112, .314,
                                       .32241, .32273, .32443, .45
  —Documents, sources, etc.   D505, Z733   940.3082
  —Drama   PN1997   791.437
  —Economic aspects   HC56-7, D635   334, 338
    —Canada   HC56
    —France   HC56   334+
    —Germany   HC286   940.31, 330.904
    —Great Britain   HC256, HC56, HD8390   330.942, 940.3113, 338.16
    —Russia
    —Scandinavia
    —Turkey
    —United States   HC56, HC106, HD8057, JX1416, JX5270   327.73,
                         330.973, 338.0973, 341+, 940.37305
  —Education and the war   D639   379.151
  —Engineering and construction   D607 940.4
  —England   D547   940.342393
  —Fiction
    —Bibliography   Z6207   016.823081
    —History and criticism   PR6011 (Eng.)   823.912
  —Finance   HJ8011, HJ8117   940.3144, 336.4, .3094
    —France
    —Great Britain   HJ1023   336.42. 940.34205
    —Russia
    —United States   HJ257, HJ8117, HJ8011   336.73

306

European War, 1914-1918
 —Food question D637, HD9007 940.4778
  —Congresses HD9000 338.19
  —France   HC56 338.10944
  —Germany HD9613
  —Great Britain HC56
  —Russia   HC56 338.10947
  —United States HD9005, HD9435
 —France   D509, D548 940.344
  —Historiography D522 940.4144072
  —Paris D544 940.4341
 —Germany D515, D531, DD228, DD231, UA712   355.00943,
    .3310924, 940.32443, .343, .40943, .41343, .4512, 943.084-085
  —Addresses, essays, lectures D515 940.311
 —Gift-books
 —Great Britain D517, D546, D651, DA577, DA68-9 320.942,
    354.42066, 923.542, 940.32242, .40942, .342, 942.082
  —London
 —Greece DF832, D616 949.506
 —Hawaii (Territory)
 —Historiography D522 940.322
 —Hospitals D638-9 940.477
 —Hospitals, charities, etc. D628-9, D638-9, UH537, HV575 360.6273,
    940.47642, .477873, .4779+
 —Humor, caricatures, etc. D526 940.30207, .496-497
 —Iconography D503
 —Illinois
 —Indiana
 —Influence and results D511, D523, D610, D643, D653, HC56 940.3144,
    .3148, 330.9436
 —Italy D523, D560, D640, DG570 940.32, .481, .401245, 945+
 —Jews D639.J4 940.478
 —Juvenile literature
 —Kansas
 —Language (New words, slang, etc.) D523, PE1689, PE3727 427.09, 428+
 —Latin America D520 940.38
 —Law and legislation
  —France
  —United States JX5270 341+
 —Libraries (in camps, etc.) Z675 026+, 027.652
 —Literature and the war D509, PR478 (Eng.), PS221 (US) 810.9005,
    820.900912
 —Maps G1037 912.4
 —Massachusetts
 —Medical and sanitary affairs D629-30, UH274, UH400 940.475+,
    .47573 (U.S.), .47634+
 —Mennonites BX8116
 —Mesopotamia D566 940.415
 —Miscellanea PR2771, D619, D523 822.33
 —Moral aspects HQ16 940.3183926
 —Museums and libraries

European War, 1914-1918
    —Naval history and operations
    —Naval operations   D580-2, D591-2   940.45+, .459
    —Naval operations, American   D589   940.45
    —Naval operations, British   D581-2, D593   940.45+, .451341, .4514,
                            .455, .45941-2
    —Naval operations, German   D531, D581-2   940.45+, .45943, .545,
                            943.084
    —Naval operations—Submarine   D568, D581, D589, D591, D593, D595
                            940.451+, .4512-13, .459+
    —Negroes   D639   940.403, .477873
    —New York (State)
    —New Zealand   D547
    —North Carolina   D570   975.604
    —Norway   D621   940.325481
    —Ohio—Cleveland
    —Outlines, syllabi, etc.   D522   940.302
    —Palestine   D568
    —Peace   D523, D613, D644-6, D651, JX1906, JX1975   327.4, .73,
                            940.312+, .314
    —Peace movement   D613
    —Pennsylvania—Philadelphia
    —Periodicals
    —Personal narratives   D602, D628-9, D640   940.343, .48142, .48173
    —Personal narratives, American   CT275, D570, D606, D640   914.436,
                            940.4144, .44942, .44973, .48173, .481756
    —Personal narratives, Armenian
    —Personal narratives, Austrian
    —Personal narratives, Belgian
    —Personal narratives, British
    —Personal narratives, Canadian
    —Personal narratives, English   D602, D640, D568, DA566   823.912,
                            940.315, .40942, .4144, .44941, .48141-48142
    —Personal narratives, French   D603, D640, D548   940.48144
    —Personal narratives, German   D531, D551, D591, D640   940.422,
                            .450924, .48243
    —Personal narratives, Hungarian   D640   940.482439
    —Personal narratives, Irish   D640   940.5481415
    —Personal narratives, Italian   D569, D640   940.48145
    —Personal narratives, New Zealand   D640   940.481931
    —Personal narratives, Polish   DK440, D640   943.8
    —Personal narratives, Russian   D640, DK254, DK265   940.48147, 947.084
    —Personal narratives, Serbian   D640   940.481497
    —Pictorial works   D522, D527, NE2012   760.0924, 940.3022, .431, .49
        —Exhibitons
    —Poetry   D526, PR610, PR1226-7, PR9900, PS3503, PS3545
                    811.52, 821.0080355, 821.912+
        —History   PR605, PR6029   821.91209
    —Portraits   D507, D609
    —Postal service   HE6375   383.2209+
    —Posters   D522, D527   327.14, 741.973, 769.499403, 940.3022
        —Exhibitions   D522   769.5
    —Preparations

European War, 1914-1918
  —Prisoners and prisons   D627
  —Prisoners and prisons, British   D627   940.47242
    —Egypt
    —India   D627 365
  —Prisoners and prisons, French   D627   940.47244
  —Prisoners and prisons, German   D627   301.15, 940.47243
    —Ruhleben
  —Prisoners and prisons, Italian   D627   940.47245
  —Prisoners and prisons, Russian   D627   940.47243, .47247
  —Prisoners and prisons, Turkish   D627
  —Propaganda   D639.P7   940.488+, .5488
  —Prophecies   D524, D639   940.3181333
  —Protest movements—Great Britain   JX1961   940.3162
  —Public opinion   D511, D515, D619, D570, D632   301.15+, 940.4886+, .3778
  —Refugees   D638
  —Regimental histories
    —Canada   D547   940.41271
    —France
    —Germany
    —Great Britain   D546-7   940.41241
      —Cavalry
      —Infantry
        —Gordon Highlanders
        —Irish Guards
        —King's Own Scottish Borderers
        —Royal Munster Fusilliers
    —Royal Air Force   D547   940.44941-2
  —Newfoundland   D547   940.41271
    —Royal Newfoundland Regiment
  —United States   D570   940.41273, .4144, 355+
    —Aero Squadron   D570   940.44973
    —Ambulance Company, No. 307
    —1st Army Corps
    —Artillery
    —5th Division
    —26th (Yankee) Division
    —28th (Iron) Division
    —29th Division
    —42d (Rainbow) Division
    —77th Division   D570.3.77th
    —90th Division
    —Engineers
    —101st Engineers
    —66th Field Artillery Brigade
    —Infantry
    —320th Infantry
    —Infantry—359th—Co. L
    —2d Machine Gun Battalion
    —Machine gun battalions—305th
    —102nd Military Police
    —New York Infantry
  —Registers, lists, etc.   D589, D609, D639, E186   369.121, 940.412+,
          .41273 (US)
  —Registers of dead   D570

European War, 1914-1918
 —Religious aspects   D524, D639, BR479, BX5937, BR115   248.4,
                        940.3152, .3181331, .53, 230+, 265+, 399
 —Religious life
 —Reparations   D648-9, HC57, JX1907-8   940.31422, 943.085, 336.43
 —Rhode Island
 —Rumania   D520, DR262   923.1498
 —Russia   D550, D559, D552, D585, D651, DK265   947.084, .08,
                940.3141, .40947
    —Archangel
    —Moscow
 —Science   D639.S2
 —Secret service   D639.S7-8   940.485-486, .486437
    —Austria   D639   940.487436
    —France   D639   940.48644
    —Germany   D619, D639   940.48743
    —Great Britain   DA89, D616, D639.S7-8   940.48641-2, 923.542
    —United States   D619, D639   940.48673
 —Serbia   D561
 —Servia   D629.S4
 —Siberia   D558
 —Societies   D570   369.186-188
 —Songs and music   D526, M1629   427.09, 784+
 —Sources   D505   940.3082, 940.4
 —Spanish America   D520   980
 —Study and teaching   D570   940.3
 —Submarine operations   V210   359.4
 —Supplies   D619, UF510   355.82, 940.32
 —Sweden   D621.S5
 —Switzerland   D621.S   940.3494
 —Tasmania   D547   940.3946
 —Telephone   D639
 —Territorial questions   D650-3   940.314+
    —Armenia
    —East
    —Germany   D643, D651   940.31424
    —Hungary   D643, D651   940.3141-3142
    —Italy
    —Kamerun   D651.K3
    —Lithuania   D651
    —Poland   D651   327.730438, 940.31424
    —Rhine Valley   D650   940.3142, 944.08
    —Ruthenia
    —Thrace
    —Transylvania
    —Turkey   D651, DR584   949.6, 956.101
    —Yugoslavia
 —Texas—Houston
 —Transcaspian Province   DK265
 —Transportation   D639, HC56, HF56   334+, 385+, 940.41273 (US)
 —Treaties   D644
 —Turkey   D566, D520   327.430561, 940.32496
 —United States   D522, D544, D570, D619-20, E181, E766, E780, E802
        322.440973, 327.172, 355.2120973, 940.32273, .373, .37309, .40973,
        .41273, .4173, .4373, .45973, .314, .46573, 973.91+, 923.273, .573

France
  . Armée   DC403, D761, UA700-708   944.01, 940.540944, 355.00944, .409033, 320.944, 322.50944
    . Cavalerie
    . Escadrille Lafayette   D603.F55   940.449, .44944, .44973+
    . Groupement des Commandos de France
    —History   DC46, DC151, UA702   355.00944, 940.540944
    —Infanterie
        —Chasseurs
        —Drill and tactics
    . Légion Étrang`ere   UA703, U55, D810   355.31, .35, .3520944, 940.5405
    —Military life
  —Army—Infantry—Légion étrang`ere   D570.9
  —Colonies
  —Foreign relations
    —1870-1940   DC340-2, DC369, DC373, DC385   940.5, 944.081+, 327.44
    —1914-1940   DC369, DC373, DC389, DC393   327.440+, 940.5314, 944.081+
    —Germany   DC341   327.44043, .43044
  —History
    —Third Republic, 1870-1940   DC335-7   944.08, .081
    —20th century   DC361, DC389   944.08
    —1914-1940   DC396   944.0816
    —German occupation, 1914-1918   D548
  —History, Military   DC46, DC95, DC135   944.04
    —20th century   DC367   355.0330944
  —History, Naval   VA503   359.00944
  . Marine   D779.F7-8, VA503   359.00944, .3250924
    —History   D779, VA503   940.545944, 359.00944
      —World War, 1914-1918   D583.M33
    —Sea life
  —Politics and government
    —1870-1940   DC331, DC340-44, DC354, JN2562, UA700 320.94408+, 322.50944, 944.081
    —1914-1940   DC373, DC387-9, DC396, JN2863, JN3007 320.9440816, 944.081
  —Relations (general) with Germany   DC59   327.43044, .44043
Franchet D'Esperey, Louis Felix Francis, 1856-1942 [Fr.: Gen.]   DC373.F7, DC342.8.P4, D545.M3, D569.2   944.0810924
Francis Ferdinand, 1863-1914 [SEE 'Franz Ferdinand']
Francis Joseph I, 1830-1916   [SEE 'Franz Joseph I']
Franco-German War, 1870-1871   DC285, DC291-3, DC300, DC310, DD219 943.081-082
Franz Ferdinand, Archduke of Austria-Este, 1863-1914 [Aust.-Hung.: A.k.a. 'Francis Ferdinand']   DB89.F7, UA672   943.6040924, 940.3112, 355.309436, 364.1524
Franz Joseph I, 1830-1916   [Aust.-Hung.: A.k.a. 'Francis Joseph': Emperor of Austria, King of Hungary]   DB49, DB85-7, UA672   943.6040924, 327.436043-044, 355.309436, 940.28
Frederick, Archduke of Austria, 1856-1936 [Aust.-Hung.: Duke of Teschen, Field Marshal]   D556, CT903, CT912   940.464436
Freedom of the seas   JX4423-5 (int'nal. law), JX5203-5268   341.57

French, John Denton Pinkstone, 1852-1925 [G.B.: Field Marshal]   D521, D544,
                        D548, D569.A2   940.3, .4145, .421
Friends, Society of. American Friends Service Committee   BX7635, BX7747,
                        JX1953   172.4, 267.1896+, 289.6
Frigates   V767
Fuses (Ordnance)   UF780   353.00712, 623.4542

Gallieni, Joseph Simon, 1849-1916   [Fr.: Gen., Min. of War]   D507, D545.V3,
                        D548, DC387, U55.G3   940.410922, .427, 944.08
Gamelin, Maurice Gustave, 1872-1958 [Fr.: Gen.]   D761.G, UA702.G   940.5344
Garand rifle   UD395   355.82
Gaza, Battles of, 1917   D568.7
Geddes, Eric Campbell, Sir, 1875-1937 [G.B.: 1st Lord o/t Adm'ty.]   D611,
                        VA454   940.45, 359.00941
General strike   HD5307   331.892, .89201, .8925
Generals   U51-4 (biog.)
   —[Austria, France, etc.]—Biography
   —Australia—Biography   DU116.2
   —Germany—Biography   DD247   943.0860924
   —Great Britain—Biography   DA68-9, DA407, DA426, DA455   355.00924,
            .3310924, 940.54250924, 941.0660922-0660924, 942.060924
   —Russia   DK169   355.3310924
   —South Africa—Biography   DT764.5
   —United States   E181, E207, E467, E745, U52   973.730120922, .741,
            .330924, 355.3310924, .3320922-3320924
      —Biography—Correspondence   E207   973.3330924
Genocide   JX5418, JX6731   301.592, 341.4, .77, 364.151
George II, 1889-1947   [Greece: King]
George V, 1865-1936   [G.B.: King of G.B., Emperor of India]   DA573, D412.6,
                        D546   942.0830924, 920.02, 923.142
Gerard, James Watson, 1867-1951 [U.S.: Ambass. to Ger.]   D515, D611   940.45
German Library of Information
Germans in Poland
Germany   DD   943, 914.3
   —Air defenses, Military
   —Armed Forces   D757   940.5443
      —Ordnance and ordnance stores—History   UF525   623.0943
      —Organization   UA710   355.00943
      —Uniforms   UC485.G   355.140943
      —Weapons systems UG635   355.82
   —Bibliography   Z2249   016.914303
   —Biography   DD231, CT1098   920.043, 940.531620924
   —Boundaries   D821.A-Z, D821.G4
      —Czechoslovakia
      —France
      —Poland
   —Civilization   DD61-7   914.3032, 943.07-08
   —Colonies   JV2017-8, JV2027   325.343, .43, 940.5314
      —Africa   DT34   916.6
      —Africa, Southwest   JV2018   325.343068
   —Description and travel—1919-1945   DD43   914.3+
   —Economic conditions—1918-1945   DD237, DD247, HC286
                        943.085, 330.943, 332.110943, 338.0943, 940.5343
   —Emigration and immigration
   —Exiles

314

Great Britain   [SEE ALSO 'England', 'Scotland', 'Ireland']   DA, DA11   941-2
. Admiralty
—Air defenses, Military
. Army
    —Fifth Army, 1915-1918   D546.5.5th   940.41242
    —Eighth Army
    —Australian and New Zealand Army Corps—History   D547.A8, D568
                                                 940.322931
    —Biography   DA69.3
    —Black Watch (Royal Highlanders)   UA652.B6   356.110942, 355.31
    —Boys' units   U549.2
    —British Expeditionary Force   D541.A, D547.B74
    —Colonial forces
    . Field Security Personnel
    —Firearms   UD385   355.82
    . Grenadier Guards. 2d Battalion   D547   940.41241
    —History   UA649, UA853   355.00942, .02130942, .30941, .310941
    . 2d King Edward VII's Own Gurkha Rifles
    —Military life   DA68, DA566   923.242
    . Royal Fusiliers (City of London Regiment)   D568   940.41242
    . Royal Regiment of Artillery   D547.R5
    . Royal Tank Corps   D608   940.412
    —Scottish regiments
    —Uniforms—History   UC485   355.140941-140942, 356.110942
    . Welsh Regiment   D640   940.48142
    —Welsh regiments   UA663
    . Zion Mule Corps   DS125.5 [WWI]
—Biography   CB19, CT774-5, CT781-3, DA28, DA566, DA568, DA585
. British Information Services   Z2009
—Civilization—20th century   DA566   914.2, 941.082-083
—Coast defenses   UG429   355.450942
. Colonial Office
—Colonies   D413, DA16, DA563, HC256, JV1009-1018, JV1026-7
               320.9171241, 325.342, 326.342, 327.20924, 382.0942, .
               30942, 909.0971242, 914.203
    —Administration
      —Documents, sources, etc.
    —Africa   DT32   325.34206, .342096
    —Africa, Eastern   DT423   916.7
    —Asia
    —Economic conditions
    —Economic policy   HC259   338.9142, 382.0942
    —Emigration and immigration   JV1041   325.341-2
    —History   DA16-17, DA505, DA566, JV1011   325.34209,
               909.0971242, 923.242, 942.08
    —Race question
    —Tropics
—Commerce   HF3503   330.942, 382.0942, .50942, .60942
    —Europe   HF3508   382.094204
    —History
. Committee of Imperial Defence   UA647   355.033542, .0942
—Defenses   DA585, DA592, U55, UA647   355.0309171242,
               .033041-033042, .033542, .20942, .450942
—Description and travel—1901-1945   DA630   914.2, .20383, .20484
—Diplomatic and consular service   JX1783   327.42

Great Britain
—Economic conditions
—20th century HC256 330.942
—1918-1945 HC256 330.941083, .942083
—Foreign economic relations HF1533, HC256 337.9142, 382,0942, .10942
—Foreign relations
—1901-1910 DA570 327.41
—1910-1936 DA566, DA576-8 327.42, 940.31206342
—East (Far East) DA47, DS518 327.4105, .42051
—Europe DA47 327.4204, .4042
—France
—Germany DA47 327.42043, .43042
—Russia
—Treaties
—United States DA47, E183 327.42073, .73042
—History DA, DA16, DA30-2, DA40, DA45 914.1-2, 941-2
—Victoria, 1837-1901 DA16, DA536, DA550-4, DA550-4, DA560-6
942.08-081, 914.20381
—20th century DA16, DA566, DA588 941.082-085, 942.08-082,
914.20382, 909.0971242+
—Edward VII, 1901-1910 DA567-70 941.082, 942.082, 914.20382
—George V, 1910-1936 DA577-8 942.083, 914.20383
—History, Military DA50, DA65, DA68, UA649 355.00942,
.30941, .310941
—20th century DA69 942.084
—History, Naval DA70, DA85, DA88, VA454 359.00941-00942,
.030941-030942
—20th century DA89, D770 359.0942, .33109, .00941
. H.M. Stationery Office [SEE ALSO 'Great Britain. Stationery Office']
—Kings and rulers DA28, DA177, JN331 321.60942, 914.2030922-
2030924, 942.00922, .09231
. Ministry of Defence
. Ministry of Economic Warfare
. Ministry of War Transport
. Navy [SEE ALSO 'Great Britain. Royal Navy'] V163, V767, V820-5, V820,
V825, V859, VA454-6, D581 359.00941-00942, .0942, .10942,
.32520942, .32530942, .32570942, .942, 623.8250942, .82540942
—Aviation—History VG95 358.4183
—Biography DA87-8 359.00922, 923.542
—Bibliography Z2021 016.35900942
. Tenth Cruiser Squadron D581 940.45941+
. Fleet Air Arm VG95 358.40942, 623.746
—History DA70-89, V750, V800, V825, VA454-7 359.00941-00942,
.120941-120942, .13320941, .30942, .3250942, .32520942,
.32540941, 940.545941
—Lists of vessels VA40, VA456 359.320941-320942
—Regulations V167 359.00942, .40942, .420942
—Sea life DA88 359.10942, .12
—Politics and government
—20th century
—1901-1910
—1910-1936
—Public Record Office CD1048 016.95127
—Relations (military)—Germany

318

Great Britain
    . Royal Air Force   UG635, UG1245, D568, D602, D756   358.40942,
                    .420941, .430941-430942, 623.7460941, .74630942,
                    940.44942, .5421
        —Biography   D568.4, D602   940.440924
        . Fighter Command   UG635   358.414
        —History   DA585, UG635   940.44942, 358.400941-400942,
                    .4135, .4183, .430942
        . 617 Squadron
    . Royal Navy   [SEE ALSO 'Great Britain. Navy']
        —Aviation   VG695.G7
        —Biography   DA70, DA74, DA88.1
        . Coastal forces
        . Fleet Air Arm   VG95.G7
        —History   DA70, VA454   359.3510942
        —Lists of vessels   VA454-6   359.320942
        —Medals, badges, decorations, etc.   VB335, UB435, CJ6113
        —Officers   VB315.G7   355.220942
        —Records and correspondence
        —Registers   V11.G7
        —Sea life   V737
        —Uniforms   VC305.G7
        —Yearbooks   V10
    . Stationery Office   [SEE ALSO 'Great Britain. H.M. Stationery Office']
    . War Office   D546, D759   942.084, 354.42066
        . General Staff   UB225, UA647   355.3310942, .30924
        . Intelligence Division
        —Manuscripts
Greece, Modern
    —History
        —George I, 1863-1913   DF831   949.507
        —1917-1944
Grenades   UF765   623.42
Grey, Edward, Sir, 1862-1933 [G.B.: Sec. of State for For. Aff.]   DA566.9.G8, .A1,
        D517, D546   942.0820924, 940.311, .342, 920.042
Grigorovich, Ivan Konstantinovich, 1853-1930   [Rus.: Adm., Min. o/t Navy] D580,
        D585, DE98.H3, DK260, DK265.35.B3   320.947, 359.0091822,
        940.45947, 947.08, .0841
Guam   DU647   919.67, 996.7
Guerrilla warfare   U240, U210   355.02184, .425, .425098, 356.15, 335.438+
Guillaumat, Marie-Louis Adolfe, 1863-1940 [Fr.: Gen.]   D548, D569.2, DC387
                    940.414, 944.08
Gunboats   V880, V895   359.3262+
Gunnery   UF800, UF150-302 (manuals), VF144-7, VF150-302
Gunpowder   TP268, TP272 (chem.), HD9663 (industry)   662.26-3
Gurko, Vasily Iosifovich, 1864-1937   [Rus.: Gen.]   D550, DK265.19,
                    DK265.9.A6   940.40947, .4147, 947.0841

Haakon VII, 1872-1957   [Norway: King]   DL530
Haig, Douglas, Sir, 1861-1928 [G.B.: Field Marshal]   DA69.3.H3, D507, D521,
                    D544.A2, D546, D546.5.2d, D569.A2
                    940.41440924, .410922, .4145,   355.3310924
Half-track vehicles, Military   UG446   355.83
Hamilton, Ian Standish Monteith ('Johnny'), Sir, 1853-1947   [G.B.: Gen.]
        DA88.1.H25, D523, D568.3, DT930   923.542, 968.3

Hand-to-hand fighting   GV1111-1141, U167   796.8+, 355.348, .548, .82
Harbord, James Guthrie, 1866-1947   [U.S.: Gen.] E745.H3, D570   940.41273
Harmsworth, Alfred Charles William, Viscount Northcliffe ('King Alfred') [G.B.: Dir. of
     Enemy Propaganda]   D546, D611, DA566.9.N7   940.45, 920.5
Haus, Anton Baron von, 1851-1917   [Aust.-Hung.: Grand Adm.]   D556, D583
                                                          940.464436

Hawaiian Islands
Heads of state
     —Biography   D412   920.02
     —(country)—Biography
Heinkel aeroplanes   TL686   629.13334
Helfferich, Karl, 1872-1924   [Ger.: Dep. Chanc.]   DD231.H35, D521   330.0924
Helgoland, Battle of, 1914   D580-2
Henry, Prince of Prussia, 1862-1929 [Ger.: Grand Adm.] DD106, VA513
                                                          359.00943, .030943
Hentsch, Richard, 1869-1918 [Ger.: Col.]   D521, D530, D545.M3, CR5327 929.71,
                                                          940.30922, .4140922

Herbicides—War use
Heroes
Hindenburg, Paul von Beneckendorf und von, 1847-1934 [Ger.: Field Marshal, Pres.]
     DD231.H5, DD228, D531.H4813   943.0850924, .085, 923.143,
     940.343, .41430922
Hinzert (Germany: Concentration camp)
Hipper, Franz Ritter von, 1863-1932   [Ger.: Adm.]   DD231.H53, DD106,
                                             VA513   359.00943, 923.543
History, Modern—20th century   D421, D398, D415, D422-9, D443-5, D643, D720
Hoffmann, Max, 1869-1927   [Ger.: Gen.]   DD231.H5-6, D531, D551
                                             943.0850924, 940.343
Holtzendorff, Henning von, 1853-1919 [Ger.: Grand Adm.]   D591, VA513
                                             940.45943, 359.00943
Hong Kong—History   DS796   951.25, 915.125
Horthy, Miklos, 1868-1957   [Sometimes 'Horthy de Nagybánya, Miklos': Aust.-
     Hung.: Vice Adm., Adm., Regent of Hung.]   DB950.H6, DB955, D556,
     D583   943.9050924, .9105, 940.464436, .5324439
Hospitals, Military   UH460-85   355.345, .92, 353.007+, .008+, 362.11+
Hospitals, Naval and marine   RA975, RA980-93, VG410-50, VG463   616.98024
Hot pursuit (International law)
House, Edward Mandell, 1858-1938   [U.S.: Pres. Adviser]   E766.H85, E748,
                                   D611   973.9130924, 940.45, 923.273
Houthulst, Battle of, 1918   D541-2
Howitzers   UF470-5, UF560-5, VF390-5 (naval)
Hungary
     —History   DB925   943.9+
          —20th century   DB950   943.91
          —Revolution, 1918-1919 DB955   943.905, .9105
Hymans, Paul, 1865-1941   [Belg.: For. Aff. Min.] DH685.H9, DH620   949.3,
                                                          327.493, 923.2493

Imperial War Museum (Great Britain)   N9145.I
Incendiary bombs
Incendiary weapons   UG447   358.34
Indemnity—Periodicals   D649.G31.A5 (WWI)

India
—Armed forces
——Monuments   D547.I5 (WWI)
. Army   D767, UA842   940.540954, 355.00954
——History   UA842   355.00954, .352, 356.110954
——History
——1765-1947   DS463-79   954.029-031, .79
——British occupation, 1765-1947
Indians of North America as seamen
Indians of North America as soldiers
Indochina, French—History   DS550   959.7+
Indochina—History   DS550   959.7+
Indonesia—History
——1798-1942   DS643   959.008
Industrial mobilization   UA18   355.26
Industry and state   HD3611-3790   330.08, 338.0186, .091724
Industry
——Defense measures
——Germany
——Russia
——United States   UA929   363.35+
Infantry   UD
Infantry drill and tactics   UD157-302
Infantry—History   UD15   356.109
Integrated logistic[s] support   UC263   355.621
Intelligence service   UB250   355.3432, 353.0089
——France
——Germany
——Great Britain   D810, JN329   355.34320942, 940.548642
——Japan
——Russia
——Soviet Union
——United States   D767, UB251, UG633   353.0074, .0081, .00892,
                                  940.5426, .548673
Inter-allied Commission on Mandates in Turkey. American Section   D651   956.102
Inter-allied Games, 1919   GV721
Inter-allied Military Mission to Hungary, 1919-1920   DB955   943.905+
Inter-allied Rhineland High Commission   D650.M5
International Labor Office   HD2755, HD7801   341.5, .763, 658.3
International organization   D815   940.5304
International trusteeships   JX1977, JX4021   321.027, 325.21, .31, 341.132, .27
Intrenchments   UG403 (field fortification), UG446 (trench warfare)
Invincible (Cruiser)
Iran—History—1909-1945   DS315-18   955.05+
Ireland
——History
———20th century   DA959-60   941.59
———1910-1921   DA960-65   941.50821, .59
——Neutrality   D754.I6   940.54874309415
——Politics and government—1910-   DA959   941.591
Iron Duke (Warship)
Ironside, Edmund, Sir, 1880-1959 [G.B.: Field Marshal]   DA69.3.I7, D559
                                  942.0840924, 940.4147

Japan
—Foreign economic relations
 —Asia
 —United States   HF1602   338.9152073, 382.095201812
—Foreign opinion, American
—Foreign relations
 —1868-1912   DS845, DS881-4   327.52, 952.03
 —1912-1945   DS845, DS885-8, JX1975   327.52, 341.2252, 952.033
 —China   327.52051, .51052
 —Germany   DS849   327.52043
 —Russia   DS849   327.52047
 —United States   E183   327.52073, .73052
—History
 —1868-   DS881-5   952.03+
 —Meiji period, 1868-1912 DS881-5   952.031, 915.20431+
 —20th century   DS885   952.03
 —1912-1945   DS888   952.033
 —Taisho period, 1912-1926   DS886   952.032, 309.152032
—History, Military—1868-
—History, Naval—1868-
—Industries
. Kaigun   [Navy]   VA653, D777, D777.5.A-Z (by ship)   359.030952,
                       .052, .3250952, 623.8250952, 940.545952
 —Appropriations and expenditures
 —History   D742, D777, VA653   940.53112, .545952
 . Kokutai   VG95 [Aerial ops.]   358.4183, 623.74630952
 . Lists of vessels   VA653   359.320952
 . Ordnance and ordnance stores
 . Organization
—Military policy   UA845, VA50, VA653   355.033552, .33552, 359.030952
—Politics and government
 —20th century
 —1912-1945   DS845, DS885-9   320.952032-952033, 329.951,
                        940.5352, 952.033
—Relations (general) with the East (Far East)
—Relations (general) with the United States   E183   301.2952073, 327.73052
—Relations (military) with the United States
. Rikugen   D767, UA845-7   355.30952, 940.541352, 355.00952
 —Armored troops   UG446   358.180952
 . Kokutai   UG635, UG1242   358.4183, 623.74640952
 —Military life   U773   355.00952
—Social life and customs—1912-1945   DS821   915.20333
—Territorial expansion
Japanese in the United States—History   E184   917.306956
Jaroslawice, Battle of, 1914   D551-2
Jebel Musa (Syria), Defense of, 1915   D568.6
Jellicoe, John Rushworth Jellicoe, 1st Earl, 1859-1935   [G.B.: Adm. o/t Fleet]
                  DA89.1.J4, DA70, D580-1   940.45942

Jewish Legion   D568   940.41242, .416
Jewish question   DS141-51   909.0974924, 910.03924, 956.93-94+
Jewish soldiers
Jews as soldiers   DS119   355.30922
Jews
   —History—1789-1945   DS125-6, DS107, DS140-3   909.0492408, 956.93-4
Jews in Hungary   DS135   940.5405, .53439
Jews in Europe
   —History   DS135   301.45192404, 914.04
   —Persecutions   DS135, DD247   341.41, 940.5405, 943.086
Jews in Germany
   —History
      —1800-1933
Jews in Russia—History   DS135   323.11924047, 914.706924, 947.004924
Jews
   —Legal status, laws, etc.
   —Germany
   —Persecutions   DS102, DS116, DS145   301.45192404, 956.93
Jiu River (Romania), Battle of, 1916   D565
Jiul River, Battle of, 1916   D565.J
Joffre, Joseph Jacques Césaire, 1852-1931   [Fr.: Field Marshal]   DC342.8.J6,
                              D507, D511, D530, D545.M3, .V3, D548,
                              D568.3, JN2562   944.081,
                              940.410922, .4144, .425, .427, 327.42044
Joseph, Archduke, 1872-1962 [Aust.-Hung.: Gen.]   D556, UA672   940.464436,
                              355.309436
Joseph Ferdinand, Archduke, 1872-1942 [Aust.-Hung.: Gen.] UA672   355.309436
Journalism, Military
Jungle warfare   U167.5.J
Junkers airplanes   TL686   623.7463
Just war doctrine   B105, BT736   261.873
Jutland, Battle of, 1916   D580-1, D582.J8   940.456

Kamio, Mitsuomi, 1876-1925   [Japan: Gen.]   D572.T75, DA47.9.J3, UA847
                              940.423, 355.00952, 327.42052
Karl I, 1887-1922   [Aust.-Hung.: Emperor of Austria]   DB92
Károli von Nagykároly, Mihály Count, 1875-1955 [Aust.-Hung.: Pr. Min. of Hung.]
      DB950.K3, DB925, DB65   943.603, .9
Kato, Takaaki, 1860-1926   [Japan: For. Aff. Min.]   DS518.4, DS740.4,
                     DS886, DA47.9.J3   327.51, .42051, 329.951
Kemal Atatürk, 1881-1938   [Tur.: Gen., Pres.]   DR592.K4, DR589, D568.3, .7,
                     DK511.C2   956.1, 940.425, .438, 923.1561
Kemal Pasa, Mustafa   [SEE Kemal Atatürk]
Kemmel, Battles of, 1918   D541-2
Kerensky, Aleksandr Fedorovich, 1881-1970   [Rus.: Min. of Justice, ...War,
      Politician] DK254.K3, DK264.8, DK265.19, DK265.8.L4   947.0841,
      947.450841, 320.947, 327.47
Keyes, Roger John Brownlow, 1872-1945   [G.B.: Adm. o/t Fleet]   DA89.1.K4,
      DA70.A1, D581, D594, VA454   359.00941, .3310924, 940.458, .45942
Kitchener, Horatio Herbert, 1850-1916   [G.B.: 1st Earl of Khartoum, Field Marshal,
      State Sec. for War]   DA68.32.K6, D546, U51, UB225.G7
                              942.080924, 355.3310942
Kites (Military and naval reconnaisance)   UG670
Kolchak, Aleksandr Vasilevich, 1874 [1873?]-1920   [Rus.: Vice Adm.]
      DK56, DK265, D585   947.0841, 940.45947

Komarów, Battle of, 1914
Konigsberg (Cruiser)   D582.K6, D576   940.416
Kornilov, Larr Georgievich, 1870-1918   [Rus.: Gen. of Infan.]   DK265, .2,
                DK265.8.L4   947.0841, .450841
Krafft von Dellmensingen, Konrad, 1862-1953   [Ger.: Gen.]   D521, D569.C3, .I7,
                CR5327   940.431, 929.71
Krivoshein, Aleksandr Vasilevich, 1858-1921   [Rus.: Min. of Agric.]   DK254.K754,
                DK260, JN6515.1907   947.08, 320.94708
Kronprinz Wilhelm (Cruiser)   D582.K7
Kühlmann, Richard von, 1873-1948   [Ger.: For. Sec.]   DD231.K85, DD120.R8,
                DD228, .8, D515   940.311, .3243, .343, 923.243

Landing craft
Landing operations
Langemarck, Battle of, 1914   D541-2
Lanrezac, Charles Louis Marie, 1852-1925   [Fr.: Gen.]   D507, D530, D542.M7,
        D544, D545.M3, D548   940.30922, .4140922, .421
Lansing, Robert, 1864-1928   [U.S.: Sec. of State]   E768.L32, E766, E780,
                D579.A2, D619, D644, D647.A2   973.913,
                940.31410922, .3142, .32273, 327.20924, .73052
Last letters before death   D811
Latvia—History
Lawrence, Thomas Edward ('Lawrence of Arabia'), 1888-1935   [G.B.: Mil. adventurer]
        D568.L421-45, DS94, U240, Z8491   941.0830924, 940.4150924,
        953.542, 355.4250922, 910.4153, 923.452, .542, 016.9404150924
Le Cateau, Battle of, 1914   D544-5
Leachman, Gerard, 1880-1920   [G.B.: Lt. Col.]   U55.L347
Leadership   UB210 (mil.), VB203 (naval)   355.4, 359.6
Leaflets dropped from aircraft   HE9739
League of Nations   JX1974-5, D442, D642, D644, D650, D727   309.1043,
                327.116, .170973 (U.S.), 341.08, .1209, .22, .26, 963.056
Lee-Enfield rifle   UD395   623.442
Legates, Papal   BX1908
Leipzig Trials, 1921
Lemborg, Battle of, 1914   D556, D557.L4
Lenin, Vladimir Ilich, 1870-1924   [Orig. 'Bronshtein, Lev Davidovich': Rus.: Head
        of the U.S.S.R.]   DK254.L4, DK246, DK262, DK265, DK267-8, D412, B4249,
        HF1028, HX40, HX312, JN6598   947.08410924, .8410924, 320.53220947,
        .947084, 322.4209, 329.947, 331.880947, 335.43082, .430947, 923.247
Leopold, 1846-1930   [Ger.: Prince of Bavaria, Field Marshal on the Eastern
        Front]   DD85, DD120.R8   940.3243, 920.043
Lettow-Vorbeck, Paul von, 1870-1964   [Ger.: Gen. in E. Africa]   DD231.L4,
                D576.G3, D651.G3   940.31424, .91
Letts   [Latvia: post-WWI terr. ?]   DK511.L17, D561.L4
Lewis machine-gun   UF620.L   355.82
Liberator pistol   UD413   355.82
Libya—History   DT224-235   961.2-203
Liechtenstein—History   DB540.5   943.648
Liggett, Hunter, 1857-1935   [U.S.: Gen.]   D570, .2, .27.1st   940.412
Liman von Sanders, Otto, 1855-1929   [Ger.: Gen. at Gallipoli]   D566, DD120.G3,
                DR588   327.430561
Limanova, Battle of, 1914   D551-2
Limited war   UA11   355.0215
Lithuania—History

Lloyd George, David, 1863-1945 [G.B.: Prime Min.] D546.L5, D517, DA566,
    DA577, HN385   941.0830924, .0930924, 942.0810924,
    .0830924, 940.341, .40942, 309.142082, 923.242
Lodge, Henry Cabot, 1850-1924 [U.S.: Sen.]   E664.L7, D643, JX1975
                     973.90924, 328.730924, 923.273
Lodz, Battle of, 1914   D551-2
Logistics   U168   355.411, .621, 658.7
Logistics, Naval   V179, VE353   359.41, .621+, 355.41
London
    —Air defenses, Military
    —Bombardment, 1917-1918   D547   940.44943
    —History—1800-1950   DA683   914.210373
Loos-en-Gohelle (France), Battleof, 1915   D544-5   940.424
Ludendorff, Erich, 1865-1937 [Ger.: Gen.]   DD231.L8, D531.L75-818, D507
                     943.0840924, 940.40943, .410922, .4143, 355.3310924
Luger pistol   TS537   623.443, 683.43
Lusitania (Passenger ship)
Lusitania (Steamship)   D592   940.308, .4514, .454
Lutsk (Ukraine), Battle of, 1916
Luxembourg   [SEE ALSO 'Luxemburg']   DH916   949.35
Luxemburg   [SEE ALSO 'Luxembourg']   DH916   949.35
Lys, Battle of the, 1918   D544-5
Macedonia—History—1912-1945   D562.M32
Macedonian question   DR2242, DR381, DR701   320.94976, 949.7
Machine-guns   UF620, VF410 (naval)   355.547, .82+, 623.4424
Mackensen, August von, 1849-1945 [Ger.: Field Marshal]   DD231.M2, DD85,
                     D557.G6, CR5327   920.043, 929.71
Madagascar   DT468-9   916.91+, 969.1+
Malinov, Alexander, 1867-1938   [Bulg.: Min., Pres.]   DR87.7, D20, HD815.S74,
                     JN9609.A8   322.440924, 329.94977
Manila (Philippine Islands)
Mannerheim, Carl Gustav Emil von, 1867-1951 [Fin.: Marshal]   DK461.M32,
                     DL1067.5.M36   948.97030924, 947.1030922, 923.5471
Mannerheim Cross
Maps, Military   UA985-97 (mil. geog.), UG470 (topog., surveys), U408, UC30
                     526.8, 623.71
    —Symbols   UG470-3
Marasesti, Battle of, 1917   D565
Marasesti (Romania), Battle of, 1917   D565
March, Peyton Conway, 1864-1955   [U.S.: Gen.] D570.M35, U53.M35
                     355.3310924, 940.373, .41273
Marghiloman, Alexandru, 1854-1925   [Rum.: Pr. Min.]   DR217, D651.R6   949.8
Mariana Islands   DU645   996.7
Maritime law   JX4408-49 (int'nal. law), JX6311 (private), HE585-7 (shipping laws)
                     333.9164+, 341.448, .45-762+, 343.096+, 347.75+
Marne, Battle of the, 1914   D544, D545.M3, D515   940.421
Marne, 2d Battle of the, 1918   D544-5
Marshall, William, Sir, 1865-1939 [G.B.: Gen.]   D521, D546   940.4
Marshall Islands
Martial law   JX4595 (int'nal. law)
    —United States   JX343-55, KF223, KF5063   342.73062, 344.0973,
                     345.730231
Marwitz, Georg von der, 1856-1929 [Ger.: Gen.]   D507, D530   940.30922,
                     .4140922

Masaryk, Tomas [Thomas] Garrigue, 1850-1937   [Aust.-Hung.: Pres. of Czech.]
   DB217.M3, DB215, DB2191.M38, D521.M43, D558, D619, DS141.M33
   943.7020922-7030922, 940.32273, 320.50924, 923.1437
Mass casualties   355.48
Massachusetts—History—1865-1950
Massaua, Eritrea—Harbor
Masurenland, Battles of, 1914-1915   D551-2
Maude, Frederick Stanley, Sir, 1864-1917 [G.B.: Gen.]   DA69.3.M3, D507, D546
                              940.3-4
Mauser rifle   UD395, TS536   623.44231, 683.42
Max, Prince of Baden, 1867-1929 [Ger.: Chanc.]   DD231.M3, DD85, DD248
                             943.085, 920.043, 940.4
Mayo, Henry Thomas, 1856-1937 [U.S.: Adm] D611   940.45
McAdoo, William Gibbs, 1863-1941   [U.S.: Sec. of State] E748.M14, HJ8117
                                973.9130924, 923.273
Mechanization, Military—Germany
Medals, Military and naval   UB430-5 (mil.), VB330-5 (naval), UC530, NK6302
           355.134, .134075, .13409, 737.2
Medicine, Military   RC970-1 (med. practice), UH223 (mil. sci.), UH393
Medicine, Naval   RC981-6, VG228   614.864, 616.98024
Mediterranean region—Strategic aspects
Melanesia—History
Memorials
Merchant marine
   —France   D779.F8   940.545944
   —Great Britain   HE823, HF3505   382.0941-0942, 387.5142, .70942, .506541
   —Norway   D779.N6
   —Russia   D779.R9
   —United States   HD6976, HE741-6, VK23, VK160   343.7309602632,
           353.008775, .82, 387.50973, .5173, .5440973
Merchant seamen   VK221   658.373875
Merchant ships, American   VM7   387.24
Merchant ships—United States
Mercier, Désiré Joseph, 1851-1926   [Belg.: Cardinal] BX4705.M5   922.2493
Merkem (Belgium), Battle of, 1918   D541-2
Meteorology, Military
Meuse-Argonne American Cemetery, France   D639 940.46544
Mexico—History—1910-1946 F1208-34   972.081-082
Michel (Cruiser)
Micheler, Joseph Alfred, 1861-1931   [Fr.: Gen.]   D548, DC17.9.C7, DC342.P4,
                        DC387   944.08, .0810924, 929.1
Micronesia—History   DU500   996.5, 919.65
Midshipmen   V415, VB315.G7 (GB)   359.071173 (US)
Militarism   JX1937-64, U21, UA10   355.01-02, .082, .09
Military administration   UB87, UB145, UA649   355.609+, 355+
Military architecture   NA490-7 (architec.), UG460 (mil. sci.)   725.180902
Military art and science   U, U43, U102-4   355, 355.009+, .02, .109+
   —Abbreviations   U26   355.00148
   —Dictionaries   U24-6   355.003, 623.03
   —History   U27-43, U823, U873, UA702, UG320, V33   355.009,
           .009+, .0209+, .09+, .409+
   —Terminology   U26
Military assistance, American   UA12, UA23   355.00715, .0320973,
           343.73019, .73074, 338.473550320973
Military assistance, British

Military attachés   UB260   355.3432
Military attachés, American
Military attachés, British
Military bases, American
Military biography   U51-5, CT220, CT6900   355.00922, .330922,
       .3310922, .3320922, 923.2
Military bridges   UG335   623.6709+
Military calls   M1270, UH40-5
Military ceremonies, honors, and salutes   U350-65, U353 (US), U408 (US),
       U766 (US)   355.00973 (US), .1709+
Military courts   [For martial law]   341.32
Military departments and divisions—United States
Military dependents   UB400-405
Military discipline   UB790-5, KF7590 (US)   343.73014 (US)
Military education   U400-714   355.0007, .07
  —United States   U408-10, U429   355.0071173, .071173, .11520973,
       613.7071173
Military engineering   UG
Military ethics   U22
Military field engineering   UG360-90
Military funerals—United States   UG633   355.17
Military geography   UA985-97   355.47
Military geology   UG465
Military government   JF1820, JX5003   322.5, 341.32, .320991
Military helicopters   TL716, UC333, VG93   353.007232, 355.83, 358.4183
Military history   D25, U27-43 (mil. sci.)   904.7, 940.28, 355.0009,
       .033,.43, .48, 909
  —Bibliography   Z6724, D25, U27-43   016.355009, 355.009, .0009
Military history, Modern   U39-42, D295, D361, D217   904.7, 940.28
  —19th century   D396   355.48, 904, 909.8
  —20th century   D431   909.824
Military intelligence   UB250-70, U220   355.34, .3432, .34320904, .43, 342.73085
Military law   UB461-736   343+
  —United States   KF26-7, KF7204-7210, KF7250, KF7305, KF7606-7609
       343.7301-730184, 355.000973, .133
Military libraries   Z675.M5   026.355, 027.65
Military maneuvers   UD250-5, UD460-5, U250   355.5
Military miniatures   NK494, NK8475, TT154, U311   745.59, .592, .59282,
       .59282075
Military missions   UA16
Military museums   U13   355.0074013 (US)
Military music   M1270
Military music, American [English, German, etc.]
Military music, American   ML1311, ML3930   784.71973, 785.0671, .130973
Military music, English—History and criticism   ML1331   784.71942
Military music, German
Military music, Russian
Military necessity   JX5135.M5
Military nursing   UH347, UH495   355.345+
Military occupation   JX4093, JX5003, U408   341.32, .63, .66, 355.4
Military occupation damages
Military oceanography   V396-396.5   551.46
Military offenses
  —United States   KF7609   343.7301+

Military paraphernalia
   —Collectors and collecting   U790   355.14075, .8075, .80942
   —Germany   UC465   329.943
   —Prices—Great Britain   U790   355.82
Military planning
   —Germany—History—20th century   U162
   —Soviet Union
Military policy   UA11, HC101, U104, VA19   355.00184, .0215-02184,
    .03301821, .0335, .03350904, .4307, .4509485, 358.39, 623.4
Military posts
   —California   F862   979.4
   —United States   UA26, VE422   355.70973, 359.96
Military railroads   UG345, UG128, UC313   355.27, 358.25, 625.27
Military reconnaisance   U220   355.413
Military research   U390-5   353.00711
   —Indexes   016.3550973 (US)
   —United States   U393, UG633, VE353   355.0072073, .033573, .070973,
    358.4070973, 359.96, 623.072
Military reservations—United States
Military roads   UG330
Military service as a profession   U53, UB147, UB323, UB413   355.0023,
    .0071173, .069, .1023, .220973
Military service, Compulsory   UB340-55   355.2250973 (US)
   —Draft resisters   UB341-5   355.22509+, .2236+
   —United States   UB323, UB343, UB353   343.73012, 355.220973,
    .2230973, .22360973, .2250973
Military service, Voluntary   UB320-5   355.2236
Military social work   UH750-69
Military supplies   UC260-7   355.6213+, 620.0045, 623.75
Military symbols   U26
Military telephone   UG620
Military topography   UG470
Military training camps
Miliukov, Paul Nikolaevich, 1859-1943   [Rus.: Min. of For. Aff.]   DK254.M52,
    DK260, DK63, JN6598.K95   947.080924, 329.947
Millerand, Alexandre, 1859-1943   [Fr.: Min. of War]   D548, D568.3, DC342.8.J4,
    DC373.S3, HX263.M57   944.08150924, 940.425, 320.944081, 923.244
Milne, Archibald Berkeley ('Arky Barky'), Sir, 1855-192?   [G.B.: Adm.]   D580,
    D582.G7, VA454   359.00941
Milne, George Francis, 1866-1948   [G.B.: Baron, Field Marshal]   D546, D569.2,
    DA69   940.41496, 355.3310924
Milner, Alfred, 1854-1925   [G.B.: Viscount, Sec. of State]   DA566.9.M5,
    DA18.M5, DT776, DT927, JN276   941.0830924,
    942.083, 325.3106341, .310968, .34209687, 923.242, 968.04
Mine sweepers
Mines, Military   UG490
Mines, Submarine   UG490-7
Miniature heraldic porcelain   NK4210   738.27
Misi´c, Zivojin, 1855-1921 [Serbia: Field Marshal]   DR359.M58, DR2012.5.M58,
    D561, D569.2   940.41496, .42
Mitchell, William ('Billy'), 1879-1936   [U.S.: Gen.]   UG633.M45, D606
    358.413320924, 355.3320924, 940.44973, 923.573
Mobile communication systems   TK6570   384.5453, 621.38413, 629.277
Mojkovac (Montenegro), Battle of, 1916

Moltke, Helmuth von ('The Younger'), 1848-1916 [Ger.: Gen.]   DD231.M8, D507,
                    D515, D531   943.0810924, 940.311, .410922
Monetary gold confiscations
Monro, Charles Carmichael, Sir, 1860-1929 [G.B.: Gen.]   DA69.3.M54, D546
                                                            923.242
Mons, Battle of, 1914   D541, D542.M7   940.421
Montdidier (Somme, France), Battle of, 1918   D544-5
Monte Cimone, Battle of, 1916   D569.M
Monte Novegno, Battle of, 1916   D569.M
Monte Piano, Battles of, 1915-1917   D569.M
Montecuccoli degli Erri, Rudolf Count von, 1843-1922   [Aust.-Hung.: Adm.]
                    VA454   359.00943+, .00941
Montello, Battle of, 1918   D569.M
Monuments
Moral rearmament   BJ10.M6   248.2508, .25081
Morale   HM291, D810.P6, D810.U22   301.1522, 355.123
Morocco—History—20th century   DT317, DT324   964.03-04
Mortars (Ordnance)   UF560-5
Motor-boats   D771, VM341, VM357, VM771   623.8231, .82314-82315,
                    .8723, .88, .8823
Motor-trucks, Military   UG615-20   623.7472
Motor vehicles, Amphibious   TL229.A (technology), V880 (naval sci.)   623.747
Motorization, Military   UC340-5
Mountain guns   UF440-5
Mountain warfare   U240
Moving-pictures in propaganda
Müller, Georg Alexander von, 1854-1940   [Ger.: Adm.]   D531, D581, DD228-9,
                    VA513   359.00943, 030943, 943.084
Munitions   HD9743 (econ.), JX5390 (int'nal. law), UF530-7 (manufacture), JX1907,
          U102, UF520   338.4735582, .476234, 382.4535582, .453583
     —Germany   UF535   623.0943
     —United States   HD9743, UF533   338.476230973, 343.73025,
                    355.033573, .62110973, 382.456234, 658.80935582
Music and war
Mutiny
     —Germany   D639   940.45943

National cemeteries—United States   E160, E494, UB393-4   343.73025,
                    353.00866, 355.115, .69, 362.8
National characteristics   CB197, CB203, D443   914.03, 940.5, 901.9
National characteristics, American   E169, E173, E784, B1649, BF755
               917.3039+, .303917-303918, 136.4973, 155.8973, 301.3260973
National characteristics, British   DA110   914.2
National characteristics, English   DA118   914.203+
National characteristics, German   DD76, DD256   914.30631, 155.8943, 320.943
National characteristics, Russian   DK32, DK268, DK276   914.7+
National German-American Alliance   D620   940.31530145343073
National security   UA10   355.0335
National Service Board for Religious Objectors   UB342.U5.N2
National War College (U.S.)

Naval architecture   VM, VM15, VM142, VM162   623.8, .81082, .8122, .84,
                      .88, .891
  —Bibliography   Z6834   623.8016
Naval art and science   V, V103, V107, V143, V163, VA50   359, .03+, .4, .43
  —Dictionaries   V23-4   359.003, .03, 387.03, 623.803, .8903
  —History   V25-55   359.009, .00904, .009046, .0091822, 623.82
Naval auxiliary vessels   V865
Naval aviation   VG90-5
Naval battles   D27, D436, V163   359.00903, 359.48, 904.7, 940.2
Naval biography   V61-5, D-F (partic. #s by country)   359.09, .33109+
Naval ceremonies, honors, and salutes   V310
Naval convoys—History—20th century   D771
Naval discipline
  —United States   359.1334
Naval districts
  —United States   VA62.5-7
Naval education   V400-695
  —United States   V411   359.54
Naval gunnery   VF, VF145, VF160   359.82, 623.418
Naval history   D27, D362, VA573   359.009, 904, 909, 940.2
Naval history, Modern   D27, D215, D436   359, 359.03, .40903, 909
Naval history—Sources—Bibliography   Z6616   016.35900722
Naval law   VB350-785
  —United States   KF7368   343.73019
Naval maneuvers   V245
Naval museums   V13
Naval offenses   VB850-80
  —United States   VB853   359.1332
Naval prints
Naval prints, American   NE957   769.49359
Naval reconnaisance   V190
Naval research
  —United States   V393   623.808
Naval reserves   VA
Naval stores
Naval strategy   V160-5, V103   359.43
Naval tactics   V167-78   359.42+
Naval War College (U.S.)
Navies   VA10, VA40   359.009+, .03, .1409+, 623.825
Navies and warships   623.825058
Navies, Cost of
Navies
  —History—Congresses   V51   359.009
  —Officers   VB310   355.33023
  —Yearbooks   V10   623.82505
Navigation   VK145, VK149, VK555, VK559, VM341   623.8, .89, .892, 629,
                      629.045, .89
Navigation (Aeronautics)   TL586-9, TL507, TL521, TL546   629.125, .1325,
                      .13251, .1351
  —Handbooks   TL586   629.13251
Navy-yards and naval stations   V22-40, VA67-7 (by country)
Navy-yards and naval stations, American
Navy-yards and naval stations
  —California—San Diego
  —United States

Negro soldiers
　—United States　[SEE 'Afro-American soldiers' for titles after about 1969]
　　　　　　　　　E185　　　355.00917496, .330973, 973.0496073, .893
Negroes as soldiers
Netherlands
　—History—Wilhelmina, 1898-1948
Neufchâteau, Battle of, 1914　　　D544-5
Neurath, Konstantin von, 1873-1956　　[Ger.: For. Min. (1932-8), Reich Protector of
　Bohemia-Moravia]　　DD247.N4　　943.0860924
Neutrality　　JX5355-97, JA37　　341.3, .35, .64, 327.09045, .091716
Neutrality, Armed　　JX5383, D295　　940.25
New Britain (Island)
New Guinea　　DU740　　919.5, 995, .3
New York (State)—History—1865-1950　　F119-120+　　917.4703, 974.7
New Zealand
　. Army
　—History　　DU418-427+　　919.31, 993.1+, .102, .1022, .10333+
　　—1870-
　　—1876-1918
Newfoundland—History　　F1122-3　　971.8
Nicholas II, 1868-1918　　[Rus.: Czar]　DK254.A, DK258-9, DK262, D511,
　D741, DD228.7.R8　　947.080922, .080924, 940.311, 923.147, 364.131
Nicholas Petrovi'c-Njegos, 1841-1921　[Montenegro: King]　DR341, DR360,
　DR2030, D511, D561, D741　　949.7101, 940.42, .311
Niedermayer, Oskar von, 1885-1948　　D568.8.V63, D640.N
Night fighting (Military science)　　U167
Night flying　　TL711　　629.132+, .1325212
Nikolai Nikolaevich ('The Younger'), Grand Duke of Russia, 1856-1929[Rus.: Gen. of
　Cav.]　DK254.N5, DK265.19, D550　　947.0841, 940.4147
Nitti, Francesco Saverio, 1868-1953　　[It.: Politician, Min. o/t Treasury]　　DG555,
　DG570, D643.A7, D651.I6, UA742　　945.08-09, 940.3141, 320.94509, 327.45
Nivelle, Robert, 1856-1924　　[Fr.: Gen.]　D544, D545.V3, D548, DC342.8.P4,
　　　　　　　　　　DC387　　944.08, .0810924, .427
Nixon, John Eccles, Sir, 1857-1921　　[G.B.: Gen.]　　D521, D546　　940.3-4
North Atlantic region—Strategic aspects
Norway
　—Foreign relations
　—History　　DL449-534+　　914.81, 948.1+
　　—1905-1940
Noske, Gustav, 1868-1946　[Ger.: Socialist politician]　　DD247.N63, DD85
　　　　　　　　　　　　　　　　　　　920.043
Noyon (France), Battle of, 1917-1918　　D544-5
Nuncios, Papal

Obstacles (Military science)
Occupation currency　　H31　　940.53144
Oceania　　[SEE ALSO 'Oceanica']　　DU, DU15-28+　　919, 990-999
Oceanica　　[SEE ALSO 'Oceania']　　DU, DU15-28+　　919, 990-999
Oder-Neisse area　　DD801.O35　　943.805
Oder-Neisse Line (Germany and Poland)
Offensive (Military strategy)—History—20th century U162
Official secrets
　—Great Britain　KD8024　　345.420231
　—United States　KF26　　342.7305
Operational rations (Military supplies)

Orden Pour Le Merite   D604
Ordnance   UF520-630   355.82+, 356.186+, 623.4
Ordnance, Coast
—Manufacture   UF530-45   623.4+, .41
Ordnance, Naval   VF15, VF23, VF353   359.82+, 623.4+
Orlando, Vittorio Emanuele, 1860-1952 [It.: Pr. Min.]   DG555, DG570, D520.I7,
     D569.I8, .A2, D617, D643.A7   945.09, 940.3141, 327.45
Orphans
Orphans and orphan asylums
Orphans
     —Europe
     —Great Britain   HV1148   362.73
Ortigara, Battle of, 1917   D569.O

Pacifism—History   BX7635, BX7748, JX1938, JX1944, JX1961
     261.873, 289.6, .673 (US), 327.172+
Page, Walter Hines, 1855-1918   [U.S.: Ambass. to G.B.]   E664.P15, D611
          973.80924, 940.45, 070.40924, 327.20924
Painlevé, Paul, 1863-1933   [Fr.: Min. of War, Prem.]   DC342.8.P4, DC373.S3,
          DC385, D548   944.0810922-0810924,
     320.944081
Paléologue, Georges Maurice, 1859-1944   [Fr.: Ambass. to Russia]   DC385,
     DK265.P255, D453, D741   944.08, 940.311, .3112, 320.94708
Papacy—History—20th century   BX1389   262.130904, 282, 327.45634
Paris
     —History
     . Peace Conference, 1919   D619, D643-7, D651   940.3141+, .3142, .32273
          . Hungary   D651   940.3142
          . Italy   D651   940.3141
          . Rumania   D651.R6   327.498
          . Russia   D651.R8   940.3141
          . U.S. Territorial Section   D644   940.312
     . Peace Conference, 1919-. Yugoslavia   D651   940.31425
     . Peace Conference (1919-1920)   D647.A2   940.3141
Partizanski spomenik (Mostar, Bosnia and Hercegovina)
Pasic, Nikola, 1845-1926 [Serbia: Pr. Min.]   DR359.P283, DR341, DB91, D741,
          DJK4   949.71020924, .7101, .6, 940.311, 943.604
Pasubio, Battles of, 1916-1918   D569.P
Payer, Friedrich von, 1847-1931   [Ger.: Vice Chanc.]   DD231.P3, DD228.8
          943.0840924, 940.343
Peace   JX1901-99 (int'nal. law)   172.4+, 309.2206, 320.94+, 322.43-44,
     327.17+, .172+, 341.1+, 355.027, 940.51
Peace treaties   JX5181
Pensions, Military   UB370-5 & UB400-5 (army), VB280-5 & VB340-5 (navy),
          E255 (pension rolls)
Pensions, Military and naval—United States
Pensions, Military
     —United States   UB373, UB403, KF26-7   355.115, .11510973,
          .11560973, 343.73011, 344.73011
     —European War, 1914-1918
Pershing, John Joseph ('Black Jack'), 1860-1948   [U.S.: Gen., A.E.F.
     Commander]   E181.P575, D521, D570, U53, F1234   973.913,
          940.41273, .4173, 355.3310924, .3320924, 923.573, 972.081

Psychiatry, Military   D807.U6, UB323, UH629   616.8, .89, 355.22
Psychological warfare   UB275-7, U22   355.3434, .42-3, 301.1523
Psychology, Military   U22.3, U15, UH629, HQ797   355.0019, .1156, .22,
                    .6133, 301.593, 155.93
Psychology, Naval
Public opinion   D810.P85 (WWII)
    —Germany   DD117, DD228   329.050943
    —United States   D810.P85.U5+   301.1540973
Public shelters
Putnik, Radomir, 1847-1917 [Serbia: Field Marshal]   DR360, D521, D561
                    949.7101, 940.3, .42

Queen Mary (Cruiser)

Radio in propaganda   JF1525, HE8696   327.1409+, 301.154
Radio, Military   UG610
Radoslavov, Vasil, 1854-1929   [Bulg.: Min.-Pres.]   DR72, DR217, DD120.G7
                    949.8, 327.430436
Railroads
Railroads and state   HE1051-1081, HE2757 (US), HE2801-3600 (other countries)
                    385+
    —Italy
Railroads
    —Europe   HE3004-8   385.094, .2094
    —Germany
    —Great Britain   HE3015-3020, TF57, TF64   385.0941-0942, .142, 625.18,
                    912.138531
    —History—Europe
    —Russia   HE3135-8   380.50947, 385.0947
Railway artillery   UF490-5   358.12, 623.412
Rasputin, Grigorii [Grigory] Efimovich, 1864?[1871?]-1916   [Rus.: Imper. Advisor
    & Confidant]   DK254.R3, DK262   947.080924, .0830924,
                    281.90924, 922.147
Rathenau, Walther, 1867-1922   [Ger.: Chief of Raw Mater's. Office]
                    DD231.R3, D649, DS135.G5   943.0850924, 940.31422
Rationing, Consumer
Rawlinson, Henry Seymour, Sir, 1864-1925 [G.B.: Baron Rawlinson, Gen.]
                    DA68.32.R3, D521   940.4144
Reconnaisance aircraft
Reconstruction (1914-1939)   D653-9, D638
    —Germany   D659   330.94308
    —Sources   E802   940.531440922
Red Cross   HV560-83, HV568, UH535-7 (army), VG457 (navy)   361.506, .53
    —Germany
    . U.S. American National Red Cross   UC74.R4, HV576-8, HV640   361.506,
                    .77, 362.7
Refugee property
Refugees, Political   JX4292.P6 (int'nal. law), HV640 (relief), D842, JV6477,
                    JX1907   325.21, 341.51, 361.53, 940.53159
Rennenkampf, Pavel Karlovich von, 1854-1918 [Rus.: Gen. of Cav.] DK265.2,
                    D521. D550   947.0841, 940.4147
Renunciation of war treaty, Paris, Aug. 27, 1928 [A.k.a. Treaty of Paris (1928)]
          JX1987, E748   341.2, .52, .6, .73, 923.273
Reparations
Repatriation   JX4231

Russia
—Foreign economic relations
—Germany
—United States
—Foreign relations
—1917-1945   DK63, DK66, DK265-274   327.09042, .20924, .470+,
                         341.2247, 940.532247, 947.0841

—France
—Germany   327.47043
—Great Britain   327.47041
—Japan   DK68.7.J3, DS783, DS849   327.47052
—United States E183, JX1555   327.47073, .73047
—History
—20th century   DK246, DK268, DK275   947.08+, .084-085, 914.7038
—History, Military   UA772, DK268, D550   355.00947, 940.40947,
                         355.4300924

—Politics and government—1936-1953   DK254-268, JN6598   947.0842,
                         .085, 320.9470842

—Relations (military) with Germany
. Voenno-morskoi Flot   VA573, D779.R9   359.00947, .320947, 940.545947
Russo-Japanese War, 1904-1905   DS517   952.031, .03185
Ruzsky, Nikolai Vladimirovich, 1854-1918   [Rus.: Gen. of Infan.]
                         DK265.19, .2, DK265.9.A6   947.0841

Saint-Mihiel (France), Battle of, 1918   D544-5, D548-9
Salandra, Antonio, 1853-1931   [It.: Pr. Min.]   DG575.S25, DG555, DG568.5,
                         D617, UA742   945.08-09, 327.45, 940.32245, .34502
Salazar, Antonio, 1889-1972   [Port.: Pr. Min.]   DP676.S25, DP680
                         946.9040924, 320.9469
Sapping   UG510-15
Sardar-Abad, Battle of, 1918
Sarkotic von Lovcen, Stephan, 1858-1939   [Aust.-Hung.: Baron, Gen.]   DB249,
                         UA672 355.309436
Sarrail, Maurice Paul Emmanuel, 1856-1929 [Fr.: Gen.]   DC373.S3, D545.M3,
                         D548, D569.2   944.08, 940.414, 320.944081
Sazonov, Sergei Dmitrievich, 1860-1927   [Rus.: Min. of For. Affairs]DK254.S35,
      DK260, DK264.8, DR48.5   940.311, 320.947, 327.47
Scapa Flow   D581, V65   940.453094112, .5451
Scapa Flow Scuttling, Scotland, 1919
Scharnhorst (Battleship)   [WWI (armoured cruiser) & II (battle cruiser): 2 ships]
                         D771, D772.S35   940.545, .5459, .545941-3
Scheer, Reinhard, 1863-1928 [Ger.: Adm.]   D581, VA454   940.45
Schleissheim (Displaced persons camp)
Schlieffen Plan
Schmidt, Battle of, 1944
Schmidt von Knobelsdorf, Constantin, 1860-1936   [Ger.: Gen.] DD231.F3, D531
Science and state—Germany—History—20th century   D804.G4   940.5405
Scotland—History—20th century

Sea control
Sea-power   V25, V17, VA10, VA50, VA513, VA573   359.0309, .409, .43,
     355.0308, 327.1109, 325.308
Seamanship—History   VK541   623.809
Seamen   G225, G545   359.109
Seamen
    —[country]—Biography
    —Great Britain—Biography
    —United States—Biography   E207, V63   359.3380924, 973.350924
Seaplanes   TL684   629.13334709, 387.733470904
Search and rescue operations   TL553.8, VG55   353.0075, 359.9709
Search, Right of   JX5268   323.4
Security classification (Government documents)
    —United States   JK468, KF26-7, KF4774, KF7695   342.7304, .73068,
     .73085, 343.73013, .730531, 353.00714, 355.61, 364.131, 328.7305-07
Seeckt, Hans von, 1866-1936 [Ger.: Gen.]   DD231.S47, U55.S38
     355.3320924
Seicheprey, Battle of, 1918   D544-5
Seizure of vessels and cargoes   HJ6645   353.0074
Self-determination, National   JX4054   320.13, .158, 323.1, 341.26, .52
Senussite Rebellion, 1916-1918
Serbia   DR317, DR360   949.71
    —Foreign relations
      —Europe
      —Russia   DR327   327.4704971
    —History—1804-1918   DR341, DR360   949.7101
Shcherbachev, Dmitry Grigorevich, 1857-1932   [Rus.: Gen. of Infan.]
     DK265.2, D550   947.0841, 940.4147
Ship-building   VM, VM15, VM144-6, VM298   623.8, .823, .809, 387.209
    —United States—History   VM23, VM140, VM299   623.8203, 387.50973,
     359.830973, 338.4762382
Ship-building workers
Ships—History   VM15-23, VM121, VM307, VK20   387.209, .2074013,
     .20977, .09687, 623.82009, .821
Ships' stores and Navy exchanges (United States Navy)   VC393   646.024359
Shipwrecks   JX4436 (int'nal. law), G525-30 (narratives), VK1250-99 (reports)
     910.091636, .45, .453, .45308, 904.5
Shipyards   VM12-124   623.809, .8309+, .830973 (US), 338.476238309
Shooting, Military   UD330-5, UD383   356.162, 623.442, .5, 683.409+
Sieges   JX5117 (int'nal. law)
Signals and signaling   UG570-82 (mil.), V280-5 (naval), VK385   359.983, 384.9
Signals and signaling, Submarine   VK388
Silesia, Upper (Poland and Czechoslovakia)—History—Partition, 1919-1922
Sims, William Sowden, 1858-1936   [U.S.: Adm.]   E748.S52, D589.U6
     359.3310924, 940.45973, 923.573
Singapore—History   DS598   959.5, .52, 915.952
Slavic countries—History
Slavs—History   D147   930.04918
Smith and Wesson firearms   TS537   623.443, .4434, 683.43
Smith-Dorrien, Horace Lockwood, Sir, 1858-1930   [G.B.: Gen.]   DA68.32.S5,
     D521, D544   940.4144
Smoke screens   UG447.7
Smuts, Jan Christiaan, 1870-1950 [S.Afr.: Gen., Brit. War Cabinet member (WWI);
    Pr. Min. (WWII)]   DT779.8.S6, D517   968.050924, 923.568, 940.304
Sociology, Military   U21, UA25   355.009, .022, .1209, .3, .61, 301.593

Spring Rice, Cecil Arthur, Sir, 1859-1918   [G.B.: Ambass. to the U.S.]
                              DA566.9.S65, D611   327.20924, 940.45
Springfield rifle   UD395   623.4421
Spy films—Catalogs   PN1998   016.79143
Spy stories   [fiction]
St. Mihiel, Battle of, 1918   D544-5
Stalin, Joseph [Iosif] ('Uncle Joe'), 1879-1953   [U.S.S.R.: Dictator, Comm. in Chief
     o/t Armed Forces]   DK268.S8, DK267, DK274, D764, D16, DS740, HX40
                             947.080924, .08420924, .085, 940.540947, 320.9470842,
                             335.4, 355.4300924, 923.247, 951.042
Stamboliski, Alexander, 1879-1923   [Bulg.: Politician]   DR88.S77, D643.B6,
     HD815.S74, JN9609.A8   320.94977, 322.440924, 329.94977
Stanley, Edward George Villiers, 1865-1948 [G.B.: Earl of Derby, Sec. of State for
     War, Ambass. to Fr.]   DA574.D4, D546   940.40942
Sten machine carbine   UF620.S8
Strategic materials
     —United States   HC110, UA23   333.80973, 355.240973, .6213, .75
Strategy   U161-3 (mil.), V160-5 (naval), UA11   355.021, .0217, .03, .4,
                .43, .4301-07, 359.43
Stream-crossing, Military   U205, UG335   623.65
Street fighting (Military science)   U167   355.426
Stresemann, Gustav, 1878-1929   [Ger.: Politician]   DD231.S83, DD901
                             943.085, 320.94382, 940.3141, .32443
Sturdee, Frederick Charles Doveton, Sir, 1859-1925 [G.B.: Adm. o/t Fleet]
Sturgkh, Karl Count von, 1859-1916   [Aust.-Hung.: Min.-Pres.]   DB90.S8, DB80
                             943.604
Sturmer, Boris Vladimirovich, 1848-1917   [Rus.: Chair. o/t Council of Min's.]
Submachine guns   UF620.A2   355.82, 623.4424
Submarine boats   V858-9 (by country), VM365 (construc.), V210 (war use), V857
                 359.3257+, .325709, .92, 355.03+, 623.82, .825, .8257,
                 .82572+, .825720943 (Ger.), 940.5451
     —Bibliography   Z6834, V857-9   016.623825
     —History   V857-9, V210, VM365   359.325709, .3257209+, .83, 387.257
Submarine chasers   D590 (WWI)
Submarine disasters   VK1265   613.69
Submarine warfare   V210, VB230, JX1295   359.32, .3257, .4, .83, 623.825,
                 .8257, 940.451
Sugiyama, Hajime, 1880-1945 [Japan: Gen.]
Sukhomlinov, Vladimir Aleksandrovich, 1848-1926   [Rus.: Gen. of Cav., Min. of
     War]   DK254.S6, DK265.19, D550   947.0841, 940.4147
Surgery, Military   RD151-498   617.02, .99
Surgery, Naval   RD151-498
Surplus military property   UC260-5
Surplus military property, American   KF26-7   353.00713, 355.6213
Survival (after airplane accidents, shipwrecks, etc.)   TL553.7, U408, VK1259,
     VK1447, G525-40   613.69, 623.865, 629.13443, 910.091641, .09165, .453
Suzuki, Kantaro, 1867-1948   [Japan: Pr. Min., 5 Apr-Aug 1945]

Sweden
    —Foreign relations—1905-1950   DL658   327.485
    —History
        —1905-   DL658+
        —Gustavus V, 1907-1950
    —Politics and government—1905-1950
Switzerland
    —History—20th century
    —Politics and government—20th century

Tactics   U133, U164-5   355.402, .42
    —Bibliography   Z6724   016.35542
Taiwan—History—1895-1945   DS799   951.24904, 320.95124904, 915.124904
Talât Pasa, Mehmed, 1874-1921   [Tur.: Min. o/t Inter., Grand Viz.]   DR584,
    DD120.G3, DS195, DS589   956.101, .62, 327.430561, 923.1561
Tank gunnery
Tank warfare   UG446, U55, D608   358.1809, .180904, 355.331+,
        623.438, 940.412
Tanks (Military science)   UG446.5, UF537   358.18, .1809+, .180941 (GB),
        .180943 (Ger.), .180973 (US), 623.7475+, 355.621, .8209, .83, 356.5
    —Pictorial works
Tannenberg, Battle of, 1914   D551, D552.T3   940.422
Telephone—Defense measures
Telescopic sights
Terrain study (Military science)
Texas (Battleship)   [WWI & II]   VA65   623.82520973
Theater in propaganda
Theater of war
Thomas, Albert, 1878-1932   [Fr.: Munitions Min., Ambass. to Rus.]   DC373.T5,
    HV28.T361, D516, D548, DK265.19   944.08, 940.344, 947.0841
Thompson submachine gun   UF620   623.4424, 683.4
Tirpitz, Alfred Peter Friedrich von, 1849-1930   [Ger.: Grand Adm.]   DD231.T5,
    VA513   359.00943, 940.45120924
Tirpitz (Battleship)   D772.T5   940.5421, .544942, .545
Tisza de Boros-Jëno, Istvan Count, 1861-1918   [Aust.-Hung.: Pr. Min.]
    DB950.T5, DB65   943.603, 923.24391
Tokyo—History   DS896-7   952.135
Torpedo-boat destroyers
Torpedo-boats   V830-8   359.32, .3254, 359.83, 940.5459+
Torpedo bombers
Torpedoes   V850-5   359.4, .82
Totalitarianism   JC481, JC233   320.53-533, 321.6-6082, .64, .9, 335.4-6
Townshend, Charles Vere Ferrers, Sir, 1861-1924   [G.B.: Gen.]   D568.5.T7
Trading with the enemy   JX5270-1   341.3, 343.73087
    —History—20th century
Transportation and state   HE148-51, HE193   350.87, 380.5, 388.109+
Transportation, Military   UC270-360, UH500-505 (med.), VC550-5   355.27,
    .341, .8309+, 623.746
    —Cold weather conditions
Tre Cime di Lavaredo, Battles of, 1915-1917   D569.T

Treason   HV6275, JC328 (polit. theory) 364.13
 —France
 —Germany
 —Great Britain 343.41
 —South Africa
 —United States KF9392, E179 343.3, 345.73023108, 351.74, 364.131
Treaties JX4161-71, JX120-191 (collections), JX235-6, JX351-1195, JA40
    341.026, .2, .273, .2016
 —Catalogs
 —Collections
Treaty of Trianon (1920) D643.H9
Trench mortars
Trials (Crimes against humanity)
Trials (Genocide)
Trials (Military offenses) 355.1332+
Trials (Naval offenses)
Trials (Political crimes and offenses) KF221 (US) 345.730231 (US),
    .47023 (Russia), .023
Trianon, Treaty of, June 4, 1920
Trianon, Treaty of, June 4, 1920 (Hungary) D651.H7, D643 940.3141-3142
Trieste
 —History DB321 943.68
 —Politics and government DB321, DG975 320.945393, 327.450497
Trophies, Military
Trotha, Adolf von, 1868-1940 [Ger.: Adm.] DD231.T86, V65.T7, VA513
    359.030943, .00943
Trotsky, Leon, 1879-1940 [A.k.a. 'Trotskii, Lev': Rus.: Politician] DK254.T6,
   DK265, HC335, HX312 947.083, .0840924, 327.47,
   330.947084, 335.433, 345.470231, 347.9947, 349.4704, 923.247
Trowbridge, Ernest Charles Thomas, 1862-1926 [G.B.: Adm.] DA565.T7, D580
Tunisia—History—French occupation, 1881-1956 DT264 961.1
Turkey
 —Foreign relations
  —Europe
  —Germany
  —Great Britain DR562 327.4961042
 —Politics and government—1909-1918 DR584 956.101
Turret ships V860
Twentieth century CB425-7 (civiliz.), D401-725 (hist.), D421, D840
    940.5, 914.035, 901.904, .94, .946, 909.82, 301.24
Twentieth Century Fund. Labor Committee HD8072 331.0973
Tyrwhitt, Reginald Yorke, Sir, 1870-1951 [G.B.: Adm.]

Ukraine
 —History DK508 947.7, .71
  —German occupation, 1941-1944 D764 947.7
Unified operations (Military science) U260 (jt. ops. of one nation's service branches)
Uniforms, Military UC480-5, UA712, UE445, VC300 355.14, .1409+, .14094,
    .81, 357.1, 359.14094
United Nations—History JX1976-7 341.1309, .23, .2309+

United States
. Army   U716, UA22-7   355.00973, .033573, .10973, .30973
  . 12th
  . A.E.F., 1917-1920   [SEE ALSO 'U.S. Army. American Expeditionary
         Forces']   D570   940.40973, .412, .41273, .431
    . Air Service   D606   940.44973
    . Games Committee   GV721
    . Services of Supply   D570.75
  . Aero Squadron
    —103d (Lafayette Flying Corps)
  . 95th Aero Squadron   D570   940.44973
    . 104th Aero Squadron   D606   940.44973
  —Afro-American troops   [SEE ALSO '...—Negro troops']   D639, E185
         917.80696, 355.330973, .61330973, 356.110973
  . Air Corps   UG633, D606, E745   358.400973, .413320924,
         940.44973, 973.913
. Army Air Forces   UG633, UG1242, D790   358.4, .4030973,
         .4140973, 940.544973

. Army
  —Ambulances   UH503
  . American Expeditionary Forces   [SEE ALSO 'U.S. Army. A.E.F.']
    —History   D570, D528
  . American Forces in Germany, 1918-1923   D650.M5
  —Anecdotes, facetiae, satire, etc.
. Army and Navy Munitions Board. Industrial Mobilization Plan   UA23, HB195
         355.20973

. Army
  —Appointments and retirements   UB413
  —Appropriations and expenditures   UA24.A7, UA25   353.62
  . Armored Force   UA30   358.180973
  —Armored troops
  . First Army   D570.2, D763   940.41273, .53493
  . 2d Army
  . Artillery   UA32-3, UF23, UF153   358.10973, 356.4
    —Drill and tactics   UE160
  —Barracks and quarters   UC403-4   355.6220973
  —Bibliography   Z6725   016.35560973, .940540973
  —Biography   E181, E840.5.A-Z, U11, U52   355.30922, .330973
  . Cavalry   UA30, UE23   357.10973
  . Chaplain Corps   UH23   355.34, .3470973
  . Coast Artillery   UF453, UF625
  . Corps of Engineers   UG23   355.6213, 356.94, 358.20973
  . Corps of Military Police
  . Demobilization
  . 42d Division   [Rainbow Division]
  . 101st Division
  —Drill manuals
  . European Theater of Operations
  —Examinations   U408, UG610   355.07, .338076, 623.7348
  . Field Artillery   UF403   358.12
  —Finance   UC23
  —Firearms   UD383-4, UD395 (rifles)   355.62120973, .82, 623.440973,
         .4420973, .4425
  —Foreign Service

United States
  —Army
    . 1st Gas Regiment. Company E
    . General Hospital No. 30   D629   940.547673
    —Guard duty   U193
    —Handbooks, manuals, etc.   U113, U133, U408, UB413
        355.00911, .0973, .4209597
    —History   UA23-5, E181   355.00973, .033573, .30973, .3510973,
        .1150973
      —Bibliography   Z1249   106.355
      —Sources—Bibliography   Z6725, CD3033   106.97389
      —World War, 1939-1945
    —Indian troops   E99   970.3
    . Infantry   UA28-9, UD23   356.110973, 959.7043373, .70434
    . 107th Infantry   D570   940.4143
    . Infantry, 339th—History [Exped. force in N. Russia, 1918-19]
                                            D570.33.339th
    . 369th Infantry (Colored)   D570.33.369th   940.41273
    . 371st Infantry (Colored)   D570   940.41273
    . Infantry Division, 42nd—History   ['Rainbow Division']   D570.3.42d
    . Infantry
      —Drill and tactics   UD160, U15   355.54, 356.10973, .18
      —History   UA28, D769   940.541273
    . Infantry Regiment, 369th   [Afro-Am. unit from N.Y.]   D570.33.369th
                                            940.41273
    . Judge Advocate General
    —Maneuvers   U253
    —Medals, badges, decorations, etc.   UC533, CR4509
  . Army Medical Department   UH223   355.3450973
  . Army Medical Service
  . Army
    —Military construction operations
    —Military life   U766, UA25, D570, E745   355.00973, .10973,
        .12920924, .3380973, .54097
    . Military Railway Service   UG523   356.95, 358.2
    —Mobilization   UA913   355.280973
    —Negro troops   [SEE ALSO '...Afro-Am. troops']   D639, E185, U21
        940.403, 917.80696, 355.00917496, .30978, .330973,
        .61330973, 356.110973
    —Non-commissioned officers UB210   355.547
    —Officers UB412-14, UB210   355.0023, .33, .332019,
        301.1543355332
    —Officers' handbooks   U133   355.02, 356.3
    —Ordnance and ordnance stores   UF523-63, UF753, U897
        355.830973, .820973, 343.73025, 623.40973, .440973
    —Organization UA23-33   355.00973, .3
    —Pay, allowances, etc. UC70-5, UB403   355.135, .640973
    —Physical training U323, U408
    —Pictorial works
    —Political activity
    —Postal service
    —Prisons   KF7675   355.71
    —Procurement   UC263-7, UF780   355.62120973, .82, 358.18,
        .4183, 338.43641371, 343.73013
    —Promotions   UB412-14

United States
—Defenses   UA23   355.02130973, .033273, .033573, .6220973,
              358.4030973, 327.730599, 353.00895, .60924
. Department of State   JK851, JX1293, JX1417, JX1428, JX1705-6
                          327.072073, .6073, .73, 353.00712, .007232
    . Historical Office
    —History
    . Office of Public Affairs
    —Records and correspondence
. Department of the Army
    . General Staff—History   UB200   355.3310973
    . Office of Military History   D570   940.41273
—Diplomatic and consular service   JX1705-6, JK851   327.20973,
                                      341.70973, 353.00892, 355.033573

    —Germany
    —Great Britain
    —Italy
    —Russia
—Economic conditions
    —1865-1918   E661, HC105-6, HD8051   917.3038, 330.97308,
                   .9730913, 309.17308, 333.70973, 339.20973
    —1918-1945   HC106.3-4, HC101, E801   330.973091, 339.20973,
                   309.1730917
. Embassy
    . Germany
    . Great Britain
    . Russia
    . Soviet Union
—Emigration and immigration   JV6403-7127, E158, E184
                325.7309, 301.3230973, .32845073, .32847073,
                .4534073, 331.880973, 917.30356, .309749162
. Employment Service   HC101, HD5873-5   330.973, 331.1106173,
                         .110973, .13770973, 353.008485
—Executive departments   JK631-821 328.7307+, 342.730602+, .73064,
                           353.0002-0003, .00722, .008236, .01-09
    —Records and correspondence   CD3030-3041, KF5101   342.73066,
                                    353.0372
. Food Administration   D637   940.477873
. Foreign Claims Settlement Commission [WWII]   KF27   341.55, 353.00892
—Foreign economic relations HF1455-6, HF73, HC106   330.973, 337.9173,
                338.9173, .973, 343.73+, 353.008, 382.0973, .10973
    —Germany   HF1456   338.9173043, 382.0973043
    —Great Britain   382.0973042
    —Russia
—Foreign relations   JX1405-28, JX1971, JX1987, E183, E713
                       320.973, 341.2373, 343.73+, 909.82
    —20th century   JX1416-17, JX1916, D413, D570, E173, E744-8, E840
                      327.062073, .20973, .730+, 330.973, 973.92+
    —Germany   E183, E748   327.73043, .43073, .9613,
                 943.086, 973.917+
    —Great Britain   E183, E664   327.73041-2, .42073
    —Italy   327.73045
    —Japan   E183, DS518, JX233   327.73052, .52073, .5073,
               301.15439152, 940.5312
    —Law and legislation KF4650-1   328.730765, 342.7306-73064, 353.00892

United States
—Foreign relations
    —Russia   E173, E183, E744, E748, JX1974-81, D651, DK69
        327.73047, .47073
    —Speeches in Congress   E173 (collections)
    —Treaties   JX570-3, JX235-6 (texts), JX1407   341.273, .762026,
        .7304, 328.7307+
. General Staff
—Government publications   Z1223 (bibliog.), Z208, Z695, Z7164   015.73,
        016320973, .01573, .309173, .320973, .32873
—Historical geography—Maps
—History   E, F1-975+ (local), E178   973+, 974-9 (local)
    —20th century   E740-2, E173   973.9, .9082, .91, .916
    —1901-1953   E740-1, E766   973.9, .91, .913
    —1913-1921   E766, E780   973.91, .913
    —1919-1933   E741, E784-91, E806   973.91, .914-15, .917,
        .9108, 917.303915, 309.173091
      —Sources   E743, E784-5, E791   973.9108, .914-17
    —Addresses, essays, lectures
    —Anecdotes, facetiae, satire, etc.   E178-9   973.08, 917.30308
    —Bibliography   Z1215, Z1236, Z8462   016.9173, .917303
      —Catalogs
    —Chronology   E174.5   973.0202, .03
—History, Comic, satirical, etc.   E178.4, NC1427   973.0207, 741.5973
—History
    —Dictionaries   E174, E18   973.03, 917.30303
    —Fiction
    —Historiography   E175   973.07
—History, Local   E175, E180, F1-970   974-9, 917.303
—History, Military   E181, E183, U133   355.420973, 357.10924, 923.573
    —20th century   E745, E840   901.9
    —Bibliography   Z1249   016.355
    —Chronology   E181   355.00973
—History, Naval   E182, E746, VA58-63   359.00973, .0973, .310973,
        .325, 387.20973
    —20th century   E746-8, E182   359.009, .3310924
    —Bibliography   Z6835   016.35900973, .35930973
    —Sources   E182   359.332+
      —Bibliography—Catalogs   Z1249, Z6616, Z6835
      016.3593310924, .359, .35900973
—History
    —Philosophy   E175.9, E179   973.01, .04, .072, 917.303013
    —Sources   E173, E178, E183   973.08, .082, .908, 917.303, .
        30308, 320.973
      —Bibliography   Z1236, Z6616, CD3027, CD3049   016.9739,
        .917303, .301450973
    —Directories   E175   973.02573
. Joint Army-Navy Assessment Committee
. Mare Island Naval Shipyard, Vallejo, Calif.   VA70.M3

United States
  . Marine Corps   UB210, UG632, VE23, VE422, D570, D767, D769,
                                  D821, TL685   359.96, .9609, .960973, 629.1339,
                                  940.45973, .5412730952, .5426, .544973, .545
     . Aviation—History   VG93, UG633   358.41830973
     —Biography   E182   359.960973, 923.573
     —History   VE23, VE21-3, E746, D767   359.960973, 940.5426
        —Anecdotes   VE500   359.960973
        —World War, 1914-1918
     . History and Museums Division
     —Insignia   VE403
     —Medals, badges, decorations, etc.   VE23
     —Military life   VE23   359.96
United States Marine Corps Reserve   VE23.3   359.960973
United States
  . Marine Corps
     —Target-practice   VE333
     —Uniforms   VE403, UC483   359.960973, 355.14, 646.47
     —Women
United States Military Academy, West Point   U408-10
     —Biography   U410   355.0071174731
     —History   U410, U408   355.0071173, .0071174731, .02130973
     . Library
     —Registers
     —Songs and music
United States Military Mission to Russia
United States
     —Military policy   UA23, UA25, UA646, V63, VE23   355.033073,
                      .0330973, .0335182, .033573, .0973, .430973, .820973,
                      .02130973, 358.4030973, 359.960973, 327.1740973, .10973
     —Bibliography   Z1215, KF7201   016.3550330973
     —Case studies   UA23   355.033573
     —History   UA23, UA25   355.00973, .033573
     —Militia   UA42   355.35
     . National Archives   CD3028, E179   016.6314, .911777, .91273, 344.73092
     —National Guard   UA42-3, U230   355.3510973, .370973, .4260973, .54,
                      343.73013
     —National security   UA23, JK1051   355.033073, .033573, 328.7307412
     . National War College   355.622, .0711753
     . National War Labor Board   [1942-5]
United States Naval Academy (Annapolis)
       . Alumni Association
       —Buildings
       . Dept. of Engineering and Aeronautics
       . Dept. of Seamanship and Navigation
       —Examinations   V415   359.071175256, 355.071173
       —History   V415, U408
       . Library
       . Museum
       —Registers
       —Songs and music
       .Trident Society
United States Naval Academy, Annapolis   V415
United States Naval Hospital, Norfolk, Va.   VG425.N6
United States Naval Institute, Annapolis

United States Naval Medical Research Institute, Bethesda, Md.
United States Naval Medical School, Bethesda, Md.
United States—Naval militia   VA80
United States Naval Observatory   QB82, Z5156   353.00855
United States Naval Photographic Interpretation Center
United States Naval Postgraduate School, Monterey, Calif.
United States Naval Research Laboratory, Washington, D.C.
United States Naval Reserve   VA80   359.370973
          —Registers
United States Naval Training Station, San Diego, Calif.
United States
     . Navy   V25, V133, V399, V736, V825, V858, V874-80, VA49-58, VB23, VM470
               359, 359.00973, .030973, .12920973, .32520973, .32540973,
                    .32620973, .830973, 623.8250973, .8257, .8433, 940.545973
          —Accounting   VC503   359.6223
          —Afro-Americans   [SEE ALSO '...—Negroes']   VB853   359.1332
          —Airmen
          —Anecdotes, facetiae, satire, etc.   E182, V736   359.00973, .10973
          —Appropriations and expenditures   VA53, V858   359.83, 343.73013
          —Artificers' handbooks   VG603   535.33
          . Asiatic Fleet   VA63.A78   359.310973
          . Atlantic Fleet   D770, VA63   940.545973, 359.310973
          —Aviation   VG93, TL685, TL721   358.400973, .41, .4183, .4140973,
                              623.4519, .74607, .7460973, .74640973, 629.130911
               —Job descriptions
          —Barracks and quarters   VC423
          —Bibliography   Z6835, E182   016.35930973, .35900973
          —Biography   E182, V23, V62-3   359.310922, .3310922,
                              .3320922, 923.573
               —Dictionaries
          —Boats   V880
          —Boatswains   VG953   623.825
          —Boatswain's mates
          . Bombing squadron 109   D790   940.544
          . Chaplain Corps   VG23
          . Civil Engineer Corps
          —Communication systems   VG77, V283   359.983, 623.8560973
          —Congresses
          . Construction battalions   [Seabees]   VG597, D769.55   359.982
               —Handbooks, manuals, etc.   VG597
          —Demobilization
     . Navy Department
               —Appropriations and expenditures
                    . Board on Regular and Reserve Aviation Personnel of the Navy and
                         Marine Corps
                    . Board on Submarine, Destroyer, Mine, and Naval Air Bases
               —History   VB23
                    . Office of Industrial Relations
                    . Office of Public Relations
               —Officials and employees   VB183
               —Personnel management

United States
. Navy
. Destroyer Forces   D773   940.545973
—Drill manuals   VD160 (seamen), VE160 (Marines), VF160 (ordnance)
—Engineering aids   VG923   526.9024359
—Examinations   V411, VB273   359.0076, .338076, 371.2640715
—Facilities
—Fiction
—Field Service   V175
—Finance   VA60   359.620973
—Firearms   VF23 (ordnance), VF353-420, VD363-90 (small arms)
                      623.440973, .442
—Firing regulations   VD333
—Flags
—Flight officers
—Fuel   VC276.A47   338.82, 359.83
—Gunners
—Gunner's mates
—Handbooks, manuals, etc.   V113, V123, V133, V143 (officers, seamen,
                      etc.), V310 (ceremonies), VA55, VB200, VM605
                      359.00202, 623.872
—History   E182, V767, V833, V874, VA55-8, VB23, D773, E746
                      359.30973, .310973, .32550973, .3320924, .370973,
                      .621, 623.82530973, 940.542, .545973, 973.75
    —Addresses, essays, lectures   VA58 359.070973
    —Bibliography   Z6835   016.35900973
    —World War, 1914-1918
    —World War, 1939-1945
. Hospital Corps   VG320   359.3450973
—Hospital Corps—Drill regulations   VG320   359.34, 610.2
—Illustrations   VA59   359.3250973
—Indians
—Insignia   VC345, UC530-3
—Job descriptions   VB258
. Judge Advocate General's Corps   KF26   332.6323
—Lawyers
—Lists of vessels   VA61   359.32, .320973, .3250973
—Management   VB203, VG593, VK1474, VM147   359.31, .621,
                      .9820973
—Maneuvers   V245, V169, VK597   359.5
—Medals, badges, decorations, etc.   VB333 (medals, decorations),
          VC345 (badges, insignia), UB433, UC533-5, CR4651   355.134
. Medical Corps   VG425
. Medical Dept.   VG123, R847, D807.U6   359.3450973, 610.71073
—Messes   VC383
—Military construction operations   VA68   341.725
. Mobile base hospital no. 3   D807.U6-8+   940.547673
—Negroes   [SEE ALSO '...—Afro-Americans']   E185, D810
          325.260973, 940.54516
—Officers   VB313-14, VB203, UA23   359.3320973, 353.00895,
                      343.73019
    —Classification   VB313   359.332
    —Correspondence, reminiscences, etc.
—Officers' handbooks   V133, VM600   359.00973, .02, .31, .33, 623.87

War damage compensation   [indemnification to property owners by their gov. for
    damage suffered from attacks]   341.3
War damage, Industrial   UA929.5-9, HD28   355.26, 658.28, .401
War
    —Economic aspects   HB195, HC110   330.9, .973092, 338.9, 355.02,
        .0273 (US), .027309034, .26, .03, 940.531
    —Film catalogs   U21   016.35502
War films—History and criticism   PN1995   791.4309093, .437
War games   U310, UA673, V250, V253   355.02, .08, .4, .48, .48094,
        .5, .54, 356.11+, 904.7, 940.541241
War games, Naval   V250   793.9
War in art   N330, N8260, NC968, NX650   704.949399, .9499047, 741.65, 769.973
War in literature
War (International law)   JX68, JX1907, JX1916, JX4505, JX4508, JX4511,
        JX4521, JX5001   341.3, .31, .5, .6026, .65-67, .30902
War libraries   Z675.W2
War, Maritime (International law)   JX5203-5268
War—Medical aspects
War memorials   NA9325
        —Europe—Guide-books   D663   914.0455
War neuroses   RC550   616.85, .852109
War (Philosophy)
War poetry   PN6110.W28 (gen.), PR1195.H5 (Eng.), PS595.H5 (Am.)
        808.8193, 821.00803 (Eng.)
War poetry, American
War poetry, English [British]
War Poetry, French
War —Protection of civilians   JX5144 (int'nal' law)   341.481
    —Psychological aspects   U22   355.02019, 150.194, 155.935, 172.4, 301.2
    —Quotations, maxims, etc.   PN6084   808.882
War relief—Case studies   HV639   361.53
War—Relief of sick and wounded   UH201-551
War-ships   V800   623.825
War ships, Scuttling of
War-songs
War-songs, American   M1628   784.71973, .68973
War-songs, English
War-songs, French
War-songs, German
War stories
War stories, American
War stories, English
War stories, French
War stories, German
War victims
    —Law and legislation
War wounds   RD156   617.1
War—Women's work
Warfare, Conventional
Warsaw—History

Warships   V750-980 (construc.), VA (naval organiz.), V750-800, VA40-61,
                  VA454- 6, VA503, VA513, VA653, VA700   359.325+, .32,
                  .83+, 623.825+, .8252, .82509+, 940.5459+
—Camouflage   V215
—Costs
—Handling   VK545   623.88, .8825
—History   V750, V765, VA456, VA513   359.325+, .32509+,
                  .3250942 (GB), .3254+, .83, 623.82509, .8250904
   —Collected works
Warships, Internment of
Warships
   —Models   VM298   623.82015
   —Recognition   V767   623.825, 359.3250222
Warships, Scuttling of
Warships
   —Turrets   VF440
   —Visits to foreign ports
Warspite (Battleship) [WWI & II]
Washburn, Stanley, 1878-1950   [U.S.: Correspondent]   D550.W28   940.4147
Washington, D.C.—History   F191-205   917.53, .5303, .303, 975.3
Washington naval treaty (1922)
Weizmann, Chaim, Dr., 1874-1952 [G.B., Israel: Zionist leader, scientist, chem.
   advisor to G.B., 1st Pres. of Israel (1948)]   DS125.3.W45, DS151.W4, DS126,
   DS149   956.94050924, 922.96, 923.15694
Wekerle, Alexander, 1848-1921   [Aust.-Hung.: Min.-Pres.]   DB65, DB91, UA672
                                      943.603-604, 355.309436
Wemyss, Rosslyn Erskine, 1864-1933 [G.B.: Baron, Adm.]   DA89.1.W4, D568.3,
                  D580, VA454   359.00941, 923.542
Westarp, Kuno Count von, 1864-1945   [Ger.: Politician]   DD228.5-8, D515
                                            940.343
Weygand, Maxime, 1867-1965   [Fr.: Gen. (WWI & II), Supr. Allied Comm.
   (1940)]   U55.W45, .F6, D530.F, D761.W, D811.W443, DC342.8.F6
                  944.0810924, 940.5344, 928.544
Wielkopolska (Poland)—History—Uprising, 1918-1919   D651.P7
Wilhelm, Crown Prince of Prussia and Germany, 1882-1951   [Ger.: Gen.]
   DD229.8.W5, D531.W   923.243
Wilhelm II, 1859-1941   [Ger.: Kaiser, Emperor-King]   DD218, DD228.5, DD229,
                                D531   943.0840924, 923.143
William and Mary College, Williamsburg, Va. Hampton Roads-Peninsular War Studies
   Committee   HC107.V82.H48   309.1755
Wills, Military
Wilson, Henry Hughes, Sir, 1864-1922 [G.B.: Field Marshal] DA69.3.W5,
                  U55.W536, D546   923.542, 355.00924
Wilson, Woodrow, 1856-1924 [U.S.: Pres.]   E765-768, E780, D570, D611,
                  D619, D644, D651, E780   973.0992, .80924,
                  .912-913, .9130924, 940.3141, .32273, .373, .45,
                  327.7304+, 378.74967, 923.173
Winter warfare   U167.5.W5   355.423
World politics   D, J, D21, D105, D363, D397, D413, D421, D443, D455, D720,
                  D727, JC251-2, JX1315, JX1395, UA11, UA646   940.28, .51, .55,
                  301.1523, 327.0904, 341.09, .1818+, 901.9, 909.82
   —19th century D363, D397   327.09034, 320.94028, 335.4, 909.81
   —20th century D440-72, D419, JC252   320.904, 327.0904, 330.15, 909.82
   —1900-1945   D413, D443, D450   940.531, 901.94, 327.14
   —1900-1918   940.312

World War, 1914-1918   [For older books prior to around 1982, SEE 'European
                             War, 1914-1918'. Subdivisions listed in either area may be
                             found under either heading]   D501-680, D511,
                             D521-3, D639, D644, JX1952-3   940.3-940.499,
                             940.3+, 940.4+
—Addresses, essays, lectures   AC8, D509, D525, D523   940.308, .31
—Addresses, sermons, etc.   B945, D443, PS2120   301.593, .953,
                             940.308, .34208
—Aerial operations   D600-607, D788, DA89, TL515, TL540, UG633   358.43,
                             623.746, 923.542, 940.44, .54
—Aerial operations, American   UG633, D606
—Aerial operations, Australian   D792.A8, UG635.A8
—Aerial operations, Austrian
—Aerial operations—Bibliography   Z6207.E8
—Aerial operations, British   UG635.G7, D786, D602, D545
                             940.48142, .447
—Aerial operations, Canadian   UG635.C2
—Aerial operations—Chronology
—Aerial operations, French   D603, UG635.F8   940.44944
—Aerial operations, German   D546, D604, UG635.G3-4   940.44943
—Aerial operations, Italian
—Aerial operations, Russian
—Aerial operations, Serbian
—Africa   D651.A4, DT31-4
—Africa, French-speaking West   DT532.5
—Africa, German East   D640, D627.A3, D576.G3   940.48168
—Africa, German Southwest   D576.G5, D640   940.48248, .41688, .48168
—Africa, North   DT204, HC56.C38
—Afro-Americans   D639.N4, D570.33.369th   940.403, .41273
—Algeria   DT295
—Alsace-Lorraine   DD801.A57, D548
—American republics   F3097.3
—Anecdotes   D509, D523   940.48
—Angola   DT604, DT611
—Arab countries   DA47.9.S4
—Arabia   D568.4, D568.4.L43 (T.E. Lawrence)   940.4153
—Argentina   D621.A8, F2846-8
—Armenia   DS195.5, D651.A7, D638.A7, DS195.3.A65   947.92
—Armistices   D641, D509   940.452, .43, .439
—Art and the war   NX543, N9145, N6848-9, NC266, N9150, D527.1
                             745.09041, 709.43
     —Exhibitions   N9150
     —Periodicals   N9150
—Asia, Western   D566
—Atrocities   D625-6, JX1906, DS195.5, DH682, D626.G3 (Ger.),
                             D520.T8 (Turkish), D638.A7 (Armenians)   940.488
     —Sources   DS195.5
—Australia   D520.A9, D568.2-7, DU116, DU212, DU161, D547.A8,
                             D568.A2, DU110, D609.A8   919.4034, 940.41294, .394
     —Biography   D609.A8
     —Fiction
     —Periodicals   D501, D501.C13
     —Tasmania   D547.T3
—Austria   D621.A9, DB86-93, D539.A5, DB48, DB98, D512
                             940.41436

World War, 1914-1918
  —Automobiles   UC10
  —Balkan Peninsula   D562.M32, D560-1   940.3496
  —Baltic States   DK511, DK511.L17, D633
  —Battlefields   D521, D527-8, D542-5, D542.Y7 (Ypres), DC16, DH416,
                DR416.E45-49t (Gallipoli)
    —Guide-books
  —Battles, sieges, etc.   [SEE 'World War, 1914-1918—Aerial ops.'; '...—
          Campaigns'; '...—Naval ops.' and specific battle names]
  —Bavaria   D604, DD801.B41
  —Belgium   D526.2, D626.B4 or .G3, D651, D541, DH681-82, DH401,
                DH523, D623.B4   923.1493, 940.3493, .4313
    —Antwerp   DH811.A58-68
    —Dinant
    —Flanders, West
    —Louvain   D542.L7, D626.B4
    —Spa   D542.S6
    —Ypres   D542.Y7
  —Bibliography   Z6207.E8, D613, D570.1, D509   016.9403
    —Catalogs   Z1035.B77, Z6207.E8
  —Biography   D530, D507, DD231.A2   940.315355
  —Blockades   D580-1, JX5225   940.322, .3481, .452
  —Bohemia   DB215, D521
  —Brazil   D621.B8, F2537, VA422
  —Bulgaria   D621.B9, D643.B6, DR72   940.31412
  —California   D570.85.C2
  —Campaigns   D529-78, D511, D521-3, U738, U162   940.4+, .413-414+
    —Afghanistan   D568.8.V63
    —Africa   D573-6
      —Cameroon   D576.C3
    —Africa, East   D576, D576.G3
    —Africa—German East   D576.G3
      —German Southwest   D576.G5, DT779.8
    —Africa—Mozambique   D576.G3, D549.P82
    —Africa, North   D766.82
    —Africa
      —Southwest   DT715
      —Tanganyika   D576.G3, D576.G3.L5-6   940.41676
      —Togoland
    —Alsace
    —Angola
    —Arab countries   D568.4, U55.L347
    —Arabian Peninsula   D568.4
    —Armenian S.S.R.
    —Balkan Peninsula   D569.2, D560-3   940.41496
      —Fiction   PA5610.M99
    —Belgium   D541-2   940.481
    —Bibliography   Z6207.E8
    —Black Sea region   D583
    —Bulgaria   D640.M3648
    —Cameroon   D576.C3
    —Champagne   D527
    —Czechoslovakia

World War, 1914-1918
—Campaigns
——Dardanelles   [SEE 'World War, 1914-1918—Campaigns—Turkey—
                  Gallipoli Peninsula', '...—Campaigns—Turkey and the
                  Near East', etc.]
——Eastern   D550-569.5, D539.5   940.4147
——Egypt   D629.E3, D568.2, D566
——Far East   D520.O8, D574
——France   D544-5, D548-9, D570.9, D629.F8, D640, D541, U53.P4,
             DC342.8.F6   940.4144, .48144, .457
———Chronology   D548.F55, D548
———Hartsmannswillerkopf D545.H25
——German East Africa   D576.G3
——Greece
——Iran   D568.8
——Iraq   D568.5
——Italo-Austrian   D569, D569.A2   940.481
——Italy   D569
——Lithuania
——Macedonia   D562.M32
——Maps   G1037
——Near East   DS125.5, D566, D640, D568.4
——New Guinea (Territory)   D578.N4
——North Sea   D581
——Palestine   D568.7, D566
——Picardy
——Poland   D550-2
——Romania   D565
——Serbia   D561   940.4256
——Soviet Union   D550
——Syria   D568.6
——Tanzania   D576.G3
——Transcaucasia   D567.C3
——Turkey   D566-8, D581
——Turkey and the Near East   D568+, DR448, DS315, D566, D651+
                                 940.415
———Afghanistan   D568.8
———Caucasus   D567.C3, DR588
———Egypt   D629.E3, D568.2
———Gallipoli   D526.2, D568.3, DR592, DU114   940.425-26, .4259
———Poetry
———Iran   D568.8
———Iraq   D568.5
———Palestine D568.7, DS125.5, DA69.3.A6
———Persia   D568.8
———Sources   DR588
—Turkey
——Gallipoli Peninsula   D568.3, D547.A, DR592, DR592.K4

World War, 1914-1918
—Campaigns
    —Ukraine   D550-7
    —Western   D530-549.5, D663, D640, D570   940.34, .343, .344, .4
    —Yugoslavia   D560-4
       —Dalmatia (Croatia)   D562.D3
       —Montenegro
       —Serbia   D561.S21, D562.M32
—Canada   D520.C2, D547.C2, D640, F1027   971.4, 940.31412
   —Addresses, essays, lectures   D547.C2   309.1705
—Caricatures and cartoons   D526, D526.2, D526.5
—Casualties (Statistics, etc.)   HB871.H47, HB881, HB3607, D635, D609,
        UG447   940.37305, .34705, 312.0947
—Catholic Church   D622
—Causes   D511, D501-515, DD228.5-6, DB89.F7, D465, JX1906,
        DD232.5, DD221   940.3112, .311208, .311, 944.08, 332.09
   —Addresses, essays, lectures
   —Bibliography   Z6207.E8   016.947
   —Collected works   D511, D515
   —Congresses   D511
   —Sources   D511
—Cavalry operations
—Censorship   D631-2
   —France
   —Germany
   —Great Britain
   —United States
—Chemical warfare   UG447   623.45-452
—Chemistry   UG447
—Children
—Chile   D621.C5
—China   DS721, D549.C5, DS774-5   940.345102, .32251
—Chronology   D522.5   940.34205
—Church of England   D639.C54   261.873
—Civilian relief   BX7635.A, D637-9, D639.W7, D809   940.3144
   —Belgium   D638.B4
   —France   D638.F8
   —Great Britain   D638.G7
   —Russia
   —Serbia   D638.S48
   —Sources   —Bibliography   Z6616.H588.H
   —Soviet Union   DK188
—Claims   JX5326, JX5483   341.3
—Collectibles
—Concentration camps   D627
   —[country]
—Confiscations and contributions
   —Austria   JX5313.G7
   —Bulgaria
   —Germany   JX5313.G3-7
   —Great Britain   JX5313.G7
   —United States   JX5313.U5-6, JX238.N83   341.3
—Congresses   D504, DR504-15, D570.8
—Conscientious objectors   UB342
   —Great Britain   UB342.G7, B1649.R91   355.2240942

World War, 1914-1918
   —Economic aspects
      —Scandinavia   HC345   330.948, 940.34805
      —Scotland   HC257
      —Serbia
      —South Africa   HC517.S7
      —Soviet Union
      —Spain
      —Sweden   HC375
      —Switzerland   HC397
      —United States   D635, HD6095, HD9074, HC106.2, HB236.U5, HD9914,
            HD8072, D619   338.50973, 331.0973, 330.973
   —Ecuador
   —Education and the war   D639.E3
   —Egypt   D568.2
      —Prisoners and prisons, British   D627.E3
   —England   D640, DA690
      —Bristol   D547.8.B8
   —Equipment and supplies   D639.S9
   —Europe, Eastern   D639, DJK48, D645
   —Exhibitions   D675
   —Fiction
      —Bibliography   Z5917.W33
      —History and criticism
   —Finance   D635, HJ8011, HC56-7, JX1315, HC240   940.31422, 336.3, .34
      —Austria   HG3020, HJ1063
      —Canada   HC115   330.971
      —England
      —Europe
      —France   HJ1091
      —Germany   HJ1119
      —Great Britain   HC256.2, HJ1023, HG1586, D505, HJ8627, D635, HB195,
            HJ1015, HJ2619   336.41-2, .20942, 330.19355, 940.34205
      —Hungary   HJ1063
      —Italy   HC305, HJ2765
      —Netherlands   HC325, HJ1202
      —Russia   HJ1207
      —Soviet Union   HJ1207
      —United States   HC56.C33, HC106.2, HJ257, HJ8117, D570.15,
            D570.85   940.37305, 336.73, .30973, 330.973
   —Finland   D621.F5, DD120.F49, DK446-59, DK265   327.430471, 330.9471
   —Food question   HD9000-9049, D637   940.477873
      —Austria   HC265   330.9436
      —Belgium
      —Canada
      —Congresses
      —Europe   HD1917
      —France   HD9012.5   338.10944
      —Germany   D581, D641, HD9013.6   940.452, .3141
      —Great Britain   HD9011.6
      —Hungary   HC265   330.9436
      —Italy   HD9015.I8
      —Russia   HD9015.R9   338.10947
      —United States   HD9005-6, HD1765, SB83, HD9035   940.37305

World War, 1914-1918
  —Food supply   D570.1
    —Germany   D581
    —Great Britain   HD9011.6
    —Russia
  —France   D516, D548, D520.F8, DC387-9, DC367, DC373   940.405,
                    .431, .344, 320.944081, 944.0815
    —Arras   DC801.A79   944.27
    —Bordeaux
    —Bourges
    —Briey
    —Brittany   DC611.B916
    —Colonial troops
      —Senegalese   D548.9.S4
    —Congresses   D621.F8
    —Épernay   DC801.E63
    —Lille   D545.L5, D541
    —Loire-Atlantique (Dept.)   D545.L65
    —Lyons
    —Marseille
    —Metz   D545.M5
      —Sources
    —Moselle   D545.M5+
    —Moselle (Dept.)
    —Naval operations
    —Noyon   D545.N7
    —Paris   DC736, D544-8, D640   914.436
    —Registers, lists, etc.
    —Rouen   DC801.R85
    —Saint-Quentin
    —Toulouse
    —Tours   D545.T6
    —Verdun
  —Georgia—Troup Co.   D570.85.G4
  —German-Americans   E184.G3, F475.G3
  —German East Africa   D576.G3
  —Germany   D515, D531, D609-13, DD231-232.5, DD221.5,
                    DD228.6-8, DD229.8, U738, UA647, UA712
                    940.53112, .4886, .32443, .343, 327.43+
    —Berlin
    —Bibliography   Z6207.E8
    —Bremen   DD901.B78
    —Collected works
    —Fiction
    —Nuremberg   DD901.N94   943.32
    —Periodicals
    —Sources
  —Giftbooks   D526.2, D568.2-3, D638.A-Z, AY14

World War, 1914-1918
  —Great Britain   D546, D544-7, D517, D521, D547.8, D611, D645,
              DA68.32, DA566.9.A-Z, DA577   942.083, 940.342, .31, .41241-
              41242, .34207, 923.542
      —Bibliography   CD1047   354.4205
      —Biography   D609.G7
      —Dorset   DA670.D7
      —London   D547.8.L7
      —Periodicals   D501, D501.W19
  —Greece   DF838, D616, D610, DF833-8
  —Greece, Modern   DF837   327.495
  —Handbooks, manuals, etc.   D525
  —Hawaii (Territory)   DU620
  —Historiography   D515, D522.42, D743.42, DB36.8, DD86, U21
  —History—Sources
  —Hospitals   D629.G7
  —Hospitals, charities, etc.   D638, D541, D629, D640, D809   360.6273,
                        940.47709+, .4771, .34207, 352.047
  —Humor   D526.2, .2-7
  —Humor, caricatures, etc.   D526.2, .2-7, NC1479, DK188
  —Humor—Periodicals
  —Hungarian participation DB953
  —Hungary   D643.H9, D539-40, D651.H7, DB947-55
      —Budapest
  —Iconography   D503, CJ6170, Z1009
World War, 1914-1918, in art   N6888, ND623
World War, 1914-1918, in literature PR605.W3
World War, 1914-1918, in motion pictures   PN1993.5.U6, D522.33
World War, 1914-1918
  —India   D520.I6, D547.I5
      —Punjab   DS485.P2
  —Indiana   F521
  —Influence   D509-23, D511, D443, D643, D727, D741, E768
  —Influence and results   D443, D511, D523, D639.D45, D643.A7, D653,
                      D741, CB155   940.5, .51, .314, .3149+, 909.82
  —Influence—Pictorials   TR820.5
  —Intelligence service
      —France
      —Germany
      —Great Britain
      —Russia
  —Iowa   D570.85.I8
  —Iran   D640, DS315
  —Iraq   D566
  —Ireland   DA952-62
  —Islands of the Baltic   D764.7.B3 (also WWII)
  —Italy   DG568.5, DG570, DG799, D520.I7, D526.7.I8, D569.A2, D617,
              D621, D640, D651.I6, DB879   940.32245, .345, .34502, .4145
      —Congresses
      —Pictorial works
      —Rome
      —Venice
  —Japan   D520.O8, DS518, DS845

World War, 1914-1918
    —Jews   DS135.G33, DS135, D609.G3, D639.J4   940.315296
        —Bibliography   Z6207.E8
        —Germany
    —Journalism, Military   PN5247.M5
        —United States   D501.S725
    —Journalists   PN4815, D546
    —Juvenile fiction
    —Juvenile literature
    —Language (New words, slang, etc.)   D526.2, PE3727.S6, PC1977.S6,
                                   PC3747.S6   427.09, 821.04
    —Latin America   D520.S8
    —Law and legislation   JX5003   341.3
        —Austria   HC265, HD7880
        —Belgium   D623.B4
        —Great Britain   HC256.2, D505.G77
        —Sweden   HC375
        —United States   JC599.U5, JX5270
    —Lebanon   DS85
    —Libraries (in camps, etc.)   Z675.W2   027.652, .777829
    —Literary collections   PN6071.E8
    —Literature and the war   PN56.W1, PN3448, PN3503, PR106, PR478.E8,
                              PR605.W3+ (Brit. poetry), PR610, PR888.E9, PR2976.H385,
                              PS228.W37 (US), PT405, PT553 (Grmn. poetry), PT772,
                              PQ307.W3 (Fr.)   810.9005, 809.33
        —Addresses, essays, lectures
        —Bibliography
    —Lithuania   DK511.L2
    —Louisiana   D570.85.L8   940.37303
    —Macedonia   D629.G8
    —Maine
    —Manpower   UA18
        —United States   UA18.U5
    —Manscripts
        —Catalogs   Z6611.H5
    —Maps   G1037, D521, D540   912.4
        —Bibliography
    —Massachusetts   D570.85.M41
    —Medical and sanitary affairs   D628-30   940.5476+, .475+
        —France   D629.F8
    —Medical care   D629-30
        —France   D629.F8
        —Great Britain   D629.G7
    —Mexico   F1234, E183.8.M5
    —Michigan   D570.85.M5
    —Military operations   [SEE 'World War, 1914-1918—Aerial ops.; '... —
                              Campaigns'; '... —Naval ops.']
    —Minnesota   D570.85.M6+   940.3776
        —St. Paul   D570.85.M61
    —Miscellanea
    —Missouri
    —Montenegro   D564.A2, D561
    —Monuments   D663
    —Moral and ethical aspects   D523-4
    —Moral aspects

World War, 1914-1918
—Morocco   D547.M6, DT317
—Motion pictures and the war   D522.23, D639.P7, PN1993.5, PN1995.9
—Museums
—Naval operations   D580-9, VA40, VA454   359.3252, 940.45+, .485,
          .454-459+
—Naval operations, American   D589.U6   940.45
—Naval operations, Australian
—Naval operations, Austrian   D583
—Naval operations, British   D581-2, D593, DA89.1, VA456, D771
          359.3320924, 940.455
—Naval operations, French   D583, VA503
—Naval operations, German   D581-2, D591, VA513, D639.M82, D640
          940.45943
—Naval operations, Italian
—Naval operations, Russian   D585, DK265
—Naval operations—Submarine   D580, D589-90, D591-5, D619-21, V210,
          V859, JX5244.A7   940.451+
—Netherlands   DJ281-5, D621.N4   940.3492
—New Mexico   F791
—New York   D570.85.N
—New Zealand   D547.N5, D501.K53, D568.3, D629.N4
—Nigeria   D547.N57
—North Dakota
—Norway
—Ontario   F1056-1059.7
—Outlines, syllabi, etc.   D522.5   940.302
—Pacific Ocean   D581-2
—Palestine   D568.7, DS125+, DS125.5   956.9
—Panama   TC774.B88
—Paraguay   D525
—Participation, Jewish
—Peace   D610-14, D642-50, D443, D523, JX1907, JX5181, JX1952
          940.31+, .312, .3141, .3162, .318331, 341.1
    —Bibliography   Z6207.E8
    —Periodicals   HX1.U71
—Pennsylvania—Philadelphia   D570.85.P41, F158.5
—Periodicals   D501.A-Z
—Personal narratives   D568.3, D640   940.481+, .476+
—Personal narratives, American   D570+, D570.9, D603, D629, D640
          940.48173, .4144, .4771
—Personal narratives, Armenian
—Personal narratives, Australian   D640, D568.3, D547, D630
—Personal narratives, Austrian   D640, D643   940.482436
—Personal narratives, Belgian   D541-2, D627.G3
—Personal narratives, British   D640, D545   940.48141-48142
—Personal narratives, Canadian   D640   940.48171
—Personal narratives, Croatian
—Personal narratives, Czech   D640, DB217
—Personal narratives, English   D639-40, D530, D541-5, D568.7, D569.2,
          D576, D582, D602, D627, DA566.9.A-Z, PR6013.G78
          940.414409+, .48141-48142
—Personal narratives, Estonian

World War, 1914-1918
—Prisoners and prisons, Russian   D627.R8-9   940.47247
—Prisoners and prisons, Serbian
—Prisoners and prisons, Swiss   D627.S9
—Prisoners and prisons, Turkish   D627.T8   940.47256
—Prizes, etc.   JX5251
—Propaganda   D639.P6-7, D632, UB275   940.4886+, .3152, .322+, .488642
—Prophecies   BF1815.N8, D523
—Protest movements   D639.P77   940.3162
    —Germany   D639.P77
    —Great Britain   JX1961.G7
—Prussia, East (Province)   DD491, DD491.O42
—Psychological aspects   D523, D525
—Public opinion   D639.P88, .R4, D509, D523, D570.1, D619, D639
    940.3152, .37+, .4886-4887+
    —Australia   D639.P88.A8+
    —Europe   D639.P88.E85+
—Quotations, maxims, etc.   PN6084.W35
—Refugees   D637-8   940.3159+
    —France   D638.F8   940.315944
    —Russia   D638.R9
    —Sources
—Regimental histories   D547.A-Z   940.409+, .412+
    —Africa, South   D547.A4
    —Australia   D547.A8, D568.A2   940.41294
        —6th Light Horse Regiment
        —22d Battalion
        —48th Battalion
        —A.I.F. Camel Corps
        —Flying Corps. 1 Squadron   D607.A8
    —Austria
    —Canada   D547.C2   940.40971
    —France
        —Escadrille Lafayette   D603
        —Infantry—Periodicals   D501.R49
        —Service aéronautique
            —Escadrille n. 124   D603   940.44944
    —Germany   D609.G3, D534.3
        —Südarmee (1915-1918)
    —Great Britain   D547.B74, .G7, D546   940.41242
        —Australian and New Zealand Army Corps   D568.3
        —Cavalry—Desert mounted corps   D568.7
        —Infantry
            —Cheshire Volunteer Regiment   D547.8.C5
            —Irish Guards   D547.I6
        —Royal Scots (The Royal Regiment)   D547.R8
        —King's Royal Rifle Corps   D547.K5
        —Royal Fusiliers (City of London Regiment)   D568.7, DS125.5
        —Royal Regiment of Artillery   D547.R5
        —309 (H.A.C.) siege battery   D547.L6
        —West African Frontier Force—Nigeria Regiment   D576.G3
    —India   D547.I5
    —Ireland   D547.I6
    —Italy   D569.A2

World War, 1914-1918
—Regimental histories
——New Zealand   D547.N5
———Auckland infantry   D547.N5
———Machine Gun Corps
———Wellington Mounted Rifles
——Russia   UA774, D552
———Kavalergardskii polk
——Saxony
——Serbia
——United States   D570.3-33. D570-570.9   940.41273
———1st Division   D570.9, D570.3.1st
———3rd Division
———26th Division   D570.3.26th
———26th Infantry   D570.33.26th
———42d Division   D570.3.42d   940.41273
———91st Division
———Engineers—105th   D570.31.105th
———Infantry
————308th   D570.33.308th
————369th (Colored)
———347th Machine Gun Battalion   D570.34.347th
——Yugoslavia—Serbia
—Registers, lists, etc.   D639.E4, D547, D570.85
—Registers of dead   D609, D639.E
——France   D609.F8
——Italy
——United States   D609.U6, D570.A2, D639.D4
—Religious aspects   D639.R4   940.3152, .3182
——Germany
—Reparations   D648-9, D644, DC59.8.G3, HG186.F8, HG1997.I6,
        HG3949, HJ8654, HJ8751, JX1908   940.31422,
        330.904, 336.309, .30943, .497
——Periodicals   D649.G31.A5
—Romania   D520.R8, DR205, D651.R6   940.3498, .482+, 949.8
—Russia   DK265, DK254, D646, D514, D550, D585   940.347,
        .34705, .4147, 947.08
——Archangel   D559   940.7374
—Russia, Asiatic   D567.A2
—Russia
——Bibliography   Z6207.E8   016.947
——Caucasus   DK511.C3
——Congresses
——Miscellanea
——Moscow (Province)   DK188.R92, D639.S9
—Russian S.F.S.R.
——Arkhangel'sk
——Murmansk
——Siberia
—Samoa   DU813, D578.S19
—Science

World War, 1914-1918
—Secret service   D639.S7-8, .C75, D619.3, UB250, UB271   940.486-487+
    —Austria   D639.S7   940.487436
    —France   D639.S7   940.48644
    —Germany   D639.S7-8, D619.3   940.48743
    —Great Britain   D639.S7, D616   940.48642
    —Jews   DS125.5
    —United States   D639.S7, D619.3   940.48673
—Serbia   D629.S4, D561, D569.2, D651.Y8, DR363   940.477, 330.9497
—Siberia   DK265, D558, DB215   940.482
—Slovenia   D621.Y8, DR381
—Social aspects
    —Germany
—Societies
—Songs and music   D526.2, M1646   427.09, 821.04
    —Discography   ML156   016.789912
    —History and criticism
—Sound, The (Denmark and Sweden)   D581
—Sources   D505-9   940.31412, .4, 943.084 (Ger.)
    —Bibliography   Z6207.E8   016.9403141
—South Africa
—South Dakota   D570.85.S7   940.41273
—Soviet Union   DK254-65, D639.S9, D521
    —Congresses
—Soviet Union, Northern
—Soviet Union
    —Periodicals
—Spain   D621.S73
    —Catalonia
—Statistics   D521, D550, D570.1.U
—Supplies   D639.SS9, UD390   355.82
—Sweden   D621.S5, DL658
—Switzerland   D621.S8, DQ48, DQ69   940.3494
—Syria   DS98
—Tank warfare   UG446.5
—Tasmania   D547.T3
—Territorial questions   D650.T4, D651.A-Z, D645, D443, JV2018, JX1975
                940.314+, .3141, .31424, 943.91, 321.07, 325.343, 341.1
    —Africa   D651.A4, DT32.5   309.16, 333.096
    —Africa, East   D651.A41
    —Albania   DR701.S5-7   914.965
    —Armenia   D651.A7   327.56620+
    —Austria   D645, D651.A95   940.31424
        —Tyrol   D643.A9, D651.A
        —Vorarlberg
    —Baltic Provinces   DK511.L17, D651.L4
    —Belgium
    —Besserabia (Moldavian S.S.R. and Ukraine)   D651.B4, DK511.B4   949.8
    —Bibliography   Z6207.E8   016.321027
    —Bulgaria   D651.B8   323.1497
    —Cameroon   DT574, D651.K3
    —Carinthia
    —China   DS793, DS793.S4
    —Czechoslovakia   D651.C9, DB205.8, DB215
    —Czechs

World War, 1914-1918
 —Territorial questions
  —Dalmatia
  —Dobruja (Romania and Bulgaria)
  —Egypt   D651.E3
  —Estonia
  —Finland DK451, DK459.3
  —Fiume   D651.I6
  —Galicia (Poland and Ukraine) D520.U35, D651.G18, .P7
  —Georgia (Transcaucasia) DK511.G3
  —Germany D651.G3, D643-4 940.31424
  —Greece   DF701
  —Hungary D651.H7, D643.H9, DB215, DB917, DB955 940.31412,
       943.91
  —Istria   D651.I5
  —Italy   D520.I7, D651.I6-7, D617 940.5082, .31424, .32245,
       .34502, 949.6
   —Gorizia
   —Trieste
  —Karelia   DK451
  —Ladrone Islands
  —Latvia   D651.L3-4
  —Lebanon D651.S9
  —Levant DC59.8
  —Lithuania DK511.L26-273, D651.L5-7, .V4, .P7 940.31424
  —Macedonia D651.M3, DR701.M4
  —Mesopotamia
  —Montenegro D651.M7
  —Palestine
  —Periodicals D650.T4.E13
  —Poland D651.P7, .L5, DD901.D25, .D28, DA578, DB215, DK440,
       DK511.L273, JX1907 940.31424, 943.12, .8, 341.6082
  —Prussia, East D651.P7+, DD247.W5-7 940.31424, 943.8
  —Prussia, East (Province)
  —Rhine River Valley D650.M5, DD801.R75
  —Romania DB48
  —Rumania
  —Ruthenia D651.R9, .P7
  —Saar River Valley (France and Germany) DD801.S13, D651.S13 943.42
  —Saar Valley DD801.S13
  —Samoan Islands
  —Saudi Arabia D651.S32
  —Schleswig DD491.S622
  —Shantung DS845
  —Silesia   DD491.S53, D651.S5 943.14
  —Silesia, Upper (Poland and Czechoslovakia) D651.S5
  —Syria   D651.S9, DS98
  —Thrace   D651.T5
  —Togoland D651.T7
  —Transylvania D643.H9, D651.T8, DB730.7, DR281.T7 943.91-2,
       323.1094392
  —Trieste D651.T85
  —Turkey DR477, DR584, D651.T9, D610, DF833, DS63 949.6, 956.101
  —Tyrol   DB779, D651.T95 943.64
  —Ukraine D651.U6, DK508.8

World War, 1914-1918
—Territorial questions
    —Yemen   D651.S32
    —Yugoslavia   D651.Y8-9, D465, D561, DR317   940.322497
        —Dalmatia (Croatia)
        —Istria (Croatia and Slovenia)
        —Montenegro
        —Rijeka (Croatia)   D651.I8
        —Rijeka, Croatia (City)
—Thailand   DS578
—Theater and the war   PN2641   792.09+
—Togoland   D626.K1
—Transcaucasia   D567.C3, DK511.T65
—Transportation   D568.5, D639.T8   940.41242, .453
—Treaties   D650.T4, D450, D644, JX846   940.31424
    —Bibliography
    —Sources
—Trench warfare   D523, D530
—Turkey   D520.T8, D568.4, D587, DR448, DR584-92   940.4153, 949.6,
                956.101, 327.430561
    —Atrocities   DS195.5
—Turkmen S.S.R.   DK858
—Ukraine   D520.U35, D614.B5, DK188, DK265.8.U3-4, DK508
—Underground movements   DC611
—United States   D570-570.7, D619, D632, D639, E664, E743-5, E766-7,
                E780, E784, E802, JK464   940.373, .5373,
                .32273, .3141, .488673, .48743, 973.913, 355.0973
    —Addresses, essays, lectures
    —Bibliography   Z6207.E8, D570, D570.A2
    —Congresses   D570.1, E768
    —Fiction   PS3539
    —107th Infantry   D570.33.107th
    —Periodicals   D570.A2, D570.8.C7
    —Posters   D522.25
    —Societies, etc.   D570.A15
—Uruguay   F2726
—Vorarlberg   D539.5.V91
—War work   D570.85, U766
    —Great Britain
    —Mennonites   BX8116
    —Red Cross   D639.R, D640
    —Salvation Army   D639.S15
    —Schools   D639.E3-4
    —Society of Friends   D637, BX7675   940.4777, .477873
    —Young Men's Christian Associations   D639.Y7
—Washington, D.C.   F199
—West Virginia   D570.85.W4
—Women   D639.W7
—Women's work   D639.W7, HD6093   940.477842, .3161
    —Bibliography   Z6207.E8

World War, 1914-1918
—Y.M.C.A.   D639.Y7, .J4, UB342, U5, D627.G3
—Yugoslavia   DR363, DB215, D651.Y8
    —Bosnia and Hercegovina
    —Montenegro   D564.A2, DR158
    —Serbia   D626.B8, DR363
—Zaire   DT657
—Zimbabwe   D530
World War, 1918-1945
World War, 1939-1945   [For contemporary works early in the period SEE
                    'European War, 1939-' and 'World War, 1939-'. Some titles may
                    ALSO be found under 'World War, 1930-1945', '...1935-1945',
                    '...1936-1945', '...1930-', etc.]   D731-838, D741 (overall works),
                    D743-4, D755, D757   940.53-5499, .53, .54
—Aerial operations   [SEE ALSO 'Bombardment' under names of cities]
                    D785-7, D767, D790, D811, TL685.7, UG630   623.746,
                         940.544, .5449+, 358.4+
—Asia   DS518
—Atlantic Ocean   D770-1, D781, VM395   940.5429, .5459
—Atrocities   D803-5, D804.G3, D805.G3, D810.J4, DD247.E34, DD253,
                    DD253.6, DS135.P63   940.54056, .547243,
                         .5472475, .54724972, .5405+, 943.086
—Australia   D754.A, D742.A8, D767, D767.8-95, D767.95.A8, D779.A9,
                    DU107-110, DU116-17   940.5394, .5304, 330.994
—Battlefields
—Bibliography   Z6207.W8, Z6725, D731-838, D734, D746
                    016.94053-94054, .36, 940.52-4
—Blacks   [SEE ALSO '...—Negroes']   D810.N4   940.5403, .541273, .54516
—Campaigns   D743-4, D755-7, DA69, E836   940.53-4, .5401,
                         .5408-5409, .541-2, 923.542
    —Atlantic Ocean
    —Eastern   D755.1, D757+, D764, D764.6, D765.13, D787-8, DK4185,
                    UG633   940.541244, .5421, .54210924
        —Public opinion   D764
    —Europe   [SEE ALSO 'World War, 1939-1945—Campaigns—Eastern'
                    and '...—Campaigns—Western']   D756.5, D769,
                    D769.31, DD256.5
    —France   D743, D755.2, D756, D761-2   940.540944, .5421
    —Germany   D755.7, D757, .9, D769.U   940.5401, .542
    —Great Britain
    —Italy   D763.I8+, D768.15-3, D769.A or U (U.S. Army)
                    940.5421, .548173
    —Near East   D766
    —Poland   D765, D765.13, D765.2, D764.7, UA772, UA829.P7
                    940.542, .5421, .544, 943.804
    —Russia   D764, D757.32, .85, D764+, DK266-8, UA770   940.5421,
                         .5481438
    —Soviet Union   D757, D764+, DK268   947.0842
    —Western   D756-763, D756, D756.3, D743, D768-9+, E836
                    940.53-5421, .549
—Canada   D742.C2, D754.C2, D768.15, D769.2, F1034, F1008,
                    UG635.C2   940.532, .5371, .541271
—Casualties (Statistics, etc.)   D797, D797.U (US), D820.P72   940.5467,
                    .546773 (US)

World War, 1939-1945
—Catholic Church   D810.C3-6, .J4 (Jews), D807.I8, BX1378, BX1536,
          BX1566   940.531522, .53152208, .5478, .54824563, 327.45634
—Causes   D727, D741-2, D748, D753, D816.5, E806   940.5311+,
          .53112, .53114, .5312, .532244, .532443, .5352, .5373, .5375,
          943.086, 973.917, 327.4104, .43073
—Censorship   D798-9+   940.5405
—Children   D810.C4, .J4 (Jewish), D811.5, HQ784.W3, HQ792, HV741,
          LC4069.W3   940.53161, 943.8405+, 362.7061+, .71063+, .74, 371.9
—Chronology   D743.5, D743   940.53, .5302, .5373, .540202, .542,
          .545973 (U.S. Navy)
—Dictionaries   D740, D744   940.53, .5303, 411.5
—Diplomatic history   D748-754, D748, D754, D735, DB955, DD256+, DD523,
          DK268, E744, E183.8.A-Z (U.S.-other places)   940.430+,
          .520+, .5314, .5322, .5324, .5332, .5373, .542, .582, 327.73081
—Documents, sources, etc.   D735   940.53082, .5322, .5332, .52
—Economic aspects   D800, HB195, HC58, HC101, HC286.4, D785.U
          940.5485, .53144, .531833, 330.19355, .5452, .904
—Europe   D755-7, D802.A2, D785.U (bombing), D922   940.5337, .544, .5308
—Finance   D800, HC57, HJ8011   336, 336.34
—Food question   [SEE ALSO '...—Food supply']   HC101, HD1761 (agric.),
          HD9000.1, .5, .62, HD9015, HF5415 (rationing), TX357, TX551,
          D410, D808   306.273, 338.1, .10611, .10631-10637+, .18355,
          612.39082, 940.53144, .5318338, .53405
—France   D742.F8, D752, D761, D802.F8+ (underground occupied terr.),
          D811, D819.F, DC340, DC373, DC389, DC396-7   940.5344,
          .540944, .5421, .548144, .5486, .5311, .532244, 944.081, 923.544
     —Paris   D762.P2-3, D802.F82.P375-376 (underground), D809.F8
          (evac. of civilians)   940.5344, .534436
—Germany   D735-7, D741, D742.G3, D751, D757+, D764,
          D781 (naval ops.), D785.U5-6 (bombing of), D804.G3 (atrocities),
          D809.G3(refugees), D811, D819.G3, D821, DD94, DD232,
          DD247, DD247.H5 (Hitler), DD253, DD256+   940.5314, .5343,
          .54013, .540943, .541343, .5421, .5440943, .5482, .548743,
          943.086, .1087, 355.331, 623.194
     —Berlin   D757.9.B4, DD256.3, DD880-81
—Great Britain   D742.G7, D743, D750, D755, D759, D786, D810-811.5,
          DA566, DA566.9.C4 (Churchill), DA586-7   940.342, .5304,
          .532, .532241, .5341-5342, .540942, .542, .5421, .544, .548142,
          .548173, .548642, .5842, 941.084, 942.084, .0840922, 923.242
          (biog.), 320.942, 327.420+ (for. rel'ns.), .42043 (for. rel'ns. w.
          Ger.), .42073 (w. U.S.), 355.480942 (generals)
     —London   D760.8.L7, D811.5   940.534203, .53421, .54422
—Italy   D742.I7, D754.I8, D763.I8, D802.I8 (underground), D813.I8,
          D829.I8, DG498, DG571-2, DG575   940.5320924, .5345,
          .5421, 945.091
—Medical and sanitary affairs   D806-7, D807.A-Z (by place or by country
          responsible), D807.B8 (Burma), .U5-6+ (U.S. medical work), D629,
          D769, .A or U, D785.U5-6+ (U.S. bombing), D805, D811, R722,
          RA776, RA790, RC971   940.5475+, .54752, .547542 (GB),
          .547547 (Rus.), .547573 (US), .547643 (Ger. hospitals),
          .5476732 (U.S. hospitals)
—Moral and ethical aspects   D744.4, D790 (bombing), UA26

World War, 1939-1945
—Naval operations   [SEE ALSO names of individual ships, e.g. 'Hotspur
    (Destroyer)]   D770-784, D767, D769, D770, D773, D779, D786,
    D811, UG1240+ (aviation), V767, VA58   940.542, .545+, 359+,
    359.32, .3252, .3255+
—Naval operations, Submarine   D780-4, D782 (Ger.), D782.U15 (U-99),
    D783 (US), D783.5.A-Z (names etc.), D784.A-Z (misc. countries),
    .F7 (Fr.), .G7 (GB), D771-3, V859.A-Z, .G3 (Ger.)
    940.5451, .54513+, .5451342 (GB), .5451373 (US), .54516,
    .545943 (Ger.), .5465756
—Near East   D766, D731, D754, D769.U or A, DS63.2.A-Z   940.542
—Negroes   [SEE ALSO '...—Blacks']   D810.N   940.5403, .541273, .54516
—Prisoners and prisons   D763, D804 (war crimes & atrocities), D805.A2,
    D806 (Red Cross etc.), D811+ (personal narratives)
    940.5472+, .547252 (Jpns.), .547243 (Ger.), .5315
—Propaganda   D639.P7 (WWI & II), D810.P6-7, D810.P7.A-Z (by origin),
    .P7.F73 (Fr.), .P7.G3+ (Ger.), .P7.G7 (Brit.), .P7.J3 (Jpns.),
    .P7.U39-5 (US), DD256.5 (Ger.)   940.4886+,
    .4889+, .534886+, .5486+, .5488, .54886+, .5488642 (Brit.),
    .5488673 (US), .54887+, .5488743 (Ger.), .5488752
    (Jpns.), .54889+, .5488973
—Public opinion   D810.P85, .P7+, HM261   940.5342
—Refugees   [SEE ALSO '...—Displaced persons']   D809.A-Z (by place),
    .C2 (Canada), .E8+ (Europe), .F7 (Fr.), .G3 (Ger.), .S65 (Sov. Un.),
    .S9 (in Switz.), D806, D808, D810.J4 (Jews), D820.P72.A-Z (pop.
    transfers by country), JV6601   940.53159+, .5315943 (Ger.),
    .5315944 (Fr.), .5344, .5486+, .548673, 301.3284
—Regimental histories   [Subdivided by country, regiment, division, etc.: SEE
    ALSO names of individual units by country, branch, then specific unit
    name as alternative entries]
—Registers, lists, etc.   D797.A-Z (by place), D810.J4 (Jews)
    940.5467+, .546773 (US), .5404, .541273
—Registers of dead   [SEE ALSO 'Registers of dead' as subdiv. of military
    branches {e.g. 'U.S. Army—Registers of dead'}]   D797.A-Z
—Reparations   [In general, SEE ALSO 'War damage compensation' and
    'Restitution and indemnification...']   D818-19, D819.A-Z (by place),
    .G3 (Ger.), .J3 (Japan), D821, HC337   940.531422, .53144,
    .5315296 (Jews), 330.9471, 338.943
—Russia   [SEE ALSO '...—Soviet Union']   D735.R9, D736, D742.R9,
    D753.2.R9, D764+, DK265-8, DK273, UA772+   940.5347,
    .540947, .548147, .532, .5322, .5421+, 947.084, 327.47+ (for.
    relns.), 330.947 (econ. conditions)
—Secret service   D810.S7-8, .S7 (gen.), .S8.A-Z (by biog. name),
    D810.C88 (cryptography), D802.A-Z (underground), DD247 (Ger.),
    E748.D665 (Donovan, Wm.), UB250   940.5485-5487+,
    .548642 (Brit. spies), .548644 (Fr.), .548647 (Rus.), .548673 (US),
    940.548743 (Ger.), .548752 (Jpns.), .485, 327.120924 (biog.),
    351.742, 355.34
—Social aspects
—Sources   [SEE ALSO numbers for countries or other topics]   D734,
    D735, D735.A (official), D814 (peace)   940.52, .5308+,
    .5314+ (peace), .5322, 940.54012-54013, .5408
—Soviet Union   [SEE ALSO '...—Russia']   D764, D754.S65 (diplomacy),
    D804.G3.R9 (atrocities by Ger.), DB2207, DK68.7.A-Z (for. relns.
    by place), DK268, DK273, DK651, UA772 (Red Army)

World War, 1939-1945
    —Territorial questions   D820-1, D821.A-Z (by place), D644 (WWI),
                D734.A-Z, D748   940.531, .5314, .531424, .31412 (WWI)
    —Transportation   D810.T8, HE823 (merch. marine: G.B.),
                HE2751 (railroads: U.S.), HE3018 (r.r.'s: G.B.), TF23, UG523
                940.531838+, .5318385, .5412+, .5425, .5441, .545, 356.95,
                358.2, 385, 387.5
    —Treaties   D814 (peace), D814.55, D735, JX1963   940.53141, .5322
    —United States [SEE ALSO '...—U.S.]   D769+, D731, D742-3, D742.U5,
                D753+ (diplomacy), D749, D761, D767, E173, E744, E806-7
                940.5312, .532, .532273, .5373, .53973, .540973, .541273,
                973.917, .92, 327.73 (for. relns.)
    —War work   [Civilian participation]   D769.85.A-Z (U.S.: by state),
                D807-810, BX7749 (Am. Friends)   940.5477-5478,
                .5477873 (US), .5481497
    —Women   D810.W7, DK4419 (underground: Poland), HQ1420, HQ1623
                940.53161, .5485
    —Women's work   D810.W7, D769, HD6093-5   940.5315396, .5318396,
                .541273, 306.27471, 331.112, .406173 (US), .48219
Woyrsch, Remus von, 1847-1920   [Ger.: Field Marshal]   DD231.W65, DD85,
                                CR5327   920.043, 929.7
Wyoming (Battleship)

Yanushkevich, Nikolai Nikolaevich, 1868-1918   [Rus.: Gen. of Infan.]   DK260,
                D550   940.4147, 947.08, 320.947
Young Men's Christian Associations   BV1030, BV1090, BV1172, BV1185
                267.3063771, .341082, .369, .3973
Young Women's Christian Associations   BV1340, BV1375, BV1392
                267.5, .5973
Ypres, Battles of, 1914-1917   D541, D542.Y5
Ypres, 1st Battle of, 1914   D542.Y6   940.421
Ypres, 2d Battle of, 1915   D542.Y7
Ypres, 3d Battle of, 1917   D542.Y72
Yser, Battle of, 1914   D541, D542.Y8
Yudenich, Nikolai Nikolaevich, 1862-1933   [Rus.: Gen. of Infan.]   DK254.I69,
                DK511.C2, D550   940.4147, 947.9
Yugoslavia
    . Armija
    —Boundaries
Yugoslavia
    —Foreign relations
    —History
        —1918-1941   DR366-9   949.702

Zborov, Battle of, 1917
Zeebrugge-Ostend Raids, 1918   D580-89, D594   940.458
Zhekov, Nikola Todorov, 1864-1949   [Bulg.: Gen.]   DR55, D360, D569.2,
                HD815.S74   940.414, 322.440924, 914.977032, 949.7
Zimmermann, Arthur, 1864-1940   [Ger.: For. Sec.]   JX1796.Z7, D511, Z103
                354.4300892, 940.3112

ABOUT THE AUTHOR

BUCKLEY BARRETT commenced his career as a librarian in 1973 after received a master's degree from the University of Southern California. He held a number of professional positions at the South Dakota State Library and the California State Library, and served as Library Director at Marymount College in Rancho Palos Verdes from 1979-1982. During the latter period he also provided part-time library reference assistance for CSU, Fullerton and CSU, Dominguez Hills. Since 1982 Mr. Barrett has worked as a library faculty member at California State University, San Bernardino. He was Head of Technical Services from 1987-1994, and then became Head of Automation Services.

Barrett wrote *The Barstow Printer: A Personal Name and Subject Index to the Years 1910-1920* (Borgo Press, 1985), and co-authored with Marty Bloomberg two evaluative, abstracted bibliographies: *Stalin: An Annotated Guide to Books in English* (Borgo Press, 1993) and *The Jewish Holocaust: An Annotated Guide to Books in English* (Second Edition, Borgo Press, 1995). Mr. Barrett has in press with Borgo a companion volume to his work on World War I, *World War II: A Cataloging Reference Guide*. In process is an annotated bibliography on books by and about Winston S. Churchill.

The author lives in San Bernardino with Nannette Bricher, his librarian wife; and the couple has two children who are not librarians.

www.ingramcontent.com/pod-product-compliance
Lightning Source LLC
Chambersburg PA
CBHW031231090426
42742CB00007B/158